FV

President and Publisher
Ira Shapiro

Senior Vice President
Wendl Kornfeld

Vice President Sales and Marketing
Marie-Christine Matter

Production Director
Karen M. Bochow

Marketing Director
Ann Middlebrook

Data Systems Manager/
Distribution/Grey Pages
Scott Holden

Marketing
Promotion/Editorial Manager
Mitchell Hinz
Marketing Coordinator
Lisa Wilker
Book Sales Coordinator
Cynthia Breneman

Advertising Sales
Advertising Coordinator
Shana Ovitz
Sales Representatives:
John Bergstrom
Kate Hoffman
Ellen Kasemeier
Barbara Preminger
Joe Safferson
Dave Tabler

Administration
Controller
Joel Kopel
Office Manager
Elaine Morrell
Accounts Manager
Connie Malloy
Accounting Assistants
Myron Yang
Mila Livshits
Administrative Assistant
Paula Cohen

Published by:
American Showcase, Inc.
915 Broadway, 14th Floor
New York, New York 10010
(212) 673-6600
FAX: (212) 673-9795

American Illustration
Showcase 15 Book 2 of 2
ISBN 0-931144-71-X
ISSN 0278-8128

Cover Credits:
Front Cover Illustration:
Rob Day
Lead Page Illustration:
David Wink

Production
Production Manager
Chuck Rosenow
Art Director/Studio Manager
Marjorie Finer
Production Coordinators
Zulema Rodriguez
Tracy Russek
Production Administrator
Pamela Schechter
Traffic Coordinator
Sandra Sierra

Grey Pages
Data Systems Assistant
Julia Curry

Special Thanks to:
Elizabeth Atkeson
Ron Canagata
Ken Crouch
Jeffrey Gorney
Hardy Hyppolite
Amir Iravani
Rita Muncie
Anne Newhall
George Phillips
Tina Sher

U.S. Book Trade Distribution:
Watson-Guptill Publications
1515 Broadway
New York, New York 10036
(212) 764-7300

For Sales outside the U.S.:
Rotovision S.A.
9 Route Suisse
1295 Mies, Switzerland
Telephone: 022-755-3055
Telex: 419246 ROVI
FAX: 022-755-4072

Mechanical Production:
American Showcase, Inc.

Typesetting:
The Ace Group, Inc.

Color Separation:
Universal Colour Scanning Ltd.

Printing and Binding:
Everbest Printing Co., Ltd.

ILLUSTRATION 2 OF 2

AMERICAN
SHOWCASE

CONTENTS

V I E W P O I N T S

G R A P H I C A R T S
O R G A N I Z A T I O N S

I N D E X

G R E Y P A G E S

Illustrators &
Photographers
at
Work

SHARP WORK AHEAD.

To find the right creative solutions, you've got to know where to look.

And when you own Corporate Showcase 10 you'll have access to the best photographers and illustrators working in America's corporate arena.

Not only that, you'll have a rich creative source-book for ideas and inspiration, offering the widest selections of styles and talent appropriate to every type of corporate communications.

And because Corporate Showcase 10 is a handy one-volume book, you'll slow down the traffic jam of portfolios and briefcases in your office.

So order Corporate Showcase 10 today. Send a check for $37.50 + $4.00 postage and handling for your paperback copy. Or call 212-673-6600.

And enter the fast lane of corporate work.

CORPORATE
SHOWCASE 10
The Work's Great

Published by American Showcase, 915 Broadway,
New York, NY 10010 212-673-6600.

Gal, Susan
San Francisco, CA 1002
Garbot, Dave
Tinley Park, IL 1003
Garland, Michael
Patterson, NY 1004
Garner, David
NYC 860
Garvie, Ben
San Francisco, CA 884
Gay-Kassel, Doreen
Princeton, NJ 1005
Gieseke, Thomas A.
Merriam, KS 1006
Gillies, Chuck Troy, MI 1140
Goldberg, Richard A.
Boston, MA 764,765
Goldman, Bart NYC 1007
Goldrick, Lisa
Ridgewood, NJ 1009
Goodrich, Carter
Stonington, CT 1010,1011
Gordon, David
Oakland, CA 1012
Gormady, Thomas
Austin, TX 1013
GrandPré, Mary
Saint Paul, MN 1014
Graphic Chart & Map Co., Inc. NYC 1015
Graves, David
Gloucester, MA 1016
Gregoretti, Rob
Woodside, NY 1017
Grimes Design, Inc., Don
Dallas, TX 885
Grimes, Rebecca
Westminster, MD 1018
Guitteau, Jud
Portland, OR 821
Gurney, John Steven
Brooklyn, NY 1019
Hahn, Marika
Palisades, NY 852
Haimowitz, Steve
Forest Hills, NY 1020
Halbert, Michael
Saint Louis, MO 1021
Hall, Bill
Arlington, TX 780,781
Hall, Joan
NYC 1022,1023
Hall, Kate Brennan
Saint Paul, MN 823
Hamilton, Ken
West Orange, NJ 1024
Hampton, Gerry
Huntington Harbour, CA 1025

Hansen, Biruta Akerbergs
Liverpool, PA 864
Hantel, Johanna
Nazareth, PA 1027
Harris, Leslie
Atlanta, GA 891
Harrison, Wm
Chicago, IL 832
Hart, John
Brooklyn, NY 1028,1029
Hayes, John
Chicago, IL 882
Healy, Deborah
Upper Montclair, NJ 817
Hendrix, Bryan
Atlanta, GA 1030
Henrie, Cary NYC 756,757
Henry-May, Rosemary
Washington, DC 1031
Herbert, Jonathan
NYC 829
Hess, Rob
East Greenwich, RI 1032
Hewitson, Jennifer
Cardiff, CA 1033
Hewitt, Margaret
Huntington, NY 1034
Hewitt/Low Studios
Huntington, NY 1034,1035
Higgins, Dave
Troy, MI 1140
Hill, Henry
Tucson, AZ 1036
Hoffman, Kate
Fort Collins, CO 1037
Holmes, Matthew
Carmichael, CA 844
Hong, Min Jae
Warwick, NY 776,777
Horjus, Peter
San Diego, CA 1038
Hovland, Gary
Manhattan Beach, CA 1039
Hubbard, Marcie Wolf
Silver Spring, MD 1040
Huerta, Gerard
Darien, CT Back Flap Book 1
Hughes, Dralene "Red"
New Berlin, WI 1041
Hutchinson, Bruce
Southboro, MA 889
Huyssen, Roger
Darien, CT Back Flap Book 2
Jaben, Seth NYC 774,775
Jareaux, Robin
Boston, MA 1042
Jarecka, Danuta
NYC 826

Jastrzebski, Zbigniew T.
Chicago, IL 1180
Jeffers, Kathy
NYC 1043
Jensen, Bruce
Woodside, NY 1044
Jinks, John NYC 786,787
Johnson, Steve
Minneapolis, MN 1045
Joyner, Eric
San Anselmo, CA 1046
Kachik, John
Baltimore, MD 1047
Kann, Victoria NYC 1048
Ketler, Ruth Sofair
Silver Spring, MD 1049
Kimball, Anton
Portland, OR 888
Kolosta, Darrel
San Francisco, CA 1050
Koster, Aaron
Manalapan, NJ 1051
Kotik, Kenneth William
Saint Peters, MO 1052,1053
Kovalcik, Terry NYC 1054
Krovatin, Dan
Monmouth Junction, NJ 1055
Kueker, Don
Saint Louis, MO 1056
Lackow, Andy
Guttenberg, NJ 843
Lawson, Pamela
Redlands, CA 881
LeBlanc, Terry
Newton, MA 1057
Lee, Jared D.
Lebanon, OH 839
Lee, Tim
Atlanta, GA 833
Leer, Rebecca J.
NYC 1058
Leonardo, Todd
Castro Valley, CA 1059
Lester, Mike
Duluth, GA 1060,1061
Levine, Andy
Long Island City, NY 1063
Lewis, H.B. NYC 1064,1065
Long, Suzanne M.
San Francisco, CA 1066
Löse, Hal
Philadelphia, PA 887
Low, William
Huntington, NY 1035
Lyhus, Randy
Bethesda, MD 1067
Lytle, John
Sonora, CA 1068

MacLeod, Ainslie
London, England 1069
Madrid, Carlos NYC 820
Mahoney, Katherine
Belmont, MA 836
Maisner, Bernard
NYC 857
Mannes, Don NYC 1070
Marden, Phil NYC 828
Marinelli, Jeff
Canandaigua, NY 1071
Marinsky, Jane
Buffalo, NY 1072
Marion, Bruce
Half Moon Bay, CA 1073
Mark, Roger
Lenexa, KS 1074
Marsh, James
London, England 1075
Marshall, Craig
San Francisco, CA 815
Martin, Gregory
Cardiff, CA 1077
Maslen, Barbara
Sag Harbor, NY 1078,1079
Masuda, Coco NYC 782
Masuda/Salerno
NYC 782,783
Mattos, John
San Francisco, CA 772,773
May, Jeff
Saint Louis, MO 1081
Mayer, Bill
Decatur, GA 758,759
McLoughlin, Wayne
NYC 861
McManus, Tom
Montclair, NJ 856
McNamara Associates Inc.
Troy, MI 806,807
Merrell, Patrick
NYC 1082,1083
Mezzapelle, Bruno
San Francisco, CA 859
Milgrim, David NYC 1084
Miliano, Ed NYC 1085
Mitchell, Celia
Astoria, NY 1086
Mitsuhashi, Yoko
NYC 1087
Monley, Jerry
Troy, MI 1138
Moonlight Press Studio
Ocean Breeze, NY 1088,1089
Moorhead, Meg Ann
NYC 1090
Morgan, Jacqui
NYC 778,779

212·243·7688

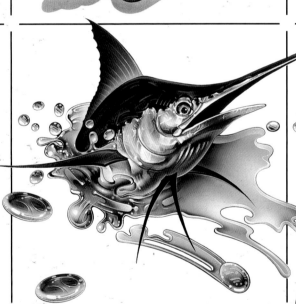

212·243·7688

Cary Henrie

310 EAST 46 STREET #5H, N.Y., N.Y. 10017 212 · 986 · 0299

Cary Henrie

310 EAST 46 STREET #5H, N.Y., N.Y. 10017 212 · 986 · 0299

Clients Include: TIME WARNER, AT&T, APPLE COMPUTER, LOTUS, SAMSUNG, MERRILL LYNCH, RJR NABISCO, NEW YORK LIFE, THE NEW YORK TIMES, BUSINESS WEEK, FORBES, ESQUIRE, SPORTS ILLUSTRATED, CONDÉ NAST TRAVELER, SCRIBNER'S, ST. MARTIN'S PRESS.

BILL MAYER INC., 240 FORKNER DRIVE, DECATUR, GA 30030 404-378-0686 FAX 404-373-1759

Excited

Petrified

Bored

Curious

Intimidated

Proud

Worried

Determined

Sleazy

Furious

Seething

Consoling

Sad

Adoring

Happy

STEVE BJÖRKMAN
Studio: 714·261·1411 FAX: 714·261·7528

New York
Madeline Renard 212·490·2450
FAX 212·697·6828

Chicago
Vincent Kamin 312·787·8834
FAX 312·787·8172

Los Angeles
Laurie Pribble 818·574·0288
FAX 818·574·3940

San Francisco
David Wiley 415·989·2023
FAX 415·989·6265

Delighted.

STEVE BJÖRKMAN
Studio: 714·261·1411 FAX: 714·261·7528

CATHLEEN TOELKE

RHINEBECK

NEW YORK

·

914 · 876 · 8776

·

FAX IN STUDIO

·

PORTFOLIOS

AVAILABLE IN

MANHATTAN

·

INQUIRE ABOUT

STOCK IMAGES

Global and Environmentally Safe

RICHARD A. GOLDBERG

368 Congress Street, 5th Floor
Boston, MA 02210
(617) 646-1041
(617) 646-0956 FAX

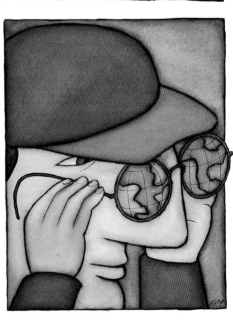

Global and Environmentally Safe

RICHARD A. GOLDBERG

368 Congress Street, 5th Floor
Boston, MA 02210
(617) 646-1041
(617) 646-0956 FAX

MICHAEL
DORET
Say "Door-ett"

310 - 376 - 2275

212 - 929 - 1688

TEST YOUR PROFIT Ability

WORTE DIE WIR SETZEN Stehen BESSER Da TypoPress

The GLOBAL PLANNER

NBA HERITAGE COLLECTION ESTD 1946

"His highly tuned linear skills are inspired by a childlike sensibility," *Innovators of American Illustration.*

ALAN E. COBER

95 Croton Dam Road, Ossining, New York 10562   914-941-8696

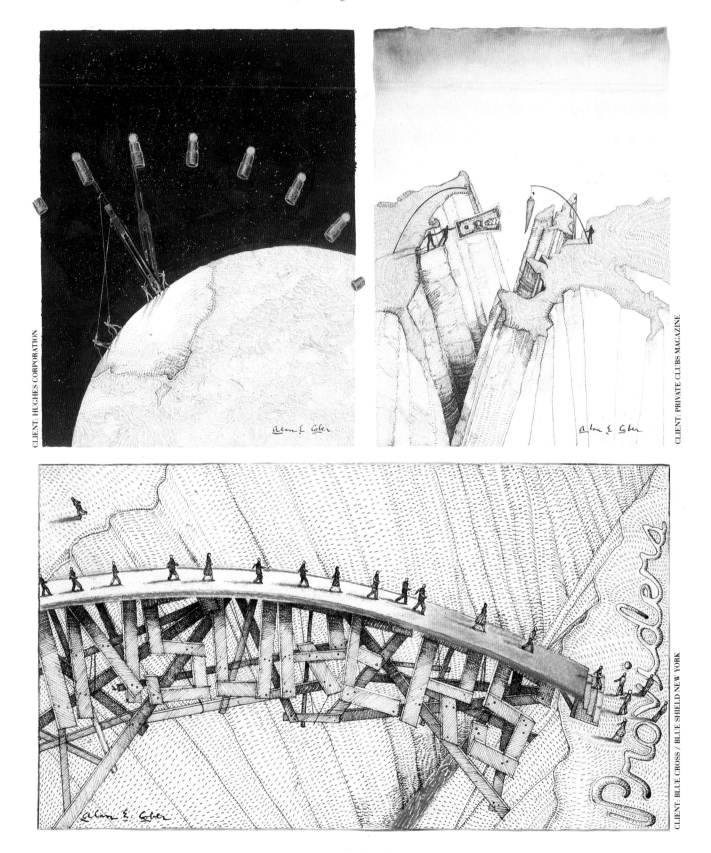

CLIENT: HUGHES CORPORATION

CLIENT: PRIVATE CLUBS MAGAZINE

CLIENT: BLUE CROSS / BLUE SHIELD NEW YORK

He has recently illustrated annual reports for Republic Bank, Squibb, Warner-Lambert, American International Group, Chicago Merchantile Exchange,
Equitable, 3-Com, Case-Western University and McKesson, and corporate literature for many of the Fortune 500. His work has
appeared in every major magazine, he has created sketchbooks of presidential campaigns for TIME, the space shuttle for NASA, and the great cities
of Europe for American Airlines. Included in over 300 awards are Artist of the Year, 11 medals including the Hamilton King Award
from the Society of Illustrators, NY, and 6 gold medals from the NYADC.

CA magazine said, "he draws the way he speaks." *Graphis* called him "the natural."

CORPORATE COBER

95 Croton Dam Road, Ossining, New York 10562   914-941-8696

CLIENT: MANAGING AUTOMATION

Call him! He'll Listen.

JOHN

ILLUSTRATION

MATTOS

415.397.2138

SETH JABEN™

Illustration

New York 212 • 673 • 5631

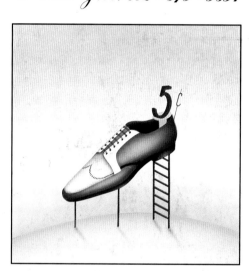

E. G. SMITH

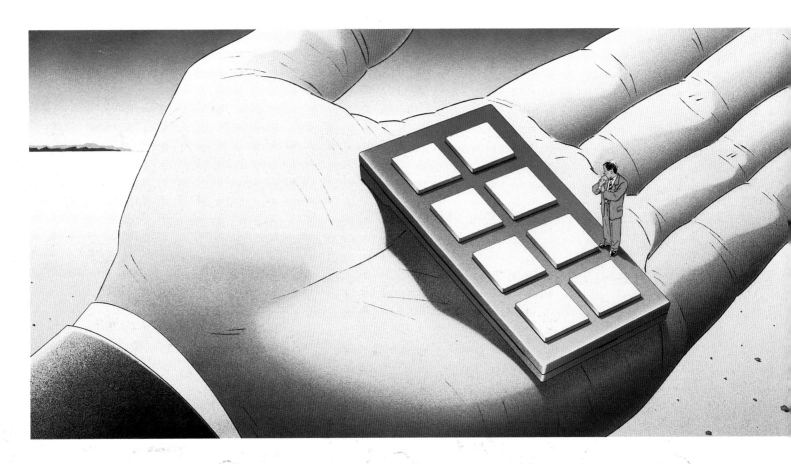

JACQUI MORGAN

Clients include: American Express, Architectural Digest, AT&T, Black Enterprise, Booz-Allen & Hamilton, CPC Int'l, Champion Papers, Citibank, Colgate Palmolive, Eli Lilly, Family Circle, First National Supermarkets, General Foods, Hilton Int'l, IBM, ITC, ITT Sheraton, Kellogg's, Kinney Shoes, Kmart, Kraft, Lear's, New Woman, New York Hospital for Special Surgery, New York Mag., Nuveen, Outdoor Life, Oxford University Press, Pfizer, Proctor & Gamble, St. Francis College, Scott Paper Co., Seiko, Self Magazine, Southern Bell, Stolichnaya, TIAA-CREF, Woman's Day.

JACQUI MORGAN STUDIO • 692 GREENWICH STREET • NEW YORK, NY 10014 • 212 • 463 • 8488 • FAX • 463 • 8688

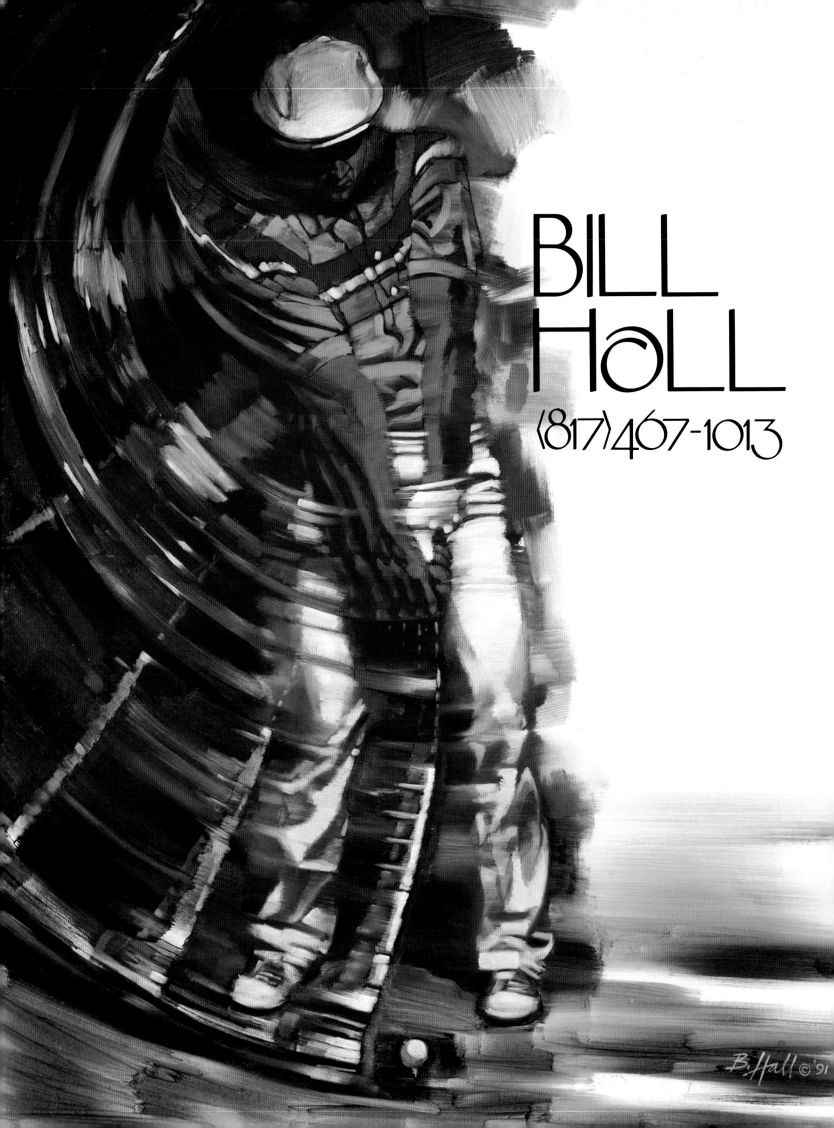

BILL
HaLL
(817) 467-1013

COCO MASUDA

Illustration &   *Design In Style*

MASUDA / SALERNO **212.727.1599** Fax: 212.727.2650

STEVEN SALERNO

Illustration &

Calligraphy

Hot Artists · Visual Arts · Movies · Theatre · Dance · Jazz · Classical Music

MASUDA / SALERNO **212.727.1599** Fax: 212.727.2650

ZIEMIENSKI

JIM LILIE 415 441·4384

JIM LILIE 415 441·4384

ZIELIENSKI

Kazuhiko Sano

Studio (415) 381-6377   Fax (415) 381-3847

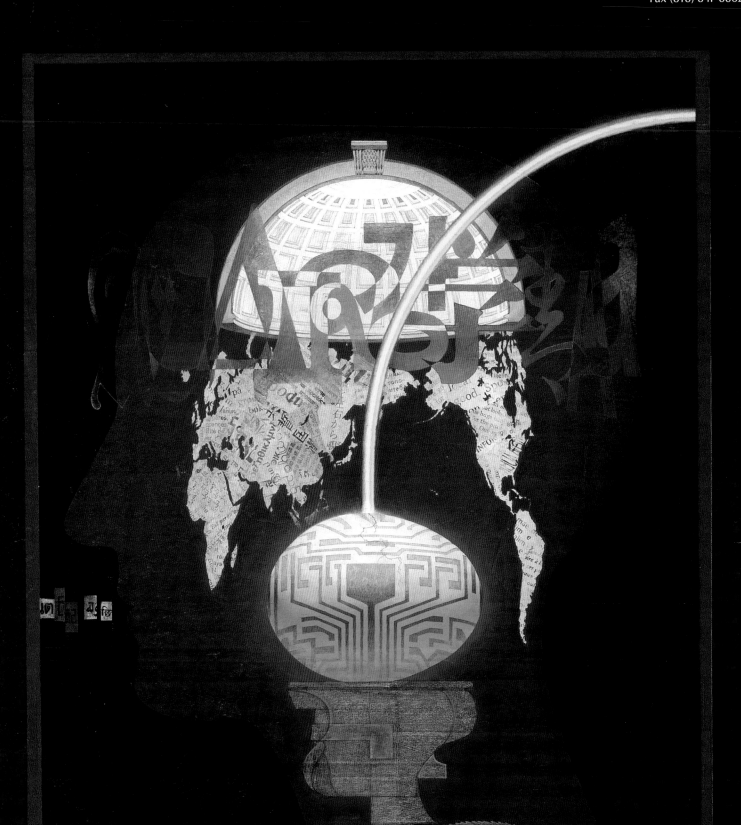

Acer Computer Corp./Global potentials in computer communication.

Kazuhiko Sano   Studio: (415) 381-6377   New York: (212) 490-2450   Los Angeles: (818) 985-8181

neiman-marcus

rolling stone

© 1992 the walt disney company

*from the book
'the art of mickey mouse'*

g e capital

Terry

Allen

164 daniel low terrace si ny 10301   *(718) 727 0723   fax (718) 727 0927*

the boston globe magazine

the society of publication designers

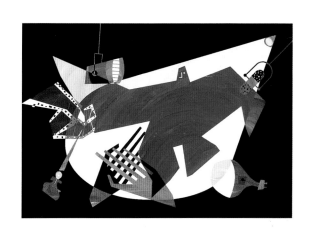

time-warner annual report

rolling stone

KEVIN SPROULS

"Kevin's wonderful illustrations speak for themselves.
But I'll speak for Kevin:
He's about the most worry-free illustrator
I've ever worked with."
-Colt Givner, Scali, McCabe & Sloves, New York

"A delight to work with, Kevin turned car parts into
wonderfully detailed works of art."
-Dria Hill, Hal Riney & Partners, San Francisco

jözef sumichrast

708 295 0255

jözef

jözef sumichrast

RENARD REPRESENTS
NEW YORK
212 490 2450

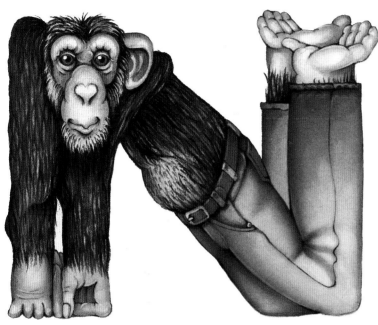

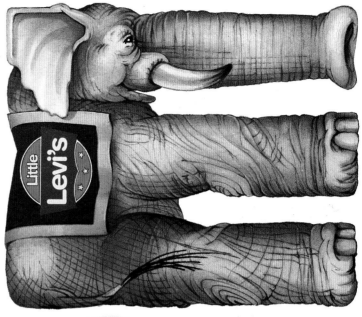

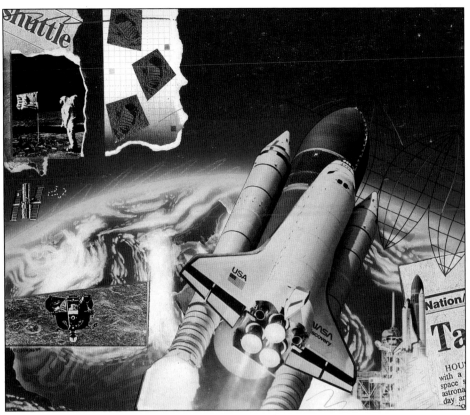

U.S. POSTAL SERVICE - GUIDE TO STAMPS: COVER ART

STUDIO

818.301.9662

FAX

818.303.1123

CHICAGO

RANDI FIAT & ASSOC.
312.664.8322

LOS ANGELES

REPERTORY
213.931.7449

SAN FRANCISCO

JAMES CONRAD
415.921.7140

JON CONRAD

STRAND LIGHTING - CAPABILITIES BROCHURE

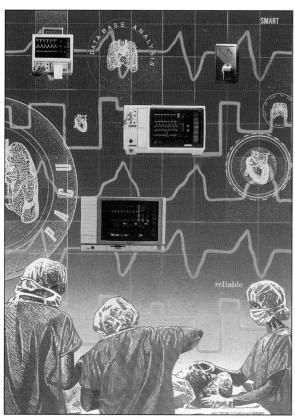

SPACE LABS - CAPABILITIES BROCHURE

DUGAN FARLEY ADVERTISING - SELF PROMOTION

STUDIO

818
301
9662

FAX

818
303
1123

JON CONRAD

HONDA GOLF CLASSIC - BOY SCOUTS OF AMERICA

ANTAR DAYAL

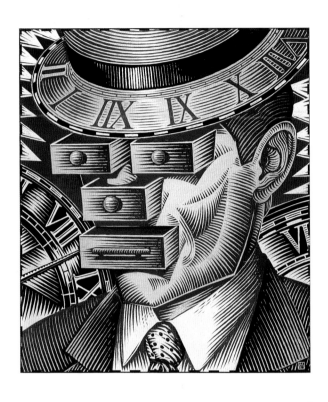

EAST

IRMELI HOLMBERG

212.545.9155   FAX 545.9462

STUDIO

707.544.8103

FAX 544.9340

WEST

JOANNE HEDGE

213.874.1661   FAX 874.0136

ANTAR DAYAL

EAST

212.545.9155 FAX 545.9462

STUDIO

707.544.8103

FAX 544.9340

WEST

213.874.1661 FAX 874.0136

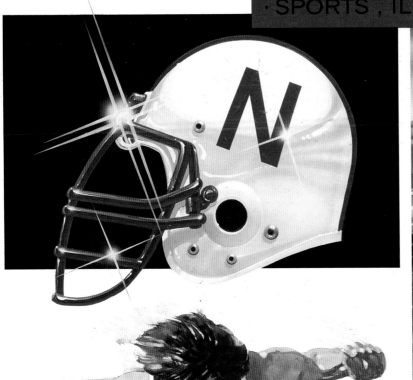

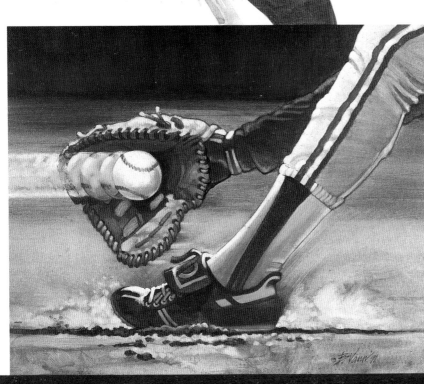

Joe Saffold

719 Martina Drive, N.E. ▪ Atlanta, GA 30305 ▪ FAX 404·364·9014 ▪ **404·231·2168**

Joe Saffold

719 Martina Drive, N.E. ▪ Atlanta, GA 30305 ▪ FAX 404·364·9014 ▪ **404·231·2168**

McNamara
Associates inc.

Advertising Artists

Over four decades of commitment
to the Advertising community.

1250 Stephenson Highway
Troy, Michigan 48083
313-583-9200
313-583-3033 fax

Please Contact:
James Maniere
Bruce MacDonald
Lou DeMaris

California Office
3858 Carson Street, Suite 105
Torrance, California 90503
213-540-6223
213-540-6303 fax

Please Contact:
Jim Coburn
Nereus Dastur

Other Representatives:
John Kubista
4 Park Avenue
New York, New York 10016
212-889-7787
212-759-5910

Will Sumpter & Associates
1728 North Springs Road
Atlanta, Georgia 30324
404-874-2014
404-874-8173 fax

The Willson Creative Group
355 North Ashland Avenue
Chicago, Illinois 60607
312-738-3555
312-738-4982 fax

T.D.F. Artists, Ltd
980 Yonge Street
Toronto, Ontario, Canada M4W-2J9
416-924-3371
419-924-7001 fax

STEPHEN
FOSTER inc.
ILLUSTRATION
STUDIO: (708)·835·2741
FAX: (708)·835·2783

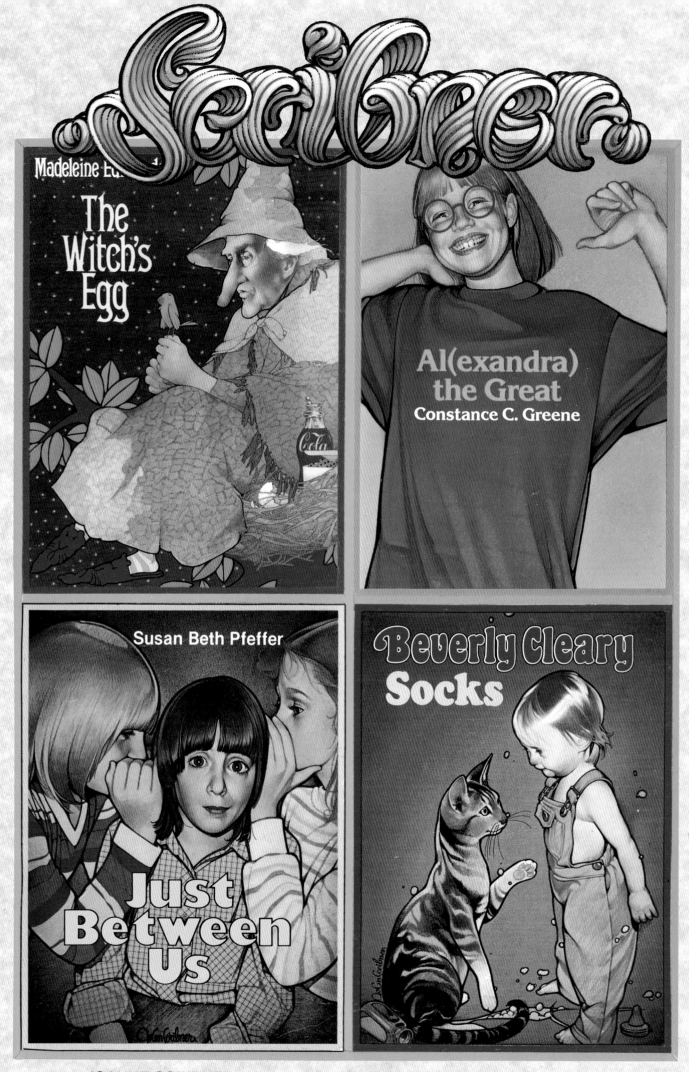

New York Studio
Telephone: (212) 533 2648
Fax: (212) 353 0131

California (Agent)
MARTHA PRODUCTIONS INC.
Telephone: (213) 204 1771

EQUILIBRIUM
Stanislaw Fernandes

London Studio
Telephone: (071) 352 3845
Fax: (071) 351 2677

Bologna (Agent)
MARIA-LUISA NERI
Telephone: (51) 261253

Illustration, images and lettering
for advertising, corporate,
and publishing

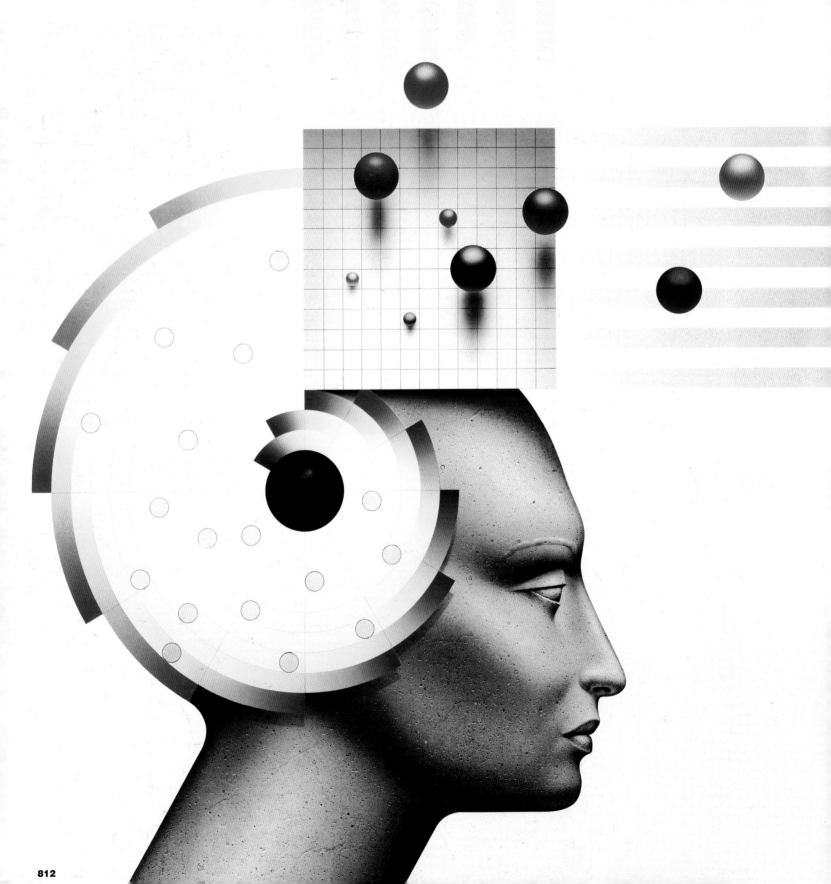

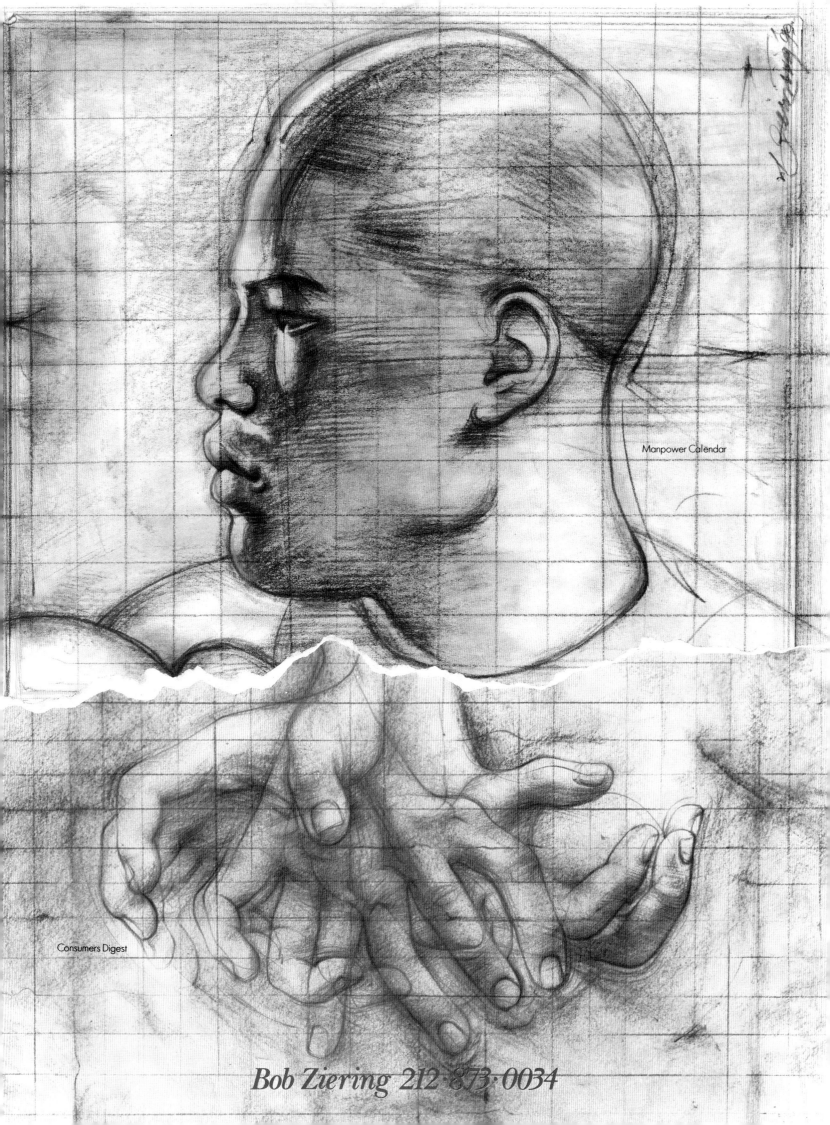

Manpower Calendar

Consumers Digest

Bob Ziering 212·873·0034

CRAIG MARSHALL

Represented By
Jim Lilie
(415) 441·4384

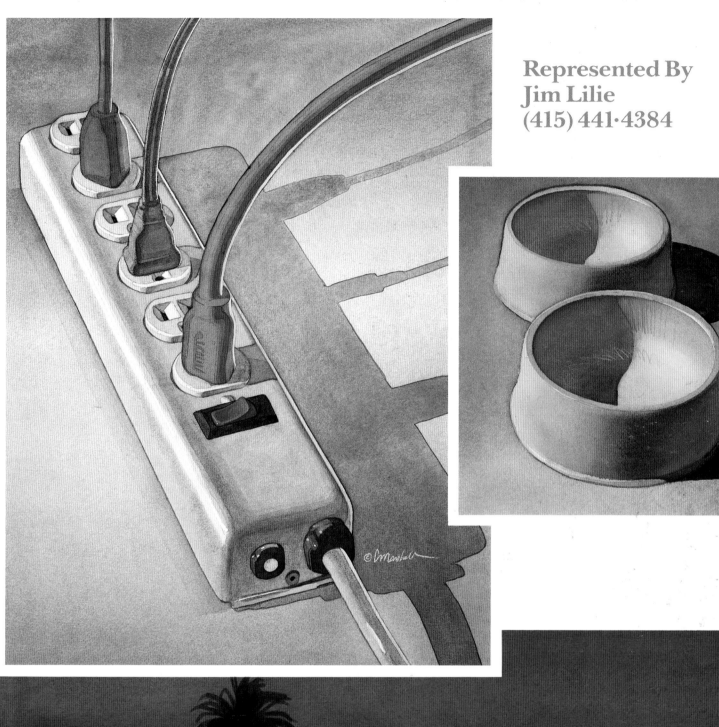

william RieSer

fax [312] 883 0375

[312] 222 0337

DEBORAH HEALY
201 746 2549

ARDEN VON HAEGER
ILLUSTRATION

DUGALD STERMER
Represented by Jim Lilie

[415] 777-0110
[415] 441-4384

HOT · DOG

approx 5"

The BASEBALL

Made by Rawlings
108 stitches
Weight: 5–5¼ ounces
Cowhide cover

First yarn winding
Cushioned cork center
Second yarn winding
Third yarn winding
Fourth yarn winding

Circumference: 9–9¼"

JOHN (HONUS) WAGNER

"THE FLYING DUTCHMAN"

"...And it turned out that while Honus was the best third baseman in the league, he was also the best first baseman, the best second baseman, the best shortstop and the best outfielder; that was in fielding. And since he led the league in batting eight times between 1900 and 1911, you knew that he was the best hitter, too...as well as the best base runner."

—TOMMY LEACH
Pittsburgh Pirate

AFRICAN ELEPHANT

PEREGRINE FALCON

MISSION BLUE

CALIFORNIA CONDOR

FLORIDA PANTHER

MANATEE

HUMPBACK WHALE

BLACK RHINOCEROS

LOGGERHEAD TURTLE

SAN FRANCISCO GARTER SNAKE

CARLOS MADRID

ILLUSTRATION

212·541·5797

DESIGN

JUD GUITTEAU

Studio
Tel: (503) 282-0445
Fax: (503) 282-0445

Renard Represents
Tel: (212) 490-2450
Fax: (212) 697-6828

JOHN JUDE PALENCAR

▼ FLOATING INVESTMENTS ▲ POSTGRADUATE MEDICINE / WATERCOLOR ▼ANHEUSER BUSCH ▼ EARTH CAPITOL / MIXED MEDIA

6763 MIDDLEBROOK BLVD. MIDDLEBURG HTS., OHIO 44130 • (216) 676-8839 • STUDIO (216)845-8163

KATE BRENNAN HALL

PHIL SCHEUER 126 FIFTH AVENUE NY NY 10011 212·620·0728

DANUTA JARECKA

ILLUSTRATOR

114 EAST 7 STREET #15

NEW YORK. NY 10009

212 ●. 353 3298

CARMELA  EMERSON

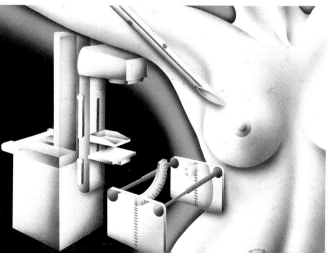

PHIL MARDEN ILLUSTRATION

Studio:
28 East 21st St., #2B
New York, NY 10010
(212) 260-7646
FAX: (212) 260-7701

Represented By:
David Starr
(212) 254-0321

Jonathan Herbert **COMPUTER** Illustration

SCOTT SAWYER

508 4th Street, San Francisco, California 94107   (415) 227-0539

CATHY SAKSA

SPECIALIZING IN COLLAGE, PHOTOMONTAGE, HAND-COLORING, AND CUT PAPER ILLUSTRATION

41 UNION SQUARE W.

NEW YORK CITY

NEW YORK, 10003

SUITE 1001

TEL. (212) 255-5539

FAX. (212) 243-4571

TO SEE MORE WORK

PLEASE CALL!

W^M HARRISON

I L L U S T R A T I O N

NEW YORK:
RENARD REPRESENTS   212·490·2450

CHICAGO:
DAN SELL   312·565·2701

LOS ANGELES:
JAE WAGONER   213·392·4877

IF YOU HAVE GOOD NEWS, OR MONEY:
BILL HARRISON   708·232·7733

To see more of this
illustrator's work,
please consult index
for Book 1.

TIM LEE

I L L U S T R A T I O N

404-938-8829
1715 Brantford Dr.
Atlanta, GA
30084

BALVIS RUBESS

260 Brunswick Avenue, Toronto, Ontario, Canada, M5S 2M7 (416) 927-7071

RON CHAN

REPRESENTED BY JIM LILIE   TEL 415.441.4384   FAX 415.395.9809

KATHERINE MAHONEY
617·868·7877
617·489·0406

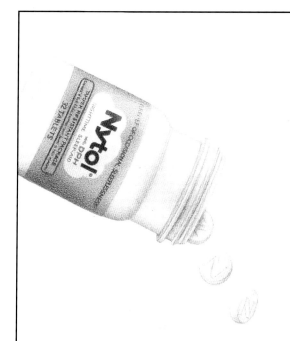

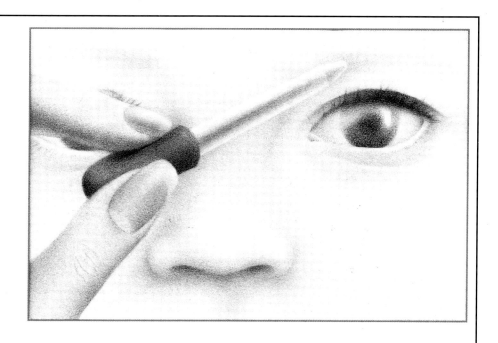

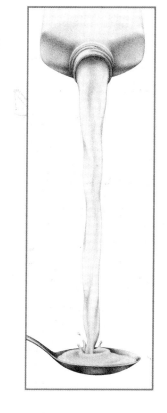

A Delicious, Healthy Combination!

Burton Morris

-ILLUSTRATION-

Telephone (412) 441-2740 or Fax (412) 661-2898

Represented in the Midwest by David Montagano (312) 527-3283

Viking / Penquin Press

More Direct

Kelly Michener

Folio Magazine

DAVID BISHOP

ILLUSTRATION

DAVID BISHOP

610 22ND ST. #311

SAN FRANCISCO

CALIFORNIA 94107

415·558·9532

JOSÉ ORTEGA   212 · 772 · 3329

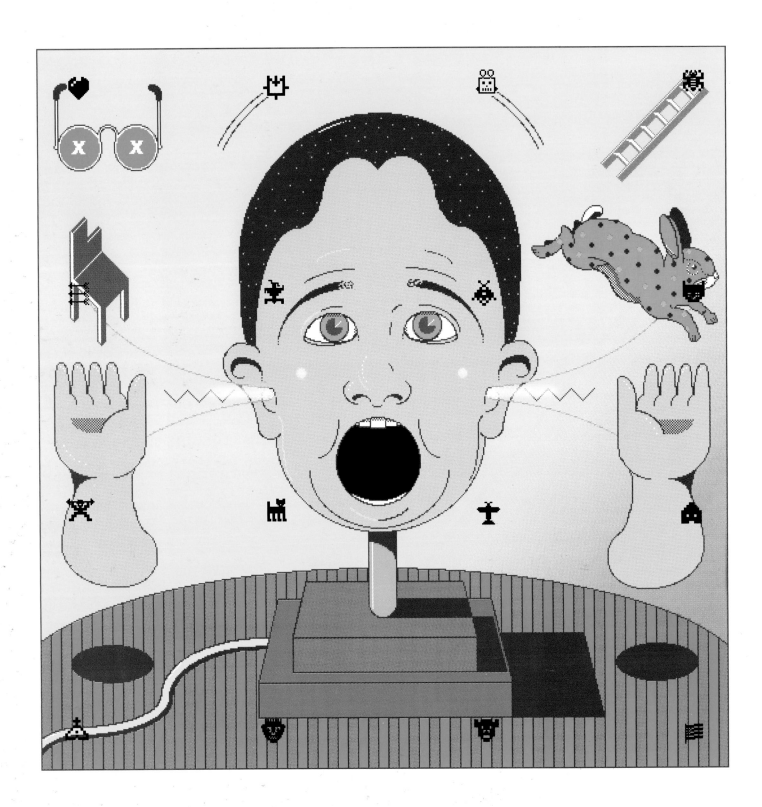

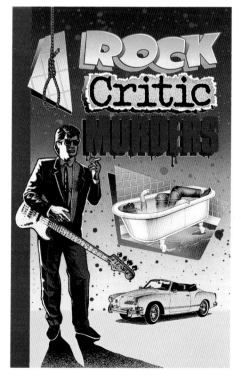

PRICE WATERHOUSE/"GLOBAL BANKING"

ROSANNE PERCIVALLE

212·633·2480

CLIENTS INCLUDE: ATLANTIC RECORDS NBC RANDOM HOUSE

GRAPHIC ARTS MONTHLY CHANGING TIMES

LEADERS ELECTRA/ASYLUM RECORDS PRICE WATERHOUSE

JSB JAPAN SATELLITE BROADCASTING TIMES BOOKS WORKING MOTHER

DEC PROFESSIONAL BOOK OF THE MONTH CLUB

RICE WATERHOUSE/"BANKING"

DOING OUR PART FOR OUR PART OF THE WORLD

ANNUAL REPORT COVER/DELMARVA POWER COMPANY/PHOTOGRAPHY BY: CARLOS ALEJANDRO

©ROSANNE PERCIVALLE '91

RAWSON
illustration

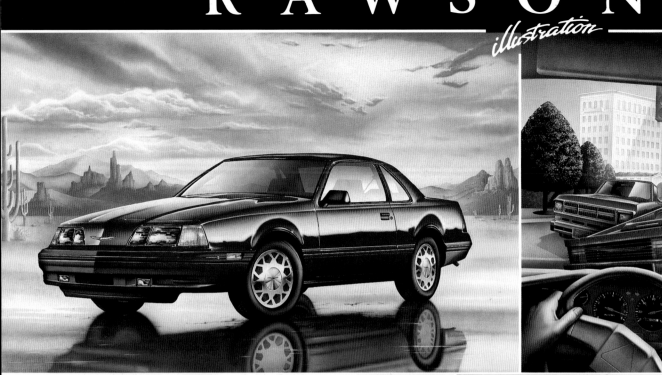

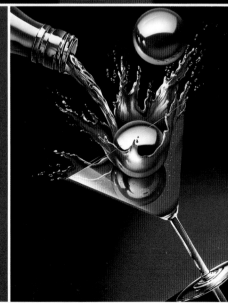

RAWSON ILLUSTRATION
1225 SOUTH HAMILTON, LOCKPORT, ILLINOIS 60441 (815) 838-4462 / (312) 266-4884
FAX (815) 838-4463

Holler, scream, vociferate, yell, get on the horn, buzz, dial, bellow, fax, phone or shout for J.W. Burkey.

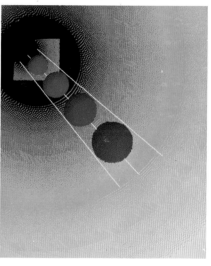

• For effective, award-winning digitized photo illustration, do any or all of the above. • Burkey Studios in Dallas: phone Kathy Jane Hill at 214-559-0802 or fax 214-559-3688. On the West Coast, phone Maria Piscopo at 714-556-8133 or fax 714-556-0899 • Clients include: Pepsi-Cola, American Express, Frito-Lay, Apple Computer, IBM, American Airlines and Taco Bell

D E B R A   W H I T E

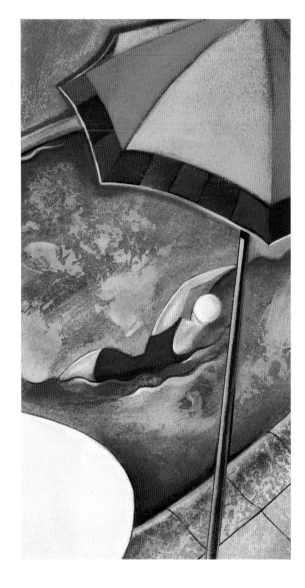

BILL CIGLIANO

To see more of this
illustrator's work,
please consult index
for Book 1.

Renard Represents
Tel: (212) 490-2450
Fax: (212) 697-6828

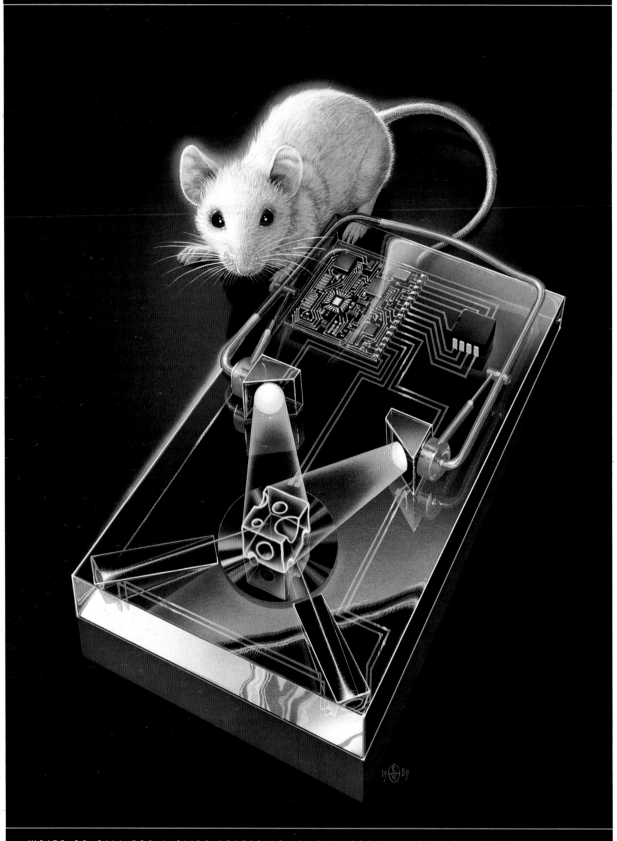

WRITE OR CALL FOR A SLIDE PORTFOLIO   247 N. GOODMAN ST. ROCHESTER, NY 14607

RICHARD WEHRMAN

THE BOB WRIGHT CREATIVE GROUP INC.

716 · 271 · 2280

DAVID CAIN
ABLE ILLUSTRATOR

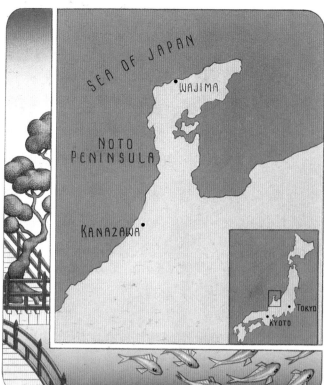

200 WEST 20 ST. #607

NEW YORK, N.Y. 10011

2 1 2 6 3 3 0 2 5 8

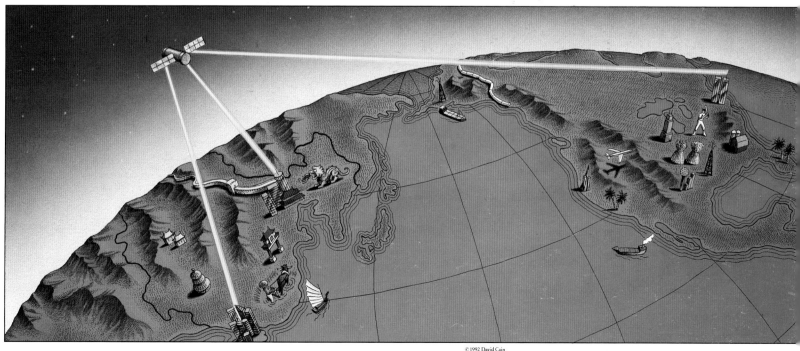

MARIKA HAHN 914.365.3317

THEO RUDNAK

To see more of this
illustrator's work,
please consult index
for Book 1.

Renard Represents

Tel: (212) 490-2450
Fax: (212) 697-6828

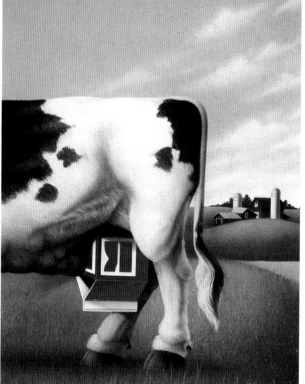

G R E G
COUCH
51 SEVENTH AVE #2
BROOKLYN • NY • 11217
718 • 789 • 9276

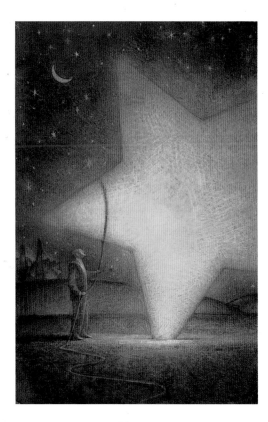

Gary Zamchick

DAdA BASE DESIGN

155 East 23rd Street
New York NY 10010
212.473.0363

BELL ATLANTIC

THE NEW YORK TIMES

NATIONAL CAR RENTAL

SAKS FIFTH AVENUE

TIME MAGAZINE

BUSINESS WEEK MAGAZINE

AT&T

CHASE MANHATTEN BANK

855

McManus

BERNARD MAISNER • The "Zelig" of Hand-Lettering.

BERNARD MAISNER HAND LETTERING

Represented by
GERALD & CULLEN RAPP, INC.
108 East 35 St. ◇ New York 10016
(212) 889-3337 • Fax (212) 889-3341

TIM BARRALL

372 BLEECKER STREET, NYC, 10014 TEL: 212-243-9003 FAX: 212-675-1939

WAYNE McLOUGHLIN

To see more of this
illustrator's work,
please consult index
for Book 1.

Renard Represents

Tel: (212) 490-2450
Fax: (212) 697-6828

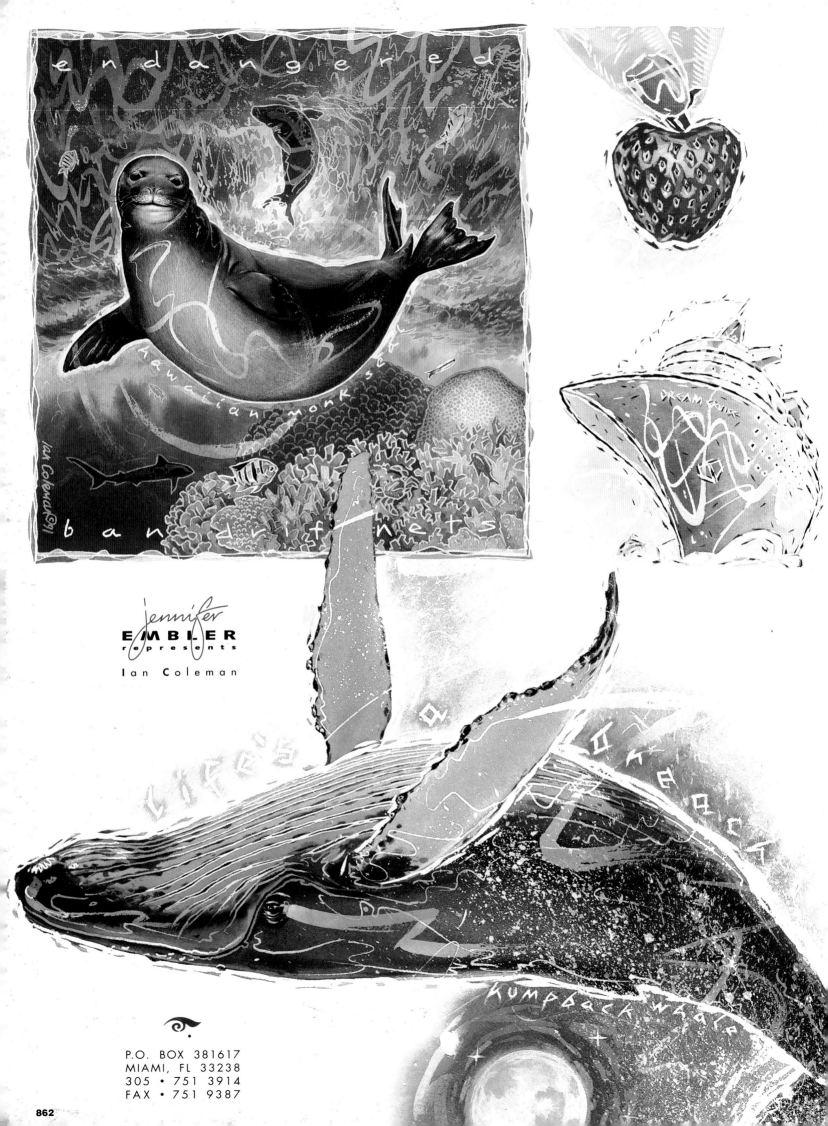

Jennifer
EMBLER
represents

Ian Coleman

JEFFREY OH 410-661-6064
FAX AVAILABLE

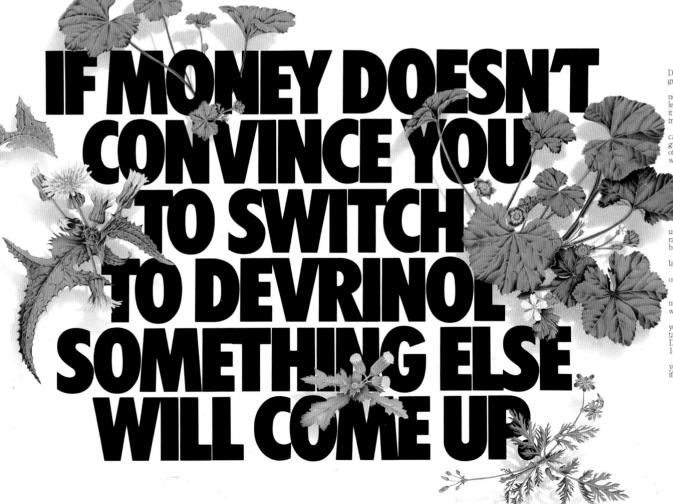

IF MONEY DOESN'T CONVINCE YOU TO SWITCH TO DEVRINOL SOMETHING ELSE WILL COME UP

The reasons to switch to DEVRINOL® herbicide keep growing.

Because DEVRINOL is not only, pound for pound, less expensive than Surflan, it's far more effective in controlling tough weeds.

Consider this: One application of DEVRINOL will give you long lasting control of more than 40 broadleaf weeds and grasses.

Including tough, problem weeds like groundsel, malva, sow thistle, filaree, purple cudweed and pineappleweed.

Six weeds that Surflan can't control.

And DEVRINOL can be used effectively with a wide range of tank-mixes. Even burndown herbicides.

Yet it's perfectly safe for labeled young plantings.

But if you're still not sold on DEVRINOL, look at it this way:

Surflan is costing you more money to control fewer weeds.

Figure that one out. If you can't, maybe you should talk to your dealer about DEVRINOL. Or call ICI at 1-800-759-2500.

But do it today. Because you know what will come up if you don't.

DEVRINOL
Herbicide

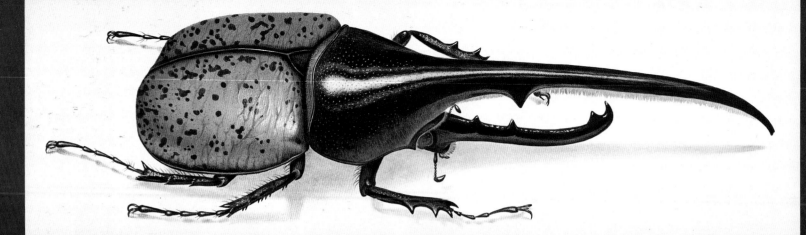

Biruta Akerbergs Hansen

SUN HILL
RD 1, Box 39G
Liverpool, PA 17045

(717) 444-3682
FAX (717) 444-7483

Clients include:
- American Family Physician
- Ciba-Geigy
- Discover
- Harper & Row
- Marriott
- National Wildlife Federation
- Pittman-Moore
- Pop-Shots
- Random House
- Reader's Digest
- Scientific American
- Smithsonian Institution
- Smithsonian Magazine
- Time-Life Books
- Union Carbide/Rhone-
  Poulenc
- Yankee
- Zoobooks

Pop-up books:
- Simon & Schuster, Inc.
- Stewart, Tabori & Chang
- National Geographic Soc.

Additional work:
- The Artist's Magazine,
  July 1988
- American Showcase 13, 14
- Society of Illustrators 32

It's no accident that Mother Nature put her most prized foods in hard-to-open containers.

Support North Carolina Shell Fishermen and taste the freshness of homegrown.

Baby Gap

Poster/ The Washington Market School

Poster/ Decus Convention

Times Mirror

DAVID RICKERD

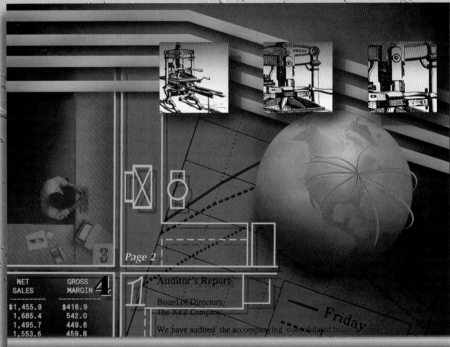

Represented by **SuperStudio**
Digital Photo-illustration and Retouching
50 West 23rd Street, New York, NY 10010 Tel: 212.627.4111

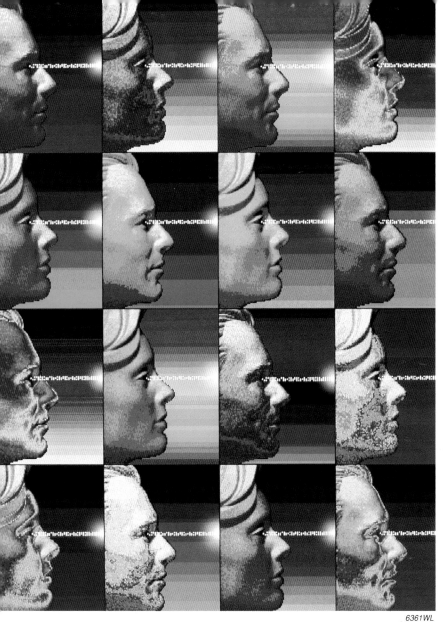

6361WL

Choices...

Westlight offers you total creative freedom with unsurpassed variety. And, Westlight stays on the edge by adding thousands of new images each month including:

Maps

World global, polar and flat plane views; North America, USA, European and Pacific Rim countries, all with a full spectrum of color choices.

Special Effects

Special effects covering a wide range of styles from color palettes to explosions.

Computer Graphics

Covering all styles, with many surprising colors and textures.

5974WL

8432WL

5249W.

Westlight®

1-800-872-7872

FAX 1-310-820-2687

Overnight Delivery — Standard Industry Practices and Terms

8431WL

PAULA · COHEN

524 Henry Street • Brooklyn, N.Y. 11231 • 718 852 7496

STUDIO
312.404.0375
312.404.0377 FAX

JERRY ANTON
EAST COAST REPRESENTATIVE
119 WEST 23RD STREET
NEW YORK, NEW YORK 10011
212.633.9880
212.691.1685 FAX

MARTHA PRODUCTIONS
WEST COAST REPRESENTATIVE
4445 OVERLAND AVENUE
CULVER CITY, CALIFORNIA 90230
213.204.1771
213.204.4598 FAX

JOHN S. DYKES

17 Morningside Dr. S. □ Westport, CT 06880 □ (203) 222-8150 Fax 222-8155

Client: Businessweek

Client: Network Computing

JAMES CHAFFEE

Represented By

David Wiley
Artists' Representative
415.989.2023   Fax 415.989.6265

STUDIO (916) 348-6345

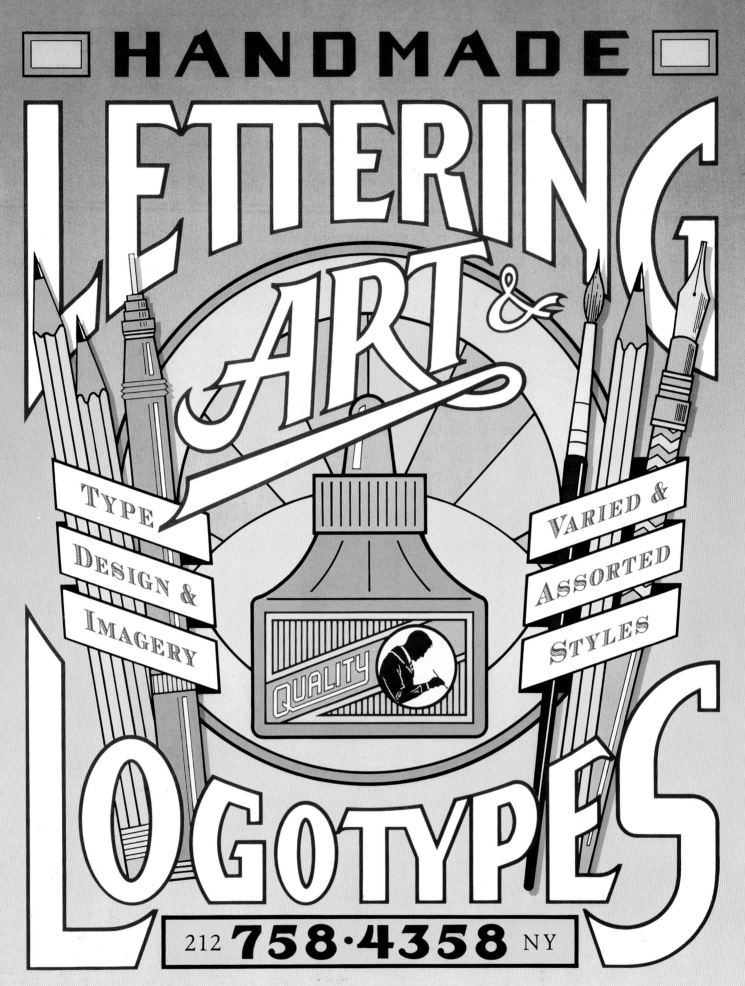

HANDMADE LETTERING ART & LOGOTYPES

TYPE DESIGN & IMAGERY

VARIED & ASSORTED STYLES

QUALITY

212 **758·4358** NY

 Paul Perlow Design • 123 East 54 Street, NY, NY 10022 • 212 758 4358
Represented in Paris, France • Hugo Weinberg Associés • 1-4 266 6200

DAVID AUSTIN CLAR

104 Loyalist Avenue

Rochester, NY 14624

PHONE 716 • 247-2050

FAX 716 • 426-4467

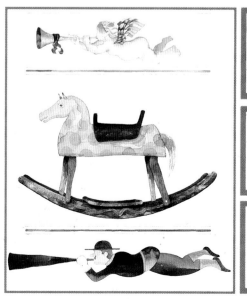

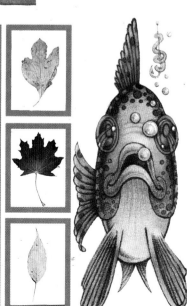

AndreaBrooks
ILLUSTRATION

99 BANK ST./3G, NYC 10014, (212) 633-1477

Clients include:

Continental Airlines
Spiedel
Presbyterian Church
U.S.A.
Scott Paper Co.
Avon Products Inc.
Charles of the Ritz
Revlon
Coty
Elizabeth Arden
International Wildlife
Redbook
J.P. Stevens & Co.
Little Brown & Co.
Random House
Western Publishing
Putnam Publishing Group
The Scribner Book
Companies
W. Atlee Burpee Co.

Member:

Graphic Artists Guild
Society of Illustrators

874

Bill Farnsworth

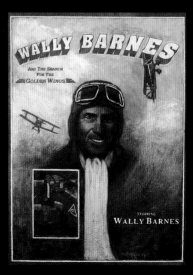

(203) 355-1649 PO BOX 653 NEW MILFORD, CT 06776

EZRA
©1992

EZRA TUCKER
REPRESENTED BY
JIM LILIE
(415) 441-4384

BETSY SCHELD

212 465 9945

RAY VELLA

20 NORTH BROADWAY
BLDG. I - 240
WHITE PLAINS, N.Y. 10601

PHONE: 914-997-1424
FAX/MODEM: 914-686-0538

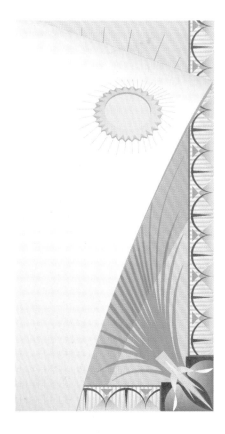

Business Week Magazine
The New York Times
Manufacturers Hanover Trust
McCall's
Gannett Newspapers
Syracuse University
The National Law Journal
Mullen Advertising
American Express
Knight Ridder Newspapers
P.C. Magazine
Fairchild Publications
Washington University
Newhouse Communications
Ziff-Davis Publications
Communications Week Magazine
San Francisco Examiner
Scholastic Magazines

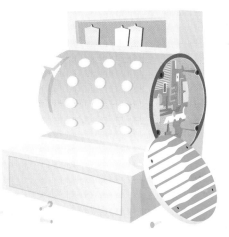

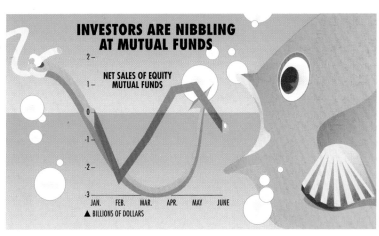

INVESTORS ARE NIBBLING
AT MUTUAL FUNDS

NET SALES OF EQUITY
MUTUAL FUNDS

JAN. FEB. MAR. APR. MAY JUNE
▲ BILLIONS OF DOLLARS

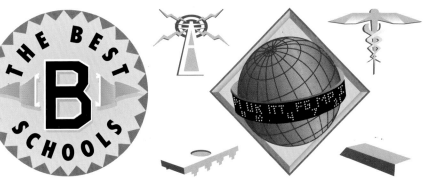

ROB WESTERBERG

34 Hillside Avenue, 4v
New York, New York 10040
212 · 567 · 1884
Humorous Illustration

"Hey, listen...
what's
black, white,
and
colored
all over?"

(714)-792-9245

REDLANDS, CA

PAUL WILEY
800 627 8071
212 EAST AND WEST COASTS

BEN GARVIE

Don Grimes Design, Inc.
3514 Oak Grove
Dallas, TX 75204
214 526 0040

MARX BROTHERS
FRESH SWEET FRUITS

Jack the Ripper is looking for you

Release me!

Pool Patrol

Mexico's fiesta of the senses

Expressions

Arkansas

Heart & Soul

CAREER
GAME

A Stroke of Genius

AT&T, American Airlines, Benson & Hedges, Maybelline, Miller Brewing, PBS, Schenley Industries, Sea Ray,
Southwestern Bell, Sports Illustrated, Steak & Ale, Stouffer Hotels, Texas Instruments, Tropical Blend and Zales

To see more, refer to American Showcase volumes 7, 8, 9, 10, 11, 12, 13, and 14.

Donna Ruff

Studio 203.866.8626 • 212.580.9056   Fax 203.866.8005

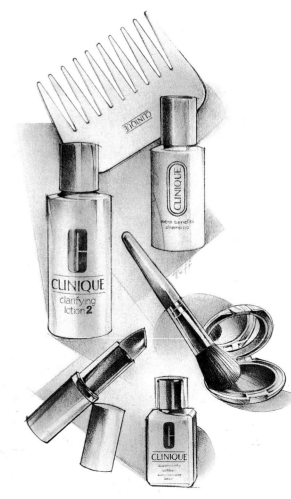

886

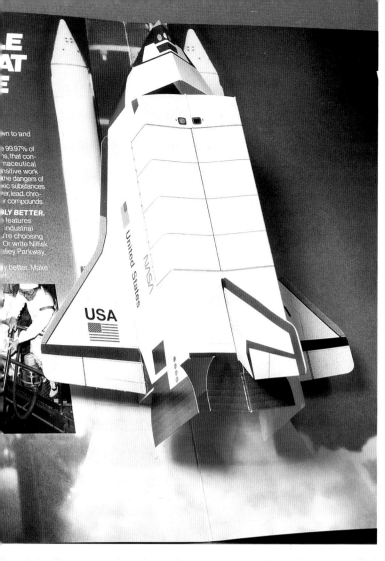

HAL LŌSE   (215) 849-7635
PAPER SCULPTURE / POP-UPS

ANTON KIMBALL DESIGN

820 SE SANDY BOULEVARD

PORTLAND OREGON 97214

503 234-4777 FAX 234-4687

VAMPIRES

192 SOUTHVILLE ROAD
508·872·4549
SOUTHBORO, MA 01772

BRUCE HUTCHISON

REPRESENTED BY SHARON KURLANSKY

PORTLAND PIPE LINE
Une Source de Fierté Depuis 50 Ans
1941 LES PIPE·LINE MONTRÉAL 1991

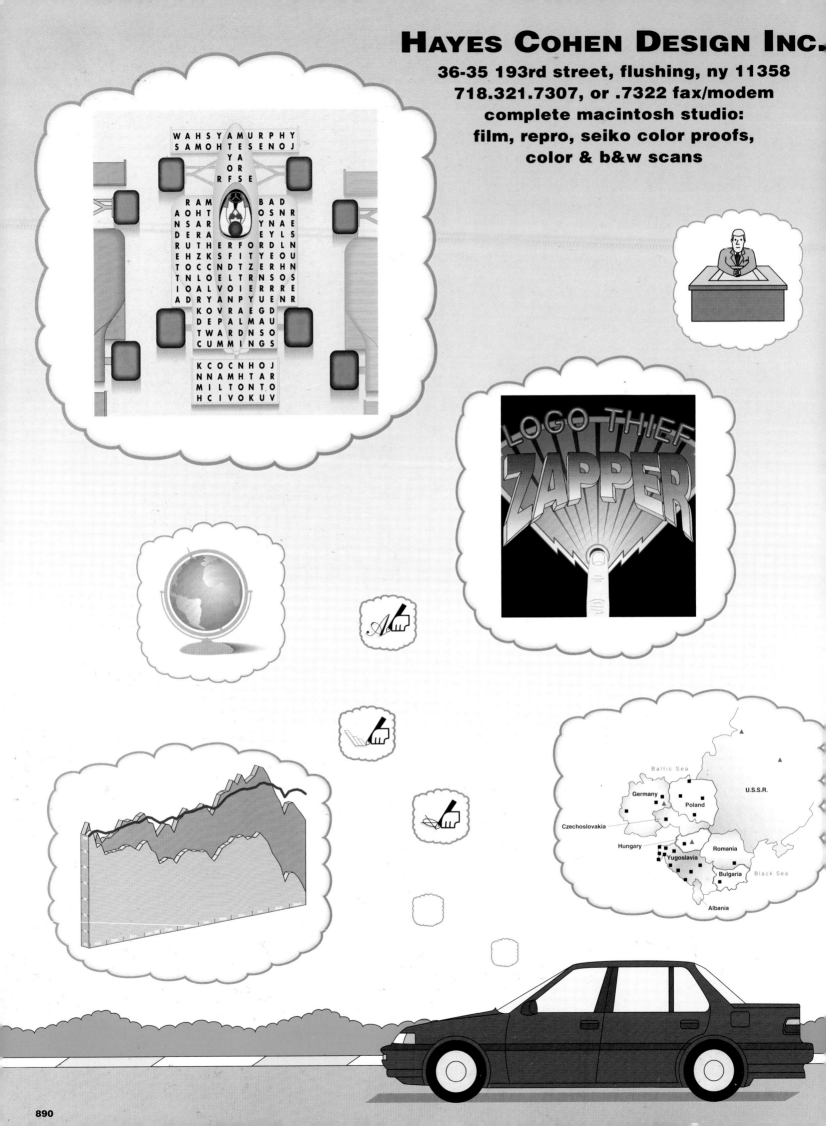

LESLIE HARRIS

(404) 872-7163 FAX IN STUDIO

TED GADECKI

NATIONAL SAFETY COUNCIL

NATIONAL SAFETY COUNCIL

RHEA + KAISER ADV.

708·213·9003

FAX IN STUDIO

ILLUSTRATION

STORM

PHONE: (708) 369-0164
FAX: (708) 369-4004

6293 SURREY RIDGE ROAD
LISLE, IL 60532

J e a n - F r a n c o i s **PODEVIN**

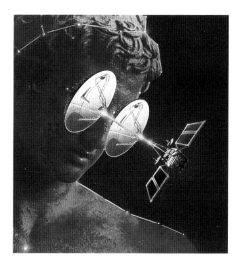

L.A. : (2 1 3) 9 4 5 - 9 6 1 3 , **N.Y.** : (2 1 2) 9 6 4 - 4 2 4 4 , *Fax* : (2 1 3) 9 4 5 - 9 6 1 4

Lisa Adams
100 West 12th Street
Studio 4H
New York, New York 10011
(212) 691-3238
FAX: (212) 691-3238

Represented in London:
Tony Parsons
011-44-71-833-9292

Clients include: Adweek; AC&R; Ally & Gargano; BusinessWeek; Hill, Holliday; Lotus; Lord & Taylor; Little, Brown; Macy's; NY Times; McCalls; New York Woman; New Yorker; MacDougall Co.; Penthouse; People; Random House; Revlon; Saatchi & Saatchi; Spring

O'Brien; Sports Illustrated for Kids; Simon & Schuster; Whittle Communications.

Additional work refer to Showcase 13, 14

Member Graphic Artist Guild
Member Society of Publication Designers

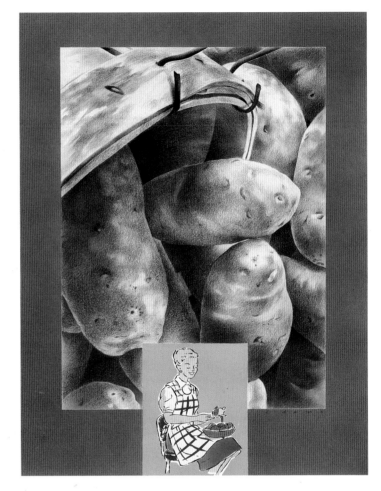

Steven Adler

Contact:
**Frank & Jeff Lavaty
& Associates**
509 Madison Avenue
New York, New York 10022
(212) 355-0910   FAX in studio

John Allison
3747 Washington
Kansas City, Missouri 64111
(816) 561-7782

Thomas Amorosi
6 Compton Street
East Rockaway, New York 11518
(516) 596-0160 Studio
(516) 593-3845 Messages

Color and B/W conceptual, editorial, medical and scientific illustration. Work appears in AS 14, Illustrators 33, Dir. of Illustration #8 and 1991 Medical Illustration Source Book.

Clients: Insurance Review;Cosmopolitan; Annual Review Inc.; Hunter College,

CUNY; NYU; Bryn Mawr College.

Awards: Society of Illustrators 33rd Annual National Exhibition.

Affiliations: Graphic Artist Guild Association of Medical Illustrators Guild of Natural Science Illustrators

Philip Anderson
245 Broadway
Arlington, Massachusetts 02174
(617) 641-3823
FAX in studio

Lori Anzalone
35-02 Berdan Avenue
Fair Lawn, New Jersey 07410
(201) 796-5588
(201) 796-5960
FAX: (201) 796-2698

Clients Include:
AT&T, Agfa, Becton Dickinson, Bic, Ciba-Geigy, Colgate/Palmolive, Elizabeth Arden, General Foods, Gloria Vanderbilt, Grand Union, Letraset, Lipton, Maxell, Molson, NJ Bell, NJ Lottery, Panasonic, Pathmark, Prudential, Port Authority of NY & NJ, Ralph Lauren, Random House/Knopf, Siemens, Schering Plough, Sharp, Squibb, Subaru, Warner Lampert, Winsor & Newton.

For additional work, see:
American Showcase 14, pg. 901
NJ Source 4, pg. 190
NJ Source 5, pg. 147

DO WE KNOW WHAT MAKES ADVERTISING COMMUNICATE?

After intimate contact with 25,000 commercials, I can't have helped developing some fairly unshakable conclusions, if only implicitly, about which messages communicate and which of them don't.

Over the years, Miner Raymond Associates has consulted for a gratifyingly large number of America's most successful advertisers, each of which seems disposed toward a different method of copy research (ASI, ASI-Plus, Burke, ARS, McCollum-Spielman, Clucas, Phase One, CW1 and a dozen other techniques). This huge database of research methods and results led to an interesting observation: Irrespective of methodology, the same factors keep cropping up again and again as having positive effects on both recall and persuasion scores. A cardinal principle as an example: Visualizing a product's end-result benefit in an interesting and memorable way inevitably leads to enhanced recall and persuasion scores. Yet over half the commercials on today's television fail to Visualize the End Result Benefit (VERB) .

To be sure, no one knows precisely what sort of advertising actually moves goods or alters perceptions. But I'd have to have been deaf, blind and distracted not to have noted those factors that enrich recall and persuasion results, irrespective of research method used for testing.

I grew even more interested in the subject when it became utterly conclusive that the research-derived factors boosting recall and persuasion mirror absolutely classic principles of selling. Lessons I learned about copy strategy, execution, and communication, growing out of a lifetime of writing, reviewing, and producing commercials, are the same ones that show up in research reports and analyses. What all researchers are reconfirming across the board is exactly what has been the advertising writer's instinctive and empirical creative stock-in-trade for years.

Magazine readers and television viewers in 1989 respond to approximately the same appeals (measured by ARS) as when Burke DAR research measured viewer responses in 1960. Burke's results, in turn, showed up the same as those articulated in CSMI principles (Compton Sales Message Index) in 1953. The same notions as to what interests and motivates consumers surface about every 15 years, regular as clockwork.

These same selling principles were also expressed clearly and vividly in the work of David Ogilvy, who received most of his confirmatory research training through the Starch and Gallup organizations; and they echo Rosser Reeves, whose Reality in Advertising was a seminal book of the 1960s (if a much maligned, misunderstood and unread text by subsequent generations). Reeves based most of his inferences and conclusions on solid research results .

Everybody seems to be espousing the same principles. That shouldn't be surprising. If each research method produced a different set of conclusions as to what seems to work and what doesn't, we'd have no concordance of principle. On top of that, if the empirical experience of successful writers and producers were then at variance with all other accumulated knowledge about communication, the advertising world would wobble wildly on its axis, and we'd have marketing anarchy. We've a full supply of that already; we needn't create any more.

One questionably-scientific (but plenty persuasive) technique for convincing yourself that advertising appeals really don't change much over the decades, is to go to your corporate library and pull out any magazine published in the 1950s or 1960s.

continued on page 908

Fian Arroyo
(305) 663-1224
FAX Telecopier in studio

Color scratchboard samples available
upon request

© Fian Arroyo 1991

Thanks to my family, friends and all my
clients, who have made this the greatest
job in the world. Where else can you go
to work in your underwear, draw
pictures all day and get paid for it?

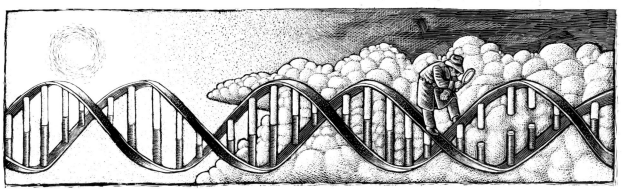

Zita Asbaghi
104-40 Queens Boulevard
Apartment #12X
Forest Hills, New York 11375
(718) 275-1995

Clockwise from top left: Cannes
Advertising Film Festival, Sports
Illustrated Magazine, CBS Records

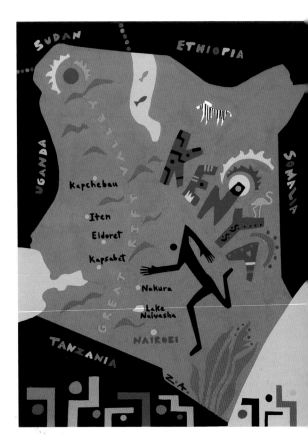

Zita Asbaghi
104-40 Queens Boulevard
Apartment #12X
Forest Hills, New York 11375
(718) 275-1995

Clients Include:
Adweek, The Atlantic Monthly, Atlantic Records, Audio, Avon Books, Business Week, CBS Records, Condé Nast, Family Circle, Fortune Magazine, Harper & Row, Hixo Design, GE Capital, Landscape Architecture, Lederle, Macmillan Publishing Co., MTV

Networks, New York Magazine, Pepsi Cola, Pentagram, Pfizer, Polygram Records, Premier Magazine, Random House, Sports Illustrated, Time Magazine, Whittles Communications

Clockwise from top left: Book cover for Billboard Publications, American College of Physicians, Whittles Communications, BusinessWeek, Promo., Promo., BusinessWeek

Susan Harriet Baker
315 West Side Drive 303
Gaithersburg, Maryland 20878
(301) 258-0126
call for FAX

clients:
American Academy of Combat
Choreographers; Arena Stage; Beanie's
Baskets; Catholics for a Free Choice;

Hard Times Cafe; The Journal
Newspapers; Outdoor Impressions;
Round Fiddle Records; Sears, Roebuck
& Company; The Unicorn Times

memberships:
Washington, DC Illustrators' Club
The Cultural Alliance of Greater
Washington

David Barnett
41 Hidcote Road
Oadby, Leicester
England LE2 5PG
533 717658
FAX available

Clients: Beechams Research, British Gas, British Rail, British Shoe Corp., David C. Cook (Chicago), Electrolux, Epson Computers, EMI Security, Fison Chemicals, Fuji Film, Glass & Glazing Fed., Guiness, Hamlyn, Heinemann Int., Jersey Tourist Board, Kodak, Lloyds Bank, Milk Marketing Board, Nabisco, National Holidays, Norwich Union, P&O Cruises, Portals Water Treatment, Royal Insurance, Sanatogen, TNT, TWA, Tea Council, USA MIlk, Walkers Crisps, Weetabix.

Milk. What more could a body ask for?

continued from page 902

If you also pull the equivalent publication for a comparable month this year, you'll find the call-outs on the front covers - the come-ons for stories inside which publishers depend on to sell issues off the stands - really haven't changed.

Family Circle still promises "Five Easy Recipes Your Family Will Love." Summertime issues of *Cosmo* and *Redbook* are still promising readers they can "Lose Eight Pounds by Swim Suit Weather"; or that their readers can "Meet and Hold a Man" - even in this age of elevated consciousness.

Consumers haven't changed in any of their basic needs or wants during the hundred years advertising has been functioning in its relatively modern state. Some superficial executional techniques have been updated to reflect contemporary tastes, but advertising's basic hierarchy of needs - security, love, health, a sense of worth, opportunity for self-improvement, hints on leading a full and rewarding life, avoidance of extravagance - all the basic appeals remain essentially the same.

Man has not altered in any fundamental way in 50,000 years, except that today's feed-lot beef has seven times as much saturated fat as that of the wooly mammoth. We still live in condoed "caves", although the mortgage payments are steeper; and, unlike the Victorians (but like the Cro-Magnons), both husband and wife work these days in order to meet the modern tax bite.

You can count on the conclusion: People haven't changed much. They love each other, fight each other, love their children, worry about incomes and expenses, and generally struggle to do their best.

Also unchanging in any essential way, are the techniques of communicating through advertising. The first jingle-driven, quick-cut commercial may have attracted some attention simply by being itself; but by now there are jingle-driven commercials on the air for insurance companies and lunch-pail snacks; and automobiles and soft drinks; and beers and chewing gum; and savings and loans and local television stations. The genre has lost its specificity, its distinctiveness and capacity to differentiate - and, therefore, its ability to command attention and send a brand-specific message.

A cogent, dramatic appeal to health, or safety, or comfort - those never change. So, worry - worry a lot and earnestly - if your agency skips over the meat of the sale and starts expounding at length about, and in love with, the execution. Really start to panic if they say, "This commercial will come off only in production. The 'magic moments' are everything." What that unquestionably means is: You don't have much of a strategy or selling idea. You've got a lot of razzle-dazzle, which is terribly expensive and may not improve research scores one whit or iota.

Another essential communication problem that makes commercials relatively indistinguishable from one another is that copywriters and Product Managers, living for the most part in urban areas, tend to think everybody in America is exactly like they are. Young Urban Professional creative people and account execs convince fledgling Product Managers to make a commercial about themselves. Doesn't anyone do store checks any more? Or find out who the consumers really are and what they want?

In my intemperate earlier days, I used to threaten to send every New York or West Coast art director and copywriter to the Ohio State Fair for three days late in August, where they would discover what "sweats" really are. Or to the Hampstead, North Carolina, Spot Festival, where the Volunteer Fire Department sponsors its annual stand-up oyster roast - complete with a precision parachute landing exhibition direct from Camp Lejeune. It's the biggest show in Hampstead, and you meet some wonderful people.

continued on page 912

Tom Barrett
81 Mount Vernon Street
Boston, Massachusetts 02108
(617) 523-4072

Andrea Baruffi
341 Hudson Terrace
Piermont, New York 10968
(914) 359-9542
FAX in office

Andrea Baruffi
341 Hudson Terrace
Piermont, New York 10968
(914) 359-9542
FAX in office

V
I
E
W
P
O
I
N
T
S

continued from page 908

Real consumers live in in Columbus, Ohio, and in Hampstead, North Carolina. They work, and strive, and go to church, and bowl, and love their children.

They also buy one hell of a lot of beer and cat food and Chevrolets and insurance policies.

If all this is common knowledge, why continue to reinvent patently lumpy or eccentric wheels? We buy trouble in big quantities every time we disregard the basics of selling.

Every writer in America should have been as lucky as I was, some time ago, to be in Salem, Oregon, on the Fourth of July. I was sitting in the local university stadium, waiting for the sky to darken enough for the fireworks to begin. In front of me, resting patiently in the fading light, was a dirt farmer in tattered overalls (nothing "design" about his jeans; you'd have to run them through the lava rock wash for 20 years to match that honorable patina). In his callused hands, nails cracked and split from handling the tools of the earth, was a book of Tennyson's poems. He was reading, as long as the light held.

I frequently think of that farmer when I'm asked to look at yet another commercial involving yuppies at play. I know that my farmer is there in front of his TV set, muting out foolishness and executional fripperies, waiting for an advertiser to say, "Here's how to make your savings safe." When he hears something like that, which really gathers him in, he might even put down his Tennyson.

From *Advertising That Sells*
by **Miner Raymond**
Miner Raymond Associates
Cincinnati, Ohio
© 1990 by Miner Raymond
Published by Black Rose Inc.
and reproduced with permission.

Stephen Bauer
3000 Chestnut Avenue
Suite 340
Baltimore, Maryland 21211
(301) 243-0643
FAX: (301) 243-1116

Gary Bennett
Illustrations
(502) 458-0338

Represented by:
Clare Jett & Associates
Artist Representative
(502) 561-0737

BENNETT

BENNETT

John Berg
110 Cottage Street
Buffalo, New York 14201
(716) 884-8003
FAX: (716) 885-4281

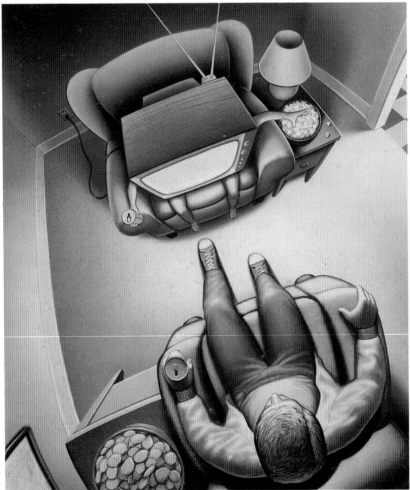

Kieran Bergin
41 Stevenson Place
Kearny, New Jersey 07032
(212) 340-4158
(201) 998-1901
FAX in studio

Member of Graphic Artist Guild
Partial client list:
Frito-Lay; Dreyfus; Sony; DCA; Slater
Hanft Martin; Levine, Huntley, Vick and
Beaver; First Nationwide Bank; Simon &
Schuster; American Druggist; Cruise &
Vacation; Montcalm Publishing;
Emerge; High School Sports.

KIERAN
BERGIN

Eliot Bergman, Inc.
362 West 20th Street
New York, New York 10011
(212) 645-0414 • FAX: (212) 633-6654
(212) 645-0414 Modem

Eliot Bergman creates original
computer-generated infographics for
magazines, annual reports, corporate
literature, advertising and publishing.

Clients include: Allied Signal, Amax,
AT&T, Avnet, CompuServe, Grumman,
Liz Claiborne, MHT, McGraw-Hill, Ogilvy
& Mather, Paramount, Random House,
Time Warner, Whittle Communications

Additional work:
American Showcase 12, 13, 14
Corporate Showcase 8, 9, 10

Eliot Bergman, Inc.
362 West 20th Street
New York, New York 10011
(212) 645-0414 • FAX: (212) 633-6654
(212) 645-0414 Modem

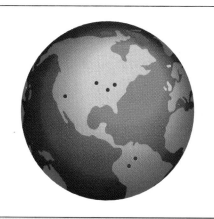

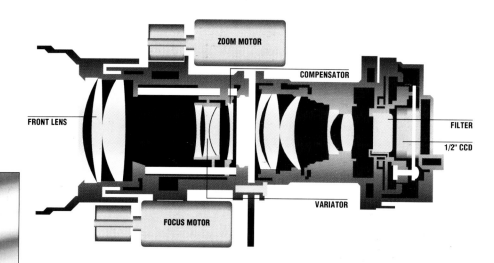

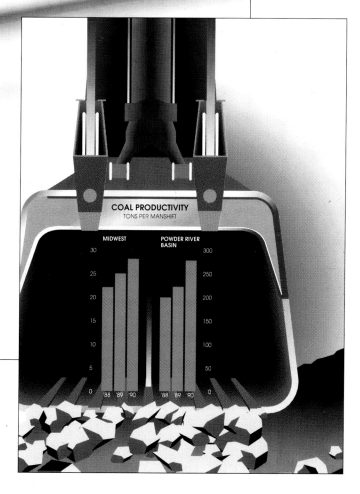

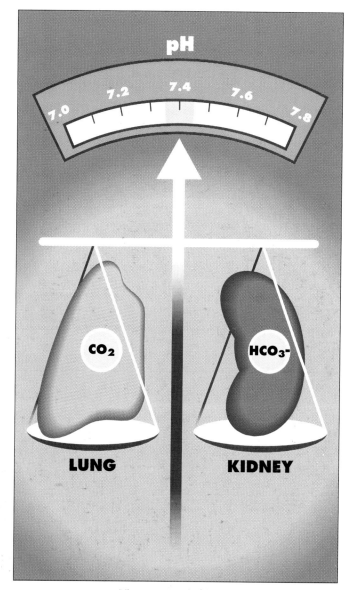

David Biedrzycki
8 Pilgrim Lane
Medfield, Massachusetts 02052
(508) 359-6276
In Studio FAX

Clients include:
After The Fall Juices
Avon Books
Baxter
Digital
Gillette

Honeywell
Kodak
New England Aquarium
Newsweek
Ocean Spray
Seagrams

Simon & Schuster
Timberland
Tropicana Juices
W.R. Grace
Yankee Magazine

Paul Blakey
2910 Caribou Trail
Atlanta, Georgia 30066
(404) 977-7669
FAX: (404) 565-5468

Clients include: Advico Young &
Rubicam, Barker Campbell & Farley,
Celestial Seasonings, East West
Creative, Harrowsmith Country Life,
Knouse Foods, Prentice Hall, Price
Waterhouse, Simon & Schuster, Yankee
Magazine, Readers Digest, Welch's.

HARROWSMITH COUNTRY LIFE

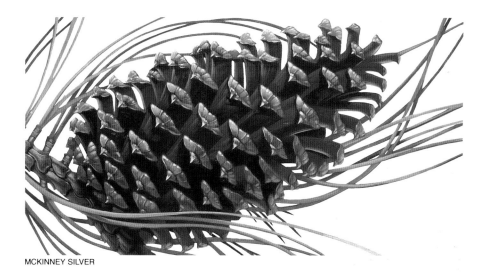

MCKINNEY SILVER

GRAY KIRK & EVANS

HOWARD MERRELL & PARTNERS

BARKER CAMPBELL & FARLEY

READERS DIGEST

Mary Lynn Blasutta
Rider Hollow Road
Arkville, New York 12406
(914) 586-4899
FAX: (914) 586-2312

IBM
New York Times
Barney's New York
Gap
Disney
Fresca
Chevron

Westinghouse
Grey Advertising
DDB Needham
Chiat Day
California State Lottery
Colossal Pictures
Scholastic

Random House
Boston Globe
Money Magazine
Premiere Magazine
Esquire
Atlantic Magazine
Family Circle

Linda Bleck
2739 North Hampden Court #1S
Chicago, Illinois 60614
(312) 281-0286
FAX: (312) 281-4955

Represented in Dallas by
Celeste Cuomo
(214) 443-9111
FAX: (214) 443-9112

See additional work in
Creative Illustration Book 1992
American Showcase 14
American Illustration 8
Samples available upon request

Susan M. Blubaugh
165 Church Street, 4-S
New York, New York 10007
(212) 406-3652

Rob Bolster
7 Hope Street
Walpole, Massachusetts 02081
(508) 660-1751
FAX in studio

Xerox, Nynex, New England Telephone, Digital Equipment Corporation, Wang Laboratories, Dunkin' Donuts, American Tourister, Ocean Spray, Boston Globe, Bank of Boston, Bank of New England, Boston Edison, Converse, Etonic, Dexter, Rockport Shoe, Massachusetts State Lottery, Boston Museum of Science, Boston Museum of Fine Arts.

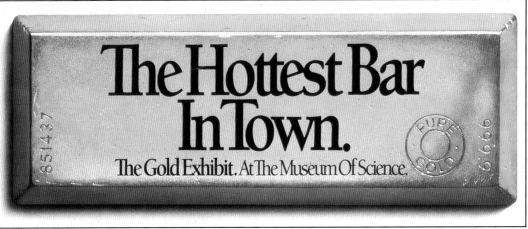

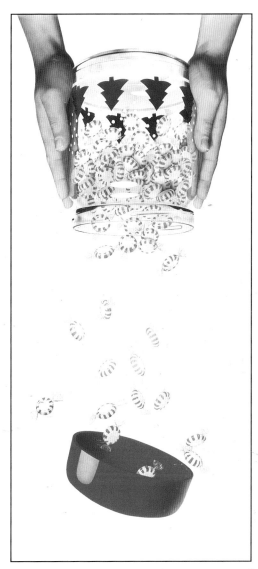

Denny Bond
6481 Miriam Circle
East Petersburg, Pennsylvania 17520
(717) 569-5823
FAX: (717) 569-5823

For additional work:
American Showcase 14, page 930

D E N N Y   B O N D

Tim Bower
141 Sullivan Street #12
New York, New York 10012
(212) 982-0032
FAX: (212) 982-0032

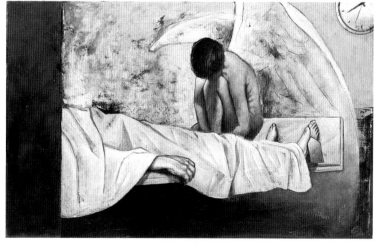

Douglas Bowman

The Creative Dept., Inc.
(405) 942-4868

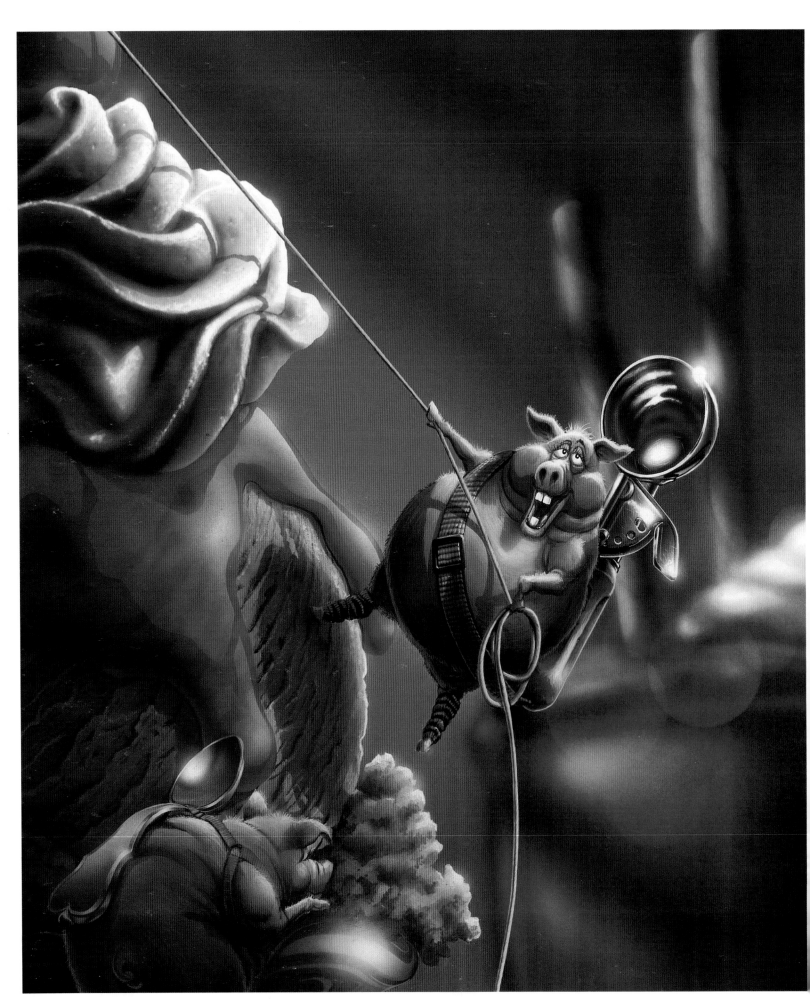

Dave Bramsen
644 North Hope Avenue
Santa Barbara, California 93110
(805) 566-8246
FAX in Studio

Illustration work includes:
Levi's, Hot Sessions, Ocean Pacific,
Newport Blue, Teenage Mutant Ninja
Turtles, National Football League.

We have resources, photos, sketches,
and ideas, from travels in 34 countries.
We also have several pencils and
erasers.

Ron Brancato
333 North Plymouth Avenue
Rochester, New York 14608
(716) 262-4450
FAX: (716) 262-3022

Represented in Western New York by
Linda Jagow
Illustrators Quorum
PO Box 425
Rochester, New York 14603
(716) 546-7606

Krista Brauckmann
10 South 260 Havens Drive
Downers Grove, Illinois 60516
(708) 985-1803
FAX in studio

Clients include: American Express, Bank of Boston, Bennigans, Brookfield Zoo, Burger King, Chicago Sun-Times, Citibank, DeKuyper, General Foods, Honeywell, Hyatt-Hotels, Iams, Illinois State Lottery, Kraft, McDonalds, NYNEX, Seven-Up, United Airlines

To view additional work:

American Showcase
Volumes 10 and 14
The SourceBook 1989
Society of Illustrators Annual 32

Steve Brodner
120 Cabrini Boulevard #116
New York, New York 10033
(212) 740-8174

MAKE THE BEST ADDRESSED LIST WITH

Yehlen Brooks

(800) 999-ARTS
(913) 273-5379
FAX: (913) 273-0466

Commissioned Portraits include, among many others: Kansas Governors Mike Hayden and Joan Finney • US Member of Congress Dick Nichols

Partial Client List: Kansas State Government Agencies - Banking

Department; Dept. of Commerce; Dept. of Administration; Corporation Commission; Secretary of State; State Treasurer's Office; Governor's Chief of Staff • Local bank branches: Capitol Federal Savings; Capital City Bank & Trust Company.

Science Diet • Hills Pet Products • Colgate-Palmolive.

To see additional work in full color and black & white, call me toll-free, Mon-Sun, 9am to 9pm, CST.
I will Mail-A-Folio.

935

**Lou Brooks
Productions, Inc.**
415 West 55th Street
New York, New York 10019
(212) 245-3632 • FAX: (212) 489-6360

Representing:
Clare Vanacore Brooks

Acrylic paintings and illustrations
of technological and architectural
landscapes.

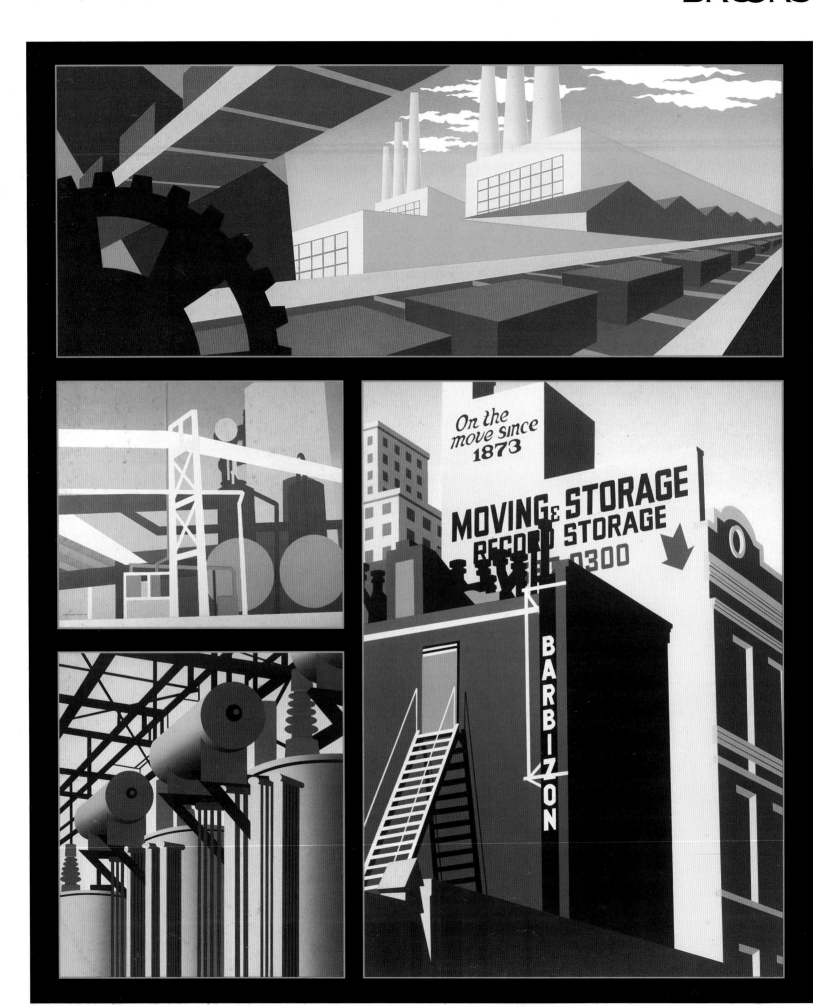

**Lou Brooks
Productions, Inc.**
415 West 55th Street
New York, New York 10019
(212) 245-3632 • FAX: (212) 489-6360

Representing:
Clare Vanacore Brooks

Acrylic paintings and illustrations
of technological and architectural
landscapes.

CLARE
VANACORE
BROOKS

Lou Brooks Productions, Inc.
415 West 55th Street
New York, New York 10019
(212) 245-3632 • FAX: (212) 489-6360

Representing:
Lou Brooks

Illustration, Design,
Lettering and Animation

WHERE MOVERS AND SHAKERS BECOME SITTING DUCKS.

Targeting the rich is easy. Simply track them to where they gather, like clockwork, to feed on information: The Wall Street Journal Broadcast Networks.℠

Throughout each business day, our financial/economic news briefs zero in on a higher concentration of upscale and executive listeners than all major networks combined. And that's just on radio.

On television, our weekly ½-hour Wall Street Journal℠ Report enables you to successfully reach the same group of affluent decision makers in their other arena of influence: the home.

We invite you to call Bob Rush at (800) 828-6397, and discover the difference between media that merely takes aim at the rich and powerful. And programming that makes them easy pickings.

THE WALL STREET JOURNAL
BROADCAST NETWORKS

Great Summer Reading

**Lou Brooks
Productions, Inc.**
415 West 55th Street
New York, New York 10019
(212) 245-3632 • FAX: (212) 489-6360

Representing:
Lou Brooks

Illustration, Design,
Lettering and Animation

Lee Brubaker
212 North Clay
Kirkwood, Missouri 63122
(314) 965-5608
FAX: (314) 966-6649

Additional Work Exhibited In:
Illustrators Annual #32
American Artists Jan. 1990
Contemporary Western Artists 1982
Art Of The West Nov./Dec. 1988
Art Of The West July/Aug. 1989

Send For Free Personal Full
Color Portfolio.

Taylor Bruce
946 B Street
Petaluma, California 94952
(707) 765-6744

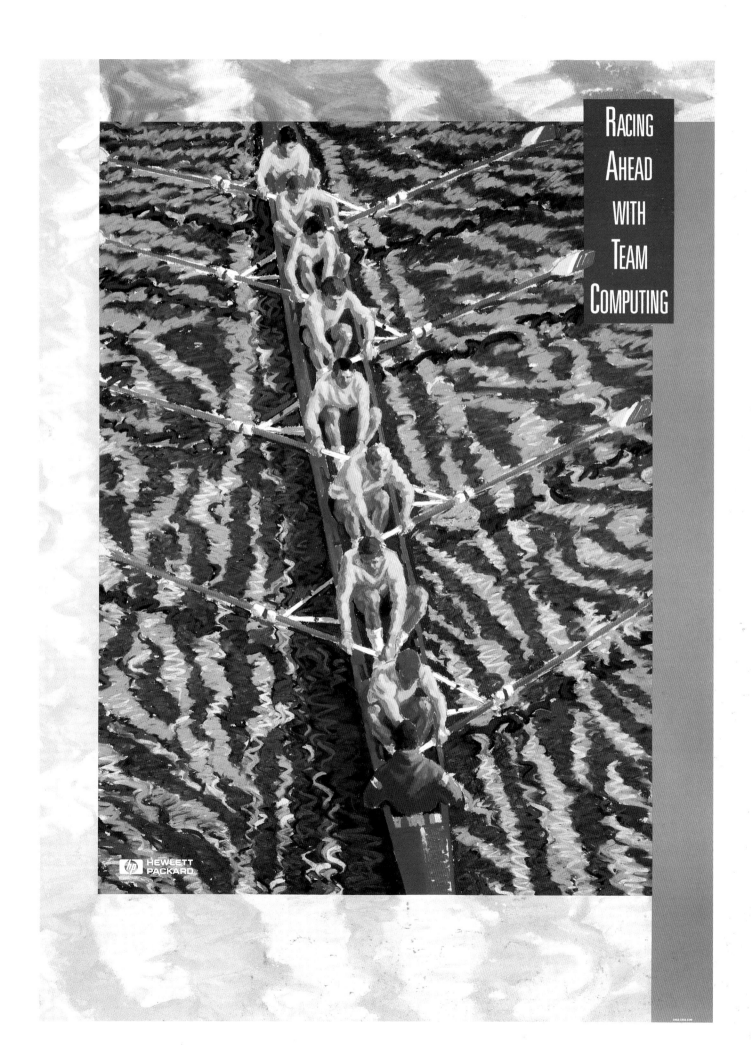

RACING AHEAD WITH TEAM COMPUTING

HEWLETT PACKARD

Callie Butler
2670 Del Mar Heights Road, #295
Del Mar, California 92014
(619) 755-5539
FAX in studio

Dave Calver
70 Stoneham Drive
Rochester, New York 14625
(716) 383-8996
FAX: (716) 385-8706

Clients Include:
AT&T
Bloomingdales
BusinessWeek
Caesars Palace
CBS
Esquire
Fortune

HBO
Mobil
Money
Newsweek
New York Times
Playboy
Random House
Rolling Stone

Sports Illustrated
Time, Inc.
TWA
United Airlines
U.S. News
Vanity Fair
Vogue
Warner Brothers

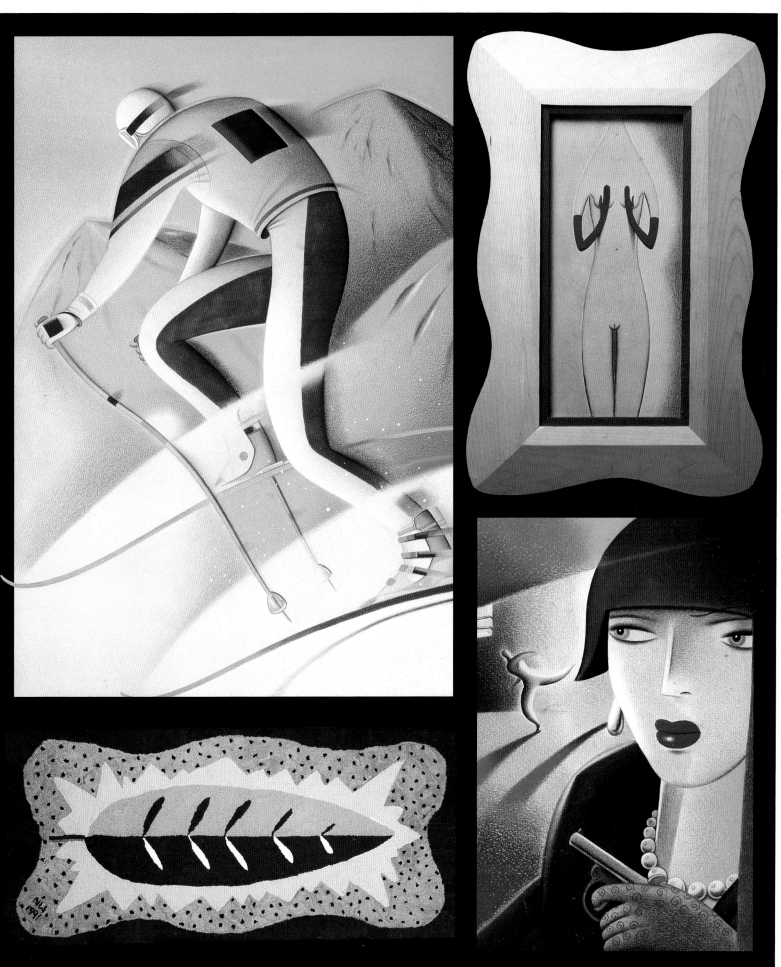

Elaine Cardella
116 Clinton Street
Hoboken, New Jersey 07030
(201) 656-3244
FAX: (201) 798-2848

Partial Client List: Adweek • Atlantic Monthly • BusinessWeek • Connoisseur • CMP Publications • Detroit Free Press • FCB/Leber Katz Partners: Colgate-Palmolive • Glamour • Health • Inc • Jordache • Lear's • Modern Bride •

Manhattan Inc • New England Business • New Woman • Reebok • Scholastic • San Antonio Light • Star Ledger • Twin Cities Reader • Washington Post • Weight Watchers • Whittle Communications

Additional work may be seen in Art Direction: "Upcoming Illustrator," July 1988; Adweek Portfolios: Publication Art & Design 1988; Adweek Portfolios: Advertising Illustration & Photography 1989; Print's Regional Design Annual/ 1990; American Showcase #14

C A R D E L L A

Lee Carlson
1500 Massachusetts Avenue, NW
Apartment 143
Washington, DC 20005
(202) 429-9823

Professional memberships include the Society of Illustrators, National Cartoonists Society and ASIFA (The International Film Animators Association).

Twenty years as an illustrator, cartoonist, designer, and art director has involved me in a wide variety of projects with an equally wide selection of clients and employers. From book, magazine and record covers to posters.

From editorial illustration and cartoons to animated films (as animator and background painter) and restaurant menus. Commercial art offers the variety to keep it interesting.

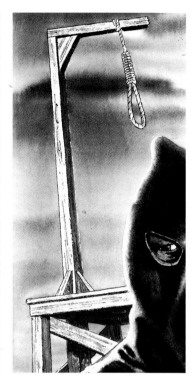

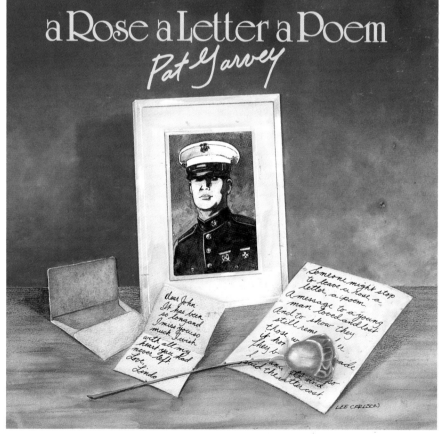

945

American Showcase Illustration II

Printed by *Everbest* : The choice of excellence

Everbest Printing Co. Ltd Block C5 • 10/F
Ko Fai Industrial Building • 7 Ko Fai Road
Yau Tong • Kowloon • Hong Kong •
Tel 852 727 4433 • Fax 852 772 7687

Aprinco 30 Casebridge Court • Scarborough
Ontario • M1B 3M5 • Canada
Tel 416 286 6688 • Fax 416 286 4931

AsiaPrint/Everbest Ltd Suite 310
26522 La Alameda • Mission Viejo
California 92691 • USA
Tel 714 348 1192 • Fax 714 348 1189

Four Colour Imports Ltd Suite 102
2843 Brownsboro Road
Louisville • KY 40206 • USA
Tel 502 896 9644 • Fax 502 896 9594

Chuck Carlton
Axiom, Inc.
(502) 584-7666
FAX: (502) 581-0024

Dimensional Illustration involving scale models, computer designed or enhanced images, with painted or real backdrops combined on 8 x 10 transparency to best portray your product or service.

Clients have included Blue Cross & Blue Shield, Sports Illustrated, Texas Instruments, Eli Lily & Co., Glaxo, General Electric, RCA, American Express, Tonka, Hilton, American Airlines, Kentucky Fried Chicken, RJR (Doral), Hanes, SwatchWatch, Macy's and a plethora of others.

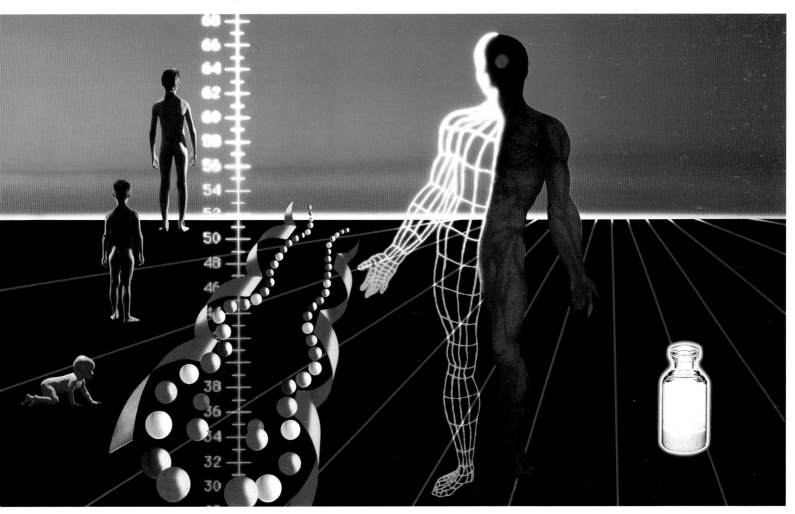

Don Cassity
207 Pine Street
Bonner Springs, Kansas 66012

Linda Pool
7216 East 99 Street
Kansas City, Missouri 64134
(816) 761-7314

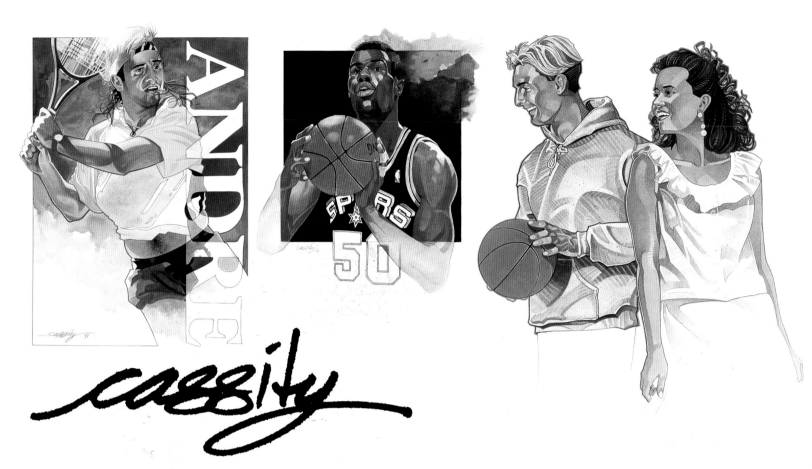

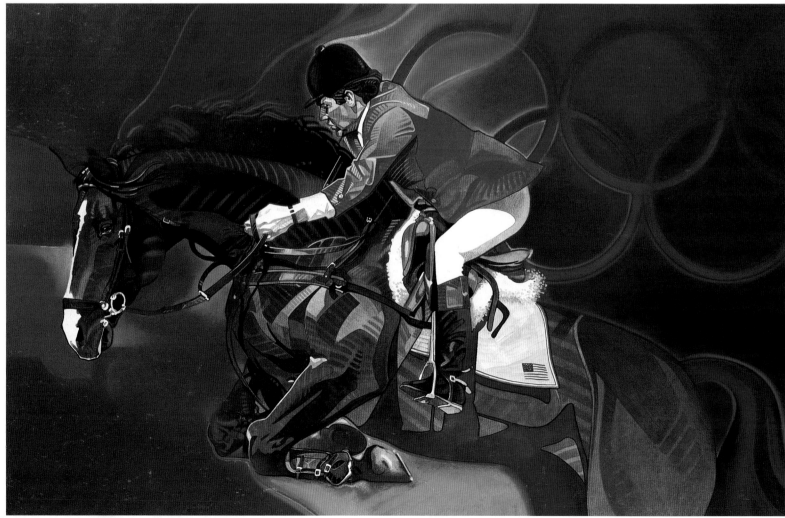

Don Cassity
207 Pine Street
Bonner Springs, Kansas 66012

Linda Pool
7216 East 99 Street
Kansas City, Missouri 64134
(816) 761-7314

**Carlos Castellanos
Illustration, Inc.**
20150-08 Northeast 3rd Court
Miami, Florida 33179
(305) 651-9524
FAX/Telecopier in studio

© Carlos Castellanos 1992
Member Graphic Artist Guild

P.S. Tight deadlines welcomed, I don't
go out much anyway.

Chandler
80 Lattingtown Road
Locust Valley, New York 11560
(516) 671-0388

Represented by:
Barbara Gordon Associates
165 East 32nd Street
New York, NY 10016
(212) 686-3514

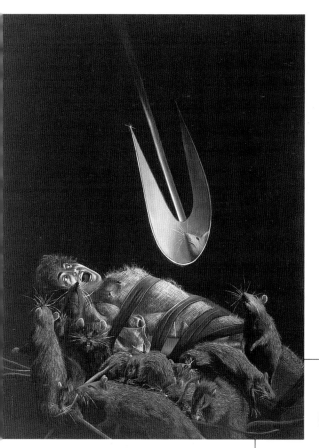

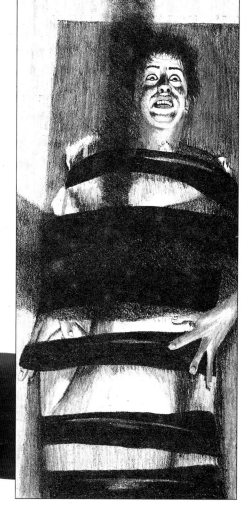

Fay Chandler
Engine House Studios
444 Western Avenue
Brighton, Massachusetts 02135
(617) 254-0428
FAX: (617) 868-2708

For further examples of work, see
American Showcase 12, page 654
American Showcase 14, page 952
New York Art Review 1988-89,
pages 351 and 385

Animation demo available on request

Bruce Hamilton, photographer
Engine House Studies

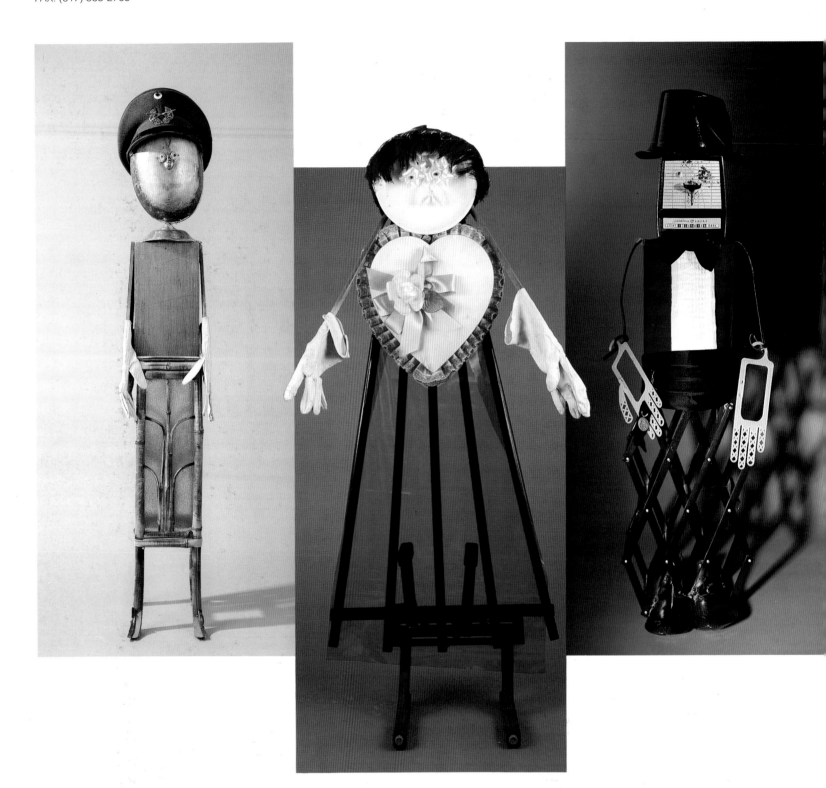

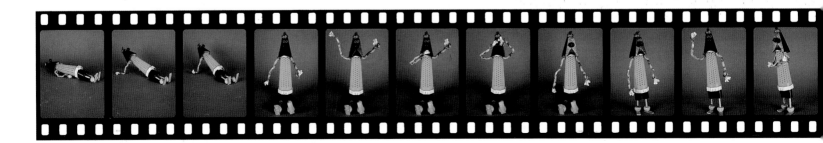

Mark Chickinelli
6348 Pierce Street
Omaha, Nebraska 68106
(402) 551-6829
FAX in Studio

Work can also be seen in
Showcase 14, Page 954

Ronald Chironna
122 Slosson Avenue, 2nd floor
Staten Island, New York 10314
(718) 720-6142

Clients: American Bankers Association,
American Journal of Nursing, Chapman
Direct Advertising, David C. Cook Pub.
Co., Houghton Mifflin Co.

Illustrations in pen & ink and pencil.

Kent Christensen
320 East 50th Street
New York, New York 10022
(212) 754-3017
FAX: (212) 754-3017

John Churchman
4 Howard Street
Burlington, Vermont 05401
(802) 863-4627
FAX: (802) 658-2151

Airbrush and photographic illustration
Technical to fantastical

Clients have included:
Academy Entertainment, Artec,
Barrecrafters, Consumer Reports,
Dynastar, Elan, General Electric,
IBM, Karhu, Lange, Merrell, National

Gardening, Science and Mechanics
and Vermont Microsystems.

Additional images available in
Image Bank Illustration Catalog #4.

All photography by John Churchman

Joe Ciardiello
2182 Clove Road
Staten Island, New York 10305
(718) 727-4757
FAX in studio

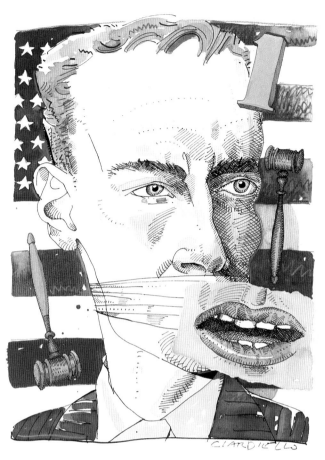

Graham Greene

Rusty has A Dream

Bradley H. Clark
36 Haggerty Hill Road
Rhinebeck, New York 12572
(914) 876-2615
FAX: (914) 876-2950

Clients Include:
American Express
Cahners
Conde Nast's Traveler
Grey Advertising
Harper & Row
NY Times Magazine

Ogilvy & Mather
Random House
Redbook
Scali, McCabe, Sloves
Simon & Schuster
Travel Holiday
Zeckendorf

See Additional Work:
American Showcase 10, pg. 471
American Showcase 11, pg. 115
American Showcase 12, pg. 116
American Showcase 13, pg. 81
American Showcase 14, pgs. 88-89

Greg Clarke
844 Ninth Street, #10
Santa Monica, California 90403
(213) 395-7958
FAX: (213) 395-7958

Clients include:
Adweek
The Atlantic
Altman & Manley
BusinessWeek
California Business

Esquire
Fox Television
Hixo, Inc.
Home Magazine
L.A. Style
Los Angeles Times

Mother Jones
Newsweek
New York Magazine
Time
The Washington Post
Wigwag

Leslie Cober
150 Huntington Avenue, #NE-11
Boston, Massachusetts 02115
(617) 266-0228

Clients Include:
Air & Space Magazine; American
Health; Barney's New York; Bell
Communications; Bergdorf Goodman;
Boston Globe; Bristol-Myers;
BusinessWeek; Franklin Library; G.E.;

How Magazine; Little, Brown, & Co.,
Mademoiselle; McDougall, Littel, & Co.;
McGraw-Hill Books; Monsanto; NCR;
New York Times; Outside Magazine;
Postgraduate Medicine Magazine;
Washington Post; Working Woman.

Additional work may be seen in:
American Showcase 13, page 725
American Showcase 14, page 962

Adam Cohen
74 Charles Street #2B
New York, New York 10014
(212) 691-4074

McGraw-Hill, Bantam Doubleday Dell,
Cosmopolitan, The New York Times,
St. Martin's Press, Time-Life, Adweek,
Scholastic Inc., Insurance Information
Inst., Grau Publications, Sloan-Millman
Productions, East-West Network

Sharon Cohen
20200 Shipley Terrace, #202
Germantown, Maryland 20874
(301) 540-3466
FAX Available

SHARON ○ COHEN
I·L·L·U·S·T·R·A·T·O·R

Sally Wern Comport
241 Central Avenue
St. Petersburg, Florida 33701
(813) 821-9050
FAX: (813) 821-8945

Represented by:
Florida: W/C Studio Inc. (813) 821-9050
Chicago: Sell Inc. (312) 565-2701
Carolinas: Kerry Reilly (704) 372-6007
Mich.: The Neis Group (616) 672-5756
Atlanta: Alexander/Pollard (404) 875-1363

Thoughtful Illustration.

Condon & White
Suburban Drive
Ashfield, Massachusetts 01330
(413) 628-4042
FAX: (413) 628-4043

Call for more samples and see:
American Showcase #10 and 12
and the Graphic Artists Guild's Directory
#5 and 6.

© Ken Condon 1992

KEN CONDON

413-628-4042

Condon & White
Suburban Drive
Ashfield, Massachusetts 01330
(413) 628-4042
FAX: (413) 628-4043

Call for more samples and see:
American Showcase #12

CAROLINE WHITE

413-628-4042

Bob Conge
28 Harper Street
Rochester, New York 14607
(716) 473-0291

AIR CANADA / ENROUTE MAGAZINE: "THE ANYWHERE OFFICE"

Bob Conge
28 Harper Street
Rochester, New York 14607
(716) 473-0291

FRITO LAY / PERSPECTIVES BROCHURE: "DREAMING OF SUCCESS"

Gwen Connelly

(312) 943-4477

Hyatt, Libbys, Mott's, McDonalds, Lands' End, Quaker Oats, Boise Cascade, Illinois State Tourism, Shoneys, Burger King, Tonka, Hasbro, Silver Burdett Ginn, Western Publishing,

Harper & Row, Harcourt Brace Jovanovich, Houghton Mifflin Co., JTG Nashville, McGraw Hill Publishing, Scott Foresman & Co., Sunrise, Crayola, Purina, Worldbook/Childcraft.

MCDONALDS

AMERICAN GRAPHICS

HYATT

NEWMARKET

Mona Conner
One Montgomery Place, #8
Brooklyn, New York 11215
(718) 636-1527
FAX # upon request

Clients: Lenox, Mobil, Letraset, FCB
Leber/Katz, Victoria Magazine, Arista
Records, Book-of-the-Month Club,
High-Tech Marketing, American
Druggist, Ms., HarperCollins, Alfred A.
Knopf, Macmillan, McGraw-Hill, Viking
Penguin, Scholastic, St. Martin's Press,
The New York Daily News, and more.

see also: Creative Illustration Book
1991; Graphic Artists Guild's Directory
5, 6; RSVP 9, 11, 13; Communication
Arts Illustration Annnual 1984

© Mona Conner 1991
Member, Graphic Artists Guild

Mona Conner

Some, therefore, have imagined the spiritual to be like a bird flying above the air in an ether to which the sight of the eye does not reach; when yet it is like a bird of paradise, which flies near the eye, even touching the pupil with its beautiful wings and longing to be seen. —— *Swedenborg*

POSTER PROMOTING THE WORK OF 18TH CENTURY THEOLOGIAN EMANUEL SWEDENBORG

BETTER HEALTH MAGAZINE

John P. Courtney
779 11th Avenue, Apartment 5-D
Paterson, New Jersey 07514
(201) 345-7652

Member Graphic Artist Guild

Neverne Covington
241 Central Avenue, #A
St. Petersburg, Florida 33701
(813) 822-1267
FAX: (813) 821-8945

Represented in FL by
WC Studio
(813) 821-9050
Represented in the midwest by
The Schuna Group
(612) 343-0432

Additional work can be seen in
Showcase 11, Showcase 14 and the
Creative Illustration Book 1991-92

Reddish Egret   Rosette Spoonbill   Whooping Crane   Snowy Egret

Paul Cozzolino
New York City
(212) 969-8680
(718) 728-2729

Partial client list:
St. Martin's Press
Little, Brown and Co.
Grove Weidenfeld
Simon & Schuster
Penguin USA

New York Times
Print
Adweek
Byte
BusinessWeek
Newsday

Member Graphic Artists Guild

© 1992 Paul Cozzolino

ST. MARTIN'S PRESS

GROVE WEIDENFELD

BUSINESSWEEK

Peter Cunis
Hoboken, New Jersey
(201) 792-5164
FAX in Studio

Andre Deutsch
Art Direction
Atlantic Monthly Press
AT&T
BusinessWeek
Chemical Engineering
Duke Communications International

Eastern Review
Flying
Forbes
Golf Illustrated
Inx
New Jersey Monthly
New York Newsday Magazine

New York Times
New York Times Book Review
1,001 Home Ideas
Publishers Weekly
St. Martin's Press
Seventeen
World Tennis

Margaret Cusack

124 Hoyt Street in Boerum Hill
Brooklyn, New York 11217-2215
(718) 237-0145
FAX: (718) 237-0145

Hand-stitched samplers, quilts, soft sculpture, props, fabric collage and mixed media.

Margaret Cusack has been creating stitched artwork since 1972. Timing and pricing are comparable to other .more conventional styles.

Photography of the artwork is included.

Clients include: American Express, Aunt Millie's, Avon, Bloomingdale's, Chemical Bank, Dell, HBJ, Howard Johnson, Little Brown & Co., Lysol, Macy's, Maxwell House Coffee, The New York Times, Peek Freans Cookies, Perrier, RCA, Reader's Digest, Seagram's, Singer, Texaco, Thai Airlines.

For additional work: American Showcase 14, page 975; AS 13, page 734; AS 12, page 669; AS 11, page 590; AS 10, page 487; AS 9, page 312; AS 8, page 215.

Member: Graphic Artists Guild

FINAST-EDWARDS

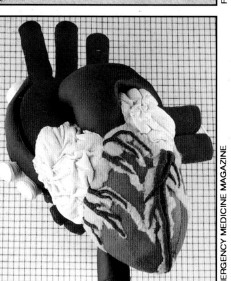

EMERGENCY MEDICINE MAGAZINE

ACTION

PRENTICE HALL
SIMON & SCHUSTER

COLORADO STATE LOTTERY

Steven R. Cusano
30 Talbot Court
Media, Pennsylvania 19063
(215) 565-8829

Clients Include: Sports Illustrated, The Upper Deck Co., IBM, AT&T, NYNEX, Johnson & Johnson, Scott Paper Co., SD Warren, Smithkline, Dupont, TV Guide, Nike, Pepsico, The Franklin Mint,

The Wall Street Journal, The Philadelphia Flyers, The Boston Bruins, The Washington Redskins, The Special Olympics

Member:
Society of Illustrators
Graphic Artists Guild

For Additional Work:
American Showcase 9, 11, 12, 13, 14
Art Directors Index 11

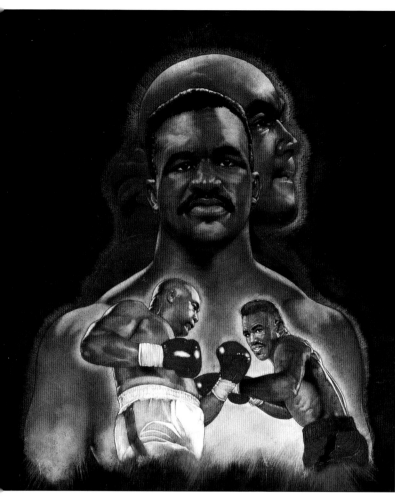

Dave Cutler
7 Sunrise Ridge
Florida, New York 10921
(914) 651-1580
FAX: (914) 651-1590

Outside the Northeast represented by:
Friend & Johnson
Call (214) 855-0055

Clients include: AT&T, IBM, Citibank,
Philip Morris, Champion International,
Monsanto, GM, Unisys, BusinessWeek,
Forbes, U.S. News & World Report,
Changing Times, NY Times, Wall Street
Journal, Washington Post, Boston
Globe, Detroit Free Press, NY Woman,

Adweek, Byte, Lotus, Golf Digest,
Simon & Schuster, Scholastic, Oxford
University Press

Also in Showcase 13 & 14, Illustrators
30 & 33, NY Art Directors Club Show
'91, SND Annual 10 & 11

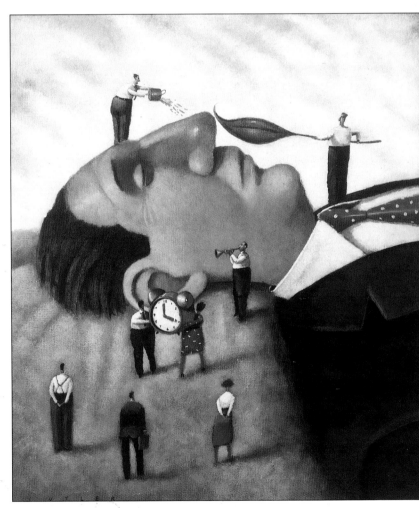

Georgan Damore
200 East Delaware Place
Suite 14A
Chicago, Illinois 60611
(312) 266-9451

New Barry Publications
New York Times
Pierre Cardin International
Spiegel Corporation

BBDO New York
Chicago Tribune
Hartmarx Corporation
Helene Curtis

Member:
Graphic Artist Guild
Chicago Artist Coalition
Fashion Group International

Harry R. Davis
189 East 3rd Street, Apartment #15
New York, New York 10009
(212) 674-5832

For additional work, please see:
American Showcase Volumes 8, 13, 14
Graphic Artists Guild's Directory of
Illustration 5

Rob Day
6095 Ralston Avenue
Indianapolis, Indiana 46220
(317) 253-9469
FAX in studio

CLIENT, GRAPHIC ARTISTS GUILD NATIONAL CONFERENCE

CLIENT, ROLLING STONE; ART DIRECTOR, FRED WOODWARD

CLIENT, BACARDI IMPORTS, INC.; AGENCY, MCKINNEY & SILVER

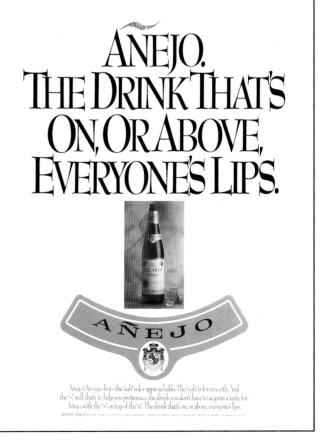

TYPE
AS
DESIGN

I think of type as the bridge between word and picture. Abstract shapes in the form of single letters combine to make words, and words conjure up imagery. Type can function as design in two ways. The first is where the letter forms themselves become illustrative elements. Early books used illuminated initials; the title page of Shakespeare's First Folio, the Gutenberg Bible, the Book of Hours. Or type can assume literal meaning as imagery, as in a book jacket I designed where the second "O" in the word "moon" became a representation of the moon.

These images differ greatly from person to person. I look at the word "war" in print, and it brings back images that I actually saw during World War II. What pictures appear to someone who has never seen a war? I once gave a lecture addressing this idea, that a three-letter word can generate so many images, and called it "A word is worth a thousand pictures."

On returning from a visit to Jerusalem, I described that fabled city in a letter to a friend who had never been there. As I wrote, I wondered what imagery my words would create in her mind. Would this added information about Jerusalem change the stereotypes she had already formed from reading other words and seeing other pictures ?

I have always believed that designers who cannot express themselves in words cannot be very good at designing, either. They certainly would not make good art directors, because an art director has to be able to convey- in words written or spoken- the content and mood of an assignment to another artist for execution. In explaining the assignment, he should also consider the bias that artist will bring to it, and fit his description around those perceived prejudices .

Reading, especially early on in life, trains you to be able to translate imaginatively from word to picture. Sitting in your room reading *A Passage to India* is a much more participatory and creative activity than watching the movie, which forces the director's particular translation, brilliant as it may be, onto every viewer. I am afraid that television, which now does this translation for most children for many hours each day, may be responsible in two or three generations for a severe shortage of adults with the ability to make these translations with any individuality.

Sometimes type itself can also become the design, the illustration, or can, by its physical aspect, reinforce the literal message. Who hasn't wondered at the beauty of Japanese calligraphy-or even the Japanese type forms in a booklet for Honda? Because most of us are unable to read the message, we see the beauty of its abstract design without distraction.

In this century, Western poets like Apollinaire and Christian Morgenstern and e.e. cummings used typographic forms as pictorial elements to complement their writing. I have always loved a design solution where the visual aspect of the type itself acquires literal meaning. Type reaches its highest potential when doing double duty.

From *Visual Thinking*
by **Henry Wolf**
Henry Wolf Productions
(photo and design studio)
New York City

Robert de Michiell
26 West 78 Street #2G
New York, New York 10024
(212) 769-9192
FAX: (212) 874-3747

Clients include:
Premiere, The New Yorker, Esquire,
GQ, HG, BusinessWeek, Working
Woman, Mademoiselle, Adweek, Child,
Scholastic, Sports Illustrated for Kids,
Computer World, New York, Utne
Reader, Travel Life, Whittle Special
Reports, Health, The Washington
Post, Simon & Schuster, MCI, ABC-TV,
New York City Opera.

Roger T. De Muth
De Muth Illustration / Design Studio
4103 Chenago Street
Cazenovia, New York 13035
(315) 655-8599
FAX in Studio

"Wild Bird Seed"- new Product from De Muth Design
(makes a great gift.)

"Road kill Bingo", the game. Ask for one for your car!

"Linhoff, the Cat Photographer." Ray Beale/ client.

·From the Mini-book "Wild Birds" by Roger DeMuth·
·Portfolio on request·

Peter de Sève
25 Park Place
Brooklyn, New York 11217
(718) 398-8099
FAX: (718) 622-0121

Animation reel and portfolio available
upon request.

Jim Deal
3451 24th Avenue West
Seattle, Washington 98199
(206) 285-2986

Represented in the Northeast by:
S.I. International
(212) 254-4996

Represented in the Northwest by:
Santee Lehmen Dabney Inc.
(206) 467-1616

Clients Include: CMP Publications, Computer Dealer, Harley Davidson, Houghton Mifflin, Medical Economics, Northrop, Pepsico, Tenera Corp., Time-Life Books, 3M Corp., Western Publishing, Whittle Communications, The Rockefeller Foundation, Illustrators 31.

CONCEPT; SOFTWARE CHOICE

CONCEPT; SOFTWARE LANGUAGE

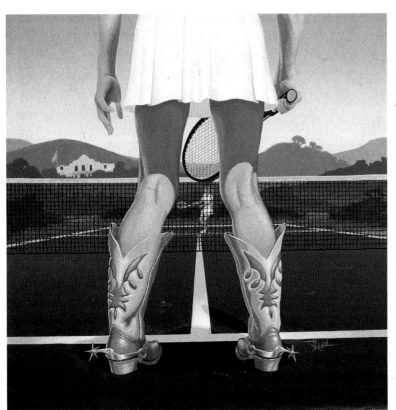

CONCEPT; HIGH NOON SHOOTOUT IN SAN ANTONIO

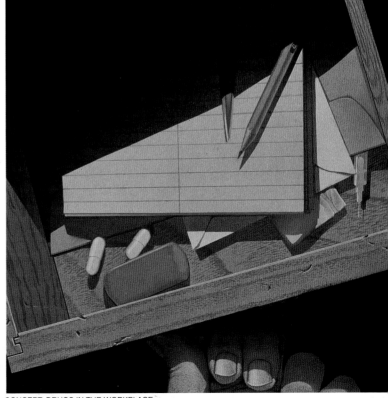

CONCEPT; DRUGS IN THE WORKPLACE

Charles J. Demorat
305 Cornelia Drive
Graham, North Carolina 27253
(919) 229-7359

"I can draw people and animals that dress like people."

"Editorial Illustration with imagination plus."

D E M O R A T

Mike Dietz
PO Box 3145
San Clemente, California 92674
(714) 496-3021

John Edwards
2356 East Broadway
Tucson, Arizona 85719
(602) 623-4325

Represented by
Marla Matson
(602) 252-5072

Richard Elmer
504 East 11th Street
New York, New York 10009
(212) 598-4024
FAX: (212) 473-1655

Glenn Elson
303-A Market Street
Roanoke, Virginia 24011
(703) 343-3385
FAX in studio

Betsy Everitt
582 Santa Rosa Avenue
Berkeley, California 94707
(510) 527-3239
FAX: (510) 525-3987

Clients: Adweek, American Express Publishing, AT&T, Bantam Books, Children's Television Workshop, Detroit Free Press, Esprit, General Foods, Grey Advertising, Harcourt Brace Jovanovich Inc., Joyce Theatre, MCI,

New York Magazine, NYC Museum of Natural History, Ogilvy & Mather Direct, PC Resource, San Francisco Focus, Scholastic Inc., Thompson Recruitment Advertising, Time Inc., Whittle Communications, Unix Review.

Children's Books: Frida The Wondercat, Mean Soup, The Happy Hippopotami

See also: American Showcase Volume 12, 13 and 14.

Matt Faulkner
35 Pineapple Street, #1-A
Brooklyn, New York 11201
(718) 797-2784

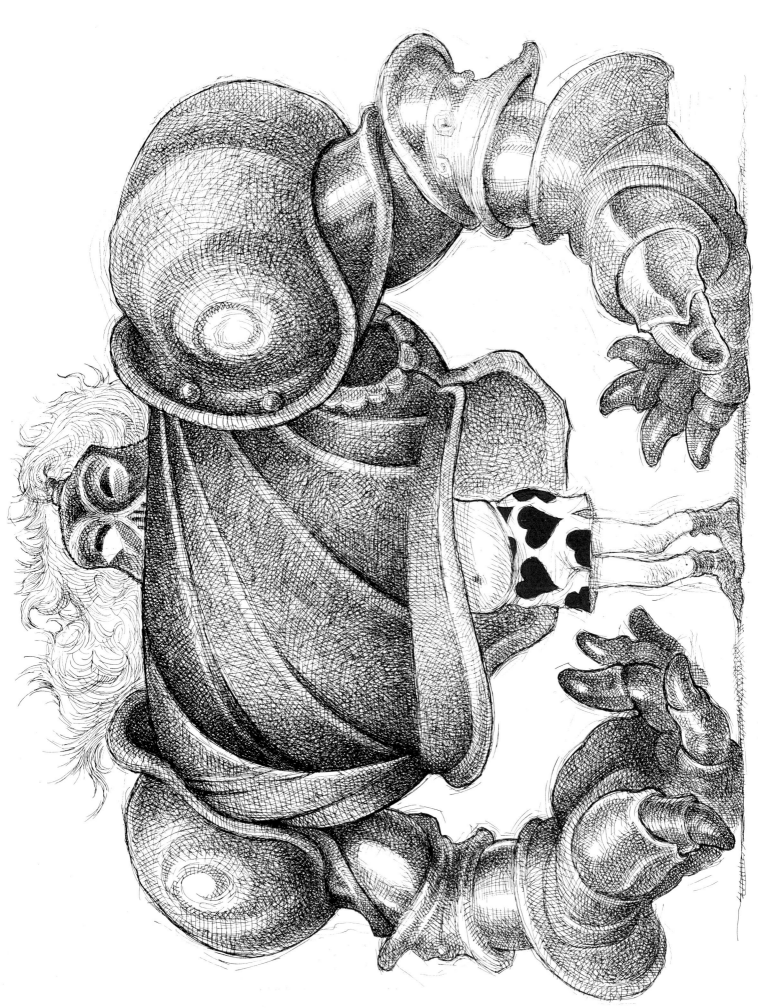

David FeBland
105 West 13th Street, 6C
New York, New York 10011
(212) 645-4190 Studio
FAX: (212) 366-5735

THE **DAVID FeBLAND**

IMAGE BOOK

INCLUDING HUNDREDS
OF BLACK AND WHITE
STOCK ILLUSTRATIONS
FOR REPRODUCTION

CALL FOR A
FREE CATALOGUE
OF HUNDREDS OF
BLACK & WHITE
STOCK ILLUSTRATIONS
AVAILABLE FOR SALE

Lori Nelson Field
860 West 181st Street,
Apartment #41A
New York, New York 10033
(212) 795-4281

Clients Include:
Fitz & Floyd
The Bradford Exchange
Vanity Fair
Barton-Cotton
Dupont Corporation

Ogilvy & Mather
Lears Magazine
Marcel Schurman
Museum Bookmarks
Gerber Products
Evenflo
Jayne Mauborgne Asso.

Mike Fisher
510 Turquoise Street
New Orleans, Louisiana 70124
(504) 288-4860
FAX in Studio

Clients: American Express, Bantam Books, Bordens, Coca Cola, EyeMasters, FoxMeyer Drug Co., Hyatt Hotels, Lord & Taylor, Midway Airlines, JC Penney, Lockheed Corp., Pepsi, Reebok, and Warner Books.

Judy Francis
110 West 96th Street, #2C
New York, New York 10025
(212) 866-7204
FAX: (212) 866-7911

Illustration for Print and Animatics

Member Society of Illustrators
Member Graphic Artists Guild

© 1991 Judy Francis

Clients include:
Grey Advertising
Peartree Advertising
The MacDougall Company
Triton Advertising
Warwick Baker & Fiore
Wells Rich Greene
Young & Rubicam

Good Housekeeping
Milady Publishing Company
McGraw-Hill Inc.
Time Inc.
Chesebrough-Pond's Inc.
Ms. Foundation for Women
Charlex
Napoleon Videographics

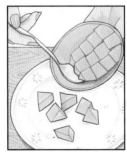

Barbara Friedman
New York, New York
(212) 242-4951
FAX in studio

Client listing available up

To receive additional san
view the portfolio please

Frank Frisari
95-08 112th Street
Richmond Hill, New York 11419
(718) 441-0919
FAX In Studio

"Frank is a great friend, with this natural ability to create unique images. He makes me want to throw my scratchboard out the window!"

–Jose Ortega,
illustrator

Frank Frisari
95-08 112th Street
Richmond Hill, New York 11419
(718) 441-0919
FAX In Studio

"Sometimes Frank's work is psychically unhinging....
I'm glad to see he's painting thinner people."

–Victor Stabin,
    illustrator

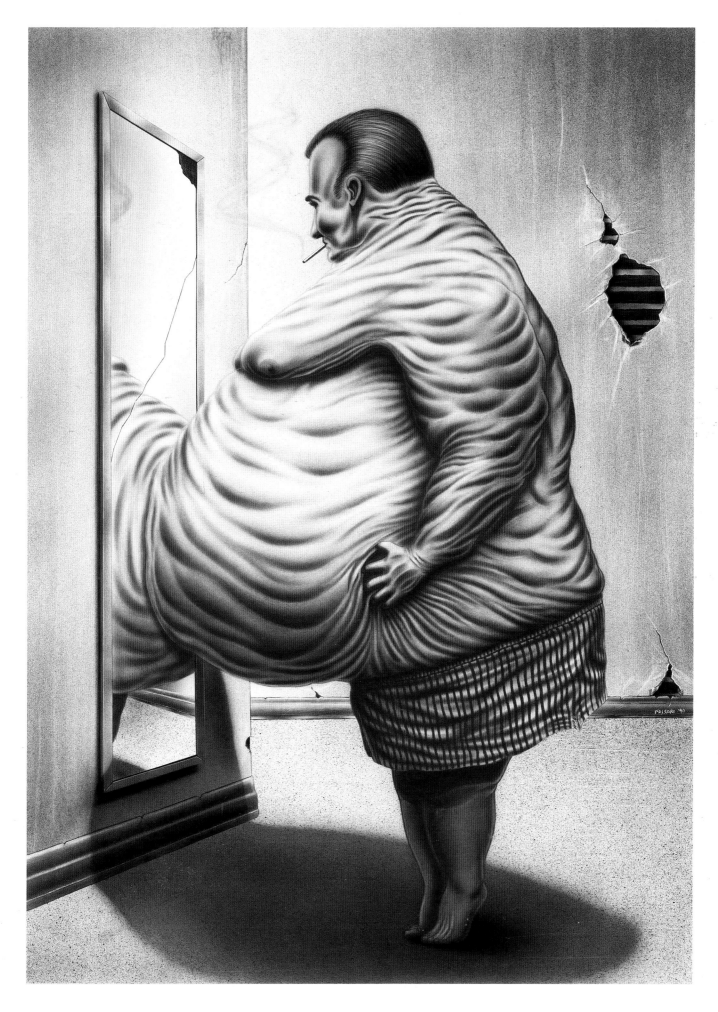

Susan Gal Illustration
689 Third Avenue
San Francisco, California 94118
(415) 668-9262
FAX: (415) 668-0125

Beware
of the
Stain Gang

Dave Garbot
8422 Westberry Lane
Tinley Park, Illinois 60477
(708) 532-8722
FAX: (708) 532-8725

Michael Garland
19 Manor Road, RR #2
Patterson, New York 12563
(914) 878-4347
FAX: (914) 878-4349

Work appears in:
Illustrators 23, 24, 25, 26, 27, 28,
29, 30, 32, 33
American Showcase 9, 10, 11, 13, 14
Adweek Portfolio of Illustration 1987
The Creative Illustration Book 1989

Clients include: J. Walter Thompson,
AT&T, Hartford Insurance, IBM,
General Electric, Forbes, Ladies'
Home Journal, Muir Cornelius Moore,
Avon, Cosmopolitan, Fortune, New York
Magazine, Simon & Schuster, Crown
Publishers, Scribner/Atheneum

Publishers, Harper & Row, Bantam
Books, Ballantine Books, Random
House, ABC, NY Ayer, Playboy,
Woman's Day, Saatchi & Saatchi
Compton, CBS Records, Dell Books,
RJ Reynolds, NBC, Pocket Books.

Doreen Gay-Kassel
24a Chestnut Court
Princeton, New Jersey 08540
(609) 497-0783
FAX: (609) 252-0857

Clients include:
AT&T, National Geographic, Donvier,
HBO, Woman's Day, Newsweek
International, Nation's Business, Whittle
Communications, Travel Weekly,
Cahner's Publishing, Houghton Mifflin,
Macmillan, Prentice-Hall, Silver Burdett
& Ginn, Oracle Magazine.

More work can be seen in
Showcase 10, 12 and 13.

3-D ILLUSTRATION, ALL CLAY.

Thomas A. Gieseke
7909 West 61st Street
Merriam, Kansas 66202
(913) 677-4593
FAX in Studio

See American Showcase, Volumes
10 through 14 for more of my work. Or
write or call for reprints of those pages.

Bart Goldman
360 West 36th Street
Suite 8NW
New York, New York 10018
(212) 239-0047
FAX: (212) 239-0062

Clients:
Ogilvy and Mather
Sony
St. Martin's Press
The New Yorker
The New York Times

Scali, McCabe, Sloves
BusinessWeek
Money
AT&T
The Los Angeles Times
Scholastic

Annuals:
Society of Illustrators 27, 29, 31
American Illustration 1, 4

THE AESTHETES
OF ADBIZ
OR
WEARING
CUTOFFS ON
MOUNT OLYMPUS

Flip through the pages of this book. Dazzling, are they not? And who created all this sleek, gorgeous stuff? Illustrators and photographers, of course. But who hired these people? Who phoned them 11 hours before deadline, wheedled them down to half their fee, and dangled the phony carrot of big future assignments before them?

Art Directors. The pampered aesthetes of advertising. The acclaimed Matisses of Mad Avenue. The finicky hothouse plants who can perch high on a chrome stool, sucking yesterday's garlic soup out of their beards while green flies swarm at their underarms, and tell you with a straight face that the idea of grey for the agency stationery makes them nauseous.

But hey, despite the general view, I happen to believe that art directors should not be rounded up and exterminated en masse. I take the more liberal view: Daily flogging and seven-to-ten without probation might suffice.

Let us be kind to art directors. A majority, scientists tell us, are human beings like you and me.

Human beings? Okay, I can buy that.

But like you and me? People who put their pants on one leg at a time? Alas, no. We are talking major-league exotic here. I have it on good authority that certain art directors leap into their pants from feathery nests high within spacious Soho lofts. Others cram both legs into one pant and hop to work, daring anyone to question or snicker. The point is, art directors are not keen on doing the expected, and we mere mortals had better get used to it. As a first step, let's dispel a few myths about art directors once and for all.

Myth 1: *Art directors can be identified by their creative manner of dress.* Creative my foot! What they do is dress unexpectedly. Consider that critical event, the client presentation. If your clients wear mousy blue suits with red paisley ties (as is their custom), count on it- your art director will show up in faded Levi's with slashes below the knees, a rumpled silk shirt, and possibly a faint glint of gold at one earlobe. If, on the other hand, the clients go casual, your art director instinctively knows to show up in a loosely draped Armani suit with an outrageously graphic tie and....Reeboks. With dirty, broken laces. Unmatched. (Matched, you see, would be boring.)

Myth 2: *Art directors eat.* No, they only drink. Coffee til 5, vodka after. When they do pretend to eat, it's only to assemble things that are guaranteed to spill on mechanicals-greasy things like peanut butter, steak tartare, or tuna salad. Try presenting a comp sometime with a huge kosher pickle smudge and a ring of Folger's Instant obscuring the body copy. (I once had a client who thought these additions were part of the design and got huffy when they didn't show up in the finished ad! But clients are a story for another time- the witching hour, perhaps.)

continued on page 1026

Lisa Goldrick
738 Hillcrest Road
Ridgewood, New Jersey 07450
(201) 702-1328 or (201) 652-3835

Guaranteed happy results
for the busy art director!

Portfolio or further
samples await your call.

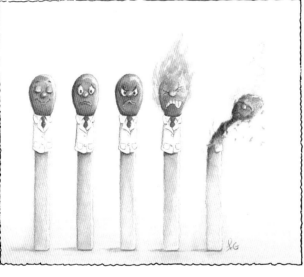

ILLUSTRATOR EXTRAORDINAIRE!

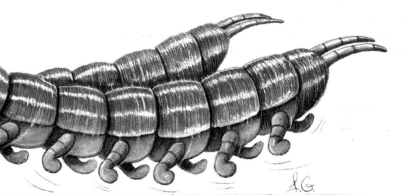

Carter Goodrich
137 Water Street
Stonington, Connecticut 06378
(203) 535-1141
(800) 992-4552
FAX # upon request

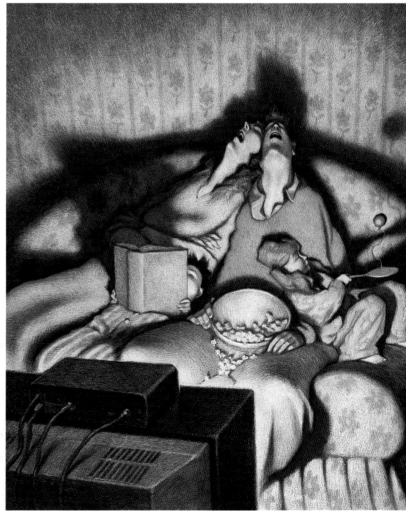

Carter Goodrich
137 Water Street
Stonington, Connecticut 06378
(203) 535-1141
(800) 992-4552
FAX # upon request

David Gordon
4120 Emerald Street, #3
Oakland, California 94609
(415) 954-1240

Clients Include:
New York Tmes, The New Yorker,
Sports Illustrated, Colossal Pictures,
CMP Publications, Washington
Journalism Review, Pentagram,
Amblin and Universal Pictures.

Thomas Gormady

Out-of-my-Mind / Illustration
1221 West Ben White Boulevard
#208A
Austin, Texas 78704
(512) 326-8383
FAX: (512) 326-8889

Clients include: Fisher Price, Dunlop
Sports, Mentholatum, Libby's, Welch's,
Hyatt Regency/Buffalo, Owen/GALDERMA
Matrix Medical, Ellio's Pizza, Buffalo Eve.
News, Quaker Oats, Marcus James
Wines, Mrs. Richardson's Toppings,
Nance's, Crystal Beach Amusement
Park, Canterbury of New Zealand.

G T O h R o M m A a D s Y

Mary GrandPré
475 Cleveland Avenue North
Suite 222
St. Paul, Minnesota 55104
(612) 645-3463
FAX: (612) 645-5118

Tel : 612/645-3463

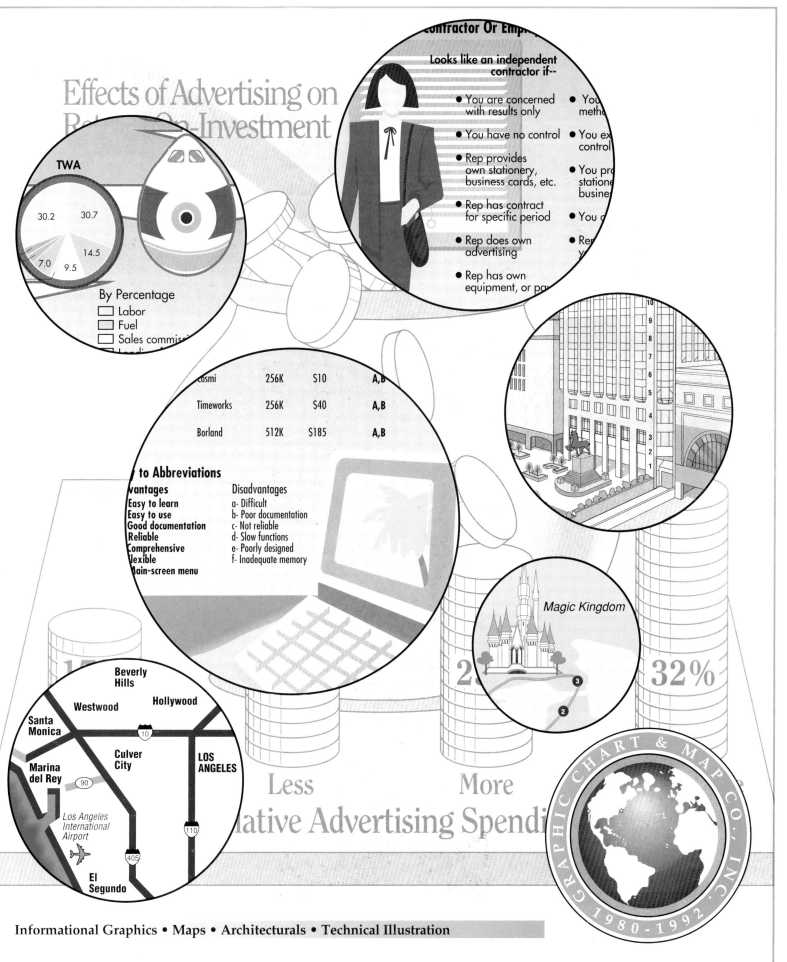

Effects of Advertising on Return-On-Investment

TWA

30.2 30.7
7.0 9.5 14.5

By Percentage
- Labor
- Fuel
- Sales commissi
- Landi

Contractor Or Empl

Looks like an independent contractor if--

- You are concerned with results only
- You have no control
- Rep provides own stationery, business cards, etc.
- Rep has contract for specific period
- Rep does own advertising
- Rep has own equipment, or pa

- You meth
- You ex control
- You pro statione busine
- You c
- Rep y

Cosmi	256K	$10	A,B
Timeworks	256K	$40	A,B
Borland	512K	$185	A,B

to Abbreviations

vantages
Easy to learn
Easy to use
Good documentation
Reliable
Comprehensive
Flexible
Main-screen menu

Disadvantages
a- Difficult
b- Poor documentation
c- Not reliable
d- Slow functions
e- Poorly designed
f- Inadequate memory

Magic Kingdom

3
2

2 32%

Beverly Hills
Westwood **Hollywood**
Santa Monica
Culver City **LOS ANGELES**
Marina del Rey
Los Angeles International Airport
El Segundo

Less More

lative Advertising Spendi

David Graves
133 RR Wheeler Street
Gloucester, Massachusetts 01930
(508) 283-2335
(508) 281-7874

Clients Include: Disney Productions, Disney/Spielberg Productions, Hasbro Toys, Parker Bros. Games, Mullen Adv., HBM Creamer, Doerr Assoc., Jim Cross Design, Whitaker Corp., Epsilon, Pacific Gas, Boston Gas, United Engineers, Peterson Griffin, Womens Sports Mag., Clarion Car Stereos, Emerson, Lane & Fortuna, Cosmoplus, Crowley & Daly, Carney Mohlin & Co., Houghton Mifflin Pub., GTE.

Rob Gregoretti
41-07 56th Street
Woodside, New York 11377
(718) 779-7913

Clients include:
CBS Records
RCA/BMG Records
Lifetime Television
Arnell/Bickford Associates Marketing

Additional work appears in
American Showcase 14

Rebecca Grimes
936 Stone Road
Westminster, Maryland 21158
(410) 857-1675
(410) 848-4472
FAX

Dimensional Illustration

Additional Samples:
American Showcase 13

John Steven Gurney
261 Marlborough Road
Brooklyn, New York 11226
(718) 462-5073
FAX service available

Clients include:
Ace Berkley Publishing
Ariel Books
Atheneum Publishing
The Bradford Exchange
CMP Publications
Contemporary Books

Field Publications
Houghton Mifflin
Jim Henson Productions
MacMillan Publishing
Molson's Golden Ale
National Lampoon Mag.
Orchard Books

Rumple Minze
Peppermint Schnapps
Scholastic Publishing
Simon & Schuster
Sunrise Publications
Wills & Evans Adv.
Workman Publishing

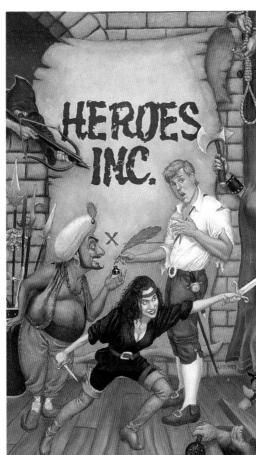

Steve Haimowitz
67-40 Yellowstone Boulevard
Forest Hills, New York 11375
(718) 520-1461
FAX: (718) 897-4740

Member Graphic Artists Guild

IBM • McGraw-Hill • Russ Berrie and Co.
Inc. • The National Theatre of the Deaf •
The Equitable Life Insurance Co •Whittle
Communications • Tennis Magazine •
Games Magazine • Scholastic • Spy

Michael Halbert
2419 Big Bend
St. Louis, Missouri 63143
(314) 645-6480
FAX: (314) 645-6480

Black and white and color
portfolio available

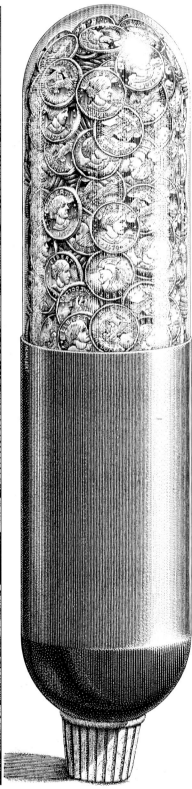

Joan Hall
155 Bank Street
Studio H954
New York, New York 10014
(212) 243-6059
FAX: (212) 924-8560

2 and 3 Dimensional Collage Illustration

Clients include: Adweek; Atlantic Records; The Bank of New York; CBS; Cunard Lines, Ltd.; Doubleday; Estee Lauder; Gourmet; GTE

Telecommunications; HBO; IBM; International Paper Co.; L'Express; Macy's; Merrill Lynch; New York Magazine; NYNEX; Omni; Popular Computing; RCA; Remy Martin; Simon & Schuster; Sofitel Hotels; Sony;

Stanford Medicine; The New York Times; Time/Life Inc.; Vogue; Warner Communications; WPLJ.

Instructor of "Collage Now", The School of Visual Arts, New York

JOAN HALL

10th Anniversary Fair 3/16 – 5/6

壮大な物語が始まる。

TOKYO-BAY LaLaport

Ken Hamilton
16 Helen Avenue
West Orange, New Jersey 07052
(201) 736-6532

Addison Wesley; Arbor House; Crown
Publishing; Daily News; Design Office;
Doubleday; Farrar Straus & Giroux;
Foltz/Wessinger, Inc.; The Food Group;
Freundlich Books; Kamber Group;
Inc. Life; McCann Erickson; Ogilvy
& Mather; Pittman Learning; Putnam;
SSC&B Lintas; J. Walter Thompson.

Member Graphic Arts Guild
Illustrators 23, 28
Showcase 12, 13, 14

Gerry Hampton
4792 Tiara Drive, Suite 204
Huntington Harbour, California 92649
(714) 840-8239
FAX in studio.

Clients Include: Armstrong/Pirelli;
Butterfield S&L; CA Federal S&L;
CA Trans; Church's Chicken; C Itoh;
Cooper Vision; CO State Lottery;
Disney Channel; 1st Interstate Bank;
Honda; Insight Magazine; ITT/Cannon;
KCET; Magnavox; Mattel; McDonnell
Douglas; Monex; NCR; New World
Pictures; Nissan; Paper Moon; Redkin
Labs; RJ Reynolds; SC Edison; Security
Savings Bank; Shape Magazine; Sony;
Syntex; Tomy Toys; TRW; Warner Bros.;
Yaesu; AC&R/CCL; BBDO; BGM;
Chiat/Day; Della Famina;
Flynn/Sabatino; Foote, Cone & Belding;
Grey; J Walter Thompson; Karsh &
Hagan; Marcoa DR; McCann-Erickson;
NW Ayer; Ogilvy & Mather; William Esty;
York Alpern.

Member:
Society of Illustrators LA
Graphic Artists Guild

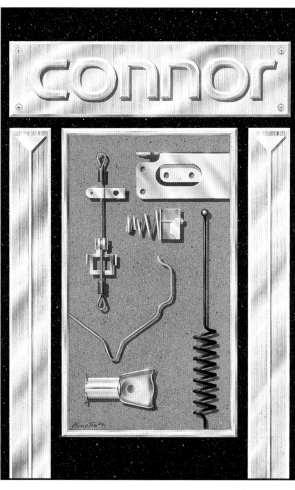

continued from page 1008

Myth 3: *Art directors work from 9 til 5.* Baloney! Art directors waft in by 10 on a good day, take 3-hour lunches, rant about their unfair workloads until 5, then settle back and create magic well into the night. What they do after that is unknown to mere writers (we religiously depart at 5), but Stolichnaya definitely plays a role.

Myth 4: *Art directors make good spouses.* True, art directors often marry- and marry often. (Why else would divorce lawyers send them Dom Perignon every Christmas?) There is, in fact, a politically active support group for ex-spouses of cardiovascular surgeons, art directors, and serial killers. (I know of one despairing wife who informed her art director husband that their marriage was finito- no response. She threatened to leave and take the Alfa- still nothing. Finally, as she began flinging clothes into a suitcase, the man looked up from his comic book: "You're taking all the wrong things. That blue with that red? Puh-leez!")

Myth 5: *Art directors are rational about color.* Art directors are, in fact, totally irrational about color; ask any printer. (Obituary columns herald the names of printers who didn't get the blacks black enough or the blues blue enough.) And white? Art directors see 50 whites where sane people see one, and only the right one will do. And they fuss constantly over PMS colors, scattering little chips of colored paper over their offices like confetti. Despite evidence to the contrary, PMS doesn't stand for what you think.

Myth 6: *Art directors are literate.* Huh! Ask any copywriter. Art directors never, never read a word of copy, and cannot spell. Or if they can, they do not. This enables them to foul up your headlines, thus expressing their lofty disdain for mere words. A single good image, they remind you, is worth ten thousand words. The only thing they read is telegrams, which is why they insist that all copy be written in the style of a pauper attempting to telegraph disaster in eight words or less.

They insist your 50-word copy is interminable. You cut. Still too long. You chip away until it is distilled to its barest essence: a mere 17 monosyllabic words. But lo, when the mechanical is unveiled before the client- surprise! Your bare essence has been mysteriously truncated to 12 words, three of which are grossly misspelled. What do you do? You thank the art director, of course. After all, it might have been worse: ten words, five misspellings would not have been out of the question.

Myth 7: *Art directors work with copywriters.* Come, now. Did you really think they did? Have you considered institutional care? When copywriters hunker down with art directors to spawn a "concept", it goes like this. Writer says gently, "Hey, how about this one?" Art director scratches nose and gazes out window. "This?" Art director emits yodeling yawn. Beginning to sweat, writer tries a third time: "Or this one, maybe?" Art director idly swats mosquito and tries to match corpse with PMS chip. Finally, when writer- bone-dry and spent- drops head onto desk and whimpers for death to come, behold! Suddenly both headline and art spring fully formed from art director's brain, like Athena from forehead of Zeus, and art director adds in afterthought, "I see it in plum and charcoal grey." At such moments, a rare intrepid writer occasionally protests, "But...hey, that idea is a mile off strategy ! " Art director sends a withering glare. "Then change the strategy!" he sniffs as he stalks off to create. (The worst of it is, the client will love it. And later it will win an award.)

Oh. One more thing about art directors: Maddening, obstreperous, haughty, crazed though they may be, they are the undisputed geniuses of our industry.

(Okay, I said it. I said it. Now will you fix my headline, for chrissake?)

Frank Murphy
Vice President/Group Copy Supervisor
Klemtner Advertising (Saatchi & Saatchi)
New York City

Johanna Hantel
437 East Belvidere Street; F-8
Nazareth, Pennsylvania 18064
215) 759-2025
201) 635-5264

John Hart
494 State Street
Brooklyn, New York 11217
(718) 852-6708
FAX: (718) 643-1755

Bryan Hendrix
777 Ponce de Leon Terrace
Atlanta, Georgia 30306
(404) 875-4290
FAX: (404) 875-5098

Clients:
The American Kennel Club
Benton & Bowles
Cambridge University Press
Cato Johnson, Y & R
Children's Television Workshop
Macmillan

Parents Magazine
Random House/ Knopf
Scholastic, Inc.
Sports Illustrated
Topps, Inc.

Member, Graphic Artists Guild

Rosemary Henry-May
2625 Garfield Street NW
Washington, DC 20008
(202) 667-0455
FAX: (202) 328-2057

Clients include
Smithsonian Institution
The World Bank
Trust House Forte
Maryland National Bank
Association of Landscape Architects

Mid-Atlantic Country Magazine
American Land Title Association
The Times Journal Co.
National School Board Association
Waste Age Magazine
Nature Conservancy

For additional work please see
Showcase Volume 14 page 1038

AIR AND SPACE MUSEUM

TITLE News
JANUARY · FEBRUARY 1991

San Diego
1991 ALTA Mid-Year
Convention

Rob Hess
63 Littlefield Road
East Greenwich, Rhode Island 02818
(401) 885-0331
FAX in studio

Technical and realistic illustration, rendered from blueprints, photographic references or product samples. Services include color, B&W photo retouching.

Clients include: Anderson-Little, AT&T, Autolite, Cahners Publishing, DCA, Fram, Hewlett-Packard, Keds, North Safety Equipment, Norton Company, Spalding.

Additional samples in American Showcase Volumes 12, 13, 14.

Member Graphic Artists Guild
© 1991 Rob Hess

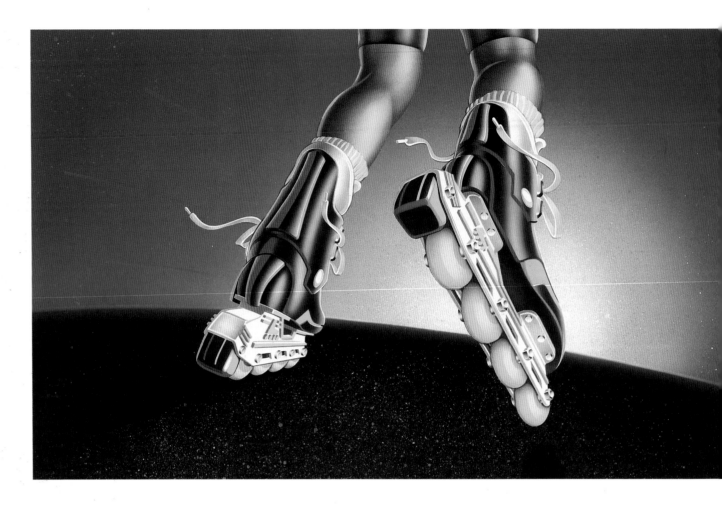

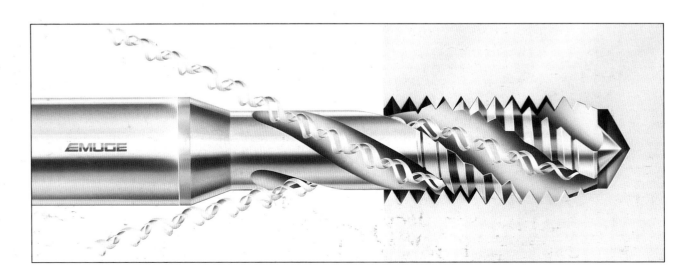

Jennifer Hewitson
859 Sandcastle Drive
Cardiff, California
(619) 944-6154
FAX upon request

Clients include:
Adweek
Disney
Harcourt Brace Jovanovich
Houghton Mifflin Co.

MCI
Macmillan/McGraw Hill
San Diego Union/Tribune
San Diego Zoo
Simon & Schuster

Scholastic
Whittle Communications
Yankee Magazine
To view more work:
American Showcase 14
Adweek Portfolios '87, '88

Hewitt/Low Studios
144 Soundview Road
Huntington, New York 11743
(516) 427-1404

Representing:
Margaret Hewitt

Clients include: Grey Entertainment
+ Media, Woman's Day, Scholastic,
Washington Post, Food Science
Associates and Viking USA

Hewitt/Low Studios
144 Soundview Road
Huntington, New York 11743
(516) 427-1404

Representing:
William Low

Clients include: New York Magazine,
Corporate Annual Reports, Hill and
Knowlton, Esquire, Corporate Graphics
London and Henry Holt/Books for
Young Readers

Henry Hill
2356 East Broadway
Tucson, Arizona 85719
(602) 623-4325

Represented by
Marla Matson
(602) 252-5072

Marla Matson
R E P R E S E N T S

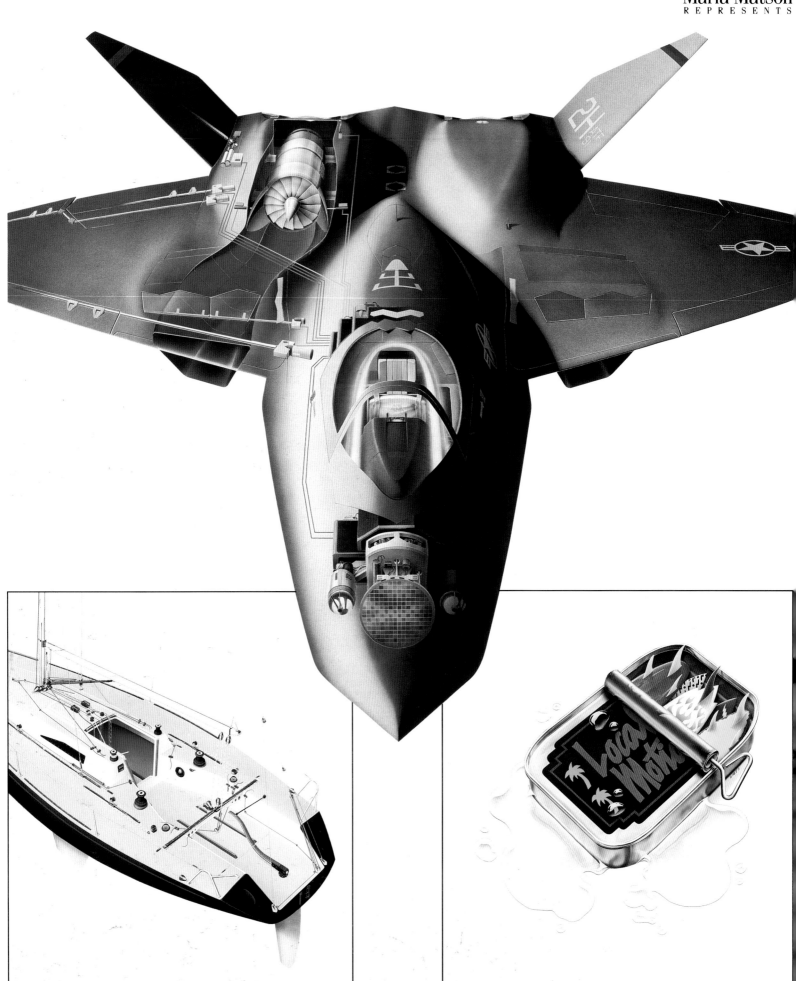

Kate Hoffman
(303) 493-1492
FAX: (303) 493-4807

People, places and things for print ads, annual reports, capabilities brochures and editorial.

Mini-portfolio available on request.

Peter Horjus
3647 India Street, Suite 1
San Diego, California 92103
(619) 299-0729
FAX: (619) 574-7774

Clients Include: ARCO; Carl's Jr.;
Coldwell Banker; Harcourt, Brace,
Jovanovich, Inc.; Kaiser Permanente;
Prudential Realty; San Diego Home/
Garden Magazine; San Diego
Magazine; San Diego Union/Tribune;
U.S. Grant Hotel.

Member: AIGA

Awards:
Print's Regional Design Annual '89, '90
SanDi Awards '87, '88, '90

Gary Hovland
3408 Crest Drive
Manhattan Beach, California 90266
(310) 545-6808

Clients include: The New York Times,
Conde Nast Traveler, Forbes,
Connoisseur, Time, Newsweek,
BusinessWeek, The Washington Post,
The Los Angeles Times, The San
Francisco Chronicle, Simon & Schuster,
Random House, Ogilvy and Mather
Advertising and Grey Advertising.

Marcie Wolf Hubbard
1507 Ballard Street
Silver Spring, Maryland 20910
(301) 585-5815

Top: Corporate Brochure, Robbins Gioia, Inc. Photographed by Charles Rumph. Lower Left: Promotional Collaboration. Barbara Tyroler, photographer. Lower Right: Magazine Cover, The Madeira School.

Clients include: Century 21, League of Women Voters, Manufacturers Hanover, National Institute of Health, Oliver Carr Company, Review & Herald Publishers, Washington Post, WJLA-TV7, and WTTG-TV5.

Dralene "Red" Hughes
9750 West Observatory Road
New Berlin, Wisconsin 53146
(414) 542-5547
FAX in Studio

Computer Creative: Illustration, Design,
Layout, Lettering, Desktop Publishing,
Formatting, Production, & Photo
Retouching/Manipulation.

Plus, regular boardwork: Illustrations,
Design, Layout, Lettering, & Production.

redgrafix

PROMOTIONAL

RESCUE
DESIGN
FIRST AID
414-542 CALL 5547!!!!

Robin Jareaux
(617) 524-3099

Kathy Jeffers
51 West 19th Street, 3rd floor
New York, New York 10011
(212) 255-5196
FAX: (212) 675-1206

Dimensional illustration, props, and prototypes

Clients include:
Ogilvy Mather, NW Ayer, Saatchi & Saatchi, Reader's Digest, Ralston Purina, AT&T, Hasbro, Avon Products, Modern Maturity, Chemical Bank, and New Age Journal

For additional work:
American Showcase 14, pages 522-23; AS 13, pages 374-75; AS 12, pages 312-13; AS 11, pages 264-65; AS 10, page 572; AS 8, page 189

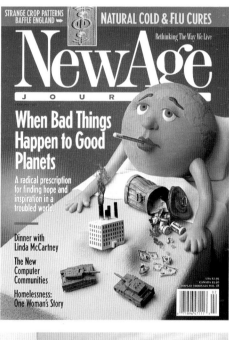

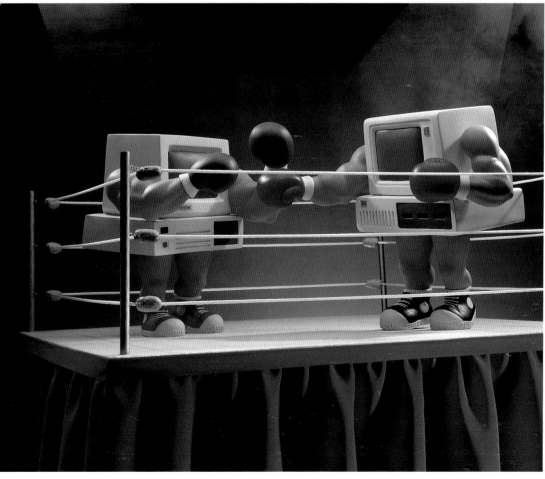

Bruce Jensen
41-61 53rd Street
Woodside, New York 11377
(718) 898-1887

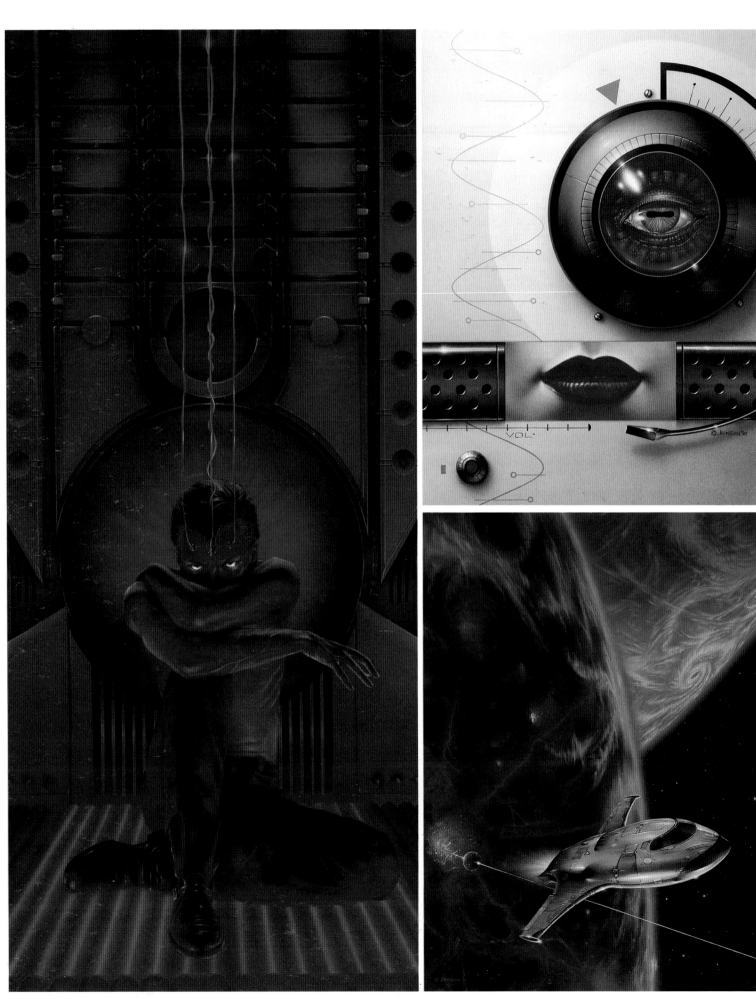

Steve Johnson
Johnson/Fancher Illustration

Lou Fancher, Associate
440 Sheridan Avenue South
Minneapolis, Minnesota 55405
(612) 377-8728

Represented in Los Angeles by:
France Aline, Inc.
(213) 933-2500

All concepts: Steve Johnson/Lou Fancher
Clockwise from top:
-Book Cover: The Brave Cowboy
-Annual Report: TCI's government and
 community affairs division.
-Editorial: Space, Politics and the
 Next President.
-Capability Brochure: International Law

Additional Work in:
Illustrators 27, 29, 30, 31, 32, 33
CA Illustration Annuals '86, '87,
'89, '90, '91
American Illustration 6

Eric Joyner
425 The Alameda
San Anselmo, California 94960
(415) 459-1448

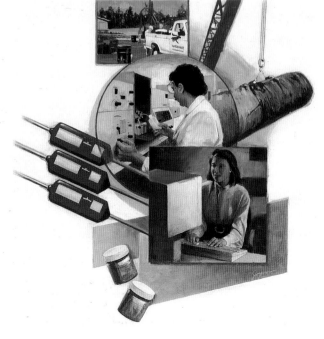

John Kachik
3000 Chestnut Avenue
Baltimore, Maryland 21211
(301) 467-7916
FAX: (301) 243-8239

KACHIK

Victoria Kann
336 East 22nd Street
New York, New York 10010
(212) 979-0988
FAX in studio

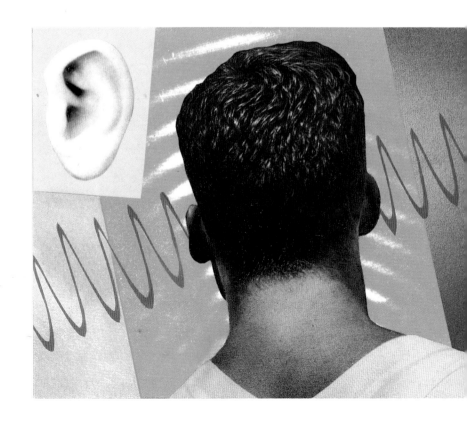

Ruth Sofair Ketler
101 Bluff Terrace
Silver Spring, Maryland 20902
(301) 593-6059
FAX in Studio

Clients include: Amiga World, Book-of-the-Month, Export Today, National Geographic, Legal Times of Washington, The Scientist, Society of American Foresters, Washington Post.
See also American Showcase 14.

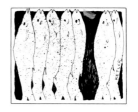

WASTE AGE

Darrel Kolosta
San Francisco, California
(415) 641-8119

KOLOSTA

Darrel Kolosta. Illustrator. 415.641.8119

Aaron Koster
2 Yeoman Way
Manalapan, New Jersey 07726
(908) 536-2815
FAX in Studio

Kenneth William Kotik
9 Last Chance Court
St. Peters, Missouri 63376
(314) 441-1091 (303) 799-3714
FAX Available

Clients: McDonnell Douglas Corp., Sabreliner, TRW, Falcon Jet International, Fairchild Aviation, Butler Aviation, Crown Publishing Group, National Air and Space Museum, U.S. Navy Blue Angels, U.S. Air Force Academy, Air Forces of Israel, Spain, Great Britain, Saudi Arabia, United States, Japan, St. Louis Aviation Museum, Experimental Aircraft Association.

Large format color brochure available.

Kenneth William Kotik
9 Last Chance Court
St. Peters, Missouri 63376
(314) 441-1091 (303) 799-3714
FAX Available

Clients: McDonnell Douglas Corp., Sabreliner, TRW, Falcon Jet International, Fairchild Aviation, Butler Aviation, Crown Publishing Group, National Air and Space Museum, U.S. Navy Blue Angels, U.S. Air Force Academy, Air Forces of Israel, Spain, Great Britain, Saudi Arabia, United States, Japan, St. Louis Aviation Museum, Experimental Aircraft Association.

Large format color brochure available.

Terry Kovalcik
124 West 18th Street
New York, New York 10011
(212) 620-7772
(201) 942-9359
FAX: (212) 620-7778

Looking to see more?
See AS Vols. 10,11,12,13,14;
Workbook 1991, 1992;
Single Image 4, 5, 6.

Clients include: AT&T, Bantam Books,
Discover Mag., Field & Stream,
Howard Savings, Lipton Soup, LIRR,
MCI, Macmillan Publ., Metro North,
Scholastic Inc., Warner Home Video,
and Welsh Farms.

Dan Krovatin
702 Oak Court
Monmouth Junction, New Jersey 08852
(908) 274-2363

Clients include:
New York Magazine, New Jersey
Monthly, Chermayeff & Geismar, Saatchi
& Saatchi, Houghton Mifflin, Doubleday,
The American Prospect, National
Review, Citibank, Manufacturers
Hanover Trust, Careers Magazine,
Writer's Digest, Home Life Insurance,
Northwest Airlines, West Point
Pepperel, Crane Paper.

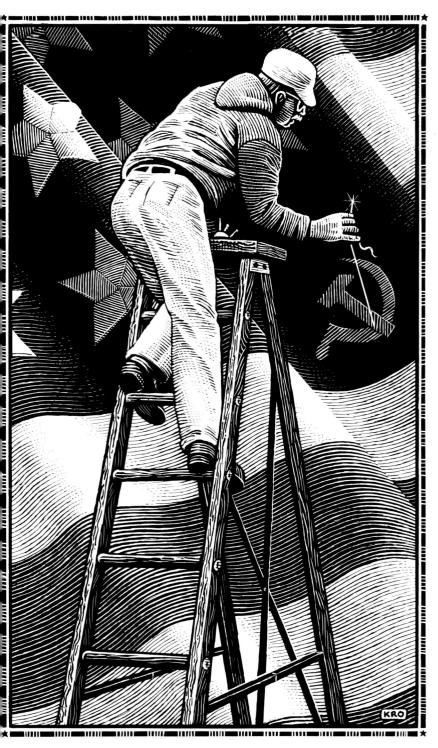

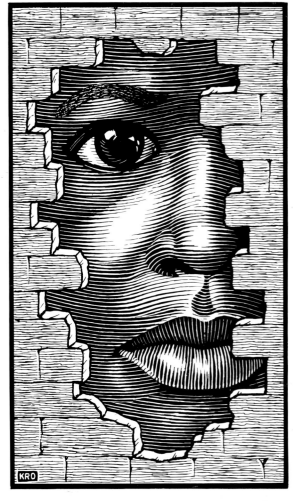

Don Kueker
829 Ginger Wood Court
St. Louis, Missouri 63021
(314) 225-1566
FAX in studio

Additional Work Exhibited In:
Work Book Volume Eleven
American Showcase volume Twelve
American Showcase volume Thirteen
and Fourteen (Illustration Volume)

Transparencies available on a wide
variety of subjects. The dynamic and
animated look in my painting is a
specialty.

Send for free personal full color
portfolio.

Client list on request.

Terry LeBlanc
25 Watertown Street
Newton, Massachusetts 02158
(617) 969-4886
FAX: (617) 969-4478

Product/Technical Illustration
• Color: pencil and markers
• Precision B/W: ink, computer
  art or pencil
• Cut-away, exploded, x-ray views
• Solutions that show how things
  function

Clients include:
Aerospace Museum (CA) • Alfa Laval •
Boston Whaler • Camp Dresser &
McKee • Ciba Corning Diagnostics •
Country Journal • Cruising World •
Doremus/Boston • Draper Lab (Apollo,
Polaris) • Dynatech • EG&G • Hasbro
Industries • HBM/Creamer • Ilex •

Instron • ITP/Boston • Laser Science •
Lexicon • Peckham • Polaroid • Raben
Publishing • Raytheon • Sanborn • Thermo
Electron • Wetzel Assoc. • WGBH

Member
Graphic Artists Guild, Boston

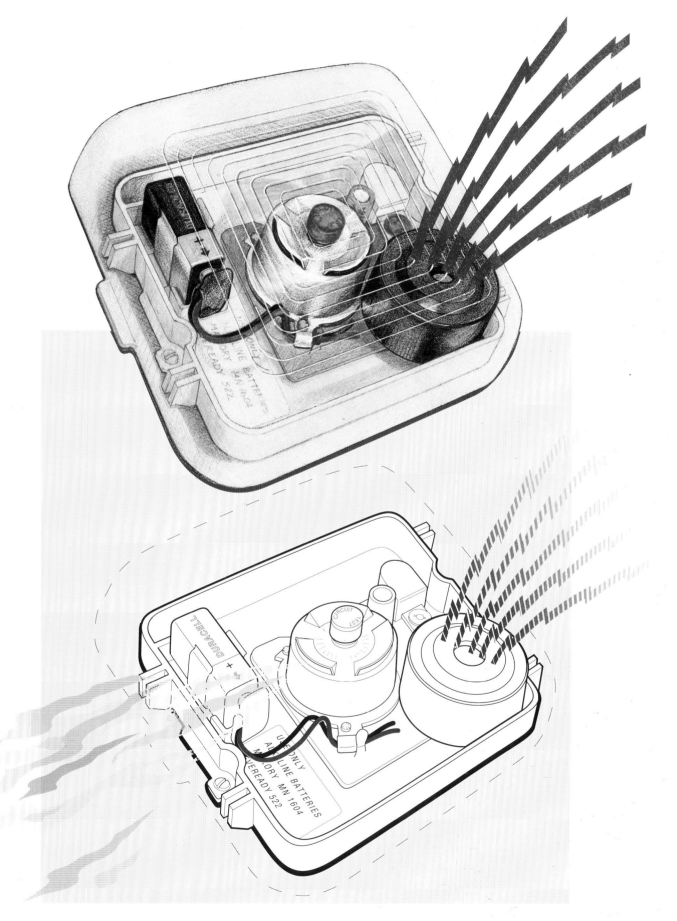

Rebecca J. Leer
560 West 43rd Street, 11-K
New York, New York 10036
(212) 563-4980
FAX: (212) 563-5253

Clients include:
Mortgage Banking
Prentice Hall
USIA
Corporate Finance
Baltimore Sun
Washington Post
Apple

Bon Appetit
Cahners Publishing
Washingtonian
U.S. Department of Justice
Nation's Business
Brunner Mazel, Inc.
Wickham & Assoc.
Franklin Institute Museum

Awards:
LA Society of Illustrators
DC Society of Illustrators

Additional work in American
Showcase 14

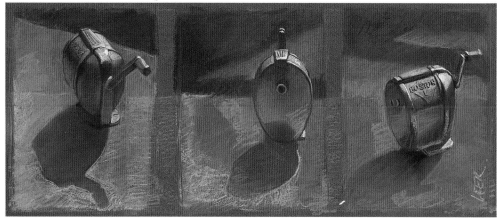

▲ POINTS OF VIEW

▲ THE RELATIONSHIP

▲ A TRUE OPTIMIST

odd Leonardo

Represented by:
Sara Reitz
PO Box 845
Half Moon Bay, California 94019
(415) 728-0424
FAX: (415) 728-5010

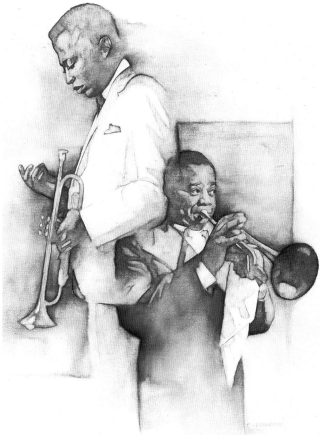

Mike Lester
(404) 447-5332
FAX: (404) 447-9559

HAY.

A free catalog of idiot-proof line art is now available for the asking. For your copy, call or fax today.

Mike Lester
(404) 447-5332
FAX: (404) 447-9559

Andy Levine
23-30 24th Street
Long Island City, New York
(718) 956-8539

H. B. Lewis
P.O. Box 1177
Old Chelsea Station
New York, New York 10011
(401) 539-0467 Direct
(800) 522-1377 Studio
FAX: (401) 539-0445

Clients include; A.B.C.; American Express; British Air; C.B.S.; Dancer, Fitzgerald & Sample; D.D.B.& Needham; Esquire; Forbes; Grey Advertising; Harcourt, Brace, Jovanovich; Hershey Foods; J. Walter Thompson; Kelloggs Food Corp.; Metropolitan Life; Metropolitan Transit Authority; McCann-Erickson Advertising; Money Magazine; National Geographic; Newsweek; New York Magazine; New York Times; Perrier; Ogilvy & Mather; Time Magazine; U.S. Air; Westinghouse; W. B. Doner & Co.; AT&T.

H. B. Lewis
P.O. Box 1177
Old Chelsea Station
New York, New York 10011
(401) 539-0467 Direct
(800) 522-1377 Studio
FAX: (401) 539-0445

Suzanne M. Long
1430 Pacific Avenue, #5
San Francisco, California 94109
(415) 776-3487

Randy Lyhus
4853 Cordell Avenue, #3
Bethesda, Maryland 20814
(301) 986-0036
FAX: (301) 907-4653

John Lytle
17130 Yosemite Road
Sonora, California 95370
(209) 928-4849 (delivery)
PO Box 5155
Sonora, California 95370
(mailing)

Additional Illustrations may be seen in:
American Showcase Vols. 5-7 & 10-14
Graphic Artist Guild Directory of
Illustration Vols. 5, 7 & 8

Clients include:
ABC Sports, American Express, Ampex,
AT&T, Atari, Bank of America, CitiBank,
CBS Sports, Edelbrock, Goodyear,
Hewlett-Packard, Jaguar, Levi-Strauss,
Eli Lilly, Nike, New York Telephone,

NFL Films, PG&E, Reebok, R.J.
Reynolds, Ryder Trucks, Seagrams,
Visa, Yamaha Motorcycles.

Member Society of Illustrators

THE ALL-STAR GAME ON CBS SPORTS.
CATCH TOMORROW'S LEGENDS TONIGHT.

CHICAGO 1990 All-Star Game

WRIGLEY FIELD
HOME OF
CHICAGO CUBS

TONIGHT 8:00 PM ET.
8:40 PM ET FIRST PITCH

Don Mannes
325 East 77th Street, #5D
New York, New York 10021
(212) 288-1661 Phone/FAX

Fine airbrush illustrations and technical art. Phantoms, explodes, and cutaways to show your product inside and out. Will work from any reference materials.

Member Graphic Artists Guild

Additional artwork in Showcase 14.

Partial client list: Hearst Corporation, Popular Mechanics, DMB&B, Norelco, The Family Handyman, Times Mirror Inc., Home Mechanix, Field & Stream, Skiing, Workbench, American Home, Greenstone Roberts Adv., Steigler Wells & Brunswick, Grolier Books, CBS Publications.

DON MANNES
TECH ART • ILLUSTRATION • DESIGN

Jeff Marinelli
4 South Main Street
2nd Floor, #3B
Canandaigua, New York 14424
(716) 394-2856
FAX in Studio

In Western New York,
call Linda Jagow at Illustrator's Quorum
(716) 546-7606

Clients: Yes.

Please call for more samples.
© 1991 Jeff Marinelli

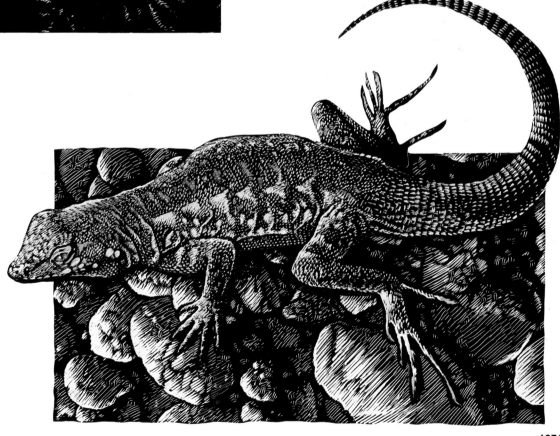

Jane Marinsky
63 Cleveland Avenue
Buffalo, New York 14222
(716) 881-3138
Call for FAX

Clients include: Changing Times,
Computer Task Group, Buffalo News,
Detroit News, Health Magazine,
National Fuel Gas, New York Woman,
New Woman, Postgraduate Medicine,
Rich Products Texas Restaurant Assoc.,
Toronto Life, Travel & Leisure

COMPUTER TASK GROUP, "THE INTEGRATED MANUFACTURING ENTERPRISE"

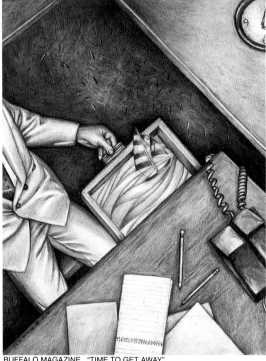

BUFFALO MAGAZINE, "TIME TO GET AWAY"

FOOD & SERVICE MAGAZINE, "EMPLOYEE OLYMPICS"

Bruce Marion
507 Highland Avenue
Half Moon Bay, California 94019
(415) 726-0595
FAX upon request

Clients include: University Games, Investment Vision, American Way, Image Magazine, Red Rose Naturals, Warner Brothers Records, Brentwood Publishing, Art Direct, Creative Edge, The Summit Organization, Inc., Fog Press, Steccone Products Co.

Member of the San Francisco Society of Illustrators and the Western Art Directors Club.

©1991 Bruce Marion

COVER FOR THE GAME "PENGUIN FREEZE-TAG" ©1991 UNIVERSITY GAMES

Roger Mark Illustration
8518 Alden
Lenexa, Kansas 66215
(913) 492-4444
FAX: (913) 492-4528

Represented by:
Helen Ravenhill
(913) 677-0028

Partial Client List: Arthur Andersen Consulting, Banquet Foods, Con-Agra, Cramer Sports Products, Fairbanks-Morse, Marley Corporation, Mobay Chemical (Cutter Div.), Montague-Sherry Adv. Agency, Multivac, Noble & Associates, Shell Oil, Stephens Adv. Agency, TWA-Pars, Tyson Foods.

James Marsh
21 Elms Road
London, England
SW4 9ER
01144 71 622 9530
FAX: 01144 71 498 6851

TDK TAPES

BATA POSTER

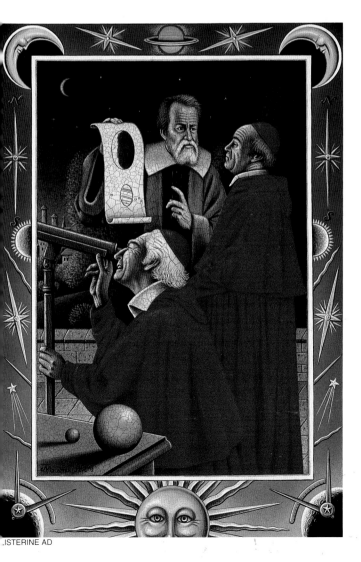

LISTERINE AD

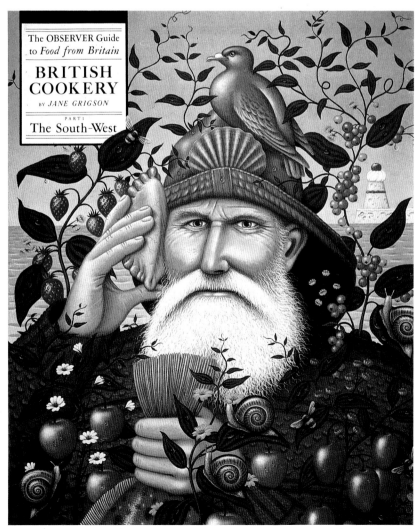

Do it by the book.

How do you decide on an appropriate fee for artwork you sell or buy? How do you write a contract that's fair to both artist and buyer? What are the implications of new technologies in the art marketplace? If you're an artist, what business practices should you expect from your clients? And if you're a buyer, what should you expect from a professional artist?

Artists and buyers alike will find good answers to questions like these in *Pricing and Ethical Guidelines,* 7th Edition. Published by The Graphic Artists Guild, the *Guidelines* contains the result of the Guild's extensive survey of pricing levels in every branch of the graphic arts, as well as a wealth of information on estimates, proposals, contracts, copyrights, and many other aspects of the business relationship between artist and buyer.

To order your copy of this indispensable reference, send $22.95 plus $3.50 shipping and handling, along with your name and address, to the **Graphic Artists Guild, 11 West 20th St., New York, NY 10011.** New York residents please add 8¼% sales tax (total $28.63).

GREGORY MARTIN

MARTIN
ILLUSTRATION

1307 GREENLAKE DR. CARDIFF, CA 92007 · TEL: 619 753 4073 FAX: 619 436 6931

Barbara Maslen
216 Suffolk Street
Sag Harbor, New York 11963
(516) 725-3121 Studio
FAX: (516) 725-4608
(212) 645-5325 NYC

Additional work appears in:
American Showcase: volumes 8-14
Adweek Portfolio: '88, '89, '90
Workbook: 13

BARBARA·MASLEN
ILLUSTRATION
216 SUFFOLK STREET
SAG HARBOR · NY · 11963
516·725·3121 · FAX·4608

WANTED

Problem-solvers.
Sages.
Wits.
Philosophers.
Boat-rockers.

■

We hope you've enjoyed reading the **VIEWPOINTS** in American Showcase 15. This popular feature is designed to enlighten and entertain our readers by providing unique insights on the current state of photography, graphic design, illustration, advertising, and corporate marketing.

We'd like to take this opportunity to invite you to share your own thoughts, opinions and methods with thousands of your colleagues worldwide.

The average **VIEWPOINT** is 1,000 words but we'll consider longer (or shorter) pieces. Have the article titled, typed double-space, and be sure to include your own name, job title, company and address. If we publish your submission in our next Showcase, you will receive a copy of the book, 500 reprints of your article and our eternal gratitude.

(Of course, we can't guarantee that yours will be published, but we do promise to acknowledge and read every submission.)

Go ahead, write down all those things you've always wanted to get off your chest. Speak out to those photographers, illustrators and designers you hire . . . share confidences with your colleagues . . . tell off your boss. Do it while you're feeling outraged/ satisfied/ frustrated about the work you create. Do it today and mail it to:

Cynthia Breneman
Viewpoints Editor
American Showcase, Inc.
915 Broadway
New York, New York 10010

Thanks a lot. We're looking forward to hearing from you and hope to see you in **AMERICAN SHOWCASE VOLUME 16!**

Jeff May
7351 Tulane Avenue
St. Louis, Missouri 63130
(314) 727-1476
In-studio FAX available

4-color original illustrations, tight black & white renderings, photo-illustration, design.
Portfolio available upon request.

Partial Client List: Anheuser-Busch, Anheuser-Busch Promotional Products Grp., City Corp., Hazel Atapco, Noble Broadcast, Ralston Purina.

Vision Statement: Visualizing the client's concepts by using my background in fine arts, design & art direction to create dynamic, energized illustrations that captivate the designated target audience. The images on this page represent a commitment to that unique sense of vision.

Patrick Merrell
124 West 18th Street
New York, New York 10011
(212) 620-7777
FAX: (212) 620-7778

10 ways to identify a Patrick Merrell illustration:
1. The signature.
2. The signature is spelled correctly.
3. It's on your desk before it's due.
4. It has a Patrick Merrell invoice attached to it.
5. Compare it to all the other ones he's done for all those other top clients.
6. Ask him.
7. There's a free Patrick Merrell calendar with it.
8. You hired him to draw it.
9. From the rubber stamp on the back with his name and address on it.
10. People see it and say, "Aaahhh."

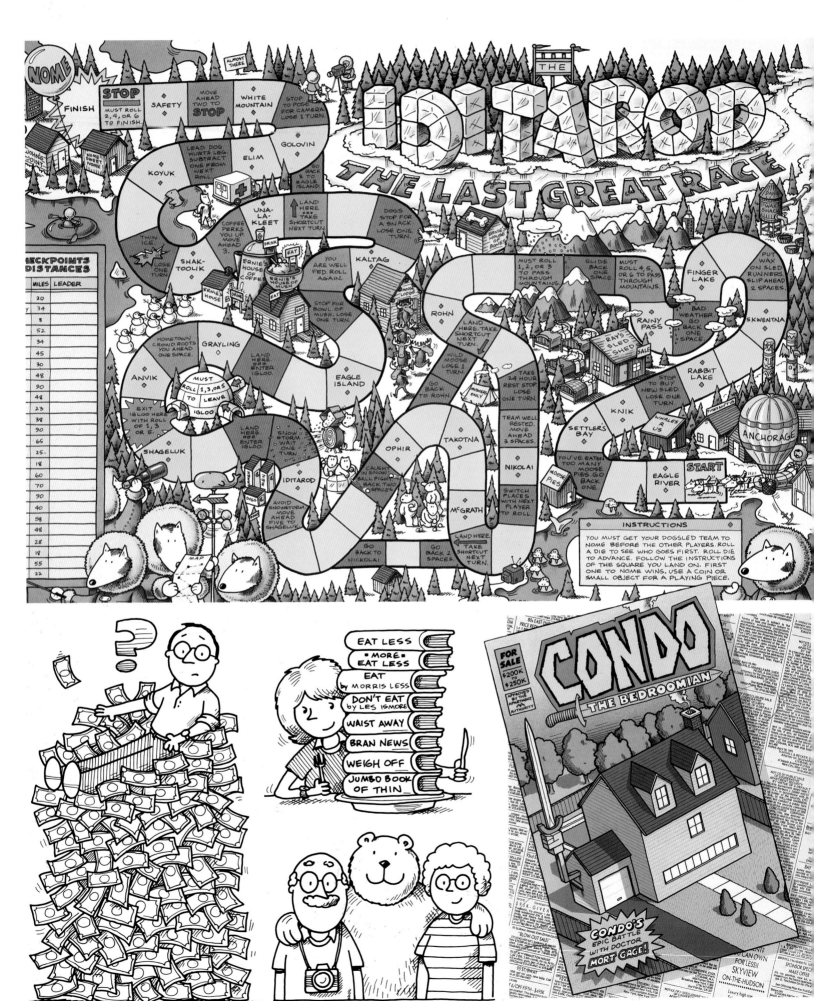

Patrick Merrell
124 West 18th Street
New York, New York 10011
(212) 620-7777
FAX: (212) 620-7778

Full-size portfolio or 35mm mailable
portfolio available.

More samples can be seen in
American Showcase 11, 12, 13 and 14.

David Milgrim
8 Gramercy Park South
Apartment 2G
New York, New York 10003
(212) 673-1432

Some clients:
Adweek, Hallmark, Parents Magazine,
Weight Watchers Magazine, Seventeen,
Gruner + Jahr, First Magazine, Pentech.

Call to see more.

Also see Showcase 14 and
RSVP 15, 16 and 17.

Ed Miliano

In USA contact
Frank Tagariello
(212) 889-2298

In Ireland contact
Mairéad Hennigan
01-2807626

Clients include: Audio, BusinessWeek, CBS Records, New York Woman, The New York Times, Premiere Magazine, Time, Travel & Leisure, Travel Holiday, Working Mother and Warner Books.

Celia Mitchell
(718) 626-4095
(814) 765-6339

Yoko Mitsuhashi
27 East 20th Street
New York, New York 10003
(212) 979-1266
FAX: (212) 979-5158

Partial Client List:
Aesop; Doubleday Publishing; Good Housekeeping; Harcourt, Brace & Jovanovich; Harper & Row Publishing; Johnson & Johnson; Kodansha and Kodansha International; MacMillan; Magazine House; McCalls; McGraw

Hill Publications; Ms. Magazine; NBC; New York Magazine; OCS News; Parents Magazine; Parke-Davis; Redbook; Scholastic Publications; Sesame Street Magazine and U.S. News.

Also Featured in These Magazines: Art Direction; Brain; Design; Graphic; Graphis; Idea; Illustration; New York, and Print.

Poster for Artist's Retrospective Exhibition

"The Silent Concert" children's book

"Haloween" Sesame Street Magazine

The Spiritual Drum" children's book

"Cats" OCS News

"Poppy" OCS News

"Aesop's Fables" magazine cover

Moonlight Press Studio
Chris Spollen
362 Cromwell Avenue
Ocean Breeze. New York 10305
(718) 979-9695
FAX: (718) 979-8919

Design illustration for agencies, design firms and magazines, worldwide. Mini Portfolio of 4/C and B/W. Samples available on request.

Moonlight Press Studio
Chris Spollen
362 Cromwell Avenue
Ocean Breeze. New York 10305
(718) 979-9695
FAX: (718) 979-8919

Design illustration for agencies, design firms and magazines, worldwide. Mini Portfolio of 4/C and B/W. Samples available on request.

READERS DIGEST

TEXAS BANK

BANK ONE

OHIO BANK

WILLIAM DOUGLAS MCADAMS

C.B.S. SPORTS

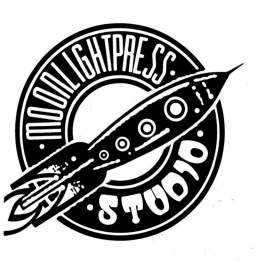

MOONLIGHTPRESS STUDIO

PHILIP MORRIS

AUDI USA

Meg Ann Moorhead
205 East 77th Street
New York, New York 10021
(212) 628-4285

Donald Mulligan
418 Central Park West, Suite 81
New York, New York 10025
(212) 666-6079
FAX available

Illustration and award-winning design.
Mac-equipped.
Further examples please refer to
Showcase 12, 13, and 14 and
Adweek Portfolio.
Mini-portfolio on request.

Some clients - Avenue, Chocolatier,
Diversion, MD, Life Today, Wall Street
Journal, Fodor, John Wiley, Dow
Chemical, Mount Sinai, Villeroy & Boch,
South Street Seaport, Harcourt, Brace.

Bottom- Poster, 18x24 for South Street
Seaport Museum, N.Y. Top Left -. Real
Estate Campaign for Classic Properties.
Agency; Shaw & Dugow. Top Right;
Villeroy & Boch Campaign. Agency;
Bergelt, Litchfield, Raboy & Tsao.

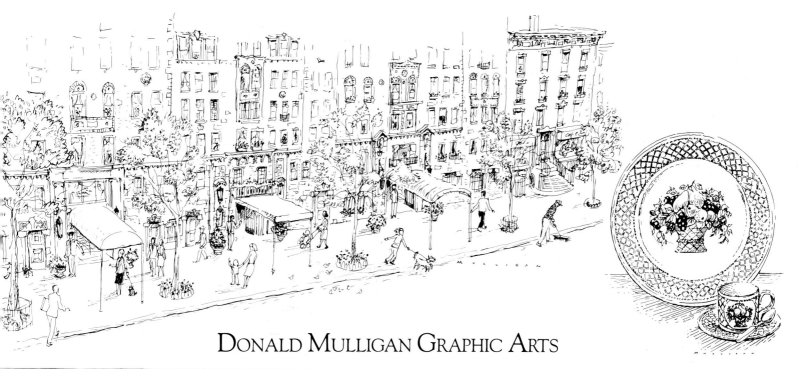

DONALD MULLIGAN GRAPHIC ARTS

John Murray
Illustration/Graphics
(617) 424-0024
FAX: (617) 424-8650

ILLUSTRATION

ILLUSTRATION

John Murray
Illustration/Graphics
(617) 424-0024
FAX: (617) 424-8650

PEPSI **Boston Music Awards**
TUESDAY, APRIL 16, 1991 8:00 PM
THE WANG CENTER FOR THE PERFORMING ARTS

STRAWBERRIES · BOSTON HERALD · ASCAP · THE WANG CENTER · TWA

IN MEMORIAM
UNIVERSAL WIDGET CORP.
1975 - 1990
virus infection, 1990

Ann Neumann
78 Franklin Street
Jersey City, New Jersey 07307
(201) 420-1137
FAX: (201) 653-3092

Work appears in:
Illustrators 31
American Illustration 2
American Showcase 6,7,10,11,12,13
Adweek Art Directors Index 11
Adweek Portfolio 1986

Clients Include:
Aris Isotoner
Atlantic Monthly
Chemical Bank
J Walter Thompson
Macmillan Publishing
Manufacturers Hanover
Medical Economics

New York Times
New York Zoological Society
Ogilvy & Mather
Psychology Today
Washington Post
William Morrow & Company
Viking Penguin

Rosemary Nothwanger
7604 Shadywood Road
Bethesda, Maryland 20817
(301) 469-7130

Clients include: Smithsonian Institution, National Wildlife Federation, National Institute of Health, Woods Hole Oceanographic Institution, US Dept. of State, Clorox Co., National Science Teachers Assoc., Hazelton-Webb Design, Garden Design Magazine, Studio Grapic, Potomac Almanac.

Further work seen in: Creative Source Directory Vols., One & Two, American References 2nd Edition, Artists of the Chesapeake Bay, 1st Edition, Wildlife Art News 1990-91, National Wildlife Magazines.

Bob Novak
6878 Fry Road
Middleburg Heights, Ohio 44130
(216) 234-1808
FAX in Studio

My partial client list and other samples
are available in American Showcase
12, page 814 and 14, page 1116.

Erik Olson
616 9th Street
Brooklyn, New York 11215
(718) 965-0914

Clients include:
DHL Express, Walt Disney, Nintendo,
Paramount Pictures, Emerald Pictures,
Doubleday Books, Avon Books,
DAW Books, TSR Inc., Pop-shots Inc.

Portfolio available upon request.

ILLUSTRATION
ERIK
OLSON
718 965 0914

Lori Osiecki
123 West 2nd Street
Mesa, Arizona 85201
(602) 962-5233
FAX: (602) 962-5233

Patrick S. Owsley
1 Buckingham Court, #5
Michigan City, Indiana 46360
(219) 872-6570
FAX: (219) 872-6570

Cartoon illustration.

Call for additional samples!

© 1992 Patrick S. Owsley.

John Pack
2342 North Fillmore Street
Arlington, Virginia 22207
(703) 243-4024
FAX: (703) 243-4024

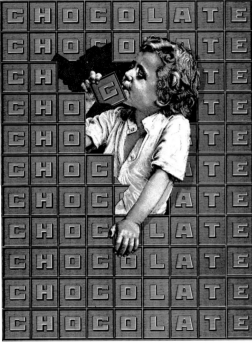
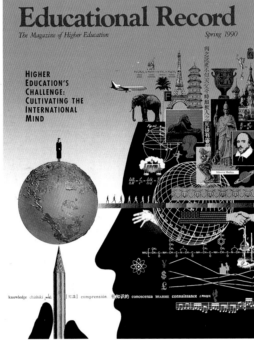

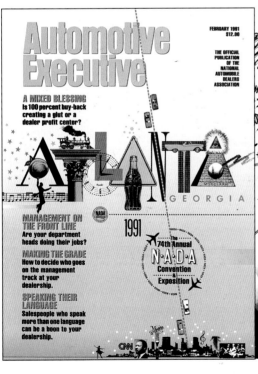

Melanie Marder Parks

5 Broadview Lane
Red Hook, New York 12571
(914) 758-0656
FAX: (914) 758-0656

Clients Include:
Bloomingdale's
Book-of-the-Month Club, Inc.
CBS Records
Condé Nast
Franklin Library
Grove Weidenfeld
Harper Collins

Houghton Mifflin
Lincoln Center
Macy's
Money Magazine
New York Times
Nonesuch Records
Oxford University Press
Penguin USA

Prentice Hall
Random House
St. Martin's Press
Shearson's of London Food
Simon and Schuster
University of Pennsylvania
Walt Disney Publications
Whittle Communications

Pearlray Illustration
James J. Garcia
430 Dongan Hills Avenue
Staten Island, New York 10305
(718) 351-3071
FAX: (718) 980-1630

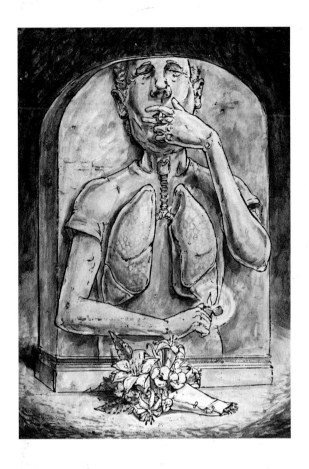

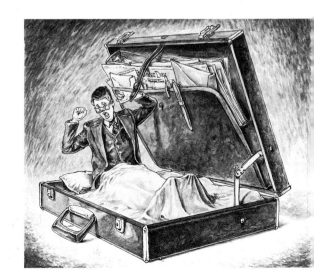

Joe Peery
3561 Ebenezer Road
Marietta, Georgia 30066
(404) 973-0010

Specializing in caricature and humorous illustration. Also experienced in rendering backgrounds and creating character designs for animation. Video reel available.

Clients include: Disney, Delta, Kellogg's, Orkin, CNN, WTBS, PBA, DuPont, Contel, General Electric, Atlantic Steel, Gates, and Southern Homes magazine.

Daniel Pelavin
80 Varick Street Suite 3B
New York, New York 10013
(212) 941-7418
FAX: (212) 431-7138

Illustration

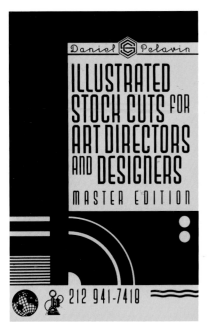

ASK FOR YOUR FREE CATALOG OF B/W STOCK
ILLUSTRATION FROM THE EVER-EXPANDING
STOCK CUTS COLLECTION

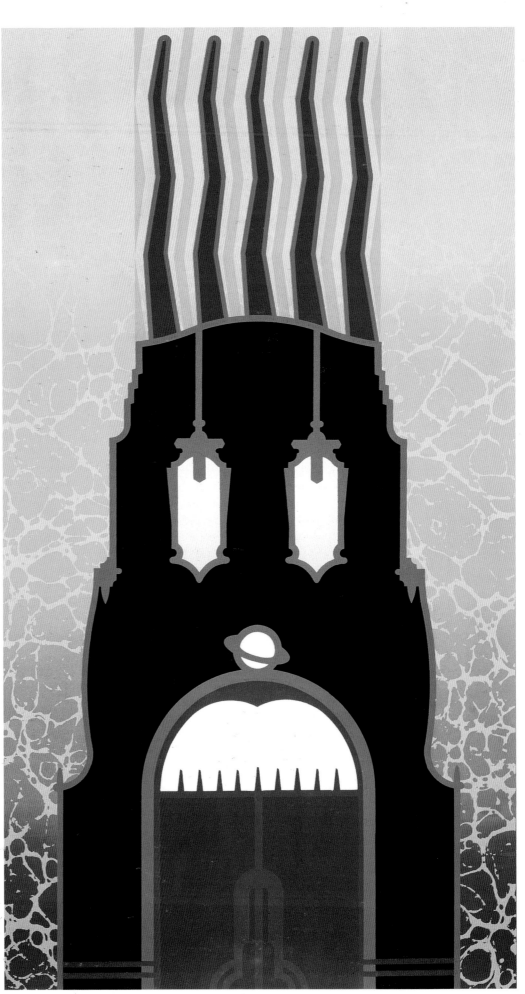

Daniel Pelavin
80 Varick Street Suite 3B
New York, New York 10013
(212) 941-7418
FAX: (212) 431-7138

Lettering and typographic design

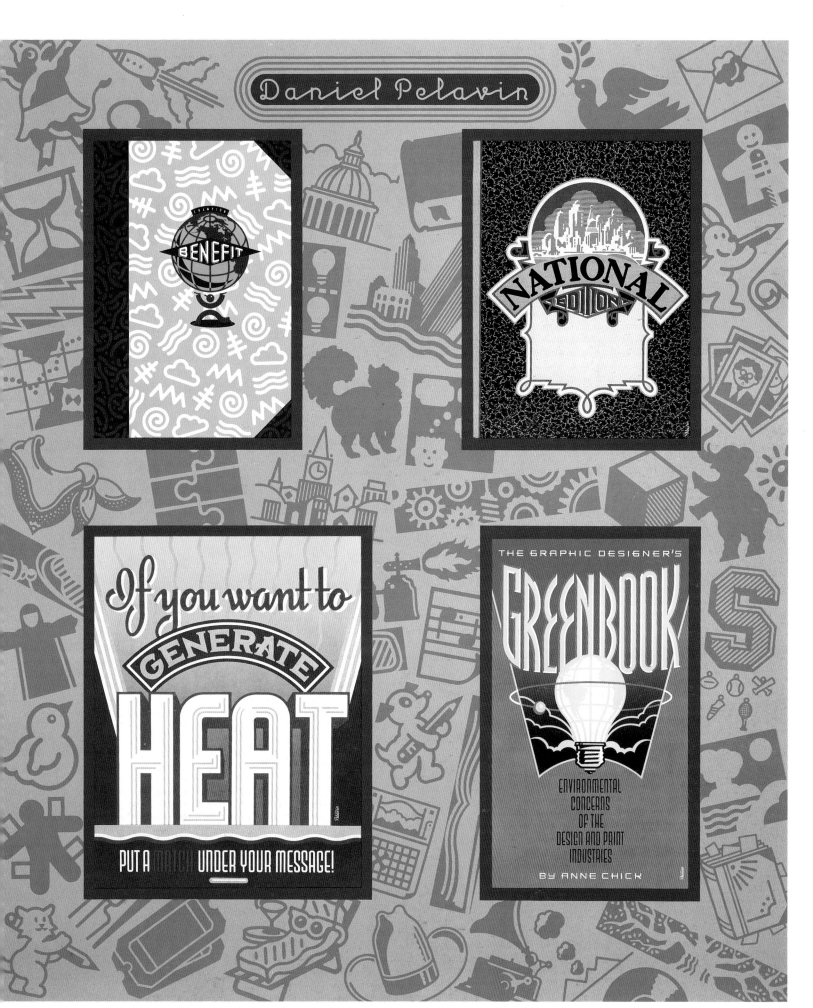

Joanne Pendola
2 Sutherland Road, #34
Boston, Massachusetts 02146
(617) 566-4252
FAX Available

Clients include:

Bostonia
Dell
Details
Macmillan
Ms.

NAL/Plume
Penguin USA
PC Computing
Rizzoli International
St. Martin's Press
Worldwide Publications
Ziff Davis

PENDOLA
ILLUSTRATION

Al Pisano
22 West 38 Street, Suite 600
New York, New York 10018
(212) 730-7666

Al Pisano is a Multi-award-winning, Three-dimensional Artist/Designer, who works in Wood, Leather, paper sculpture, collage and clay. He services a wide variety of clients world-wide, and has received recognition for his talents both in Design and Typography, as well as in illustration.

Clients include: American Express, Avon, Exxon, Seagram National Distillers, Citicorp, Reader's Digest, Purina, Schweppes, Bantam Books, Simon & Schuster, Berkeley, Dell Books, Time-Life, Newsweek, General Foods Corporation, Turner Broadcasting and many others.

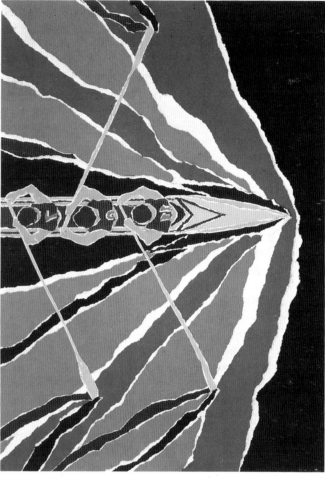

Colin Poole
817 Mackall Avenue
McLean, Virginia 22101
(703) 893-0759
FAX: (703) 448-1270

Walter Porter
4010 West El Camino del Cerro
Tucson, Arizona 85745
(602) 743-9821
FAX: (602) 743-9821

Marla Matson Represents
(602) 252-5072
FAX: (602) 252-5073

America West Airlines, American Rifle
Assoc., Arizona Highways Magazine,
Arizona Lottery, Canyon Ranch Resort,
Dail Corp., Emerald Homes, IBM, Merit
Software, Park Hyatt Hotels, Phoenix
Cardinals, Tempe Historical Museum,
University Medical Center Corp., U.S.
West Communications

Rodica Prato
Studio One Two Three
154 West 57th Street
New York, New York 10019
(212) 245-5854
FAX in studio

**Mike Quon
Design Office, Inc.**
568 Broadway, Suite 703
New York, New York 10012
(212) 226-6024
FAX: (212) 219-0331

Design and Illustration for Advertising.

Clients include:
Clairol, Inc., DuPont, Macy's, Merrill Lynch, New York State Lottery, Showtime, United Parcel Service, Pepsi, Hersheys, Chemlawn, Dunkin' Donuts, Marlboro, Central Park Zoo, Foot Quarters, American Express, Roy Rogers, Home Box Office, McDonalds, Pampers, Philip Morris.

DEPT. OF CONSUMER AFFAIRS

THE IMAGE BANK

HACHETTE MAGAZINES

CLAIROL OPTION CHALLENGE

CLAIROL

BELL ATLANTIC

Mike Quon
Design Office, Inc.

568 Broadway, Suite 703
New York, New York 10012
(212) 226-6024
FAX: (212) 219-0331

Design and Illustration for Advertising.

Clients include:
Amtrak National Railroad, Burger King, Chase Manhattan Bank, Foot Locker, National Football League, New York Times, WNET Thirteen, World Trade Center, NYNEX, Hanes, Sports Illustrated, Ortho Pharmaceutical, Cinemax, Quasar, T.G.I. Fridays, Teleport Communications, Coca-Cola.

TYPE DIRECTORS CLUB/PROMOTION

SPORTS MARKETING

HACHETTE MAGAZINES

APPLE COMPUTERS

PARSONS SCHOOL OF DESIGN

RadenStudio
3016 Cherry
Kansas City, Missouri 64108
(816) 756-1992
FAX: (816) 756-1186

East Coast Rep:
Mendola Ltd.
(212) 986-5680

Midwest and West Coast Rep:
Linda Pool
(816) 761-7314

Clients include:
United Parcel Service
TV Guide
Amway International
Simon & Schuster
Activision
AT&T

Peterbilt Trucks
Citibank
Hyatt Hotels
MacMillan Books
Doubleday
Shell Oil
Johnson & Johnson

RadenStudio
3016 Cherry
Kansas City, Missouri 64108
(816) 756-1992
FAX: (816) 756-1186

East Coast Rep:
Mendola, Ltd.
(212) 986-5680

Midwest and West Coast Rep:
Linda Pool
(816) 761-7314

Clients include:
United Parcel Service
TV Guide
Amway International
Simon & Schuster
Activision
AT&T

Peterbilt Trucks
Citibank
Hyatt Hotels
Macmillan Books
Doubleday
Shell Oil
Johnson & Johnson

Lyne Raff
9501 Rolling Oaks Trail
Austin, Texas 78750
(512) 219-1208

Frank Riley
108 Bamford Avenue
Hawthorne, New Jersey 07506
(201) 423-2659
FAX Available

© FRANK RILEY

Harry Roolaart
6449 Montpelier Road
Charlotte, North Carolina 28210
(704) 552-6311

Represented by:
Trlica/Reilly:Reps
Post Office Box 13025
Charlotte, North Carolina 28270
(704) 372-6007
(704) 365-6111
FAX available

For additional work, see:
American Showcase 14, page 733

B&W PHOTO BY JIM McGUIRE

B&W PHOTO BY HOWARD BEMUS

Bob Rose
873 Broadway
Room 406
New York, New York 10003
(212) 982-9535
(201) 378-8376
FAX: (201) 378-8376

Marc Rosenthal
#8 Route 66
Malden Bridge, New York 12115
(518) 766-4191
FAX: (518) 766-4191

clients include:
Altman & Manley/Eagle Advertising,
Time, Fortune, Newsweek, US
News & World Report, Playboy,
Vanity Fair, New York Magazine, ATT,
Whittle Communications, The Boston
Globe, The New York Times, The
Philadelphia Inquirer

Barry Ross
12 Fruit Street
Northampton, Massachusetts 01060
(413) 585-8993

Illustrating To Explain

My paintings take complex technological processes and presents them to the layperson in terms that are simple, understandable, and aesthetic.

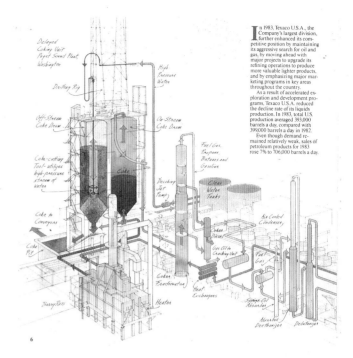

In 1983, Texaco U.S.A., the Company's largest division, further enhanced its competitive position by maintaining its aggressive search for oil and gas, by moving ahead with major projects to upgrade its refining operations to produce more valuable lighter products, and by emphasizing major marketing programs in key areas throughout the country.

As a result of accelerated exploration and development programs, Texaco U.S.A. reduced the decline rate of its liquids production. In 1983, total U.S. production averaged 393,000 barrels a day, compared with 399,000 barrels a day in 1982.

Even though demand remained relatively weak, sales of petroleum products for 1983 rose 7% to 706,000 barrels a day.

6

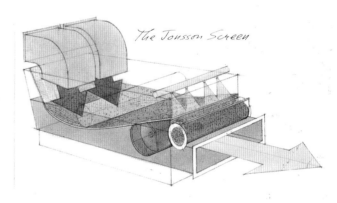

The Jonsson Screen

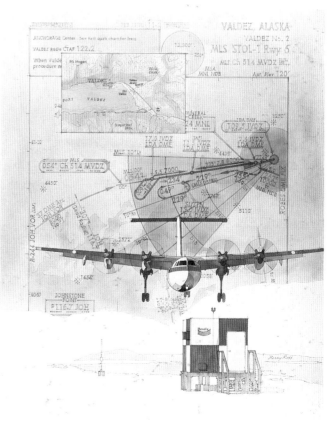

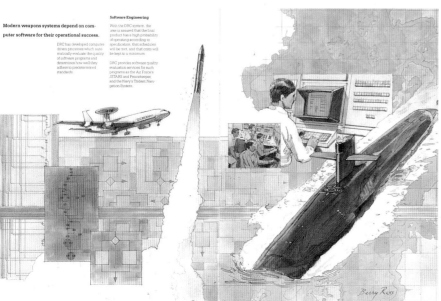

Modern weapons systems depend on computer software for their operational success.

DRC has developed computer driven processes which automatically evaluate the quality of software programs and determines how well they adhere to predetermined standards.

Software Engineering

With the DRC system, the user is assured that the final product has a high probability of operating according to specification, that schedules will be met, and that costs will be kept to a minimum.

DRC provides software quality evaluation services for such programs as the Air Force's JSTARS and Peacekeeper, and the Navy's Trident Navigation System.

Michael Sabanosh
433 West 34 Street, #18B
New York, New York 10001
(212) 947-8161

Lettering/Illustration
Clients: Berkley Publishing • Book-of-
the-Month-Club • Cahners Publishing •
Carnegie Hall (100 Anniversary Logo) •
Crown Publishers • Doubleday • Ellen
Tracy (logo) • Harper Collins • Klemtner
Adv • Lerner NY • St. Martin's Press •

Simon & Schuster/Pocket Books
"Shadows in Bronze"--Crown
"Eagle Knight"--Harper Collins

SABANOSH

JULIE GARWOOD
THE PRIZE

Linda Allard for ELLEN TRACY

Collections

MASTER OF BLACKWOOD

the Saloon

Forever My Love

HENRI BENDEL

Brief Candle

Prairie Bouquet

SHADOWS IN BRONZE

SUSAN BOWDEN
TOUCHED BY THORNS

Treasure of the Sun

EAGLE KNIGHT

433 WEST 34

GEORGETTE HEYER

Michael Sabanosh
433 West 34 Street, #18B
New York, New York 10001
(212) 947-8161

Illustration/Lettering
Clients: Berkley Publishing • Crown
Publishers • Delacorte • Harper Collins •
Hodder & Stoughton Publishers •
Lerner NY • St. Martin's Press

Left: "Eric & Julia Roberts"--Unpublished
Right: Above--Delacorte;
Below--St. Martin's Press

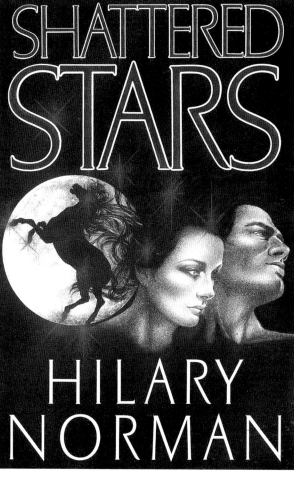

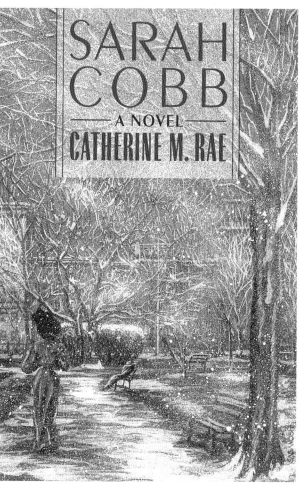

P R A Y

IT'S A MYSTERY, A LEGEND, A WORK OF ART. It's everywhere in New York City, yet very nearly invisible. If you ask people if they've seen the PRAY graffiti campaign, you are asking if they have looked at almost any street-level door frame in New York. There, and on every other window frame and phone booth and subway column and railing and lamp post, PRAY quietly chants its message.

A whisper is often louder than a shout. Especially when it's repeated thousands of times. This is a brilliant strategy accomplished with the simplest, most direct means. The word is always scratched with a stylus, always vertically, in crude half-inch caps. Considering that the distance for legibility of the message is quite close, it assumes your eyes are focused on the foreground, that you are momentarily myopic (a dangerous thing on the street). If lost in thought, you are predisposed to this message. You will only physically "discover" it at the time you are psychologically open to it. In their sophisticated simplicity, the signs could be the result of years of psychological testing and focus groups.

The message itself could have been brainstormed at the conference table of an advertising agency. It is immediate, memorable and universal. It is nondenominational (pray to whom?) and vague (pray for what?) but there is no mistaking its earnestness and emotional impact. The message dovetails placement to its target audience: There are few better locations than at eye-level on the streets of New York to invoke this ancient placebo.

The longevity of the program looms legendary. I first discovered it nine years ago; some say it's older than that. Like any good legend, it seems it's always been there, and judging from the fresh applications still being sighted, it always will be there. One day I hope to see the writer in action.

What have we really got here? I doubt there were any brainstorming sessions, any focus groups or psychological studies. I think it is actually the work of a single obsessed person and a few imitators. But to discount the program as vandalism or a cry in the dark is to miss some important lessons. If painters trained in academic traditions can look at the work of Grandma Moses and find Beauty and Truth, then designers can look at PRAY and feel we have found our first anonymous genius of "folk" environmental graphic design.

Tom Wojciechowski
Wojciechowski Design
(environmental and communication graphics)
New York City
He has been heard to confess that the job he's
always wanted is writing headlines for the
New York Post-or being a scribe in a monastery.

Rob Saunders
34 Station Street
Brookline, Massachusetts 02146
(617) 566-4464
FAX # upon request

Best of Show: New England Press Assn
Awards '87, Ad Club of Boston Hatch
Silver award '90, NY Art Directors Club
'88, Creative Club of Boston '84, '86-'89,
'91 Merits

Additional work: American Showcase
11, Adweek Portfolios '87 and '89, GAG
Directory of Illustration 5 & 6,
Designsource/ Worksource '85-'89,
Print's Regional Design Annual '88-'90

Member Graphic Artists Guild

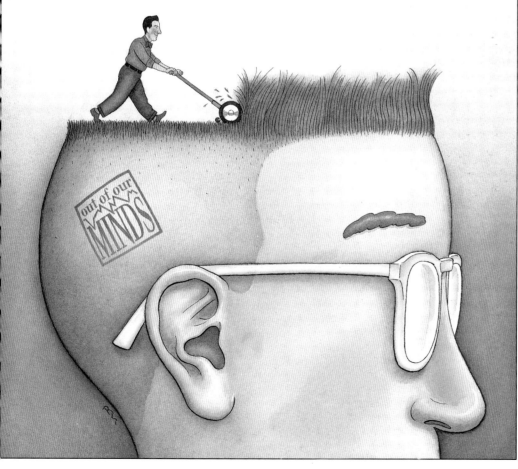

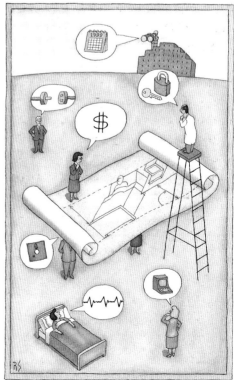

Paul Schulenburg
11 Park Street, #4
Brookline, Massachusetts 02146
(617) 734-0548
FAX in studio

Clients include: Bank of Boston, Boston
Globe, Cahners, Citibank, Harper
Collins, Hewlett Packard, Lotus, Money
Magazine, Open Software Foundation,
Philadelphia Inquirer, Polaroid, Simon &
Schuster, Ziff Davis.

See also: Humor (1987), Society of
Illustrators 31, Print Design Annual
1989, American Showcase 13, 14.

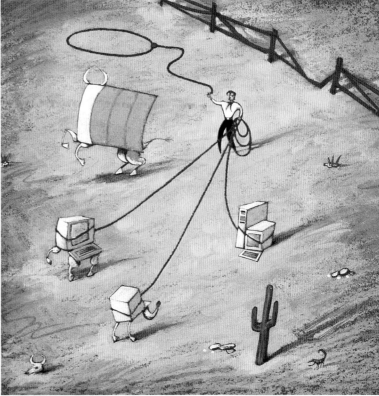

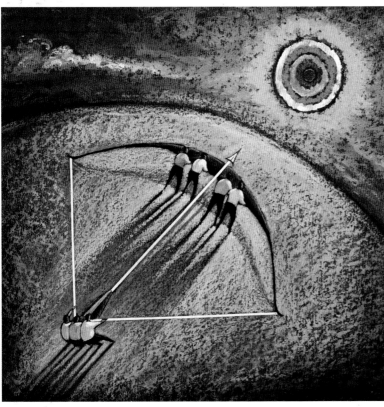

Paul Schulenburg
1 Park Street, #4
Brookline, Massachusetts 02146
(617) 734-0548
FAX in studio

Clients include: Bank of Boston, Boston Globe, Cahners, Citibank, Harper Collins, Hewlett Packard, Lotus, Money Magazine, Open Software Foundation, Philadelphia Inquirer, Polaroid, Simon & Schuster, Ziff Davis.

See also: Humor(1987), Society of Illustrators 31, Print Design Annual 1989, American Showcase 13, 14.

Bob Scott
4108 Forest Hill Avenue
Richmond, Virginia 23225
(804) 232-1627
FAX: (804) 233-7737

In The Midwest Contact:
Koralik Assoc.
(312) 944-5680

Graphic Airbrush Illustration

Additional work can be seen in
American Showcase, Volumes 10-14
Graphic Artists' Guild Directory,
Volume 5

Jeffrey Seaver
130 West 24th Street, #4B
New York, New York 10011-1906
(212) 741-2279
FAX: (212) 255-3823

Ned Shaw
2770 North Smith Pike
Bloomington, Indiana 47404
(812) 333-2181
FAX: (812) 331-0420

Warner Bros., Citibank, Ralston-Purina,
Forbes, BusinessWeek, Random House,
Macmillan, New York Times, Washington
Post, Travel and Leisure, Children's
Television Workshop

Silver Funnybone Award, Society of
Illustrators; Silver Award, Florida
Magazine Association; Silver Award,
Art Directors Club of Indiana; Print
Design Annual: 86, 89, 91

Member Graphic Artists Guild
Artwork © 1991 Ned Shaw

R. J. Shay
3301 South Jefferson Avenue
St. Louis, Missouri 63118
(314) 773-9989
FAX: (314) 773-6406

Other examples may be seen in
Showcase #13 p. 939 and #14 p. 1159.

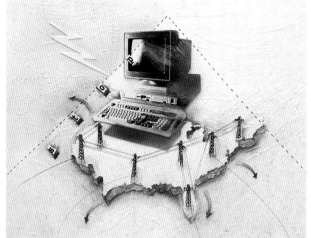

Chris Sheban
1807 West Sunnyside, 1G
Chicago, Illinois 60640
(312) 271-2720
FAX: (312) 271-5213

Represented by:
Emily Inman
(312) 525-4955
FAX: (312) 525-0244

CHRIS SHEBAN

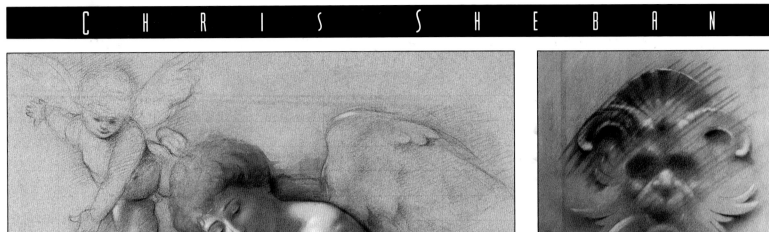

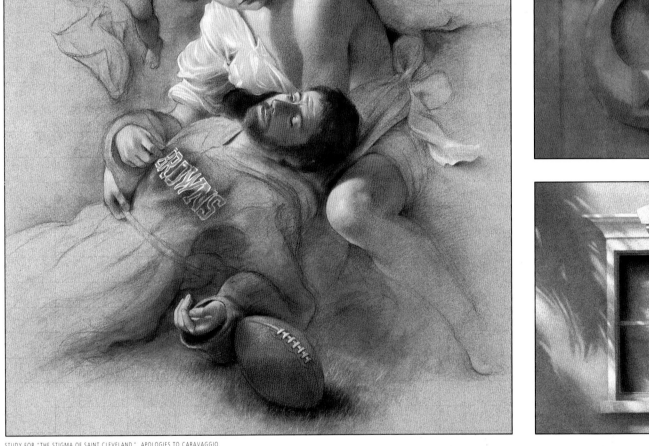

STUDY FOR "THE STIGMA OF SAINT CLEVELAND." APOLOGIES TO CARAVAGGIO.

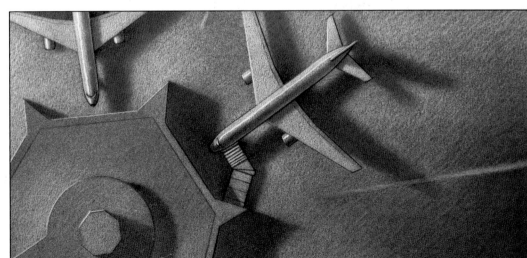

Marti Shohet
41 Union Square West
New York, New York 10003
(212) 627-1299
FAX in studio

Clients include:
American Pharmacist, Calet, Hirsch &
Spector, Health Magazine, McCaffrey
McCall, Macmillan, Lintas: Muir Cornelius
Moore, Newbridge Communications,
New York Times, Warick Baker & Fiore

Silver Medal 2nd Dimensional
Illustrators Show

Cut paper portfolio also available

Michael Shumate
198 Chelsea Road
Kingston, Ontario K7M 3Y8
(613) 384-5019
FAX Available

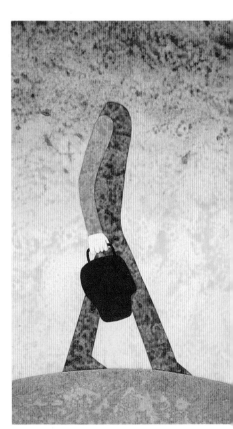

Carla Siboldi
252 Juanita Way
San Francisco, California 94127
(415) 681-4731

In Los Angeles contact:
Cornell/Agents
Kathleen Cornell
(310) 301-8059

Skidmore Sahratian Inc.
2100 West Big Beaver Road
Troy, Michigan 48084
(313) 643-6000
FAX: (313) 643-7799
(313) 548-5996 Toll free

Illustrators and designers
For additional examples of our
work see Illustrators Showcase:
No. 10, pages 672-675
No. 11, pages 766-769
No. 12, pages 866-867
No. 13, pages 948-949
No. 14, pages 1168-1169

Chicago representative:
Tom Maloney & Associates
(312) 704-0500
FAX: (312) 236-5752

West Coast representative:
Lee & Lou
(213) 287-1542
FAX: (213) 287-1814

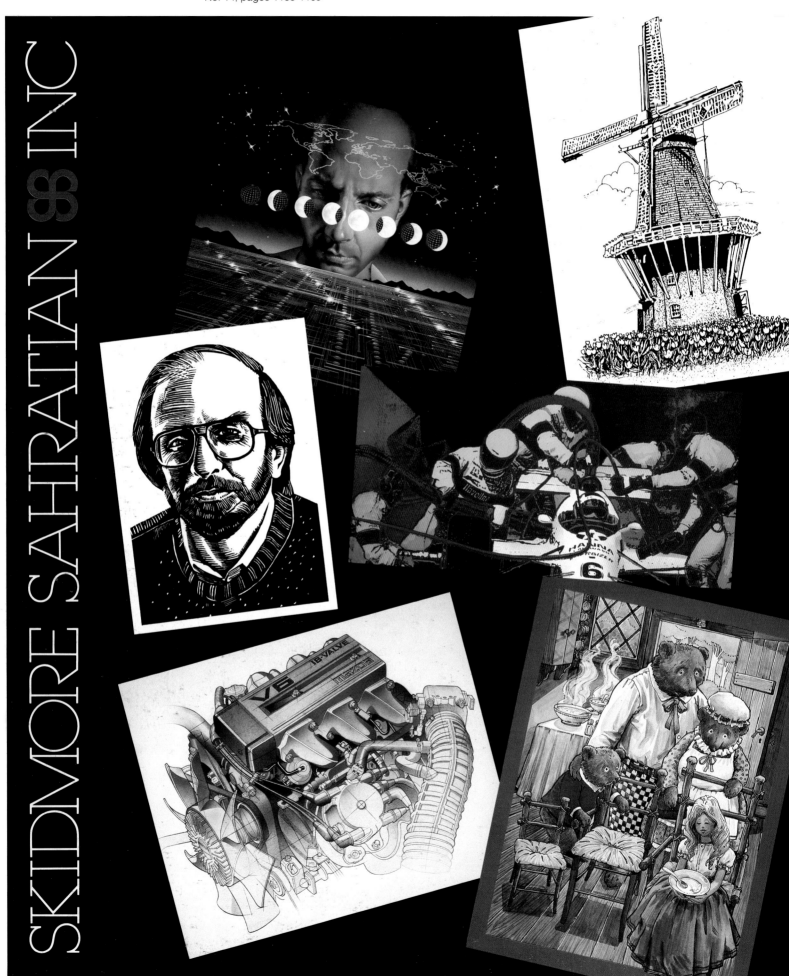

SKIDMORE SAHRATIAN INC

Skidmore Sahratian Inc.
2100 West Big Beaver Road
Troy, Michigan 48084
(313) 643-6000
FAX: (313) 643-7799
(313) 548-5996 Toll free

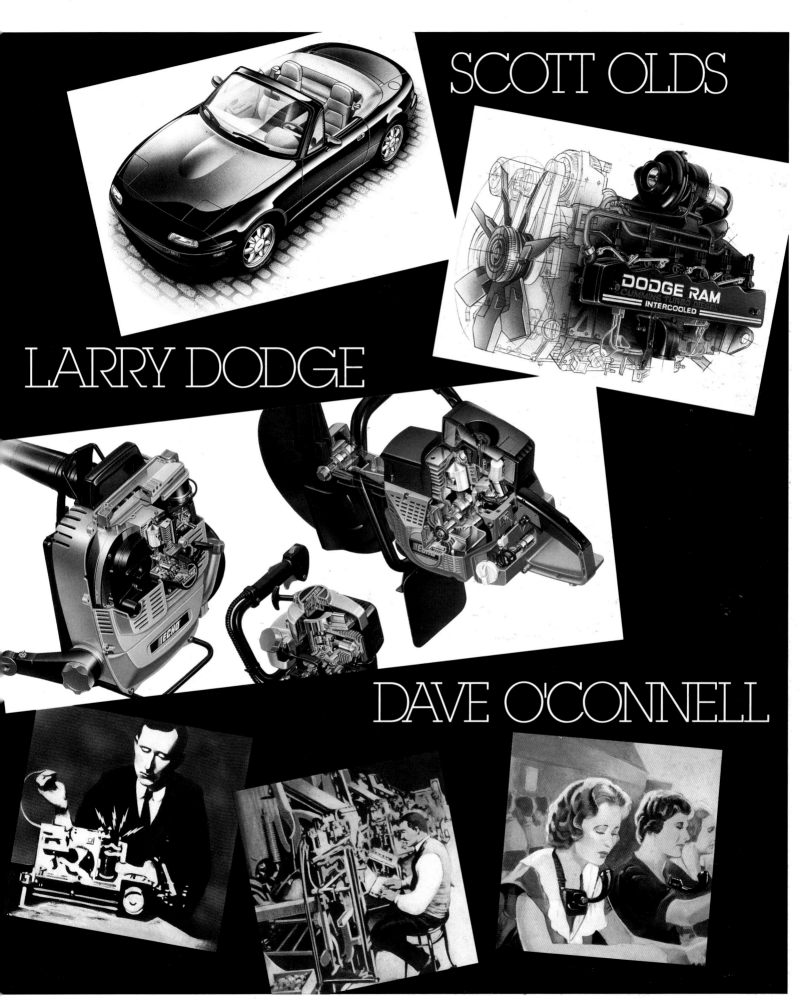

SCOTT OLDS

LARRY DODGE

DAVE O'CONNELL

Skidmore Sahratian Inc.
2100 West Big Beaver Road
Troy, Michigan 48084
(313) 643-6000
FAX: (313) 643-7799
(313) 548-5996 Toll free

Illustrators and designers
For additional examples of our
work see Illustrators Showcase:
No. 10, pages 672-675
No. 11, pages 766-769
No. 12, pages 866-867
No. 13, pages 948-949
No. 14, pages 1168-1169

Chicago representative:
Tom Maloney & Associates
(312) 704-0500
FAX: (312) 236-5752

West Coast representative:
Lee & Lou
(213) 287-1542
FAX: (213) 287-1814

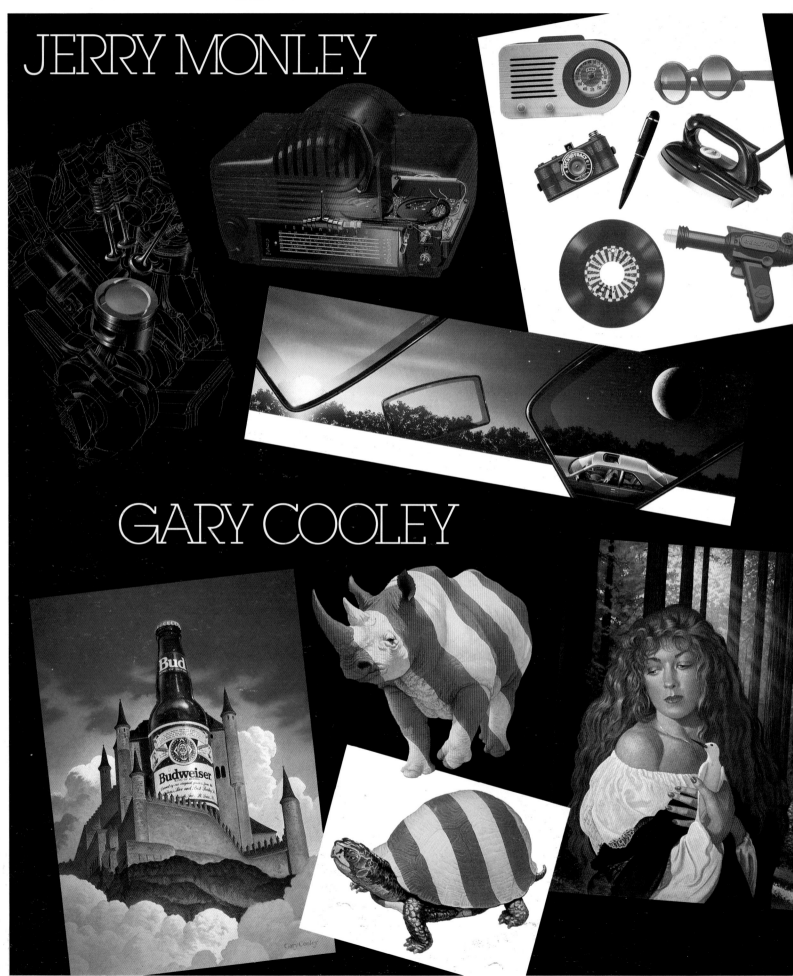

JERRY MONLEY

GARY COOLEY

Skidmore Sahratian Inc.
2100 West Big Beaver Road
Troy, Michigan 48084
(313) 643-6000
FAX: (313) 643-7799
(313) 548-5996 Toll free

BOB ANDREWS

ROB BURMAN

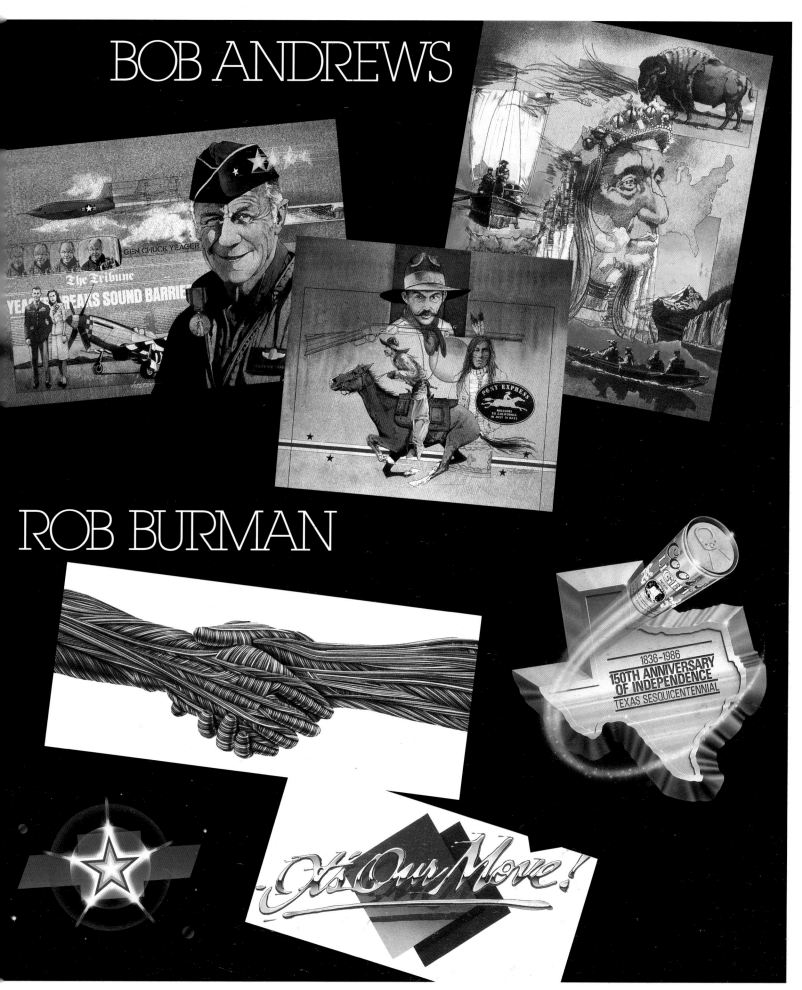

Skidmore Sahratian Inc.
2100 West Big Beaver Road
Troy, Michigan 48084
(313) 643-6000
FAX: (313) 643-7799
(313) 548-5996 Toll free

Illustrators and designers
For additional examples of our
work see Illustrators Showcase:
No. 10, pages 672-675
No. 11, pages 766-769
No. 12, pages 866-867
No. 13, pages 948-949
No. 14, pages 1168-1169

Chicago representative:
Tom Maloney & Associates
(312) 704-0500
FAX: (312) 236-5752

West Coast representative:
Lee & Lou
(213) 287-1542
FAX: (213) 287-1814

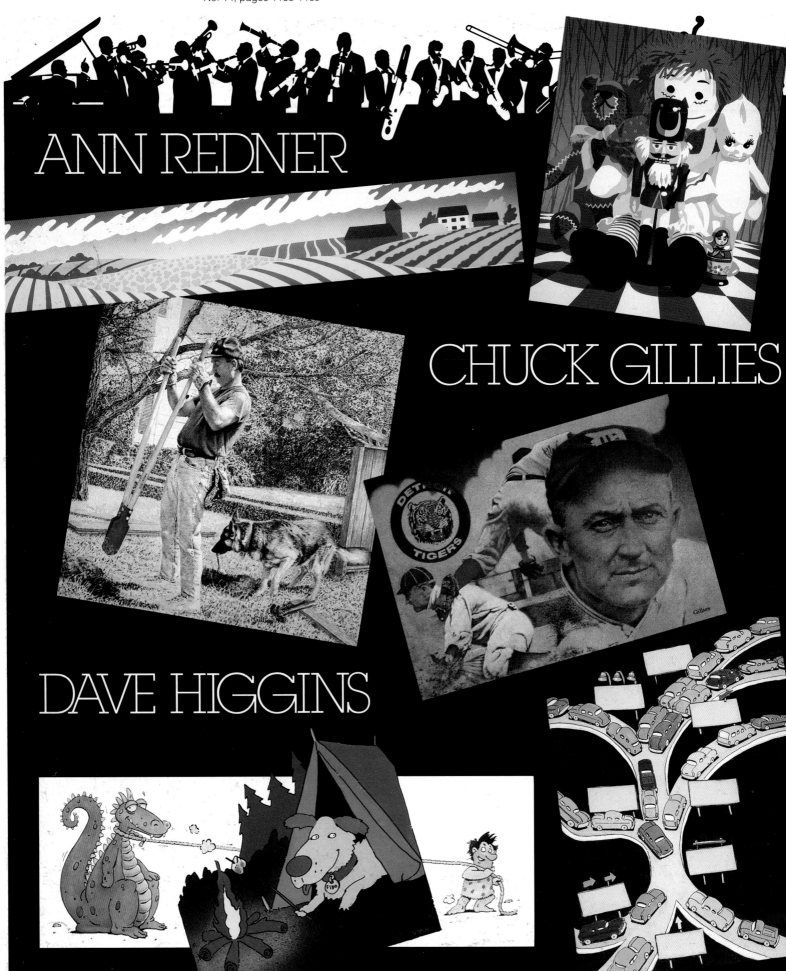

ANN REDNER

CHUCK GILLIES

DAVE HIGGINS

Skidmore Sahratian Inc.
2100 West Big Beaver Road
Troy, Michigan 48084
(313) 643-6000
FAX: (313) 643-7799
(313) 548-5996 Toll free

JOHN BALL

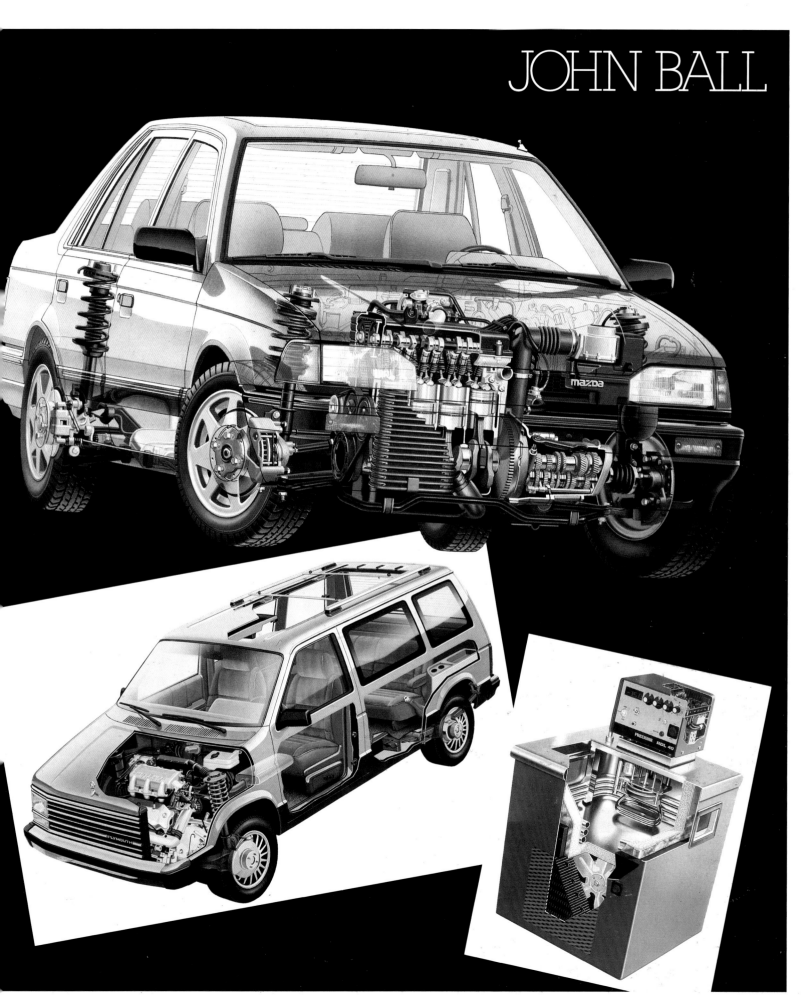

William A. Sloan
(212) 463-7025 in New York
(215) 766-7335 in Pennsylvania
FAX: (212) 727-7961

David Slonim
232 South Street
Chesterfield, Indiana 46017
(317) 378-6511
FAX in studio

Sports Illustrated VIDEO

P R E S E N T S

TRICK PLAYS

The sneakiest, most sensational sleight-of-hand plays in all of sport

Elwood H. Smith
2 Locust Grove Road
Rhinebeck, New York 12572

Maggie Pickard
(914) 876-2358
FAX: (914) 876-5931

Raymond E. Smith
606 Jersey Avenue
Jersey City, New Jersey 07302
(201) 653-6638
FAX: (201) 795-2087

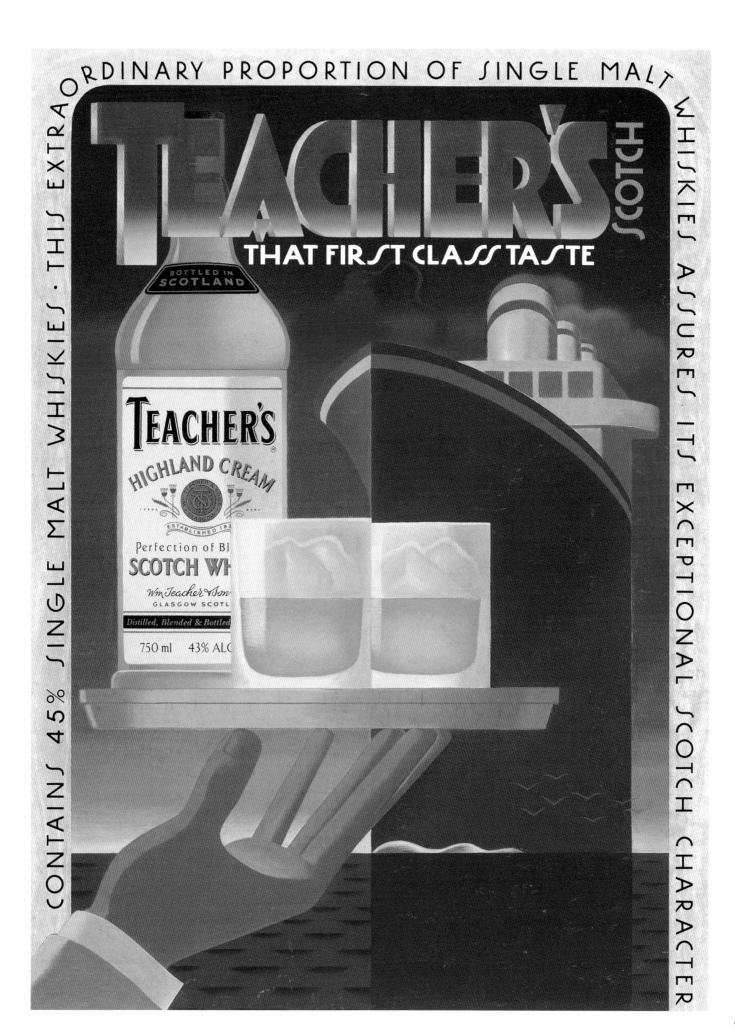

Susan Smith
66 Clarendon Street
Boston, Massachusetts 02116
(617) 266-4441
FAX: (617) 536-2563

Clients Include:
AT&T, Boston Globe, Proctor &
Gamble, Altos Computers, Lotus
Development, MetLife, MCI, Houghton-
Mifflin, Progress Software, Unisys

Corporation, Entertainment Weekly,
Southwestern Bell, Fidelity Investments,
Computerworld, Digital Equipment
Corporation, GTE, Data General

Danny Smythe
6103 Knight Arnold
Memphis, Tennessee 38115
(901) 794-5883

West Coast representative:
Rita Marie & Friends
183 N. Martel, Suite 240
Los Angeles, CA 90036
(213) 934-3395
Chicago:
Rodney Ray
(312) 222-0337

East Coast representative:
The Williams Group
1270 W. Peachtree, Suite 8C
Atlanta, GA 30309
(404) 873-2287
New York City:
Tricia Weber
(212) 799-6532

ALASKA
Alaska Artists Guild
PO Box 91982
Anchorage, AK 99059-1982
(907) 248-4818

ARIZONA
Arizona Artists Guild
8912 North Fourth Street
Phoenix, AZ 85020
(602) 944-9713

CALIFORNIA
Advertising Club of Los Angeles
3600 Wilshire Boulevard, Suite 432
Los Angeles, CA 90010
(213) 382-1228
APA Los Angeles, Inc.
7201 Melrose Avenue
Los Angeles, CA 90046
(213) 935-7283
APA San Francisco
22 Cleveland Street
San Francisco, CA 94103
(415) 621-3915
Art Directors and Artists Club
2791 24th Street
Sacramento, CA 95818
(916) 731-8802
Book Club of California
312 Sutter Street, Suite 510
San Francisco, CA 94108
(415) 781-7532
Los Angeles Advertising Women
3900 West Alameida
The Tower Building, 17th Floor
Burbank, CA 91505
(818) 972-1771
San Francisco Art Directors Club
Box 410387
San Francisco, CA 94141-0387
(415) 387-4040
San Francisco Creative Alliance
Box 410387
San Francisco, CA 94141-0387
(415) 387-4040
Society of Illustrators of Los Angeles
5000 Van Nuys Boulevard, Suite 300
Sherman Oaks, CA 91403-1717
(818) 784-0588
Society of Motion Pictures & TV Art Directors
11365 Ventura Boulevard, #315
Studio City, CA 91604
(818) 762-9995
Visual Artists Association
2550 Beverly Boulevard
Los Angeles, CA 90057
(213) 388-0477

Western Art Directors Club
PO Box 996
Palo Alto, CA 94302
(408) 998-7058
Women's Graphic Commission
1126 Highpoint Street
Los Angeles, CA 90035
(213) 935-1568

COLORADO
Art Directors Club of Denver
1900 Grant Street
Denver, CO 80203
(303) 830-7888
International Design Conference in Aspen
Box 664
Aspen, CO 81612
(303) 925-2257

CONNECTICUT
Connecticut Art Directors Club
PO Box 639
Avon, CT 06001
(203) 651-0886

DISTRICT OF COLUMBIA
American Advertising Federation
1400 K Street NW, Suite 1000
Washington, DC 20005
(202) 898-0089
American Institute of Architects
1735 New York Avenue, NW
Washington, DC 20006
(202) 626-7300
American Society of Interior Designers/National Headquarters
608 Massachusetts Avenue NE
Washington, DC 20002
(202) 546-3480
Art Directors Club of Metropolitan Washington
1420 K Street NW, Suite 500
Washington, DC 20005
(202) 842-4177
NEA: Design Arts Program
1100 Pennsylvania Avenue, NW
Washington, DC 20506
(202) 682-5437

FLORIDA
APA Miami
2545 Tiger Tail Avenue
Coconut Grove, FL 33033
(305) 856-8336

continued on page 1162

Mark and Erin Sparacio
Waterworks Studio
30 Rover Lane
Hicksville, New York 11801
(516) 579-6679
FAX: (516) 735-8474

Represented Outside N.Y.C. by:
Wendy Morgan
Network Studios
(516) 757-5609
FAX: (516) 261-6584

See previous ads in:
American Showcase 10 pg.697
American Showcase 11 pg.799
American Showcase 12 pg.480
American Showcase 13 pg.530
American Showcase 14 pg.1177

Member Graphic Artist Guild

If extruded aluminum display systems were sandwiches, would you send to Switzerland for your next lunch?

Of course not! The same logic applies to buying a modular display system. Foga extrudes and stocks all their aluminum profiles here, in the United States. This translates into big savings, of both time and money. Forget ordering from a European manufacturer. That takes weeks to process and an indefinite amount of time to get through customs. Foga stocks over 60 profiles that are ready to customize to your exact specifications for immediate delivery. And, if needed, we have CAD operators on-hand ready to assist you with your design. So, the next time you're in the market for a new modular display system, call Foga Systems for immediate attention and satisfaction at 1-800-488-FOGA, in California 805-988-FOGA, or Fax us at 805-988-1254. Foga Systems 800 Del Norte Boulevard., Oxnard, California 93030.

FOGA

1149

Jane Sterrett
160 Fifth Avenue
New York, New York 10010
(212) 929-2566
FAX: (212) 929-2566

Clients include: Anheuser Busch, Atlantic Records, AT&T, Barnwell Industries, Book-of-the-Month Club, Booz Allen & Hamilton, Chief Executive, Consolidated Gas, BusinessWeek, Dell, Dillon Reed, Dow B. Hickham, European Travel & Life, Exxon, Food & Wine, Grove Weidenfeld,

Health Progress, Hoechst, IBM, J.C. Penney, Macmillan, Mars-Snickers, McGraw Hill, Money Magazine, NatWest Bank, New American Library, N.Y. Life, Paine Webber, Peat-Marwick, Price-Waterhouse, Printing News, Salvation Army, Tylenol, United Jewish Appeal.

Also see: Showcase 8-14, Creative Illustration Book 1 & 2, Society of Illustrators Annual 17, 19, 22, 25, 26, 28, 30, 31; C.A. Illustration Annual 1990

Jane Sterrett
160 Fifth Avenue
New York, New York 10010
(212) 929-2566
FAX: (212) 929-2566

Clients include: Anheuser Busch, Atlantic Records, AT&T, Barnwell Industries, Book of the Month Club, Booz Allen & Hamilton, Chief Executive, Consolidated Gas, BusinessWeek, Dell, Dillon Reed, Dow B. Hickham, European Travel & Life, Exxon, Food & Wine, Grove Weidenfeld,

Health Progress, Hoechst, IBM, J.C. Penney, Macmillan, Mars-Snickers, McGraw Hill, Money Magazine, NatWest Bank, New American Library, N.Y. Life, Paine Webber, Peat-Marwick, Price-Waterhouse, Printing News, Salvation Army ,Tylenol, United Jewish Appeal.

Also see: Showcase 8-14, Creative Illustration Book 1 & 2, Society of Illustrators Annual 17, 19, 22, 25, 26, 28, 30, 31; C.A. Illustration Annual 1990.

Sturdivant Design
4114 McMillan Avenue
Dallas, Texas 75206
(214) 821-8111
FAX: (214) 823-6082

James Sullivan
253½ Fifth Street, #2
Jersey City, New Jersey 07302
(201) 963-6670

Partial List of Clients:
Macmillan Publishing, St. Martin's
Press, Henry Holt, Harper Collins,
Scribner's, Viking Press, Penguin
Books, UNICEF

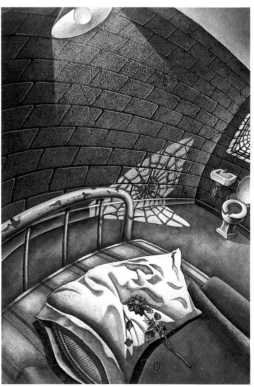

Sara Swan
5904 West 2nd Street, Apartment B
Los Angeles, California 90036
(213) 935-4781 Los Angeles
(212) 206-6780 New York
FAX: (213) 935-5095

Clients:
Pantheon Books
Viking/Penguin
Harcourt Brace Jovanovich
Los Angeles Times
Chicago Tribune

Boston Globe
Washington Post
Cosmopolitan
Metropolitan Home
American Illustration 4

Susan Swan
83 Saugatuck Avenue
Westport, Connecticut 06880
(203) 226-9104
FAX: (203) 454-7956

Clients:
Publisher's Weekly; Chemical Bank;
CMP Publications; Harcourt Brace
Jovanovich; Scholastic; Houghton
Mifflin; Holt Rinehart Winston; Bantam
Doubleday Dell; Silver Burdett and
Ginn; Putnam; Macmillan; Walker;

Scott Foresman; Harper and Row;
Children's Television Workshop.

See also:
Creative Illustration Book 1992;
Corporate Showcase #10;
GAG Directory #5, 6, 8.

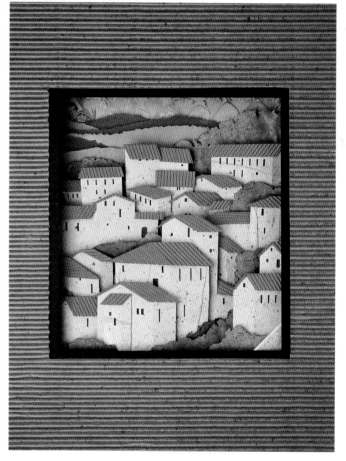

James Swanson
815 North Marion
Oak Park, Illinois 60302
(708) 383-0141

Gustav Szabo
380 Riverside Drive
New York, New York 10025
(212) 663-1106
FAX: (212) 663-6729

David Tamura
153 East 26th Street
New York, New York 10010
(212) 686-4559
FAX: (212) 213-3253

Awards:
Society of Illustrators
American Illustration
Communications Arts
New York Art Director's Club
Print Regional Design Annual

Clients:
Random House
MacMillan Publishing
Warner Books
St. Martin's Press

OLIN MARINE PRODUCTS   SLATTER DEAN & DAHMS

MACMILLAN PUBLISHING

DAVID R. GODINE PUBLISHERS

Joseph Taylor
2117 Ewing Avenue
Evanston, Illinois 60201
(708) 328-2454
FAX available

JOSEPH TAYLOR
ILLUSTRATION

Jack Tom
80 Varick Street
Suite 3-B
New York, New York 10013
(212) 941-1860
FAX: (212) 431-7138

Clients: American Express; Backer Spielvogel & Bates; Burger King; Citibank; CBS Inc.; Chase Manhattan Bank; Chemical Bank; Crossland Savings Bank; Disney Channel; Greer Dubois Inc.; HBO; Letraset; Lois/GGK; McCaffrey & McCalls; McGraw Hill; Merrill-Lynch; Mercedes-Benz; New York Times; Newsweek; Ogilvy & Mather Direct; Random House; Rockefeller Foundation; Saatchi & Saatchi; Scali, McCabe, Sloves, Inc.; Simon & Schuster; Time/Warner, Inc.; U.S. News & World Report; Wall Street Journal; Warwick; Baker & Fiore; Volkswagen. Also see American Showcase 13 & 14

Ket Tom
736 West Micheltorena Street
Santa Barbara, California 93101
(805) 965-0994
(619) 292-4866

Clients Include: Boston Globe, Changing Times Magazine, Confetti Magazine, Cross & Associates, Disney Adventures, Eating Well Magazine, Harrowsmith Magazine, Outside Magazine, Physician's Weekly, Post Graduate Medicine, Simpson Papers, Seymour Duncan Guitars & Pickups, Scholastic Magazine, Security Pacific Bank, Toy & Hobby World, Wadsworth Publishing.

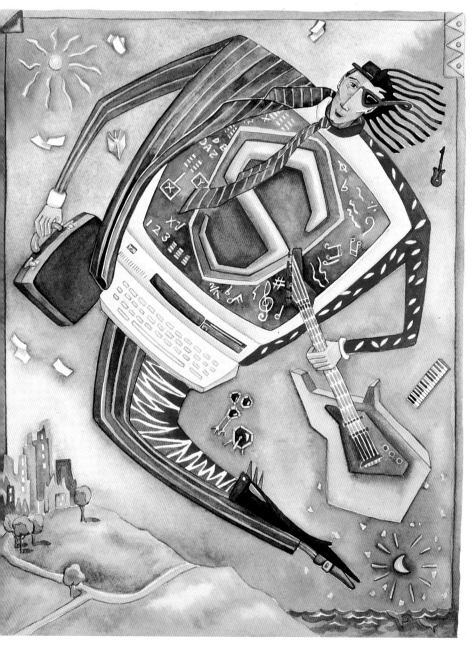

continued from page 1148

GEORGIA

APA Atlanta
PO Box 20471
Atlanta, GA 30325-1471
(404) 881-1616

Creative Club of Atlanta
PO Box 12483
Atlanta, GA 30355
(404) 266-8192

Atlanta Art Papers, Inc.
PO Box 77348
Atlanta, GA 30357
(404) 588-1837

Creative Arts Guild
PO Box 1485
Dalton, GA 30722-1485
(404) 278-0168

HAWAII

APA Hawaii
733 Auani Street
Honolulu, HI 96813
(808) 524-8269

ILLINOIS

APA Chicago
1725 West North Avenue, #2D2
Chicago, IL 60622
(312) 342-1717

Institute of Business Designers
341 Merchandise Mart
Chicago, IL 60654
(312) 467-1950

American Center For Design
233 East Ontario Street, Suite 500
Chicago, IL 60611
(312) 787-2018

Women in Design
2 North Riverside Plaza, Suite 2400
Chicago, IL 60606
(312) 648-1874

INDIANA

Advertising Club of Indianapolis
3833 North Meridian, Suite 305 B
Indianapolis, IN 46208
(317) 924-5577

IOWA

Art Guild of Burlington
Arts for Living Center
PO Box 5
Burlington, IA 52601
(319) 754-8069

MAINE

APA Portland
PO Box 10190
Portland, ME 04104
(207) 773-3771

MASSACHUSETTS

Boston Visual Artists Union
33 Harrison Avenue
Boston, MA 02111
(617) 695-1266

Creative Club of Boston
155 Massachusetts Avenue
Boston, MA 02115
(617) 338-6452

Center for Design of Industrial Schedules
221 Longwood Avenue
Boston, MA 02115
(617) 734-2163

Graphic Artists Guild
425 Watertown Street
Newton, MA 02158
(617) 244-2110

Guild of Boston Artists
162 Newbury Street
Boston, MA 02116
(617) 536-7660

Society of Environmental Graphic Designers
47 Third Street
Cambridge, MA 02141
(617) 577-8225

MICHIGAN

APA Detroit
32588 Dequindre
Warren, MI 48092
(313) 795-3540

Michigan Guild of Artists and Artisans
118 North Fourth Avenue
Ann Arbor, MI 48104
(313) 662-3382

MINNESOTA

Advertising Federation of Minnesota
4248 Park Glen Road
Minneapolis, MN 55416
(612) 929-1445

continued on page 1170

Carlos Torres
192 17th Street
Brooklyn, New York 11215
(718) 768-3296
FAX on premises

Client List Includes:
United Feature Syndicate, Topper
Books, Pharos Books, Adweek, Times-
Mirror, Bullet Publicity, R.H. Macy's,
Scholastic, Golf Magazine, Modern
Bride and The Leukemia Society of
America.

David Uhl
1501 Boulder Street
Denver, Colorado 80211
(303) 455-3535
FAX: (303) 455-1603

David Uhl
1501 Boulder Street
Denver, Colorado 80211
(303) 455-3535
FAX: (303) 455-1603

Lauren Uram
838 Carroll Street
Brooklyn, New York 11215
(718) 789-7717

Lauren Uram
338 Carroll Street
Brooklyn, New York
(718) 789-7717

Victor Vaccaro
1037 Seventh Street
West Babylon, New York 11704
(516) 888-2637
Studio FAX

Additional work may be seen in
American Showcase Volumes 13 and 14.

Gregg Valley
128 Thomas Road
McMurray, Pennsylvania 15317
(412) 941-4662
FAX: (412) 941-3490

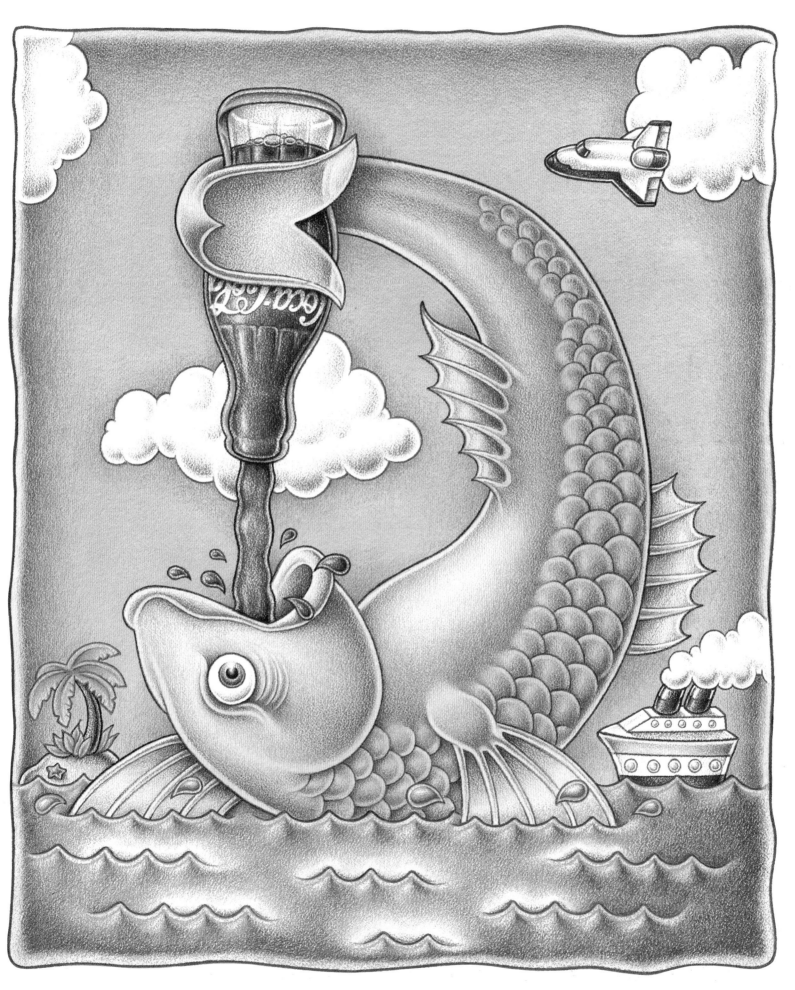

continued from page 1162

MISSOURI

Advertising Club of Greater St. Louis
10 Broadway, #150-A
St. Louis, MO 63102
(314) 231-4185

Advertising Club of Kansas City
9229 Ward Parkway, Suite 260
Kansas City, MO 64114
(816) 822-0300

American Institute of Graphic Arts
112 West Ninth
Kansas City, MO 64105
(816) 474-1983

NEW JERSEY

Federated Art Associations of New Jersey, Inc.
PO Box 2195
Westfield, NJ 07091
(908) 232-7623

Point-of-Purchase Advertising Institute
66 North Van Brunt Street
Englewood, NJ 07631
(201) 894-8899

NEW YORK

The Advertising Club of New York
155 East 55th Street
New York, NY 10022
(212) 935-8080

The Advertising Council, Inc.
261 Madison Avenue, 11th Floor
New York, NY 10016
(212) 922-1500

APA
Advertising Photographers of America, Inc.
27 West 20th Street, Room 601
New York, NY 10011
(212) 807-0399

Advertising Production Club of NY
60 East 42nd Street, Suite 1416
New York, NY 10165
(212) 983-6042

TANY Inc.
408 8th Avenue, #10A
New York, NY 10001
(212) 629-3232

Advertising Women of New York Foundation, Inc.
153 East 57th Street
New York, NY 10022
(212) 593-1950

A.A.A.A.
American Association of Advertising Agencies
666 Third Avenue, 13th Floor
New York, NY 10017
(212) 682-2500

American Booksellers Association, Inc.
137 West 25th Street
New York, NY 10001
(212) 463-8450

American Council for the Arts
1285 Avenue of the Americas, 3rd Floor
New York, NY 10019
(212) 245-4510

The American Institute of Graphic Arts
1059 Third Avenue, 3rd Floor
New York, NY 10021
(212) 752-0813

American Society of Interior Designers
New York Metro Chapter
200 Lexington Avenue
New York, NY 10016
(212) 685-3480

American Society of Magazine Photographers, Inc.
419 Park Avenue South, #1407
New York, NY 10016
(212) 889-9144

Art Directors Club of New York
250 Park Avenue South
New York, NY 10003
(212) 674-0500

Association of American Publishers
220 East 23rd Street
New York, NY 10010
(212) 689-8920

Association of the Graphic Arts
5 Penn Plaza, 20th Floor
New York, NY 10001
(212) 279-2100

The Children's Book Council, Inc.
568 Broadway, #404
New York, NY 10012
(212) 966-1990

CLIO
336 East 59th Street
New York, NY 10022
(212) 593-1900

Graphic Artists Guild
11 West 20th Street, 8th Floor
New York, NY 10011
(212) 463-7730

Guild of Book Workers
521 Fifth Avenue, 17th Floor
New York, NY 10175
(212) 757-6454

Institute of Outdoor Advertising
342 Madison Avenue, #702
New York, NY 10173
(212) 986-5920

International Advertising Association, Inc.
342 Madison Avenue, Suite 2000
New York, NY 10173
(212) 557-1133

continued on page 1186

Carolyn Vibbert
3911 Bagley Avenue North
Seattle, Washington 98103
(206) 634-3473
FAX number on request

Represented by:
Freda Scott
244 Ninth Street
San Francisco, California 94103-9879
(415) 621-2992
FAX: (415) 621-5202

Additional work:
American Showcase Vol.13,14
Adweek Portfolios '87,'88

Portfolio on request.

Sam Viviano
25 West 13th Street
New York, New York 10011
(212) 242-1471
FAX: (212) 691-4271

Clients include: ABC, BBD&O, Billboard Publications, CBS, CTW, Cahners Publishing, Cambridge University Press, Citibank, DFS Dorland, Diener/Hauser/Bates, DDB Needham Worldwide, Golf Digest, Institutional Investor, Mad Magazine, McCaffrey & McCall, McCann-Erickson, NBC, NW Ayer, New American Library, Ogilvy & Mather, PBS, People, RCA, Reader's Digest, Rolling Stone, Scholastic, Tennis, J. Walter Thompson, United Artists, Ziff-Davis.

Member Graphic Artists Guild

© Sam Viviano 1991

Pictured below:
Presidential masks commissioned by Time, Inc.
NBA/Comic Relief video package for CBS/Fox Video
Pictionary advertisement for Toys "R" Us
Humorous illustration for Field & Stream

Shari Warren
Humorous Illustration
San Francisco
(415) 591-1558
FAX Available

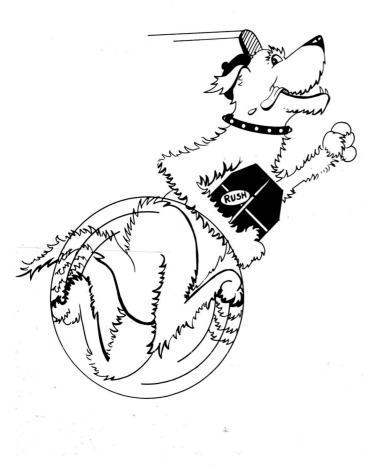

Cameron Wasson
4 South Portland Avenue
Brooklyn, New York 11217
(718) 875-8277
FAX In Studio

Clients Include: American Express, AT&T, Compaq Computer, General Foods, Johnson & Johnson, Cannon Mills, Pepsi Cola, Southwestern Bell, Nat West Bank, Barnett Bank, Time Inc., Dell Publishing, Westvaco Corp, Crown Publishing, McGraw-Hill, Ladies Home Journal, Reader's Digest Assoc. Inc., St. Martin's Press, Woman's Day, McCall's, Seventeen, and Working Woman.

READER'S DIGEST

COMPAQ COMPUTER

ST. MARTIN'S PRESS

ST. MARTIN'S PRESS

WESTVACO CORP.

DELL PUBLISHING

Rosemary Webber
644 Noank Road
Mystic, Connecticut 06355
(203) 536-3091

Garison Weiland
(617) 983-9251

To view more work see The Graphic
Artists Guild's Directory of Illustration,
Vols. 6 & 8.

Eric Westbrook
2830 27th Street, NW
Washington, DC 20008
(202) 328-8593
FAX in studio

Clients include:
U.S. News & World Report
Psychology Today
The Washington Post
Bell Atlantic

McDonald's
DDB Needham Worldwide
Mortgage Banking
State of Maryland
AARP

S.B. Whitehead
397 First Street
Brooklyn, New York 11215
(718) 768-0803
FAX: (718) 788-2328

Recent Clients:
Entertainment Weekly
Reader's Digest
Sports Illustrated for Kids
The Village Voice
Times Mirror Magazines
NFL Properties

Ally & Gargano
Arista Records
Simon & Schuster
Warner Books
The Topps Magazine (Back
Page Extra Feature)

THE VILLAGE VOICE

READER'S DIGEST

READER'S DIGEST

ENTERTAINMENT WEEKLY

Wild Onion Studio
Amy Paluch Epton and
Zbigniew T. Jastrzebski
431 South Dearborn Street
Suite 403
Chicago, Illinois 60605
(312) 663-5595
FAX: (312) 663-5383

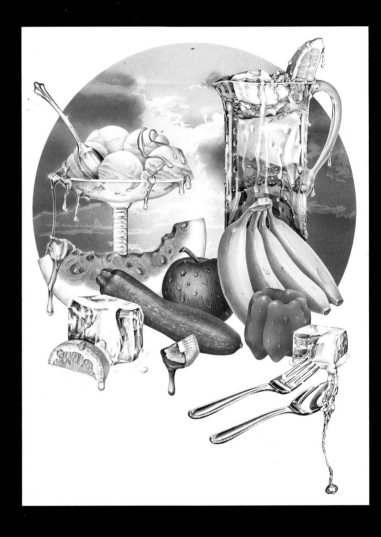

Chuck Wimmer
7760 Oakhurst Circle
Cleveland, Ohio 44141
(216) 526-2820
FAX: (216) 526-1809

David Wink
(404) 874-3389

Represented in New York by:
Creative Freelancers
(212) 398-9540

Portfolio available upon request

To view more work: RSVP 15,16, 17
Illustrators 28

**Michael James
Winterbauer**
1220 Lyndon Street #22
South Pasadena, California 91030
(818) 799-4998

Partial Client List:
American Video Entertainment, Bandai
America, Cannon Films, Cosmi
Entertainment, CSG Imagesoft, DLM
Publishing, Glencoe Publishing,
International Video Entertainment, ITC
Entertainment, Media Home
Entertainment, Mindcraft Software,
Muscle and Fitness Magazine,
Paramount Pictures, Prism
Entertainment, RCA Columbia Home
Pictures, Taito Software, Taskforce
Games, Transworld Entertainment,
Video Gems, Warner Brothers Feature
Film, Workhouse U.S.A.

-Pasadena Art Center College of
 Design Alumnus
-Work exhibited in Illustration West 29
 (1990)
-See also L.A. Workbook, 1987, p. 460;
 L.A. Workbook, 1989, p. 483; American
 Showcase vol. 11, p. 836.

Carol Way Wood
569 Barney's Joy Road
So. Dartmouth, Massachusetts 02748
(508) 636-2404
FAX: (508) 636-4446

Clients Include:
Wells, Rich, Greene, Inc.
IBM
Houghton Mifflin
D.C. Heath
Travel Holiday
Scholastic Magazine

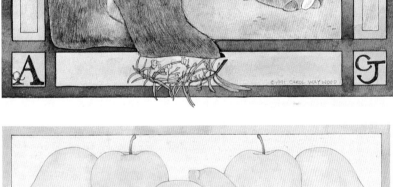

Leslie Wu
36 Harwood Lane
East Rochester, New York 14445
(716) 385-3722
FAX: (716) 232-2849

Represented in the Southwest by
Linda Ryan
(214) 826-8118
FAX: (214) 328-6662

©1992 Leslie Wu

ART AUCTION
To Benefit The Sojourner House

Saturday, Sept. 23, 1989
Wilson Art Gallery of The Harley School

continued from page 1170

The One Club
3 West 18th Street
New York, NY 10011
(212) 255-7070

The Public Relations Society of America, Inc.
33 Irving Place
New York, NY 10003
(212) 995-2230

Society of American Graphic Artists
32 Union Square, Room 1214
New York, NY 10003
(212) 260-5706

Society of Illustrators
128 East 63rd Street
New York, NY 10021
(212) 838-2560

Society of Photographers and Artists Representatives
1123 Broadway, Room 914
New York, NY 10010
(212) 924-6023

Society of Publication Designers
60 East 42nd Street, Suite 1416
New York, NY 10165
(212) 983-8585

Television Bureau of Advertising
477 Madison Avenue, 10th Floor
New York, NY 10022
(212) 486-1111

Type Directors Club of New York
60 East 42nd Street, Suite 1416
New York, NY 10165
(212) 983-6042

U.S. Trademark Association
6 East 45th Street
New York, NY 10017
(212) 986-5880

Volunteer Lawyers for the Arts
1285 Avenue of the Americas, 3rd Floor
New York, NY 10019
(212) 977-9270

Women in the Arts
c/o Roberta Crown
1175 York Avenue, #2G
New York, NY 10021
(212) 751-1915

NORTH CAROLINA

Davidson County Art Guild
224 South Main Street
Lexington, NC 27292
(704) 249-2742

OHIO

Advertising Club of Cincinnati
PO Box 43252
Cincinnati, OH 45243
(513) 576-6068

Design Collective
D.F. Cooke
130 East Chestnut Street
Columbus, OH 43215
(614) 464-2883

PENNSYLVANIA

Art Directors Club of Philadelphia
2017 Walnut Street
Philadelphia, PA 19103
(215) 569-3650

TEXAS

Advertising Club of Fort Worth
1801 Oak Knoll
Colleyville, TX 76034
(817) 283-3615

Art Directors Club of Houston
PO Box 271137
Houston, TX 77277
(713) 961-3434

Dallas Society of Visual Communications
3530 High Mesa Drive
Dallas, TX 75234
(214) 241-2017

VIRGINIA

Industrial Designers Society of America
1142-E Walker Road
Great Falls, VA 22066
(703) 759-0100

National Association of Schools of Art and Design
11250 Roger Bacon Drive, #21
Reston, VA 22090
(703) 437-0700

WASHINGTON

Allied Arts of Seattle, Inc.
107 South Main Street, Rm 201
Seattle, WA 98121
(206) 624-0432

Seattle Ad Federation
2033 6th Avenue, #804
Seattle, WA 98121
(206) 448-4481

WISCONSIN

Coalition of Women's Art Organizations
123 East Beutel Road
Port Washington, WI 53074
(414) 284-4458

Milwaukee Advertising Club
231 West Wisconsin Avenue
Milwaukee, WI 53203
(414) 271-7351

Jeffrey York
111 East Chestnut, Apartment 18J
Chicago, Illinois 60611
(312) 664-8849

PHONE LISTINGS & ADDRESSES OF REPRESENTATIVES, VISUAL ARTISTS & SUPPLIERS

CONTENTS

REGIONS

New York City

Northeast
Connecticut
Delaware
Maine
Maryland
Massachusetts
New Hampshire
New Jersey
New York State
Pennsylvania
Rhode Island
Vermont
Washington, D.C.
West Virginia

Southeast
Alabama
Florida
Georgia
Kentucky
Louisiana
Mississippi
North Carolina
South Carolina
Tennessee
Virginia

Midwest
Illinios
Indiana
Iowa
Kansas

Miichigan
Minnesota
Missouri
Nebraska
North Dakota
Ohio
South Dakota
Wisconsin

Southwest
Arizona
Arkansas
New Mexico
Oklahoma
Texas

Rocky Mountain
Colorado
Idaho
Montana
Utah
Wyoming

West Coast
Alaska
California
Hawaii
Nevada
Oregon
Washington

International

R E P S

N Y C

A

Altamore, Bob/237 W 54th St 4th Fl......212-977-4300
Cailor/Resnick, (P)

American Artists/353 W 53rd St #1W (P 409-421).......212-682-2462
Keith Batcheller, (I), Bart Bemus, (I), Roger Bergendorff, (I), Robert Burger, (I), Chris Butler, (I), Gary Ciccarelli, (I), Jim Deigan, (I), Jacques Devaud, (I), Bob Dorsey, (I), Lane DuPont, (I), Michael Elins, (I), Malcolm Farley, (I), Russell Farrell, (I), George Gaadt, (I), Rob Gage, (P), Bill Garland, (I), Jackie Geyer, (I), John Hamagami, (I), Pam Hamilton, (I), Steve Hendricks, (I), Doug Henry, (I), Michael Hill, (I), John Holm, (I), Mitch Hyatt, (I), Richard Kriegler, (I), Alan Leiner, (I), Maurice Lewis, (I), Ed Lindlof, (I), Jerry LoFaro, (I), Ron Mahoney, (I), Mick McGinty, (I), Jean-Claude Michel, (I), David Noyes, (I), Erik Olson, (I), Jim Owens, (I), Charles Passarelli, (I), Tony Randazzo, (I), Jan Sawka, (I), Todd Schorr, (I), Michael Schumacher, (I), Joe Scrofani, (I), Jim Starr, (I), Mike Steirnagle, (I), Thomas Tonkin, (I), Stan Watts, (I), Will Weston, (I), Ron Wolin, (I), Jonathan Wright, (I), Gary Yealdhall, (I), Andy Zito, (I)

Anton, Jerry/119 W 23rd St #203 (P 588,589)......212-633-9880
Bobbye Cochran, (I), Abe Echevarria, (I), Norman Green, (I), Aaron Rezny, (P), Chris Vincent, (P), Oliver Williams, (I)

Arnold, Peter Inc/1181 Broadway 4th Fl......212-481-1190
Yann Arthus-Bertrand, (P), Fred Bavendam, (P), Dieter Blum, (P), Herb Comess, (P), Martha Cooper, (P), Dennis diCicco, (P), Bob Evans, (P), Helmut Gritscaher, (P), Jacques Jangoux, (P), Manfred Kage, (P), Steve Kaufman, (P), Stephen Krasemann, (P), Werner Muller, (P), Jim Olive, (P), Hans Pfletschinger, (P), Jeffrey L Rotman, (P), Galen Rowell, (P), David Scharf, (P), Erika Stone, (P), Bruno Zehnder, (P)

Art & Commerce/108 W 18th St......212-206-0737
William Claxton, (P), Clint Clemens, (P)

Artco/232 Madison Ave #402 (P 312-351)......212-889-8777
Ed Acuna, (I), Alexander & Turner, (I), Edmund Alexander, (I), George Angelini, (I), Gene Boyer, (I), Dan Brown, (I), Alain Chang, (I), Anne Cook, (I), Jeff Cornell, (I), Joann Daley, (I), Beau & Alan Daniels, (I), Mort Drucker, (I), Ed Gazsi, (I), Michael Helsop, (I), Lisa Henderling, (I), Kathy Jeffers, (I), David Loew, (I), Rick McCollum, (I), Jean Restivo Monti, (I), Susan Richman, (P), Marcel Rozenberg, (I), Paul Sheldon, (I), Oren Sherman, (I), Mark Smollin, (I), Cynthia Turner, (I), Sally Vitsky, (I), Rob Zuckerman, (P)

Artists Associates/211 E 51st St #5F (P 516-519)......212-755-1365
Norman Adams, (I), Don Brautigam, (I), Michael Deas, (I), C Michael Dudash, (I), Mark English, (I), Alex Gnidziejko, (I), Robert Heindel, (I), Steve Karchin, (I), Dick Krepel, (I), Skip Liepke, (I), Fred Otnes, (I), Daniel Schwartz, (I), Norman Walker, (I)

Artworks Illustration/270 Park Ave S #10B (P 538-542)......212-260-4153
Paul Bachem, (I), Linda M Benson, (I), Sterling Brown, (I), Jim Campbell, (I), Deborah Chabrian, (I), Donna Diamond, (I), Richard Dickens, (I), Sandra Filippucci, (I), Peter Fiore, (I), Enid Hatton, (I), Bob Jones, (I), Michael Koester, (I), Rudy Laslo, (I), Dennis Lyall, (I), Patrick Milbourn, (I), Lisa Palombo, (I), Marcia Pyner, (I), Romas, (I), Mort Rosenfeld, (I), Larry Schwinger, (I), Jim Sharpe, (I), Philip Singer, (I), Broeck Steadman, (I), Evan T Steadman, (I), Tom Stimpson, (I), Michael Storrings, (I), Brad Teare, (I)

Asciutto Art Reps/19 E 48th St......212-838-0050
Anthony Accardo, (I), Eliot Bergman, (I), Alex Bloch, (I), Deborah Borgo, (I), Olivia Cole, (I), Mark Corcoran, (I), Daniel Delvalle, (I), Suzanne DeMarco, (I), Len Epstein, (I), Gershom Griffith, (I), Meryl Henderson, (I), Al Leiner, (I), Morissa Lipstein, (I), Loreta Lustig, (I), James Needham, (I), Sherry Niedigh, (I), Charles Peale, (I), Jan Pyk, (I)

B

Badd, Linda/568 Broadway #601......212-431-3377

Tom Clayton, (P)
Badin, Andy/15 W 38th St......212-532-1222
Bahm, Darwin/6 Jane St......212-989-7074
Harry DeZitter, (P), Gordon Kibbe, (I), Joan Landis, (I), Rick Meyerowitz, (I), Don Ivan Punchatz, (I), Arno Sternglass, (I), John Thompson, (I), Robert Weaver, (I), Chuck Wilkinson, (I)
Baker, Valerie/152 W 25th St 12th Fl......212-807-7113
Skylite Photo Productions, (P)
Barboza, Ken Assoc/853 Broadway #1603......212-505-8635
Anthony Barboza, (P), Leonard Jenkins, (I), Peter Morehand, (P), Man Tooth, (P), Marcus Tullis, (P)
Barnes, Fran/25 Fifth Ave #9B......212-505-2720
Barracca, Sal/381 Park Ave S #919......212-889-2400
Becker, Erika/150 W 55th St......212-757-898
Esther Larson, (I)
Becker, Noel/150 W 55th St......212-757-898
Sy Vinopoll, (P)
Beidler, Barbara/648 Broadway #506......212-979-6990
Richard Dunkley, (P), Bob Hiemstra, (I), Robert Levin, (P), Nana Watanabe, (P)
Beilin, Frank/405 E 56th St......212-751-307
Bernstein & Andriulli/60 E 42nd St #505 (P 14-49)......212-682-1490
Tony Antonios, (I), Pat Bailey, (I), Jim Balog, (P), Garie Blackwell, (I), Rick Brown, (I), Daniel Craig, (I), Creative Capers, (I), Everett Davidson, (I), Jon Ellis, (I), Ron Finger, (I), Ron Fleming, (I), Brett Froomer, (P), Victor Gadino, (I), Joe Genova, (I), Christina Ghergo, (P), John Harwood, (I), Bryan Haynes, (I), Frank Herholdt, (P), Kevin Hulsey, (I), Tim Jessell, (I), Alan Kaplan, (I), Hiro Kimura, (I), Daniel Kirk, (I), Peter Kramer, (I), Mary Ann Lasher, (I), John Lawrence, (I), Bette Levine, (I), Todd Lockwood, (I), Hakan Ludwigsson, (P), Lee MacLeod, (I), Greg J Martin, (I), Tom McCavera, (P), David B McMacken, (I), Christian Moore, (I), Bill Morse, (I), Pete Mueller, (I), Craig Nelson, (I), Jeff Nishinaka, (I), Greg J Petan, (I), Laura Phillips, (I), Gunther Raupp, (P), Mike Rider, (I), Peggi Roberts, (I), Ray Roberts, (I), Vittorio Sacco, (P), Goro Sasaki, (I), Marla Shega, (I), Gunar Skillins, (I), Chuck Slack, (I), Peter Stallard, (I), David Harry Stewart, (P), John Stoddart, (P), Tommy Stubbs, (I), Thomas Szumowski, (I), Peter Van Ryzin, (I), Pam Wall, (I), Richard Warren, (P), Brent Watkinson, (I), Matthew Zumbo, (I)
Big City Prodctns/5 E 19th St #303......212-473-336
Earl Culberson, (P), Tony DiOrio, (P), David Massey, (P), Pete Stone, (P), Dan Weaks, (P)
Black Star/116 E 27th St......212-679-328
John W. Alexanders, (P), Nancy Rica Schiff, (P), Arnold Zann, (P)
Black, Fran/116 E 27th St 12th fl......212-725-380
Rob Blackard, (I), Dennis Murphy, (P), Jose Ortega, (I), Aernout Overbeeke, (P), Roger Tully, (P), Kenneth Willardt, (P), Tom Zimberoff, (P)
Black, Pamela/73 W Broadway......212-385-066
William Heuberger, (P), Irada Icaza, (P), Rick Young, (P)
Blanchard, Jean/1175 York Ave #10M......212-371-144
Ellen Denuto, (P)
Bloncourt, Nelson/666 Greenwich St......212-924-225
Chris Dawes, (P), Jim Huibregtse, (P), Joyce Tenneson, (P)
Boghosian, Marty/201 E 21st St #10M......212-353-1313
James Salzano, (P)
Booth, Tom Inc/425 W 23rd St #17A......212-243-275
Thom Gilbert, (P), Joshua Greene, (P), Thibault Jeanson, (P), Charles Lamb, (P), Gordon Munro, (P), Robert Reed, (P), Lara Rossignol, (P)
Brackman, Henrietta/415 E 52nd St......212-753-648
Brennan, Dan/568 Broadway #1005......212-925-833
Knut Bry, (P), Mark Bugzester, (P), Charles Ford, (P), Scott Hagendorf, (P), Anthony Horth, (P), Kenji Toma, (P), Claus Wickrath, (P)
Brindle, Carolyn/203 E 89th St #3D......212-534-417
Brody, Sam/12 E 46th St #402......212-758-064
Fred Hilliard, (I), Allen Lieberman, (P), Jacques Lowe, (P), Steve Peringer, (I), Carroll Seghers, (P), Elsa Warnick, (I)
Brown, Deborah & Assoc/1133 Broadway #1508......212-463-773
Brown, Doug/17 E 45th St #1008......212-953-008
Dennis Blachut, (P), Abe Seltzer, (P)
Bruck, Nancy & Eileen Moss/333 E 49th St (P 592-603)......212-982-6533
Tom Curry, (I), Warren Gelbert, (I), Ken Goldammer, (I), Joel Peter Johnson, (I), Lionsgate, (I), Robert Neubecker, (I), Adam

Niklewicz, (I), Pamela Patrick, (I), Ben Perini, (I), Robert Pizzo, (I), Scott Pollack, (I), Rebecca Ruegger, (I), Mark Yankus, (I)

Bruml, Kathy/201 W 77th St 212-874-5659
Grant Peterson, (P)

**Buck, Sid & Kane, Barney/566 Seventh Ave #603
(P 576-577)** **212-221-8090**
Jacques Alschech, (I), Ken Call, (I), Claudia Callander, (I), Joseph Denaro, (I), Ann Fox, (I), Nate Giorgio, (I), Laura Hesse, (I), John Hickey, (I), David Jarvis, (I), Mark Kaufman, (I), Steven Keyes, (I), Bob Labsley, (I), Saul Lambert, (I), Dan Lavigne, (I), Peter Lloyd, (I), Robert Melendez, (I), Jess Nicholas, (I), Gary Nichols, (I), Wally Niebart, (I), Paul Palnik, (I), Ric Powell, (I), Jerry Schurr, (I), Joseph Sellers, (I), Tad Skozynski, (I), Lynn Stephens, (I), Bill Thomson, (I), Vahid, (I)

Burris, Jim/350 W 39th St 212-239-6767
Bush, Nan/135 Watts St 212-226-0814
Barry Lategan, (P), Bruce Weber, (P)
Byrnes, Charles/435 W 19th St 212-473-3366
Steve Steigman, (P)

C

Cahill, Joe/43 W 24th St #9A 212-924-4744
Shig Ikeda, (P), Brad Miller, (P)
Camp, Woodfin & Assoc/116 E 27th St 212-481-6900
Kip Brundage, (P), Jason Laure, (P)
Caputo, Elise & Assoc/PO Box 6898/Grand Central Stn.........212-725-0503
Becker/Bishop, (P), Steve Brady, (P), Didier Dorot, (P), James Kozyra, (P), Steve Prezant, (P), Sean Smith, (P), Pete Turner, (P)
Carp, Stan/2166 Broadway 212-362-4000
Dick Frank, (P), Dennis Gray, (P), Dennis Kitchen, (P)
Casey and Sturdevant/245 E 63rd St #201 212-486-9575
Jade Albert, (P), Albaino Ballerini, (P), Geoffrey Clifford, (P), Thomas Hooper, (P), Michael Luppino, (P), Zeva Oelbaum, (P), Louis Wallach, (P)
Casey, Judy/96 Fifth Ave 212-255-3252
Richard Bailey, (P), Calliope, (P), William Garrett, (P), Torkil Gudnason, (P), Christopher Micaud, (P), Jim Reiher, (P), Tim Simmons, (P)
Chislovsky, Carol/853 Broadway #1201 (P 604-609) **212-677-9100**
Karen Bell, (I), Taylor Bruce, (I), Russell Cobane, (I), Jim Cohen, (I), Jon Conrad, (I), Scott Ernster, (I), Jan Evans, (I), Chris Gall, (I), Jeff George, (I), Bob Gleason, (I), Ignacio Gomez, (I), Ken Graning, (I), Steve Gray, (I), Mark Herman, (I), Oscar Hernandez, (I), Greg Huber, (I), Mike Kowalski, (I), Joe Lapinski, (I), Leo Monahan, (I), Joe Ovies, (I), Julie Pace, (I), Chuck Schmidt, (I), Rick Schneider, (I), Sandra Shap, (I), Randy South, (I), C A Trachok, (I)
Collignon, Daniele/200 W 15th St (P 452-458) **212-243-4209**
Diane Bennett, (I), Dan Cosgrove, (I), Bill Frampton, (I), David Gambale, (I), Steve Lyons, (I), Dennis Mukai, (I), Mitch O'Connell, (I), Cindy Pardy, (I), Irena Roman, (I), Hisashi Sekine, (I), Doug Suma, (I), Alex Tiani, (I), Don Weller, (I)
Conlon, Jean/461 Broome St 212-966-9897
Elizabeth Brady, (I), Roberto Brosan, (P), Kenro Izu, (P), Ivano Piza, (P), Evan Polenghi, (I)
Connections Unlimited/37 E 28th St #506
(P 570,571) **212-696-4120**
Robert Buchanan, (P), Randy Douglas, (I), Ian Ross, (I)
Cornelia/232 Front St 212-732-6240
Tom Fogliani, (P), Richard Pierce, (P), Peter Zander, (P)
Creative Freelancers/25 W 45th St (P 459-469) **212-398-9540**
Peter Angelo, (I), Gil Ashby, (I), Philip Bliss, (I), Wende Caporale, (I), Karen Chandler, (I), Heidi Chang, (I), Judith Cheng, (I), Dan Cooper, (I), Howard Darden, (I), Joseph DeCerchio, (I), Jim DeLapine, (I), Steve Dinnino, (I), Glenn Dodds, (I), Peggy Dressel, (I), John Duncan, (I), Steven Duquette, (I), John Dzedzy, (I), John Edens, (I), Gregg Fitzhugh, (I), Stephen Fritsch, (I), Gretta Gallivan, (I), Rick Geary, (I), Cameron Gerlach, (I), Blake Hampton, (I), Gary Hanna, (I), Traci Harmon, (I), R Mark Heath, (I), Amy Huelsman, (I), Chet Jezierski, (I), Kid Kane, (I), Barbara Kiwak, (I), Salem Krieger, (I), Tim Lee, (I), James Martin, (I), Susan Melrath, (I), A J Miller, (I), Burton Morris, (I), Michael Ng, (I), Jan North, (I), Russ North, (I), Greg Olanoff, (I), Jim Owens, (I), Richard Parisi, (I), Robert Pasternak, (I), Elena Poladian, (I), Girair Poladian, (I), Meryl Rosner, (I), Barry Ross, (I), Joanna Roy, (I), Glen Schofield, (I), Clare Sieffert, (I), Tom Starace, (I),

Wayne Anthony Still, (I), Steve Sullivan, (I), Stephen Sweny, (I), Glen Tarnowski, (I), Bill Teodecki, (I), Kurt Wallace, (I), Roger White, (I), David Wink, (I)

Creative Workforce/270 Lafayette #401 212-925-1111
Ashkan Sahihi, (P)
Cuevas, Robert/118 E 28th St #306 212-679-0622
Ron Brown, (P), Barnett Plotkin, (I)
Cullom, Ellen/55 E 9th St 212-777-1749
Robert Grant, (P)

D

Dagrosa, Terry/12 E 22nd St 212-254-4254
Davies, Nora/370 E 76th St #C103 212-628-6657
Michael Pateman, (P)
Dedell, Jacqueline Inc/58 W 15th St 6th Fl (P 50-71)...**212-741-2539**
Scott Baldwin, (I), Cathie Bleck, (I), Ivan Chermayeff, (I), Teresa Fasolino, (I), David Frampton, (I), Griesbach/Martucci, (I), Hiroko, (I), Paula Munck, (I), Merle Nacht, (I), Edward Parker, (I), Barry Root, (I), Kimberly B Root, (I), Marco Ventura, (I), Mick Wiggins, (I), Richard Williams, (I), Heidi Younger, (I)
Des Verges, Diana/73 Fifth Ave 212-691-8674
Paccione Photography, (P)
DiBartolo/Lemkowitz/310 Madison Ave 212-297-0041
Chris Collins, (P), Steve Krongard, (P), Gary Kufner, (P), Nancy Moran, (P), Michael O'Neill, (P), James Porto, (P), Jerry Simpson, (P)
DiParisi, Peter/250 W 99th St #3A 212-663-8330
Gary Buss, (P), Ellen Denuto, (P), Lucille Khornack, (P), Cyndy Warwick, (P)
Dorman, Paul/430 E 57th St 212-826-6737
Studio DGM, (P)
Dorr, Chuck/1123 Broadway #1015 212-627-9871
John Bean, (P), Robert Carroll, (P), Robert Farber, (P), Michael Gerger, (P)
Drexler, Sharon/451 Westminster Rd, Brooklyn 718-284-4779
Les Katz, (I)
DuCane, Alex/111 E 64th St 212-772-2840
Tony Kent, (P), Niel Kirk, (P), Cheryl Koralik, (P), Christopher Micaud, (P), Maria Robledo, (P)

EF

Erlacher, Bill/Artists Assoc/211 E 51st St #5F
(P 516-519) **212-755-1365**
Michael Deas, (I), C Michael Dudash, (I), Mark English, (I), Alex Gnidziejko, (I), Dick Krepel, (I), Skip Liepke, (I), Fred Otnes, (I), Daniel Schwartz, (I), Norman Walker, (I)
Feinstein, Ron/312 E 9th St 212-353-8100
Feldman, Robert/133 W 17th St #5A 212-243-7319
Brian Hagiwara, (P), Lizzie Himmel, (P), Alen MacWeeney, (P)
Fischer, Bob/135 E 54th St 212-755-2131
Alex Chatelain, (P), James Moore, (P)
Fishback, Lee/350 W 21st St 212-929-2951
JAEL, (I)
Foster, Pat Artists Rep/6 E 36th St #1R (P 532-537) **212-685-4580**
Sandro Biffignandi, (I), Ken Birdsong, (I), Dru Blair, (I), Lina Chesak, (I), David Cook, (I), Louis Henderson, (I), Ken Otsuka, (I), Keith Simmons, (I)
Foster, Peter/870 UN Plaza 212-593-0793
Donald Penny, (P), Charles Tracey, (P)

G

Gaynin, Gail/241 Central Park West 212-580-3141
Karen Cipolla, (P), Terry Clough, (P)
Gebbia, Doreen/501 Cathedral Pkwy....................................212-678-0160
Ginsberg, Michael/407 Park Ave S #25F 212-679-8881
Godfrey, Dennis/231 W 25th St #6E 212-807-0840
Jeffrey Adams, (I), Daryl Cagle, (I), Dean Flemming, (I), Joel Nakamura, (I), Wendy Popp, (I), David Stimson, (I)
Goldman, David Agency/41 Union Sq W #918
(P 622-632) **212-807-6627**
Michele Barnes, (I), Norm Bendell, (I), Keith Bendis, (I), Rosemary Fox, (I), Kazu Shite Nitta, (I), Mitch Rigle, (I), David Anson Russo, (I), James Yang, (I), Kang Yi, (I)
Gomberg, Susan/41 Union Sq W #636 (P 431-443)........**212-206-0066**
Marty Blake, (I), Neil Brennan, (I), Steve Carver, (I), Robert

Dale, (I), G Allen Garns, (I), Ralph Giguere, (I), Franklin Hammond, (I), Scott Hunt, (I), Jacobson/Fernandez, (I), Laurie LaFrance, (I), Jeff Leedy, (I), Daniel McGowan, (I), Enzo & Schmidt, Urs Messi, (I), Marti Shohet, (I), James Tughan, (I), Jack Unruh, (I), Mark Weakley, (I)

Goodwin, Phyllis A/10 E 81st St #5 212-570-6021
Whistl'n Dixie, (I), John Paul Endress, (P), Carl Furuta, (P), Dennis Gottlieb, (P), Howard Menken, (P), Carl Zapp, (P)

Gordon, Barbara Assoc/165 E 32nd St (P 636-642) **212-686-3514**
Craig Bakley, (I), Ron Barry, (I), Bob Clarke, (I), Jim Dietz, (I), Wendy Grossman, (I), Glenn Harrington, (I), Robert Hunt, (I), Nenad Jakesevic, (I), Jackie Jasper, (I), Sonja Lamut, (I), Jacquie Marie Vaux, (I)

Gotham Art Agency/1123 Broadway #600 212-989-2737
Manuel Boix, (I), Petra Mathers, (I), JJ Sempe, (I), Peter Sis, (I), Tomi Ungerer, (I), F K Waechter, (P)

Grande, Carla/444 W 52nd St 212-977-9214
John Dugdale, (P), Helen Norman, (I)

Grant, Lucchi/800 West End Ave #15C 212-663-1460
Claire Phipps, (I)

Green, Anita/718 Broadway 212-674-4788
Bret Lopez, (P), Rita Maas, (P), Michael Molkenthin, (P)

Grien, Anita/155 E 38th St (P 650,651) **212-697-6170**
Dolores Bego, (I), Fanny Mellet Berry, (I), Julie Johnson, (I), Hal Just, (I), Jerry McDaniel, (I), Don Morrison, (I), Alan Reingold, (I), Alex Zwarenstein, (I)

H

Hankins & Tegenborg/60 E 42nd St #1940 212-867-8092
Bob Berran, (I), Ralph Brillhart, (I), Joe Burleson, (I), Michael Cassidy, (I), Jamie Cavaliere, (I), Jim Cherry, (I), Mac Conner, (I), Guy Deel, (I), John Taylor Dismukes, (I), Bill Dodge, (I), Danilo Ducak, (I), Marc Ericksen, (I), Robert Evans, (I), George Fernandez, (I), David Gaadt, (I), Steve Gardner, (I), James Griffin, (I), Ray Harvey, (I), Edwin Herder, (I), Michael Herring, (I), Aleta Jenks, (I), Rick Johnson, (I), Mia Joung, (I), Tom Kasperski, (I), Dave Kilmer, (I), Uldis Klavins, (I), Bob Maguire, (I), Neal McPheeters, (I), Cliff Miller, (I), Wendell Minor, (I), Miro, (I), Mitzura, (I), Walter Rane, (I), Kirk Reinert, (I), Frank Riley, (I), Don Rodell, (I), Sergio Roffo, (I), Kenneth Rosenberg, (I), Ron Runda, (I), Peter Van Ryzin, (I), Harry Schaare, (I), Bill Schmidt, (I), Diane Slavec, (I), Dan Sneberger, (I), Frank Steiner, (I), Jeff Walker, (I), Romeo Washington, (I), John Youssi, (I)

Hansen, Wendy/126 Madison Ave 212-684-7139
Metin Enderi, (P), Jon Holderer, (P), Masaaki Takenaka, (P)

Hardy, Allen/121 W 27 St #703 212-986-8441
Phillip Dixon, (P), Mike Russ, (I), Thomas Schenk, (P), Steven Wight, (I)

Hayes, Kathy Associates/131 Spring St 3rd Fl
(P 655-657) **212-925-4340**
Derek Buckner, (I), James Ennis Kirkland, (I), Christie Kitchens, (I), Ken Krafchek, (I), Ruth Lozner, (I), David Moyers, (I)

Head, Olive/155 Riverside Dr #10C 212-580-3323
Lauren Hammer, (P), Nesti Mendoza, (P), Jackie Nickerson, (P), Thomas Sullivan, (P), Frans Van Der Heyden, (P)

Henderson, Akemi/44 W 54th St 212-581-3630
Hitoshi Fugo, (P), Sonia Katchian, (P), Bob Osborn, (P), Liu Chung Ren, (P), Toshiro Yoshida, (P)

Henry, John/237 E 31st St 212-686-6883
Amos Chan, (P), Lois Greenfield, (P), Irutchka, (P), Eric Jacobson, (P), Eric Jacobson, (P)

Herron, Pat/80 Madison Ave 212-753-0462
Larry Dale Gordon, (P), Malcolm Kirk, (P), Kep Meyer, (P)

Heyl, Fran/230 Park Ave #2525 212-581-6470
Hill, Lilian/107 W 25th St #3A 212-627-5460
Holmberg, Irmeli/280 Madison Ave #1402 (P 378-393) ...**212-545-9155**
Gary Aagaard, (I), Jenny Adams, (I), Pat Alexander, (I), Toyce Anderson, (I), Alexander Barsky, (I), Dan Bridy, (I), Bob Byrd, (I), Lindy Chambers, (I), Rita Chow, (I), Henk Haselaar, (I), Deborah Healy, (I), Stephen Johnson, (I), Barbara Kelley, (I), Sue Llewellyn, (I), John Martinez, (I), Lu Matthews, (I), Marilyn Montgomery, (I), Cyd Moore, (I), John Nelson, (I), Jacqueline Osborn, (I), Judy Pedersen, (I), Deborah Pinkney, (I), Karen Pritchett, (I), Nikolai Punin, (I), Bob Radigan, (I), Donald Ranaldi, (I), Lilla Rogers, (I), Pat Thacker, (I), Randie Wasserman, (I), Cindy Wrobel, (I)

Hovde, Nob/1438 Third Ave 212-753-0462

Larry Dale Gordon, (P), Hiro, (P), Malcolm Kirk, (P)

Hurewitz, Gary/38 Greene St 212-925-2999
Howard Berman, (P), Steve Bronstein, (P)

I

In Focus Assoc/21 E 40th St #903 212-779-3600
Andrew Eccles, (P), Mark Hill, (P), Raul Vega, (P)

Indre, Christina/26 E 81st St 3N 212-794-7110
Ivy League of Artists/156 Fifth Ave #617 (P 658, 659) **212-243-1333**
Ernest Albanese, (I), Ivey Barry, (I), Cheryl Chalmers, (I), William Colrus, (I), Ric Del Rossi, (I), John Dyess, (I), Paula Goodman, (I), David Klein, (I), Chris Murphy, (I), Justin Novack, (I), Frederick Porter, (I), Tom Powers, (I), Tanya Rebelo, (I), Herb Reed, (I), John Rice, (I), B K Taylor, (I), Kyuzo Tsugami, (I), Allen Welkis, (I), Amy Zimmerman, (I)

J

Jedell, Joan/370 E 76th St 212-861-7861
George Agalias, (P), Charles Bush, (P), Ken Chung, (P), Marty Evans, (P), David Guilbert, (P), Elyse Lewin, (P), Malyszko Photography, (P), Tom McCarthy, (P), James Moore, (P), Jeff Nadler, (P), Michael Pruzan, (P), John Stember, (P)

Johnson, Arlene/5 E 19th St 212-725-4520
Johnson, Bud & Evelyne/201 E 28th St 212-532-0928
Kathy Allert, (I), Irene Astrahan, (I), Cathy Beylon, (I), Lisa Bonforte, (I), Carolyn Bracken, (I), Frank Daniel, (I), Larry Daste, (I), Betty de Araujo, (I), Jill Dubin, (I), Ted Enik, (I), Carolyn Ewing, (I), Bill Finewood, (I), George Ford, (I), Robert Gunn, (I), Erasmo Hernandez, (I), Tien Ho, (I), Mei-ku Huang, (I), Yukio Kondo, (I), Tom LaPadula, (I), Turi MacCombie, (I), Darcy May, (I), Eileen McKeating, (I), John O'Brien, (I), Heidi Petach, (I), Steven Petruccio, (I), Frank Remkiewicz, (I), Christopher Santoro, (I), Stan Skardinski, (I), Barbara Steadman, (I), Tom Tierney, (I)

Joyce, Tricia/342 W 84th St 212-962-0728
Reuven Afanador, (P), Michaela Davis, (S), Sara Feldmann, (S), Barry Harris, (P), Pat Lacroix, (P), Wei Lang, (MU), Sam Pellesier, (P), Peter Sakas, (P), Jeffrey Thomas, (S), Betty Wilson, (S)

K

Kahn, Harvey Assoc Inc/14 E 52nd St (P 501-507) **212-752-8490**
Bernie Fuchs, (I), Nick Gaetano, (I), Gerald Gersten, (I), Robert Peak, (I), Bill Sienkiewicz, (I), Joel Spector, (I),

Kane, Odette/236 W 27th St 10th Fl 212-807-8730
Richard Atlan, (I), Albano Guatti, (P), Maria Perez, (I), Charles Seesselberg, (P)

Kapune, Laurel/370 Central Park West 212-222-2378
Steven Randazzo, (P)

Kauss, Jean-Gabriel/235 E 40th St 212-370-4300
Serge Barbeau, (P), Gianpaolo Barbieri, (P), Karel Fonteyne, (P), Jesse Gerstein, (P), Francois Halard, (P), Mark Hispard, (P), Dominique Isserman, (P), Mark Kayne, (P), Jean La Riviere, (P), Isabel Snyder, (P), Lance Staedler, (P)

Kenney, John Assoc/145 E 49th St 212-758-4545
Gary Hanlon, (P), Elizabeth Heyert, (P)

Ketcham, Laurie/210 E 36th St #6C 212-481-9592
Timothy Hill, (P), Victoria Luggo, (P), Gerard Musy, (P), Dick Nystrom, (P), David O'Connor, (P)

Kim/137 E 25th St 11 Fl 212-679-5628
Carl Shiraishi, (P)

Kimche, Tania/425 W 23rd St #10F (P 669-677) **212-242-6367**
Paul Blakey, (I), Kirk Caldwell, (I), Rob Colvin, (I), Joe Fleming, (I), Hom & Hom, (I), Rafal Olbinski, (I), Miriam Schottland, (I), Christopher Zacharow, (I)

Kirchoff-Wohlberg Inc/866 UN Plaza #525
(P 678, 679) 212-644-2020
Angela Adams, (I), Esther Baran, (I), Bob Barner, (I), Maryjane Begin, (I), Liz Callen, (I), Steve Cieslawski, (I), Brian Cody, (I), Gwen Connelly, (I), Donald Cook, (I), Floyd Cooper, (I), Betsy Day, (I), Rae Ecklund, (I), Lois Ehlert, (I), Al Fiorentino, (I), Frank Fretz, (I), Jon Friedman, (I), Dara Goldman, (I), Jeremy Guitar, (I), Konrad Hack, (I), Ron Himler, (I), Rosekrans Hoffman, (I), Kathleen Howell, (I), Chris Kalle, (I), Mark Kelley, (I), Christa Kieffer, (I), Dora Leder, (I), Tom Leonard, (I), Susan

Lexa, (I), Don Madden, (I), Susan Magurn, (I), Jane McCreary, (I), Lyle Miller, (I), Carol Nicklaus, (I), Sharon O'Neil, (I), Robin Oz, (I), Diane Paterson, (I), Jim Pearson, (I), J Brian Pinkney, (I), James Ransome, (I), Charles Robinson, (I), Bronwen Ross, (I), Andy San Diego, (I), Mary Beth Schwark, (I), Robert Gantt Steele, (I), Arvis Stewart, (I), Dorothy Stott, (I), Pat Traub, (I), Lou Vaccaro, (I), Joe Veno, (I), Alexandra Wallner, (I), John Wallner, (I), Fred Winkowski, (I), Arieh Zeldich, (I)

Klein, Leslie D/255 Sherman St, Brooklyn...............718-435-6541
Klimt, Bill & Maurine/15 W 72nd St......................212-799-2231
Randy Berrett, (I), Wil Cormier, (I), Jamie DeJesus, (I), Steve Ferris, (I), Mark Heath, (I), Paul Henry, (I), Jeffrey Lindberg, (I), Frank Morris, (I), Shusei Nagaoka, (I), Alan Neider, (I), Frank Ordaz, (I), Gary Penca, (I), Rob Sauber, (I), Mark Skolsky, (I), Carla Sormanti, (I), Charles Tang, (I), Susan Tang, (I)
Knight, Harrison/1043 Lexington Ave #4................212-288-9777
Barbara Campbell, (I)
Korman, Alison/95 Horatio St.............................212-633-8407
David Bishop, (P), Dana Buckley, (P)
Korn, Elaine Assoc/234 Fifth Ave 4th fl................212-679-6739
Klaus Laubmayer, (P), Francis Murphy, (P), Jim Varriale, (P), Jim Wood, (P), Frank Yarborough, (P)
Korn, Pamela & Assoc/32 W 40th St #9B (P 686-691)....**212-819-9084**
Brian Ajhar, (I), Jeff Moores, (I), Kurt Vargo, (I)
Kramer, Ina/61 Lexington Ave #1H........................212-779-7632
Lewis Calver, (I), Sharon Ellis, (I), Ken & Carl Fischer, (P), Jeffrey Holewski, (I), Ellen G Jacobs, (I), Lauren Keswick, (I), Randee Ladden, (I), Stan Sholik, (P)
Kramer, Joan & Assoc/49 E 21 St........................212-567-5545
Richard Apple, (P), Bill Bachmann, (P), Roberto Brosan, (P), David Cornwell, (P), Micheal DeVecka, (P), Clark Dunbar, (P), Stan Flint, (P), Stephen Frink, (P), Peter Kane, (P), John Lawlor, (P), Roger Marschutz, (P), James McLoughlin, (P), Ralf Merlino, (P), Frank Moscati, (P), Bill Nation, (P), John Russell, (P), Ed Simpson, (P), Roger Smith, (P), Glen Steiner, (P), Janice Travia, (P), Ken Whitmore, (P), Gary Wunderwald, (P), Edward Young, (P), Eric Zucker, (P)
Kreis, Ursula G/63 Adrian Ave, Bronx...................212-562-8931
Bill Farrell, (P), George Kamper, (P)
Krongard, Paula/210 Fifth Ave #301.....................212-683-1020
Douglas Foulke, (P), Bill White, (P)

L

Lada, Joe/330 E 19th St....................................212-475-3647
Lamont, Mary/56 Washington Ave, Brentwood...........212-242-1087
Jim Marchese, (P)
Lane, Judy/444 E 82nd St..................................212-861-7225
Larkin, Mary/308 E 59th St................................212-832-8116
Lynn St John, (P), Mort Klein, (MM), Charles Masters, (P)
Lavaty, Frank & Jeff/509 Madison Ave 10th Fl (P 548)....**212-355-0910**
Steve Adler, (I), John Burkey, (I), Jim Butcher, (I), Bernard D'Andrea, (I), Domenick D'Andrea, (I), Don Daily, (I), Donald Demers, (I), Roland DesCombes, (I), Chris Duke, (I), Bruce Emmett, (I), Gervasio Gallardo, (I), Tim Hildebrandt, (I), Martin Hoffman, (I), Stan Hunter, (I), Chet Jezierski, (I), David McCall Johnston, (I), Mort Kunstler, (I), Paul Lehr, (I), Lemuel Line, (I), Robert LoGrippo, (I), Carlos Ochagavia, (I), Ben Verkaaik, (I)
Lee, Alan/33 E 22nd St #5D................................212-673-2484
Jim Barber, (P)
Leff, Jerry Assoc Inc/420 Lexington Ave #2760 (P 212-237)....**212-697-8525**
Franco Accornero, (I), Lisa Adams, (I), Roger Barcilon, (I), Ken Barr, (I), Semyon Bilmes, (I), Alex Boies, (I), Tracy Britt, (I), Ron Broda, (I), Bradford Brown, (I), Mike Bryan, (I), Michael Bull, (I), Brian Callanan, (I), Gwen Connelly, (I), Denise Chapman Crawford, (I), Ron DiCianni, (I), Bill Donovan, (I), Norm Eastman, (I), Charles Gehm, (I), Penelope Gottlieb, (I), Kate Brennan Hall, (I), Richard High, (I), Fred Hilliard, (I), Terry Hoff, (I), Lars Justinen, (I), Armen Kojoyian, (I), Lingta Kung, (I), Ron Lesser, (I), Francis Livingston, (I), Steven Mach, (I), Kelly Maddox, (I), Dennis Magdich, (I), Michele Manning, (I), Frank Marciuliano, (I), Alan Mazzetti, (I), Gary McLaughlin, (I), Celia Mitchell, (I), Rick Ormond, (I), John Parsons, (I), Kenn Richards, (I), Sue Rother, (I), Rob Ruppel, (I), John Sayles, (I), Jackie Snider, (I,G), Mary Thelen, (I), James Woodend, (I), Judy York, (I)
Leone, Mindy/381 Park Ave S #710......................212-696-5674

Bill Kouirinis, (P)
Leonlan, Edith/220 E 23rd St..............................212-989-7670
Philip Leonian, (P)
Lerman, Gary/113 E 31st St #4D.........................212-683-5777
John Bechtold, (P), Jan Cobb, (P)
Levin, Bruce/1123 Broadway.............................212-243-3810
Levy, Leila/4523 Broadway #7G...........................212-942-8185
David Bishop, (P), Yoav Levy, (P)
Lewin, Betsy/152 Willoughby Ave, Brooklyn.............718-622-3882
Ted Lewin, (P)
LGI/241 W 36th St 7th Fl..................................212-736-4602
John Bellissimo, (P), Bruce Birmelin, (P), Peter Dokus, (P), Douglas Dubler, (P), Lynn Goldsmith, (P), Jim Graham, (P), Todd Gray, (P), Stephen Harvey, (P), Marc Hauser, (P), Christopher Kehoe, (P), Richard Pasley, (P), Don Weinstein, (P)
Lindgren & Smith/41 Union Sq W #1228 (P 188-211)....**212-929-5590**
Julian Allen, (I), Barbara Banthien, (I), Harry Bliss, (I), Bradley Clark, (I), Regan Dunnick, (I), Cameron Eagle, (I), Douglas Fraser, (I), Jan Grashow, (I), Joe & Kathy Heiner, (I), Lori Lohstoeter, (I), Richard Mantel, (I), John Mattos, (I), Yan Nascimbene, (I), Kathy O'Brien, (I), Michael Paraskevas, (I), Charles S Pyle, (I), Tim Raglin, (I), Robert Gantt Steele, (I), Cynthia Torp, (I), Stefano Vitale, (I), Jean Wisenbaugh, (I)
Liz-Li/260 Fifth Ave...212-889-7067
Martin Mistretta, (P), Roy Volkmann, (P)
Locke, John Studios Inc/15 E 76th St....................212-288-8010
Avoine, (I), Tudor Banus, (I), John Cayea, (I), Andre Dahan, (I), Oscar DeMejo, (I), Jean-Pierre Desclozeaux, (I), James Endicott, (I), Jean Michel Folon, (I), Michael Foreman, (I), Andre Francois, (I), Edward Gorey, (I), Dale Gottlieb, (I), Michel Granger, (I), Catherine Kanner, (I), Peter Lippman, (I), Richard Oden, (I), William Bryan Park, (I), Robert Pryor, (I), Hans-Georg Raugh, (I), Victoria Roberts, (I), Fernando Puig Rosado, (I), Ronald Searle, (I), Peter Sis, (I), Tim, (I), Roland Topor, (I), Carol Wald, (I)
Lott, Peter & George/60 E 42nd St #1146 (P 496-500)....**212-953-7088**
Juan C Barberis, (I), Ted Chambers, (I), Tony Cove, (I), Keith Hoover, (I), Ed Kurtzman, (I), Eric J W Lee, (I), Wendell McClintock, (I), Mark Nagata, (I), Tim O'Brien, (I), Marie Peppard, (I), John Suh, (I), Barbara Tyler, (I)
Lynch, Alan/155 Ave of Americas 10th Fl (P 693-695)....**212-255-6530**
Michael Armson, (I), Jim Burns, (I), John Clementson, (I), Merritt Dekle, (I), Stephen Hall, (I), John Harris, (I), Jane Human, (I), Mark Oldroyd, (I), Liane Payne, (I), Daniel Torres, (I), Jenny Tylden-Wright, (I), Jim Warren, (I), Janet Woolley, (I)
Lysohir, Chris/80 8th Ave.................................212-741-3187
Leland Bobbe, (P), John Uher, (P)

M

Mahar, Therese Ryan/233 E 50th St #2F................212-753-7033
Mark Platt, (P)
Mandell, Ilene/61 E 86th St...............................212-860-3148
Mann & Dictenberg Reps/20 W 46th St.................212-944-2853
Terry Heffernan, (P), Brian Lanker, (P), Ulf Skogsbergh, (P)
Marek & Assoc Inc/160 Fifth Ave #914..................212-924-6760
Chase Aston, (MU), Susan Breindel, (S), David Cameron, (F), Pascal Chevallier, (P), Walter Chin, (P), Gad Cohen, (H), Hans Feurer, (P), BJ Gillian, (MU), Sonia Kashuk, (MU), Eddy Kohli, (P), Just Loomis, (P), Andrew MacPherson, (P), Nori, (MU), Mel Rau, (MU), Roseann Repetti, (S), Francesco Scavullo, (P), Ronnie Stam, (H), Edward Tricomi, (H), Deborah Turbeville, (P), Basia Zamorska, (S)
Marlon Inc/115 Fourth Ave #8C..........................212-777-5757
Tierney Gearon, (P), Piero Gemelli, (P), Marco Glaviano, (P), Dominique Guillemot, (P), Christophe Jouany, (P)
Marshall, Mel & Edith/40 W 77th St.....................212-877-3921
Marzena/229 E 79th St....................................212-772-2522
Chris Callis, (P)
Mason, Pauline/267 Wycoff St, Brooklyn................718-624-1906
Clifford Harper, (I), Peter Knock, (I), Peter Till, (I)
Mattelson Assoc Ltd/ (P 696,697)......................**212-684-2974**
Karen Kluglein, (I), Marvin Mattelson, (I)
McKay, Colleen/229 E 5th St #2..........................212-598-0469
Marili Forastieri, (P), Russell Porcas, (P), Lilo Raymond, (P), Robert Tardio, (P)
Mendola Ltd/420 Lexington Ave #PH4,5 (P 157-187)....**212-986-5680**
Gus Alavezos, (I), Paul R Alexander, (I), Steve Brennan, (I), Ellis Chappell, (I), Garry Colby, (I), Jim Deneen, (I), Vincent

DiFate, (I), John Eggert, (I), Dominick Finelle, (I), Phil Franke, (I), Tom Gala, (I), Hector Garrido, (I), Elaine Gignilliat, (I), Chuck Gillies, (I), Dale Gustafson, (I), Michael Halbert, (I), Chuck Hamrick, (I), Attila Hejja, (I), Dave Henderson, (I), Mitchell Hooks, (I), James Ibusuki, (I), Bill James, (I), Dean Kennedy, (I), Alfons Kiefer, (I), Joyce Kitchell, (I), Ashley Lonsdale, (I), Dennis Luzak, (I), Jeffrey Lynch, (I), Jeffrey Mangiat, (I), Edward Martinez, (I), Bill Maughan, (I), Geoffrey McCormack, (I), Michael McGovern, (I), Mark McMahon, (I), Ann Meisel, (I), Roger Metcalf, (I), Ted Michener, (I), Mike Mikos, (I), William Miller, (I), Tom Newsome, (I), Chris Notarile, (I), RadenStudio, (I), Phil Roberts, (I), Brian Sauriol, (I), David Schleinkofer, (I), Bill Silvers, (I), Mike Smollin, (I), Kipp Soldwedel, (I), John Solie, (I), George Sottung, (I), Cliff Spohn, (I), Robert Tanenbaum, (I), Jeffrey Terreson, (I), Thierry Thompson, (I), Mark Watts, (I), Don Wieland, (I), Mike Wimmer, (I), Larry Winborg, (I), David Womersley, (I), Ray Yeldham, (I)
Mennemeyer, Ralph/364 W 18 St...................................212-691-4277
Les Jorgenson, (P), Steve Robb, (P), David Weiss, (P)
Meo, Frank/220 E 4th St #510.....................................212-353-0907
Miller, Susan/1641 Third Ave #29A..............................212-427-9604
Desmond Burdon, (P), Bill Frakes, (P), Ainslie MacLeod, (I), Michael Questa, (P), Bill Robbins, (P), Richard Hamilton Smith, (P)
Mintz, Les/111 Wooster St #PH C (P 422-430)......**212-925-0491**
Istvan Banyai, (I), Robert Bergin, (I), Bernard Bonhomme, (I), Grace DeVito, (I), Curt Doty, (I), Mark Fisher, (I), Phil Franke, (I), Oscar Hernandez, (I), Amy Hill, (I), Elizabeth Lennard, (I), Roberta Ludlow, (I), David Lui, (I), Julia McLain, (I), Bobbie Moline-Kramer, (I), Rodica Prato, (I), Tommy Soloski, (I), Barton Stabler, (I), Maria Stroster, (I), Randall Zwingler, (I)
Monaco Reps/280 Park Ave S.....................................212-979-5533
Hans Gissinger, (P), Gabriella Imperatori, (P), Roger Neve, (P), John Peden, (P), Danny Sit, (P), Otto Stupakoff, (P)
Morgan, Vicki Assoc/194 Third Ave (P 100-113)...........**212-475-0440**
Nanette Biers, (I), Ray Cruz, (I), Patty Dryden, (I), Vivienne Flesher, (I), Joyce Patti, (I), Joanie Schwarz, (I), Kirsten Soderlind, (I), Nancy Stahl, (I), Steam/Dave Willardson, (I), Dahl Taylor, (I), Bruce Wolfe, (I), Wendy Wray, (I)
Mosel, Sue/310 E 46th St...212-599-1806
Moses, Janice/155 E 31st St #20H...............................212-779-7929
Brad Guice, (P), Karen Kuehn, (P)
Moskowitz, Marion/315 E 68 St #9F (P 698-699)...........**212-517-4919**
Dianne Bennett, (I), Diane Teske Harris, (I), Arnie Levin, (I), Geoffrey Moss, (I)
Moss & Meixler/36 W 37th St.....................................212-868-0078
Moss, Eileen & Nancy Bruck/333 E 49th St #3J (P 592-603)...**212-980-8061**
Tom Curry, (I), Warren Gelbert, (I), Ken Goldhammer, (I), Joel Peter Johnson, (I), Lionsgate, (I), Robert Neubecker, (I), Adam Niklewicz, (I), Pamela Patrick, (I), Ben Perini, (I), Robert Pizzo, (I), Scott Pollack, (I), Rebecca Reugger, (I), Mark Yankus, (I)
Muth, John/37 W 26th St...212-532-3479
Pat Hill, (P)

N

Neail, Pamela R Assoc/27 Bleecker St..........................212-673-1600
Margaret Brown, (I), Greg Dearth, (I), David Guinn, (I), Celeste Henriquez, (I), Thea Kliros, (I), Michele Laporte, (I), Marina Levikova, (I), Tony Mascio, (I), Peter McCaffery, (I), Cary McKiver, (I), CB Mordan, (I), Manuel Nunez, (I), Brenda Pepper, (I), Janet Recchia, (I), Linda Richards, (I), Kenneth Spengler, (I), Glenn Tunstull, (I), Jenny Vainisi, (I), Vicki Yiannias, (I)
Network Representatives/206 W 15th St 4th Fl...............212-727-0044
Philippe Gamand, (P), Ross Whitaker, (P)
Newborn, Milton/135 E 54th St...................................212-421-0050
John Alcorn, (I), Stephen Alcorn, (I), Braldt Bralds, (I), Robert Giusti, (I), Dick Hess, (I), Mark Hess, (I), Victor Juhasz, (I), Simms Taback, (I), David Wilcox, (I)

P

Page Assoc/219 E 69th St..212-772-0346
Bob Abraham, (P), David Cornwell, (P), John Curtis, (P), Sam Haskins, (P), Michael Horikawa, (P), Rick Peterson, (P), Lincoln Potter, (P), Franco Salmoiraghi, (P), Ford Smith, (P), William Sumner, (P), Phil Uhl, (P), Gert Wagner, (P), William Waterfall, (P), Steve Wilkings, (P), John Zimmerman, (P)

Palmer-Smith, Glenn Assoc/150 W 82 St......................212-769-3940
John Manno, (P), Charles Nesbitt, (P)
Parallax Artist's Reps/350 Fifth Ave...........................212-695-0445
Adah, (MU), Aragao, (P), Patti Dubroff, (MU), Marc Gourou, (P), Christian Kettiger, (P), Hilmar Meyer-Bosse, (P), Pauline St Denis, (P)
Penny & Stermer Group/31 W 21st St 7th Fl Rear (P 520)..**212-243-4412**
Manos Angelakis, (F), Doug Archer, (I), Ron Becker, (I), Scott Gordley, (I), Mike Hodges, (I), Don Kahn, (I), Julia Noonan, (I), Thomas Payne, (I), Deborah Bazzel Pogue, (I), Terri Starrett, (I), James Turgeon, (I), Judy Unger, (I)
Photography Bureau/400 Lafayette St #4G.....................212-255-3333
Pierce, Jennifer/1376 York Ave....................................212-744-3810
Pinkstaff, Marsha/25 W 81st St 15th Fl.........................212-799-1500
Neal Barr, (P)
Polizzi, Antonia/125 Watts St.....................................212-925-1571
Mark Lyon, (P)
Pritchett, Tom/130 Barrow St #316..............................212-688-1080
George Kanelous, (I), George Parrish, (I), Terry Ryan, (I)
Pushpin Assoc/215 Park Ave S #1300 (P 707-713)......**212-674-8080**
Elliott Banfield, (I), Lou Beach, (I), Eve Chwast, (I), Seymour Chwast, (I), Alicia Czechowski, (I), Michael A Donato, (I), Moira Hahn, (I), Dave Jonason, (I), R Kenton Nelson, (I), Nishi, (I), Roy Pendleton, (I)

R

Rapp, Gerald & Cullen Inc/108 E 35th St (P 114-156;Back Cover/Books 1&2)...........**212-889-3337**
Ray Ameijide, (I), Emmanuel Amit, (I), Michael David Brown, (I), Lon Busch, (I), Jose Cruz, (I), Ken Dallison, (I), Jack Davis, (I), Bob Deschamps, (I), Bill Devlin, (I), Ray Domingo, (I), Lee Duggan, (I), Dynamic Duo Studio, (I), Randy Glass, (I), Thomas Hart, (I), Lionel Kalish, (I), Laszlo Kubinyi, (I), Sharmen Liao, (I), Lee Lorenz, (I), Bernard Maisner, (I), Allan Mardon, (I), Hal Mayforth, (I), Elwyn Mehlman, (I), Alex Murawski, (I), Lou Myers, (I), Marlies Merk Najaka, (I), Bob Peters, (I), Sigmund Pifko, (I), Jerry Pinkney, (I), Camille Przewodek, (I), Deborah Roundtree, (I,P), David Art Sales, (I), Charles Santore, (I), Nora Scarlett, (P), Steve Spelman, (I,P), Drew Struzan, (I), Michael Witte, (I)
Ray, Marlys/350 Central Pk W.....................................212-222-7680
Bill Ray, (P)
Reactor Worldwide Inc/156 Fifth Ave #508.....................212-967-7699
Jamie Bennett, (I), Federico Botana, (I), Blair Brawson, (I), Henrik Drescher, (I), Bob Fortier, (I), Gail Geltner, (I), Carolyn Gowdy, (I), Steven Guarnaccia, (I), Jeff Jackson, (I), Jerzy Kolacz, (I), Ross MacDonald, (I), James Marsh, (I), Simon Ng, (I), Tomio Nitto, (I), Bill Russell, (I), Joe Salina, (I), Fiona Smyth, (I), Jean Tuttle, (I), Maurice Vellekoop, (I), Rene Zamic, (I)
Reese, Kay Assoc/225 Central Park West.......................212-799-1133
Lee Baltimore, (P), Paul Cranham, (P), Ashvin Gatha, (P), Lowell Georgia, (P), Peter Gullers, (P), Arno Hammacher, (P), Dellan Haun, (P), Sergio Jorge, (P), Simpson Kalisher, (P), Jay Leviton, (P), Tim Long, (P), Jonathan Love, (P), Ben Martin, (P), Lynn Pelham, (P), T Tanuma, (P)
Reid, Pamela/66 Crosby St..212-925-5909
Thierry des Fontaines, (P), Bert Stern, (P)
Renard Represents/501 Fifth Ave #1407 (P 72-99;Inside Front Flap/Bk 1)...........**212-490-2450**
Steve Bjorkman, (I), Joseph Cellini, (I), William Cigliano, (I), Glenn Dean, (I), Carol Donner, (I), Bart Forbes, (I), Dan Garrow, (I), Tim Girvin, (I), Jud Guitteau, (I), William Harrison, (I), Matthew Holmes, (I), Jane Hurd, (I), Hideaki Kodama, (I), Lamb & Hall, (P), John Martin, (I), Wayne McLoughlin, (I), Richard Newton, (I), Robert Rodriguez, (I), Theo Rudnak, (I), Maso Saito, (I), Kazuhiko Sano, (I), Michael Schwab, (I), Valerie Sinclair, (I), Doug Struthers, (I), Jozef Sumichrast, (I), Kim Whitesides, (I)
Rep Rep/211 Thompson St #1E.....................................212-475-5911
Rob Fraser, (P), Bernard Maisner, (I), Marcus Tullis, (P)
Ridgeway, Karen/330 W 42nd St #3200NE.....................212-714-0130
Ronald Ridgeway, (I)
Riley Illustration/81 Greene St (P 566,567)...............**212-925-3053**
Benoit, (I), Quentin Blake, (I), William Bramhall, (I), CESC, (I), Paul Degen, (I), Chris DeMarest, (I), Jeffrey Fisher, (I), Paul Hogarth, (I), Benoit Van Innis, (I), Pierre Le-Tan, (I), Paul Meisel, (I), Jim Parkinson, (I), Cheryl Peterson, (I), J J Sempe, (I), David Small, (I)

Riley, Catherine/12 E 37th St.................................212-532-8326
Riley & Riley Photo, (P)
Robinson, Madeleine/31 W 21st St.......................212-243-3138
Jamie Hankin, (P), Russell Kirk, (P), Chuck Kuhn, (P), Michel
Tcherevkoff, (P)
Roderick-Payne, Jennifer/80 Varick St #6A..........212-268-1788
Brian Goble, (P), Deborah Klesenski, (P), Bob Ward, (P)
Roman, Helen Assoc/140 West End Ave #9H.........212-874-7074
Lou Carbone, (I), Roger T De Muth, (I), Mena Dolobowsky, (I),
Naiad Einsel, (I), Walter Einsel, (I), Myron Grossman, (I), Jeff
Lloyd, (I), Sandra Marziali, (I), Andrea Mistretta, (I)

S

S I International/43 East 19th St...........................212-254-4996
Jack Brusca, (I), Oscar Chichoni, (I), Daniela Codarcea, (I),
Richard Corben, (I), Richard Courtney, (I), Bob Cowan, (I),
Robin Cuddy, (I), Dennis Davidson, (I), Allen Davis, (I), Andre
Debarros, (I), Ted Enik, (I), Blas Gallego, (I), Vicente Gonzalez,
(I), Mel Grant, (I), Devis Grebu, (I), Oscar Guell, (I), Steve
Haefele, (I), Sherri Hoover, (I), Susi Kilgore, (I), Richard
Leonard, (I), Sergio Martinez, (I), Fred Marvin, (I), Francesc
Mateu, (I), Jose Miralles, (I), Isidre Mones, (I), Steve Parton, (I),
Joan Pelaez, (I), Jordi Penalva, (I), Vince Perez, (I), Martin Rigo,
(I), Melodye Rosales, (I), Aristides Ruiz, (I), Paul Wenzel, (I)
Sacramone, Dario/302 W 12th St.........................212-929-0487
Tracy Aiken, (P), Marty Umans, (P)
Samuels, Rosemary/14 Prince St #5E...................212-477-3567
Beth Galton, (P), Chris Sanders, (P)
Sander, Vicki/155 E 29th St #28G.........................212-683-7835
John Manno, (P)
Santa-Donato, Paul/25 W 39th St #1001..............212-921-1550
Saunders, Gayle/145 E 36th St #2.......................212-481-3860
Tiziano Magni, (P), Dewy Nicks, (P), Michael O'Brien, (P)
Saunders, Michele/84 Riverside Dr #5.................212-496-0268
Ricardo Bertancourt, (P), Francis Giacobetti, (P), David
Hamilton, (P), Cheryl Koralik, (P), Uwe Ommer, (P)
Schecter Group, Ron Long/212 E 49th St.............212-752-4400
Scher, Dotty/235 E 22nd St...................................212-689-7273
Harry Benson, (P), David Katzenstein, (P), Frank Spinelli, (P),
Elizabeth Watt, (P), Denis Waugh, (P)
Schneider, Jonathan/175 Fifth Ave #2291.............212-459-4325
Dennis Dittrich, (I), Mike Kreffel, (I), Adam Max, (I), Harley
Schwadron, (I), Steve Smallwood, (I), Jay Taylor, (I)
Schochat, Kevin R/150 E 18th St #14N.................212-475-7068
Thom DeSanto, (P), Mark Ferri, (P)
Schramm, Emily/167 Perry St...............................212-620-0284
Schub, Peter & Robert Bear/136 E 57th #1702.....212-246-0679
Robert Freson, (P), Irving Penn, (P), Rico Puhlmann, (P)
Seigel, Fran/515 Madison Ave 22nd Fl.................212-486-9644
Kinuko Craft, (I), John Dawson, (I), Catherine Deeter, (I), Lars
Hokanson, (I), Mirko Ili'c, (I), Earl Keleny, (I), Larry McEntire, (I)
Shamilzadeh, Sol/214 E 24th St #3D....................212-532-1977
Strobe Studio, (P)
Sharlowe Assoc/275 Madison Ave........................212-288-8910
Claus Eggers, (P), Nesti Mendoza, (P)
Sheer, Doug/59 Grand St......................................212-274-8446
Siegel, Tema/234 Fifth Ave 4th Fl........................212-696-4680
Susan David, (I), Loretta Krupinski, (I)
Sigman, Joan/336 E 54th St...................................212-832-7980
Robert Goldstrom, (I), John H Howard, (I)
Smith, Emily/30 E 21st St......................................212-674-8383
Jeff Smith, (P)
Solomon, Richard/121 Madison Ave (P 238-263)..........**212-683-1362**
Kent Barton, (I), Tom Blackshear, (I), Steve Brodner, (I), John
Collier, (I), Paul Cox, (I), Jack E Davis, (F), David A Johnson,
(I), Gary Kelley, (I), Greg Manchess, (I), Bill Nelson, (I), C. F.
Payne, (I), Douglas Smith, (I), Mark Summers, (I)
Speart, Jessica/150 E 18th St #1F........................212-673-2289
Stein, Jonathan & Assoc/353 E 77th St...............212-517-3648
Roy Wright, (P)
Stevens, Norma/1075 Park Ave.............................212-427-7235
Richard Avedon, (P)
Stockland-Martel Inc/5 Union Sq W 6th Fl.............212-727-1400
Joel Baldwin, (P), Hank Benson, (P), Hank Benson, (P),
Richard Corman, (P), Anthony Gordon, (P), Tim Greenfield-
Sanders, (P), Hashi, (P), Reudi Hoffman, (P), Walter looss, (P),
Nadav Kander, (P), Eric Meola, (P), Sheila Metzner, (P), Tim

Mitchell, (P), Claude Mougin, (P), Michael Pruzan, (P), Timothy
White, (P), Bruce Wolf, (P)

T

Testino, Giovanni/251 Fifth Ave............................212-889-8891
Enrique Badulescu, (P), Martin Brady, (P), Franck Dieleman,
(P), Stephane Gerbier, (P), Arnold Hugh, (P), Wayne Stambler,
(P), Mario Testino, (P), Alberto Tolot, (P), Javier Valhonrat, (P)
The Art Farm/163 Amsterdam Ave........................212-873-2227
Bruce Aruffenbart, (I), Mona Mark, (I), Linda Pascual, (I), Bob
Walker, (I), Bill Zdinak, (I)
The Organisation/267 Wyckoff St, Brooklyn..........718-624-1906
Grahame Baker, (I), Enikoe Bakti, (I), Zafer Baran, (I), Yvonne
Chambers, (I), Emma Chichester Clark, (I), David Eaton, (I),
Mark Entwisle, (I), Michael Frith, (I), Peter Goodfellow, (I), Glyn
Goodwin, (I), Neil Gower, (I), Susan Hellard, (I), M Hill, (), Rod
Holt, (I), Leslie Howell, (I), Nicholas Hely Hutchinson, (I),
Natacha Ledwidge, (I), Toby Leetham, (I), Alan McGowan, (I),
Alan Morrison, (I), Lawrence Mynott, (I), Kevin O'Brien, (I),
Michael O'Shaughnessy, (I), Janet Pontin, (I), Fred Preston, (I),
Mark Reddy, (I), Ruth Rivers, (I), Max Schindler, (I),
Christopher Sharrock, (I), Jane Smith, (I), Linda Smith, (I),
Amanda Ward, (I), Paul Wearing, (I), Nadine Wickenden, (I),
Nick Williams, (I), Chris Winn, (I), Alison Wisenfeld, (I)
Thomas, Pamela/254 Park Ave S #5D....................212-529-4033
Three/236 W 26th St #805......................................212-463-7025
Frank Marchese, (G), William Sloan, (I)
Tise, Katherine/200 E 78th St (P 521-523)....................**212-570-9069**
Raphael Boguslav, (I), John Burgoyne, (I), Bunny Carter, (I),
Judy Pelikan, (I)
Torzecka, Marlena/531 E 81st St #1C (P 492-495)........**212-861-9892**
Andrzei Czeczot, (I), Tomek Olbinski, (I), Voytek Wolynski, (I),
Paul Zwolak, (I)
Tralongo, Katrin/144 W 27th St.............................212-255-1976
Mickey Kaufman, (P)
Turk, Melissa/370 Lexington Ave #1002 (P 572, 573)..**212-953-2177**
Juan Barberis, (I), Barbara Bash, (I), Ka Botzis, (I), Susan
Johnston Carlson, (I), Paul Casale, (I), Nancy Didion, (I),
Robert Frank, (I), Susan Johnston Carlson, (I), Kevin O'Malley,
(I), Wendy Smith-Griswold, (I)
Turner, John/55 Bethune St...................................212 243 6373
Troy Word, (P)

UV

Umlas, Barbara/131 E 93rd St...............................212-534-4008
Hunter Freeman, (P), Nora Scarlett, (P)
Vallon, Arlene/47-37 45th St #4K, Long Island City..........718-706-8112
Van Arnam, Lewis/881 7th Ave #405.....................212-541-4787
Paul Amato, (P), Mike Reinhardt, (P)
Van Orden, Yvonne/119 W 57th St.......................212-265-1223
Von Schreiber, Barbara/315 Central Park West #4N..........212-580-7044
Josef Astor, (P), Oberto Gili, (P), Tim Gummer, (P), Dennis
Manarchy, (P), Sarah Moon, (P), Jean Pagliuso, (P), Neal
Slavin, (P)

WYZ

Wainman, Rick/341 W 11th St #4D........................212-360-2518
Ward, Wendy/200 Madison Ave #2402.................212-684-0590
Mel Odom, (I)
Wasserman, Ted..212-867-5360
Michael Watson, (P)
Wayne, Philip/66 Madison Ave #9C.......................212-696-5215
Denes Petoe, (P), Douglas Whyte, (P)
Weber, Tricia Group/125 W 77th St (P 732,733)............**212-799-6532**
Raul Colon, (I), Abe Gurvin, (I), Seth Jaben, (I), Bill Mayer, (I),
David McKelvey, (I), Pat Mollica, (I), John Robinette, (I), Jim
Salvati, (I), Danny Smythe, (I), Dale Verzaal, (I)
Weissberg, Elyse/299 Pearl St #5E.......................212-406-2566
Michael Mazzel, (P), Jack Reznicki, (P)
Wilson, Scott/160 Fifth Ave #906...........................212-633-0105
Salvatore Baiano, (P), John Falocco, (P), Rolf Juario, (P),
Greg Weiner, (P)
Yellen/Lachapelle/420 E 54th St #21E....................212-838-3170
Joe Francki, (P), Tim Geaney, (P), Thom Jackson, (P),
Palmer Kolansky, (P), Olaf Wahlund, (P)

NORTHEAST

A

Ackermann, Marjorie/2112 Goodwin Lane, North Wales, PA.........215-646-1745
H Mark Weidman, (P)
Anderson, Laurel/5-A Pirates Lane, Gloucester, MA........................508-281-6880
John Curtis, (P), Elizabeth Henderson, (P)
Artco/227 Godfrey Rd, Weston, CT (P 312-351) **203-222-8777**
Artists International/7 Dublin Hill Dr, Greenwich, CT....................203-869-8010
Tony Chen, (I), David Chestnut, (I), Eric D'Zenis, (I), Gino, (I),
Michael Hampshire, (I), Paul Lopez, (I), John Nez, (I), Earl
Parker, (I), Paul Vaccarello, (I)

B

Bancroft, Carol & Friends/7 Ivy Hill Rd/Box 959, Ridgefield, CT......203-438-8386
Lori Anderson, (I), Mary Bausman, (I), Kristine Bollinger, (I),
Stephanie Britt, (I), Chi Chung, (I), Jim Cummins, (I), Susan
Dodge, (I), Andrea Eberbach, (I), Barbara Garrison, (I), Toni
Goffe, (I), Ethel Gold, (I), Mark Graham, (I), Linda Graves, (I),
Fred Harsh, (I), Ann Iosa, (I), Laurie Jordan, (I), Ketti Kupper,
(I), Karen Loccisano, (I), Laura Lydecker, (I), Steve Marchesi,
(I), Kathleen McCarthy, (I), Elizabeth Miles, (I), Yoshi Miyake,
(I), Steven Moore, (I), Rodney Pate, (I), Cathy Pavia, (I), Ondre
Pettingill, (I), Larry Raymond, (I), Beverly Rich, (I), Gail Roth,
(I), Sandra Shields, (I), Cindy Spencer, (I), Linda Boehm
Weller, (I), Ann Wilson, (I)
Beranbaum, Sheryl/115 Newbury St, Boston, MA...........................617-437-9459
David Barber, (I), Ronald Dellicolli, (I), James Edwards, (I),
Bob Eggleton, (I), Mike Gardner, (I), Michael Joyce, (I), Manuel
King, (I), Greg Mackey, (I), Michael McLaughlin, (I), Stephen
Moscowitz, (I), Matthew Pippin, (I)
Birenbaum, Molly/7 Williamsburg Dr, Cheshire, CT 203-272-9253
Peter Beach, (I), Alice Coxe, (I), W E Duke, (I), Sean Kernan,
(P), Joanne Schmaltz, (P), Paul Selwyn, (I), Bill Thomson, (I)
Bogner, Fred/911 State St, Lancaster, PA.....................................717-393-0918
brt Photo Illustration, (P)
Bookmakers Ltd/25-Q Sylvan Rd S, Westport, CT.........................203-226-4293
David Bolinsky, (I), Steve Botts, (I), Dawn DeRosa, (I), George
Guzzi, (I), Lydia Halverson, (I), Keith LoBue, (I), Judith Lombardi,
(I), Kathy McCord, (I), David Neuhaus, (I), Karen Pellaton, (I),
Marsha Serafin, (I), Dick Smolinski, (I), Harriet Sullivan, (I)
**Brewster, John Creative Services/597 Riverside Ave,
Westport, CT (P 590)**...**203-226-4724**
Don Almquist, (I), Mike Brent, (I), Wende L Caporale, (I), Lane
Dupont, (I), Tom Garcia, (I), Glen Gustafson, (I), Steve
Harrington, (I), Seth Larson, (I), Dolph LeMoult, (I), Howard
Munce, (I), Alan Neider, (I), Nan Parsons, (I), Rick Schneider,
(I), Richard Sparks, (I), Steven Stroud, (I), Al Weston, (I)
Breza-Collier, Susan/235 South 15, Philadelphia, PA......................215-790-1014
Vince Cucinotta, (I), Nancy Johnston, (I), Frank Margasak, (I),
Bot Roda, (I), Meryl Treatner, (I), Lane Yerkes, (I)
Brigitte Inc/202 48th St, Union City, NJ.....................................201-867-4846
Peter Castellano, (P), Robert DiScalfani, (P), Alan Messer, (P),
David Stetson, (P), Christopher Von Hohenberg, (P)
Browne, Pema Ltd/Pine Rd HCR Box 104B, Neversink, NY...........914-985-2936
Robert Barrett, (I), Todd Doney, (I), Richard Hull, (I), Ron
Jones, (I), Kathy Krantz, (I), John Rush, (I), John Sandford, (I)

C

Cadenbach, Marilyn/149 Oakley Rd, Belmont, MA 617-484-7437
Susie Cushner, (P), John Huet, (P), Jack Richmond, (P)
Campbell, Rita/129 Valerie Ct, Cranston, RI....................................401-826-0606
Caton, Chip/15 Warrenton Ave, Hartford, CT...................................203-523-4562
Bob Durham, (I), Phillip Dvorak, (I), Mike Eagle, (I), Andy
Giarnella, (I), Simpson Kalisher, (P), Kathleen Keifer, (I), Joe
Klim, (I), David Mendelsohn, (P), Diana Minisci, (I), Mark
Panioto, (P), Aina Roman, (I), Linda Schiwall-Gallo, (F),
Frederick Schneider, (I), Shaffer-Smith Photo, (P), Marc Sitkin,
(P), Janet Street, (I), Andy Yelenak, (I)
City Limits/80 Wheeler Ave, Pleasantville, NY 914-747-1422
Colucci, Lou/POB 2069/86 Lachawanna Ave, W Patterson, NJ........201-890-5770
Joe Colucci, (P)
Conn, Adina/3130 Wisconsin Ave NW #413, Washington, DC 202-296-3671
Rosemary Henry-May, (I), Carl Schoanberger, (I), Peter Steiner, (I)

Cornell/McCarthy/2-D Cross Hwy, Westport, CT.....................203-454-4210
**Creative Advantage Inc/620 Union St,
Schenectady, NY (P 610)** **518-370-0312**
Jack Graber, (I)
**Creative Arts International Inc/1024 Adams St,
Hoboken, NJ (P 611-615)** **201-659-7711**
Scott Bryant, (P), Ralph Butler, (I), Stephanie Causey, (I), David
Chen, (I), Gene Garbowski, (I), Richard LaLiberte, (I), Scott
Mutter, (P), Wayne Parmenter, (I), Jerry Pavey, (I), Michael
Powell, (I), Mark Seidler, (I), Tibor Toth, (I)
Creative Option/50 Washington St, S Norwalk, CT..........................203-854-9393

DE

D'Angelo, Victoria/620 Centre Ave, Reading, PA 215-376-1100
Andy D'Angelo, (P)
Disckind, Barbara/2939 Van Ness St NW, Washington, DC, ...202-362-0448
Ella/229 Berkeley #52, Boston, MA (P 524-531)............**617-266-3858**
Anatoly, (I), Krista Brauckman, (I), Rob Cline, (I), Scott Gordley,
(I), Robert Gunn, (I), Kevin Hawkes, (I), Doug Henry, (I), Roger
Leyonmark, (I), William L Petersen, (I), Kathy Petrauskas, (I),
Philip Porcella, (P), Jim Raycroft, (P), Cheryl Roberts, (I),
Robert Roth, (I), Bruce Sanders, (I), Ron Toelke, (I), Rhonda
Voo, (I), Bryan Wiggins, (I), Francine Zaslow, (P)
Ennis Inc/78 Florence Ave, Arlington, MA......................................617-643-2656
Erwin, Robin/54 Applecross Cir, Chalfont, PA.................................215-822-8258
Callaghan Photography, (P)
Esto Photographics/222 Valley Pl, Mamaroneck, NY.....................914-698-4060
Peter Aaron, (P), Scott Frances, (P), Jeff Goldberg, (P), John
Margolies, (P), Jock Pottle, (P), Ezra Stoller, (P)

G

Geng, Maud/25 Gray St, Boston, MA..617-236-1920
Caroline Alterio, (I), Julie Fillipo, (I), Robert Kasper, (I), Jon
McIntosh, (I), Glenn Robert Reid, (I), Michael Ryan, (P), Vicki
Smith, (I)
Giandomenico, Bob/13 Fern Ave, Collingswood, NJ.....................609-854-2222
Giannini & Talent/201 Tulip Ave, Takoma Park, MD......................301-565-0275
Mark Daniels, (P), Sheldon Greenberg, (I), Breton Littlehales,
(P), Mark Segal, (P), Joyce Tenneson, (P)
Giraldi, Tina/42 Harmon Pl, N Haledon, NJ 201-423-5115
Frank Giraldi, (P)
Goldstein, Gwen/8 Cranberry Lane, Dover, MA 508-785-1513
Cathy Diefendorf, (I), Steve Fuller, (I), Lane Gregory, (I),
Marcus Hamilton, (I), Gary Phillips, (I), Terry Presnall, (I),
Patrick Soper, (I), Susan Spellman, (I), Gary Torrisi, (I), Joe
Veno, (I), Mel Williges, (I)
Goodman, Tom/1424 South Broad St, Philadelphia, PA...................215-468-5842
Barney Leonard, (P), Steven Pollock, (P), Matt Wargo, (P)

H

Heisey, Betsy/109 Somerstown Rd, Ossining, NY 914-762-5335
Whitney Lane, (P)
HK Portfolio/458 Newtown Trnpk, Weston, CT 203-454-4687
Anthony Carnabuci, (I), Abby Carter, (I), Randy Chewning, (I),
Carolyn Croll, (I), Bert Dodson, (I), Eldon Doty, (I), JAK
Graphics, (I), Anne Kennedy, (I), Benton Mahan, (I), Susan
Miller, (I), Stephanie O'Shaughnessy, (I), Jan Palmer, (I),
Sandra Speidel, (I), Peggy Tagel, (I), Jean & Mou-sein Tseng,
(I), George Ulrich, (I), Randy Verougstraete, (I), Scott Webber,
(I), David Wenzel, (I)
Holt, Rita/920 Main St, Fords, NJ..212-683-2002
David Burnett, (P), Glen Daly, (P), Chuck Ealovega, (P),
Rodney Rascona, (P)
Hone, Claire/859 N 28th St, Philadelphia, PA...............................215-765-6900
Stephen Hone, (P)
Hurewitx, Barbara Talent/72 Williamson Ave, Hillside, NJ...........201-923-0011
Hyams, Ron/185 Moseman Ave, Katonah, NY...............................914-962-5777

IJK

ICON Graphics/34 Elton St, Rochester, NY...................................716-271-7020
Jagow, Linda/PO Box 425, Rochester, NY....................................716-546-7606
Ron Brancato, (I), Bob Conge, (I), Susan Covert, (I), Bob
Dorsey, (I), Paul Alois Jutton, (I), Malik Maliki, (I), Jeff Marinelli,
(I), Jean K Stephens, (I)

Kerr, Ralph/239 Chestnut St, Philadelphia, PA 215-592-1359
Joseph Mulligan, (P)
**Knecht, Cliff/309 Walnut Rd, Pittsburgh, PA
(P 681-685)** **412-761-5666**
David Bowers, (I), Janet Darby, (I), Jim Deigan, (I), Jackie
Geyer, (I), Deborah Pinkney, (I), George Schill, (I), Greg
Schooley, (I), Lee Steadman, (I), Jim Trusilo, (I), Phil Wilson, (I)
Kurlansky, Sharon/192 Southville Rd, Southborough, MA...............508-872-4549
Colleen, (I), John Gamache, (I), Peter Harris, (I), Geoffrey
Hodgkinson, (I), Bruce Hutchison, (I), Donald Langosy, (I),
Julia Talcott, (I)

M

Manasse, Michele/200 Acuetone Rd, New Hope, PA......................215-862-2091
Traian Alexandru-Filip, (I), Maxine Boll, (I), Sheldon Greenberg,
(I), Carol Inouye, (I), Narda Lebo, (I), Cathy Christi O'Connor,
(I), Terry Widener, (I)
Marc, Stephen/1301 Veto St, Pittsburgh, PA..................................412-231-5160
AD-1 Ad Agency, (GD), Markpoint Creative, (I), Mirage Visuals,
(AV), Mike Robinson, (P)
**Mattelson Associates Ltd/37 Cary Rd,
Great Neck, NY (P 696, 697)** **212-684-2974**
Karen Kluglein, (I), Marvin Mattelson, (I)
McConnell McNamara & Co/182 Broad St, Wethersfield, CT.......203-563-6154
Jack McConnell, (P)
Metzger, Rick/5 Tsienneto Rd, Derry, NH.......................................603-432-3356
Jon Chomitz, (P), Dave Deacon, (R)
Monahan, Terry/16 Kinsman Pl, Natick, MA..................................508-651-0671
Fabia DePonte, (I), Sara DePonte, (I)
Morgan, Wendy/5 Logan Hill Rd, Northport, NY............................516-757-5609
Karl Edwards, (I), Brad Gaber, (I), Scott Gordley, (I), Fred
Labitzke, (I), Al Margolis, (I), ParaShoot, (P), Fred Schrier, (I),
Mark Sparacio, (I)
Murphy, Brenda/72 High St #2, Topsfield, MA...............................508-887-3528
Diane Bigda, (I), Joe Goebel, (I), Howie Green, (I), William Kurt
Lumpkins, (I), Valentine Sahleanu, (I), Mark Seppala, (I), Paul
Wasserboehr, (I), Richard Watzulik, (I)

OP

O'Connor, Leighton/15 Ives St, Beverly, MA................................508-922-9478
Jeffrey Coolidge, (P), Joe Veno, (I)
Oreman, Linda/22 Nelson St, Rochester, NY.................................716-244-6956
Nick Agnello, (I), Jim Bliss, (I), Roger DeMuth, (I), Paul Facklam,
(I), Bill Finewood, (I), Peter Lautenslager, (I), Bob Radigan, (I),
Pete Smith, (I), Karen Tomaselli, (I), Vicki Wehrman, (I)
**Palulian, Joanne Reps/18 McKinley St, Rowayton,
CT (P 470-475)** **203-866-3734**
M John English, (I), Bonnie Hofkin, (I), Gayle Kabaker, (I),
David Lesh, (I), Kirk Moldoff, (I), Dickran Palulian, (I),
Bonnie Timmons, (I)
Publishers Graphics/251 Greenwood Ave, Bethel, CT 203-797-8188
Robert Alley, (I), Dan Andreasen, (I), Ellen Beier, (I), Paige Billin-
Frye, (I), Deborah Borgo, (I), Patti Boyd, (I), Robin Brickman, (I),
Ray Burns, (I), Jean Cassels, (I), Eulala Conner, (I), Kees de
Kiefte, (I), Marie DeJohn, (I), Leslie Dunlap, (I), Julie Durrell, (I),
Allan Eitzen, (I), Marlene Ekman, (I), Gioia Fiammenghi, (I),
Fuka, (I), T R Garcia, (I), Patrick Girouard, (I), Paul Harvey, (I),
Benrei Huang, (I), Pamela Johnson, (I), Brian Karas, (I), Kathie
Kelleher, (I), Robin Kramer, (I), Barbara Lanza, (I), Gary
Lippincott, (I), Bob Marstall, (I), Lisa McCue, (I), Peter
Palagonia, (I), Robert A Parker, (I), Larry Raymond, (I), Dana
Regan, (I), David Rickman, (I), S D Schindler, (I), Joel Snyder,
(I), Barbara Todd, (I), James Watling, (I), Kathy Wilburn, (I)
Putscher, Terri/1214 Locust St, Philadelphia, PA.............................215-569-8890
Bob Byrd, (I), Tom Herbert, (I), Bob Jones, (I), Adam
Matthews, (I), Kimmerle Milnazik, (I), Bob Neumann, (I),
Andrew Nitzberg, (I), Gary Undercuffler, (I)

RS

Redmond, Sharon/8634 Chelsea Bridge Way, Lutherville, MD 301-823-7422
Jim Owens, (I)
Reese-Gibson, Jean/4 Puritan Rd, N Beverly, MA 508-927-5006
Dennis Helmar, (P), Dan Morrill, (P), Steve Rubican, (P)
Reitmeyer, Roxanne/2016 Walnut St, Philadelphia, PA....................215-972-1543
Terrence McBride, (P)

Roland, Rochel/20150 Locust Dale Terrace, Germantown, MD.......301-353-9431
Tom Engeman, (I), Mike Mitchell, (I), Michael Pohuski, (P), Jim
Sloane, (P)
Satterthwaite, Victoria/115 Arch St, Philadelphia, PA...................215-925-4233
Michael Furman, (P)
Schnitzel, Gary/PO Box 297, Pineville, PA.....................................215-598-0214
Sheehan, Betsy/7928 Ruxway Rd, Baltimore, MD...........................410-828-4020
Shokie Bragg, (I), Gary Crane, (I), Don Dudley, (I), RJ Shay, (I),
Steve Uzzell, (P)
Skeans, Hillary/PO Box 158, Miquon, PA.......................................215-825-1047
Sonneville, Dane/PO Box 155, Passaic, NJ....................................201-472-1225
Bryn Barnard, (I), Tim Barrall, (I), Barry Blackman, (P), DL
Creamer, (I), Sid Evans, (I), Ken Korsh, (P), Art Kretzchmar, (I),
Sergio Levin, (P), Angelo Santeniello, (P), Stuart Simons, (P),
Art Thompson, (I), Bill Truran, (P), Greg Voth, (I), Pam Voth, (I)
Soodak, Arlene/11135 Korman Dr, Potomac, MD..........................301-983-2343
Renee Comet, (P), Anthony Edgeworth, (P), Martin Rogers,
(P), Scott Sanders, (I)
Star, Lorraine/1 Canterbury Circle, Kennebunk, ME.......................207-967-5319
Hank Gans, (P)
Stemrich, J David/213 N 12th St, Allentown, PA 215-776-0825
Mark Bray, (I), Bob Hahn, (P)
Stockwell, Jehremy/97 Highwood Ave, Englewood, NJ 201-567-3069
Michael Conway, (I)
Studioworks/237 Hopmeadow St, Simsbury, CT...............................203-658-2583

TU

Talbot & Assoc, TJ/3101 New Mexico Ave, Washington, DC, ...202-364-1947
The Art Source/444 Bedford Rd/PO Box 257, Pleasantville, NY......914-747-2220
James Barkley, (I), Karen Bell, (I), Liz Conrad, (I), Hui Han Lui,
(I), Richard Redowl, (I)
TVI Creative Specialists/1146 19th St NW, Washington, DC........202-331-7722
June Chaplin, (P), Mark Freeman, (I), Isaac Jones, (P),
Eucalyptus Tree Studio, (I)
Unicorn/120 American Rd, Morris Plains, NJ 201-292-6852
Greg Hildebrandt, (I)

VW

Veloric, Philip M/128 Beechtree Dr, Broomall, PA 215-356-0362
Michael W Adams, (I), Deb Troyer Bunnell, (I), Suzanne K Clee,
(I), Rick L Cooley, (I), Don Dyen, (I), Len Ebert, (I), Kathy
Hendrickson, (I), Patricia Gural Hinton, (I), John Holder, (I), Robert
R Jackson, (I), Polly Krumbhaar Lewis, (I), Richard Loehle, (I),
Laurie Marks, (I), Eileen Rosen, (I), Ed Sauk, (I), Nancy Schill, (I),
Dennis Schofield, (I), Samantha Carol Smith, (I), Wayne Anthony
Still, (I), Brad Strode, (I), Gary Undercuffler, (I), Lane Yerkes, (I)
Warner, Bob/1425 Belleview Ave, Plainfield, NJ.............................908-755-7236
Phil Harrington, (P), Lester Lefkowitz, (P), Hank Morgan, (P),
Tomo Narashina, (I), Lou Odor, (P), Victor Valla, (I)
**Wolfe, Deborah Ltd/731 North 24th St, Philadelphia,
PA (P 363-377)** **215-232-6666**
Skip Baker, (I), Robert Burger, (I), Richard Buterbaugh, (I), Dia
Calhoun, (I), Jenny Campbell, (I), Dave Christiana, (I), Jeff
Cook, (I), Bob Cooper, (I), Ray Dallasta, (I), Jeff Fitz-Maurice,
(I), John Paul Genzo, (I), Patrick Gnan, (I), Randy Hamblin, (I),
Jim Himmsworth, 3rd (I), Michael Hostovich, (I), Robin
Hotchkiss, (I), Marianne Hughes, (I), Neal Hughes, (I), John
Huxtable, (I), Scott Johnston, (I), Tony Mascio, (I), Joe
Masterson, (I), Tom Miller, (I), Verlin Miller, (I), Bill Morse, (I),
Andy Myer, (I), Steven Nau, (I), Lisa Pomerantz, (I), Richard
Waldrep, (I), Bea Weidner, (I), Larry Winborg, (I)
Wolff, Timmi/1509 Park Ave, Baltimore, MD 410-383-7059
Steven Biver, (P), Burgess Blevins, (P), R Mark Heath, (I), Meg
Kratz, (P), Ron Solomon, (P), Richard Ustinich, (P)

S O U T H E A S T

ABC

Addison Paramount Images/1416 Forest Hills Dr,
Winter Springs, FL..407-339-1711
**Aldridge, Donna Reps Inc/755 Virginia Ave NE,
Atlanta, GA (P 584-586)**...**404-872-7980**
Catpack, (I), Thomas Gonzalez, (I), Bill Jenkins, (I), Chris

Lewis, (I), Carol H Norby, (I), Marcia Wetzel, (I)
Anders, Phil/704 Churchill Dr, Chapel Hill, NC 919-929-0011
Ray Dugas, (I), Dan Johnson, (I), Jan Lukens, (I), Bob Murray,
(I), Chuck Primeau, (I), Keith Simmons, (I), Elizabeth Traynor, (I)
Beck, Susanne/2721 Cherokee Rd, Birmingham, AL 205-871-6632
Charles Beck, (P)
Brenner, Harriet/901 Martin Downs Blvd, Palm City, FL..................407-283-9945
Dick Krueger, (P), Erich Schremp, (P), Tony Soluri, (P)
Burnett, Yolanda/571 Dutch Vall Rd, Atlanta, GA 404-881-6627
**Cary & Co/666 Bantry Lane, Stone Mountain, GA
(P 543-547)** **404-296-9666**
Robert August, (I), Johnna Bandle, (I), Kathi Brown, (I), Mike
Hodges, (I), Kevin Hulsey, (I), David Marks, (I), Shawn
McKelvey, (I), Charlie Mitchell, (I), Greg Olsen, (I), John
Sommerfeld, (P)
Comport, Allan/241 Central Ave, St Petersburg, FL......................813-821-9050
Sally Wern Comport, (I), Neverne Covington, (I), Chris Coxwell,
(P), Vicki Gullickson, (I), Douglas Studio Johns, (P), Berney
Knox, (I), Jim Lange, (I), Dick Loader, (I)
Cuneo, Jim/5620 Executive Dr, New Port Richey, FL 813-848-8931
Eric Oxendorf, (P)

EF

Embler, Jennifer/738 NE 74th St, Miami , FL........................305-372-9425
Forbes, Pat/11459 Waterview Cluster, Reston, VA 703-478-0434
Kay Chernush, (P), Lautman Photography, (P), Claude
Vasquez, (P), Taren Z, (P)

GJ

Gaffney, Steve/PO Box 9285, Alexandria, VA....................................703-751-1991
Lee Anderson, (P), Paul Fetters, (P), Lightscapes Photo, (P),
Lisa Masson, (P), Len Rizzi, (P)
Green, Cindy/772 Edgewood Ave NE, Atlanta, GA...........................404-525-1333
Kurt Fisher, (P)
**Jett & Assoc Inc/1408 S Sixth St, Louisville, KY
(P 660-668)** **502-561-0737**
Ron Bell, (I), Gary Bennett, (I), Dan H Brawner, (I), Annette
Cable, (I), Mark Cable, (I), Toby Lay, (I), John Mattos, (I), Mario
Noche, (I), Cynthia Torp, (I), David Wariner, (I), Roy Wiemann,
(I), Paul Wolf, (I)

KLM

Klinko, Julia/2843 S Bayshore Dr #11E, Coconut Grove, FL............305-445-5540
Lee, Wanda/3647 Cedar Ridge Dr, Atlanta, GA 404-432-6309
Flying Photo Factory, (A)
Linden, Tamara/3490 Piedmont Rd #1200, Atlanta, GA..................404-262-1209
Gail Chirko, (I), Tom Fleck, (I), Joe Ovies, (I), Charles
Passarelli, (I), Larry Tople, (I)
McGee, Linda/1816 Briarwood Ind Ct, Atlanta, GA..........................404-633-1286
Alan McGee, (P)
McLean & Friends/571 Dutch Valley Rd, Atlanta, GA......................404-881-6627
Al Clayton, (P), Michael Harrel, (I), Mitch Hyatt, (I), Martin Pate,
(I), Joe Sapphold, (I), Steve Spetseris, (I), Pamela Trowe, (I),
Michael West, (P)
McPheeters, Wilson/3737 Orange St, Norfolk, VA..........................804-966-5889
Moore, Carolyn/PO Box 37108, Charlotte, NC 704-335-1733
Joseph Ciarlante, (P), Judy Nemeth, (P)

PS

Pollard, Kiki/848 Greenwood Ave NE, Atlanta, GA..........................404-875-1363
Betsy Alexander, (G), Dianne Borowski, (I), Lindy Burnett, (I),
Cheryl Cooper, (I), David Guggenheim, (P), Leslie Harris, (I),
Allen Hashimoto, (I), Kathy Lengyel, (I), Pat Magers, (I), Julie
Muller-Brown, (I), Brian Otto, (I), Frank Saso, (I), James
Soukup, (I), Elizabeth Traynor, (I)
Prentice, Nancy/919 Collier Rd NW, Atlanta, GA...........................404-351-5090
Rene Faure, (I), Pat Harrington, (I), Kenny Higdon, (I), Ed
Horlbeck, (I), Robbie Short, (I), Derek Yanicer, (I), Bruce
Young, (I)
Satterwhite, Joy/PO Box 398, Concord, VA.....................................212-219-0808
Al Satterwhite, (P)
St John, Julia/5730 Arlington Blvd, Arlington, VA 703-845-5831
David Hathcox, (P)
Stock South/75 Bennett St, Atlanta, GA..404-352-0538

Sumpter, Will/1728 N Rock Springs Rd, Atlanta, GA 404-874-2014
Charles Cashwell, (I), Flip Chalfant, (P), Brit Taylor Collins, (I),
Bob Cooper, (I), David Gaadt, (I), Brenda Losey, (I), David
Moses, (I), Jackie Pitman, (I), Drew Rose, (I), R M Schnieder,
(I), Garcia Studios, (P), Clark Tate, (I), Phil Wende, (I)

TW

Trlica/Reilly: Reps/7436 Leharne Court, Charlotte, NC 704-372-6007
Tim Anderson, (I), Tim Bruce, (I), Gerin Choiniere, (P), Sally
Wern Comport, (I), Gary Crane, (I), Laura Gardner, (I), Marcus
Hamilton, (I), Steve Knight, (P), Jim McGuire, (P), Mike
McMahon, (I), Gary Palmer, (I), Harry Roolaart, (I), Greg Rudd,
(I), Walter Stanford, (I), David Taylor, (I), Jack Vaughan, (I),
John White, (I), Robin Wilgus, (I)
Wells, Susan/5134 Timber Trail NE, Atlanta, GA..............................404-255-1430
Paul Blakey, (I), Ted Burn, (I), Tom Cain, (I), David Clegg, (I),
Elaine Dillard, (L), John Findley, (I), Alex Hackworth, (I), Laura
Hesse, (I), Bob Hogan, (I), Keith Kohler, (I), Don Loehle, (I),
Kelley Maddox, (I), Randall McKissick, (I), Christine Mull, (I),
John Nelson, (I), Bob Pitt, (I), Bob Radigan, (I), Tommy Stubbs,
(I), Monte Varah, (I), Janie Wright, (I)
Williams Group, The/1270 W Peachtree St #8C,
Atlanta, GA (P 734-739)...**404-873-2287**
Boris/Pittman, (G), Luis Fernandez, (I), Abe Gurvin, (I), Jack
Jones, (I), Rick Lovell, (I), Bill Mayer, (I), David McKelvey, (I),
Pat Mollica, (I), Tom Nikosey, (I), John Robinette, (I), Danny
Smythe, (I), Dale Verzaal, (I)

MIDWEST

A

Altman, Elizabeth/1420 W Dickens, Chicago, IL 312-404-0133
Ben Altman, (P), Don DuBroff, (P), Jack Perno, (P), Abby
Sadin, (P)
Art Staff Inc/1000 John R Rd #110, Troy, MI...................................313-583-6070
John Arvan, (I), Joy Brosious, (I), Larry Cory, (I), Caryl
Cunningham, (I), Brian Foley, (I), Jim Gutheil, (I), Vicki Hayes, (I),
Ben Jaroslaw, (I), Dan Kistler, (I), John Martin, (I), Dick Meissner,
(I), Jerry Monteleon, (I), Linda Nagle, (I), Jeff Ridky, (I), Jody
Ridky, (I), Al Schrank, (I), Ken Taylor, (I), Alan Wilson, (I)
Atols, Mary/405 N Wabash #1305, Chicago, IL 312-222-0504

B

Ball, John/203 N Wabash, Chicago, IL...312-332-6041
Wilson-Griak Inc, (P)
**Bartels, Ceci Assoc/3286 Ivanhoe, St Louis, MO
(P 394-408)** **314-781-7377**
Bill Bruning, (I), Lindy Burnett, (I), Justin Carroll, (I), Gary
Ciccarelli, (I), Robert Craig, (I), David Davis, (I), Paul Elledge,
(P), Mark Fredrickson, (I), Michael Halbert, (I), Bill Jenkins, (I),
Keith Kasnot, (I), Leland Klanderman, (I), Shannon
Kriegshauser, (I), Greg MacNair, (I), Pete Mueller, (I), John
Nelson, (I), Kevin Pope, (I), Guy Porfirio, (I), Jean Probert, (I),
Mike Randal, (I), B B Sams, (C), Todd Schorr, (I), Terry Sirrell,
(I), Terry Speer, (I), Judy Unger, (I), Wayne Watford, (I), Morgan
Weistling, (I), Linden Wilson, (I), Ted Wright, (I)
Bauer, Frank/6641 W Burleigh St, Milwaukee, WI............................414-449-2081
Bryan Peterson, (I)
**Bernstein, Joanie/PO Box 3635, Minneapolis, MN
(P 509-515)** **612-374-3169**
Lee Christiansen, (I), Tom Garrett, (I), Eric Hanson, (I), Todd
Jones, (L), Jack A Molloy, (I), Stan Olson, (I), Dan Picasso, (I)
Blue Sky Projects/1237 Chicago Rd, Troy, MI 313-583-2828
Steve Jungquist, (P), Tom Kirby, (P), Glen Rohde, (P)
Bracken, Laura/215 W Illinois, Chicago, IL....................................312-644-7108
William Sladcik, (P), James Wheeler, (I)
Brenna, Allen Represents/112 N Third St #204, Minneapolis, MN ...612-349-3805
Don Ellwood, (I), Lou Flores, (I), Christy Krames, (I), Richard
Kriegler, (I), Lynn Tanaka, (I), Judy Unger, (I)
Brooks & Assoc/855 W Blackhawk St, Chicago, IL..........................312-642-3208
Nancy Brown, (P), David Kogan, (P), Deborah VanKirk, (P)
Burchill, Linda/680 N Lakeshore Dr, Chicago, IL.............................312-664-4703
Bussler, Tom/1728 N Wood St #2F, Chicago, IL...............................312-649-5553

Sid Evans, (I), Frank Kasy, (I), Phoenix Studio, (I)

CD

Coleman, Woody/490 Rockside Rd, Cleveland, OH..........................216-661-4222
Eric Apel, (I), Jeffrey Bedrick, (I), Alex Bostic, (I), Larry Elmore, (I), Jack Jones, (I), Michael Koester, (I), Vladimir Kordic, (I), John Letostak, (I), Jeff Lloyd, (I), Charles Manus, (I), Al Margolis, (I), Manuel Morales, (I), Bill Morse, (I), David Moses, (I), Ernest Norcia, (I), Vincent Perez, (I), Bob Radigan, (I), James Seward, (I), Marla Shegal, (I), Tom Shephard, (I), Bill Silvers, (I), David Taylor, (I), Ezra Tucker, (I), Tom Utley, (I), Monte Varah, (I), Chuck Wimmer, (I), Tom Yurcich, (I)
Cowan, Pat/604 Division Rd, Valparaiso, IN......................................219-462-0199
Ralph Cowan, (P)
Creative Network/3313 Croft Dr, Minneapolis, MN........................612-781-7385
DeWalt & Assoc/210 E Michigan St #403, Milwaukee, WI.............414-276-7990
Craig Calsbeek, (I), Tom Fritz, (P), Rick Karpinski, (I), Chris Krenzke, (I), Mark Mille, (I), Brian Otto, (I)
Dodge Account Services/301 N Waters St, Milwaukee, WI..........414-271-3388
Ken Hanson, (G), Dave Vander Veen, (P), Matthew Zumbo, (I)
Dolby, Karen/333 N Michigan #2711, Chicago, IL..........................312-855-9336
Sandra Bruce, (I), Cam Chapman, (P), Diane Davis, (I), Jan Jones, (I), Julie Pace, (I), Fran Vuksanovich, (I), Eddie Yip, (I)

EF

Edsey, Steve/520 N Michigan Ave #706, Chicago, IL 312-527-0351
Stuart Block, (P), Michael Carroll, (I), Wil Cormier, (I), Deszo Csanady, (I), Mike Dammer, (I), Tom Durfee, (I), Richard Erickson, (I), Mike Hagel, (I), Lou Heiser, (I), Kelly Hume, (L), Keith Jay, (P), Al Lipson, (I), Rob Magiera, (I), Betty Maxey, (I), Tom McKee, (I), Manny Morales, (I), Mike Phillips, (I), John Rau, (I), Joe Sapulich, (I), Harlan Scheffler, (I), Shanoor, (P), Sue Shipley, (I), Mike Sobey, (I), Sam Thiewe, (I), Bobbi Tull, (I), Terry Wickart, (I)
Eldridge Corp/916 Olive St #300, St Louis, MO..............................314-231-6800
Gayle Asch, (I), Jana Brunner, (I), Rob Cline, (I), Bob Commander, (I), David FeBland, (I), Ted Fuka, (I), Kuni Hagio, (I), John Hanley, (I), Bud Kemper, (I), Tom Killeen, (I), Doug Klauba, (I), Nora Koerber, (I), Gary Krejca, (I), David Larks, (I), Greg Litwicki, (I), Tom Lungstrom, (I), Jane Meredith, (I), Bill Miller, (I), Dean Mitchell, (I), Marilyn Montgomery, (I), Garry Nichols, (I), Ernest Norcia, (I), Virginia Peck, (I), Eduardo Reyes, (I), Carol Robbins, (I), Ed Scarisbrick, (I), William Simon, (I), John Van Hamersveld, (I), Jay Vigon, (I), Charles White III, (I)
Erdos, Kitty/210 W Chicago, Chicago, IL 312-787-4976
Finished Art, (I)
Feldman, Kenneth/333 E Ontario #2011B, Chicago, IL................312-337-0447
Fiat, Randi & Assoc/211 E Ohio #621, Chicago, IL (P 562,563) **312-784-2343**
David Csicsko, (I), Marc Hauser, (P), John Kleber, (I)
Foster Represents, Teenuh/4200 Flad Ave, St Louis, MO............314-436-1121
Sandy Appleoff, (I), Brian Battles, (I), Sandra Filippucci, (I), Jim Hancock, (I), Bryan Haynes, (I), Michael P. Haynes, (I), Daphne Hewett, (I), Warren Hile, (I), Kelly Hume, (I), Mark Langeneckert, (I), Mike Lynch, (I), Jeff May, (I), James Olvera, (P), Joe Saffold, (I), Frank Steiner, (I), Beth Tipton, (I)
Frazier, Bob/617 W Fulton St #2, Chicago, IL.................................312-845-9650

GHI

Graphic Access/401 E Illinois #310, Chicago, IL.........................312-222-0087
Gregg & Assoc/112 W 9th St 2nd Fl, Kansas City, MO 816-421-4473
Hahn, Holly/770 N Halstead #102, Chicago, IL.............................312-243-5356
Nan Brooks, (I), Lina Chesak, (I), Dan Coha, (P), Jane Dierksen, (I), Ted Fuka, (I), Doug Githens, (I), Tom Lindfors, (P), Wendell McClintock, (I), Steve Snodgrass, (I), Dan Zaitz, (P)
Handelan-Pedersen/1165 North Clark, Chicago, IL 312-664-1200
Hanson, Jim and Talent/777 North Michigan Ave #706, Chicago, IL (P 652-654) **312-337-7770**
Sandi Fellman, (P), Glen Gyssler, (P), Maria Krajcirovic, (P), Rob Porazinski, (I), Hannes Schmid, (P), Craig Smallish, (I), Christian Vogt, (P), Richard Wahlstrom, (P), Harry K Whitver, (I)
Harlib, Joel Assoc/405 N Wabash #3203, Chicago, IL (P 549-553) **312-329-1370**
Richard Anderson, (I), Nick Backes, (I), Michael Backus, (I),

Bart Bemus, (I), Tim Bieber, (P), Al Brandtner, (I), Russell Cobane, (I), Esky Cook, (I), Mike Dean, (I), Lawrence Duke, (I), Chuck Eckart, (I), Paul Elledge, (P), Robert Farber, (P), Abe Gurvin, (I), Scott Harris, (I), Karel Havlicek, (I), Barbara Higgins-Bond, (I), Roger Hill, (I), David McCall Johnston, (I), Tim Langenderfer, (I), Richard Leech, (I), Peter Lloyd, (I), Albert Lorenz, (I), Kenvin Lyman, (I), Don Margolis, (I), Bill Morse, (I), Dennis Mukai, (I), Steve Nozicka, (P), Fred Pepera, (I), Kevin Pope, (I), Ray Roberts, (I), Buc Rogers, (I), Delro Rosco, (I), Boris Vallejo, (I), Bill Vann, (I), Ron Villani, (I), Kim Whitesides, (I), Michael Witte, (I), Bruce Wolfe, (I), Jonathan Wright, (I), Bob Ziering, (I)
Harmon, Ellen & Michaline Siera/950 W Lake St, Chicago, IL...312-829-8201
Harry Przekop, (P)
Harris, Gretchen & Assoc/5230 13th Ave S, Minneapolis, MN.....612-822-0650
Ken Jacobsen, (I), Nathan Jarvis, (I), Jim Rownd, (I), Mary Worcester, (I)
Hartig, Michael/3602 Pacific, Omaha, NE....................................402-345-2164
Hellman Assoc Inc/1225 W 4th St, Waterloo, IA (P 352-362) **319-234-7055**
Kim Behm, (I), Deb Bovy, (I), Greg Hargreaves, (I), Dan Hatala, (I), Mitchell Heinze, (I), Steve Hunter, (I), Doug Knutson, (I), Paul Lackner, (I), Pat Muchmore, (I), David Olsson, (I), John Thompson, (I), Todd Treadway, (I)
Hogan, Myrna & Assoc/333 N Michigan, Chicago, IL....................312-372-1616
Horton, Nancy/939 Sanborn, Palatine, IL....................................708-934-8966
Hull, Scott Assoc/68 E Franklin St, Dayton, OH (P 264-287) **513-433-8383**
Mark Braught, (I), Tracy Britt, (I), Andy Buttram, (I), John Buxton, (I), John Ceballos, (I), Greg Dearth, (I), Andrea Eberbach, (I), Josef Gast, (I), David Groff, (I), Peter Harritos, (I), Julie Hodde, (I), Bill James, (I), Bob James, (I), Greg LaFever, (I), John Maggard, (I), Gregory Manchess, (I), Larry Martin, (I), Evangelia Philippidis, (I), Ted Pitts, (I), Mark Riedy, (I), Don Vanderbeek, (I)
Image Source, The/801 Front St, Toledo, OH 419-697-1111
Jay Langlois, (P), Joe Sharp, (P)
In Flight Productions/3114 St Mary's Ave, Omaha, NE.................402-345-2164
Inman, Emily/2149 N Kenmore, Chicago, IL..................................312-525-4955
Inman, J W/2149 N Kenmore, Chicago, IL.....................................312-525-4955
Rose Divita, (I), Ilene Ehrlich, (P), Barbara Karant, (P), Chris Shoban, (I), Russell Thurston, (I)

K

Kamin, Vince & Assoc/111 E Chestnut, Chicago, IL 312-787-8834
Sara Anderson, (I), Tom Berthiaume, (P), Steve Bjorkman, (I), Dave Jordano, (P), Mary Anne Shea, (I), Dale Windham, (P)
Kastaris, Harriet & Assoc/3301-A S Jefferson Ave, St Louis, MO (P 483-491) **314-773-2600**
Creative Partners NY, (F), Eric Dinyer, (I), Jason Dowd, (I), John Dyess, (I), Dan Erdmann, (I), Mike Fehar, (P), Steve Hix, (P), April Goodman Willy, (I), Greg Johannes, (I), Rip Kastaris, (I), Tony Ravenelli, (P), Tracy Rea, (I), Greg Spalenka, (P), Jeff Tull, (I), Arden Von Haeger, (I)
Keltsch, Ann/9257 Castlegate Dr, Indianapolis, IN 317-849-7723
Kleber, Gordon/1711 N Honore, Chicago, IL..................................312-276-4419
Knutsen, Jan/10740 Toledo Ct, Bloomington, MN...........................612-884-8083
Kogen, Judi/315 W Walton, Chicago, IL.......................................312-266-8029
Richard Izui, (P)
Koralik, Connie/900 West Jackson Blvd #7W, Chicago, IL.............312-944-5680
Ron Criswell, (I), Ted Gadecki, (I), Myron Grossman, (I), Robert Keeling, (P), Chuck Ludecke, (I), David Lyles, (P), Michelle Noiset, (I), Bob Scott, (I), Scott Smudsky, (P), Bill Weston, (I), Andy Zito, (I)
Kuehnel, Peter & Assoc/30 E Huron Plaza #2108, Chicago, IL...312-642-6499
Ted Carr, (I), Dan Hurley, (I), Racer & Reynolds, (P), Phoenix Studio, (I), Jim Weiner, (P)

LM

Langley, Sharon/770 N Halstead #P-102, Chicago, IL....................312-243-8580
Zack Burris, (P), Vince Chiaramonte, (I), Eddie Corkery, (I), Roxanne Donnelli, (I), Dale Fleming, (I), Diane Johnson, (I), Tim Jonke, (I), Don Margolis, (I), Dave Rotoloni, (I)
Lawrence, Lydia/1250 N La Salle Dr #1001, Chicago, IL 415-267-3087
Lux & Associates, Frank/20 W Hubbard #3E, Chicago, IL..........312-222-1361
Maloney, Tom & Assoc/307 N Michigan Ave, Chicago, IL............312-704-0500

Dave Allen, (I), Scott Ernster, (I), John Hamagami, (I), Mitch O'Connell, (I), Stephen Rybka, (I), Skidmore Sahratian, (I), John Schmelzer, (I), John Youssi, (I)

Marie, Rita & Friends/405 N Wabash Ave #2709, Chicago, IL (P 288-311) 312-222-0337
Bob August, (I), David Beck, (I), James Bradley, (I), Chris Consani, (I), Todd Dorey, (I), Mort Drucker, (I), Jim Endicott, (I), Rick Farrell, (I), Marla Frazee, (I), Mark Frueh, (I), Ken Goldammer, (I), Rick Gonnella, (I), Robert Gunn, (I), Karel Havlicek, (I), Dave Jonason, (I), Robert Krogle, (I), Robert Pryor, (I), Renwick, (I), Paul Rogers, (I), Dick Sakahara, (I), Tim Schultz, (P), Danny Smythe, (I), Jackson Vereen, (P), Bill Wilson, (I), Greg Wray, (I)

Masheris, R Assoc Inc/1338 Hazel Ave, Deerfield, IL.....................708-945-2055
McGrath, Judy/612 N Michigan Ave 4th Fl, Chicago, IL...................312-944-5116
Sandi Appleoff, (I), Bob Bullivant, (P), Joanne Carney, (P), Bret Lopez, (P)

McNamara Associates/1250 Stephenson Hwy, Troy, MI (P 806,807) 313-583-9200
Max Altekruse, (I), Perry Cooper, (I), Garth Glazier, (I), Hank Kolodziej, (I), Kurt Krebs, (I), Jack Pennington, (I), Tony Randazzo, (I), Gary Richardson, (I), Don Wieland, (I)

McNaughton, Toni/233 E Wacker #2904, Chicago, IL 312-938-2148
Pam Haller, (P), Rodica Prato, (I), James B. Wood, (P)

Miller, Richard Assoc/405 N Wabash #1204, Chicago, IL..............312-527-0444
Montagano, David/405 N Wabash #1606, Chicago, IL..................312-527-3283
Munro Goodman Reps/405 N Wabash #3112, Chicago, IL (P 633-635) 312-321-1336
Tom Bookwalter, (I), Chris Butler, (I), Bill Cigliano, (I), Pat Dypold, (I), Malcolm Farley, (I), Clint Hansen, (I), Quang Ho, (I), Mike Kasun, (I), Ben Luce, (I), Randy Nelsen, (I), David Schweitzer, (I), Michael Steirnagle, (I)

NOP

Neis, The Group/11440 Oak Drive, Shelbyville, MI (P 700-705) 616-672-5756
Bender + Bender, (P), Tom Bookwalter, (I), Liz Conrad, (I), Gary Eldridge, (I), Clint Hansen, (I), William Hosner, (I), Rainey Kirk, (I), Nancy Munger, (I), Bill Ross, (I), David Schweitzer, (I), Rick Thrun, (I)

Nicholson, Richard B/2310 Denison Ave, Cleveland, OH 216-398-1494
Mark Molesky, (P), Mike Steinberg, (P)

Nicolini, Sandra/230 N Michigan #523, Chicago, IL 312-871-5819
Elizabeth Ernst, (P), Tom Petroff, (P)

O'Grady Advertising Arts/111 E Wacker Dr #3000, Chicago, IL...312-565-2535
Jerry Dunn, (P)

Ores, Kathy, Frank Lux & Assoc/21 W Hubbard, Chicago, IL....312-222-1361
Osler, Spike/2616 Industrial Row, Troy, MI.....................................313-280-0640
Madison Ford, (P), Rob Gage, (P), Mark Harmer, (P), Eric W Perry, (P), Dennis Wiand, (P)

Paisley, Shari/402 Newberry Ave, La Grange Park, IL (P 583) 708-482-9060
Peterson, Vicki/211 E Ohio, Chicago, IL..312-467-0780
John Cascarano, (P), Whistl'n Dixie, (P), Elyse Lewin, (P), Howard Menken, (P), Garrick Peterson, (P)

Pool, Linda/7216 E 99th St, Kansas City, MO...............................816-761-7314
Don Cassity, (P), Rosanne W Olson, (P), Michael Radencich, (P)

Potts, Carolyn & Assoc/4 E Ohio #11, Chicago, IL (P 564,565) 312-944-1130
Mark Battrell, (P), Karen Bell, (I), John Craig, (I), Alan Dolgins, (P), Byron Gin, (I), Bob Gleason, (I), Alan Kaplan, (P), Don Loehle, (I), John McCallum, (P), Susan Nees, (I), Joe Ovies, (I), Stacey Previn, (I), Donna Ruff, (I), Jack Slattery, (I), Rhonda Voo, (I), Tim Walters, (P), Leslie Wolf, (I)

Potts, Vicki/PO Box 31279, Chicago, IL 312-631-0301
Preston, Lori/449 W Belden Ave #1F, Chicago, IL...........................312-528-5483

R

Rabin, Bill & Assoc/680 N Lake Shore Dr #1020, Chicago, IL........312-944-6655
John Alcorn, (I), Steve Alcorn, (I), Joel Baldwin, (P), Joe Baraban, (P), Roger Beerworth, (I), Michael Bennallack-Hart, (I), Hank Benson, (P), Guy Billout, (I), Howard Bjornson, (P), Thomas Blackshear, (I), Charles William Bush, (P), Richard Corman, (P), Etienne Delessert, (I), Anthony Gordon, (P), Tim Greenfield-Sanders, (P), Robert Guisti, (I), Lamb & Hall, (P), Min Jae Hong, (I), Walter Iooss, (P), Victor Juhasz, (I), Art

Kane, (P), Steve Mayse, (I), Sheila Metzner, (P), Jonathan Milne, (I), Claude Mougin, (P), Robert Rodriguez, (I), Michael Schwab, (I), David Wilcox, (I), Bruce Wolf, (P)

Ramin, Linda/6239 Elizabeth Ave, St Louis, MO (P 714-716) 314-781-8851
Phil Benson, (I), Richard Bernal, (I), Don Curran, (I), Richelle Fleck, (I), Pam King, (I), Starr Mahoney, (I), David Niehaus, (I), William O'Donnell, (I), Roy Smith, (I), Jack Whitney, (I), Mike Whitney, (I), John Zilinski, (I)

Ray, Rodney/405 N Wabash #2709, Chicago, IL (P 288-311) 312-222-0337
David Beck, (I), James Bradley, (I), Chris Consani, (I), Mort Drucker, (I), Jim Endicott, (I), Rick Farrell, (I), Marla Frazee, (I), Mark Frueh, (I), Ken Goldammer, (I), Rick Gonnella, (I), Robert Gunn, (I), Karel Havlicek, (I), Dave Jonason, (I), Robert Krogle, (I), Robert Pryor, (I), Renwick, (I), Paul Rogers, (I), Gary Ruddell, (I), Dick Sakahara, (I), Tim Schultz, (P), Danny Smythe, (I), Jackson Vereen, (I), Bill Wilson, (I), Greg Wray, (I)

Ridgeway Artists Rep/444 Lentz Ct, Lansing, MI 517-371-3086
Darwin Dale, (P), Barbara Hranilouish, (I), Kim Kauffman, (P)

S

Sell, Dan/233 E Wacker, Chicago, IL 312-565-2701
Bob Boyd, (I), Lee Lee Brazeal, (I), Daryll Cagle, (I), Kirk Caldwell, (I), Wayne Carey, (I), Bobbye Cochran, (I), Sally Wern Comport, (I), Lee Dugan, (I), Mike Elins, (I), Christian Ellithorpe, (I), Bill Ersland, (I), Eucalyptus Tree Studio, (I), Dick Flood, (I), Alex Gross, (I), Bill Harrison, (I), Dave Kilmer, (I), Tom Lochray, (I), Gregory Manchess, (I), Bill Mayer, (I), Frank Morris, (I), Stanley Olson, (I), WB Park, (I), Ian Ross, (I), Mark Schuler, (I), R J Shay, (I), Dave Stevenson, (I), Dale Verzaal, (I), Arden Von Haeger, (I), Phil Wendy, (I), Jody Winger, (I), Paul Wolf, (I), John Zielinski, (I)

Shulman, Salo/215 W Ohio, Chicago, IL 312-337-3245
Stan Stansfield, (P)

Skillicorn, Roy/233 E Wacker #1209, Chicago, IL 312-856-1626
Tom Curry, (I), David Scanlon, (I)

Spectrum Reps/206 N 1st St, Minneapolis, MN 612-332-2361
Steiber, Doug/405 N Wabash #1503, Chicago, IL..........................312-222-9595
Sullivan, Tom/3805 Maple Court, Marietta, GA 404-971-6782
Terry Buchanan, (I), John Burns, (I), Alan David, (P), Clinton Davies, (P), Ralph Frost, (I), Jay Greer, (I), Ray Herbert, (P), Richard Hicks, (I), Bruce Hull, (I), Mark Kiesgen, (I), Sylvia Martin, (I), Harrison Northcutt, (I), Darrell Odom, (P), Charles Scogins, (I), Hart Shardin, (I), Philip Shore, (I), George Sipp, (I), Mark & Laura Stutzman, (I), Top Drawer Design, (I), Ed Wolkis, (P), Art Woodle, (I)

TVW

Tuke, Joni/325 W Huron #310, Chicago, IL......................................312-787-6826
Dan Blanchette, (I), Steven Chorney, (I), Mary Grandpre, (I), John Hull, (I), Susan Kinast, (P), Cyd Moore, (I), Michel Tcherevkoff, (P), Bill Thomson, (I), Pam Wall, (I), John Welzenbach, (P), Ken Westphal, (I)

Virnig, Janet/2116 E 32nd St, Minneapolis, MN (P 730,731) 612-721-8832
Rick Allen, (I), Mary Grandpre, (I), Dean Kennedy, (I), Robin Moline, (I), Brian Otto, (I), Kate Thomssen, (I)

Wolff, Carol/655 W Irving Park Rd #4602, Chicago, IL 312-871-5359

SOUTHWEST

AB

Art Rep Inc/3525 Mockingbird Lane, Dallas, TX (P 568,569) 214-521-5156
Sara Anderson, (I), Lee Lee Brazeal, (I), Kirk Caldwell, (I), Lindy Chambers, (I), Ellis Chappell, (I), Tom Curry, (I), Jay Dickman, (P), M John English, (I), Tim Girvin, (I), Janie Hughes, (I), Jim Jacobs, (I), Greg King, (I), Kent Kirkley, (P), Matthew Savins, (P), Elle Schuster, (P), Stephen Turk, (I), Andrew Vracin, (P), Terry Widener, (I)

Brooke & Company/4323 Bluffview Blvd, Dallas, TX.....................214-969-0034
Sandy Appleoff, (I), Robin Brisker, (I), David Chasey, (P), Bryan Haynes, (I), Michael P Haynes, (I), Gary Head, (I), Mike

Hodges, (I), Lynn McClain, (I), Cap Pannell, (I), Al Pisano, (I), Alain Redder, (P), Mike Reed, (I), Sherie Stevens, (I), Joe Viesti, (P), Benjamin Vincent, (I), Paul Wolf, (I), Keith Wood Photography Inc, (P)

Butler Creative Resources/7041 E Orange Blossom Lane, Scottsdale, AZ 602-941-5216
Rand Carlson, (I), Robert Case, (I), Jeff Dorgay, (P), Michael Hale, (I), RB Photographic, (P), Peggi Roberts, (I), Ray Roberts, (I), Jerry Roethig, (I)

C

Campbell, Pamela/314 N Rock Island, Angleton, TX 713-523-5328
Richard Anderson, (I), Mark Busacca, (I), George Campbell, (I), Frankie Flores, (I), Ralph Hughes, (I), Don McQueen, (I), Alexander Molinello, (I), Tom Nikosey, (I), Kevin Phillips, (I), Kevin Richert, (I)

Cedeno, Lucy/PO Box 254, Cerrillos, NM 505-473-2745
David Michael Kennedy, (P)

Creative Connections of Dallas/1505 Bella Vista, Dallas, TX......214-327-7889
Dana Adams, (I), Matt Bowman, (P), Marc Burckhardt, (I), Curtis Eaves, (I), Ed Holmes, (I), Matthew McFarren, (I), Randy Nelson, (I), Peter Papadopolous, (I)

Creative Department Inc, The/3030 NW Expwy, Ok City, OK 405-942-4868
Douglas Bowman, (I)

Creative Services/233 Yorktown, Dallas, TX................................214-748-8663
John Cook, (I), Glenn David, (I), Richard Deweese, (P), Tim McClure, (I), Dave Miller, (I), Tina Rosenbaum, (I), Terry Sollenberger, (I), Michael Sours, (I), Sharon Watts, (I), Roger Xavier, (I)

Cuomo, Celeste/3311 Oaklawn Ave #300, Dallas, TX 214-443-9111
Linda Bleck, (I), Lynn Rowe Reed, (I), Roxanne Villa, (I), David Yuhl, (I)

DF

DiOrio, Diana/2829 Timmons Ln, Houston, TX...................................713-960-0393
Justin Carroll, (I), John Collier, (I), Chris Consani, (I), Mike Dean, (I), Michael Elins, (I), John Hamagami, (I), Larry Keith, (I), Dennis Mukai, (I), William Rieser, (I), Steven Scott, (I), Bruce Wolfe, (I)

Freeman, Sandra/3333 Elm St #202, Dallas, TX................................214-871-1956
Jennifer Harris, (I), Mary Haverfield, (I), Gretchen Shields, (I)

Friend & Johnson/2811 McKinney Ave #206, Dallas, TX (P 616-621)..**214-855-0055**
Kent Barker, (P), Connie Connally, (I), Ray-Mel Cornelius, (I), Dave Cutler, (I), Robert Forsbach, (I), Michael Johnson, (P), Margaret Kasahara, (I), Donald Keene, (I), Robb Kendrick, (P), Geof Kern, (P), Mercedes McDonald, (I), Michael McGar, (I), Hilary Mosberg, (I), Richard Myers, (P), R Kenton Nelson, (I), Steve Pietzsch, (I), Theo Rudnak, (I), Tom Ryan, (P), Jim Sims, (P), James Noel Smith, (I), Joel Spector, (I), Kelly Stribling, (I), Michele Warner, (I), Neill Whitlock, (P)

KL

KJ Reps/4527 Travis #200, Dallas, TX 214-559-0805
Kline, Sandy/637 Hawthorne, Houston, TX 713-522-1862
Tom Bookwalter, (I), Lee Lee Brazeal, (I), Mark Chickinelli, (I), Keith Graves, (I), Clint Hansen, (I), Rolf Laub, (I), Dave Maloney, (I), Jimmy Margulies, (I), Mike Robins, (I), Denise Watt, (I)

Lynch, Larry & Andrea/5521 Greenville #104-338, Dallas, TX.......214-369-6990
Amy Bryant, (I), Charles William Bush, (P), Denise Chapman Crawford, (I), Diane Kay Davis, (I), Bob Depew, (I), Glenn Gustafson, (I), Kate Brennan Hall, (I), Dan Ham, (P), Aaron Jones, (P), Christopher Kean, (P), Jeff Kosta, (P), Ron Lieberman, (I), Gary Nolton, (P), Brian Otto, (I), Ambrose Rivera, (I), John Saxon, (P), Mike Wimmer, (I)

PRS

Photocom Inc/3005 Maple Ave #104, Dallas, TX 214-720-2272
Robb Depenport, (P), Phillip Esparza, (P), Bart Forbes, (I), Iskra Johnson, (I), Claude Mougin, (P), Tom Nikosey, (I), Andy Post, (P), Rick Smith, (I), Michael Steirnagle, (I), Richard Wahlstrom, (P), Gordon Willis, (P)

Production Services/1711 Hazard, Houston, TX...........................713-529-7916
Wright Banks Films, (F)

Ryan St Clair Ltd/7028 Wabash Circle, Dallas, TX............................214-826-8118
Dean St Clair, (I), Becky Cutler, (I), Faith DeLong, (I), Laura Hesse, (I), Chris Hoover, (I), Mark Mroz, (I), John Nelson, (I), Bob Radigan, (I), Kevin Short, (I), Leslie Wu, (I)

Simpson, Elizabeth/1415 Slocum St #105, Dallas, TX....................214-761-0001
Jeff Baker, (P), Kathleen Kinkopf, (I), John Parrish, (P), Michael Simpson, (P)

TW

Those Three Reps/2909 Cole #118, Dallas, TX 214-871-1316
Dave Albers, (I), Diane Bennett, (I), Gary Blockley, (P), Phil Boatwright, (I), Tim Boole, (P), Steve Brady, (P), Gary Ciccarelli, (I), Bill Debold, (P), Regan Dunnick, (I), Mike Fisher, (I), Ted Gadecki, (I), Myron Grossman, (I), Rick Kroninger, (P), Larry Martin, (I), Richard Reens, (P), George Toomer, (I), Ka Yeung, (P)

Washington, Dick/4901 Broadway #152, San Antonio, TX 512-822-1336
Patti Bonham, (I), Larry Brooks, (I), Ken Coffelt, (I), Joseph DeCerchio, (I), Darius Detwiler, (I), Stephen Durke, (I), Cameron Eagle, (I), Kari Kaplan, (I), Rick Kroninger, (P), Mark Mroz, (I), Reuben Njaa, (P), Terry Powell, (I), Dan Soder, (I), Mark Weakley, (I)

Whalen, Judy/2336 Farrington St, Dallas, TX...................................214-630-8977
Robert LaTorre, (P)

Willard, Paul Assoc/217 E McKinley #4, Phoenix, AZ 602-257-0097
Jim Bolek, (I), Jack Graham, (I), Mike Gushock, (I), Liz Kenyon, (I), Gary Krejca, (I), Kevin MacPherson, (I), Frank Mendeola, (I), Jan Nelson, (I), Curtis Parker, (I), Nancy Pendleton, (I), Sharon Singley, (I), Wayne Watford, (I), Anne Romney Weaver, (I), Jean Wong, (I)

R O C K Y   M T N

C

Carol Guenzi Agents Inc/130 Pearl St #1602, Denver, CO............303-733-0128
Gus Alavezos, (I), John Ceballos, (I), Frank Cruz, (P), Eldridge Corporation, (I), Phillip Fickling, (I), Hellman Animates, (FA), Jeff Lauwers, (I), Bill Lesniewski, (I), Todd Lockwood, (I), Brian Mark, (P), Dan McGowan, (I), Greg Michaels, (I), Prism Productions, (FA), Jill Sabella, (I), Don Sullivan, (I), Carl Yarbrough, (P)

Comedia/1664 Lafayette St, Denver, CO 303-832-2299
Larry Laszlo, (P)

MN

Matson, Marla/74 W Culver St, Phoenix, AZ 602-252-5072
Kent Knudson, (P), David Schmidt, (P)

No Coast Graphics/2629 18th St, Denver, CO 303-458-7086
Robert August, (I), John Cuneo, (I), Bill Kastan, (I), Patrick Merewether, (I), Tom Nikosey, (I), C F Payne, (I), Jim Salvati, (I)

W E S T   C O A S T

AB

April & Wong/41 Sutter St #1151, San Francisco, CA 415-398-6542
Ayerst, Deborah/2546 Sutter St, San Francisco, CA........................415-567-3570
Tom Bonauro, (P), Robert Cardellino, (P), Charlie Brown & Co, (M), Ann Field, (I), Jeffrey Newbury, (P), Thea Schrack, (P), Malcolm Tarlofsky, (PI)

Baker, Kolea/2125 Western Ave #400, Seattle, WA (P 444-451) **206-443-0326**
George Abe, (I), Don Baker, (I), Jeff Brice, (I), Elaine Cohen, (I), Tom Collicott, (P), Tim Lord, (I), Pete Saloutos, (P), Bruce Sharp, (I), Al Skaar, (I), Jere Smith, (I), Kris Wiltse, (I)

Braun, Kathy/75 Water St, San Francisco, CA.................................415-775-3366
Pat Allen, (PS), Laurence Bartone, (P), Steve Bonini, (P), Sandra Bruce, (L), Michael Bull, (I), Eldon Doty, (I), Lamb & Hall, (P), John Huxtable, (I), Bob Johnson, (I), Sudi McCollom, (I), Jaqueline Osborn, (I), Stephen Osborn, (I), Gary Pierazzi, (AB), Doug Schneider, (I), Koji Takei, (P)

Brenneman, Cindy/1856 Elba Cir, Costa Mesa, CA 714-641-9700
Dean Armstrong, (P), Steve Ellis, (I), Pierre Kopp, (P), Gregory
Miller, (I), Brian Murray, (I), Jim Stefl, (I)

**Brock, Melissa Represents/43 Buena Vista
Terrace, San Francisco, CA (P 591)** **415-255-7393**
Franklin Avery, (P), Barbara Callow, (C), Michele Collier, (I),
John Cuneo, (I), Miriam Fabbri, (I), Shelby Hammond, (I), Mike
Kowalski, (I), Chuck Pyle, (I), David Wasserman, (P), Dave
Wilhelm, (P)

Brown, Dianne/402 N Windsor Blvd, Los Angeles, CA.................213-462-5598

Burlingham, Tricia/9538 Brighton Way #318, Beverly Hills, CA 213-271-3982
Greg Gorman, (P), Robert Grigg, (P), Kam Hinatsu, (P),
Charles Hopkins, (P), John Konkal, (P), Karen Krasner, (P),
Dennis Manarchy, (P), Peggy Sirota, (P)

Busacca, Mary/1335 Union St, San Francisco, CA.........................415-776-4247
Richard Anderson, (I), Willardson & Assoc, (I), Olden Budwine,
(I), Mark Busacca, (I), Ignacio Gomez, (I), Paul Hoffman, (P),
John Lund, (P), Tom Nikosey, (I), Michael Pearce, (I), Jack
Slattery, (I)

C

Campbell, Marianne/Pier 9 Embarcadaro, San Francisco, CA 415-433-0353
Michael Lamotte, (P), Will Mosgrove, (P)

Carriere, Lydia/PO Box 8382, Santa Cruz, CA...............................408-425-1090
Don Faia, (GD), Danilo Gonzalez, (I), Glenn Harvey, (I), Steve
Hathaway, (P), Jeff Hicks, (P), Steve Kurtz, (P), John Sutton, (P)

Collier, Jan/166 South Park, San Francisco, CA 415-552-4252
Barbara Banthien, (I), Gary Baseman, (I), Bunny Carter, (I),
Chuck Eckart, (I), Rae Ecklund, (I), Douglas Fraser, (I), Yan
Nascimbene, (I), Kathy O'Brien, (I), David Rawcliffe, (P),
Robert Gantt Steele, (I), Peter Sui, (I), Cynthia Torp, (I), Vahid,
(I), Don Weller, (I)

Conrad, James/2149 Lyon #5, San Francisco, CA 415-921-7140
Patrick Cone, (P), Jon Conrad, (I), Tom Curry, (I), Andrzej
Dudzinski, (I), Jack Eadon, (P), David Fisher, (P), Ron
Flemming, (I), Nick Gaetano, (I), Tim Jessell, (I), John Jinks, (I),
Charles Kemper, (P), Leland Klanderman, (I), Bret Lopez, (P),
Rafael Lopez, (I), Michael Maydak, (I), Gregory Miller, (I),
Robin Moline, (I), Kim Scholle, (I), Michael Steirnagle, (I), Dave
Stevenson, (I), Brenda Walton, (I)

Cook, Warren/PO Box 2159, Laguna Hills, CA 714-770-4619
Kathleen Norris Cook, (P)

Cormany, Tom Reps/7740 Manchester Ave, Playa Del Rey, CA 213-578-2191
Mark Busacca, (I), Greg Call, (I), Dave Clemons, (I), Jim
Heimann, (I), Rich Mahon, (I), Penina Meisels, (P), Gary
Norman, (I), Ted Swanson, (I), Stan Watts, (I), Will Weston, (I),
Dick Wilson, (I), Andy Zito, (I)

Cornell, Kathleen/741 Millwold Ave, Venice, CA 213-301-8059
Hank Benson, (P), John Cuneo, (I), Nancy Duell, (I), Seith
Erlich, (P), John Jones, (I), Joe Saputo, (I), Glen Wexler, (P)

Creative Resource/12056 Summit Circle, Beverly Hills, CA 213-276-5282
Bill Atkins, (I), Colin James Birdseye, (I), Bonsey, (P), Eldon
Doty, (I), Nancy French, (P), Herve Grison, (P), Toni Hanson-
Kurrasch, (I), Hal Jurcik, (P), Wendy Lagerstrom, (I), Jean-
Claude Maillard, (P), Darlene McElroy, (I), Mercier/Wimberg,
(P), Karen Miller, (P), Levon Parion, (P), Tony Ratiner, (P), Robin
Riggs, (P), Norman Stevens, (P), Dave Stevenson, (I), Thom
Tatku, (I), Anne Teisher, (I), Sandi Turchyn, (I), Brett Wagner, (I),
Dave Wilhelm, (P), Greg Winters, (I)

DEF

DeMoreta, Linda/PO Box 587/1839 9th St, Alameda, CA 415-769-1421
Sam Allen, (I), Piet Halberstadt, (I), Ron Miller, (P), Diane
Naugle, (I), Steven Nicodemus, (I), Michael Pierazzi, (P), Zhee
Singer, (I), Steven Underwood, (P)

Dodge, Sharon/3033 13th Ave W, Seattle, WA...............................206-284-4701
Robin Bartholick, (P), Maggie Bellis, (I), Bart Bemus, (I),
George Cribs, (G), Nancy Davis, (I), John Fortune, (L), Lani
Fortune, (I), Jud Guitteau, (I), Jim Henkens, (P), G Brian Karas,
(I), Mike Kowalski, (I), Jerry Nelson, (I), Ken Orvidas, (I), Frank
Renlei, (I), Patricia Ridenour, (P), John Schilling, (I), Paul
Schmid, (I), Keith Witmer, (I)

Epstein, Rhoni/Photo Rep/3814 Franklin Ave, Los Angeles, CA 213-663-2388
Charles Bush, (P), Cheryl Mader, (P), Bill Robins, (P), Stuart
Watson, (P)

Ericson, William/1024 Mission St, South Pasadena, CA..................213-461-4969

Feliciano, Terrianne/16812 Red Hill #B, Irvine, CA.........................714-250-3377
Michael Jarrett, (P)

Fleming, Laird Tyler/5820 Valley Oak Dr, Los Angeles, CA 213-469-3007

Fox & Spencer/8350 Melrose Ave #201, Los Angeles, CA 213-653-6484
Jody Dole, (P), David FeBland, (I), Raphaelle Goethals, (I),
Larry Dale Gordon, (P), Abe Gurvin, (I), William Hawkes, (P),
Bo Hylen, (P), Michael Manoogian, (I), Bill Mather, (I), Sue
Rother, (I), Steven Rothfeld, (P), Joe Spencer Design, (I), Trudi
Unger, (P)

France Aline Inc/1076 S Ogden Dr, Los Angeles, CA 213-933-2500
Daniel E Arsenault, (P), Guy Billout, (I), Thomas Blackshear, (I),
Elisa Cohen, (I), Pierre Yves Goavec, (P), Peter Greco, (L),
Thomas Hennessy, (I), Steve Huston, (I), Steve Johnson, (I),
John Mattos, (I), Jacqui Morgan, (I), Craig Mullins, (I), Jesse
Reisch, (I), Ezra Tucker, (I), Steve Umland, (P), Kim
Whitesides, (I), Bruce Wolfe, (I)

G

Gardner, Jean/348 N Norton Ave, Los Angeles, CA 213-464-2492
John Reed Forsman, (P), Richard Hume, (P), Brian Leatart, (P),
Rick Rusing, (P), Steve Smith, (P), Tim Street-Porter, (P)

George, Nancy/302 N LaBrea Ave #116, Los Angeles, CA.............213-655-0998
Dianne Bennett, (I), Robert Cooper, (I), Daniels & Daniels, (I),
Diane Davis, (I), Bruce Dean, (I), Richard Drayton, (I), Dean
Foster, (I), Penelope Gottlieb, (I), Steve Hendricks, (I), Hank
Hinton, (I), Gary Hoover, (I), Richard Kriegler, (I), Gary Lund,
(I), Julie Pace, (I), Jeremy Thornton, (I), Jeannie Winston, (I),
Corey Wolfe, (I)

Glick, Ivy/350 Townsend St #426, San Francisco, CA....................415-543-6056
Jerry Dadds, (I), Jane Dill, (I), Malcolm Farley, (I), Martin
French, (I), Raphaelle Goethals, (I), Derek Grinnell, (I),
Matthew Holmes, (I), Dean Kennedy, (I), Rhonda Voo, (I)

Goldman, Caren/4504 36th St, San Diego, CA 619-284-8339
Pete Evaristo, (I), Susie McKig, (I), Gary Norman, (I), Mark GW
Smith, (I)

**Graham, Corey/Pier 33 North, San Francisco, CA
(P 643-649)** **415-956-4750**
Frank Ansley, (I), Roger C Boehm, (I), Byron Coons, (I), Steve
Dininno, (I), Gordon Edwards, (P), Betsy Everett, (I), Bob
Gleason, (I), Peg Magovern, (I), Patricia Mahoney, (I), Joel
Nakamura, (I), Gretchen Schields, (I), Doug Suma, (I), David
Tillinghast, (I)

Group West Inc/5455 Wilshire Blvd #1212, Los Angeles, CA 213-937-4472
Kathleen Hession, (R), Larry Salk, (I), Ren Wicks, (I)

H

Hackett, Pat/101 Yesler #502, Seattle, WA...................................206-447-1600
Bill Cannon, (P), Jonathan Combs, (I), Steve Coppin, (I), Eldon
Doty, (I), Larry Duke, (I), Bill Evans, (I), Martin French, (I),
David Harto, (I), Gary Jacobsen, (I), Larry Lubeck, (R), Dan
McGowan, (I), Bill Meyer, (I), Leo Monahan, (I), Bruce Morser,
(I), Dennis Ochsner, (I), Chuck Pyle, (I), Jill Sabella, (P), Yutaka
Sasaki, (I), Michael Schumacher, (I), John C Smith, (I), Kelly
Smith, (I), Chuck Solway, (I), Bobbi Tull, (I), Dean Williams, (I)

Hall, Marni & Assoc/1010 S Robertson Blvd #10, LA, CA.............213-652-7322
Kevin Aguilar, (I), Dave Arkle, (I), Gary Baseman, (I), Dave
Erramouste, (I), Stan Grant, (I), Dennis Gray, (P), Pam
Hamilton, (I), Miles Hardiman, (I), Fred Hilliard, (I), John Holm,
(I), Elyse Lewin, (P), Peggi Roberts, (I), Ray Roberts, (I), Ken
Sabatini, (P), Nancy Santullo, (P), John Turner, (P), Perry Van
Shelt, (I), James Wood, (P)

Hardy, Allen/1680 N Vine #1000, Los Angeles, CA 213-466-775
Phillip Dixon, (P), Mike Russ, (P), Thomas Schenk, (P), Steven
Wight, (P)

Hart, Vikki/780 Bryant St, San Francisco, CA 415-495-4278
Jan Evans, (I), G K Hart, (P), Kevin Hulsey, (I), Aleta Jenks, (I),
Tom Kamifuji, (I), Julie Tsuchiya, (I), Jonathan Wright, (I)

Hedge, Joanne/1838 El Cerrito Pl #3, Hollywood, CA.....................213-874-166
Antar Dayal, (I), Cathy Deeter, (I), Tom Dillon, (I), Future Fonts,
(L), Rick McCollum, (I), David McMacken, (I), Ken Perkins, (I),
Laura Phillips, (I), Jim Salvati, (I), Dave Schweitzer, (I), Julie
Tsuchiya, (I), Brent Watkinson, (I)

Hillman, Betsy/Pier 33 North, San Francisco, CA 415-391-118
Istvan Banyai, (I), Hank Benson, (P), Greg Couch, (I), Jud
Guitteau, (I), John Hyatt, (I), John Marriott, (P), Randy South,
(I), Greg Spalenka, (I), Kevin Spaulding, (I), Joe Spencer, (I),

Jeremy Thornton, (I), Trudi Unger, (P)
Hodges, Jeanette/12401 Bellwood, Los Alamitos, CA 213-431-4343
Ken Hodges, (I)
Hunter, Nadine/80 Wellington Ave/Box 307, Ross, CA 415-456-7711
Jeanette Adams, (I), Rebecca Archey, (I), Charles Bush, (P),
Mercedes McDonald, (I), Cristine Mortensen, (I), Alan Ross,
(P), Jill Sabella, (P), Jan Schockner, (L), Liz Wheaton, (I)

JK

Jaz, Jerry/223 Prospect St, Seattle, WA 206-783-5373
Jorgensen, Donna/PO Box 19412, Seattle, WA 206-634-1880
Susan Marie Anderson, (P), Mel Curtis, (P), Sandra Dean, (I),
Steve Firebaugh, (P), Fred Hilliard, (I), Dale Jorgenson, (I), Mits
Katayama, (I), Richard Kehl, (I), Doug Keith, (I), Tim Kilian, (I),
David Lund, (I), Greg McDonald, (I), Cheri Ryan, (I), Nancy
Stentz, (I)
Karpe, Michele/6671 Sunset Blvd #1592, Los Angeles, CA 818-760-0491
Carol Ford, (P), Claude Morigin, (P), Victoria Pearson-
Cameron, (P), Mike Reinhardt, (P), Joyce Tenneson, (P)
**Kirsch Represents/7316 Pyramid Dr, Los Angeles,
CA (P 559-561)**..**213-651-3706**
David Kimble, (I), Joyce Kitchell, (I), Royce McClure, (I), Todd
Smith, (P), Jeff Wack, (I)
Knable, Ellen/1233 S La Cienega Blvd, Los Angeles, CA 213-855-8855
Roger Chouinard, (I), Bob Commander, (I), John Dearstyne,
(I), Coppos Films, (F), Randy Glass, (I), Bob Gleason, (I), Jeff
Kosta, (P), Lamb & Hall, (P), Bret Lopez, (P), James Skistimas,
(I), Jonathan Wright, (I), Brian Zick, (I)
Koeffler, Ann/5015 Clinton St #306, Los Angeles, CA......................213-957-2327
Istvan Banyai, (I), Karen Bell, (I), Dick Cole, (I), Byron Coons,
(I), Jan Evans, (I), Chuck Kuhn, (P), Rik Olson, (I), Frank
Ordaz, (I), Dan Picasso, (I), Katherine Salentine, (I), Sandra
Speidel, (I), James Stagg, (I), Pam Wall, (I)
Kramer, Joan & Assoc/LA/10490 Wilshire Blvd #605, LA, CA 213-446-1866
Richard Apple, (P), Bill Bachmann, (P), Roberto Brosan, (P),
David Cornwell, (P), Micheal DeVecka, (P), Clark Dunbar, (P),
Stan Flint, (P), Stephen Frink, (P), Peter Kane, (P), John Lawlor,
(P), Roger Marschutz, (P), James McLoughlin, (P), Ralf
Merlino, (P), Frank Moscati, (P), Bill Nalton, (P), Bill Nation, (P),
John Russell, (P), Ed Simpson, (P), Roger Smith, (P), Glen
Steiner, (P), Janice Travia, (P), Ken Whitmore, (P), Gary
Wunderwald, (P), Edward Young, (P), Eric Zucker, (P)

L

Laycock, Louise/1351 Ocean Frt Walk #106, Santa Monica, CA 213-204-6401
Lesli-Art Inc/PO Box 6693, Woodland Hills, CA 818-999-9228
Lilie, Jim/251 Kearny St #510, San Francisco, CA...........................415-441-4384
Ron Chan, (I), Craig Marshall, (I), Bruno Mezzapelle, (I),
Dugald Stermer, (I), Ezra Tucker, (I), Sarah Waldron, (I), Stan
Watts, (I), Dennis Ziemienski, (I)
London, Valerie/9301 Alcott St, Los Angeles, CA............................213-278-6633
Neal Brown, (I), Ann Cutting, (I), Diego Uchitel, (P)
Ludlow, Catherine/1632 S Sherburne Dr, Los Angeles, CA 213-859-9222
James Calderara, (P), John Colao, (P), Amanda Freeman, (P),
Chris Haylett, (P), Michael Miller, (P), Dewy Nicks, (P)
Luna, Tony/39 E Walnut St, Pasadena, CA.......................................818-584-4000

MN

**Marie, Rita & Friends/183 N Martel Ave #240,
Los Angeles, CA (P 288-311)**...**213-934-3395**
Bob August, (I), David Beck, (I), James Bradley, (I), Chris
Consani, (I), Todd L W Doney, (I), Mort Drucker, (I), Jim
Endicott, (I), Rick Farrell, (I), Marla Frazee, (I), Mark Frueh, (I),
Ken Goldammer, (I), Rick Gonnella, (I), Robert Gunn, (I), Karel
Havlicek, (I), Dave Jonason, (I), Robert Krogle, (I), Robert
Pryor, (I), Renwick, (I), Paul Rogers, (I), Dick Sakahara, (I), Tim
Schultz, (P), Danny Smythe, (I), Jackson Vereen, (P), Bill
Wilson, (I), Greg Wray, (I)
Martha Productions/4445 Overland Ave, Culver City, CA................213-204-1771
Pearl Beach, (I), Bob Brugger, (I), Kirk Caldwell, (I), Bobbye
Cochran, (I), Stan Evenson Dsgn, (GD), Mike Elins, (I), Allen
Garns, (I), Jeff George, (I), Bryon Gin, (I), Joe & Kathy Heiner, (I),
Mark Jasin, (I), John Kleber, (I), Dan Lavigne, (I), Catherine Leary,
(I), R Kenton Nelson, (I), Cathy Pavia, (I), Delro Rosco, (I), Kevin
Short, (I), Steve Vance, (I), Rhonda Voo, (I), Wayne Watford, (I)

Mix, Eva/2129 Grahn Dr, Santa Rosa, CA 707-579-1535
Morgan, Michele/4621 Teller #108, Newport Beach, CA 714-474-6002
Bill Brown, (I), Rob Court, (I), Elaine DaVault, (I), Kevin
Davidson, (I), Diane Davis, (I), Shelby Hammond, (I), Mark
McIntosh, (I), Morgan Pickard, (I)
Newman, Carol/1119 Colorado Ave #23, Santa Monica, CA 213-394-5031
Karen Anderson, (P), Ted Burns, (I), Paul Conrath, (P), David
Fairman, (P), Tim Huhn, (I), Michael Humphries, (I), Paul
Janovsky, (I), Patty McClosky, (I), Kim Passey, (I), Ken Tiesson,
(I), Tom Slacky/Outerspace, (R), James Wolnick, (I), Eddie
Young, (I)

OP

Onyx/7515 Beverley Blvd, Los Angeles, CA.....................................213-965-0899
Max Aguilera-Hellweg, (P), Eika Aoshima, (P), Fredrich Cantor,
(P), Davies & Starr, (P), Nancy Ellison, (P), Darryl Estrine, (P),
Michael Garland, (P), D Gorton, (P), Mark Hanauer, (P), Aaron
Rapoport, (P), Joyce Ravid, (P), Tim Redel, (P), Philip
Saltonstall, (P), Bonnie Schiffman, (P), Mark Sennet, (P), Brian
Smale, (P), David Strick, (P), Bob Wagoner, (P), Barbra Walz,
(P), Timothy White, (P), Tom Wolff, (P), Firooz Zahedi, (P)
Parrish, Dave/Photopia/PO Box 2309, San Francisco, CA 415-441-5611
Curtis Degler, (P), Rick Kaylin, (P), Curtis Martin, (P), Jeff
Richey, (P), Vince Valdes, (P)
Partners & Artists Assoc/13480 Contour, Sherman Oaks, CA.....818-995-6883
Pate, Randy/3408 W Burbank Blvd, Burbank, CA 818-985-8181
Capstone Studios, (I), Chris Dellorco, (I), John Taylor
Dismukes, (I), Robert Florczak, (I), Kunio Hagio, (I), Bryan
Haynes, (I), Robert Hunt, (I), Marvin Mattelson, (I), Mick
McGinty, (I), Kazuhiko Sano, (I), Hugh Syme, (I)
Peek, Pamela/10834 Blix #116, Toluca Lake, CA.............................818-760-0746
Randy Berrett, (I), David Hanover, (P), Patrick James, (IP), Ann
Mitchel, (P), Chuck Pyle, (I), Leonard Robledo, (I), Greg Alan
Rowe, (I), Gretchen Schields, (I), Randy South, (I), Harry
Vamos, (P), Jim Warren, (I)
Pelkin, Christine/1962 San Pablo Ave #3, Berkeley, CA.................415-841-2238
Rob Barber, (I), John Chui, (I), Penina Meisels, (P), Frank
Remkiewicz, (I), Cathy Trachok, (I), Mark Trousdale, (P)
Peterson, Linda/310 1st Ave S #333, Seattle, WA 206-624-7344
Piscopo, Maria/2038 Calvert Ave, Costa Mesa, CA........................714-556-8332
Jack Boyd, (P), J W Burkey, (P), John Connell, (P), Yuri Dojc,
(P), Stan Sholik, (P)
Prentice Assoc Inc, Vicki/1245 McClellan Dr #314, LA, CA.........213-305-7143
Pribble, Laurie/911 Victoria Dr, Arcadia, CA (P 508) **818-574-0288**
Dave Albers, (I), Steve Bjorkman, (I), Greg Hally, (I), John Hull,
(I), John Huxtable, (I), Catherine Kanner, (I), Ken Rosenberg,
(I), Andrea Tachiera, (I)

R

Rappaport, Jodi/5410 Wilshire Blvd #1008, Los Angeles, CA..........213-934-8633
Glen Erler, (P), Guzman, (P), David Jensen, (I), Lauren
Landau, (P), Meryl Rosenberg, (P)
**Repertory/6010 Wilshire Blvd #505,
Los Angeles, CA (P 476-482)** **213-931-7449**
Kaz Aizawa, (I), Richard Arruda, (I), Jim Britt, (P), Rhonda
Burns, (I), Craig Calsbeek, (I), Jon Conrad, (I), Laurie Gerns,
(I), Scott Hensey, (MM), Hom & Hom, (I), Haruo Ishioka, (I),
Rob Kline, (I), Paul Kratter, (I), Gary Krejca, (I), Ling-ta Kung,
(I), Russell Kurt, (P), Bob Maile, (L), Joel Nakamura, (I), Karl
Parry, (P), Teresa Powers, (I), Robert Schaefer, (I), Steve
Walters, (I)
Rosenthal Represents/3443 Wade St, Los Angeles, CA 213-390-9595
Dave Allen, (I), Joel Barbee, (I), Jody Eastman, (I), Marc
Erickson, (I), Robert Evans, (I), Bill Hall, (I), R Mark Heath, (I),
Jim Henry, (I), Reggie Holladay, (I), Mia Joung, (I), Dennis
Kendrick, (I), Rick Kinetader, (I), Kyounja Lee, (I), Roger
Leyonmark, (I), Roger Loveless, (I), David Mann, (I), Roger
Marchutz, (P), Kathleen McCarthy, (I), Erik Olsen, (I), Tom
Pansini, (I), Kim Passey, (I), Stephen Peringer, (I), Bob
Radigan, (I), Ed Renfro, (I), Ching Reyes, (I), Scott Ross, (I),
Larry Salk, (I), Chris Tuveson, (I), Erik Van der Palen, (I), Bill
Vann, (I), Ren Wicks, (I), Larry Winborg, (I), Kenny Yamada, (I),
Allen Yamashiro, (I)

S

Salzman, Richard W/716 Sanchez St, San Francisco, CA (P 718-725)..........................**415-285-8267**
Doug Bowles, (I), Kristen Funkhouser, (I), Manuel Garcia, (I), Marty Gunsaullus, (I), Denise Hilton-Putnam, (I), Jewell Homad, (I), Dan Jones, (I), Chris McAllister, (I), David Mollering, (I), Everett Peck, (I), Greg Shed, (I), Walter Stuart, (I)

Santee Lehmen Dabney Inc/900 1st Ave S #404, Seattle, WA (P 727-729) **206-467-1616**
Fred Birchman, (I), Laurine Bowerman, (J), Raymond Gendreau, (P), Peter Goetzinger, (I), Rolf Goetzinger, (I), Linnea Granryd, (I), Obadinah Heavner, (I), Chuck Kuhn, (P), Anita Lehmann, (I), Jim Linna, (P), Kong Lu, (I), Matt Myers, (I), Rosanne W Olson, (P), Julie Pace, (I), Stan Shaw, (I), Allen Yamashiro, (I)

Scott, Freda/244 Ninth St, San Francisco, CA 415-621-2992
Sherry Bringham, (I), Ed Carey, (P), Lon Clark, (P), Terry Hoff, (I), Scott Johnson, (I), Francis Livingston, (I), Alan Mazzetti, (I), R J Muna, (P), Sue Rother, (I), Susan Schelling, (P), William Thompson, (P), Carolyn Vibbert, (I), Pam Wall, (I), Elisabet Zeilon, (I)

Scroggy, David/2124 Froude St, San Diego, CA (P 578)..**619-222-2476**
Ed Abrams, (I), Jodell D Abrams, (I), Willardson + Assoc, (I), Rick Geary, (I), Jean "Moevius" Giraud, (I), Jack Molloy, (I), Hal Scroggy, (I), Lionel Talaro, (I)

Shaffer, Barry/PO Box 48665, Los Angeles, CA....................213-939-2527
Ann Bogart, (P), Wayne Clark, (I), Todd Curtis, (I), Doug Day, (I)

Sharpe & Assoc/3952 W 59th St, Los Angeles, CA..........................213-290-1430
Alan Dockery, (P), Lois Frank, (P), Hugh Kretschmer, (P), John LeCoq, (P), Paul Maxon, (P), Bob McMahon, (I), Greg Moraes, (I), C David Pina, (L), Judy Reed, (I), Lionel Talaro, (I)

Slobodian, Barbara/745 N Alta Vista Blvd, Hollywood, CA 213-935-6668
Pearl Beach, (I), Bob Greisen, (I), Scott Slobodian, (P)

Sobol, Lynne/4302 Melrose Ave, Los Angeles, CA............................213-665-5141
Laura Manriquez, (I), Arthur Montes de Oca, (P)

Stefanski, Janice Represents/2022 Jones St, San Francisco, CA (P 579-581) **415-928-0457**
Jeffrey Bedrick, (I), Adrian Day, (I), Karl Edwards, (I), Emily Gordon, (I), Gary Hanna, (I), Barbara Kelley, (I), Laurie La France, (I), Beth Whybrow Leeds, (I), Katherine Salentine, (I)

Studio Artists/638 S Van Ness Ave, Los Angeles, CA.....................213-385-4585
Chuck Coppock, (I), George Francuch, (I), Bill Franks, (I), Joe Garnett, (I), George Williams, (I)

Susan & Company/2717 Western Ave, Seattle, WA.........................206-728-1300
Bryn Barnard, (I), David M Davis, (I), Gary Eldridge, (I), Jeff Foster, (I), Craig Holmes, (I), Linda Holt-Ayrris, (I), Iskra Johnson, (I), Larry Jost, (I), Kristin Knutson, (I), Nina Laden, (I), Don Mason, (I), Karen Moskowitz, (P), Stephen Peringer, (I), Joe Saputo, (I), John Schmelzer, (I), Teresa Snyder, (I), Karl Weatherly, (P)

Sweeney, Karen/1345 Chautauqua Blvd, Pacific Palisades, CA 213-459-0331
Karen Knauer, (P), Jeff Nadler, (P), Nancy Stahl, (P)

Sweet, Ron/716 Montgomery St, San Francisco, CA........................415-433-1222
Randy Barrett, (I), Charles Brown, (I), Randy Glass, (I), Richard Leech, (I), Tom Lochray, (I), Steve Mayse, (I), Will Nelson, (I), Chris Shorten, (P), Darrell Tank, (I), Jeffrey Terreson, (I), Jack Unruh, (I), Bruce Wolfe, (I), James B Wood, (P)

TVW

Thornby, Kirk/611 S Burlington, Los Angeles, CA.............................213-933-9883
Myron Beck, (P), Darryl Estrine, (PP)

Valen Assocs/950 Klish Way, Del Mar, CA (P 558).........**619-259-5774**
Booth, (C), Richard Cline, (C), Whitney Darrow, (C), Eldon Dedini, (I), Joe Farris, (C), Mort Gerberg, (C), Bud Handelsman, (C), Stan Hunt, (C), Henry Martin, (C), Warren Miller, (C), Frank Modell, (C), Mischa Richter, (C), Mick Stevens, (C), Henry Syverson, (C), Weber, (C), Gahan Wilson, (C), Bill Woodman, (C), Jack Ziegler, (C)

Vandamme, Vicki/35 Stillman #206, San Francisco, CA..................415-543-6881
Lee Lee Brazeal, (I), Kirk Caldwell, (I), John Collier, (I), Flatland Studios, (I), Kathy & Joe Heiner, (I), Alan Krosnick, (P), Steve Lyons, (I), Rik Olson, (I), Jennie Oppenheimer, (I), Will Rieser, (I), Kim Whitesides, (I), Nic Wilton, (I)

Wagoner, Jae/654 Pier Ave #C, Santa Monica, CA 213-392-4877
David Edward Byrd, (I), David Danz, (I), Dennis Doheny, (I),

Stephen Durke, (I), Ken Durkin, (I), William Harrison, (I), Steve Jones, (I), Nobee Kanayama, (I), Maurice Lewis, (I), Leo Monahan, (I), Jeff Nishinaka, (I), Doug Suma, (I), Joan Weber, (I), Don Weller, (I)

Wiley, David/251 Kearny St #510, San Francisco, CA 415-989-2023
Steve Bjorkman, (I), Chris Consani, (I), Richard Eskite, (P), Ben Garvie, (I), Scott Sawyer, (I), Keith Witmer, (I), Paul Wolf, (I)

Winston, Bonnie/195 S Beverly Dr #400, Beverly Hills, CA.............213-275-2858
Eshel Ezer, (P), Marco Franchina, (P), Joe Hill, (P), Mark Kayne, (P), Neil Kirk, (P), Susan Shacter, (P)

I N T E R N A T I O N A L

Durcher, Marcel/512 Richmond St E, Toronto, ON...........................416-367-2446
Kane, Dennis/135 Rose Ave, Toronto, ON 416-323-3677
Link/Diane Jameson/2 Silver Ave, Toronto, ON (P 554-557) **416-530-1500**
Nina Berkson, (I), Normand Cousineau, (I), Pierre Pratt, (I), Paul Rivoche, (I)

Miller + Comstock Inc/180 Bloor St W #1102, Toronto, ON 416-925-4323
Organisation, The/69 Caledonian Rd, London, England, ...44-071-281-5176
Grahame Baker, (I), Emma Chichester Clark, (I), Neil Gower, (I), Michael O'Shaughnessy, (I), Max Schindler, (I)

Osner, Margrit/, Toronto, ON (P 574,575) **416-961-5767**
Audra Geras,

Sharp Shooter/524 Queen St E, Toronto, ON (P 574,575) **416-860-0300**
Three in a Box/512 Richmond St E, Toronto, ON 416-367-2446
Vernell, Maureen/128 Fieldgate Dr, Nepean, ON.............................613-825-4740

ILLUSTRATORS

NYC

A

Aagaard, Gary/280 Madison Ave #1402 (P 388) **212-545-9155**
Abraham, Daniel E/Box 2528/Rockefeller Sta 718-499-4006
Abrams, Kathie/548 Ninth St, Brooklyn....................718-499-4408
Accardo, Anthony/19 E 48th St 3rd Fl....................212-838-0050
Accornero, Franco/420 Lexington Ave (P 219) **212-697-8525**
Acuna, Ed/232 Madison Ave #402 (P 312,313) **212-889-8777**
Adams, Angela/866 UN Plaza #525....................212-644-2020
Adams, Jeanette/261 Broadway....................212-732-3878
Adams, Jeffrey/231 W 25th St #6E....................212-807-0840
Adams, Jenny/280 Madison Ave #1402 (P 391) **212-545-9155**
Adams, Lisa/100 W 12th St #4H (P 896) **212-691-3238**
Adams, Norman/211 E 51st St #5F....................212-755-1365
Adelman, Morton/144-69 28th Ave....................718-961-5072
Adler, Steve/509 Madison Ave 10th Fl (P 897) **212-355-0910**
Aiese, Bob/60 Pineapple St, Brooklyn....................718-596-2240
Ajhar, Brian/32 W 40th St #9B (P 686,687) **212-819-9084**
Alavezos, Gus/420 Lexington Ave #PH4,5 (P 174) **212-986-5680**
Albahae, Andrea/2364 Brigham St 1st Fl, Brooklyn 718-934-7004
Alcorn, John/135 E 54th St....................212-421-0050
Alcorn, Stephen/135 E 54th St....................212-421-0050
Alexander & Turner/232 Madison Ave #402
(P 314,315) **212-889-8777**
Alexander, Pat/280 Madison Ave #1402 (P 392) **212-545-9155**
Allaux, Jean Francois/21 W 86th St....................212-496-8593
Allen, Julian/41 Union Sq W (P 208) **212-929-5590**
Allen, Michael Illus/89 Fifth Ave....................212-924-3432
Allen, Terry/164 Daniel Low Terr, Staten Island,
(P 790,791) **718-727-0723**
Allert, Kathy/201 E 28th St....................212-532-0928
Aloisio, Richard/145 E 16th St....................212-473-5635
Alper, A J/224 Elizabeth St #19....................212-935-0039
Alpert, Alan/405 E 54th St....................212-741-1631
Alpert, Olive/9511 Shore Rd, Brooklyn....................718-833-3092
Ameijide, Ray/108 E 35th St #1C (P 148) **212-889-3337**
Amicosante, Vincent/280 Madison Ave #1402....................212-545-9155
Amit, Emmanuel/108 E 35th St #1C (P 149) **212-889-3337**
Amrine, Cynthia/240 E 27th St....................716-374-5847
Anderson, Rolf/45 W 84th St....................212-787-3305
Anderson, Toyce/280 Madison Ave #1402....................212-545-9155
Angelakis, Manos/31 W 21st St 7th Fl Rear....................212-243-4412
Angelini, George/232 Madison Ave #402 (P 316,317) **212-889-8777**
Angelo, Peter/500 W 43rd St #7G (P 469) **212-947-7454**
Antonios, Tony/60 E 42nd St #505 (P 34) **212-682-1490**
Arcelle, Joan/430 W 24th St....................212-924-1865
Archer, Doug/31 W 21st St 7th Fl Rear (P 520) **212-243-4412**
Arisman, Marshall/314 W 100th St....................212-662-2289
Aristovulos, Nick/16 E 30th St....................212-725-2454
Arnold, Robert/149 W 14th St....................212-989-7049
Arnoldi, Per/60 E 42nd St #505....................212-682-1490
Asbaghi, Zita/104-40 Queens Blvd, Forest Hills,
(P 904,905) **718-275-1995**
Assel, Steven/472 Myrtle Ave, Brooklyn....................718-789-1725
Astrahan, Irene/201 E 28th St....................212-532-0928

B

Bacall, Aaron/204 Arlene St, Staten Island....................718-494-0711
Bachem, Paul/270 Park Ave S #10B (P 542) **212-260-4153**
Bailer, Brent/104 E 40th St....................212-661-0257
Bailey, Pat/60 E 42nd St #505 (P 30) **212-682-1490**
Baker, Garin/60 E 42nd St #505....................212-682-1490
Baker, Grahame/267 Wyckoff St, Brooklyn....................718-624-1906
Banfield, Elliott/215 Park Ave So S #1300 (P 711) **212-674-8080**
Banner, Shawn/170 Broadway #201....................212-312-6447
Banthien, Barbara/41 Union Sq W (P 204, 205) **212-929-5590**
Baradat, Sergio/210 W 70th St....................212-721-2588
Baran, Esther/866 UN Plaza #525 (P 679) **212-644-2020**
Baran, Zafer/267 Wycoff St, Brooklyn....................718-624-1906

Barancik, Cathy/18 E 78th St....................212-472-3838
Barberis, Juan C/60 E 42nd St #1146....................212-953-7088
Barbour, Karen/51 Warren St 5th Fl....................212-619-6790
Barcilon, Roger/420 Lexington Ave #2760 (P 220) **212-697-8525**
Barner, Bob/866 UN Plaza #525....................212-644-2020
Barnes, Michele/111 Sullivan St #3B (P 630) **212-219-9269**
Barr, Ken/420 Lexington Ave #2760....................212-697-8525
Barrall, Tim/372 Bleecker St #2 (P 858) **212-243-9003**
Barrera, Alberto/463 West St #1017D....................212-645-2544
Barrett, Ron/2112 Broadway #402A....................212-874-1370
Barritt, Randi/240 W 15th St....................212-255-5333
Barry, Ivey/156 Fifth Ave #617 (P 658) **212-243-1333**
Barry, Ron/165 E 32nd St (P 642) **212-686-3514**
Barsky, Alexander/280 Madison Ave #1402 (P 384) **212-545-9155**
Bartholomew, Caty/721 Carroll St #3, Brooklyn....................718-636-1252
Barton, Kent/121 Madison Ave (P 256,257) **212-683-1362**
Baseman, Gary/443 12th St #2D, Brooklyn
(P 768,769) **718-499-9358**
Bates, Harry....................718-693-6304
Battaglia, Denise/1073 First Ave #34....................212-838-2990
Bauer, Carla Studio/156 Fifth Ave #1100....................212-807-8305
Bauman, Jill/PO Box 152, Jamaica....................718-886-5616
Baumann, Karen/43 E 19th St....................212-688-1080
Baxter, Daniel/88 First Pl Parlr Fl, Brooklyn....................718-522-1549
Beach, Lou/215 Park Ave S #1300 (P 712) **212-674-8080**
Becker, Ron/265 E 78th St....................212-535-8052
Beckerman, Richard/326 E 13th St #18....................212-228-3465
Beecham, Tom/420 Lexington Ave #2738....................212-697-8525
Begin, Maryjane/866 UN Plaza #525 (P 678) **212-644-2020**
Bego, Dolores/155 E 38th St (P 650) **212-697-6170**
Belair & Inoue Visual Comm/323 Park Ave S....................212-473-8330
Belcastro, Mario/1650 Third Ave #4A....................212-534-6688
Bemus, Bart/353 W 53rd St #1W....................212-682-2462
Bendell, Norm/41 Union Sq W #918 (P 622,623) **212-807-6627**
Bennett, Dianne/200 W 15th St (P 458) **212-243-4209**
Benney, Robert/50 W 96th St....................212-222-6605
Benoit/81 Greene St (P 566) **212-925-3053**
Benson, Linda M/270 Park Ave S #10B (P 542) **212-260-4153**
Berger, Stephen/43 E 19th St....................212-254-4996
Bergin, Robert/111 Wooster St #PH C (P 422) **212-925-0491**
Bergman, Eliot/362 W 20th St #201 (P 918,919) **212-645-0414**
Berkey, John/509 Madison Ave 10th Fl....................212-355-0910
Berran, Bob/60 E 42nd St #1940....................212-867-8092
Berrett, Randy/15 W 72nd St....................212-799-2231
Berry, Fanny Mellet/155 E 38th St (P 651) **212-697-6170**
Beylon, Cathy/201 E 28th St....................212-532-0928
Bianco, Gerard/1040 82nd St, Brooklyn....................718-836-8637
Biers, Nanette/194 Third Ave (P 104,105) **212-475-0440**
Billout, Guy/225 Lafayette St #1008....................212-431-6350
Bilmes, Semyon/420 Lexington Ave #2760....................212-697-8525
Biniasz, Paul/132 W 21st St 12th Fl....................212-979-0025
Birdsong, Ken/6 E 36th St #1R (P 536,537) **212-685-4580**
Bjorkman, Steve/501 Fifth Ave #1407 (P 80,760,761) **212-490-2450**
Black & White Dog Studio/3240 Henry Hudson Pkwy #6H, Bronx....................212-601-8820
Blackshear, Lisa/11 W 17th St #3....................212-675-1083
Blackshear, Thomas/121 Madison Ave (P 258,259) **212-683-1362**
Blackwell, Garie/60 E 42nd St #505....................212-682-1490
Blair, Dru/6 E 36th St #1R (P 533) **212-685-4580**
Blake, Bob/359 Ft Washington Ave #6G....................212-781-4855
Blake, Marty/41 Union Sq W #636 (P 440) **212-206-0066**
Blake, Quentin/81 Greene St....................212-925-3053
Blas, Bob/43 E 19th St....................212-254-4996
Bleck, Cathie/58 W 15th St 6th Fl (P 60-61) **212-741-2539**
Bliss, Harry/41 Union Sq W (P 194) **212-929-5590**
Bloch, Alex/19 E 48th St 3rd Fl....................212-838-0050
Bloom, Tom/235 E 84th St #17....................212-628-6861
Blubaugh, Susan M/165 Church St #4S (P 924) **212-406-3652**
Blum, Zevi/81 Greene St....................212-925-3053
Bogan, Paulette/287 W 4th St #1....................212-243-1694
Boguslav, Raphael/200 E 78th St (P 521) **212-570-9069**
Boies, Alex/420 Lexington Ave #2760 (P 237) **212-697-8525**
Bolognese, Don/19 E 48th St....................212-838-0050
Bonforte, Lisa/201 E 28th St....................212-532-0928
Bonhomme, Bernard/111 Wooster St #PH C....................212-925-0491
Bono, Mary M/288 Graham Ave, Brooklyn....................718-387-3774
Bordelon, Melinda/60 E 42nd St #505....................212-682-1490
Bornstein, Peter/474 Fifth Street #4, Brooklyn....................718-768-0443
Bornstein-Fahrer, Marguerita/1 Hudson St 4th Fl....................212-285-2905

Bostic, Alex/330 Haven Ave #4N 212-568-2848
Botana, Federico/227 W 29th St #9R 212-967-7699
Botas, Juan/110 Suffolk St #6A 212-420-5984
Botzis, Ka/370 Lexington Ave #1002 (P 572) **212-953-2177**
Bower, Tim/141 Sullivan #12 (P 927) **212-982-0032**
Bowie, Effie/152 E 94th St #12A 212-289-5469
Boyd, Harvey/24 Fifth Ave 212-475-5235
Boyer, Gene/232 Madison Ave #402 (P 320,321) **212-889-8777**
Bozzo, Frank/400 E 85th St #5J 212-535-9182
Bracchi & Beresford/152 E 33rd St 4th Fl 212-532-3298
Brachman, Richard/30-44 34th St #5F, Astoria 718-204-6879
Bracken, Carolyn/201 E 28th St 212-532-0928
Brady, Elizabeth/461 Broome St 212-966-9897
Bralds, Braldt/135 E 54th St 212-421-0050
Bramhall, William/81 Greene St (P 567) **212-925-3053**
Brandt, Joan/15 Gramercy Park S 212-473-7874
Braun, Wendy/104 W 74th St #3C 212-873-6859
Brautigam, Don/211 E 51st St #5F 212-755-1365
Breakey, John/611 Broadway #811 212-982-0188
Breinberg, Aaron/66-15 Thorton Pl, Forest Hills 718-261-2544
Brennan, Neil/41 Union Sq W #636 (P 436) **212-206-0066**
Brennan, Steve/420 Lexington Ave #PH4,5 (P 170) ...**212-986-5680**
Brillhart, Ralph/60 E 42nd St #1940 212-867-8092
Britt, Tracy/420 Lexington Ave #2760 (P 224) **212-697-8525**
Broda, Ron/420 Lexington Ave #2760 212-697-8525
Brodner, Steve/120 Cabrini Blvd #116 (P 932,933) **212-740-8174**
Brooks, Andrea/99 Bank St (P 874) **212-633-1477**
Brooks, Clare Vanacore/415 W 55th St (P 936,937) ...**212-245-3632**
Brooks, Ed/20 W 87th St #6A 212-595-5980
Brooks, Hal/20 W 87th St #6A 212-595-5980
Brooks, Leo/3039 Wallace Ave #6E, Bronx 212-882-0148
Brooks, Lou/415 W 55th St (P 938,939) **212-245-3632**
Brooks, Lou Productions/415 W 55th St (P 936-939) ..**212-245-3632**
Brothers, Barry/1922 E 18th St, Brooklyn 718-336-7540
Brown, Colin/41 Union Sq W #636 212-206-0066
Brown, Dan/232 Madison Ave #402 (P 318,319) **212-889-8777**
Brown, Donald/20 Bay St Landing #2D, Staten Island 212-532-1705
Brown, Judith Gwyn/522 E 85th St 212-288-1599
Brown, Michael David/108 E 35th St #1C
(P 118,119) **212-889-3337**
Brown, Peter D/235 E 22nd St #16R (P 875) **212-684-7080**
Brown, Rick/60 E 42nd St #505 (P 25) **212-682-1490**
Brusca, Jack/43 E 19th St 212-254-4996
Bryan, Diana/200 E 16th St #1D 212-475-7927
Bryan, Mike/420 Lexington Ave #2760 212-697-8525
Bryant, Rick J/18 W 37th St #301 212-594-6718
Buchanan, Yvonne/18 Lincoln Pl #2L, Brooklyn 718-783-6682
Buckner, Derek/131 Spring St 3rd Fl (P 656) **212-925-4340**
Bull, Michael/420 Lexington Ave #2760 (P 230,231) ...**212-697-8525**
Burgoyne, John/200 E 78th St (P 522,523) **212-570-9069**
Burns, Jim/155 Ave of Americas 10th Fl (P 695) **212-255-6530**
Busch, Lon/108 E 35th St #1C (P 120,121) **212-889-3337**
Buschman, Lynne/186 Franklin St 212-925-4701
Bush, George/60 E 42nd St #1940 212-867-8092
Byrd, Bob/280 Madison Ave #1402 212-545-9155

C

Caggiano, Tom/83-25 Dongan Ave, Elmhurst 718-651-8993
Cain, David H/200 W 20th St #607 (P 851) **212-633-0258**
Callanan, Brian/420 Lexington Ave (P 226) **212-697-8525**
Callen, Liz/866 UN Plaza #525 212-644-2020
Campbell, Jim/420 Lexington Ave #PH4,5 212-986-5680
Carbone, Kye/241 Union St, Brooklyn 718-802-9143
Carpenter, Joe/72 Spring St #1003 212-431-6666
Carpenter, Polly/72 Spring St 212-431-6666
Carr, Barbara/245 E. 40th St. 212-370-1663
Carr, Noell/30 E 14th St 212-675-1015
Carter, Bunny/200 E 78th St 212-570-9069
Carter, Penny/12 Stuyvesant Oval #4A 212-473-7965
Carver, Steve/41 Union Sq W #636 212-206-0066
Casale, Paul/5304 11th Ave, Brooklyn 718-871-6848
Cascio, Peter/810 Seventh Ave 41st Fl 212-408-2177
Cassidy, Michael/60 E 42nd St #1940 212-867-8092
Cassler, Carl/420 Lexington Ave #PH4,5 212-986-5680
Castelluccio, Frederico/60 E 42nd St #1940 212-867-8092
Catrow, David 212-627-7058
Cavaliere, Jamie/60 E 42nd St #1940 212-867-8092

Cellini, Joseph/501 Fifth Ave (P 81) **212-490-2450**
Ceribello, Jim/11 W Cedar View Ave, Staten Island 718-317-5972
Cesc/81 Greene St 212-925-3053
Chabrian, Deborah/270 Park Ave S #10B (P 539) **212-260-4153**
Chalmers, Cheryl/156 Fifth Ave #617 212-243-1333
Chambless-Rigie, Jane/64-66 Seventh Ave #3D 212-627-9821
Chang, Alain/232 Madison Ave #402 (P 322,323) **212-889-8777**
Chappell, Ellis/420 Lexington Ave #PH4,5 (P 184) ...**212-986-5680**
Charmatz, Bill/25 W 68th St 212-595-3907
Chermayeff, Ivan/58 W 15th St 6th Fl (P 68-69) **212-741-2539**
Chesak, Lina/6 E 36th St #1R (P 535) **212-685-4580**
Chester, Harry/501 Madison Ave 212-752-0570
Chironna, Ronald/122 Slosson Ave 2nd Fl,
Staten Island (P 0954) **718-720-6142**
Choi, Jae-eun/70 Clark St #C, Brooklyn 718-638-8301
Chow, Rita/280 Madison Ave #1402 (P 387) **212-545-9155**
Chow, Tad/50-44 68th St, Woodside 718-899-9813
Christensen, Kent/320 E 50th St #2C (P 955) **212-754-3017**
Chronister, Robert/3140 Rt 209, Kingston 914-687-4911
Chwast, Eve/215 Park Ave S #1300 (P 713) **212-674-8080**
Chwast, Jacqueline/23-83 37th St, Astoria, ...718-626-0840
Chwast, Seymour/215 Park Ave S #1300 (P 708) **212-674-8080**
Ciardiello, Joe/2182 Clove Rd, Staten Island,(P 957) .**718-727-4757**
Ciccarelli, Gary/353 W 53rd St #1W (P 409) **212-682-2462**
Ciesiel, Christine G/80 Pierpont St #5A, Brooklyn 718-237-6036
Cieslawski, Steve/866 UN Plaza #525 (P 679) **212-644-2020**
Cigliano, Bill/501 Fifth Ave #1407 (P 92,849) **212-490-2450**
Clark, Emma Chichester/267 Wyckoff St, Brooklyn 718-624-1906
Clarke, Robert/200 W 54th St #9C 212-581-4045
Clementson, John/155 Ave of Americas 10th Fl
(P 695) **212-255-6530**
Cody, Brian/866 UN Plaza #525 212-644-2020
Coffey, Deborah C/339 E 33rd St #1R 212-532-5205
Cohen, Adam/74 Charles St #2B (P 961) **212-691-4074**
Cohen, Hayes/36-35 193rd St #3, Flushing (P 890) ..**718-321-7307**
Cohen, M E/95 Horatio St #10M 212-627-8033
Cohen, Paula/524 Henry St, Brooklyn (P 868) **718-852-7496**
Cohen, Stacey L/252 W 76th St #3A 212-724-2774
Colby, Garry/420 Lexington Ave #PH4,5 (P 179) **212-986-5680**
Cole, Olivia/19 E 48th St 3rd Fl 212-838-0050
Collier, John/121 Madison Ave (P 250,251) **212-683-1362**
Collier, Roberta/201 E 28th St 212-532-0928
Collins, Jennifer/320 E 42nd St #112 212-297-0474
Colon, Ernie/43 E 19th St 212-254-4996
Colon, Raul/125 W 77th St (P 733) **212-799-6532**
Colrus, William/156 Fifth Ave #617 212-243-1333
Comitini, Peter/30 Waterside Plaza 212-683-5120
Confer, Mitchell/505 Court St #3A, Brooklyn 718-858-2159
Connelly, Gwen/420 Lexington Ave #2760 212-697-8525
Conner, Mona/1 Montgomery Pl #8, Brooklyn (P 969) ..**718-636-1527**
Continuity Graphics Assoc'd Inc/62 W 45th St 212-869-4170
Conway, Michael/316 E 93rd St #23 212-722-3300
Cook, Anne/232 Madison Ave #402 212-889-8777
Cook, David/60 E 42nd St #1940 212-867-8092
Cook, Donald/866 UN Plaza #525 212-644-2020
Cooper, Dana/35 E 85th St #4D 212-794-3969
Cooper, Floyd/866 UN Plaza #525 212-644-2020
Cooperstein, Sam/677 West End Ave 212-864-4064
Corben, Richard/43 E 19th St 212-254-4996
Corio, Paul/208 E 7th St #10 212-228-4630
Cormier, Wil/15 W 72nd St 212-799-2231
Cornell, Jeff/232 Madison Ave #402 (P 324,325) **212-889-8777**
Cornell, Laura/118 E 93rd St #1A 212-534-0596
Corvi, Donna/568 Broadway #604 212-925-9622
Cosgrove, Dan/200 W 15th St (P 453) **212-243-4209**
Couch, Greg/51 Seventh Ave #2, Brooklyn, (P 854) ..**718-789-9276**
Courtney, Richard/43 E 19th St 212-254-4996
Cove, Tony/60 E 42nd St #1146 212-953-7088
Cox, Paul/121 Madison Ave (P 262,263) **212-683-1362**
Cozzolino, Paul/30-01 37th St 3rd Fl, Astoria, (P 972) ..**718-728-2729**
Craig, Daniel/60 E 42nd St #505 (P 14) **212-682-1490**
Crawford, Denise Chapman/420 Lexington Ave
#2760 (P 221) **212-697-8525**
Creative Capers/60 E 42nd St #505 (P 24) **212-682-1490**
Crews, Donald/653 Carroll St, Brooklyn 718-636-5773
Cruse, Howard/88-11 34th Ave #5D, Jackson Heights ...718-639-4951
Cruz, Jose/108 E 35th St #1C (P 122,123) **212-889-3337**
Cruz, Ray/194 Third Ave 212-475-0440

Csatari, Joe/420 Lexington Ave #2911 212-986-5680
Cuevas Stillerman Plotkin/118 E 28th St #306 212-679-0622
Cummings, Pat/28 Tiffany Pl, Brooklyn, NY 718-834-8584
Cummings, Terrence/210 W 64th St #5B 212-586-4193
Cusack, Margaret/124 Hoyt St, Brooklyn, (P 974)......718-237-0145
Cushwa, Tom/303 Park Ave S #511 212-228-2615
Czechowski, Alicia/215 Park Ave S #1300 (P 708).....212-674-8080
Czeczot, Andrzei/531 E 81st St #1C (P 492)...........212-861-9892

D

D'Andrea, Bernard/509 Madison Ave 10th Fl 212-355-0910
D'Andrea, Domenick/509 Madison Ave 10th Fl 212-355-0910
D'Onofrio, Alice/866 UN Plaza #4014 212-644-2020
Dacey, Bob/232 Madison Ave #402 212-889-8777
Dale, Robert/41 Union Sq W (P 431) 212-206-0066
Daley, Joann/232 Madison Ave #402 (P 326,327)........212-889-8777
Dallison, Ken/108 E 35th St #1C 212-889-3337
Daly, Sean/85 South St 212-668-0031
Daner, Carole/200 W 20th St #101 212-243-8152
Daniel, Frank/201 E 28th St 212-532-0928
Daniels, Beau & Alan/232 Madison Ave #402
(P 328,329)...212-889-8777
Daniels, Sid/12 E 22nd St #11B 212-673-6520
Darden, Howard/25 W 45th St 212-398-9540
Daste, Larry/201 E 28th St 212-532-0928
Davidson, Dennis/43 E 19th St 212-254-4996
Davidson, Everett/60 E 42nd St #505 212-682-1490
Davis, Allen/141-10 25th Rd #3A, Flushing, NY 718-463-0966
Davis, Harry R/189 E 3rd St #15 (P 978) 212-674-5832
Davis, Jack/108 E 35th St #1C (P 124,125)............212-889-3337
Davis, Jack E/121 Madison Ave (P 244,245)............212-683-1362
Davis, Nelle/20 E 17th St 4th Fl 212-807-7737
Davis, Paul/14 E 4th St 212-420-8789
Dawson, John/515 Madison Ave 22nd Fl 212-486-9644
Day, Betsy/866 UN Plaza #525 212-644-2020
de Araujo, Betty/201 E 28th St 212-532-0928
De Seve, Peter/25 Park Pl, Brooklyn, (P 984, 985)......718-398-8099
Dean, Glenn/501 Fifth Ave #1407 (P 93)...............212-490-2450
Deas, Michael/39 Sidney Pl, Brooklyn 718-852-5630
Deca, Wanda Maioresco/510 Main St #430 212-838-2509
DeCerchio, Joe/25 W 45th St (P 465).................212-398-9540
Deel, Guy/60 E 42nd St #1940 212-867-8092
Deeter, Cathy/515 Madison Ave 22nd Fl 212-486-9644
Degen, Paul/81 Greene St (P 566)......................212-925-3053
DeGraffenried, Jack/566 Seventh Ave #603 212-221-8090
DeJesus, Jamie/15 W 72nd St 212-799-2231
Dekle, Merritt/155 Ave of Americas 10th Fl (P 693)....212-255-6530
Del Rossi, Ric/156 Fifth Ave #617 212-243-1333
Delmirenburg, Barry/301 E 38th St 212-573-9200
DeLouise, Dan/77-14 113th St #2E, Forest Hills 718-268-4847
Delvalle, Daniel/19 E 48th St 212-838-0050
Demarest, Chris/81 Greene St (P 566)................212-925-3053
DeMichiell, Robert/226 W 78th St #26 (P 981).........212-769-9192
Denaro, Joseph/566 Seventh Ave #603 212-221-8090
Deneen, Jim/420 Lexington Ave #2911 212-986-5680
DeRijk, Walt/43 E 19th St 212-254-4996
Dervaux, Isabelle/204 Ave B 212-505-0511
Deschamps, Bob/108 E 35th St #1C 212-889-3337
DesCombes, Roland/509 Madison Ave 10th Fl 212-355-0910
Design Loiminchay/503 Broadway 5th Fl 212-941-7488
Design Plus/156 Fifth Ave #1232 212-645-2686
Desimini, Lisa/532 E 82nd St #19 212-737-1535
DeSpain, Pamela Mannino/340 E 63rd St #2C 919-259-3107
Dettrich, Susan/253 Baltic St, Brooklyn 718-237-9174
Devaud, Jacques/353 W 53rd St #1W (P 418)..........212-682-2462
DeVito, Grace/111 Wooster St #PH C (P 423)..........212-925-0491
Devlin, Bill/108 E 35th St #1C (P 150)................212-889-3337
Diamantis, Kitty/19 E 48th St 3rd Fl 212-838-0050
Diamond Art Studio/11 E 36th St 212-685-6622
Diamond, Donna/420 Lexington Ave PH 212-986-5680
Diamond, Ruth/95 Horatio St #521 212-243-3188
DiCianni, Ron/420 Lexington Ave #2760 212-697-8525
DiComo Comp Art/120 E 34th St #12K-L 212-689-8670
Diehl, David/222 W 20th St #16 212-242-8897
Dietz, Jim/165 E 32nd St (P 640)......................212-686-3514
DiFabio, Jessica/301 E 75th St #20B 212-988-9623
Dilakian, Hovik/111 Wooster St #PH C 212-925-0491

Dininno, Steve/25 W 45th St 212-398-9540
Dinnerstein, Harvey/933 President St, Brooklyn 718-783-6879
Dittrich, Dennis/42 W 72nd St #12B 212-864-5971
Dixon, Ted/594 Broadway #902 212-226-5686
Dodds, Glenn/238 E 36th St 212-679-3630
Dodge, Bill/60 E 42nd St #1940 212-867-8092
Doktor, Patricia/95 Horatio St #9A 212-645-4452
Dolobowsky, Mena/140 West End Ave #9H 212-874-7074
Domingo, Ray/108 E 35th St #1C 212-889-3337
Donato, Michael A/215 Park Ave S #1300 (P 711)......212-674-8080
Doniger, Nancy/402A 19th St, Brooklyn 718-965-0284
Donner, Carol/501 Fifth Ave #1407 (P 88,89)........212-490-2450
Doret, Michael/12 E 14th St #4D (P 766)..............212-929-1688
Doret/Smith Studios/12 E 14th St #4D (P 766, 767)....212-929-1688
Doty, Curt/111 Wooster St (P 424)....................212-925-0491
Douglas, Randy/37 E 28th St #506 (P 571)............212-696-4120
Dowdy, Michael/3240 Henry Hudson Pkwy #6H, Bronx ..212-601-8820
Downes, Nicholas/PO Box 107, Brooklyn 718-875-0086
Draper, Linda/95 Horatio St #205 212-581-4609
Drescher, Henrik/151 First Ave #55 212-777-6077
Dressel, Peggy/25 W 45th St (P 468)................212-398-9540
Drovetto, Richard/355 E 72nd St 212-861-0927
Drucker, Mort/232 Madison Ave #402 (P 330,331)......212-889-8777
Dryden, Patty/194 Third Ave (P 113)..................212-475-0440
Duarte, Mary Young/350 First Ave #9E 212-674-4513
Dubanevich, Arlene/866 UN Plaza #4014 212-644-2020
Duburke, Randy/272 Wyckoff St, Brooklyn 718-522-6793
Ducak, Danilo/60 E 42nd St #1940 212-867-8092
Dudash, C Michael/211 E 51st St #5F (P 519).........212-755-1365
Dudzinski, Andrzej/52 E 81st St 212-772-3098
Duggan, Lee/108 E 35th St #1C (P 126,127)..........212-889-3337
Duke, Chris/509 Madison Ave 10th Fl 212-355-0910
Dunnick, Regan/41 Union Sq W #1228 (P 199).........212-929-5590
Duquette, Steven/25 W 45th St 212-398-9540
Duran, Nina/60 E 42nd St #505 212-682-1490
Dyess, John/156 Fifth Ave #617 (P 658,490).........212-243-1333
Dynamic Duo Studio/108 E 35th St (P 128,129).......212-889-3337

E

Eagle, Cameron/41 Union Sq W #1228 (P 209)........212-929-5590
Eastman, Norm & Bryant/420 Lexington Ave #2738 212-697-8525
Ecklund, Rae/41 Union Sq W #1228 212-929-5590
Eckstein, Linda/534 Laguardia Pl #5S 212-522-2552
Edwards, Andrew/124 E 4th St #13 212-274-1344
Eggert, John/420 Lexington Ave #PH4,5 212-986-5680
Ehlert, Lois/866 UN Plaza #525 (P 678).............212-644-2020
Eisner, Gil/310 W 86th St #11A 212-595-2023
Elins, Michael/353 W 53rd St #1W (P 414)...........212-682-2462
Ellis, Dean/31 E 12th St #5A 212-475-1483
Elmer, Richard/504 E 11th St (P 990)................212-598-4024
Ely, Richard/207 W 86th St 212-757-8987
Emerson, Carmela/217-11 54th Ave, Bayside,
(P 827)...718-224-4251
Emerson/Wajdowicz/1123 Broadway 212-807-8144
Endewelt, Jack/50 Riverside Dr 212-877-0575
Enik, Ted/82 Jane St #4A 212-431-8471
Enric/43 E 19th St 212-688-1080
Entwisle, Mark/267 Wycoff St, Brooklyn 718-624-1906
Ernster, Scott/853 Broadway #1201 (P 608).........212-677-9100
Evans, Jan/853 Broadway #1201 212-677-9100
Evcimen, Al/305 Lexington Ave #6D 212-889-2995
Eversz, Kim Wilson/268 Union St #3, Brooklyn 718-237-8546
Ewing, Carolyn/201 E 28th St 212-532-0928

F

Fabricatore, Carol/1123 Broadway #612 212-463-8950
Falkenstern, Lisa/232 Madison Ave #402 212-889-8777
Fanelli, Carolyn/19 Stuyvesant Oval 212-533-9829
Farina, Michael/566 Seventh Ave #603 212-221-8090
Farrell, Russell/353 W 53rd St 212-682-2462
Farrell, Sean/320 E 42nd St #112 212-949-6081
Fascione, Sabina/194 Third Ave 212-475-0440
Fasolino, Teresa/58 W 15th St 6th Fl (P 62, 63)......212-741-2539
Faulkner, Matt/35 Pineapple St #1A, Brooklyn,
(P 993)...718-858-1724
Faust, Clifford/322 W 57th St #42P 212-581-9461

FeBland, David/105 W 13th St #6C (P 994,995)............212-645-4190
Feingold, Deborah/430 Broome St 212-911-0018
Fennimore, Linda/808 West End Ave #801 212-866-0279
Fernandez, Fernando/43 E 19th St 212-254-4996
Fernandez, George/60 E 42nd St #1940 212-867-8092
Fernandez, Stanislaw/115 Fourth Ave #2A (P 812)......212-533-2648
Fertig, Howard/7-15 162nd St #6C, Beechhurst 718-746-6265
Fery, Guy A/117 E 57th St 212-371-9771
Fichera, Maryanne/120 E 34th St #12K-L 212-689-8670
Field, Lori Nelson/860 W 181st St #41A (P 996) 212-795-4281
Filippucci, Sandra/270 Park Ave S #10B (P 541) 212-260-4153
Fine, Robert/43 E 19th St 212-254-4996
Finelle, Dominick/420 Lexington Ave #PH4,5 (P 183) 212-986-5680
Finger, Ron/60 E 42nd St #505 (P 27) 212-682-1490
Fiore, Peter/270 Park Ave S #10B (P 539) 212-260-4153
Fiorentino, Al/866 UN Plaza #525 212-644-2020
Fisher, Jeffrey/81 Greene St (P 567) 212-925-3053
Fisher, Mark/111 Wooster St #PH C (P 425) 212-925-0491
Fitzhugh, Gregg/25 W 45th St (P 459) 212-398-9540
Flaherty, David/449 W 47th St #3 (P 865) 212-262-6536
Fleming, Joe/425 W 23rd St #10F (P 674,675) 212-242-6367
Fleming, Ron/60 E 42nd St #505 (P 35) 212-682-1490
Flesher, Vivienne/194 Third Ave (P 110) 212-475-0440
Forbes, Bart/501 Fifth Ave #1407 (P 74, 75) 212-490-2450
Forrest, Sandra/332 W 88th St #C1 212-769-4375
Foster, B Lynne/540 Ft Washington Ave #3D 212-740-7011
Fox, Barbara/301 W 53rd St 212-245-7564
Fox, Rosemary/41 Union Sq W #918 (P 631) 212-807-6627
Frampton, Bill/200 W 15th St (P 457) 212-243-4209
Frampton, David/58 W 15th St 6th Fl 212-741-2539
Francis, Judy E/110 W 96th St #2C (P 998) 212-866-7204
Frank, Robert/370 Lexington Ave #1002 (P 572) 212-953-2177
Frank, Scott J/518 E 80th St #2A 212-861-0635
Franke, Phil/420 Lexington Ave #PH4,5 (P 168) 212-986-5680
Fraser, Douglas/41 Union Sq W #1228 (P 196,197) ...212-929-5590
Freas, John/353 W 53rd St #1W 212-682-2462
Freda, Tony/36-34 30th St, Long Island City 212-529-4990
Freelance Solutions/369 Lexington Ave 18th Fl 212-490-3334
Fretz, Frank/866 UN Plaza #525 212-644-2020
Fricke, Warren/15 W 72nd St 212-799-2231
Fried, Janice/459 Ninth St, Brooklyn 718-832-0881
Friedman, Barbara A/29 Bank St (P 999) 212-242-4951
Friedman, Jon/866 UN Plaza #525 212-644-2020
Frisari, Frank/95-08 112th St, Richmond Hill,
(P 1000,1001)..718-441-0919
Frith, Michael/267 Wycoff St, Brooklyn 718-624-1906
Fuchs, Bernie/14 E 52nd St (P 503) 212-752-8490
Furukawa, Mel/116 Duane St 212-349-3225

G

Gabriel, Don/43 E 19th St...212-254-4996
Gadino, Victor/60 E 42nd St (P 36) 212-682-1490
Gaetano, Nick/14 E 52nd St (P 502) 212-752-8490
Gala, Tom/420 Lexington Ave #PH4,5 212-986-5680
Galindo, Felipe/96 Ave B 2nd Fl 212-477-2485
Galkin, Simon/19 E 48th St 3rd Fl 212-838-0050
Gall, Chris/853 Broadway #1201 (P 605) 212-677-9100
Gallardo, Gervasio/509 Madison Ave 10th Fl 212-355-0910
Gambale, David/200 W 15th St 212-243-4209
Gampert, John/PO Box 219, Kew Gardens, NY..................718-441-2321
Garcia, James J/430 Dongan Hills Ave, Staten Island,
(P 1102)..718-351-3071
Gardner, Steve/60 E 42nd St #1940 212-867-8092
Garguila, Joanna/107 St Mark's Pl #1H 212-777-0392
Garland, Bill/353 W 53rd St #1W (P 411) 212-682-2462
Garner, David/301 W 110th St #19B (P 860) 212-663-5625
Garns, G Allen/41 Union Sq W #636 (P 432,433)........212-206-0066
Garrick, Jacqueline/333 E 75th St 212-628-1018
Garrido, Hector/420 Lexington Ave #PH4,5 212-986-5680
Garrison, Barbara/12 E 87th St 212-348-6382
Garrow, Dan/501 Fifth Ave #1407 (P 90) 212-490-2450
Gartel, Laurence/270-16 B Grand Central Pkwy, Floral Park 718-229-8540
Gaszi, Edward/232 Madison Ave #402 212-889-8777
Gates, Donald/19 E 48th St 3rd Fl 212-838-0050
Gayler, Anne/320 E 86th St #4F 212-734-7060
Gazsi, Ed/232 Madison Ave #402 (P 332,333) 212-889-8777
Geary, Rick/1 Irving Pl #G24A 212-677-9045

Gebert, Warren/333 E 49th St #3J (P 592,593)............212-980-8061
Gehm, Charles/420 Lexington Ave #2760 (P 214) 212-697-8525
Geiser, Janie/340 E 9th St 212-353-5015
Gem Studio/420 Lexington Ave #220 212-687-3460
Genova, Joe/60 E 42nd St #505 (P 31) 212-682-1490
Gentile, John & Anthony/244 W 54th St 9th Fl.................212-757-1966
George, Jeff/853 Broadway #1201 212-677-9100
Gerberg, Darcy/149 W 24th St...212-243-3346
Gersten, Gerry/14 E 52nd St (P 505) 212-752-8490
Gerwitz, Rick/93 Perry St #11 212-353-9838
Giavis, Ted/420 Lexington Ave #PH 4,5 212-986-5680
Giglio, Richard/2231 Broadway #17 212-724-8118
Gignilliat, Elaine/420 Lexington Ave #PH4,5 212-986-5680
Giguere, Ralph/41 Union Sq W #636.................................212-206-0066
Gillies, Chuck/420 Lexington Ave #PH4,5 212-986-5680
Gillot, Carol/67 E 11th St #708 212-353-1174
Giorgio, Nate/566 Seventh Ave #603 212-221-8090
Giovanopoulos, Paul/119 Prince St 212-677-5919
Girvin, Tim/501 Fifth Ave #1407 (P 98,99) 212-490-2450
Giuliani, Bob/19 E 48th St 212-838-0050
Gladstone, Dale/128 N 1st St, Brooklyn 718-782-2250
Glass, Randy/108 E 35th St #1C (P 151) 212-889-3337
Glazer & Kalayjian/301 E 45th St 212-687-3099
Glick, Judith/301 E 79th St 212-734-5268
Glover, Gary/232 Madison Ave #402 212-889-8777
Gnidziejko, Alex/211 E 51st St #5F 212-755-1365
Goldin, David/111 Fourth Ave #7E 212-529-5195
Goldman, Bart/360 W 36th St #8NW (P 1007) 212-239-0047
Goldman, Dara/866 UN Plaza #525 212-644-2020
Goldstrom, Robert/471 Fifth St, Brooklyn 718-768-7367
Gomez, Ignacio/853 Broadway #1201 (P 607) 212-677-9100
Gonzalez, Pedro Julio/370 Lexington Ave (P 573)......212-953-2177
Goodell, Jon/866 UN Plaza #4014.....................................212-644-2020
Goodman, Paula/156 Fifth Ave #617 212-243-1333
Gordley, Scott/31 W 21st St 7th Fl Rear (P 520) 212-243-4412
Gore, Elissa/583 W 215th St #A3 212-567-2164
Gorton, Julia/85 South St #6N 212-825-0190
Gorton/Kirk Studio/85 South St #6N 212-825-0190
Gosfield, Josh/682 Broadway 212-254-2582
Gottfried, Max/82-60 116th St #CC3, Kew Gardens 718-441-9868
Gourley, Robin/244 Fifth Ave 11th Fl.................................212-679-4420
Gowdy, Carolyn/81 Greene St..212-925-3053
Gower, Neil/267 Wyckoff St, Brooklyn...............................718-624-1906
Grace, Alexa/70 University Pl 212-254-4424
Graham, Mariah/670 West End Ave 212-580-8061
Graham, Thomas/408 77th St #D4, Brooklyn 718-680-2975
Grajek, Tim/184 E 2nd St #4F 212-995-2129
Gran, Julia/3240 Henry Hudson Pkwy #6H, Bronx...........212-601-8820
Graphic Chart & Map Co/236 W 26th St #8SE
(P 1015) 212-463-0190
Grashow, David/81 Greene St 212-925-3053
Gray, Doug/15 W 72nd St 212-799-2231
Gray, Steve/853 Broadway (P 609) 212-677-9100
Gray, Susan/42 W 12th St #5 212-675-2242
Grebu, Devis/43 E 19th St..212-254-4996
Green, Norman/119 W 23rd St #203 (P 589)...............212-633-9880
Greenstein, Susan/4915 Surf Ave, Brooklyn....................718-373-4475
Gregoretti, Robert/41-07 56th St, Woodside, (P 1017) ...718-779-7913
Greif, Gene/270 Lafayette St #1505 212-966-0470
Greiner, Larry/236 W 26th St 8th Fl 212-982-2428
Griesbach/Martucci/58 W 15th St 6th Fl (P 54, 55)......212-741-2539
Griffel, Barbara/23-45 Bell Blvd, Bayside 718-631-1753
Griffin, James/60 E 42nd St #1940....................................212-867-8092
Grossman, Robert/19 Crosby St 212-925-1965
Grossman, Wendy/355 W 51st St #43 212-262-4497
Guarnaccia, Steven/430 W 14th St #508...........................212-645-9610
Guip, Amy/430 Lafayette St Loft 3 212-674-8166
Guitar, Jeremy/866 UN Plaza #525 212-644-2020
Guitteau, Jud/501 Fifth Ave #1407 (P 86,821)............212-490-2450
Gumen, Murad/33-25 90th St #6K, Jackson Heights........718-478-7267
Gurbo, Walter/208 E 13th St #6N.......................................718-634-0072
Gurney, John Steven/261 Marlborough Rd, Brooklyn,
(P 1019) 718-462-5073
Gustafson, Dale/420 Lexington Ave #PH4,5 (P 166)....212-986-5680
Gutierrez, Rudy/330 Haven Ave #4N..................................212-568-2840

H

Hack, Konrad/866 UN Plaza #525....................................212-644-2020
Haggland, Martin/2345 Broadway #728.............................212-727-0500
Hahn, Moira/215 Park Ave S #1300 (P 710) **212-674-8080**
Haimowitz, Steve/67-40 Yellowstone Blvd,
Forest Hills, (P 1020) **718-520-1461**
Hall, Deborah Ann/105-28 65th Ave #6B, Forest Hills........718-896-3152
Hall, Joan/155 Bank St #H954 (P 1022,1023) **212-243-6059**
Hall, Stephen/155 Ave of Americas 10th Fl........................212-255-6530
Hamann, Brad/330 Westminster Rd, Brooklyn.....................718-287-6086
Hamlin, Janet/478 Bergen St #3, Brooklyn........................718-492-4075
Hampton, Blake/25 W 45th St..212-398-9540
Hamrick, Chuck/420 Lexington Ave #PH 4,5.....................212-986-5680
Hanna, Gary/25 W 45th St (P 463) **212-398-9540**
Harmon, Traci/25 W 45th St (P 467) **212-398-9540**
Harrington, Glenn/165 E 32nd St (P 641)....................**212-686-3514**
Harris, Diane Teske/315 E 68th St #9F (P 698) **212-517-4919**
Harris, John/155 Ave of Americas 10th Fl (P 694) **212-255-6530**
Harrison, William/501 Fifth Ave #1407 (P 82,83,832) ..**212-490-2450**
Hart, John/494 State St, Brooklyn, (P 1028,1029) **718-852-6708**
Hart, Thomas/108 E 35th St #1C (P 130,131) **212-889-3337**
Hart, Veronika/60 E 42nd St #505......................................212-682-1490
Harvey, Ray/60 E 42nd St #1940..212-867-8092
Harwood, John/60 E 42nd St #505 (P 21) **212-682-1490**
Haselaar, Henk/280 Madison Ave #1402 (P 383) **212-545-9155**
Havilland, Brian/34 E 30th St..212- 481-4132
Haynes, Bryan/60 E 42nd St #505 (P 28) **212-682-1490**
Heath, R Mark/25 W 45th St...212-398-9540
Heindel, Robert/211 E 51st St #5F.....................................212-755-1365
Heiner, Joe & Kathy/41 Union Sq W (P 203) **212-929-5590**
Hejja, Attila/420 Lexington Ave #PH4,5 (P 180) **212-986-5680**
Hellard, Susan/267 Wycoff St, Brooklyn............................718-624-1906
Heller, Debbie/601 West End Ave #11B..............................212-580-0917
Helsop, Michael/232 Madison Ave #402 (P 336,337)..**212-889-8777**
Henderling, Lisa/232 Madison Ave #402 (P 334,335) ..**212-889-8777**
Hendenson, Dave/420 Lexington Ave (P 172).............**212-986-5680**
Henderson, Alan/31 Jane St #10B......................................212-243-0693
Henderson, Louis/6 E 36th St #1R (P 532) **212-685-4580**
Henderson, Meryl/19 E 48th St 3rd Fl................................212-838-0050
Henrie, Cary/310 E 46th St #5H (P 756,757) **212-986-0299**
Henriquez, Celeste/27 Bleecker St....................................212-673-1600
Henry, Paul/15 W 72nd St...212-799-2231
Hepke, Skip/211 E 51st St #5F (P 517) **212-755-1365**
Herbert, Jonathan/324 Pearl St #2G (P 829)..............**212-571-4444**
Herder, Edwin/60 E 42nd St #1940.....................................212-867-8092
Hering, Al/277 Washington Ave #3E, Brooklyn...................914-471-7326
Herman, Mark/853 Broadway #1201 (P 608) **212-677-9100**
Herman, Tim/853 Broadway...212-677-9100
Hernandez, Oscar/853 Broadway #1201 (P 604) **212-677-9100**
Hesse, Laura/566 Seventh Ave #603 (P 576) **212-221-8090**
Hickes, Andy/315 W 23rd St #3A.......................................212-989-9023
High, Richard/420 Lexington Ave #2760 (P 227) **212-697-8525**
Hill, Amy/111 Wooster St #PH C...212-925-0491
Himler, Ron/866 UN Plaza #525...212-644-2020
Hirashima, Jean/161 E 61st St #5C....................................212-593-9778
Hiroko/67-12 Yellowstone Blvd #E2, Forest Hills..............718-896-2712
Hobbs, Pamela/259 W 29th St #4W....................................212-947-0148
Hoff, Terry/420 Lexington Ave #2760 (P 222,223) **212-697-8525**
Hoffman, Ginnie/108 E 35th St #1.......................................212-889-3337
Hoffman, Martin/509 Madison Ave 10th Fl..........................212-355-0910
Hoffman, Rosekrans/866 UN Plaza #525 212-644-2020
Hofmekler, Ori/166 Second Ave #11K................................212-829-9838
Hogarth, Paul/81 Greene St...212-925-3053
Holland, Brad/96 Greene St...212-226-3675
Holm, John/353 W 53rd St #1W (P 415) **212-682-2462**
Holst, Joani/1814 Bay Ridge Pkwy, Brooklyn 718-236-6214
Holter, Susan/Goodman, Al/422 E 81st St 212-744-7870
Hom & Hom/425 W 23rd St #10F..212-242-6367
Honkanen, William/19 Stanton St #31.................................212-995-0751
Hooks, Mitchell/420 Lexington Ave (P 158) **212-986-5680**
Hoover, Duane/12 E 22nd St...212-797-2989
Hosner, William/853 Broadway (P 705) **212-677-9100**
Hostovich, Michael/127 W 82nd St #9A..............................212-580-2175
Howard, John/336 E 54th St...212-832-7980
Howell, Kathleen/866 UN Plaza #525.................................212-644-2020
Huang, Mei-ku/201 E 28th St...212-532-0928

Huber, Greg/853 Broadway #1201 (P 607) **212-677-9100**
Huerta, Catherine/337 W 20th St #4M.................................212-627-0031
Huffman, Tom/130 W 47th St #6A..212-755-3185
Hull, Cathy/165 E 66th St...212-772-7743
Human, Jane/155 Ave of Americas 10th Fl..........................212-255-6530
Hunt, Jim/853 Broadway...212-677-9100
Hunt, Robert/165 E 32nd St (P 639) **212-686-3514**
Hunt, Scott/41 Union Sq W #636 (P 437) **212-206-0066**
Hunter, Stan/509 Madison Ave 10th Fl................................212-355-0910
Hurd, Jane/501 Fifth Ave #1407 (P 96,97) **212-490-2450**
Hyden, Karen/49 Warren St 2nd Fl.....................................212-766-5064

I

Ibusuki, James/420 Lexington Ave #PH4,5 (P 185) **212-986-5680**
Ice, Monica/19 E 48th St...212-838-0050
Ilic, Mirko/95 Horatio St #526..212-645-8180
Illumination Studio/330 Haven Ave #4N.............................212-568-2848
Incandescent Ink Inc/111 Wooster St #PH C.....................212-925-0491
Incisa, Monica/300 E 40th St #7D.......................................212-986-5344
Inoue, Izumi/325 W 37th St 4F...212-643-9147
Iskowitz, Joel/420 Lexington Ave #2911.............................212-986-5680
Ivens, Rosalind/156 Prospect Park W #3L, Brooklyn 718-499-8285

J

Jaben, Seth Design/47 E 3rd St #3 (P 774,775).........**212-673-5631**
Jacobson/Fernandez/41 Union Sq W #636
(P 442,443) **212-206-0066**
Jaffee, Al/140 E 56th St #12H..212-371-5232
Jakesevic, Nenad/165 E 32nd St (P 636,637) **212-686-3514**
James, Bill/420 Lexington Ave #PH4,5................................212-986-5680
Jamieson, Doug/42-20 69th St, Woodside...........................718-565-6034
Janoff, Dean/514 W 24th St 3rd Fl......................................212-807-0816
Jarecka, Danuta/114 E 7th St #15 (P 826)..................**212-353-3298**
Jasper, Jackie/165 E 32nd St (P 638) **212-686-3514**
Jeffers, Kathy/151 W 19th St 3rd Fl (P 1043) **212-255-5196**
Jeffries, Shannon/494 State St, Brooklyn...........................718-643-1755
Jennis, Paul/420 Lexington Ave #2911................................212-986-5680
Jensen, Bruce/41-61 53rd St, Woodside, (P 1044) **718-898-1887**
Jessell, Tim/60 E 42nd St #505 (P 20) **212-682-1490**
Jetter, Frances/390 West End Ave 212-580-3720
Jewell, Philip/235 E 51st St #3A...212-758-1816
Jezierski, Chet/25 W 45th St..212-398-9540
Jinks, John/27 W 20th St (P 786,787) **212-675-2961**
Jirecke, Danusia/114 E 7th St #15.....................................212-691-1313
Jobe, Jody/875 W 181st St...212-795-4941
Johnson, David A/121 Madison Ave (P 246,247).........**212-683-1362**
Johnson, Doug/45 E 19th St...212-260-1880
Johnson, Joel Peter/333 E 49th St (P 594) **212-982-6533**
Johnson, Julie/155 E 38th St (P 650) **212-697-6170**
Johnson, Lonni Sue/11 Riverside Dr #3JW..........................212-873-7749
Johnson, Stephen/280 Madison Ave #1402 (P 1045) ..**212-545-9155**
Johnston Carlson, Susan/370 Lexington Ave #1002
(P 572) **212-953-2177**
Johnston, David McCall/509 Madison Ave 10th Fl..............212-355-0910
Jonason, Dave/215 Park Ave S #1300 (P 707,303) **212-674-8080**
Jones, Bob/270 Park Ave S #10B (P 541) **212-260-1453**
Jones, Randy/323 E 10th St..212-677-5387
Jones, Russell/199 Eighth Ave #C4, Brooklyn....................718-965-3224
Jones, Taylor/19 E 48th St 3rd Fl.......................................212-838-0050
Joung, Mia/60 E 42nd St #1940..212-867-8092
Joyce, Stephanie/425 Broome St #3M.................................212-431-1306
Julian, Claudia/301 W 45th St #7A, Brooklyn.....................718-891-7957
Just, Hal/155 E 38th St (P 651) **212-697-6170**
Justinen, Lars/420 Lexington Ave #2760.............................212-697-8525

K

Kagansky, Eugene/515 Ave I #2H, Brooklyn.......................718-253-0454
Kahn, Don/31 W 21st St 7th Fl Rear (P 520) **212-243-4412**
Kalish, Lionel/108 E 35th St #1C (P 132,133) **212-889-3337**
Kalle, Chris/866 UN Plaza #525..212-644-2020
Kaloustian, Rosanne/208-19 53rd Ave, Bayside.................718-428-4670
Kaneda, Shirley/34 W 56th St #4F......................................212-246-6335
Kanelous, George/130 Barrow St #316................................212-688-1080
Kaniliotis, Thanos/245 E 40th St #20C................................212-682-2554
Kann, Victoria/336 E 22nd St (P 1048) **212-979-0988**

Kantra, Michelle/26 W 97th St #4A 212-316-3176
Kaplan, Mark/156 Fifth Ave #617 212-243-1333
Kappes, Werner/134 W 26th St #903 212-242-6777
Karchin, Steve/55 W 92nd St #6G 212-689-6928
Karlin, Bernie/41 E 42nd St #PH 212-687-7636
Karlin, Eugene/3973 48th St, Sunnyside 714-472-4625
Karlin, Nurit/19 E 48th St 212-838-0050
Karm, Murray/120 E 86th St 212-289-9124
Katz, Les/451 Westminster Rd, Brooklyn..................... 718-284-4779
Kaufman, Mark/5123 Reeder St, Elmhurst, (P 577) **718-672-3257**
Kauftheil, Henry/220 W 19th St #1200 212-633-0222
Kazu/41 Union Sq W #918 (P 626,627) **212-807-6627**
Keleny, Earl/515 Madison Ave 22nd Fl 212-486-9644
Kelley, Barbara/280 Madison Ave #1402 (P 389) **212-545-9155**
Kelley, Gary/121 Madison Ave (P 254,255) **212-683-1362**
Kelley, Mark/866 UN Plaza #525 212-644-2020
Kelly, Kevin/601 E 11th St #3B 212-505-2711
Kendrick, Dennis/99 Bank St #3G 212-924-3085
Kernan, Patrick/413 W 48th St 212-924-7800
Keyes, Steven/566 Seventh Ave #603 212-221-8090
Kibbee, Gordon/6 Jane St 212-989-7074
Kiefer, Alfons/420 Lexington Ave #PH4,5 (P 164) **212-986-5680**
Kieffer, Christa/866 UN Plaza #525 (P 678) **212-644-2020**
Kimura, Hiro/60 E 42nd St (P 23) **212-682-1490**
King, J D/158 Sixth Ave, Brooklyn 718-636-0768
Kirk, Daniel/60 E 42nd St (P 22) **212-682-1490**
Kirkland, James Ennis/131 Spring St 3rd Fl (P 655) **212-925-4340**
Kitchens, Christie/131 Spring St 3rd Fl (P 655) **212-925-4340**
Kiwak, Barbara/25 W 45th St (P 466) **212-398-9540**
Klavins, Uldis/60 E 42nd St #1940 212-867-8092
Klein, David/156 Fifth Ave #617 (P 659) **212-243-1333**
Klein, David G/408 Seventh St, Brooklyn 718-788-1818
Klein, Hedy/111-56 76th Dr #B3, Forest Hills 718-793-0246
Klein, Renee/164 Daniel Low Terr, Staten Island 718-727-0723
Klein/Allen Studio/164 Daniel Low Terr, Staten Island 718-727-0723
Kletsky, Olga/63-89 Saunders St #5G, Rego Park 718-897-1771
Kluglein, Karen/ (P 696) **212-684-2974**
Knafo, Hai/370 Union St, Brooklyn 212-416-2469
Knettell, Sharon/108 E 35th St #1 212-889-3337
Kodama, Hideaki/501 Fifth Ave #1407 212-490-2450
Koester, Michael/270 Park Ave S #10B (P 541) **212-260-4153**
Kojoyian, Armen/52 Clark St #5K, Brooklyn 718-797-5179
Kondo, Vala/230 W 79th St #52 212-517-4052
Kondo, Yukio/201 E 28th St 212-532-0928
Koren, Edward/81 Greene St 212-925-3053
Kovalcik, Terry/124 W 18th St 5th Fl (P 1054) **212-620-7772**
Krafchek, Ken/131 Spring St 3rd Fl (P 657) **212-925-4340**
Kramer, Peter/60 E 42nd St #505 (P 15) **212-682-1490**
Krauter, George/89 Fifth Ave 212-924-3432
Krepel, Dick/211 E 51st St #5F (P 518) **212-755-1365**
Kretschmann, Karin/323 W 75th St #1A 212-724-5001
Kronen, Jeff/231 Thompson St #22 212-475-3166
Kubinyi, Laszlo/108 E 35th St #1C (P 152) **212-889-3337**
Kuchera, Kathleen/25 Prince St #5 212-873-8518
Kuester, Bob/353 W 53rd St #1W 212-682-2462
Kuhn, Grant/233 Bergen St, Brooklyn 718-596-7808
Kukalis, Romas/420 Lexington Ave #2911 212-986-5680
Kung, Lingta/420 Lexington Ave #2760 (P 236) **212-697-8525**
Kunstler, Mort/509 Madison Ave 10th Fl 212-355-0910
Kuper, Peter/250 W 99th St #9C 212-864-5729
Kurman, Miriam/422 Amsterdam #2A 212-580-1649
Kursar, Ray/1 Lincoln Plaza #43R 212-873-5605
Kurtzman, Edward/60 E 42nd St #411 212-953-7088
Kurtzman, Harvey/566 Seventh Ave #603 212-221-8090

L

Lacey, Lucille/87-25 86th St, Woodhaven 718-805-2215
Lackner, Paul/19 E 48th St (P 357) **212-838-0050**
Ladas, George/157 Prince St 212-673-2208
LaFrance, Laurie/41 Union Sq W #636 (P 441) **212-206-0066**
Lahaye, Barney/611 Broadway #610 212-505-6802
Laird, Campbell/162 E 23rd St #3B 212-505-5552
Lakeman, Steven/115 W 85th St 212-877-8888
Lamut, Sonja /165 E 32nd St (P 636,637) **212-686-3514**
Landis, Joan/6 Jane St 212-989-7074
Lang, Gary/420 Lexington Ave #2738 212-697-8525
Langenstein, Michael/56 Thomas St 2nd Fl 212-964-9637

LaPadula, Tom/201 E 28th St 212-532-0928
Lapinski, Joe/853 Broadway #1201 212-677-9100
Laporte, Michele/579 Tenth St, Brooklyn 718-499-2178
Lardy, Philippe/478 W Broadway #5A 212-473-3057
Larrain, Sally Marshall/19 E 48th St 3rd Fl 212-838-0050
Larson, Miriam/410 Riverside Dr #92 212-713-5765
Lasher, Mary Ann/60 E 42nd St #505 (P 47) **212-682-1490**
Laslo, Larry/179 E 71st St 212-737-2340
Laslo, Rudy/270 Park Ave S #10B (P 539) **212-260-4153**
Lau, Rikki/60 E 12th St #6D 212-674-5971
Lauter, Richard/381 Park Ave S #919 212-889-2400
Lavigne, Dan/566 Seventh Ave #603 212-221-8090
Law, Polly/305-A President St, Brooklyn 718-875-4425
Le-Tan, Pierre/81 Greene St (P 567) **212-925-3053**
Leder, Dora/866 UN Plaza #525 212-644-2020
Ledwidge, Natacha/267 Wycoff St, Brooklyn 718-624-1906
Lee, Bill/792 Columbus Ave #1-O 212-866-5664
Lee, Eric J W/60 E 42nd St #1146 (P 499) **212-953-7088**
Lee, Jody A/175 Ninth Ave 212-741-5192
Leech, Dorothy/1024 Ave of Amer 4th Fl 212-354-6641
Leedy, Jeff/41 Union Sq W #636 212-206-0066
Leer, Rebecca J/560 W 43rd St #11K (P 1058) **212-563-4980**
Lehr, Paul/509 Madison Ave 10th Fl 212-355-0910
Leiner, Alan/353 W 53rd St #1W 212-682-2462
Lennard, Elizabeth/111 Wooster St #PH C 212-925-0491
Leon, Karen/154-01 Barclay Ave, Flushing 718-461-2050
Leonard, Richard/212 W 17th St #2B 212-243-6613
Leonard, Tom/866 UN Plaza #525 212-644-2020
Lesser, Ron/420 Lexington Ave #2760 212-697-8525
Levin, Arnie/342 Madison Ave #469 212-719-9879
Levine, Andy/22-30 24th St, L I City, (P 1063) **718-956-8539**
Levine, Bette/60 E 42nd St #505 (P 49) **212-682-1490**
Levy, Franck/305 E 40th St #5Y 212-557-8256
Lewin, Ted/152 Willoughby Ave, Brooklyn 718-622-3882
Lewis, H. B./PO Box 1177 Old Chelsea Station
(P 1064,1065) **212-572-7771**
Lewis, Tim/184 St Johns Pl, Brooklyn 718-857-3406
Lexa, Susan/866 UN Plaza #525 212-644-2020
Liao, Sharmen/108 E 35th St #1C (P 153) **212-889-3337**
Liberatore, Gaetano/43 E 19th St 212-254-4996
Lieberman, Ron/109 W 28th St 212-947-0653
Liepke, Skip/211 E 51st St #5F 212-755-1365
Ligresti, Roberto/104 E 40th St #307 212-697-0650
Lilly, Charles/24-01 89th St, E Elmhurst 718-803-3442
Lindberg, Jeffrey/449 50th St, Brooklyn 718-492-1114
Lindeman, Nicky/548 Hudson St 212-645-8180
Lindgren, Goran/19 E 48th St 3rd Fl 212-838-0050
Lindlof, Ed/353 W 53rd St #1W 212-682-2462
Lindquist, Mark/1762 First Ave 212-534-3899
Line, Lemuel/509 Madison Ave 10th Fl 212-355-0910
Lionsgate/33 E 49th St #3J 212-980-8061
Lippman, Peter/410 Riverside Dr #134 212-865-1823
Lipstein, Morissa/19 E 48th St 212-838-0050
Little Apple Art/409 Sixth Ave, Brooklyn 718-499-7045
Littrell, Kandy/2 W 47th St 212-869-1630
Livingston, Francis/420 Lexington Ave #2760
(P 212,213) **212-697-8525**
Lloyd, Peter/566 Seventh Ave #603 212-221-8090
Lockwood, Todd/60 E 42nd St #505 (P 19) **212-682-1490**
Lodigensky, Ted/566 Seventh Ave #603 212-221-8090
Loew, David/232 Madison Ave #402 (P 338,339) **212-889-8777**
Lofaro, Gerald/353 W 53rd St (P 412,413) **212-682-2462**
LoGrippo, Robert/509 Madison Ave 10th Fl 212-355-0910
Lohstoeter, Lori, 41 Union Sq W (P 200, 201) **212-929-5590**
Lonsdale, Ashley/420 Lexington Ave #PH4,5 (P 162) **212-986-5680**
Lorenz, Lee/108 E 35th St #1C (P 0154) **212-889-3337**
Lovitt, Anita/308 E 78th St 212-628-8171
Lozner, Ruth/131 Spring St 3rd Fl (P 657) **212-925-4340**
Luce, Ben/5 E 17th St 6th Fl (P 634) **212-255-8193**
Ludlow, Roberta/111 Wooster St #PH C 212-925-0491
Ludtke, Jim/280 Park Ave S #18C 212-677-1988
Lui, David/66 Crosby St #5D (P 427) **212-941-7313**
Lulevitch, Tom/101 W 69th St #4D 212-362-3318
Lustig, Loretta/19 E 48th St 3rd Fl 212-838-0050
Lyall, Dennis/270 Park Ave S #10B (P 540) **212-260-4153**
Lynch, Jeffrey/420 Lexington Ave #PH4,5 212-986-5680

M

MacCombie, Turi/201 E 28th St 212-532-0928
MacDonald, Ross/27 1/2 Morton St #20..............212-727-8067
MacLeod, Lee/60 E 42nd St #505 (P 32) **212-682-1490**
Madden, Don/866 UN Plaza #525 212-644-2020
Maddox, Kelly/420 Lexington Ave (P 228, 229) **212-697-8525**
Madrid, Carlos/502 W 55th St #5W (P 820) **212-541-5797**
Magdich, Dennis/420 Lexington Ave #2760 212-697-8525
Magnuson, Diana/461 Park Ave S 212-696-4680
Maguire, Bob/60 E 42nd St #1940 212-867-8092
Magurn, Susan/866 UN Plaza #525 212-644-2020
Mahon, Rich/566 Seventh Ave #603 212-221-8090
Mahoney, Ron/353 W 53rd St #1W (P 420) **212-682-2462**
Maisner, Bernard/211 Thompson St (P 857) **212-475-5911**
Malonis, Tina/32-11 31st Ave #1, Astoria 718-956-7924
Manchess, Greg/121 Madison Ave (P 252,253) **212-683-1362**
Mangal/155 E 38th St 212-697-6170
Mangiat, Jeffrey/420 Lexington Ave #PH4,5 (P 167) **212-986-5680**
Mannes, Don/325 E 77th St #5D (P 1070) **212-288-1661**
Manning, Michele/420 Lexington Ave #2760 (P 216,217) **212-697-8525**
Mantel, Richard/41 Union Sq W (P 191) **212-929-5590**
Manyum, Wallop/37-40 60th St, Woodside 718-476-1478
Marchetti, Lou/420 Lexington Ave #PH 4,5 212-986-5680
Marciuliano, Frank/420 Lexington Ave #2760 212-697-8525
Marden, Phil/28 E 21st St #2B (P 828) **212-260-7646**
Mardon, Allan/108 E 35th St #1C (P 155) **212-889-3337**
Margulies, Robert/561 Broadway #10B 212-219-9621
Marich, Felix/853 Broadway 212-677-9100
Marridejos, Fernando/130 W 67th St #1B 212-724-7339
Martin, Gary/1264 Lexington Ave 212-749-3911
Martin, Greg J/60 E 42nd St #505 (P 42) **212-682-1490**
Martin, John/501 Fifth Ave #1407 (P 78, 79) **212-490-2450**
Martinez, Edward/420 Lexington Ave #PH4,5 (P 157) **212-986-5680**
Martinez, John/280 Madison Ave #1402 (P 379) **212-545-9155**
Martinez, Sergio/43 E 19th St 212-254-4996
Martinot, Claude/145 Second Ave #20 212-473-3137
Marvin, Fred/43 E 19th St 212-254-4996
Maryles, Helen/43 W 16th St #1B 212-727-1092
Marziali, Sandra/140 West End Ave #9H 212-874-7074
Masi, George/111 Wooster St #PH C 212-925-0491
Mason, Tod/19 E 48th St 3rd Fl 212-838-0050
Masuda, Coco/541 Hudson St #2 (P 782) **212-727-1599**
Masuda/Salerno/541 Hudson St #2 (P 782,783) **212-727-1599**
Matcho, Mark/352 E 8th St #3 212-529-1318
Mathieu, Joseph/81 Greene St 212-925-3053
Mattelson, Marvin/ (P 697) **212-684-2974**
Matthews, Lu/280 Madison Ave #1402 (P 380) **212-545-9155**
Maughan, Bill/420 Lexington Ave #PH4,5 (P 177) **212-986-5680**
Maxwell, Brookie/53 Irving Pl 212-475-6909
May, Darcy/201 E 28th St 212-532-0928
Mayforth, Hal/108 E 35th St #1C (P 134,135) **212-889-3337**
Mazzella, Mary Jo/541 Edison Ave, Bronx 212-862-3560
Mazzetti, Alan/420 Lexington Ave #2760 (P 218) **212-697-8525**
McArthur, Dennis/170-44 130th Ave #8D, Jamaica 718-987-3946
McCaffery, Peter/27 Bleecker St 212-673-1600
McCall, John/85 Eastern Parkway #1A, Brooklyn 212-757-1535
McClintock, Wendell/60 E 42nd St #1146 3(P 500) **212-953-7088**
McCollum, Rick/232 Madison Ave #402 (P 340,341) **212-889-8777**
McConnell, Gerald/10 E 23rd St 212-505-0950
McCormack, Geoffrey/420 Lexington Ave #PH4,5 (P 168) **212-986-5680**
McCreanor, Mike/323 E 88th St 212-427-3595
McCreary, Jane/866 UN Plaza #525 212-644-2020
McCutheon, Kathleen/261 W 19th St 212-989-3954
McDaniel, Jerry/155 E 38th St (P 650) **212-697-6170**
McDonald, Ross/27-1/2 Morton St #20 212-727-8067
McEntire, Larry/515 Madison Ave 22nd Fl 212-486-9644
McGovern, Michael/420 Lexington Ave #PH4,5 (P 170) **212-986-5680**
McGovern, Preston/157 E 3rd St 212-982-8595
McGurl, Michael/83 Eighth Ave #2B, Brooklyn 718-857-1866
McKeating, Eileen/340 W 11th St #2ER 212-627-7715
McKenzie, Crystal/30 E 20th St #502 212-598-4567
McLain, Julia/111 Wooster St #PH C (P 428) **212-925-0491**
McLaughlin, Gary/420 Lexington Ave #2760 212-697-8525

McLean, Wilson/902 Broadway #1603 212-752-8490
McLoughlin, Wayne/501 Fifth Ave #1407 (P 87,861) **212-490-2450**
McMacken, David B/60 E 42nd St #505 (P 45) **212-682-1490**
McMullan, James/222 Park Ave S #10B 212-473-5083
McPheeters, Neal/16 W 71st St 212-799-7021
Mead, Kimble Pendleton/125 Prospect Park West, Brooklyn 718-768-3632
Mehlman, Elwyn/108 E 35th St #1C 212-889-3337
Meisel, Ann/420 Lexington Ave #PH4,5 212-986-5680
Meisler, Meryl/553 8th St, Brooklyn 718-768-3991
Melendez, Robert/566 Seventh Ave #603 212-221-8090
Merrell, Patrick/124 W 18th St 5th Fl (P 1082,1083) **212-620-7777**
Messi, Enzo & Schmidt, Urs/41 Union Sq W #636 (P 434) **212-206-0066**
Meyerowitz, Rick/68 Jane St 212-989-2446
Michaels, Bob/267 Fifth Ave #402 212-532-0916
Michal, Marie/108 E 35th St #1 212-889-3337
Michel, Jean-Claude/353 W 53rd St #1W (P 417) **212-682-2462**
Michner, Ted/420 Lexington Ave #PH 4,5 212-986-5680
Midda, Sara/81 Greene St 212-925-3053
Middendorf, Frances/337 E 22nd St #2 212-473-3586
Mikos, Mike/420 Lexington Ave #PH4,5 (P 174) **212-986-5680**
Milbourn, Patrick/327 W 22nd St #3 212-989-4594
Milgrim, David/8 Grammercy Park S #2G (P 1084) **212-673-1432**
Miliano, Ed/248 West 88th #23-B (P 1085) **212-254-4996**
Miller, A J/25 W 45th St 212-398-9540
Miller, Cliff/60 E 42nd St #1940 212-867-8092
Miller, Douglas/36-34 30th St, Long Island City 212-529-4990
Miller, Elizabeth/303 W 91st St 212-877-3548
Mills, Elise/150 E 79th St #3 212-794-2042
Minor, Wendell/277 W 4th St 212-691-6925
Miro/60 E 42nd St #1940 212-867-8092
Mitchell, Celia/2229 19th St, Long Island City, (P 1086) **718-626-4095**
Mitchell, Judith/270 Riverside Dr #1D 212-666-5143
Mitsuhashi, Yoko/27 E 20th St Grnd Fl (P 1087) **212-979-1266**
Mitzura/60 E 42nd St #1940 212-867-8092
Moline-Kramer, Bobbie/111 Wooster St #PH C (P 426) **212-925-0491**
Monahan, Leo/853 Broadway #1201 (P 604) **212-677-9100**
Mones-Mateu/43 E 19th St 212-254-4996
Montesano, Sam/60 E 42nd St #1940 212-867-8092
Montgomery, Marilyn/280 Madison Ave #1402 212-545-9155
Monti, Jean Restivo/232 Madison Ave #402 (P 342,343) **212-889-8777**
Montiel, David/115 W 16th St #211 212-929-3659
Moonlight Press Studio/362 Cromwell Ave, Staten Island, (P 1088,1089) **718-979-9695**
Moore, Christian/60 E 42nd St (P 16) **212-682-1490**
Moore, Cyd/280 Madison Ave #1402 212-545-9155
Moore, Marlene/400 E 77th St #7A 212-288-3718
Moores, Jeff/32 W 40th St #9B (P 688,689) **212-819-9084**
Moorhead, Meg Ann/205 E 77th St (P 1090) **212-628-4285**
Moraes, Greg/60 E 42nd St #428 212-867-8092
Morenko, Michael/255 W 10th St #5FS 212-627-5920
Morgan, Jacqui/692 Greenwich St (P 778,779) **212-463-8488**
Moritsugu, Alison/504 W 111th St #62 212-316-5315
Morris, Frank/23 Bethune St #2 212-989-2598
Morrison, Don/155 E 38th St (P 651) **212-697-6170**
Moscarillo, Mark/800 A Church St, Bohemia 516-563-8114
Moss, Geoffrey/315 E 68th St (P 699) **212-517-4919**
Mossey, Belinda/526 2nd St, Brooklyn 718-499-2588
Moyers, David/131 Spring St 3rd Fl (P 656) **212-925-4340**
MS Design/27 W 20th St #1005 212-242-6525
Mueller, Pete/60 E 42nd St #505 (P 44) **212-682-1490**
Mulligan, Donald/418 Central Pk W #81 (P 1091) **212-666-6079**
Munck, Paula/58 W 15th St 6th Fl (P 52,53) **212-741-2539**
Munson, Don/235 W 76th St #9E 212-572-2251
Murawski, Alex/108 E 35th St #1C (P 136,137) **212-889-3337**
Murdocca, Sal/19 E 48th St 3rd Fl 212-838-0050
Murphy, Chris/156 Fifth Ave #617 212-243-1333
Myers, David/228 Bleecker St #8 212-989-5260
Myers, Lou/108 E 35th St #1C 212-889-3337
Mynott, Lawrence/267 Wyckoff St, Brooklyn 718-624-1906

N

Nacht, Merle/58 W 15th St 6th Fl (P 70,71) **212-741-2539**
Nagaoka, Shusei/15 W 72nd St 212-799-2231

Nagata, Mark/60 E 42nd St #1146 (P 498) **212-953-7088**
Nahas, Margo Z/41 Union Sq W #1228 212-929-5590
Nahigian, Alan/33-08 31st Ave #2R, Long Island City 718-274-4042
Najaka, Marlies Merk/108 E 35th St #1C (P 138,139) .. **212-889-3337**
Nakai, Michael/218 Madison Ave #5R..........................212-213-5333
Narashima, Tomo/1160 Third Ave #9K.........................212-988-3828
Nascimbene, Yan/41 Union Sq W #1228 (P 190) **212-929-5590**
Nazz, James/42 Stuyvesant St.................................212-228-9713
Needham, James/19 E 48th St.................................212-838-0050
Neff, Leland/506 Amsterdam Ave #61..........................212-724-1884
Nelson, Bill/121 Madison Ave (P 240,241) **212-683-1362**
Nelson, Craig/60 E 42nd St #505 (P 41) **212-682-1490**
Nelson, John/280 Madison Ave #1402..........................212-545-9155
Nelson, John Illus/101 N 3rd St, Brooklyn....................718-387-5168
Nelson, Lori/860 W 181st St #41A.............................212-795-4281
Nelson, R Kenton/215 Park Ave S #1300 (P 707,621) .. **212-674-8080**
Nessim, Barbara/63 Greene St.................................212-219-1111
Neubecker, Robert/333 E 49th St (P 598,599) **212-982-6533**
Neuwirth, Alan/310 E 75th St..................................212-879-8162
Neuworth, Pauline/230 Fifth Ave #2000........................212-686-3383
Newton, Richard/501 Fifth Ave #1407 (P 84,85) **212-490-2450**
Neyman-Levikova, Marina/155 E 38th St.......................212-697-6170
Ng, Michael/58-35 155th St, Flushing, NY.....................718-461-8264
Nicastre, Michael/420 Lexington Ave #2738....................212-697-8525
Nicholas, Jess/566 Seventh Ave #603..........................212-221-8090
Nicklaus, Carol/866 UN Plaza #525............................212-644-2020
Nicotra, Rosanne/420 Lexington Ave #2738.....................212-697-8525
Niklewicz, Adam/333 E 49th St (P 595) **212-982-6533**
Nishi/215 Park Ave S #1300 (P 713) **212-674-8080**
Nishinaka, Jeff/60 E 42nd St #505 (P 38) **212-682-1490**
Noftsinger, Pamela/600 W 111th St #6A.........................212-316-4241
Noome, Michael/420 Lexington Ave/Penthouse 212-986-5680
Noonan, Julia/873 President St, Brooklyn (P 520) **718-622-9268**
North, Jan Coffman/25 W 45th St...............................212-398-9540
North, Russ/5 Grammercy Park W................................212-228-8639
Notarile, Chris/420 Lexington Ave #PH4,5 (P 165) **212-986-5680**
Novak, Justin/156 Fifth Ave #617.............................212-243-1333

O

O'Brien, Kathy/41 Union Sq W (P 202) **212-929-5590**
O'Brien, Tim/60 E 42nd St #1146 (P 496,497) **212-953-7088**
O'Connell, Mitch/200 W 15th St (P 456) **212-243-4209**
O'Leary, Danny/342 E 65th St #5RW.............................212-628-5322
O'Shaughnessy, Michael/267 Wyckoff St, Brooklyn 718-624-1906
Oberheide, Heide/295 Washington Ave #5B, Brooklyn 718-622-7056
Ochagavia, Carlos/509 Madison Ave 10th Fl.....................212-355-0910
Ockenfels III, Frank/245 E 30th St............................212-683-1304
Odom, Mel/252 W 76th St #B1...................................212-724-9320
Oelbaum, Fran/196 W 10th St #2A...............................212-691-3422
Okuyan, Selime/69-01 Northern Blvd #2L, Woodside 718-476-1457
Olanoff, Greg/60 E 42nd St #1940..............................212-867-8092
Olbinski, Rafal/425 W 23rd St #10F (P 670,671) **212-242-6367**
Olbinski, Tomek/531 E 81st St #1C (P 494) **212-861-9892**
Oldroyd, Mark/155 Ave of Americas 10th Fl (P 693) **212-255-6530**
Olitsky, Eve/235 W 102nd St #12K.............................212-678-1045
Olson, Erik/516 9th St, Brooklyn, (P 1097) **718-965-0914**
Olson, Richard A/85 Grand St.................................212-925-1820
Orit Design/27 W 24th St 10th Fl.............................212-727-1140
Orita, Vilma/201 Ocean Pkwy #3A, Brooklyn....................718-851-5758
Ortega, Jose/524 E 82nd St #3 (P 841) **212-772-3329**
Ortiz, Jose Luis/66 W 77th St................................212-877-3081
Osaka, Rick/14-22 30th Dr, Long Island City..................718-956-0015
Otnes, Fred/211 E 51st St #5F (P 516) **212-755-1365**
Otsuka, Ken/6 E 36th St #1R (P 534) **212-685-4580**
Ovies, Joe/853 Broadway #1201 (P 607) **212-677-9100**
Owens, Jim/25 W 45th St (P 460) **212-398-9540**
Oz, Robin/866 UN Plaza #525..................................212-644-2020

PQ

Palombo, Lisa/270 Park Ave S #10B (P 540) **212-260-4153**
Pantuso, Mike/350 E 89th St..................................212-534-3511
Paragraphics/427 3rd St, Brooklyn............................718-965-2231
Paraskevas, Michael/41 Union Sq W #1228
(P 188,189) **212-929-5590**
Pardy, Cindy/200 W 15th St (P 454) **212-243-4209**
Parisi, Richard/25 W 45th St (P 461) **212-398-9540**

Parker, Edward/58 W 15th St 6th Fl...........................212-741-2539
Parker, Robert Andrew/81 Greene St...........................212-925-3053
Parry, Ivor/280 Madison Ave..................................212-779-1554
Parsons, John/420 Lexington Ave #2760........................212-697-8525
Parton, Steve/368 Broadway #302..............................212-766-2285
Passarelli, Charles/353 W 53rd St #1W........................212-682-2462
Pasternak, Robert/114 W 27th St #55..........................212-675-0002
Paterson, Diane/866 UN Plaza #525............................212-644-2020
Patrick, Pamela/333 E 49th St (P 603) **212-982-6533**
Patti, Joyce/194 Third Ave (P 111) **212-475-0440**
Pavlov, Elana/377 W 11th #1F.................................212-243-0939
Payne, C F/121 Madison Ave (P 248,249) **212-683-1362**
Payne, Liane/155 Ave of Americas 10th Fl (P 693) **212-255-6530**
Payne, Thomas/31 W 21st St 7th Fl Rear (P 520) **212-243-4412**
Peak, Matt/60 E 42nd St #1940................................212-867-8092
Peak, Robert/14 E 52nd St (P 501) **212-752-8490**
Peale, Charles/19 E 48th St..................................212-838-0050
Pearlray Illustration/430 Dongan Hills Ave,
Staten Island, (P 1102) **718-351-3071**
Pearson, Jim/866 UN Plaza #525...............................212-644-2020
Pechanec, Vladimir/34-43 Crescent St #4C, Long Island City 718-729-3973
Pedersen, Judy/280 Madison Ave #1402 (P 382) **212-545-9155**
Peele, Lynwood/344 W 88th St.................................212-799-3305
Pelaez, Joan/43 E 19th St....................................212-254-4996
Pelavin, Daniel/80 Varrick St (P 1104,1105) **212-941-7418**
Pelikan, Judy/200 E 78th St..................................212-570-9069
Penalva, Jordi/43 E 19th St..................................212-254-4996
Pendleton, Roy/215 Park Ave S #1300 (P 709) **212-674-8080**
Penelope/420 Lexington Ave #2738.............................212-679-8525
Peralta, Gina/39-33 57th St #2D, Woodside....................718-565-0919
Percivalle, Rosanne/430 W 14th St #413 (P 845) **212-633-2480**
Perez, Maria/236 W 27th St 10th Fl...........................212-807-8730
Perez, Vince/43 E 19th St....................................212-254-4996
Perini, Ben/333 E 49th St #3J................................212-980-8061
Perlow, Paul/123 E 54th St #6E (P 872) **212-758-4358**
Personality Inc/501 Fifth Ave #1407 (P 112) **212-490-2450**
Petan, Greg J/60 E 42nd St #505 (P 40) **212-682-1490**
Peters, Bob/108 E 35th St #1C (P 156) **212-889-3337**
Peterson, Cheryl/81 Greene St................................212-925-3053
Peterson, Robin/411 West End Ave.............................212-724-3479
Petragnani, Vincent/853 Broadway #1201 212-677-9100
Petruccio, Steven/201 E 28th St..............................212-532-0928
Pettingill, Ondre/2 Ellwood St #3U...........................212-942-1993
Phillips, Barry/232 Madison Ave #402.........................212-889-8977
Phillips, Laura/60 E 42nd St #505 (P 26) **212-682-1490**
Pifko, Sigmund/108 E 35th St #1C (P 140,141) **212-889-3337**
Piglia, Paola/28 Cliff St #3.................................212-393-9207
Pincus, Harry/160 Sixth Ave @ 210 Spring St.................212-925-8071
Pinkney, J Brian/866 UN Plaza #525...........................212-644-2020
Pinkney, Jerry/108 E 35th St #1C.............................212-889-3337
Pirman, John/57 W 28th St....................................212-679-2866
Pisano, Al/22 W 38th St (P 1107) **212-730-7666**
Pizzo, Valerie/425 W 57th St #3K.............................212-333-5402
Platinum Design/14 W 23rd St 2nd Fl..........................212-366-4000
Podwill, Jerry/108 W 14th St.................................212-255-9464
Pogue, Deborah Bazzel/31 W 21st St 7th Fl....................212-243-4412
Poladian, Elena/25 W 45th St.................................212-398-9540
Poladian, Girair/25 W 45th St................................212-398-9540
Polengi, Evan/159 25th St, Brooklyn..........................718-499-3214
Polishook, Emily/34-50 28th St #5B, Astoria..................212-705-3473
Pollack, Scott/333 E 49th St (P 600,601) **212-982-6533**
Popp, Wendy/231 W 25th St #6E................................212-807-0840
Porter, Frederick/156 Fifth Ave #617.........................212-243-1333
Powers, Tom/156 Fifth Ave #617 (P 658) **212-243-1333**
Prato, Rodica/111 Wooster St #PH C (P 1111) **212-925-0491**
Pratt, Russell E/150 E 35th St #440..........................212-685-7955
Pritchett, Karen/280 Madison Ave #1402 (P 390) **212-545-9155**
Przewodek, Camille/108 E 35th St #1C (P 142,143) **212-889-3337**
Puente, Lyle/324 E 5th St, Brooklyn..........................718-436-4447
Punin, Nikolai/280 Madison Ave #1402 (P 386) **212-545-9155**
Purdom, Bill/780 Madison Ave/Box 6...........................212-988-4566
Pyk, Jan/19 E 48th St 3rd Fl.................................212-838-0050
Pyle, Charles S/41 Union Sq W (P 207) **212-929-5590**
Quartuccio, Dom/410 W 24th St #9M............................212-727-7329
Quon, Mike Design Office/568 Broadway #703
(P 1112,1113) **212-226-6024**

R

RadenStudio/420 Lexington Ave #PH4,5
(P 171,1114,1115) **212-986-5680**
Radigan, Bob/280 Madison Ave #1402 212-545-9155
Raglin, Tim/41 Union Sq W (P 210,211) **212-929-5590**
Ranaldi, Donald/280 Madison Ave #1402 212-545-9155
Randazzo, Tony/353 W 53rd St #1W (P 421) **212-682-2462**
Rane, Walter/60 E 42nd St #1940 212-867-8092
Ransome, James/866 UN Plaza #525 (P 678) **212-644-2020**
Reay, Richard/515 W 236th St, Bronx 212-884-2317
Rebelo, Tanya/156 Fifth Ave #617 (P 658) **212-243-1333**
Reed, Herb/156 Fifth Ave #617 212-243-1333
Reim, Melanie/214 Riverside Dr #601 212-749-0177
Reingold, Alan/155 E 38th St (P 650,651) **212-697-6170**
Renfro, Ed/250 E 83rd St #4E 212-879-3823
Reynolds, Gene/71 Thompson St 212-431-3072
Reynolds, Scott/308 W 30th St #9B 212-629-5610
Rice, John/156 Fifth Ave #617 (P 658) **212-243-1333**
Richards, Kenn/420 Lexington Ave (P 225) **212-929-5590**
Richards, Linda/27 Bleecker St 212-673-1600
Richardson, Ruth/5 Ludlow St 212-219-2056
Rickerd, Dave/50 W 23rd St 5th fl (P 866) **212-627-4111**
Rider, Mike/60 E 42nd St #505 212-682-1490
Ridgeway, Ronald/330 W 42nd St #3200 NE 212-966-9696
Rigle, Mitch/41 Union Sq W #918 (P 632) **212-807-6627**
Rigo, Martin/43 E 19th St 212-254-4996
Risko, Robert/201 W 11th St #2C 212-989-6987
Rivers, Ruth/267 Wycoff St, Brooklyn 718-624-1906
Rixford, Ellen/308 W 97th St 212-865-5686
Roberts, Peggi/60 E 42nd St #505 212-682-1490
Roberts, Phil/420 Lexington Ave #PH4,5 212-986-5680
Robinson, Charles/866 UN Plaza #525 212-644-2020
Robinson, Lenor/201 E 69th St #6E 212-734-0944
Rochon, Joanne/21 Prince St #2 212-334-9120
Rodell, Don/60 E 42nd St #1940 212-867-8092
Rodriguez, Robert/501 Fifth Ave #1407 (P 72,73) ... **212-490-2450**
Rogers, Lilla/280 Madison Ave #1402 (P 381) **212-545-9155**
Rohr, Dixon/430 W 34th St #5E 212-268-6907
Roman, Barbara/345 W 88th St #5B (P 837) **212-362-1374**
Romer, Dan/125 Prospect Park W, Brooklyn 718-768-3632
Romero, Javier/9 W 19th St 5th Fl
(Inside Front Flap/Book 2) **212-727-9445**
Root, Barry/58 W 15th St 212-741-2589
Rosato, John/420 Lexington Ave PH 212-986-5680
Rose, Anne/276 Church St 212-334-0380
Rose, Bob/873 Broadway (P 1119) **212-982-9535**
Rosebush, Judson/154 W 57th St #826 212-398-6600
Rosen, Terry/101 W 81st St #508 212-580-4784
Rosenfeld, Mort/420 Lexington Ave #2911 212-986-5680
Rosenwald, Laurie/11 W 30th St 212-967-1229
Rosner, Meryl/25 W 45th St (P 464) **212-398-9540**
Ross Culbert Lavery Russman/15 W 20th St 9th Fl 212-206-0044
Ross, Bronwen/866 UN Plaza #525 212-644-2020
Ross, Ian/37 E 28th St #2A (P 570) **212-696-4120**
Ross, Richard/80 Eighth Ave #303 212-242-3900
Rother, Sue/420 Lexington Ave #2760 (P 215) ... **212-697-8525**
Roundtree, Deborah/108 E 35th St (P 114,115) .. **212-889-3337**
Roy, Joanna/25 W 45th St 212-398-9540
Rozenberg, Marcel/232 Madison Ave #402 212-889-7777
Rudnak, Theo/501 Fifth Ave #1407 (P 91,853) ... **212-490-2450**
Ruegger, Rebecca/333 E 49th St (P 602) **212-982-6533**
Ruffins, Reynold/15 W 20th St 9th Fl 212-627-5220
Ruiz, Artie/43 E 19th St 212-254-4996
Rundo, Ron/60 E 42nd St #1940 212-867-8092
Russell, Bill/227 W 29th St 9th Fl 212-967-6443
Ryan, Terry/130 Barrow St #316 212-688-1080

S

Sabanosh, Michael/433 W 34th St #18B
(P 1122,1123) **212-947-8161**
Sabin, Robert/60 E 42nd St #1940 212-867-8092
Saksa Art & Design/41 Union Sq W #1001 (P 831) ... **212-255-5539**
Sale, Graham/314 W 52nd St 212-582-7280
Salerno, Steve/541 Hudson St #2 (P 783) **212-727-1599**
Sales, David Art/108 E 35th St #1C (P 144,145) .. **212-889-3337**

Salina, Joe/60 E 42nd St #505 212-682-1490
Salvati, Jim/125 W 77th St (P 732) **212-799-6532**
Samuels, Mark/25 Minetta Ln #4A 212-777-8580
San Diego, Andy/866 UN Plaza #525 (P 679) **212-644-2020**
Sanders, Jane/47-51 40th St #6D, Sunnyside 718-786-3505
Sanjulian/43 E 19th St 212-688-1080
Santore, Charles/108 E 35th St #1C 212-889-3337
Santoro, Christopher/201 E 28th St 212-532-0928
Sargent, Claudia K/15-38 126th St, Queens 718-461-8280
Sasaki, Goro/60 E 42nd St #505 (P 18) **212-682-1490**
Sauber, Rob/10 Plaza St #12C, Brooklyn 718-636-9050
Saurda, Tomas/875 Third Ave 4th Fl 212-303-8326
Sauriol, Brian/420 Lexington Ave #2911 212-986-5680
Sawka, Jan/353 W 53rd St #1W 212-682-2462
Sayles, Elizabeth/10 E 23rd St 7th Fl 212-420-0292
Sayles, John/420 Lexington Ave #2760 (P 232,233) ... **212-697-8525**
Scarisbrick, Ed/853 Broadway #1201 212-677-9100
Schaare, Harry/60 E 42nd St #1940 212-867-8092
Schacht, Michael/925 Park Ave 212-734-5318
Schaer, Miriam/522 E 5th St 212-673-4926
Schaller, Tom/2112 Broadway #407 212-362-5524
Schanzer, Roz/461 Park Ave S 212-696-4680
Scheld, Betsy/500 W 43rd St #29H (P 878) **212-465-9945**
Scheuer, Phil/126 Fifth Ave #13B (P 824) **212-620-0728**
Schindler, Max/267 Wyckoff St, Brooklyn 718-624-1906
Schleinkofer, David/420 Lexington Ave #PH4,5
(P 173) **212-986-5680**
Schmidt, Bill/60 E 42nd St #1940 212-867-8092
Schmidt, Chuck/853 Broadway #1201 (P 604) ... **212-677-9100**
Schneegass, Martinu/241 Eldridge St #2R 212-529-7445
Schneider,RM/853 Broadway (P 606) **212-677-9100**
Schreier, Joshua/466 Washington St 212-925-0472
Schumacher, Michael/353 W 53rd St #1W 212-682-2462
Schumaker, Ward/194 Third Ave 212-475-0440
Schumer, Arlen/382 Lafayette St (P 128,129) **212-254-8242**
Schwab, Michael/501 Fifth Ave #1407 212-490-2450
Schwark, Mary Beth/866 UN Plaza #525 (P 678) .. **212-644-2020**
Schwartz, Daniel/48 E 13th St 212-533-0237
Schwartz, Judith/231 E 5th St 212-777-7533
Schwarz, Jill Karla/80 N Moore St 212-227-2444
Schwarz, Joanie/194 Third Ave (P 112) **212-475-0440**
Schwinger, Larry/270 Park Ave S #10B (P 538) .. **212-260-4153**
Scott, Bob/106 Lexington Ave #3 212-684-2409
Scrofani, Joseph/353 W 53rd St #1W (P 419) **212-682-2462**
Searle, Ronald/15 E 76th St 212-288-8010
Seaver, Jeffrey/130 W 24th St #4B (P 1129) **212-741-2279**
Segal, John/165 W 91st St #5A 212-662-3278
Seiffer, Alison/77 Hudson St 212-227-0087
Sekine, Hisashi/200 W 15th St 212-243-4209
Seltzer, Isadore/285 Riverside Dr #2B 212-666-1561
Sempe, J J/81 Greene St (P 566) **212-925-3053**
Shafer, Ginger/113 Washington Pl 212-989-7697
Shahidi, Behrooz/551 W 22nd St 212-206-8724
Shahinian, Brenda/81 Greene St 212-925-3053
Shannon, David/306 E 50th St #2 212-688-8475
Shap, Sandra/853 Broadway #1201 212-677-9100
Shega, Marla/60 E 42nd St #505 212-682-1490
Sheldon, Paul/232 Madison Ave #402 (P 344,345) .. **212-889-8777**
Shenefield, Barbara/85 Barrow St #6K 212-633-8755
Shepherd, Cameron/520 Broadway #7Rear 212-334-0962
Sherman, Maurice/209 E 23rd St 212-679-7350
Sherman, Oren/232 Madison Ave #402 (P 346,347) .. **212-889-8777**
Shohet, Marti/41 Union Sq W #1001 (P 1133) **212-627-1299**
Sieffert, Clare/25 W 45th St 212-398-9540
Sienkiewicz, Bill/14 E 52nd St (P 504) **212-752-8490**
Silva, Jorge/111 Wooster St PHC 212-925-0491
Silverman, Burt/324 W 71st St 212-799-3399
Silvers, Bill/420 Lexington Ave #PH4,5 (P 182) .. **212-986-5680**
Sinclair, Valerie/501 Fifth Ave #1407 (P 94,95) .. **212-490-2450**
Singer, Paul Design/494 14th St, Brooklyn 718-499-8172
Singer, Phillip/270 Park Ave S #10B (P 542) **212-260-4153**
Sis, Peter/10 Bleecker St #7B 212-260-0151
Skardinski, Stan/201 E 28th St 212-532-0928
Skolsky, Mark/257 12th St, Brooklyn 718-499-1148
Skopp, Jennifer/1625 Emmons Ave #6H, Brooklyn 718-646-2344
Skorodumov, Alexander/385 Ft Washington Ave 718-575-1678
Slack, Chuck/60 E 42nd St #505 (P 37) **212-682-1490**
Slackman, Charles B/320 E 57th St 212-758-8233

Viviano, Sam J/25 W 13th St (P 1172,1173) **212-242-1471**
Vollath, Guenther/156 Fifth Ave #617.................................212-243-1333
Von Ulrich, Mark/59 W 19th St #2B2 (P 842) **212-989-9325**
Vosk, Alex/521 E 82nd St #1A...212-737-2314
Voth, Gregory/67 Eighth Ave...212-807-9766

W

Wacholder, Lisa Roma/2613 Ave J, Brooklyn.....................718-951-7218
Wade, Robert/129 North 11th St, Brooklyn.......................212-677-2761
Walker & Assoc/18 E 64th St #4B.....................................212-759-5590
Walker, Jeff/60 E 42nd St #1940.....................................212-867-8092
Walker, John S/47 Jane St...212-242-3435
Wall, Pam/60 E 42nd St #505 (P 43) **212-682-1490**
Wallace, Kurt/25 W 45th St...212-398-9540
Waller, Charles/35 Bethune St PH C..................................212-989-5843
Wallner, Alexandra & John/866 UN Plaza #4014.................212-644-2020
Walsh, Terry/31 W 21st St 7th Fl......................................212-243-4412
Ward, Donna/19 E 48th St 3rd Fl......................................212-838-0050
Ward, John/43-36 Robinson St #5H, Flushing.....................718-358-6423
Warren, Jim/155 Ave of Americas 10th Fl (P 693) **212-255-6530**
Warren, Valerie/14 E 4th St #1103....................................212-505-5366
Wasserman, Randie/28 W 11th St #2B...............................212-645-7226
Wasson, Cameron/4 S Portland Ave #3, Brooklyn,
(P 1175) **718-875-8277**
Watkinson, Brent/60 E 42nd St #505 (P 33) **212-682-1490**
Watts, Mark/420 Lexington Ave #PH4,5 (P 169) **212-986-5680**
Watts, Sharon/201 Eastern Parkway, Brooklyn 718-398-0451
Weakley, Mark/41 Union Sq W #636 (P 435) **212-206-0066**
Weaver, Robert/42 E 12th St..212-254-4289
Weiman, Jon/2255 Broadway #306.....................................212-787-3184
Weiner, Jeffrey/214 E 90th St #4RE...................................212-876-2335
Weinman, Jon/2255 Broadway #306....................................212-787-3184
Weisbecker, Philippe/476 Broadway #4M............................212-966-6051
Weisser, Carl/38 Livingston St #33, Brooklyn 718-834-0952
Weissman, Sam/2510 Fenton Ave, Bronx............................212-654-5381
Weller, Don/200 W 15th St (P 455) **212-243-4209**
Westerberg, Rob/34-64 Hillside Ave #4V (P 880) **212-567-1884**
Wheeler, Jody/509 E 78th St #6E.......................................212-861-7178
White, Debra/4 South Portland Ave #4, Brooklyn,
(P 848) **718-797-5115**
White, Roger/160 West End Ave #3K...................................212-362-1848
Whitehead, Samuel B/397 First St #3R, Brooklyn,
(P 1179) **718-768-0803**
Whitehouse, Debora...212-682-1490
Whitesides, Kim/501 Fifth Ave #1407 212-490-2450
Wickenden, Nadine/267 Wycoff St, Brooklyn......................718-624-1906
Wieland, Don/420 Lexington Ave #PH4,5 (P 178) **212-986-5680**
Wiemann, Roy/PO Box 271/Prince St Sta (P 663) **212-431-3793**
Wiggins, Mick/58 W 15th St 6th Fl (P 56,57) **212-741-2539**
Wiley, Paul/410 W 24th St #121 (P 883) **212-627-8071**
Wilkinson, Bill/155 E 38th St...212-697-6170
Wilkinson, Chuck/60 E 42nd St #505.................................212-682-1490
Willardson + Assoc/194 Third Ave (P 103) **212-475-0440**
Williams, Elizabeth/349 E 82nd St #8................................212-517-4593
Williams, Oliver/119 West 23rd St (P 588) **212-633-9880**
Williams, Richard/58 W 15th St 6th Fl (P 66,67) **212-741-2539**
Williamson Janoff Aerographics/514 W 24th St 3rd Fl..........212-807-0816
Wilson, Harvey/316 Clinton Ave, Brooklyn.........................718-857-8525
Wimmer, Mike/420 Lexington Ave #PH4,5 (P176) **212-986-5680**
Winborg, Larry/420 Lexington Ave #PH4,5 (P 160) **212-986-5680**
Wind, Bodhi/43 E 19th St...212-254-4996
Winkowski, Fredric/866 UN Plaza #525 (P 679) **212-644-2020**
Winterhale, John/329 E 13th St...212-254-6665
Winterrowd, Turk/97 Union St, Brooklyn............................718-624-4452
Winterson, Finn/401 Eighth Ave #43, Brooklyn...................212-219-2711
Wisenbaugh, Jean/41 Union Sq W #1228 (P 198) **212-929-5590**
Witte, Michael/108 E 35th St #1C (P 146,147) **212-889-3337**
Wohlberg, Ben/43 Great Jones St 212-254-9663
Wolfe, Bruce/194 Third Ave 212-475-0440
Wolfgang, Sherri/382 Lafayette St (P 128,129) **212-254-8242**
Wollman, Paul/60 E 42nd St #505.....................................212-682-1490
Wolynski, Voytek/531 E 81st St #1C (P 493) **212-861-9892**
Womersley, David/420 Lexington Ave #PH4,5 212-986-5680
Wood, Clare/54 Berkeley Pl, Brooklyn................................718-783-3734
Woodend, James/420 Lexington Ave #2760........................212-697-8525
Woolley, Janet/155 Ave of Americas 10th Fl (P 694) ... **212-255-6530**
Wray, Wendy/194 Third Ave (P 106,107) **212-475-0440**

Wrobel, Cindy/280 Madison Ave #1402 (P385) **212-545-9155**
Wyatt, Kathy/43 E 19th St..212-254-4996
Wynne, Patricia/446 Central Pk West 212-865-1059

Y

Yankus, Marc/333 E 49th St (P 596,597) **212-982-6533**
Yealdhall, Gary/353 W 53rd St #1W (P 410) **212-682-2462**
Yee, Josie/211 W 20th St #6E..212-206-1260
Yeldham, Ray/420 Lexington Ave #PH4,5...........................212-986-5680
Yemi/7 E 14th St #812...212-627-1269
Yeo, Mike/94-23 Corona Ave, Elmhurst.............................718-760-3738
Yi, Kang/41 Union Sq W #918 (P 628,629) **212-807-6627**
Yiannias, Vicki/27 Bleecker St..212-673-1600
Yip, Jennie/625 E 82nd St, Brooklyn.................................718-444-6750
York, Judy/420 Lexington Ave #2760.................................212-697-8525
Younger, Heidi/58 W 15th St 6th Fl (P 64,65) **212-741-2539**
Yourke, Oliver/525-A Sixth Ave, Brooklyn 718-965-0609
Yule, Susan Hunt/176 Elizabeth St....................................212-226-0439

Z

Zacharow, Christopher/109 Waverly Pl #4R (P 677) **212-460-5739**
Zagorski, Stanislaw/142 E 35th St....................................212-532-2348
Zaid, Barry/219 W 81st..212-580-1993
Zamchick, Gary/155 E 23rd St #308 (P 855) **212-529-0363**
Zann, Nicky/155 W 68th St #1114.....................................212-724-5027
Zeldich, Arieh/866 UN Plaza #525.....................................212-644-2020
Ziegler, Gavin/PO Box 21076..212-957-8007
Ziemienski, Dennis/111 Wooster St #PH C.........................212-925-0491
Ziering, Bob/151 W 74th St #2B (P 813) **212-873-0034**
Zimmerman, Amy/156 Fifth Ave #617 (P 659) **212-243-1333**
Zimmerman, Jerry/124 W 18th St 5th Fl.............................212-620-7774
Zimmerman, Robert/530 1st St, Brooklyn, (P 814) **718-237-0699**
Zlowodzka, Joanna/321 First Ave......................................212-673-8511
Zudeck, Darryl/41 Union Sq W #1228................................212-929-5590
Zumbo, Matthew/60 E 42nd St #505 (P 17) **212-682-1490**
Zwarenstein, Alex "Mangal"/155 E 38th St (P 651) **212-697-6170**
Zwingler, Randall/111 Wooster St #PH C (P 430) **212-925-0491**
Zwolak, Paul/531 E 81st St #1C (P 495) **212-861-9892**
Cooper, Dan/25 W 45th St..212-398-9540

N O R T H E A S T

A

Abe, Yoshiko/165 Jacoby St, Maplewood, NJ......................201-378-9188
Abel, Ray/18 Vassar Pl, Scarsdale, NY..............................914-725-1899
Abell, Patrick/601 Himes Ave #107, Frederick, MD.............301-696-8545
Ackerman, Angela/11 Colonial Dr, Framingham, MA............508-788-0879
Adam Filippo & Moran/1206 Fifth Ave, Pittsburgh, PA.........412-261-3720
Adams, Michael W/3002 Fifth St, Trooper, PA 215-539-5679
Addams, Charles/PO Box 8, Westport, CT...........................203-227-7806
Ahle, Dorothy/8 Grimshaw St, Malden, MA.........................617-321-8302
Ahmed, Ghulan Hassan/1258 Walker Ave, Baltimore, MD 410-433-0478
Akgulian, Nishan/42-29 64th St, Woodside, NY...................718-565-6936
Albanese, Ernest/136 Park Ave #2, Hoboken, NJ.................201-659-9335
Alcorn, Bob/434 South Main St, Heightstown, NJ.................609-448-4448
Alde, David/1801 Clydesdale Pl NW, Washington, DC 202-234-1196
Alden, Anne/91 Dale Street, Chestnut Hill, MA 617-738-7791
Aldrich, Susan/31 Clearbrook Dr, Smithtown, NY.................516-261-6220
Alexander, Christian/566 Commonwealth Ave, Boston, MA....617-247-7443
Alexander, Paul R/37 Pine Mountain Rd, Redding, CT 203-544-9293
Alexander, Steven/113 77th St, N Bergen, NJ......................201-861-6314
Alsop, Mark/RR 5 Milltown Rd, Brewster, NY......................914-287-7352
Alterio, Caroline/25 Gray St, Boston, MA............................617-236-1920
Ames, Sharon/1017 Bellmore Rd, North Bellmore, NY 415-665-5144
Amorosi, Tom/6 Compton St, E Rockaway, NY
(P 899) **516-596-0160**
Anatoly/229 Berkeley #52, Boston, MA (P 524) **617-266-3858**
Ancas, Karen/84 Keystone St, W Roxbury, MA.....................617-323-8466
Anderson, John/501 N Calvert St, Baltimore, MD 410-332-6508
Anderson, Paul/249 Illinois Ave, Paterson, NJ.....................201-345-5763
Anderson, Philip/245 Broadway, Arlington, MA
(P 900) **617-641-3823**
Anderson, Richard/490 Bleeker Ave, Mamaroneck, NY 914-381-2682

Andri, Richard/46 Cherrywood Dr, Manhassat Hill, NY 516-358-7986
Angrisani, Chris/2825 Terrace Dr #202, Chevy Chase, MD 301-587-0378
Ansall, Joseph/70233 Cipriano Ct, Lanham, MD 301-552-4935
Anthony, Jay B/806 N Calvert St, Baltimore, MD 410-727-6764
Antkowiak, Jeff/8193 Mountain Estate Ct, Pasadena, MD 410-360-2535
Anzalone, Lori/35-02 Berdan Ave, Fairlawn, NJ (P 901) 201-796-5588
Apple, Margot/March Rd, Ashfield, MA 413-625-9514
Ardissone, Mary/PO Box 6539, Silver Spring, MD 301-209-0054
Armstrong, Stuart/1503 Dublin Dr, Silver Spring, MD 301-681-6178
Aronson, Ruth/124 Hornbeam Lane, Kinnelon, NJ 201-838-2207
Aruta, Mark/5115 41st St NW, Washington, DC 202-364-0384
Arvis, Tom/11228 Troy Rd, Rockville, MD 301-468-0828
Asmussen, Don/61 Glenridge, Portland, ME 207-871-1364
Astrachan, Michael/204 Carmalt Rd, Hamden, CT 203-498-0455
Atkinson-Mavilia, Peg/45 Captain Pierce Rd, Scituate, MA 617-545-7654
Avishai, Susan/28 Marlboro St, Newton, MA 617-969-7246

B

B&G Associates/520 Adams St, Hoboken, NJ 201-653-5542
Bach, Josh/326 S 19th St #11A, Philadelphia, PA 215-732-1359
Bailey, Brian/461 9th St, Palisades Park, NJ 201-585-2937
Bailey, Jean/49 Worcester St, Boston, MA 617-266-9723
Baird, Jack/88 Dartmouth St, Portland, ME 207-772-3992
Baiungo, Charles/61 Congress St, Bangor, ME 207-947-2966
Baker, Lori/RR 1/PO Box 880, Randolph Ctr, VT 802-426-3800
Baker, Skip/731 N 24th St, Philadelphia, PA (P 364) 215-232-6666
Baker, Susan Harriet/315 West Side Dr #303, Gaithersburg, MD (P 906) 301-258-0126
Bakley, Craig/68 Madison Ave, Cherry Hill, NJ 609-428-6310
Baldwin Jr, Gunnar/RR1 Box 3271, Plymouth, NH 603-536-1836
Baldwin, James/1467 Jordan Ave, Crofton, MD 410-721-1896
Ball, Harvey/340 Main St, Wooster, MA 617-752-9154
Bang, Molly Garrett/43 Drumlin Rd, Falmouth, MA 508-540-5174
Bangham, Richard/2006 Cascade Rd, Silver Spring, MD 301-649-4919
Banta, Susan/17 Magazine St, Cambridge, MA 617-876-8568
Baquero, George/145 Clinton Pl #2B, Hackensack, NJ 201-342-9362
Barber, David/21 Taft St, Marblehead, MA 617-631-6130
Barbier, Suzette/7 Devotion St #3, Brookline, MA 617-739-2822
Barger, Peter/25 Gray St, Boston, MA 617-236-1920
Barkley, James/444 Bedford Rd, Pleasantville, NY 914-747-2220
Barnard, Bryn/PO Box 285, Woodbury, NJ 609-853-4252
Barner, Bob/65 Mt Vernon St, Boston, MA 617-523-0953
Barnes, Ken/52 Mercator Lane, Willingboro, NJ 609-871-6051
Barnes, Kim/17 Pinewood St, Annapolis, MD 301-261-8662
Barnes, Suzanne/188 Central St #5, Somerville, MA 617-628-0837
Barr, Ken/770 Boylston St #17F, Boston, MA 617-267-5275
Barr, Loel (Ms)/22301 Flintridge Dr, Brookville, MD 301-774-4634
Barrett, Andrea/164 Elm Street, Kingston, MA 617-585-5791
Barrett, Debby/49 Hamilton St, Everett, MA 617-387-2031
Barrett, Jennifer/5510 Glenwood Rd, Bethesda, MD 301-654-4603
Barrett, Tom/81 Mt Vernon St #2, Boston, MA (P 909) 617-523-4072
Barrett, Victor/65 Ashburton St, Providence, RI 401-273-9898
Barrette, Steve/38 Quail Run, Massapequa, NY 516-797-2146
Barruso, Joe/30 Mildred Ave, Poughkeepsie, NY 813-530-4236
Bartlett, Christopher/2211B Woodbox Lane, Baltimore, MD 301-484-1906
Bartlett, David/8 E Hawthorne Dr, LaPlata, MD 301-932-0039
Baruffi, Andrea/341 Hudson Terr, Piermont, NY (P 910,911) 914-359-9542
Basso, Bill/38 Ogden Lane, Englishtown, NJ 201-431-5497
Bastas, Dimitrios/2276 Mt Carmel Ave, Glenside, PA 215-885-8227
Bauer, Brent/1830 E Monument St, Baltimore, MD 410-955-3213
Bauer, Stephen/3000 Chestnut Ave #340, Baltimore, MD (P 913) 410-243-0643
Becker, N Neesa/241 Monroe St, Philadelphia, PA 215-925-5363
Becker, Polly/591 Tremont St, Boston, MA 617-247-0469
Begin, Maryjane/87 Benefit St, Providence, RI (P 78) 401-421-2344
Beim, Judy/359 3rd St, Clifton, NJ 201-478-4309
Beisel, Dan/4713 Ribble Ct, Ellicott City, MD 410-461-6377
Belcastro, Mario/637 Baldwin, Bridgeville, PA 412-221-4512
Belove, Janice/46 Carolin Rd, Montclair, NJ 201-744-3760
Belser, Burkey/1818 N St NW #110, Washington, DC 202-775-0333
Ben-Ami, Doron/14 Fox Run Ln, Newtown, CT 203-270-1849
Bender, Mark/930 N Lincoln, Pittsburgh, PA 412-321-3266
Bendis, Keith/275 Tanglewylde Rd, Lake Peekskill, NY 914-528-7378
Benn, Nathan/913 E Capitol St SE, Washington, DC, ...202-546-6182
Bennett, James/165 Seventh St #1, Hoboken, NJ 201-963-1457
Bennett, Martin/2617 North Lovegrove St, Baltimore, MD 410-338-0785
Benshoshan, Orna (Ms)/34 Bernard St, Lexington, MA 617-863-1689
Benson, John D/2111-A Townhill Rd, Baltimore, MD 410-665-3395
Bensusen, Sally/2853 Ontario Rd NW #615, Washington, DC 202-462-0601
Berg, John/377 Hudson St, Buffalo, NY (P 916) 716-884-8003
Berg, Linda/34 Westwood Dr, E Rochester, NY 716-385-8513
Berger, Charles/53 Maplewood Dr, Plainview, NY 516-931-5085
Bergin, Kieran/41 Stevenson Pl, Kearny, NJ (P 917) 212-545-3710
Berlin Productions/200 William St, Port Chester, NY 914-937-5594
Berman, Craig/16 Taylor St, Dover, NJ 201-366-4407
Berman, Michael/49 S Cedar Brook Rd, Cedar Brook, NJ 609-561-4188
Bernard, Gary/11 Chippewa Way, Cranford, NJ 201-276-8381
Berney, Katherine/24 Cameron Ave #2, Somerville, MA 617-776-4242
Berry, Rick/93 Warren St, Arlington, MA 617-648-6375
Bersani, Shennen/14 Rockwell Ave, Brockton, MA 508-583-1648
Bianco, Peter/348 Manning St, Needham, MA 617-444-9077
Biedrzycki, David/8 Pilgrim Ln, Medfield, MA (P 920) 508-359-6276
Biegel, Michael David/61-C E Main St, Ramsey, NJ 201-825-0084
Bigda, Diane/72 High St #2, Topsfield, MA 508-887-3528
Billin-Frye, Paige/216 Walnut St NW, Washington, DC 202-291-3105
Bingham, Edith/ PO Box 255, Washington, NH 603-495-3961
Birmingham, Lloyd P/500 Peekskill Hollow Rd, Putnam Valley, NY 914-528-3207
Birnbaum, Meg/331 Harvard St #14, Cambridge, MA 617-491-7826
Blackwell, Deborah/3 River St, Sandwich, MA 508-888-4019
Blackwell, Patrick/PO Box 324, North Truro, MA 508-487-3336
Blahd, William/3717 Alton Pl NW, Washington, DC 202-686-0179
Blake, Alecia/59 Glen Ave, Fairfield, NJ 201-256-7039
Blake, Marty/PO Box 266, Jamesville, NY (P 440) 315-492-1332
Blaser, Michael/8 Cranberry Lane, Dover, MA 508-785-1513
Blasutta, Mary Lynn/Rider Hollow Rd, Arkville, NY (P 922) 914-586-4899
Blauers, Nancy/50 Walnut St, Stratford, CT 203-377-6109
Bliss, Harry/1703 South 10th St, Philadelphia, PA (P 194) 215-551-0888
Bliss, Philip/22 Briggs Ave, Fairport, NY 716-377-1609
Blum, Marianne/400 Executive Blvd, Elmsford, NY 914-592-2031
Board, Inge/3340 Bowman St, Philadelphia, PA 215-438-8422
Bochner, Nurit/5 Bayley Ave, Yonkers, NY 914-965-4827
Boger, Diane/3426 16th St NW #205, Washington, DC 202-328-2156
Bolinsky, David/350 Center St, Wallingford, CT 203-284-1224
Bollinger, Kristine/7 Ivy Hill Rd/Box 959, Ridgefield, CT 203-438-8386
Bolster, Robert/7 Hope St, Walpole, MA (P 925) 508-660-1751
Bomeisl, James/70 Madison Ave., Demarest, NJ 201-784-3480
Bonanno, Paul/142 W Golf Ave, S Plainfield, NJ 908-756-8867
Bonavita, Donna/Four Vera Place, Montclair, NJ 201-744-7159
Bond, Dennis A/6481 Miriam Circle, E Petersburg, PA (P 926) 717-569-5823
Bond, Higgins/304 Woodbine St, Teaneck, NJ 201-836-1396
Bone, Fred/28 Farm Court, New Britain, CT 203-827-8418
Bono, Peter/114 E 7th St, Clifton, NJ 201-340-1169
Bortman, Alan/355 Wood Rd, Briantree, MA 617-235-2077
Borzotta, Joseph/234 Garden St, Hoboken, NJ 201-420-0293
Botts, Steve/25-Q Sylvan Rd S, Westport, CT 203-226-4293
Bower, Steve/3000 Chestnut Ave #6, Baltimore, MD 301-243-0643
Bowers, David/309 Walnut Rd, Pittsburgh, PA (P 681) 412-761-5666
Boyd, Lizi/229 Berkeley St #52, Boston, MA 617-266-3858
Boyer, Jeff/1325 18th St NW #908, Washington, DC 202-331-7722
Bracco, Anthony/214 65th St, W New York, NJ 201-861-9098
Bradbury, Robert & Assoc/26 Halsey Lane, Closter, NJ 201-768-6395
Bradshaw, James/97 Mt Tabor Way, Ocean Grove, NJ 908-775-2798
Bragg, Sholie/5 Oklahoma Ave, Wilmington, DE 302-761-9144
Brancato, Ron/333 N Plymouth Ave, Rochester, NY (P 930) 716-262-4450
Brauckman, Krista/229 Berkeley #52, Boston, MA 617-266-3858
Bray, Mark/RD 1/Box 694/Huffs Chrch Rd, Alburtis, PA 215-845-3229
Breeden, Paul M/PO Box 40A, Sullivan Harbor, ME 207-422-3007
Bremer/Keifer Studio/250 Alewife Ln, Suffield, CT 203-749-9680
Brenner, Meryl/16 Cady Ave, Somerville, MA 617-623-2237
Brent, Mike/597 Riverside Ave, Westport, CT 203-226-4724
Brettlinger, Nancy/2121 Wisconsin Ave NW, Washington, DC 202-965-7800
Brickman, Robin/32 Fort Hoosac Pl, Williamstown, MA 413-458-9853
Bridy, Dan Visuals Inc/625 Stanwix St #2402, Pittsburgh, PA 412-531-4044
Brier, David/38 Park Ave, Rutherford, NJ 201-896-8476
Brindak, Hermine/3 Lockwood Ave, Old Greenwich, CT 203-698-1732
Bronstein, Diane/110 Strathmore Rd, Boston, MA 617-277-0757
Brown, Bradford/283 S 10th St 12th Fl, Newark, NJ 201-624-8743

Brown, Carolyn/PO Box 33, Enosbury Falls, VT 802-933-7720
Brown, Leslie/177 Congress/Box 15400, Portland, ME.....................207-282-2238
Brown, Michael D/932 Hungerford Dr #24, Rockville, MD 301-762-4474
Brown, Remi/Box 186, Roselle Park, NJ 908-245-1218
Brown, Rick Illus/PO Box 341, Furlong, PA 215-794-8186
Brown, Ron Illus/126 Haverhill Rd, Topsfield, MA 508-887-3801
Brown, William L/6704 Westmoreland Ave, Takoma Park, MD 301-270-2014
Bru, Salvador/5130 Bradley Blvd, Chevy Chase, MD 301-654-4420
Bruemmer, Betsy/Box 1743, Edgartown, MA 508-627-9264
Brun, Robert/76 State St, Newburyport, MA 508-462-1948
Brunkus, Denise/111 Perryville Rd, Pittstown, NJ 908-735-2671
Brunkus, Denise/7 Ivy Hill Rd, Ridgefield, CT 203-226-7674
Bruno, Peggy/51 Grove St/Cranberry Cove, Marshfield, MA.............617-837-6896
Bry, Kimberly/127 Washington Cir, W Hartford, CT 203-236-8112
Bryant, Web/330 Ninth St SE, Washington, DC 202-546-1433
Bryce, William/15 Goodrich St, Pittsfield, MA 413-443-6713
Buchanan, Steve/21 Sand Bank Rd, Watertown, CT 203-945-0285
Bullock, Wilbur/229 Berkeley #52, Boston, MA 617-266-3858
Bunnell, Deb Troyer/346 Lincoln St, Carlisle, PA.....................717-249-0937
Burchard, Susan Cronin/971 Main St, Hanover, MA.....................617-871-7805
Burger, Rob/731 North 24th St, Philadelphia, PA
(P 371) **215-232-6666**
Burleson, Joe/6035 Blvd East, W New York, NJ.....................201-854-6029
Burroughs, Miggs/PO Box 6, Westport, CT 203-227-9667
Burrows, Bill & Assoc/3100 Elm Ave West, Baltimore, MD.....................410-889-3288
Burton, Caroline/330 8th St, Jersey City, NJ.....................201-656-6502
Buschini, Maryanne/238 W Highland Ave, Philadelphia, PA 215-242-8517
Bush, Lorraine/570 Church Lane Rd, Reading, PA.....................215-779-8565
Buszka, Kimberly/96 W Central St, Natick, MA.....................508-655-6807
Butcher, Jim/1357 E MacPhail Rd, Bel Air, MD.....................410-879-6380
Buterbaugh, Richard/731 North 24th St,
Philadelphia, PA (P 374) **215-232-6666**
Butler, Ralph/18521 Tarragon Way, Germantown, MD 301-587-1505
Butler, Susan Plante/2345 York Rd, Timonium, MD 410-560-1018
Buxton, John/4584 Sylvan Dr, Allison Oark, PA 412-486-6588
Byram, Stephen/318 73rd St, N Bergen, NJ.....................201-555-1212
Byrd, Bob/409 Warwick Rd, Haddonfield, NJ 609-428-9627

C

Cabib, Leila/8601 Buckhannon Dr, Potomac, MD.....................301-299-4158
Cable, Jerry/133 Kuhl Rd, Flemington, NJ 908-788-6750
Cage, Carter/80 Candlewood Dr, Murray Hill, NJ 908-464-2570
Cage, Gary/34 Flamingo Rd, Levitt Town, NY 516-735-1983
Calabro, Carol/1263 Massachusetts Ave #2, Arlington, MA.............617-646-7961
Callahan, Donna/15 Connie Dr, Foxboro, MA.....................508-543-2705
Callahan, Kevin/26 France St, Norwalk, CT 203-847-2046
Callanan, Brian/5 Winston Pl, Yonkers, NY (P 226)......**914-779-4120**
Calleja, Bob/490 Elm Ave, Bogota, NJ 201-488-3028
Callier, Gregory/45 17th Ave #5A, Newark, NJ.....................201-621-9385
Calver, Dave/70 Stoneham Dr, Rochester, NY (P 943) **716-383-8996**
Calvert, Jeff/9518 Whiskey Bottom Rd, Laurel, MD.....................301-236-4139
Camejo, John/9436 Fens Hollow, Laurel, MD.....................410-332-6528
Caminos, Jane/370 Newtonville, Newtonville, MA 617-964-1863
Campbell, Harry/194 Washington St #G, Jersey City, NJ 201-434-3651
Campbell, Jenny/731 North 24th St, Philadelphia,
PA (P 369) **215-232-6666**
Canger, Joseph/52 Horizon Dr, Edison, NJ 908-248-1487
Cannizzaro, Gregory, J/107 York Rd, Towson, MD.....................410-296-2402
Cannone, Gregory/1982 Lake Wood Rd, Toms River, NJ.....................908-349-4332
Cantarella, Virginia Hoyt/PO Box 54, S Westerlo, NY.....................518-966-4419
Canty, Thomas/178 Old Country Way, Braintree, MA.....................617-843-7262
Caporale, Wende/Studio Hill Farm Rte 116, N Salem, NY 914-669-5653
Capparelli, Tony/110 Claremont St, Westwood, NJ.....................201-358-1536
Carallo, Annie/135 S Linwood Ave, Baltimore, MD 301-522-6060
Carbaga, Leslie/258 W Tulpehocken, Philadelphia, PA.....................215-438-9954
Carbone, Lou/286 Sylvan Rd, Bloomfield, NJ.....................201-338-8678
Cardella, Elaine/116 Clinton St, Hoboken, NJ (P 944)....**201-656-3244**
Cardillo, James/49-D Village Green, Budd Lake, NJ 201-691-1530
Carleton, Kim/20 Yarmouth Rd, Norwood, MA.....................617-762-3228
Carlson, Frederick H/118 Monticello Dr, Monroeville, PA.....................412-856-0982
Carlson, Jean Masseau/RR1/Box 303, Hinesburg, VT.....................802-482-2407
Carlson, Jonathan/1212 St Paul St, Baltimore, MD 410-625-5960
Carlson, Lee/1500 Massachusetts Ave NW #143,
Washington, DC (P 945) **202-429-9823**
Carr, Bill/1035 69th Ave, Philadelphia, PA 215-276-1819
Carreiro, Ron/6 Hillside Dr, Plymouth, MA 508-224-9290
Carroll, William/316 Franklin St, Quincy, MA.....................617-479-4229

Carrozza, Cynthia/127 Beacon St, Boston, MA.....................617-437-7428
Carson, Jim/11 Foch St, Cambridge, MA.....................617-661-3321
Carson, Kathleen/8484 16th St #505, Silver Spring, MD.....................301-495-0759
Carter, Abby/823 Shore Rd, Cape Elizabeth, NJ 207-767-2328
Carver, Stephen/626 W Glenside Ave, Glenside, PA 215-887-7381
Castellitto, Mark/126 Park Ave, Rutherford, NJ 201-935-2585
Catalano, Sal/114 Boyce Pl, Ridgewood, NJ 201-447-5318
Causey, Stephanie/8315 North Brook Ln, Bethesda, MD 301-907-9076
Cayea, John/39 Lafayette St, Cornwall, NY 914-534-2942
Cellini, Joseph/415 Hillside Ave, Leonia, NJ (P81) **201-944-6519**
Chadwick, Kevin/5416 30th Pl NW, Washington, DC 202-244-9588
Champagne, Marc/59 Chestnut Hill Ave, Brighton, MA.....................617-787-2631
Chandler, Fay M./1010 Memorial Dr #17E,
Cambridge, MA (P 952) **617-547-9013**
Chandler, Jean/385 Oakwood Dr, Wyckoff, NJ 201-891-2381
Chandler/80 Lattingtown Rd, Locust Valley,
NY (P 951) **516-671-0388**
Chapman, Linda/121 Bartlett Ave #3, Sharon Hill, PA.....................215-583-9806
Charles, Milton/199 Ravine Rd, Califon, NJ.....................908-832-7076
Chen, David/1024 Adams St, Hoboken, NJ (P 611)......**201-659-7711**
Chen, David/15013 Emory Lane, Rockville, MD
(P 611) **301-460-6575**
Chen, Tony/241 Bixley Heath, Lynbrook, NY 516-596-9158
Chernishov, Anatoly/4 Willow Bank Ct, Mahwah, NJ.....................201-327-2377
Chesak, Lina/1206 Girard St NW, Washington , DC.....................202-234-4611
Chessare, Michele/25 Compass Ave, W Milford, NJ.....................201-728-9685
Chestnutt, David/7 Dublin Hill Dr, Greenwich, CT 203-869-8010
Chid/55 Desmond Ave, Bronxville, NY.....................914-793-6011
Chlumecky, Danielle/35 Middlesex Rd #12, Waltham, MA.....................617-893-1596
Christe, Dory (Ms)/3950 Brooklyn Ave, Baltimore, MD.....................301-355-5503
Chui Studio/2250 Elliot St, Merrick, NY.....................516-223-8474
Churchman, John C/4 Howard St, Burlington, VT
(P 956) **802-863-4627**
Cicha, Cheryl/ Boston, MA.....................617-555-1212
Ciemny, Ray/33 Bradford St, Concord, MA.....................508-371-2222
Cincotti, Gerald/42 Freeport Dr, Burlington, MA 617-229-4974
Clar, David Austin/104 Loyalist Ave, Rochester, NY
(P 873) **716-247-2050**
Clark, Bradley H/36 Haggerty Hill Rd, Rhinebeck, NY
(P 958) **914-876-2615**
Clark, Cynthia Watts/36 Haggerty Hill Rd, Rhinebeck, NY 914-876-2615
Clark, Patricia Cullen/6201 Benalder Dr, Bethesda, MD.....................301-229-2986
Clarke, Bob/55 Brooke Rd, Pittsford, NY 716-248-8683
Cleaver, Bill/7 Dublin Hill Drive, Greenwich, CT 203-869-8010
Clee, Suzanne K/7520 Crittenden St, Philadelphia, PA.....................215-247-8883
Cline, Rob/1140 Washington St #6, Boston, MA 617-266-3858
Cober, Alan E/95 Croton Dam Rd, Ossining, NY
(P 770,771) **914-941-8696**
Cober, Leslie/150 Huntington Ave #NE-11, Boston,
MA (P 960) **617-266-0228**
Cocozza, Chris/9 Woodbury Pl, Woodbury, CT.....................203-263-2061
Codd, Mary/65 Ashburton Ave, Providence, RI 401-273-9898
Cohen, Alan R/2828 N Howard St, Baltimore, MD 410-366-3855
Cohen, Gil/8-2 Aspen Way, Doylestown, PA.....................215-348-0779
Cohen, Santiago/705 Park Ave, Hoboken, NJ.....................201-420-7275
Cohen, Sharon/20200 Shipley Terrace #202,
Germantown, MD (P 962) **301-540-3466**
Cohen, Susan D/84 1/2 Erie St, Jersey City, NJ 201-659-5472
Cole, Robin (Ms)/4 Marie Dr, Andover, MA.....................617-470-0609
Colleen/192 Southville RD, Southborough, MA 508-872-4549
Collette, Al/8 Covenger Dr, Medford, NJ 609-953-9470
Collyer, Frank/RR 1 Box 266, Stony Point, NY 914-947-3050
Commerford, Bill/55 Delle Ave, Boston, MA.....................617-445-5406
Condon & White/Suburban Drive, Ashfield, MA
(P 964,965) **413-628-4042**
Condon, Ken/Suburban Drive, Ashfield, MA (P 964)......**413-628-4042**
Conge, Bob/28 Harper St, Rochester, NY (P 966,967)....**716-473-0291**
Conley, Laurie/11412 Long Feather Court, Beltsville, MD.....................301-937-6698
Conner, Marsha/16 Douglas Pl, Verona, NJ 201-239-1408
Connolly, Jim/25 Cedar St, Hingham, MA 617-749-0825
Connolly, Karl S/217 W College Ave, Salisbury, MD.....................410-749-5698
Conrad, David/262 Main St, Watertown, MA 617-923-8129
Conrad, Melvin/1126 48th Pl NE #3, Washington, DC 202-399-4254
Console, Carmen Jr/8 Gettysburg Dr, Voorhees, NJ.....................609-424-8735
Cook, William/3804 E Northern Pkwy, Baltimore, MD.....................410-426-1130
Cooper, Robert T/731 North 24th St, Philadelphia,
PA (P 363) **215-232-6666**
Copie/286 Oakwood Dr, Paramus, NJ.....................201-265-3405

Cordes, Kathy/Baltimore, MD ... 301-467-8140
Corfield, Marie/48 Sylvan Place, Nutley, NJ ... 201-667-8071
Cornelius-Karp/26 E Maple Rd, Greenlawn, NY ... 516-466-4093
Correll, Cory/11511 Sullnick Way, Gaithersburg, MD ... 301-977-7254
Cosatt, Paulette/60 South St, Cresskill, NJ ... 201-871-3765
Costantino, Frank M/13B Pauline St, Winthrop, MA ... 617-846-4766
Costantino, Valerie/2037 New Hyde Park Rd, New Hyde Park, NY ... 516-358-9121
Costas, Laura/5726 Fourth St NW, Washington, DC ... 202-291-8757
Coto, Bob/13 Cloverhill Place, Montclair, NJ ... 201-509-8301
Courtney, John P/779 Eleventh Ave, Patterson, NJ (P 970) ... 201-345-7652
Covert, Susan/40 Matthew Dr, Fairport, NY ... 716-223-4765
Cowdrey, Richard/229 Berkeley St #52, Boston, MA ... 617-266-3858
Cox, Birck/300 West End Dr, Lancaster, PA ... 717-396-9346
Craft, Kinuko/RFD #1 PO Box 167, Norfolk, CT ... 203-542-5018
Cramer, D L/10 Beechwood Dr, Wayne, NJ ... 201-628-8793
Crawford, Robert/123 Minortown Rd, Woodbury, CT ... 203-266-0059
Crofut, Bob/8 New St, Ridgefield, CT ... 203-431-4304
Croll, Carolyn/458 Newton Trnpk, Weston, CT ... 203-454-4687
Crompton, Jack/229 Berkeley #52, Boston, MA ... 617-266-3858
Crosman, Hilarie/120 Federal St, Salem, MA ... 508-745-0431
Cross, Peter/210 Cherry St, Katonah, NY ... 914-232-3975
Crouse, Danny/24 Appleton Rd, Glen Ridge, NJ ... 201-748-1650
Crowley, David/711 Washington St, Gloucester, MA ... 508-283-7866
Csatari, Joseph/Two Snapper Ave, South River, NJ ... 908-257-4660
Cuan, Sergio/92 Edgemont Pl, Teaneck, NJ ... 201-833-4337
Cunis, Peter/204 Park Ave #4, Hoboken, NJ (P 973) ... 201-792-5164
Cunningham, Nancy/316 Regester St, Baltimore, MD ... 410-377-9254
Cunningham, Robert M/45 Cornwall Rd (Rt 45), Warren, CT ... 203-868-2702
Cusano, Steven R/80 Talbot Ct, Media, PA (P975) ... 215-565-8829
Cutler, Dave/7 Sunrise Ridge, Florida, NY (P 976) ... 914-615-1580

D

D'Allaird, John/411 Griffiths St, Syracuse, NY ... 315-425-7406
D'Entremont, John/355 Wood Rd, Braintree, MA ... 617-235-2077
D'zenis, Eric/7 Dublin Hill Dr, Greenwich, CT ... 203-869-8010
Dahm, Bob/166 Arnold Ave, Cranston, RI ... 401-781-5092
Daily, Don/57 Academy Rd, Bala Cynwyd, PA ... 215-664-5729
Dally, Lyman M/20-C Foxwood Dr, Morris Plains, NJ ... 201-292-9608
Daly, Tom/47 E Edsel Ave, Palisades Park, NJ ... 201-943-1837
Dameron, Ned/14 Manchester Pl #303, Silver Spring, MD ... 301-585-8512
Dano, Robert/129 Presidents Lane, Quincy, MA ... 617-773-9742
Darby, Janet/309 Walnut Rd, Pittsburgh, PA (P 685) ... 412-761-5666
Darden, Howard/56 Roosevelt Ave, Butler, NJ ... 201-492-1273
Dare, Auston/20-C Foxwood Dr, Morris Plains, NJ ... 201-292-9608
Dargis, Julie/6907 Dartmouth Ave, College Park, MD ... 301-277-3056
Davenport, Therese/189 Bowen St, S Boston, MA ... 617-268-7524
David, Glenn/33 Vincent St, Saugus, MA ... 617-231-3092
David, Susan/1010 Willow Ave, Hoboken, NJ ... 201-798-3062
Davidian, Anna/889 Worcester St, Wellesley, MA ... 617-655-6536
Davin-Hallet, Eleanor/73 Hunters Run, Pittsford, NY ... 716-385-4089
Davis, Gary/1 Cedar Pl, Wakefield, MA ... 617-245-2628
Davis, Glenn/223 Central St, Saugus, MA ... 617-231-3092
Davis, John/604 Ninth St, Carlstadt, NJ ... 201-460-7358
Davis, Susan/1107 Notley Dr, Silver Spring, MD ... 301-384-9426
Dawes, Joseph/20 Church Ct, Closter, NJ ... 201-767-8127
Dawson, Todd/3528 Greenly St, Wheaton, MD ... 301-933-7367
De Luz, Tony/49 Melcher St 3rd fl, Boston, MA ... 617-695-0006
De Muth, Roger T/4103 Chenango St, Cazenovia, NY (P 982,983) ... 315-655-8599
Deacon, Jim/373 Benefit St 1st Fl, Providence, RI ... 401-331-8742
DeAmicus, John/35 South Durst Dr, Milltown, NJ ... 908-249-4937
Dean, Glenn/RD #2 Box 788, Sussex, NJ (P 93) ... 212-490-2450
Decandia, Albert/Box 8566, Haledon, NJ ... 201-942-9165
DeCerchio, Joseph/62 Marlborough Ave, Marlton, NJ ... 609-596-0598
Defiebe Jr, Matthew/940 Salem Rd, Union, NJ ... 908-688-2536
DeGrandpre, Patty/27 Baker Ave, Beverly, MA ... 508-921-0410
Deigan, Jim/309 Walnut Rd, Pittsburgh, PA ... 412-761-5666
Delaney, John/14 Castle St, Saugus, MA ... 617-233-1409
DeLapine, Jim/398 31st St, Lindenhurst, NY ... 516-225-1247
Della-Piana, Elissa/201 Elm St, Medford, MA ... 671-395-2197
Dellicolli, Ronald E/1 Argilla Rd, Methuen, MA ... 617-437-9459
Delmonte, Steve/328 W Delavan Ave, Buffalo, NY ... 716-883-6086
DelRossi, Richard/8 Washington St, Hicksville, NY ... 516-939-0256
Demarest, Robert/87 Highview Terr, Hawthorne, NJ ... 201-427-9639
Demers, Donald/61 Tilton Ave, Kittery, ME ... 207-439-1463
Demorat, Chuck/305 Cornelia Dr, Graham, NC (P 987) ... 919-229-7359
Denham, Karl/155 Fifth St, Hoboken, NJ ... 201-792-6422
DePalma, Mary Newell/45 Bradfield Ave, Boston, MA ... 617-327-6241
Deponte, Fabio & Sara/PO Box 393/N Main St, Petersham, MA ... 508-724-8823
DeRosa, Dawn/25-Q Sylvan Rd S, Westport, CT ... 203-226-4293
Devaney, John/421 Broadway, Cambridge, MA ... 617-876-4046
Dever, Jeffrey L/7619 S Arbory Lane, Laurel, MD ... 301-776-2812
DeVita, Fred/5339 Randolph Rd #4, Rockville, MD ... 301-770-2237
DeVito, Grace/140 Hoyt St #4E, Stamford, CT (P 423) ... 203-967-2198
DeVito, Joe/425 Lancaster Ct, Piscataway, NJ ... 908-699-1099
Dey, Lorraine/PO Box 268, Toms River, NJ ... 908-505-1670
Dezita, Fred/5339 Randolph Rd #4, Rockville, MD ... 301-770-2237
Dibner, Martin/Mayberry Hill, Casco, ME ... 207-627-4369
Didion, Nancy/33 Moose Hill Parkway, Sharon, MA ... 617-784-1389
Diefendorf, Cathy/8 Cranberry Lane, Dover, MA ... 508-785-1513
Dillard, Sarah/31 Pleasant St, Charlestown, MA ... 617-241-0141
DiMartino, Paul/560 Mountain Ave, Washington Twnshp, NJ ... 212-764-5591
Dimensional Illustrators/362 2nd Street Pike #112, Southampton, PA ... 215-953-1415
Dininno, Steve/553 E Fulton St, Long Beach, NY (P 644) ... 516-431-1495
Dion, Madge/320 Palmer Terrace #1F, Mamaroneck ... 914-698-1027
Dior, Jerry/9 Old Hickory Ln, Edison, NJ ... 908-561-6536
Dircks, David/16 Dunford St, Melville, NY ... 516-427-9377
Dobrowolski, Chris/153 Pine Grove St, Needham, MA ... 617-444-7545
Dodge, Paul/731 N 24th St, Philadelphia, PA ... 215-232-6666
Dodson, Bert/RR 1/Box 1660, Bradford, VT ... 802-222-9384
Doggett, W Kirk/311 Walnut St, Wellesley, MA ... 617-431-7835
Donato, Michael A/4082-A Woodbridge Ave, Edison, NJ (P 711) ... 908-738-1339
Doney, Todd L W/18 Hillside Ave, Chatham, NJ (P 309) ... 201-701-1747
Donnarumma, Dom/25 Stanwood Rd, New Hyde Park, NY ... 516-248-5113
Dooling, Mike/161 Wyoming Ave, Audubon, NJ ... 609-546-6507
Dorsey, Bob/2133 Baird Rd, Penfield, NY ... 315-255-2367
Dow, Brian/115 Marshall St, Revere, MA ... 617-321-1315
Dowdle, Martha/474 Edinburgh Ct, Severna Park, MD ... 301-544-2969
Dreamer, Sue/345 Cross St, Hanson, MA ... 617-294-4508
Drescher, Joan/23 Cedar, Hingham, MA ... 617-749-5179
Dressel, Peggy/11 Rockaway Ave, Oakland, NJ (P 468) ... 201-337-2143
Drinkwine, Sharon/229 Berkeley #52, Boston, MA ... 617-266-3858
Driver, Ray/26012 Brigadier Pl Unit E, Damacus, MD ... 301-972-0556
Drummey, Jack/8 Ninth St #313, Medford, MA ... 617-395-2778
Drummond, Deborah/67 Concord Rd, Sudbury, MA ... 508-443-3160
Drury, Christian Potter/61 Colonial Rd, Providence, RI ... 404-421-3406
Dudash, C Michael/PO Box 2803, Moretown, VT (P 519) ... 802-496-6400
Dugan, Brian/544 W Meadow Ave, Rahway, NJ ... 908-499-8417
Dugan, Louise/5046 MacArthur Blvd, Washington, DC ... 202-966-7549
Duke, Chris/Maple Ave Box 471, Millbrook, NY ... 914-677-9510
Duke, W E/90 Elm St, Westfield, MA ... 413-562-8494
Dumville, Fritz/22 Edison Ave, Providence, RI ... 401-861-7629
Dunlavey, Rob/46 Hampton Ave, Needham, MA ... 617-449-7142
Dunne, Tom/16 Cherry St, Locust Valley, NY ... 919-644-1087
DuPont, Lane/20 Evergreen Ave, Westport, CT ... 203-222-1562
Durham, Bob/15 Warrenton Ave, Hartford, CT ... 203-523-4562
Durham, Ed/6308 Sword's Way, Bethesda, MD ... 301-493-4237
Dursee, Brian/514 Birch Ave, Westfield, NJ ... 908-233-8096
Dvorak, Phillip/15 Warrenton Ave, Hartford, CT ... 203-523-4562
Dwingler, Randy/124 Median Dr, Wilmington, DE ... 302-478-6063
Dyen, Don/410 Parkview Way, Newtown, PA ... 215-968-9083
Dykes, John S/17 Morningside Dr S, Westport, CT (P 870) ... 203-222-8150

E

Eagle, Mike/7 Captains Ln, Old Saybrook, CT ... 203-388-5654
Earl, James/17 Parkview Dr, Hingham, MA ... 617-749-7982
Ebert, Len/Box 530/RD #2, Douglassville, PA ... 215-689-9872
Echevarria, Abe/Memory Lane Farm, Sherman, CT ... 203-355-1254
Eckstein, Bob/107 Cherry Lane, Medford, NY ... 516-654-0291
Edens, John/2464 Turk Hill Rd, Victor, NY ... 716-425-3441
Ederer, Janet/24 Ruth Pl, Plainview, NY ... 516-931-8003
Edwards, James/7 Sherman St, Charlestown, MA ... 617-522-2656
Egan, Bobbi/10 Myrtle St, White Plains, NY ... 914-761-8650
Eggleton, Bob/597 Smith St, Providence, RI ... 401-831-5030
Eichner, Thomas/4012 Southend Rd, Rockville, MD ... 301-871-1235
Einsel, Naiad/26 Morningside Dr S, Westport, CT ... 203-226-0709

Einsel, Walter/26 Morningside Dr S, Westport, CT................203-226-0709
Elliott, Elizabeth/532 20th St NW #809, Washington, DC.................202-638-6009
Ellis, Jon/1622 Brownsville Rd, Langhorne, PA.................215-750-6180
Elvidge, Ed/PO Box 709, SW Harbor, ME.................207-244-5048
Emmett, Bruce/8 Gerard Ave, Bellport, NY.................718-636-5263
Emmons, Barbara/19 Minjow St, Portland, ME.................207-761-2472
Engeman, Tom/2801 Quebec St NW, Washington, DC.................202-363-2623
Enos, Randall/11 Court of Oaks, Westport, CT.................203-227-4785
Epstein, Aaron/2015 Aspen Dr, Plainsboro, NJ.................609-275-1034
Epstein, Edward/PO Box 1089, Montpelier, VT.................802-229-5123
Epstein, Len/720 Montgomery Ave, Narbeth, PA.................215-664-4700
Epstein, Lorraine/21 Marianne Rd, Darien, CT.................203-656-1185
Erickson, Mary Anne/7470 Glasco Trnpk, Saugerties, NY.................914-246-3804
Estey, Peg/27 Irving Terrace, Cambridge, MA.................617-876-1790
Ettlinger, Doris/RD #2/Box 6, Hampton, NJ.................908-537-6322
Eucalyptus Tree Studio/2221 Morton St, Baltimore, MD.................410-243-0211
Evans, Leslie/17 Bay St, Watertown, MA.................617-924-3058
Eveland, Russ/1103 Ralph Rd, Newark, DE.................302-737-9102
Ewers, Joseph/220 Mill St, Holliston, MA.................508-429-6375
Eynon, Debbie/118 Montgomery Ave #A3-3, Bala Cynwyd, PA.................215-668-0986

F

Fabian, Steven/17 Central Ave, Mine Hill, NJ.................201-989-0934
Fahey, Gilbert/60 Ridgewood St, Manchester, CT.................203-647-8955
Fallin, Ken/25 Windsor Rd, Milton, MA.................617-696-2677
Fallon, Douglas/50 Twin Brooks Ave, Middletown, NJ.................201-671-6064
Faraclas, Andrea/227 Chris Columbus Dr #335B, Jersey City, NJ.................201-433-3459
Faria, Jeff/937 Garden St, Hoboken, NJ.................201-656-3063
Farnham, Joe/14 Arlington St #1, Somerville, MA.................617-628-7882
**Farnsworth, Bill/PO Box 653, New Milford, CT
(P 876)**.................**203-355-1649**
Farrell, Marybeth/77 Dwight Pl, Engelwood, NJ.................201-569-1655
Fauver, Chris/3929 Madison St, Hyattsville, MD.................301-699-9227
Feinen, Jeff/4702 Sawmill Rd, Clarence, NY.................716-759-8406
Fellman, Nancy/126 Sumac St, Philadelphia, PA.................215-483-3698
Ferris, Keith/50 Moraine Rd, Morris Plains, NJ.................201-539-3363
Fiedler, Joseph D/500 Sampsonia Way, Pittsburgh, PA.................412-322-7245
Field, Bob/336 Washington St, Brookline, MA.................617-232-2230
Fifield, Lew/1300 Mt Royal Ave, Baltimore, MD.................410-669-9200
Figueroa, Rafael/176 Fairview Ave, Jersey City, NJ.................201-451-3160
Fijal, Ted/121 Carriage Rd, Chicopee, MA.................413-532-7334
Filippo, Judy/114 Jefferson St #4, Hoboken, NJ.................201-792-3290
**Filippucci, Sandra/614-C Larchmont Acres East,
Larchmont, NY (P 541)**.................**212-477-8732**
Finch, Sharon Roy/426 8th St NE, Washington, DC.................202-546-1045
Fine, Howard/330 Rolling Rock Rd, Mountainside, NJ.................908-522-1855
Finewood, Bill/605 S Main St, E Rochester, NY.................716-377-2126
Finney, Lawrence/110 Mercer St #3D, Jersey City, NJ.................201-432-8407
Fione, Dan/2276 Mt Carmel Ave, Glenside, PA.................215-885-8227
Fiore, Peter/St Rd 2355-H, Matamoras, PA (P 539).................**717-491-5002**
Fisch, Paul/5111 Coffee Tree Lane, N Syracuse, NY.................315-451-8147
Fisher, Cynthia/RFD Box 87B, Charlemont, MA.................413-625-8204
Fisher, Hyman W/121 E Northfield Rd, Livingston, NJ.................201-994-9480
Fisher, Mark S/15 Colonial Dr, Westford, MA.................508-392-0303
**Fitzhugh, Gregg/3000 Chestnut Ave #6, Baltimore,
MD (P 459)**.................**410-889-2733**
Flat Tulip Studio/Rt 1 Box 146, Marietta, PA.................717-426-1344
Fleischer, Pat/223 Katherine St, Scotch Plains, NJ.................908-889-9059
Flickinger, Tracy/20 W Emerson St, Melrose, MA.................617-662-8660
Flynn, Maura/8 George St, Manhasset, NY.................516-627-6608
Fogletto, Ben/3137 Bay Ave, Ocean City, NJ.................609-391-1537
Foley, Timothy/170 Thorndike St, E Cambridge, MA.................617-876-3536
Fondersmith, Mark/7008 Eden Brook Dr, Columbia, MD.................410-290-8127
Ford, Andrew/Box 537, Brunswick, ME.................207-725-1633
Ford, Pam/251 Greenwood Ave, Bethel, CT.................203-797-8188
Forman, James/2 Central Pl, Lynbrook, NY.................516-599-2046
Forte, Joseph/17 Parsonage Rd, E Setauket, NY.................516-941-3641
Foster, Stephen Design/17 51st St #5, Weehawken, NJ.................201-866-9040
Foster, Susan/4800 Chevy Chase Dr #500, Chevy Chase, MD.................301-652-3848
Fournier, Walter/185 Forest St, S Hamilton, MA.................508-468-2892
Fowler, Eric/411 Beatty St, Trenton, NJ.................609-695-4305
Fox, Rosemarie/PO Box 186, Bearville, NY (P 631).................**914-679-6132**
Foy, Lynne/243 Linwood Ave, Newton, MA.................617-244-3768
Francis, John/2132 N Market St 3rd Fl, Wilmington, DE.................302-655-9011
Francisco Adv & Design/126 Green Lane, Philadelphia, PA.................215-482-6610
**Franke, Phil/10 Nehring Ave, Babylon Village, NY
(P 168)**.................**516-661-5778**

Frankel, Adrian/315 Monroe St, Hoboken, NJ.................201-656-4317
Frazier, Jillian/Seven Wells Rd, Lincoln, MA.................617-259-9380
Freeman, Charles/192 Southville Rd, Southborough, MA.................617-872-4549
Freeman, Mark/1146 19th St NW, Washington, DC.................202-331-7722
Frick, Thomas/227 Doris Ave, Baltimore, MD.................410-789-3045
Fricke, Bill/426 Adamston Rd, Bricktown, NJ.................908-477-5482
Friederichs, Anni/10 Bay st #10, Westport, CT.................203-544-8924
Friedman, Marvin/17 Montague Ave, W Trenton, NJ.................609-883-1576
Frinta, Dagmar/2 College St, Providence, RI.................401-331-3511
Frizzell, Mark/P O Box 3176, Woburn, MA.................617-933-0805
Fry, Leslie/567 St Paul St #5, Burlington, VT.................802-862-4034
**Fuchs, Bernie/3 Tanglewood Ln, Westport, CT
(P 503)**.................**203-227-4644**
Fuggetta, Richard/1 Bridge St, Irvington, NY.................914-591-4645
Full Moon Creations/74 S Hamilton St, Doylestown, PA.................215-345-1233
Furgalack, Roberta/10 Maize Dr, Charlestown, RI.................401-364-3667

G

Gaadt, George/888 Thorn, Sewickley, PA.................412-741-5161
Gabor, Tim/474 Elm St, Northampton, MA.................413-585-0558
Gaines, Mark/370 S Harrison, E Orange, NJ.................201-678-5973
Gallagher, Jim/169 Northfiled Rd, Bridgewater, NJ.................908-722-5292
Gallagher, Matthew/1 Old Manor Rd, Holmdel, NJ.................908-741-0157
Gallimore, Gaylen/1802 Monmouth Blvd, Wall, NJ.................908-280-8030
Gallipoli, Wayne/12 Belmont St, Milford, CT.................203-874-6992
Gallivan, Gretta/11 North St #3, Marcellus, NY.................315-673-9123
Galup, Joan/2026 E York St, Philadelphia, PA.................215-423-6750
Gamache, John/192 Southville Rd, Southborough, MA.................508-872-4549
Garbowski, Gene/8958 Watchlight Ct, Columbia, MD.................301-596-1036
Garcia, Tom/597 Riverside Ave, Westport, CT.................203-226-4724
Gardei, Dean/617 E 34th St, Baltimore, MD.................410-235-3638
Gardner, Gail/227 Marlborough St, Boston, MA.................617-266-8626
Gardner, Mike/21 Heather Road, Watertown, MA.................617-924-4907
**Garland, Michael/19 Manor Rd/RR #2, Patterson,
NY (P 1004)**.................**914-878-4347**
Garland, Philip/717 Washington St, Newtonville, MA.................617-332-6741
Garrett, Cynthia/1 Fitchburg St, Somerville, MA.................617-628-2450
Gatto, Chris/PO Box 4041, Stamford, CT.................203-264-2400
Gavin, Bill/268 Orchard St, Millis, MA.................508-376-5727
**Gay-Kassel, Doreen/24-A Chestnut Court, Princeton,
NJ (P 1005)**.................**609-497-0783**
Gazzo, Peppi/1015 Grand St #5G, Hoboken, NJ.................201-798-6389
**Gebert, Warren/12 Stoneham Lane, New City, NY
(P 592,593)**.................**914-354-2536**
Geller, Andrea/45-B Hastings Ave, Rutherford, NJ.................201-507-5134
Gensheimer, Frank/5 Lawrence St Bldg 15, Bloomfield, NJ.................201-743-4305
Gensurowsky, Yvonne/2510-F Airy Hill Circle, Crofton, MD.................301-721-6938
Genzo, John Paul/802 Ravens Crest Dr, Plainsboro, NJ.................609-275-5601
Geogriann, Margaret/4508 West Virginia Ave, Bethesda, MD.................301-496-5566
Gerber, Mark & Stephanie/18 Oak Grove Rd, Brookfield, CT.................203-775-3658
Gerlach, Cameron/3000 Chestnut Ave #113, Baltimore, MD.................410-889-0406
Gervais, Stephen/183 Riverside Ave, Warwick, RI.................401-737-8526
Geyer, Jackie/107 6th St #207 Fulton Bldg, Pittsburgh, PA.................412-261-1111
Giana, Alan/19 Field Rock Rd, Farmington, CT.................203-678-9239
Giardina, Laura/12 Buckingham Ct, Pomona, NY.................914-354-0871
Giarnella, Andy/259 Main St, E Berlin, CT.................203-828-8410
Giedd, Richard/101 Pierce Rd, Watertown, MA.................617-924-4350
Giguere, Ralph/2220 Delancey Pl, Philadelphia, PA.................215-968-3696
Gilbert, Douglas R/8 Lafayette St, Newburyport, MA.................508-465-8285
Gilfoy, Bruce/568 Washington St, Wellesley, MA.................617-235-8977
Gilligan, Sheila/185 Highland Ave, Somerville, MA.................617-628-5144
Gilman, Mary/Star Rte 13-A, Wendell Depot, MA.................508-544-7425
Gilmour, Joni/10 Dane St, Jamaica Plain, MA.................617-524-6556
Gilroy, Robin/53 West St, Newton, MA.................617-964-6128
Gingras, Lisa/74 S Hamilton St , Doylestown, PA.................215-345-1233
Gino/7 Dublin Hill Dr, Greenwich, CT.................203-869-8010
Giordano, Edward/59B St Andrews Blvd, Clifton, NJ.................201-778-6379
Gist, Linda E/224 Madison Ave, Fort Washington, PA.................215-643-3757
Giuliani, Alfred/11 Terhune Ave, Jersey City, NJ.................201-432-0443
Giusti, Robert/340 Long Mountain Rd, New Milford, CT.................203-354-6539
Glasbergen, Randy J/PO Box 611, Sherburne, NY.................913-642-2620
Glazer, Art/2 James Rd, Mt Kisco, TX.................914-666-4554
Glazer, Ted/28 West View Rd, Spring Valley, NY.................914-354-1524
Glessner, Marc/24 Evergreen Rd, Somerset, NJ.................908-249-5038
Glidden, Althea/726 Pacific St, Baltimore, MD.................301-523-5903
**Gnan, Patrick/731 North 24th St, Philadelphia, PA
(P 372)**.................**215-232-6666**

Goebel, Joe/72 High St, Topsfield, MA......................................508-887-3528
Gold, Al/450 Valley Rd, W Orange, NJ.....................................201-673-9035
Gold, Marcy/155-L Friedman Rd, Monticello, NY....................914-794-0359
Gold, Sandi/18 High St, Westerly, RI...401-596-9195

Goldberg, Richard A/66 Walnut St,
Arlington, MA (P 764,765)....................................617-646-1041
Goldinger, Andras/215 C St SE #310, Washington, DC.........202-543-9029
Goldman, Marvin/RD 3 Gypsy Trail Rd, Carmel, NY..............914-225-8611

Goldrick, Lisa/738 Hillcrest Rd, Ridgewood , NJ
(P 1009)..201-652-3835
Gonzalez, Ray/169 Jane St, Englewood, NJ............................201-567-6208
Goode, Harley/30 Regina Dr, Monsey, NY..............................914-578-5677

Goodrich, Carter/137 Water St, Stonington, CT
(P 1010,1011)...203-535-1141
Gorski, Peter/41 Elizabeth St, Peak's Island, ME...................207-766-5593
Goryl, John/65 Robins Ave, Rockledge, PA.............................215-663-0128
Gothard, David/RD 4/Box 4301A, Bangor, ME........................215-588-4937
Goudreau, Roc/1342 Berkshire Ave, Springfield, MA..............413-543-6796

Graber, Jack/620 Union St, Schenectady, NY
(P 610)..518-370-0312
Grafica, Gergei/24 Roe park, Highland Falls, NY....................914-446-2367
Grashow, James/14 Diamond Hill Rd, W Redding, CT.............203-938-9195

Graves, David/133 RR Wheeler St, Gloucester, MA
(P 1016)..508-283-2335
Green, Howie/6 St James Ave, Boston, MA.............................617-542-6063

Green, Norman/11 Seventy Acres Rd, W Redding,
CT (P 589)..203-438-9909
Greene, Joel & Anne/70 Rocky Pond Rd, Boylston, MA..........508-869-6440
Gregory, Lane/8 Cranberry Lane, Dover, MA..........................508-785-1513
Greigg, Linda/1010 Notley Rd, Silver Spring, MD...................301-384-6340
Grewe, Nilou/4 Wakeman Pl, Larchmont, NY..........................914-834-6820
Griegg, Linda/509 Notley Rd, Silver Spring, MD.....................301-384-6340

Griesbach/Martucci/41 Twinlight Terrace,
Highlands, NJ (P 54,55)..908-291-5945
Griffo, Joseph/54 North Ave, New Rochelle, NY......................914-633-5734

Grimes, Rebecca A/936 Stone Rd, Westminster, MD
(P 1018)..410-857-1675
Gross, Steve/434 E Front St, Plainfield, NJ.............................908-755-4738
Grossman, Andrew/3912 Ingomar St NW, Washington, DC 202-686-0480
Grote, Rich/21 Tyndale Rd, Hamilton Square, NJ....................609-586-5896
Gruttola, John/4 School Ct, Coram, NY...................................516-696-7056
Guancione, Karen/262 DeWitt Ave, Belleville, NJ....................201-450-9490
Gully, Bethany/791 Tremont St, Boston, MA............................617-437-7556

Gunn, Robert/229 Berkeley #52, Boston, MA (P 527)....617-266-3858
Gunning, Kevin/37 Denison Rd, Middleton, CT.........................203-347-0688
Guran, Michael/1 Fitchburg St, Somerville, MA........................617-666-8881

Gustafson, Dale/56 Fourbrooks Rd, Stamford, CT
(P 166)..203-322-5667
Guzzi, George/11 Randlett Pk, W Newton, MA.........................617-244-2932
Gyson, Mitch/4412 Colmar Gardens Dr E, Baltimore, MD.......301-243-3430
Gyurcsak, Joe/Chestnut Willow #3A-6, Cranbury, NJ.............609-426-4119

H

Haas, Shelly/50-A Village Green, Budd Lake, NJ 201-347-8544
Haber-Schaim, Tamar/1870 Beacon St/Bldg 6 #B1, Brookline, MA 617-738-8883
Haberman, Jim/12 Cleveland St #2, Arlington, MA...................617-646-5906
Haefele, Steve/111 Heath Rd, Mahopac, NY............................914-736-0785
Haffner, Marilyn/15 Seven Pines Ave, Cambridge, MA............617-547-2034
Hafner, Marylin/185 Holworthy St, Cambridge, MA.................617-354-0696
Hahn, Eileen/8 Hillwood Rd, East Brunswick, NJ....................908-390-4188

Hahn, Marika/Oak Tree Rd/Box 670, Palisades,
NY (P 852)..914-365-3317
Hallgren, Gary/98 Laurelton Dr, Mastic Beach, NY.................516-399-5531
Hallman, Tom/38 S 17th St, Allentown, PA..............................215-776-1144
Hally, Greg/18 Kennedy Lane, Stamford, CT...........................203-967-8045
Halverson, Lydia/25-Q Sylvan Rd S, Westport, CT..................203-226-4293

Hamblin, Randy/731 North 24th St, Philadelphia,
PA (P 365)..215-232-6666

Hamilton, Ken/16 Helen Ave, West Orange, NJ
(P 1024)..201-736-6532
Hamilton, Thomas/2276 Mt Carmel Ave, Glenside, PA............215-885-8227
Hamilton, William/81 Sand Rd, Ferrisburg, VT........................802-877-6869
Hampshire, Michael/7 Dublin Hill Dr, Greenwich, CT...............203-869-8010
Haney, William/674 S Branch River Rd, Somerville, NJ............908-369-8792

Hansen, Biruta/Sun Hill/RD1/Box 39G, Liverpool, PA
(P 864)..717-444-3682
Hansen, Ken/2 Fuller Ave, Swampscott, MA............................617-598-0111

Hantel, Johanna/437 E Belvidere St #F8, Nazareth,
PA (P 1027)..215-759-2025
Harden, Laurie/121 Banta Lane, Boonton Township, NJ..........201-335-4578
Hardin, Bob/13 Parkway West, Caldwell, NJ...........................201-403-2896
Hardy, Jill/1662-D Beekman Pl NW, Washington, DC..............202-667-4245
Hardy, Neil O/2 Woods Grove, Westport, CT...........................203-226-4446
Hardy-Faraci, Cheryl/59 Pitman, Wakefield, MA.....................617-245-5315
Harlan, Steve/325 Chesapeake Ave, Prince Frederick, MD.....410-535-2514

Harmon, Traci/3000 Chestnut Ave #6, Baltimore,
MD (P 467)...410-467-7588

Harrington, Glenn/329 Twin Lear Rd, Pipersville,
PA (P 641)..215-294-8104
Harrington, Sheila/2836 27th St NW, Washington, DC.............202-328-3231

Harrington, Steve/597 Riverside Ave, Westport,
CT (P 590)..203-226-4724
Harris, Ellen/125 Pleasant St #602, Brookline, MA.................617-739-1867
Harris, Peter/18 Square St, Bellows Falls, VT.........................802-463-1477
Harrison, Hugh/314 Pavonia Ave, Jersey City, NJ...................201-798-6086
Harsh, Fred/7 Ivy Hill Rd/Box 959, Ridgefield, CT...................203-438-8386
Harte, Cheryl/48 Norfield Rd, Weston, CT...............................203-221-1691
Harty, Beth Rubin/4108 28th St, Mt Ranier, MD.......................301-927-0504
Harvey, Paul/475-B Commanche Ln, Stratford, CT.................203-381-9836
Haselbacher, Nancy/69 Park Dr, Boston, MA...........................617-424-8572
Hasto, Ray/34 1/2 State St, Pittsford, NY................................716-385-6101
Hasz, Judith Ann/89 Delmore Ave, Berkeley Hts, NJ..............908-464-2466
Hatton, Enid/46 Parkway, Fairfield, CT...................................203-259-3789
Havice, Susan/6 Roundy Lane, Lynnfield, MA..........................617-334-3976

Hawkes, Kevin/27 Pine St, Portland, ME (P 530)........207-828-0721
Hazelton, Betsey/106 Robbins Dr, Carlisle, MA.......................508-369-5309

Healy, Deborah/72 Watchung Ave, Upper Montclair,
NJ (P 817)..201-746-2549
Hearn, Diane Dawson/22 Spring St, Pauling, NY....................914-855-1152
Hearn, Walter/22 Spring St, Pauling, NY................................914-855-1152
Heath, R Mark/4338 Roland Springs Dr, Baltimore, MD..........410-366-4633
Heimann, Steve/PO Box 406, Oradell, NJ...............................201-345-9132
Heimbach, Gale/RD 1/Box 367/Washington St, Douglasville, PA....215-582-8026
Hein, Jean/2276 Mt Carmel Ave, Glenside, PA........................215-885-8227
Heitmann, Bob/9071 Millcreek RD #116, Levittown, PA..........215-946-1394
Hellmuth, James/7212 Willow Ave, Takoma Park, MD............301-270-4450

Henderson, Dave/32 James Rd/RR 5, Boonton
Twnshp, NJ (P 172)...201-402-1461
Henderson, Garnet/820 Hudson #2-7, Hoboken, NJ...............201-653-3948
Hendler, Sandra/1823 Spruce St, Philadelphia, PA................215-735-7380
Hendrickson, Kathy/856 Springfield Ave, New Providence, NJ....908-665-2192
Hennessey, Glenn/2151 California St NW #40, Washington, DC....202-483-7883

Henry, Doug/229 Berkeley #52, Boston, MA (P 530)....617-266-3858

Henry-May, Rosemary/2625 Garfield St NW,
Washington, DC (P 1031)......................................202-667-0455
Herring, Michael/RD 1 Box 205A, Cold Spring, NY 914-265-9476
Hess, Mark/88 Quicks Lane, Katonah, NY..............................914-232-5870
Hess, Richard/310 Litchfield Rd, Norfolk, CT..........................203-354-2921

Hess, Robert/63 Littlefield Rd, E Greenwich, RI
(P 1032)..401-885-0331

Hewitt, Margaret/144 Soundview Rd, Huntington,
NY (P 1034)..516-427-1404

Hewitt/Low Studios/144 Soundview Rd,
Huntington, NY (P 1034,1035).............................516-427-1404
Hidy, Lance/PO Box 806, Newburyport, MA............................508-462-6567
Hierro, Claudia & Gregory/162 Tamboer Dr, N Haledon, NJ....201-427-3647
Hierro, George/1099 Rosse Ave, New Milford, NJ...................201-907-0423
Hildebrandt, Greg/120 American Rd, Morris Plains, NJ...........201-292-6852
Hildebrandt, Tim/10 Jackson Ave, Gladstone, NJ....................908-234-2149
Hill, Michael/2433 Maryland Ave, Baltimore, MD....................410-366-8338
Hillios, Sonia/PO Box 90, Southampton, MA............................413-527-4059

Himsworth, Jim 3rd/731 North 24th St, Philadelphia,
PA (P 373)..215-232-6666
Hinlicky, Greg/PO Box 1521, Toms River, NJ.........................908-269-4867
Hobbs, Bob/515 Spring St, Newport, RI..................................401-848-5848
Hocking, Philip/1615 Manchester Lane NW, Washington, DC 202-882-8237
Hodgkinson, Geoffrey/192 Southville Rd, Southborough, MA....508-872-4549
Hoeffner, Deb/538 Cherry Tree Lane, Kinnelon, NJ................201-838-5490
Hoey, Peter/1715 15th St NW #2, Washington, DC.................202-234-2110
Hoffman, Nancy/16 Ridge Dr, Berkeley Heights, NJ................908-665-2177

Hofkin, Bonnie/18 McKinley St, Rowayton, CT
(P 473)..203-866-3734
Hokanson, Lars/PO Box 199, Hopeland, PA............................717-733-9066
Holas, Evzen/858 Broadway #2, Chelsea, MA.........................617-889-5880
Holder, John/128 Beechtree Dr, Broomall, PA.........................215-356-0362

Hong, Min Jae/54 Pts of View Dr, Warwick, NY (P 776,777) 914-986-8040
Hopp, Andrea/301 High Mountain Ln, York Town, NY 914-767-7164
Houston, Greg/412 Lyman Ave, Baltimore, MD 410-323-7130
Hovey, Jack/717 Park Ave, Baltimore, MD 410-244-7205
Howard, Rob/55 Westland Terrace, Haverville, MA 508-372-8915
Howell, Van/PO Box 812, Huntington, NY 516-424-6499
Hubbard, Marcie Wolf/1507 Ballard St, Silver Spring, MD (P 1040) 301-585-5815
Huehnergarth, John/196 Snowden Ln, Princeton, NJ 609-921-3211
Huelsman, Amy/24 S Calumet Ave, Hastings on Hudson, NY 914-478-0596
Huerta, Gerard/45 Corbin Dr, Darien, CT (Inside Back Flap/Books 1 & 2) 203-656-0505
Hugg, Martin/718 Park Ave, Hoboken, NJ 201-420-6304
Hughes, Marianne/731 North 24th St, Philadelphia, PA (P 368) 215-232-6666
Hughes, Neal/731 North 24th St, Philadelphia, PA (P 375) 215-232-6666
Hughes, Stephanie/89 Oawton St, Brookline, MA 617-277-7676
Huling, Phil/938 Bloomfield St, Hoboken, NJ 201-795-9366
Hunt, Peter/Six Paag Lane, Little Spring, NJ 908-741-1465
Hurd, Jackie/71 Lockland Ave, Framingham, MA 608-879-6319
Hurd, Jane/4002 Virginia Pl, Bethesda, MD (P 96,97) 301-229-7966
Hurd, Lauren/6701 Parkway Rd, Baltimore, MD 410-377-9084
Hurwitz, Joyce/7314 Burdette Ct, Bethesda, MD 301-365-0340
Hutchison, Bruce/192 Southville Rd, Southboro, MA (P 889) 508-872-4549
Huyssen, Roger/45 Corbin Dr, Darien, CT (Inside Back Flap/Books 1 & 2) 203-656-0200
Hynes, Robert/5215 Muncaster Mill Rd, Rockville, MD 301-926-7813

IJ

Ingraham, Erick/66 Old Jaffrey Rd, Peterborough, NH 613-924-6785
Inouye, Carol/Gulf Schoolhouse Rd, Cornwallville, NY 518-634-7589
Iosa, Ann/7 Ivy Hill Rd/Box 959, Ridgefield, CT 203-438-8386
Ippolito, Frank/361 Devon St, Kearney, NJ 201-998-0581
Irish, Gary/45 Newbury St, Boston, MA 617-247-4168
Irwin, Virginia/139 S Highland St #3, W Hartford, CT 203-232-6956
Jackson, Robert R/816 Bainbridge St, Philadelphia, PA 215-627-8413
JAEL/PO Box 11178, Fairfield, NJ 201-808-4363
JAK Graphics Ltd/458 Newtown Trnpk, Weston, CT 203-454-4687
Jakubowski, Nancy/252 Doyle Ave, Providence, RI 401-331-7858
Janesko, Lou/10400 Connecticut Ave NW, Kensington, MD 301-933-5533
Jareaux, Robin/28 Eliot St, Boston, MA (P 1042) 617-524-3099
Jauniskis, Ramune/210 Hillside Ave, Needham, MA 617-444-1185
Jazwiecki, Leonard/311 West St, Amherst, MA 413-256-0321
Jeffery, Lynn/RR4 Box 970, Stowe, VT 802-253-4767
Jennings, Beth/100 Manhattan Ave, Union City, NJ 201-601-0886
Jerome, Karen A/633 Highland Ave, Needham, MA 617-444-8667
Jig, Harold W/8421 Spruill Dr, Bowie, MD 301-262-7820
Johnson, Craig/63 Providence Ave, Doylestown, PA 215-348-2593
Johnson, D B/PO Box 360, Plainfield, NH 603-675-6113
Johnson, Glenn/76 Elm St #313, Boston, MA 617-522-0165
Johnson, Laura Stearns/13 Winter Rd, Weare, NH 603-529-7606
Johnson, Richard/PO Box 555, Cohasset, MA 617-749-7600
Johnson, Sarah/333 Wickenden St, Providence, RI 401-273-0903
Johnston Carlson, Susan/36 Overlook Dr, Hackettstown, NJ (P 572) 908-813-1113
Jonason, Dave/355 Epping Way, Annapolis, MD (P 303,707) 410-849-8880
Jones, Don/695 Sayre Ave #22, Perth Amboy, NJ 908-324-1096
Jones, Jeffrey/17 Central Ave, Mine Hill, NJ 201-989-0934
Jones, John R/335 Town St, East Haddam, CT 203-873-9950
Jones, Keith R/844 Berkeley Ave, Trenton, NJ 609-695-7448
Jones, Robert/47 W Stewart, Lansdowne, PA 215-626-1245
Jones, Roger/34 Gorham St, Cambridge, MA 617-661-8645
Jordan, Laurie/7 Ivy Hill Rd/Box 959, Ridgefield, CT 203-438-8386
Jordan, Polly/29 Warren Ave, Somerville, MA 617-776-0329
Joudrey, Ken/530 Tanager Pl, Stratford, CT 203-378-5007
Joyce, Michael/1402 Beacon St, Brookline, MA 617-734-4424
Joyner, Eric/731 North 24th St, Philadelphia, PA 215-232-6666
Joyner, Ginny/PO Box 306, Winooski, VT 802-865-9565
Juhasz, Victor/576 Westminster Ave, Elizabeth, NJ 908-351-4227

K

Kabaker, Gayle/18 McKinley St, Rowayton, CT (P 474) 203-866-3734
Kachik, John/3000 Chestnut Ave #6, Baltimore, MD (P 1047) 410-467-7916
Kaczman, James/7 Chester St, Watertown, MA 617-923-4605
Kalabokis, Peter/19 N Charlemont Ct, N Chelmsford, MA 508-251-3058
Kane, Kid/9 W Bridge St, New Hope, PA 215-862-0392
Kane, Michael/9 Holland Lane, Cranberry, NJ 609-448-0843
Kanturek, Les/63 Blumel Rd, Middletown, NY 914-692-0094
Kascht, John/635 A St NE, Washington, DC 202-546-9527
Kassel, Doreen/24-A Chestnut Ct, Princeton, NJ 609-497-0783
Kassler, Elizabeth/128 Prospect Ave, Dumont, NJ 201-385-3551
Kastner, John/158 Burwell Rd, Rochester, NY 716-328-3262
Kathan-Sayess, Shirley/205 Indian Meadow Dr, Northboro, MA 508-393-5108
Katsin, Nancy/229 Spring Garden Rd, Milford, NJ 908-995-2177
Kay, Patricia M/51 Linden Ave, Metuchen, NJ 908-549-7083
Kazi, Pat/2813 Rocks Rd, Jarrettsville, MD 410-838-9584
Keats, Debby/23 Washington Ave, Schenectady, NY 518-382-7560
Keene, Donald/191 Clove Rd, New Rochelle, NY (P 619) 914-636-2128
Kelley, Steve/3501 Windom Rd, Brentwood, MD 301-699-1766
Kelly, Sean/1622 19th St NW #3, Washington, DC 202-462-0606
Kemp, Dan/9543 Dublin Rd, Walkersville, MD 301-845-6107
Kenny, Aggie/51 King Street, Dobbs Ferry, NY 914-693-5836
Kerr, Tom/125 Bamm Hollow Rd, Middletown, NJ 908-922-6000
Ketler, Ruth Sofair/101 Bluff Terrace, Silver Spring, MD (P 1049) 301-593-6059
Keyes, Michael D/14 Lillian Ave, Providence, RI 401-467-6568
Kibiuk, Lydia V/8 F Cross Keys Rd, Baltimore, MD 410-433-1107
Kidd, Tom/59 Cross Brook Rd, New Milford, CT 203-355-1781
Kiernan, Jacquie/1 Rutgers Ct B3, Belleville, NJ 201-751-8717
Kilroy, John/28 Fairmount Way, Nantasket, MA 617-925-0582
King, Caryn/166 Ames St, Sharon, MA 617-784-2196
King, Manuel/20 Woodchuck Hill, Harvard, MA 508-456-3412
Kingsbery, Guy/305 High St, Milford, CT 203-878-8939
Kinstrey, Jim/1036 Broadway, W Longbranch, NJ 908-229-0312
Kirk Noll, Cheryl/19 Hooker St, Providence, RI 401-861-5869
Kirk, Betsy/310 St Dunstans Rd, Baltimore, MD 410-235-3154
Kiwak, Barbara/3000 Chestnut Ave #6, Baltimore, MD (P 466) 301-243-0643
Klein, Kathryn/51 Melcher St, Boston, MA 617-350-7970
Kleinsteuber, Robert/38 Nina Court, Gaithersburg, MD 301-921-4253
Klim, Joseph/PO Box 463, Avon, CT 203-676-9933
Kline, Rob/229 Berkeley #52, Boston, MA 617-266-3858
Klopp, Karyl/5209 Eighth St/Cnstitutn Qtrs, Charlestown, MA 617-242-7463
Kluglein, Karen/37 Cary Rd, Great Neck, NY (P 696) 212-684-2974
Knabel, Lonnie/34 Station St, Brookline, MA 617-566-4464
Knepp, Tim/3611 Laurel View Court, Laurel, MD 301-490-3115
Kocar, George F, Boston, MA 617-555-1212
Koeppel, Gary/258 Chestnut Ave, Jamaica Plain, MA 617-522-3051
Kohl, Joe/522 Vine Ave, Toms River, NJ 908-349-4149
Kolt-Fisher, Kathleen/RD4 Box 677, Middlebury, VT 802-462-3662
Korman, Ira/NJ 201-736-3022
Korvatin, Daniel/1702 Oak Court, Monmouth Junction, NJ 908-274-2363
Kossin, Sanford/143 Cowneck Rd, Port Washington, NY 516-883-3038
Koster, Aaron/2 Yeoman Way, Manalapan, NJ (P 1051) 908-536-2815
Kouw, Danny/1592 Panview Ave, Seaford, NY 516-221-5294
Kozlowski, Martin/141 Southside Ave 2nd Fl, Hastings, NY 914-478-7445
Kralyevich, Vincent/706 Hudson St, Hoboken, NJ 201-653-3277
Kraus, James/195 Canton St, Boston, MA 617-437-1945
Krause, Linda/390 Princeton Ave, Jersey City, NJ 201-451-5849
Krepel, Dick/288 Westbrook Rd, Essex, CT (P 518) 203-767-2864
Krieger, Salem/91 Park Ave, Hoboken, NJ 201-963-3754
Krommes, Beth/RR 1/Box 1689, Rindge, NH 603-899-6061
Krosnick Studio/686 Undercliff Ave, Edgewater, NJ 201-224-5495
Krovatin, Dan/1702 Oak Ct, Monmouth Junction, NJ (P 1055) 908-274-2363
Krupinski, Loretta/6 Coach Dr, Old Lyme, CT 203-434-0075
Kseniak, Mark/12 Navesink Ave, Navesink, NJ 908-872-1559
Kubinyi, Laszlo/115 Evergreen Pl, Teaneck, NJ (P 152) 201-833-4428
Kulczak, Frank/9 W 29th St, Baltimore , MD 410-467-7300
Kulhanek, Paul/167 Cherry St #177, Milford, CT 203-876-0697
Kunic, Diane/72 High St #2, Topsfield, MA 508-887-3528
Kupper, Ketti/3 Evergreen Ave, Wilton, CT 203-761-9454
Kutakoff, Lauren/47 Cobblewood Rd, Livingston, NJ 201-994-3569
Kyhos, Brian/4 Linwood Pl, Rochester, NY 716-454-2630
Kyle, Ron/186 Lincoln, Boston, MA 617-426-5942

L

La Grone, Roy E/25 Indiana Rd, Somerset, NJ 908-846-7959
Labrasca, Judy/7 Walcott Ave, Falmouth, ME......................207-781-3858
Lacano, Frank/336 Sherwood Rd, Union, NJ.........................908-688-9251
Lackow, Andy/7004 Boulevard E #29C, Guttenberg,
NJ (P 843) **201-854-2770**
LaCourse, Carol/Six Steppingstone Rd W, Durham, NH......................603-659-6149
Laird, Thomas/128 S Second St, Philipsburg, PA....................814-342-2935
LaLiberte, Richard/1024 Adams St, Hoboken,
NJ (P 612) **201-659-7711**
Lamb, Greg/16 Greenough Ave, Jamaica Plain, MA...............617-983-0875
Lambrenos, Jim/12 Salem Court, Atco, NJ 609-768-0580
Lane, Edmund/74 Key St, Millis, MA....................................508-376-8752
Lang, Charles/33 Harbor St #2, Salem, MA..........................508-741-0029
Lang, Glenna/42 Stearns St, Cambridge, MA.......................617-661-7591
Langdon, John/4529 Pine St, Philadelphia, PA......................215-476-4312
Langer, DC/662 Massachusetts Ave, Boston, MA..................617-536-6651
Lanier, David/1408 Fifth Ave, Albany, NY............................518-439-8766
Lansberry, Charles/PO Box 836, Ocean City, NJ..................609-399-3105
Lanza, Barbara/PO Box 118, Pine Island, NY.......................914-258-4601
Laoang, Alfred/13416 Justice Rd, Rockville, MD....................301-946-2530
Larrivee, Steven/1430 Pippin Orchard Rd, Cranston, RI.........401-821-8417
Lawrence, Julie/174 Summit Ave #306, Summit, NJ...............908-273-1934
Lawton, April/31 Hampshire Dr, Farmingdale, NY..................516-454-0868
Layman, Linda J/9 Alan Rd, South Hamilton, MA...................508-468-4297
Leaders, Marsha/20117 Laurel Hill Way, Germantown, MD.............301-540-1652
Lebbad, James A/24 Independence Way, Titusville, NJ.............212-645-5260
LeBlanc, Terry/425 Watertown St, Newton, MA
(P 1057) **617-969-4886**
Lee, Bryce/126 77th St, N Bergen, NJ..................................201-662-9106
Lee, Nan/Box 703, Easton, MD..410-822-8776
Lee, Victoria/D8 Holiday Estates, Jessup, MD.......................301-596-3532
Lee, Wangdon/2439 Maryland Ave, Baltimore, MD................410-467-5463
Lefkowitz, Mark/94 Fox Meadow Lane, Dedham, MA............617-326-2615
Lefkowitz, Steve/2276 Mt Carmel Ave, Glenside, PA............215-885-8227
Lehew, Ron/17 Chestnut St, Salem, NJ................................609-935-1422
Leigh, Tom/Rote Hill, Sheffield, MA.....................................413-229-8258
Lemelman, Martin/1286 Country Club Rd, Allentown, PA........215-395-4536
Lemieux, Margo/22 Highland Ave, Mansfield, MA..................508-339-7487
LeMoult, Dolph/597 Riverside Ave, Westport, CT..................203-226-4724
Lenar, Loci B/17 Central Ave, Mine Hill, NJ..........................201-989-0934
Leonard-Gibson, Barbara/3501 Toddsbury Lane, Olney, MD.............301-570-9480
Lesh, David/18 McKinley St, Rowayton, CT (P 471) **203-866-3734**
Lesnick, H Robert/80 Merbrook Bend, Merion Station, PA.......215-667-5395
LeVan, Susan/30 Ipswich St #211, Boston, MA.....................617-536-6828
Levee, Gayle/51 Century St, Medford, MA............................617-396-9656
Levenson, Wendy/19 Flintlock Dr, Warren Town, NJ..............908-647-0900
Levin, Mara/2 Beverly Cir, Holliston, MA..............................508-429-2790
Levine, Ned/301 Frankel Blvd, Merrick, NY...........................516-378-8122
Levinson, David/219-D Richfield Terr, Clifton, NJ...................201-614-1627
Levinson, W Jason/11625 Sun Circle Way, Columbia, MD 301-854-0406
Levy, Pamela R/7 Trapelo St, Brighton, MA..........................617-254-5779
Levy, Robert S/1023 Fairway Rd, Franklin Square, NY 516-872-3713
Lewis, Polly Krumbhaar/125 McClenaghan Mill Rd, Wynnewood, PA...215-649-1989
Leyonmark, Roger/229 Berkeley #52, Boston, MA
(P 528) **617-266-3858**
Leyshon, Judy/5606 Sonoma Rd, Bethesda, MD...................301-530-5070
Liberman, Joni Levy/14 Hill Park Terrace, Randolph, MA........617-986-4657
Lichtenfels, Lisa/146 Bay St, Springfield, MA.......................413-781-1359
Lies, Brian/9 Humboldt St, Cambridge, MA..........................617-876-0678
Life, Kay/419 Southwick Rd B7, Westfield, MA......................413-562-6418
Light Flight/3000 Chestnut Ave #338, Baltimore, MD............410-235-1558
Lindroth, David/85 Broadway, W Milford, NJ.........................201-697-1965
Linnett, Charles/99 High St, Canton, MA..............................617-828-4972
Linstromberg, Ruth/41 Congress St #27, Nashua, NH............603-882-5021
Lipczenko, S Dimitri/3901 Tunlaw Rd NW #402, Washington, DC.......202-338-1318
Lisi, Victoria Poyser/19 Krasky Lane, Bridgewater, CT 203-350-9404
Lisker, Emily/15 Island Pl, Woonsocket, RI...........................401-762-2502
Littmann, Barry/57 Overlook Dr, Hackettstown, NJ................908-850-4405
Littmann, Rosemary/299 Rutland Ave, Teaneck, NJ..............201-833-2417
Lloyd, Mary Anne/11 Higgins St, Portland, ME......................207-773-4987
LoBue, Keith/25-Q Sylvan Rd S, Westport, CT......................203-226-4293
Loccisano, Karen/7 Ivy Hill Rd/Box 959, Ridgefield, CT 203-438-8386
Logan, Ron/PO Box 306, Brentwood, NY..............................516-273-4693
Lohstoeter, Lori/8 Farm Creek Rd, Rowayton, CT
(P 200,201) **203-857-4607**

Lombardi, Judith/25-Q Sylvan Rd S, Westport, CT................203-226-4293
LoMele, Bachrun/100 Washington St, Hoboken, NJ...............201-963-4572
Long, Bruce/112-H2 Frederick Ave, Rockville, MD.................301-294-2252
Long, Paulette/728 Undercliff Ave, Edgewater, NJ................201-224-8106
Lorenz, Albert/49 Pine Ave, Floral Park, NY.........................516-354-5530
Loschiavo, Doree/2714 S Marvine St, Philadelphia, PA...........215-336-1724
Lose, Hal/533 W Hortter St-Toad Hall, Philadelphia,
PA (P 887) **215-849-7635**
Love, Judith DuFour/68 Agassiz Ave, Belmont, MA................617-484-8023
Loverro, Jeff/PO Box 346, Pocasset, MA.............................02559-0346
Low, William/144 Soundview Rd, Huntington, NY
(P 1035) **516-427-1404**
Lowry, Rose/Appleton Rd RR 1, New Ipswich, NH................603-878-3202
Lozner, Ruth/9253 Three Oaks Dr, Silver Spring, MD
(P 657) **301-587-3125**
Lubey, Dick/726 Harvard, Rochester, NY.............................716-442-6075
Lucas-Haji, Geri/2200 19th St NW, Washington, DC..............202-387-9045
Lucier, Brian/158 Highland Ave, Athol, MA...........................508-249-6419
Lumpkins, William Kurt/72 High St, Topsfield, MA.................508-887-3528
Lyhus, Randy/4853 Cordell Ave #3, Bethesda, MD
(P 1067) **301-986-0036**
Lynch, Bob/2433 Maryland Ave, Baltimore, MD....................410-366-6535
Lynch, Fred/123 Pinehurst Ave, Providence, RI....................401-351-2699
Lynn, Kathy/1741 Bainbridge, Philadelphia, PA....................215-545-5039
Lyons, Linda/515 Anderson Ave, Cliffside Park, NJ...............212-216-8063

M

Maas, Julie/PO Box 252, Moody, ME...................................207-646-2764
Macanga, Steve/20 Morgantine Rd, Roseland, NJ.................201-403-8967
MacArthur, Dave/147 E Bradford Ave #B, Cedar Grove, NJ ...201-857-1046
Mackey, Greg/32 Pleasant Ave, Portland, ME.......................207-774-2420
Mackin & Dowd/2433 Maryland Ave, Baltimore, MD..............301-366-8339
MacNeill, Scott A/74 York St, Lambertville, NJ.....................609-397-4631
Maddalone, John/81 Lindberg Blvd, Bloomfield, NJ...............201-338-1674
Maddocks, Bruce/39 Holman Rd, Auburndale, MA................617-332-7218
Maffia, Daniel/236 S Dwight Pl, Englewood, NJ....................201-871-0435
Magalos, Christopher/3308 Church Rd, Cherry Hill, NJ..........609-667-7433
Magee, Alan/Route 68 Box 132, Cushing, ME.......................207-354-8838
Maharry, Carol/11 Chenin Run, Fairport, NY.........................716-223-8996
Mahoney, John/61 Dartmouth St, Boston, MA.......................617-267-8791
Mahoney, Katherine/60 Hurd Rd, Belmont, MA
(P 836) **617-489-0406**
Maliki, Malik/PO Box 425, Rochester, NY............................716-546-7606
Mandel, Saul/163 Maytime Dr, Jericho, NY..........................516-681-3530
Mann, Sheila/89-2 Staniford St, Auburndale, MA..................617-969-2767
Manos, Jim/53 Apple Way, Evesham Township, NJ...............609-596-8843
Manter, Barry/46 Eastern Promenade, Portland, ME..............207-773-0790
Marchesi, Steve/7 Ivy Hill Rd/Box 959, Ridgefield, CT..........203-438-8386
Marconi, Gloria/2525 Musgrove Rd, Silver Spring, MD..........301-890-4615
Marek, Mark/42 Erie St, Dumont, NJ...................................201-384-1791
Margeson, John/521 1/2 Griffin Ave, Canonsburg, PA............412-281-3948
Marinelli, Jeff/74 S Main St, Canandaigua, NY
(P 1071) **716-394-2856**
Marinsky, Jane/63 Cleveland Ave, Buffalo, NY
(P 1072) **716-881-3138**
Marion, Kate/85 Columbus Ave, Greenfield, MA....................413-774-4862
Mariuzza, Pete/146 Hardscrabble Rd, Briarcliff Manor, NY 914-769-3310
Marks, Laurie/1915 Walnut St, Philadelphia, PA...................215-564-3494
Marlow, Christopher/3816 Beecher Street NW, Washington, DC.........202-625-9102
Marsella, Valerie/4 Briarwood Rd, Lincoln, RI......................401-334-3113
Marshall, Pat/33325 M St NW 3rd Fl, Washington, DC...........202-342-0222
Martin, Richard/485 Hilda St, East Meadow, NY...................516-221-3630
Martin-Garvin, Dawne/Box 227, Monponsett, MA..................617-293-3927
Maryanski, Ken/314 Chelsea St, Everett, MA........................617-381-1806
Marzullo, Michael/2827 E Northern Parkway, Baltimore, MD.............410-426-7713
Mascio, Tony/4 Teton Ct, Voorhees, NJ...............................609-424-5278
Maslen, Barbara/216 Suffolk St, Sag Harbor, NY
(P 1078,1079) **516-725-3121**
Masse, D D/81 Seward Lane, Aston, PA...............................215-494-7525
Masseau, Jean Carlson/RR 1 Box 303 Silver St, Hinesburg, VT........802-482-2407
Matheis, Shelley/534 East Passaic Ave, Bloomfield, NJ.........201-338-9506
Matsick, Anni/345 Oakley Dr, State College, PA....................814-234-4752
Mattelson, Marvin/37 Cary Rd, Great Neck, NY
(P 697) **212-684-2974**
Mattingly, David/1112 Bloomfield St, Hoboken, NJ................201-659-7404
Mattiucci, Jim/247 N Goodman St, Rochester, NY................716-271-2280
Mauro, Ray/228 Second St, Clifton, NJ................................201-546-8750

Max, Deborah Dudley/157 Newbrook Lane, Bay Shore, NY 516-968-5918

Mayforth, Hal/121 Rockingham Rd, Londonderry,
NH (P 134,135) **603-432-2873**
Mayo, Frank/265 Briar Brae Rd, Stamford, CT 203-322-3650
Mayo, Martin & Robert/9 Stanford Ave, Colonia, NJ 908-382-4730
Mazoujian, Charles/20 Brook Rd, Tenafly, NJ 201-569-8057
Mazut, Mark/PO Box M1573, Hoboken, NJ 201-656-0657
Mazzini, John/68 Grey Ln, Levittown, NY 516-579-6518
McCloskey, Kevin/140 E Main, Kutztown, PA 215-683-6546
McCord, Kathleen/25-Q Sylvan Rd S, Westport, CT 203-226-4293
McCracken, Steve/2900 Connecticut Ave NW, Washington, DC 202-332-5857
McCurdy, Michael/66 Lake Buel Rd, Great Barrington, MA 413-528-2749
McDermott, Michael/12 South Main St, Stewartstown, PA 717-993-2746
McDevitt, Bill/59 Temple Pl #449, Boston, MA 617-482-4546
McDonnell, Patrick/11 Laureldale Ave, Metuchen, NJ 908-549-9341
McEntire, Fred/538 Long Rd, Pittsburgh, PA 412-731-3025
McGovern, Michael/27 Laurel Ave, Bradford, MA
(P 170) **508-373-4877**
McGuire & McGuire/495 Old York #440, Jenkintown, PA 215-886-4084
McGuire, Rebecca/34 E Gravers Ln, Philadelphia, PA 215-248-1636
McIntosh, Jon C/17 Devon Rd, Chestnut Hill, MA 617-277-9530
McKee, Dianne/PO Box 102, Perkiomenville, PA 215-234-0377
McKie, Roy/164 Old Clinton Rd, Flemington, NJ 908-788-7996
McLaughlin, Michael/158 Kelton St #8, Boston, MA 617-232-1692
McLellan, Anne C/285 Bennett St, Wrentham, MA 508-384-7355
McLoughlin, Wayne/RR 1/ Box 818-A, Woodstock,
VT (P 861,87) **802-457-2752**
McManus, Tom/31 The Crescent St, Montclair, NJ
(P 856) **201-744-1676**
McMillan, Kenneth/702 ByBerry Rd, Philadelphia, PA 215-698-9785
McNally, Kathleen/21 North St, Saco, ME 207-282-2713
McNeel, Richard/530 Valley Rd #2G, Upper Montclair, NJ 201-509-2255
McVicker, Charles/PO Box 183, Rocky Hill, NJ 609-924-2660
Medbery, Sherrell/18 Philadelphia Ave, Takoma Park, MD 301-270-0314
Medeiros, John Adv Art/273 Peckham St, Fall River, MA 508-676-8752
Medici, Ray/16 Hawthorn St, Rosslindale, MA 617-323-0842
Medoff, Jack/14 Hillside Rd S, Weston, CT 203-454-3199
Meeker, Carlene/24 Shore Dr, Winthrop, MA 617-846-5117
Meisel, Paul/51 Obtuse Rd S, Brookfield, CT (P 567) ...**203-775-7859**
Meisner, Arnold/, Peaks Island, ME 207-766-5091
Melius, John/3028 New Oak Ln, Bowie, MD 301-249-3709
Melvin, William Jr/211 Woodpecker Lane, Mt Holly, NJ 609-267-3394
Menk, France/PO Box 350, Pound Ridge, NY 212-691-4877
Metcalf, Paul/Webber Rd/Box 35C, Brookfield, MA 508-867-7754
Meyer, Glenn/PO Box 1663, Cranford, NJ 908-241-5009
Michalski Jr, Joseph E/302 Smith Ave, Severne Park, MD 410-647-8683
Milan, Bucky/Mill Town Road, Brewster, NY 914-279-2840
Miles, Elizabeth/7 Ivy Hill Rd/Box 959, Ridgefield, CT 203-438-8386
Miller, Kurt/1818 Bolton St, Baltimore, MD 301-669-8117
Milnazik, Kim/73-2 Drexelbrook Dr, Drexel Hill, PA 215-259-1565
Mineo, Andrea/12 Lincoln Blvd, Emerson, NJ 201-265-3886
Minigiello, Paul/290 Stover Ave, N Arlington, NJ 201-955-2501
Minisci, Diana/15 Warrenton Ave, Hartford, CT 203-523-4562
Mintz, Margery/9 Cottage Ave, Somerville, MA 617-623-2291
Miserendino, Pete/1216 Kettletown Rd, Southbury, CT 203-264-0908
Mistretta, Andrea/135 E Prospect St, Waldwick, NJ 201-652-7531
Miyake, Yoshi/7 Ivy Hill Rd/Box 959, Ridgefield, CT 203-438-8386
Mladinich, Charles/7 Maspeth Dr, Melville, NY 516-271-8525
Mock, Paul/27 Old Meeting House Green, Norton, MA 508-285-8309
Modell, Frank/PO Box 8, Westport, CT 203-227-7806
Moede, Jade/96 S Main St, Lodi, NJ 201-778-4090
Molano, Gabriel/PO Box 482, Catskill, NY 518-945-2999
Moldoff, Kirk/18 McKinley St, Rowayton, CT (P 475) ...**203-866-3734**
Montana, Leslie/35 Lexington Ave, Montclair, NJ 201-744-3407
Monteiro, Mary/32 Lyng St, N Dartmouth, MA 508-999-2880
Monteleone, Patrick/Ashmill Rd/Box 213, Mechanicsville, PA 215-794-8919
Moody, Eric/1158 Shore Rd, Cape Elizabeth, ME 207-799-4882
Mooney, Gerry/2 Main St #3S, Dobbs Ferry, NY 914-693-8076
Moore, Jack/131 Cedar Lake West, Denville, NJ 201-627-6931
Moore, Jo/1314 Kearney St NE, Washington, DC 202-526-2356
Morales, Manuel/PO Box 1763, Bloomfield, NJ 201-676-8187
Moran, Michael/21 Keep St, Madison, NJ 201-966-6229
Morecraft, Ron/97 Morris Ave, Denville, NJ 201-625-5752
Morozko, Bruce/111 First St, Jersey City, NJ 201-792-5974
Morris, Burton/270 Shady Ave #14, Pittsburgh, PA
(P 838) **412-441-2740**
Morris, Marilyn/1852 Biltmore St NW, Washington, DC 202-234-2286
Morrison, Bill/68 Glandore Rd, Westwood, MA 617-329-5288

Morrison, Pat/219 Rock Creek Church Rd N, Washington, DC 202-723-1824
Morrissey, Belinda/17 Casino Dr, Saratoga Springs, NY...................201-836-7016
Morrissey, Pat/102 Maple Ave, Bellport, NY 516-286-5631
Morrissey, Robert/56 Bullard St, Norwood, MA 617-769-5256
Morrow, Skip/Ware Rd/Box 123, Wilmington, VT 802-464-5523
Morse, Bill/731 North 24th St, Philadelphia, PA
(P 376) **215-232-6666**
Morton, Frank/18 High St, Oakland, ME 207-465-3324
Moss, Donald/232 Peaceable St, Ridgefield, CT 203-438-5633
Mott, Herb/902 Broadway, Norwood, NJ 201-768-3229
Mowry, Scott/65 India Row, Boston, MA 617-742-9849
Mulholland, Kurt/4212 49th St NW, Washington, DC 202-244-4147
Muller, Bob/437 Prospect St, S Amboy, NJ 908-727-8629
Murakami, Maho/116 Brambach Rd, Scarsdale, NY 914-723-7145
Murphy, Martha/9708 Robert Jay Way, Ellicott City, MD 410-750-7222
Murphy, Peter/136 Mountain Ave, Malden, MA 617-324-6914
Murray, John/770 Boyston St #23E, Boston, MA
(P 1092,1093) **617-424-0024**
Musy, Mark/PO Box 755, Buckingham, PA 215-794-8851
Myer, Andy/731 North 24th St, Philadelphia, PA
(P 377) **215-232-6666**
Myers, Lou/58 Lakeview Ave, Peekskill, NY 914-737-2307
Myers, V Gene/41 Douglas Rd, Glen Ridge, NJ 201-429-8731

N

Nacht, Merle/374 Main St, Weathersfield, CT
(P 70,71) **203-563-7993**
Naprstek, Joel/76 Park Place, Morris Plains, NJ 201-285-0692
Nash, Bob/100 Grove St, Worcester, MA...508-791-5530
Nash, Scott/15 Alden Rd, Dedham, MA 617-924-6050
Natale, Vince/47 Ethan Dr, Murray Hill, NJ 908-464-2677
Nees, Susan/4205 Morrison Ct, Baltimore, MD 410-355-0059
Neibart, Wally/1715 Walnut St, Philadelphia, PA 215-564-5167
Neider, Alan/283 Timberline, Cheshire, CT.....................................203-250-9923
Neumann, Ann/78 Franklin St, Jersey City, NJ
(P 1094) **201-420-1137**
Newman, Barbara Johansen/45 South St, Needham, MA..................617-449-2767
Newman, Kevin/4 Larch Dr, Chester, NJ 908-879-7657
Newman, Robert/420 Springbrook Ln, Hatboro, PA 215-672-8079
Nez, John/7 Dublin Hill Dr, Greenwich, CT......................................203-869-8010
Nicholson, Trudy/7400 Arden Rd, Cabin John, MD 301-229-0195
Niland, Brian/12 Columbine Rd, Paramus, NJ 201-265-6419
Niles, David/66 Third St, Dover, NH 603-742-6499
Nishimura, Masato/229 Berkeley #52, Boston, MA 617-266-3858
Noi Viva Design/220 Ferris Ave, White Plains, NY 914-946-1951
Noiset, Michelle/551 Tremont Ave, Boston, MA 617-542-2731
Nolan, Dennis/172 Southampton Rd, Westhampton, MA 413-527-1767
Norman, Helen/80 Main St, Dennisville, NJ 609-861-2537
Norman, Marty/5 Radcliff Blvd, Glen Head, NY 516-671-4482
Northrup, Susan/14 Imperial Pl, Providence, RI 401-521-2389
Notarile, Chris/11 Hamilton Ave, Cranford, NJ
(P 165) **908-272-1696**
Nothwanger, Rosemary/7604 Shadywood Rd,
Bethesda, MD (P 1095) **301-469-7130**
Novick, Dorothy Michele/5903 62nd Ave, Riverdale, MD 301-277-3390
Noyes, David/506 Lebanon St, Melrose, MA....................................617-662-6009
Noyse, Janet/118 Woodland Rd, Wyncote, PA 215-572-6975
Nyman, Steven/10 Maywood Ct, Fairlawn, NJ 201-797-1003

O

O'Leary, John/547 N 20th St, Philadelphia, PA 215-561-7377
O'Malia, Carol/51 Dover Terrace, Westwood, MA 617-326-0908
O'Neill, Fran/PO Box 716, Boston, MA 617-267-9215
O'Rourke, Patricia/1469 Beacon St #12, Brookline, MA 617-787-9513
O'Shaughnessy, Stephanie/458 Newtown Trnpk, Weston, CT.............203-454-4687
Oesman, Carrie/34 Elizabeth Ave, Stanhope, NJ 201-347-9066
Oh, Jeffrey/2635 Ebony Rd, Baltimore, MD (P 63) **410-661-6064**
Olivieri, Tom/1126 Willow Ave, Hoboken, NJ 201-659-9152
Olsen, Jimmy/50 New York Ave, Clark, NJ 908-388-0967
Olson, Victor/Fanton Meadows, West Redding, CT 203-938-2863
Olsson, David/1423 Quinnipiac Ave #514, New
Haven, CT (P 358) **203-469-1714**
Oplinger, Barbara/46 Carlton St, Brookline, MA 617-277-5866
Orner, Eric/23 Bay St, Cambridge, MA 617-547-8371
Osser, Stephanie /150 Winding River Rd, Needham, MA 617-237-1116
Ostergren, Sherri/75 Gardner St #15, Allston, MA 617-254-1254

Ostrokolowicz, Debra/6 Malden Dr, Webster, MA 508-943-8451
Otnes, Fred/Chalburn Rd, West Redding, CT (P 516)....203-938-2829
Otto, Jeff/2276 Mt Carmel Ave, Glenside, PA.......................215-885-8227
Oughton, Taylor/Jamison, Bucks County, PA........................215-598-3246
Owens, Jim/3000 Chestnut Ave #108, Baltimore, MD
(P 460)...410-467-7588

P

Pagano, Richard/18 Cumberland St, West Babylon, NY 516-661-1459
Palmer, Carol/107 South St #203, Boston, MA.....................617-482-8938
Palmer, Jan/458 Newtown Trnpk, Weston, CT.......................203-454-4687
Palmer, Tom/40 Chicasaw Dr, Oakland, NJ 201-337-8638
Palombo, Lisa/226 Willow Ave, Hoboken, NJ (P 540).....201-653-1501
Palulian, Dickran/18 McKinley St, Rowayton, CT
(P 472)...203-866-3734
Papadics, Joel/22 Scribner Pl, Wayne, NJ 201-956-7761
Paquette, Darisse A/202 Waverly St, Arlington, MA 617-643-1154
Pardo, Jose Angel/2803 Palisade Ave, Union City, NJ 201-867-5932
Parisi, Richard/3000 Chestnut Ave Ste 6, Baltimore,
MD (P 461)..410-243-7217
Parke, Steven/1442 E Baltimore St, Baltimore, MD 410-675-9087
Parker, Earl/5 New Brooklyn Rd, Cedar Brook, NJ 609-567-2925
Parker, Edward/9 Carlisle St, Andover, MA...........................508-475-2659
Parmenter, Wayne/1024 Adams St, Hoboken, NJ
(P 613)...201-659-7711
Parsekian, John/5 Lawrence St/Bldg 15, Bloomfield, NJ 201-748-9717
Parson, Nan/597 Riverside Ave, Westport, CT.......................203-226-4724
Pasqua, Lou/309 Walnut Rd, Pittsburgh, PA 412-761-5666
Passalacqua, David/325 Versa Pl, Sayville, NY......................516-589-1663
Pate, Rodney/7 Ivy Hill Rd/Box 959, Ridgefield, CT 203-438-8386
Paterson, James/4312 Mt Olney Lane, Olney, MD.................301-774-8329
Patrick, Cyndy/71 Swan St #3, Everett, MA..........................617-387-4296
Patrick, Pamela/398-A Burrows Run, Chadds Ford,
PA (P 603)...215-444-5928
Pavey, Jerry/1024 Adams St, Hoboken, NJ (P 614) 201-659-7711
Pavia, Cathy/7 Ivy Hill Rd/Box 959, Ridgefield, CT 203-438-8386
Payne, Thomas/49 Sheridan Ave, Albany, NY (P 520)..518-426-8816
Peck, Byron/1301 20th St NW #1005, Washington, DC 202-331-1966
Peck, Virginia/73 Winthrop Rd, Brookline, MA......................617-232-1653
Pellaton, Karen/25-Q Sylvan Rd S, Westport, CT...................203-226-4293
Pendola, Joanne/2 Sutherland Rd #34, Boston,
MA (P 1106)..617-566-4252
Pentleton, Carol/685 Chestnut Hill Rd, Chepachet, RI...........401-568-0275
Perrin, Bryan/1364 Mercer St, Jersey City, NJ......................201-432-1634
Perugi, Deborah/711 Boylston St, Boston, MA......................617-241-7823
Petersen, William L/229 Berkeley #52, Boston, MA
(P 526)...617-266-3858
Petrauskas, Kathy/229 Berkeley #52, Boston, MA
(P 531)...617-266-3858
Phelps, Tim/504 Fairway Court, Towson, MD 410-955-3213
Phillips, Alan/212 S Compo Rd, Westport, CT.......................203-221-0531
Phillips, David Illus/3000 Chestnut Ave #6, Baltimore, MD ...410-467-7588
Phillips, Gary/8 Cranberry Lane, Dover, MA..........................508-785-1513
Pidgeon, Jean/38 W 25th St, Baltimore, MD 301-235-1558
Piejko, Alex/5796 Morris Rd, Marcy, NY..............................315-732-4852
Pierson, Huntley S/PO Box 14430, Hartford, CT 203-549-4863
Pierson, Mary Louise/RR 1/Box 68B, Thetford Ctr, VT...........802-333-9996
Pietrobono, Janet/165 W 26th St, Bayonne, NJ....................201-858-2394
Pinkney, Deborah/309 Walnut Rd, Pittsburgh, PA 412-761-5666
Pinkney, Jerry/41 Furnace Dock Rd, Croton-on-Hudson, NY ...914-271-5238
Pippin, Matthew/128 Warren St, Lowell, MA.........................508-453-5583
Pirk, Kathy/5112 45th St NW, Washington, DC......................202-363-5438
Pizzo, Robert/288 East Devonia Ave, Mt Vernon, NY.............914-961-5020
Pizzo, Susan/288 E Devonia Ave, Mt Vernon, NY 914-644-4423
Plotkin, Barnett/126 Wooleys Ln, Great Neck, NY.................516-487-7457
Pollack, Scott/78 Hidden Ridge Dr, Syosset, NY
(P 600,601)...212-517-3599
Polonsky, Gabriel/274 LaGrange St, Chestnut Hill, MA..........617-965-3035
Pomerantz, Lisa/731 North 24th St, Philadelphia,
PA (P 366)..215-232-6666
Popadics, Joel/336 Viveney St, Elmwood Park, NJ................201-794-1860
Porter, John/7056 Carroll Ave, Takoma Park, MD..................301-270-8990
Portwood, Andrew/18900 Germantown Rd, Germantown, MD ...301-916-2175
Porzio, Ed/600 Governors Dr #20, Winthrop, MA..................617-846-9456
Powell, Michael/813 E Haddonview, Westmont, NJ
(P 615)...609-854-7398
Pozefsky, Carol/6040 Boulevard E, W New York, NJ..............201-662-0111

Pratt, Wayne/PO Box 1421, Wilmington, VT 802-368-7207
Prendergast, Michael/12 Merrill St, Newburyport, MA............508-465-8598
Presley, Greg/20034 Frederick Rd #42, Germantown, MD......301-540-7877
Presnall, Terry/8 Cranberry Lane, Dover, MA........................508-785-1513
Prey, Barbara Ernst/RD 1/Box 100A, Prosperity, PA..............412-225-2996
Priest, Bob/42 Waltham St #410, Boston, MA 617-542-5321
Priestley, Russell T/241 W Emerson St, Melrose, MA............617-665-5892
Pritchard, Laura Robinson/8909 Carlisle Rd, Wynd Moor, PA ...215-836-7062
Prokell, Jim/307 4th Ave #1100, Pittsburgh, PA...................412-232-3636
Prosetti, Diane/10 Marne St, Newark, NJ.............................201-555-1212
Prosser, Les/3501 Windom Rd, Brenwood, MD 301-699-1766
Prowell, Denise/212 S 13th St #3, Allentown, PA..................215-435-6329

QR

Quinn, Ger/7405 Arden Rd, Cabin Road, MD 301-229-8030
Quinn, Molly/229 Berkeley #52, Boston, MA 617-266-3858
Radiomayonnaise/96 Greenwood Place, Buffalo, NY..............716-884-6007
Ramage, Alfred/5 Irwin St #7, Winthrop, MA 617-846-5955
Raneri, Marci/2035 Richmond, Philadelphia, PA....................800-522-0888
Ransome, James/94 North St #4N, Jersey City, NJ
(P 678)...201-659-3206
Raphael, Natalia/23 Parkton Rd #3, Jamaica Plain, MA.........617-524-0121
Ravel, Ken/2 Myrtle Ave, Stoney Creek, PA..........................215-779-2105
Rea, Ba/16 Thorton Rd, Scarborough, ME............................207-883-4712
Reed, Chris/17 Edgewood Rd, Edison, NJ 908-548-3927
Reed, Dan/PO Box 2363, Providence, RI..............................401-521-1395
Reeser, Tracy P (Mr)/254 Andover Rd, Glenmoore, PA...........215-649-8298
Regnier, Mark/59 Chestnut Hill Ave, Brighton, MA 617-787-2631
Reid, Barbara/106 S Broadway, White Plains, NY 914-993-9681
Reiner, John/27 Watch Way, Lloyds Neck, NY 516-385-4261
Reinert, Kirk/1314 Hudson St #11, Hoboken, NJ 201-420-8680
Reingold, Michael/310 Warwick Rd, Haddonfield, NJ 609-354-1787
Reni/PO Box 186, Roselle Park, NJ 908-245-1218
Reott, Paul/2701 Mckean St, Philadelphia, PA 718-426-1928
Reynolds, Keith/RR2/Box 387, Sanbornville, NH...................603-522-8765
Rheaume, Diane/PO Box 250, Hurlieville, NY........................914-434-2000
Rhodes, Nancy Muncie/146 Hathaway Rd, Dewitt, NY 315-446-8742
Riccio, Frank/279 Redding Rd, W Redding, CT 203-938-9707
Rich, Anna M/1821 Chelsea St, Elmont, NY 516-352-5025
Rich, Bob/15 Warrenton Ave, Hartford, CT............................203-523-4562
Richards, Kenn/3 Elwin Pl, East Northport, NY
(P 225)...516-499-7575
Rickerd, Dave/22 Canvas Back Rd, Manalapan, NJ
(P 866)...908-446-2119
Riley, Frank/108 Bamford Ave, Hawthorne, NJ
(P 1117)..201-423-2659
Riley, Kelly/213 Village St, Millis, MA..................................508-376-5477
Riskin, Marty/12 Tidewinds Terrace, Marblehead, MA............617-631-2073
Ritta, Kurt/66 Willow Ave, Hoboken, NJ...............................201-792-7422
Ritter, Lisa/Dakin Farm Rd, Ferrisburg, VT 908-788-3991
Roberts & Van Heusen/1153 Narragansett Blvd, Cranston, RI ...401-785-4490
Roberts, Cheryl/229 Berkeley #52, Boston, MA
(P 531)...617-266-3858
Roberts, Paul/914 N Charles St #3D, Baltimore, MD 301-783-8779
Roberts, Scott/2433 Maryland Ave, Baltimore, MD................410-366-0737
Robilotto, Philip/80-A Rt 9W, Glenmont, NY.........................518-767-3196
Robins, Lili P/703 Forest Glen Rd, Silver Spring, MD.............301-593-8228
Roda, Bot/78 Victoria Ln, Lancaster, PA...............................717-393-3831
Rodd, Greg/266B Main St #102, Monroe, CT 203-261-4462
Rodericks, Mike/129 Lounsbury Rd, Trumbull, CT 203-268-1551
Roffo, Sergio/42 Shepard St #3, Boston, MA........................617-787-5861
Rogers, Glenda/1 Fayette Pk #100, Syracuse, NY 315-478-4509
Rogerson, Zebulon W/1312 18th St NW 5th Fl, Washington, DC ...202-293-1687
Roldan, Jim/141 E Main St, E Hampstead, NH 603-382-1686
Rom, Holly Meeker/4 Stanley Keys Ct, Rye, NY.....................914-921-3155
Roman, Irena/369 Thom Clapp Rd Box 571, Scituate, MA......617-545-6514
Romano, Al/150 Glenwood Dr, Guilford, CT...........................203-453-9784
Romas/66 Dale Dr, Keene, NH 603-357-7306
Roper, Robert/132 E Washington Lane, Philadelphia, PA........215-438-1110
Rosen, Eileen/412 Anglesey Terrace, West Chester, PA.........215-524-8455
Rosenthal, Marc/#8 Route 66, Malden Bridge, NY
(P 1120)..518-766-4191
Ross, Barry/12 Fruit St, Northampton, MA
(P 1121)..413-585-8993
Ross, Larry/53 Fairview Ave, Madison, NJ 201-377-6859
Rossi, Joseph/45 Lockwood Dr, Clifton, NJ...........................201-278-5716
Roth, Gail/7 Ivy Hill Rd/Box 959, Ridgefield, CT 203-438-8386

Roth, Robert/148 Lakebridge Dr N, Kings Park, NY (P 525)........516-544-4232
Roth, Roger/RD 4/782 Old Rd, Princeton, NJ........908-821-1678
Rothman, Mike/62 E Ridge St, Ridgefield, CT........203-438-4954
Rothman, Sharon/112 Elmwood Ave, Bogota, NJ........201-489-8833
Rothman, Sol/112 Elmwood Ave, Bogota, NJ........201-489-8833
Rowe, Charles/133 Aronimink Dr, Newark, DE........302-738-0641
Rubin, Terry/1404 W Mount Royal Ave, Baltimore, MD........410-383-8100
Ruff, Donna/15 Vincent Pl, Rowayton, CT (P 886)........203-866-8626
Runnion, Jeff/755 Salem St, Lynnfield, MA........617-581-5066
Russill, Victoria/1620 Fuller St NW #203, Washington, DC........202-462-0592
Russo, Anthony/51 Fogland Rd, Tiverton, RI........401-351-1770
Russo, David Anson/427 Gregory Ave, Weehawken, NJ........201-330-8463
Rutt, Dick/6024 Wayne Ave #2-B, Philadelphia, PA........215-844-3689
Ryan, Carol/14 Adams St, Port Washington, NY........516-944-3953
Ryder, Jennifer/99 Amesbury St, Quincy, MA........617-479-4774

S

Safier-Kerzner, Sonia/9413 Locust Hill Rd, Bethesda, MD........301-530-5167
Sahleanu, Valentine/72 High St #2, Topsfield, MA........508-887-3528
Sahli, Barbara/8212 Flower Ave, Takoma Park, MD........301-585-5122
Saint John, Bob/320 South St, Portsmouth, NH........603-431-7345
Salamida, Dan/258 Third St, Hoboken, NJ........201-420-0589
Salfino, Samuel/57 Lakeside Dr, Nutley, NJ........201-667-5103
Salganik, Amy/527-A Allegheny Ave, Towson, MD........410-821-6681
Sanders, Bruce/229 Berkeley #52, Boston, MA........617-266-3858
Sanguedolce, Lynn/16 Encampment Dr, Bedminster, NJ........908-781-0302
Santoliquido, Delores/60 W Broad St #6H, Mt Vernon, NY........914-667-3199
Santore, Charles/138 S 20th St, Philadelphia, PA........215-563-0430
Sarecky, Melody/1010 Vermont Ave #720, Washington, DC........202-347-5276
Sauk, Ed/1220 Keystone Rd, Chester, PA........215-494-6045
Saunders, Rob/34 Station St #1, Brookline, MA (P 1125)........617-566-4464
Savadier, Elivia/45 Walnut Hill Rd, Chestnut Hill, MA........617-661-0951
Savidge, Robert T/1241 E St SE, Washington, DC........202-547-5186
Sawyer, Scott/9 W 29th St, Baltimore, MD (P 830)........410-467-7300
Scanlan, Peter/713 Willow Ave #5E, Hoboken, NJ........201-767-7342
Schall, Rene/5 Field Green Dr, Colchester, VT........802-878-1086
Scharf, Linda/240 Heath St #311, Boston, MA........617-738-9294
Schatell, Brian/180 Walnut St #B-31, Montclair, NJ........201-746-7562
Schenker, Bob/31 W Circular Ave, Paoli, PA........215-688-8771
Scheuer, Lauren/122 Brooks St, Brighton, MA........617-782-5592
Schieber, Julie/406 Cedar Street NW Ste 4, Washington, DC,........202-291-7339
Schill, George/309 Walnut Rd, Pittsburgh, PA (P 682)....412-761-5666
Schill, Nancy/235 Channing Ave, Malvern, PA........215-644-3426
Schiwall, Susan/2276 Mt Carmel Ave, Glenside, PA........215-885-8227
Schiwall-Gallo, Linda/15 Warrenton Ave, Hartford, CT........203-523-4562
Schlemme, Roy/585 Centre St, Oradell, NJ........212-921-9732
Schneider, Frederick/15 Warrenton Ave, Hartford, CT........203-523-4562
Schneider, Rick/215 Hanford Dr, Fairfield, CT........203-254-2391
Schoenberger, Carl/1925 16th St NW #701, Washington, DC........202-483-3117
Schofield, Dennis/7013 Hegerman St, Philadelphia, PA........215-624-8143
Schofield, Glen A/4 Hillside Ave, Roseland, NJ........201-226-5597
Schofield, Russ/5313 Waneta Rd, Bethesda, MD........301-320-5008
Scholberg, Barbara/169 Laurelwood Dr, Hopedale, MA........508-473-7637
Schonbach Graphics/1851 Columbia Rd NW, Washington, DC........202-265-2240
Schooley, Greg/309 Walnut Rd, Pittsburgh, PA (P 683)...412-761-5666
Schorr, Kathy Staico/PO Box 142, Roxbury, CT........203-266-4084
Schorr, Todd/PO Box 142, Roxbury, CT........203-266-4084
Schotte, Marilyn/7205 15th Ave, Takoma Park, MD........301-445-7114
Schottland, Miriam/2201 Massachusetts Ave NW, Washington, DC (P 676)........202-328-3825
Schreck, John/101 Spring Hill Rd, Fairfield, CT........203-259-6824
Schreiber, Dana/36 Center St, Collinsville, CT........203-693-6688
Schuh, Chris/414 Winter St, Holliston, MA........508-429-6928
Schulenburg, Paul/11 Park St #4, Brookline, MA (P 1126,1127)........617-734-0548
Schultz, C G/1140 West Street Rd, West Chester, PA........215-793-3622
Schuster, David/3-A Winter St, Westborough, MA........508-366-5021
Schwartz, Carol/8311 Frontwell Cir, Gaithersburg, MD........301-926-4776
Schwartz, Joanna H/51 Woodland St #4, Newburyport, MA........508-465-9635
Schwartz, Marty/18 Winfield Ct, East Norwalk, CT........203-838-9935
Schwartz, Matt/42 Jefferson St, Cambridge, MA........617-661-4671
Schwarz, Joanie/300 Grand St #400, Hoboken, NJ (P 112)........201-798-6486
Schweigert, Carol/791 Tremont St #E406, Boston, MA........617-262-8909
Scott, Margaret/1525 31st St NW, Washington, DC........202-965-0523
Scrofani, Joe/2 Akers Ave, Montvale, NJ (P 419)........201-391-3956
Sears, Elayne/90 Buck Mountain Rd, Crown Point, NY........518-597-3749
Seibert, Dave/16 Elmsgate Way, Rumford, RI........401-431-2077
Seidler, Mark/4035 Taylor Dr, Fairfax, VA........703-978-1813
Selby, Bob/159 Lyman St, Providence, RI........401-725-3327
Selewacz, Mark/24 French St, Watertown, MA........617-926-6331
Selwyn, Paul/68 Whiting Ln, W Hartford, CT........203-523-5752
Semler, Robert/308 Highland Terrace, Pitman, NJ........609-589-6495
Seppala, Mark/72 High St, Topsfield, MA........508-887-3528
Serafin, Marsha/25-Q Sylvan Rd S, Westport, CT........203-226-4293
Sese, Maria/7501 Holiday Terrace, Bethesda, MD........301-405-4619
Sharpe, Jim/21 Ten O'Clock Ln, Weston, CT........203-226-9984
Shaw, Barclay/170 East St, Sharon, CT........203-364-5974
Shaw, Fran/18 Imperial Place, Providence, RI........401-861-8002
Shaw, Kurt/2954 Sheridan Blvd, Pittsburgh, PA........412-771-7345
Sheehan, Tom/31 Marmion Rd, Melrose, MA........617-734-6038
Sheerin, Sean/106 Inman St #1, Cambridge, MA........617-661-6972
Sheild, Lori/13 Seneca St, E Northport, NY........516-261-2919
Sherbo, Dan/4208 38th St NW, Washington, DC........202-244-0474
Sherman, Gene/500 Helendale Rd, Rochester, NY........716-288-8000
Sherman, Linda/9825 Canal Rd, Gaithersburg, MD........301-590-0604
Sherman, Whitney/5101 Whiteford Ave, Baltimore, MD........410-435-2095
Shieldhouse, Stephanie/2904 Southern Ave, Baltimore, MD........410-254-7229
Shields, Sandra/62 Burton St, Bristol, RI........401-253-1922
Shiff, Andrew Z/153 Clinton St, Hopkinton, MA........508-435-3607
Shipman, Anne/43-C3 Jackson St, Essex Junctn, VT........802-878-5073
Sickbert, Jo/7 Dublin Hill Dr, Greenwich, CT........203-869-8010
Siegel, Stuart/106 High Plain St, Walpole, MA........508-668-5392
Sierra, Dorothea/192 Southville Rd, Southborough, MA........508-872-4549
Sikorski, Tony/2311 Clark Bldg, Pittsburgh, PA........412-391-8366
Simon, Dennis/16312 Yeoho Rd, Sparks, MD........410-329-3983
Simpson, Steve/PO Box 58, Belmont, MA........617-864-7360
Singer, Gloria/14 Disbrow Ct, E Brunswick, NJ........908-257-4728
Sisti, Jerald/436 Countrywood Ln, Encinitas, CA........619-944-7836
Six North Assoc/60 Dutch Hill Rd, Orangeburg, NY........914-365-3100
Skidmore, John/1112 Morefield Rd, Philadelphia, PA........215-698-9114
Skinner, Cortney (Mr)/32 Churchill Ave, Arlington, MA........617-648-2875
Sklut, Meryl/721 Pleasant Valley Way, W Orange, NJ........201-669-8078
Skypeck, George/2053-A Bedford Dr, Washington, DC........301-599-1018
Slamier, Marcia/4201 Cathedral Ave, Washington, DC........202-244-7989
Slandorn, Peggy/RR1/Box 561A, Bloomsbury, NJ........908-479-6745
Sloan, Lois/3133 Conn Ave NW #615, Washington, DC........202-387-3305
Slote, Elizabeth/9 Leonard Ave, Cambridge, MA........617-868-0824
Smith, Douglas/73 Winthrop Rd, Brookline, MA (P 242,243)........617-566-3816
Smith, Elwood H/2 Locust Grove Rd, Rhinebeck, NY (P 1144)........914-876-2358
Smith, Gail Hunter/PO Box 217, Barnegat Light, NJ........609-494-9136
Smith, Jeffrey/710 Lakeshore Drive, Hewitt, NJ........201-853-2262
Smith, Marcia/112 Linden St, Rochester, NY........716-461-9348
Smith, Raymond/606 Jersey Ave, Jersey City, NJ (P 1145)........201-653-6638
Smith, Samantha Carol/3818 Greenmount Ave, Baltimore, MD........301-243-6184
Smith, Susan B/66 Clarendon #3, Boston, MA (P 1146)........617-266-4441
Smith, Terry E/1713 Dryden Way, Crofton, MD........301-858-0734
Smith, Timothy A/PO Box 8784/JFK Station, Boston, MA........617-367-6472
Smith-Evers, Nancy/147 Franklin St, Stoneham, MA........617-438-5716
Smola, Jim/94 Maple Hill Ave, Newington, CT........203-665-0305
Smolinski, Dick/25-Q Sylvan Rd S, Westport, CT........203-226-4293
Snure, Roger/Box 1294, Orleans, MA........508-255-7069
Snyder, Emilie/50 N Pine St #107, Marietta, PA........717-426-2906
Soileau, Hodges/350 Flax Hill Rd, Norwalk, CT........203-852-0751
Sokolowski, Ted/RD #2 Box 408, Lake Ariel, PA........717-937-4527
Solari, Ed Jr/2276 Mt Carmel Ave, Glenside, PA........215-885-8227
Sollers, Jim/2 Vickery St, Augusta, ME........207-626-3131
Soloto, Susan/1 Bridge St, Irvington, NY........914-591-6909
Somerville, Kevin/18 Lakeview St, River Edge, NJ........201-488-1026
Sopin, Nan/9 Bradley Dr, Freehold, NJ........908-462-7154
Sorensen, Robert/22 Strathmore Ave, Milford, CT........203-874-6381
Soule, Robert Alan/15229 Baughman Dr, Silver Spring, MD........301-598-8883
Soyka, Ed/231 Lafayette Ave, Peekskill, NY........914-737-2230
Spain, Valerie/83 Franklin St, Watertown, MA........617-923-1989
Spanfeller, Jim/Mustato Rd, Katonah, NY........914-232-3546
Sparacio, Mark & Erin/30 Rover Ln, Hicksville, NY (P 1149)........516-579-6679
Sparkman, Gene/PO Box 644, Sandy Hook, CT........203-426-0061
Sparks, Richard/2 W Rocks Rd, Norwalk, CT........203-866-2002

Spear, Charles/456 Ninth St #2, Hoboken, NJ....201-798-6466
Spector, Joel/3 Maplewood Dr, New Milford, CT (P 506,507)....203-355-5942
Spellman, Susan/8 Cranberry Lane, Dover, MA....508-785-1513
Speulda, William/363 Diamond Bridge Ave, Hawthorne, NJ....201-427-6661
Springer, Daniel/1156 Commonwealth Ave, Allston, MA....617-739-1482
Springer, Sally/317 S Lawrence Ct, Philadelphia, PA....215-925-9697
Sprouls, Kevin/1 Schooner Ln, Sweetwater, NJ (P 792,793)....609-965-4795
Squadroni, Tony/2276 Mt Carmel Ave, Glenside, PA....215-885-8227
St Jacques, Phillip/8 High St, Morristown, NJ....908-494-4218
Staada, Glenn/490 Schooley Mt Rd, Hackettstown, NJ....908-852-4949
Stabler, Barton/229 Spring Garden Rd, Milford, NJ (P 429)....908-995-2177
Stackhouse, Donna/47-A Middle St, Portland, ME....207-774-4977
Stafford, Rod/1491 Dewey Ave, Rochester, NY....716-647-6200
Stahl, Benjamin F/18 Lowndes Ave, S Norwalk, CT....203-838-5308
Stansbury Ronsaville Wood Inc/17 Pinwood St, Annapolis, MD....301-261-8662
Stanziani, Diane/210 Fountain St, Philadelphia, PA....215-483-5317
Starr, Jim/110 W 25th St, Baltimore, MD....410-889-0703
Stasolla, Mario/37 Cedar Hill Ave, S Nyack, NY....914-353-3086
Stavrinos, George/139 Lawrence Rd, Salem, NH....212-724-1557
Steadman, E T/18 Allen St, Rumson, NJ....908-758-8535
Steadman, Lee/309 Walnut Rd, Pittsburgh, PA....412-761-5666
Steele, Mark/539 Tremont, Boston, MA....617-424-0604
Steig, William/PO Box 8, Westport, CT....203-227-7806
Steinberg, James/41 Fruit St, Worcester, MA....508-792-0372
Steiner, Joan/Rd 1 Box 292, Craryville, NY....518-966-8908
Stephens, Jean K/328 Brett Rd, Rochester, NY....716-288-8629
Sternberg, Debra/2151 California St NW #404, Washington, DC....202-483-7883
Steuer, Sharon/205 Valley Rd, Bethany, CT....203-393-3981
Stevens & Stevens/328 Brett Rd, Rochester, NY....716-288-8629
Stewart, Jonathan/1530 Spruce St, Philadelphia, PA....215-546-3649
Still, Wayne Anthony/6819 Clearview St, Philadelphia, PA....215-848-4292
Stillerman, Robbie/52 Prospect Ave, Sea Cliff, NY....516-671-5815
Stirnweis, Shannon/31 Fawn Pl, Wilton, CT....203-762-7058
Stock, Jeffrey/33 Richdale Ave #105, Cambridge, MA....617-868-8384
Storin, Joanne/145 Englewood Ave, Brookline, MA....617-731-6556
Stouffer, Stephanie/RR 1 Box 196, Belmont, VT....802-259-2686
Stout, Rex/10307 Procter St, Silver Spring, MD....301-681-8344
Strauss, Pamela/97 Winthrop Rd, Brookline, MA....617-232-5847
Strawbridge, Drew/2276 Mt Carmel Ave, Glenside, PA....215-885-8227
Street, Janet/15 Warrenton Ave, Hartford, CT....203-523-4562
Strode, Brad/236 Old Gradyville Rd, Glen Mills, PA....215-358-5088
Stroud, Steven/597 Riverside Ave, Westport, CT....203-226-4724
Stubbs, Elizabeth/27 Wyman St, Arlington, MA....617-646-0785
Studio 185/185 Forest St, S Hamilton, MA....508-468-2892
Sturrock, Walt/PO Box 734, Easton, PA....215-559-1256
Stutzman, Mark & Laura/100 G St, Mt Lake Park, MD....301-258-9383
Suchit, Stewart/88 Summit Ave #2L, Jersey City, NJ....201-860-9177
Sullivan, Harriet/25-Q Sylvan Rd S, Westport, CT....203-226-4293
Sullivan, James/253-1/2 Fifth St, Jersey City, NJ (P 1153)....201-963-6670
Sullivan, Richard/495 Hillside Ave, Needham Heights, MA....617-449-7901
Sullivan, Steve/72 Revere Dr, Ridgefield, CT....203-438-4969
Sullivan, Suzanne Hughes/30 Summit St, Eastchester, NY....914-961-6077
Swan, Susan/83 Saugatuck Ave, Westport, CT (P 1155)....203-226-9104
Sweeney, Jerry/339 Blvd of Allies, Pittsburg, PA....412-391-4471
Swenarton, Gordon/Lake Trial East, Morristown, NJ....908-953-0553
Symington, Gary/47 Middle Street, Portland, ME....207-774-4977
Syverson, Henry/PO Box 8, Westport, CT....203-227-7806

T

Taffet, Marc/1638 James St, Merrick, NY....516-623-2850
Tagel, Peggy/458 Newtown Trnpk, Weston, CT....203-454-4687
Talcott, Julia/38 Linden St #3, Brookline, MA....617-232-7306
Tanton, Dlerdre/273 Summer St, Boston, MA....617-426-2576
Tarantolla, Daniel/3 Ernest Ct, Kings Park, NY....516-544-4387
Tarca, Lisa/27 Willis St #37, Framingham, MA....508-875-2047
Tarlow, Phyllis/42 Stafford Rd, New Rochelle, NY....914-235-9473
Tatore, Paul/10 Wartburg Pl, Valhalla, NY....914-769-1061
Tauss, Herb/S Mountain Pass, Garrison, NY....914-424-3765
Taylor, Dahl/508 Grand St, Troy, NY (P 109)....518-274-6379
Taylor, Doug/PO Box 169, Guilford, NY....607-895-6062
Taylor, Tim/PO Box 591, Roseland, NJ....201-228-6869
Ten, Arnie/37 Forbus St, Poughkeepsie, NY....914-485-8419
Ternay, Bill/119 Birch Ave, Bala Cynwyd, PA....215-667-8626
Terreson, Jeffrey/206 Hack Green Rd, Pound Ridge, NY (P 186,187)....914-764-4897
Thiel, Joseph/2253 Rogene Dr #101, Baltimore, MD....410-764-2123
Thiel, Libby/Route 2/Box 181C/Fenwick, Bryan's Road, MD....301-283-6347
Thomas, Chris/PO Box 1072, Southport, CT....203-255-9620
Thomas, Linda/169 Mason St #4A, Greenwich, CT....203-622-5925
Thomas, Rod/157 Langley Rd, Newton Centre, MA....617-244-2393
Thomas, Susan C/6804 Greenvale Parkway, Riverdale, MD....301-773-6671
Thomas, Troy/1247 Portage Lane, Woodstock, IL....815-338-9455
Thompson, Arthur/39 Prospect Ave, Pompton Plains, NJ....201-835-3534
Thompson, Ellen/97 Pine Grove Ave, Somerset, NJ....908-249-8640
Thompson, John M/118 Parkview Ave, Weehawken, NJ....201-865-7853
Thompson, John R/5950 Hubbard Dr, Rockville, MD....301-984-1630
Thompson, Richard/9309 Judge Place, Gaithersburg, MD....301-948-3732
Thompson, Willam/169 Norfolk Ave #9, Boston, MA....617-445-8009
Thornburg, Bethann/1673 Columbia Rd NW, Washington, DC....202-667-0147
Thornley, Blair/60 Woodlawn St, Boston, MA....617-524-1808
Tiani, Alex/PO Box 4530, Greenwich, CT (P 452)....203-661-3891
Tierney, John P/659 Churchill St, Pittsfield, MA....413-442-8428
Tilberry, Susan C/1625 E Street SE, Washington, DC....202-547-0944
Tilden, David Anders/End of Wirt Way Box 2191, Duxbury, MA....617-934-0345
Tilney, Barnes/27 Glenville Ave, Allston, MA....617-782-5958
Timmons, Bonnie/18 McKinley St, Rowayton, CT (P 470)....203-866-3734
Timmons, Bonnie/100 West Highlands Ave, Philadelphia, PA (P 470)....215-247-3556
Tinkelman, Murray/75 Lakeview Ave W, Peekskill, NY....914-737-5960
Todd, Barbara/251 Greenwood Ave, Bethel, CT....203-797-8188
Toelke, Cathleen/PO Box 487, Rhinebeck, NY (P 762,763)....914-876-8776
Toelke, Ron/229 Berkeley #52, Boston, MA (P 530)....617-266-3858
Tomasulo, Patrick/76 Howard St, Dumont, NJ....201-385-4350
Torrisi, Gary/8 Cranberry Lane, Dover, MA....508-785-1513
Toth, Tibor/7939 Norfolk Ave, Bethesda, MD....301-656-5722
Trainor, Pete/1325 18th St NW #908, Washington, DC....202-331-7722
Trainor, Sandra/33 Montvale Ave #4, Woburn, MA....617-933-6196
Travis-Keene, Gayle/334 Swinton Way, Severne Park, MD....410-647-7220
Treatner, Meryl/239 Monroe St, Philadelphia, PA....215-627-2297
Trostli, Elisabeth/232 W Exchange St, Providence, RI....401-351-3429
Trusilo, Jim/309 Walnut Rd, Pittsburgh, PA....412-761-5666
Tseng, Jean & Mou-sein/458 Newtown Trnpk, Weston, CT....203-454-4687
Tsui, George/2250 Elliot St, Merrick, NY....516-223-8474
Tsui, Selena/2250 Elliot St, Merrick, NY....516-223-8474
Turci, Thomas P/41 Paul; Heights, Southington, CT....203-276-0458
Tuttle, Jean/136 Main St #9, Irvington, NY....914-591-4190
Two-H Studio/45 Corbin Dr, Darien, CT (Inside Back Flap/Books 1 & 2)....203-656-0200
Tyrrell, Susan/124 Watertown St #1E, Watertown, MA....617-923-9965
Tysko, Lisa/361 Nassau, Princeton, NJ....609-921-3610

UV

Ulrich, Christopher/232 W Exchange St, Providence, RI....401-272-2660
Ulrich, George/4 Evans Rd, Marblehead, MA....617-639-0539
Undercuffer, Gary/1214 Locust St, Philadelphia, PA....215-545-3973
Underhill, Gary R/340 Franklin St, Bloomfield, NJ....201-429-1400
Ursino, John/372 Chestnut Hill Ave, Brookline, MA....617-782-1809
Vaccaro, Vic/1037 7th St, West Babylon, NY (P 1168)....516-888-2637
Valk, Tinam/2111 Henderson Ave, Silver Spring, MD....301-946-6583
Valla, Victor R/19 Prospect St, Falls Village, CT....203-824-5014
Valley, Gregg/128 Thomas Rd, McMurray, PA (P 1169)....412-941-4662
Van Dusen, Chris/37 Pearl St, Camden, ME....207-236-2961
Van Horn, Michael/RD 2/Box 442/Milan Hill Rd, Red Hook, NY....914-758-8407
Van Ryzin, Peter/652 Skyline Ridge Rd, Bridgewater, CT (P 46)....203-350-6115
Van Seters, Kim/29 High St, Wayne, NJ....201-694-5502
Vance Wright Adams & Assoc/930 North Lincoln, Pittsburg, PA....412-322-1800
Vann, Bob/5306 Knox St, Philadelphia, PA....215-843-4841
Vartanoff, Ellen/4418 Renn St, Rockville, MD....301-460-7636
Vasconcellos, Daniel/225 Old Washington St, Pembroke, MA....617-599-9625
Vaughan, Martha/3751 W St NW, Washington, DC....202-333-1299
Vella, Judy/404 Washington Ave, Linden, NJ....908-486-5430
Vella, Ray/20 N Broadway Bldg I-240, White Plains, NY (P 879)....914-997-1424
Veno, Joe/20 Cutler Rd, Hamilton, MA....508-468-3165
Verhoorn, Shirley/35 River St, Raynham, MA....508-823-2457
Verkoutern, Dana/11 Froude Circle, Cabin John, MD....301-320-6010

Vernaglia, Michael/1251 Bloomfield St, Hoboken, NJ.....................201-659-7750
Verougstraete, Randy/458 Newtown Trnpk, Weston, CT.................203-454-4687
Vidinghoff, Carol/11 Lloyd Rd, Watertown, MA............................617-924-4846
Viglione & Assoc, Dawn/384 Elm St, Monroe, CT 203-452-7962
Vincent, Kathy/19 Longview Rd, Port Washington, NY 516-883-9021
Vincenti, Anna Maria/P O Box 1123, Bethlehem, PA......................215-865-0739
Viskupic, Gary/7 Westfield Dr, Center Port, NY 516-757-9021
Vissichelli, Joe/45 Queen St, Freeport, NY 516-872-3867
Vivilecchia, Lisa/3 Jefferson Ave, Everett, MA 617-389-1669
Volp, Kathleen/91 Bristers Hill Rd, Concord, MA 508-371-1389
Von Brincken, Maria/28 Village Rd, Sudbury, MA 508-443-4540
Von Eiff, Damon/2 W Argyle St, Rockville, MD 301-251-0381
Voo, Rhonda/229 Berkeley #52, Boston, MA (P 531) 617-266-3858
Vorhies, Roger/RR 1/Box 398H/Plains Rd, Jericho, VT 802-899-3741
Vu, Anh/1729 Featherwood St, Silver Spring, MD 301-680-0421

W

Waites, Joan/7004 Bybrook Lane, Chevy Chase, MD 301-657-4026
Walczak, Larry/803 Park Ave, Hoboken, NJ.................................201-798-6176
Waldman, Neil/47 Woodlands Ave, White Plains, NY......................914-693-2782
Waldrep, Richard/2220 N Charles St, Baltimore, MD.....................410-243-0211
Walker, Brian/2004 Palamar Turn, Seabrook, MD.........................301-794-4574
Walker, Norman/37 Stonehenge Rd, Weston, CT 203-226-5812
Walker, S A/8 Gifford Ct, Salem, MA 508-745-6175
Walsh, Patrick J/2276 Mt Carmel Ave, Glenside, PA.....................215-885-8227
Ward, Ray/2276 Mt Carmel Ave, Glenside, PA..............................215-885-8227
Ward, Sam/6829 Murray Lane, Annandale, VA..............................703-256-8313
Wasserboehr, Paul/72 High St #2, Topsfield, MA 508-887-3528
Wasserman, Amy/PO Box 1171, Framingham, MA 617-879-7679
Waterhouse, Charles/67 Dartmouth St, Edison, NJ........................908-738-1804
Waters, Julian/9509 Aspenwood Pl, Gaithersburg, MD 301-977-5314
Watson, Karen/100 Churchill Ave, Arlington, MA 617-641-1420
Watts, Mark/2004 Par Dr, Warrington, PA (P 169) 215-343-8490
Webber, Rosemary/644 Noank Rd, Mystic, CT
(P 1176)..203-536-3091
Wehrman, Richard/247 N Goodman St, Rochester,
NY (P 850)...716-271-2280
Weidner, Bea/731 North 24th St, Philadelphia, PA
(P 370)..215-232-6666
Weiland, Garison/9 Steadman #3, Boston, MA
(P 1177)..617-983-9251
Weisenbach, Stephen/200 Cedar Lane, Teaneck, NJ 201-836-1711
Weiss, Conrad/40 Mohawk Trail, W Milford, NJ.............................201-697-7226
Weiss, Richard/126 S 22nd St, Philadelphia, PA............................215-567-3828
Weissman, Bari/41 Atkins St, Brighton, MA..................................617-783-0230
Welker, Gaylord/30 Summit Rd, Sparta, NJ..................................201-729-5134
Welkis, Allen/53 Heights Rd, Fort Salonga, NY 516-261-4160
Weller, Linda Boehm/7 Ivy Hill Rd/Box 959, Ridgefield, CT 203-438-8386
Wells, Carol/12122 Hooper Lane, Glen Arm, MD...........................410-592-5072
Welsh, Patrick/PO Box 463, Williamstown, NJ 609-728-0264
Werner, Tom/Box 854, Northfield, NJ...609-383-1596
Westbrook, Eric C/2830 27th St NW, Washington,
DC (P 1178)...202-328-8593
Westerfield, William S/1133-A University Terrace, Linden, NJ 908-925-0695
Westlake, Laura/7 Dublin Hill Dr, Greenwich, CT 203-869-8010
Weston, Al/597 Riverside Ave, Westport, CT.................................203-226-4724
Whelan, Michael/23 Old Hayrake Rd, Danbury, CT 203-798-6063
White, Caroline/37 West St, Granby, MA (P 965)..........413-467-3792
Whiting, Ann/2627 Woodley Place NW, Washington, DC 202-462-1519
Whitman, Jim/53 Orchard St, Clifton, NJ......................................201-472-0990
Whitney, Richard/Monadnock Studio/POB 427, Marlborough, NH........603-876-4353
Wielblad, Linda/22 Notre Dame Ave, Cambridge, MA 617-661-8504
Wiggins, Bryan/30 Victory Ave, S Portland, ME
(P 529)..207-767-4181
Wilcox, David/5955 Sawmill Rd, Doylestown, PA............................908-832-7368
Wilkinson, Jeff/7011 Lachlan Circle, Baltimore, MD........................410-828-0543
Willert, Beth Ann/4 Woodland Dr, Roselle, NJ...............................908-298-1237
Williams, Arlene/7401 Oak Crest Lane, Corksville, MD....................301-498-6479
Williams, Donna/18 Battersea Lane, Ft Washington, MD..................301-292-3611
Williams, Frank/731 North 24th St, Philadelphia, PA.......................215-232-6666
Williams, M David/8409 Cunningham Dr, Berwyn Heights, MD...........301-345-4663
Williams, Marcia/84 Duncklee St, Newton Highlands, MA.................617-332-5823
Williams, Monica/418 Edgewater Rd, Pasadena , MD......................410-437-4325
Williams, Ted/170 Elder Dr, Macedon, NY....................................315-986-3770
Williams, Toby/84 Franklin St, Watertown, MA..............................617-924-2406
Williges, Mel/8 Cranberry Lane, Dover, MA..................................508-785-1513
Wilson, Barry/6541 1/2 Morton Pl Ne, Washington, DC....................202-544-2728

Wilson, Mary Lou/247 N Goodman St, Rochester, NY 716-271-2280
Wilson, Patricia/71 Hobart St, Ridgefield Park, NJ.........................201-440-9034
Wilson, Phil/309 Walnut Rd, Pittsburgh, PA (P 684).....412-761-5666
Winborg, Larry/731 North 24th St, Philadelphia, PA
(P 367)...215-232-6666
Wisnewski, Andrea/306 High St, Willimantic, CT............................203-423-9915
Wisnewski, Robert/338 Arlington St, Watertown, MA......................617-926-7949
Wisniewski, David/12415 Chalford Lane, Bowie, MD.......................301-776-1006
Wissman, Ray/3823 Maple Grove Rd, Manchester, MD 410-239-3584
Witkowski, Robert T/PO Box 8701, Boston, MA.............................617-227-5095
Witschonke, Alan/68 Agassiz Ave, Belmont, MA 617-484-8023
Wolf, Elizabeth/3717 Alton Pl NW, Washington, DC 202-686-0179
Wolfe, Jean/55 Frazier Rd Beech #222, Malverne, PA....................215-644-2941
Wolff, Punz/457 Herkimer Ave, Haworth, NJ.................................201-385-6028
Wombat Studio/10 Beechwood Dr, Wayne, NJ 201-628-8793
Woo, Karen/60 Lawton St, Brookline, MA.....................................617-277-8598
Wood, Carol Way/569 Barney's Joy Rd, S Dartmouth,
MA (P 1184)..508-636-2404
Woolf, Anatal S/3000 Conn Ave NW #303, Washington, DC..............202-667-9731
Wright, Amy/227 Old Mill Lane, Portsmouth, RI.............................401-849-4680
Wright, Bob Creative Group/247 North Goodman St, Rochester, NY....716-271-2280
Wright, Tom/9 W 29th St, Baltimore, MD......................................410-467-7300
Wu, Leslie/36 Harwood Lane, East Rochester, NY
(1185)..716-385-3722
Wunsch, Marjory/16 Crescent St, Cambridge, MA 617-492-3839

Y

Yaccarino, Dan/124 Country Lane, Clifton, NJ...............................201-473-3666
Yalowitz, Paul/598 Freeman Ave, Brentwood, NY..........................212-532-0859
Yang, James/41 Union Sq W #918 (P 624,625)............212-807-6627
Yaniv, Etty/50 Cedar Ct, Closter, NJ...201-784-8136
Yanson, John/733 15th St NW, Washington, DC 202-347-1511
Yavorsky Creative/2300 Walnut St #617, Philadelphia, PA...............215-564-6690
Yeager, Alice/3157 Rolling Rd, Edgewater, MD..............................410-261-4239
Yealdhall, Gary/110 W 25th St, Baltimore, MD (P 410)...410-889-5361
Yelenak, Andy/15 Warrenton Ave, Hartford, CT..............................203-523-4562
Yermal, William J/62 Carey Rd, Succasunna, NJ............................201-927-6740
Yi, Kang/7 Trappers Way, Pomona, NY (P 628,629) 914-354-7940
Young, Mary O'Keefe/28 Washington Ave, Irvington, NY...................914-591-5481
Young, Michael/475 Shawmut Ave, Boston, MA 617-266-0343
Young, Robert Assoc/78 North Union St, Rochester, NY 716-546-1973
Young, Wally/7 Birch Hill Rd, Weston, CT.....................................203-227-5672
Younger, Heidi/284 Fourth St, Jersey City, NJ
(P 64,65)..201-860-9177

Z

Zale, Peter/351 W River Rd North, Elyria, OH................................216-323-0455
Zammarchi, Robert/Box 1147/32 Rugg Rd, Boston, MA....................617-778-9513
Zappler, Nina/3153 Woodworth Rd, Waterloo, NY..........................315-789-5640
Zarins, Joyce Audy/19 Woodland St, Merrimac, MA........................508-346-8994
Zaruba, Ken/967 Wambler Ln, Westminster, MD 410-876-8447
Zimmerman, Bruce/7805 Old Georgetown Rd, Bethesda, MD............301-656-2787
Zingone, Robin/32 Godman Rd, Madison, CT.................................212-288-8045
Zinn, Ron/117 Village Dr, Jerico, NY...516-933-2767
Zorad, Ivan/ Edison, NJ..908-985-8771
Zuba, Bob/105 W Saylor Ave, Plains, PA......................................717-824-5665
Zuban, Kevin/34 Idelwild Rd, Edison, NJ......................................908-949-8617
Zuckerman, Robert/100 Washington St, South Norwalk, CT 203-853-2670
Zwart, Lawrence Jan/PO Box 281, Rockport, ME............................207-236-9028
Zwicker, Sara Mintz/98 Stetson St, Braintree, MA 617-848-8962
Zwingler, Randall/1106 Greenway Rd, Wilmington,
DE (P 430)..302-478-6063
Asprino, Donna/49 Warren Ave #4, Boston, MA.............................617-426-5067
Berman, Simi/Box 58, Chesterfield, NH..606-256-8477
Hanna, Kim/805 Jackson St, Falls Church, VA...............................703-532-2370
Lundgren, Timothy/4200 Torring Ford St, Torrington, CT..................203-496-7439

S O U T H E A S T

A

Adams, Dianne/129 Carlen Ave, Lexington, SC...............................803-957-7439
Adams, Rodney/847 S Church St, Burlington, NC............................919-222-9333
Anderson, Robert/4209 Canal St, New Orleans, LA 504-486-9011

Anderson, Tim/Winston-Salem, NC 919-377-9036
Anderton, John C/8714 Gateshead Rd, Alexandria, VA 703-360-3584
Andresen, Mark/6417 Gladys St, Metairie, LA 504-888-1644
Anthony, Tony/132 Rumson Rd, Atlanta, GA 404-237-9836
Architectural Art Inc/7700 Leesburg Pike Ste 401, Falls Church, VA 703-448-0704
Armstrong, Lynn/2510 Whisper Wind Ct, Roswell, GA 404-642-5512
Arroyo, Fian/7312 SW 80th St Plz #290, Miami, FL
(P 903) **305-663-1224**
Artell, Michael/PO Box 1819, Covington, LA 504-626-3420
The Artsmith/440 College Ave/Box 391, Athens, GA 404-543-5555
Attiliis, Andy/9710 Days Farm Dr, Vienna, VA 703-759-1519
August, Robert/666 Bantry Lane, Stone Mountain,
GA (P 544) **404-296-9666**
Auth, Dennis/396 S Witchduck Rd #201, Virginia Beach, VA 804-497-3913
Azar, Joe/3935 N 4th St, Arlington, VA......................................703-527-1443
Azzinaro, Lewis/11872 St Trinians Ct, Reston, VA.....................703-620-5155

B

Bailey, R C/255 Westward Dr, Miami Springs, FL 305-888-6309
Bandle, Johnna/666 Bantry Lane, Stone Mountain,
GA (P 547) **404-296-9666**
Barbie, Michael/463 Old Post Rd, Niceville, FL 904-897-3441
Barklew, Pete/110 Alpine Way, Athens, GA...............................404-546-5058
Bell, Ron/1408 S Sixth St, Louisville, KY (P 666) **502-561-0737**
Bennett, Gary/3304 Startan Ct, Louisville, KY
(P 914,915) **502-458-0338**
Beyl, Charles E/510 N Alfred St, Alexandria, VA 703-549-7824
Birch, Candace/2717 Cedar Creek Dr, Durham, NC 919-382-8051
Blakey, Paul/2910 Caribou Trail, Marietta, GA (P 921) ...**404-977-7669**
Bober, Kathleen/1408 N Fillmore St #12, Arlington, VA..............703-528-1449
Bolling, Bob/2395 NE 185th St, N Miami Beach, FL 305-931-0104
Boone, Joe/ PW Inc/PO Box 99337, Louisville, KY 502-499-9220
Bowles, Aaron/1686 Sierra Woods Ct, Reston, VA....................703-437-4102
Boyter, Charles/1135 Lanier Blvd NE, Atlanta, GA....................404-727-5665
Brauer, Fred/700 John Ringling Blvd, Sarasota, FL 813-361-7523
Brawner, Dan/1408 S Sixth St, Louisville, KY (P 668) **502-561-0737**
Bray, Robin (Mr.)/603 Oak Haven Dr, Falls Church, VA.............703-237-8653
Brennsteiner, Jim/13212 Pleasantview Lane, Fairfax, VA...........703-803-8637
Brown, David/11873 Catoctin Dr, Woodbridge, VA.....................703-490-3748
Bruce, Tim/5850 Brookway Dr, Winston-Salem, NC 919-767-8890
Bullock, Max/3064 Cedarwood Lane, Falls Church, VA.............703-534-1441
Burke, Leland/675 Drewry St #8, Atlanta, GA 404-881-8255
Burns, John/Rte 1/Box 487A, Bluemont, VA..............................703-955-4786
Butler, Mary Presters/Dale City, VA...703-590-4433
Butler, Meryl/PO Box 991, Virginia Beach, VA...........................804-491-2280

C

Cable, Annette/1408 S Sixth St, Louisville, KY 502-561-0737
Cable, Mark/1408 S Sixth St, Louisville, KY (P 664) **502-561-0737**
Cain, Thomas/2161 Peachtree Rd NE #502, Atlanta, GA..........404-355-2160
Carambat, David/21339 Wilson, Covington, LA...........................504-893-2432
Carey, Mark/3109 Pelham St, Chesapeake, VA..........................804-396-5768
Carter, Kip/225 Beaverdam Dr, Winterville, GA 404-542-5384
Carter, Zane/345 S Patrick St, Alexandria, VA...........................703-836-2900
Cassady, Jack/, Tampa, FL...813-960-9188
Castellanos, Carlos/20150-08 NE 3rd Court,
N Miami, FL (P 950) **305-651-9524**
Cathcart, Marilyn/6933 Columbia Ave, St Louis, MO 314-862-2644
Cavanagh, Tom/119 NW 93rd Terrace, Coral Sprngs, FL 305-753-1874
Chaffee, Doug/107 Shagbark Circle, Simponsville, SC 803-877-9826
Chau, Tung Wai/534 Richmar Dr, Nashville, TN..........................615-781-8607
Cheshire/Clemente Studios/16823 Francis West Ln, Dumfries, VA 703-221-8629
Clark, David/2101-B N Scott St, Arlington, VA 703-524-9076
Clark, Jennifer/4164 S 36th St, Arlington, VA.............................703-671-7187
Clegg, Dave/3571 Aaron Sosebee Rd, Cumming, GA 404-887-6306
CoConis, Ted/Airport Rd, Cedar Key, FL....................................904-543-5720
Coleman, Ian/PO Box 381617, Miami, FL (P 862) **305-751-3914**
Collins, Samuel/PO Box 73004, Birmingham, AL........................205-991-0557
Combs, R Mason/PO Box 573/Mile Branch, Pineville, KY 606-337-2012
Communication Arts/Bordeaux/129 E Pasagoula St, Jackson, MS.......601-354-7955
Comport, Sally Wern/241 Central Ave,
St Petersberg, FL (P 963) **813-821-9050**
Cooley, Rick L/Rt 1/ Box 155, Check, VA...................................703-651-4481
Cooper, Cheryl/525 22nd Ave N, St Petersburg, FL...................813-822-5805
Correnti, Sandra/4 Meadow Dr, Bristol, VA................................703-669-4924
Covington, Neverne/241-A Central Ave,

St Petersburg, FL (P 971) **813-822-1267**
Cowan, Robert/528 Shelton Dr, Aberdeen, NC 919-944-1306
Craig, Robert E/2029 Mt Hope Church Rd, Whitsett,
NC (P 403) **919-697-2220**
Crane, Gary/1511 W Little Creek Rd, Norfolk, VA 804-627-0717
Crowe, Trish/3310 N 23rd Rd, Arlington, VA...............................703-525-2084
Crowther, Will/304 Hampton Dr, Dunnwoody, GA......................404-393-8120
Cuevas, George/6337 SW 14th St, Miami, FL 305-264-7046
Curcio, Jeff/3520 3 6th St, Arlington, VA....................................703-920-7472

DEF

Dabagian, Marc/2614 Kingsley Rd, Raliegh, NC.........................919-847-0673
Dalton, Clay/939 Leeds Castle Way, Marietta, GA......................404-425-1065
DeBro, James/2725 Hayden Dr, Eastpoint, GA...........................404-344-2971
Dekle, Merritt/310 W Lafayette St, Marianna, FL
(P 693) **904-526-3319**
DeLahoussaye, Jeanne/816 Foucher, New Orleans, LA 504-581-2167
DeLoy, Dee/8166 Jellison St, Orlando, FL..................................407-273-8365
Diatz, Dianna/4629 Seminary Rd #301, Alexandria, VA..............703-751-4064
Dillingham, Jerry/5952 Kenton Dr, Kernersville, NC....................919-996-4059
Dixon, Christine/6734 Kenyon Dr, Alexandria, VA 703-660-8427
Dixon, David/PO Box 454 B/ Rte 14, Gray, TN 615-283-0484
Dodson, Dale/1255 Richfield Dr, Rosewell, GA...........................404-526-5328
Dole, Algar/PO Box 1263, Harrisonburg, VA...............................703-896-6217
Dove Design Studio/2025 Rockledge Rd NE, Atlanta, GA..........404-873-2209
Duckworth, Susie/2912 Kings Chapel Rd #7, Falls Church, VA ...703-698-8987
Dunlap, Leslie/510 Robinson Court, Alexandria, VA 703-836-9067
Dupree, Melissa/615 Fourth Ave, Opelika, AL 205-749-7166
Eddins, George/1249 East Blvd, Charlotte, NC 704-334-4543
Edgerton, Tom/911 Elizabeethan Dr, Greensboro, NC................919-854-2816
Ehrenfeld, Jane/301 St George St, Farmville, VA 804-392-6190
Eldredge, Ernie/2683 Vesclub Cir, Birmingham, AL....................205-822-3879
Ellistrations/PO Box 4567, Greensboro, NC...............................919-288-6521
Elson, Glenn/303A Market St, Roanoke,
VA (P 991) **703-343-3385**
Epperly's Art Studio/308 N Maple St, Graham, NC.....................919-227-2117
Faure, Renee/600 Second St, Neptune Beach, FL 904-246-2781
Fernandez, Luis/1270 W Peachtree St #8C, Atlanta,
GA (P 734) **404-873-2287**
Findley, John/206 Rogers St NE #204, Atlanta, GA....................404-378-8226
Firestone, Bill/4810 Bradford Dr, Alexandria, VA........................703-354-0247
Fisher, Mike/510 Turquoise St, New Orleans, LA
(P 997) **504-288-4860**
Floyd, Walt/1118 Rosedale Dr #4, Atlanta, GA...........................404-875-8061
Foster, Travis/313 Becklea Dr, Madison, TN 615-865-0811
Frank, Bill/3185 Shingle Creek Ct, Kissimmee, FL 407-846-8143
Frank, Cheryll/2216 Eastgate Way, Tallahasse, FL.....................904-668-0909

G

Gaadt, David/2103 Tennyson Dr, Greensboro, NC......................919-288-0953
Gabriele, Antonio J/931 Deep Lagoon Lane, Ft Myers, FL..........305-433-3202
Garcia, Ernie/640 NE 72nd Terrace, Miami, FL 305-754-5412
Garcia, Rick/620 NE 119th St, Miami, FL....................................407-784-6263
Gates, Donald/1552 Great Falls St, McLean, VA.........................703-442-4798
Gates, Kathleen/2019 Felix, Memphis, TN 901-725-4667
Gebhart, Bradley/8526 Forrester Dr, Springfield, VA 703-866-0531
Gignilliat, Elaine/747 Bayliss Dr, Marietta, GA 404-977-5635
Gilmore, Paulette/2860 Running Pump Ln, Herndon, VA.............703-478-0349
Glasgow, Dale/4493 Andy Court, Woodbridge, VA......................703-590-1702
Gonzalez, Thomas/755 Virginia Ave NE, Atlanta, GA
(P 584) **404-872-7980**
Goris, Dennis/901 N Washington St, Alexandria, VA...................703-739-0088
Gorman, Martha/3057 Pharr Ct Nrth NW #E6, Atlanta, GA.........404-261-5632
Grandstaff, Chris/12704 Harbor View Ct, Woodbridge, VA 703-494-0422
Graphics Group/6111 PchtreeDunwdy Rd#G101, Atlanta, GA.....404-391-9929
Graphics Illustrated/5720-E North Blvd, Raliegh, NC..................919-878-7883
Greathead, Ian/1591 Sandpoint Dr, Atlanta, GA.........................404-640-6517
Griswold, Theophilus Britt/3807 Foxfield Lane, Fairfax, VA..........703-830-7571
Gurche, John/390 N Granada, Arlington, VA...............................703-524-0066
Gurvin, Abe/1270 W Peachtree St #8C, Atlanta, GA
(P 738) **404-873-2287**
Guthrie, Dennis/1118 Franklin Ct, Atlanta, GA 404-325-6867

H

Hagen, David/14637 Stone Range Dr, Centreville, VA..........703-830-4208
Hamilton, Laurie/4200 St Charles Ave, New Orleans, LA 504-891-3138
Hamilton, Marcus/12225 Ranburne Rd, Charlotte, NC 704-545-3121
Harris, Leslie/1906 Wellbourne Dr NE, Atlanta,
GA (P 891)...**404-872-7163**
Harrison, Kenneth/4209 Canal St, New Orleans, LA...........504-486-9011
Havaway, Jane/806 Briarcliff Rd, Atlanta, GA.........404-872-7284
Heavner, Becky/202 E Raymond Ave, Alexandria, VA.........703-683-1544
Heinly, John/5939 Ridge Ford Dr, Burke, VA 703-451-7263
Helms, John/4255 Arrowhead, Memphis, TN 901-363-6589
Henderling, Lisa/10076 Bay Harbor Terrace, Bay Harbor Isl, FL.........305-866-3220
Hendrix, Bryan/777 Ponce de Leon Terrace,
Atlanta, GA (P 1030)...**404-875-4290**
Herbots, Luc/15069 Camellia Lane, Dumfries, VA 703-690-7030
Herchak, Stephen/1735 St Julian Pl, Columbia, SC 803-799-1800
Herring, David/6246 Woodlake Dr, Atlanta, GA.........404-945-8652
Hickey, John/3832 Abingdon Cir, Norfolk, VA.........804-853-2956
Hickman, Stephen/105 S Jenkins St, Alexandria, VA.........703-751-4070
Hicks, Richard Edward/3667 Vanet Rd, Chamblee, GA.........404-457-8928
Hilfer, Susan/PO Box 50552, Columbia, SC.........803-799-0689
Hinton, Patricia Gural/313 Sunset Ave, Louisburg, NC.........919-496-6486
Hobson, Ken/209 Kirk Rd, Greensboro, NC.........919-282-7789
Hodges, John/8 Sycamore Circle, Grenada, MS.........601-226-7527
Hodges, Mike/666 Bantry Lane, Stone Mountain,
GA (P 546)...**404-296-9666**
Hoff, Dana/5634 Pacific Blvd #903, Boca Raton, FL.........407-392-3849
Holladay, Reggie/7395 NW 51st St, Lauderhill, FL.........305-749-9031
Holz, Fred/8340 Greensboro Dr #51, McClean, VA.........703-442-9323
Horn, Dave/42 Breckenridge Pkwy, Ashville, NC.........704-645-6907
Howell, Troy/58 Dobson Lane, Falmouth, VA.........703-373-5199
Humphrey, John J Jr/2241 Wrightsville Ave #0, Wilmington, NC.........919-251-8222
Hunter, Alexander/Box 21 Blue Ridge Acres, Harper's Ferry, VA.........304-728-0091
Hyatt, Mitch/4171 Buckingham Ct, Marietta, GA.........404-924-1241
Hyatt, Steven/4171 Buckingham Ct, Marietta, GA.........404-924-1241

IJK

Image Electronic Inc/3525 Piedmont Rd NE #110, Atlanta, GA.........404-262-7610
Ingram, David/7536 Ambergate Place, McLean, VA.........703-847-6136
Irvin, Trevor/330 Southerland Terrace, Atlanta, GA.........404-377-4754
James, Bill/15840 SW 79th Ct, Miami, FL.........305-238-5709
Jamison, Alex/713 S Glebe Rd, Arlington, VA.........703-486-2690
Jarvis, David/200 S Banana River Rd #1802, Coco Beach, FL.........407-784-6263
Jepsen, Deirdre/Rte 1, Box 307E, Leesburg, VA.........703-471-5468
Joffrion, Kathleen/4209 Canal St, New Orleans, LA.........504-486-9011
Johnna/666 Bantry Lane, Stone Mountain, GA (P 547).........**404-296-9666**
Johnson, Pamela R/1415 N Key Blvd, Arlington, VA.........703-525-5012
Jones, Jack/571 Dutch Valley Rd, Atlanta, GA.........404-881-6627
Jones, Karen/3985 Evans Rd, Atlanta, GA.........404-938-8829
Kanelous, George/2864 Lake Valencia Blvd E, Palm Harbor, FL.........813-784-8528
Kasso, Larry/PO Box 40461, Baton Rouge, LA.........504-295-1644
Katzowitz, Joel/3355 Atlanta Indstrl Dr, Atlanta, GA.........404-641-9718
Kaufman, Robert J/3200 Libeth St, Charlotte, NC.........704-568-3417
Kennedy, Dean/Mary Dell Lane, Louisville, KY.........502-239-1407
Kent, Derek/1081 Woodland Ave #4, Atlanta, GA.........404-325-1565
Kettler, Al/1420 Prince St #202, Alexandria, VA.........703-548-8040
Keys, Watt/612 E Tremont Ave, Charlotte, NC.........704-332-6576
Kilgore, Susi/2905 Bay Villa, Tampa, FL.........813-837-9759
Klioze, Marcia/2409 Andorra Pl, Reston, VA.........703-620-4922
Knowles, Eric/PO Box 43, Charlottesville, VA.........804-296-3862
Kovach, Joe/3100 N Elm St, Greensboro, NC.........919-545-1788
Krafchek, Ken/815 S Lincoln St, Arlington, VA (P 657).........**703-553-0469**
Kriese, Penny/6019 Waterbury Ct, Springfield, VA.........703-644-8478
Kristoff, Dante/13835 Springstone Dr, Clifton, VA.........703-818-2799

L

Lacz, John/c/o Concepts 2840 Somerset Dr, Ft Lauderdale, FL.........305-735-0752
Laden, Nina/1517 McLendon Ave NE, Atlanta, GA.........404-371-0052
Landis, Jeff/1372 50th Ave NE, St Petersburg, FL.........813-525-0757
Lang, Cecily/250 E Royal Palm Rd #1A, Boca Raton, NY.........407-392-5860
Lay, Toby/1408 S Sixth St, Louisville, KY (P 667).........**502-561-0737**
Lee, Kelly/3511 N 22nd St, Arlington, VA.........703-527-4089
Lee, Tim/1715 Brantford Dr, Atlanta, GA (P 833).........**404-938-8829**
Left, Stephen/1351 S Dixie Hwy #E8, Pompano Beach, FL.........305-946-7485

Leiner, Alan/3265 Nocturne Rd, Venice, FL.........813-493-6754
Leister, Bryan/202 E Raymond Ave, Alexandria, VA.........703-683-1544
Lengyel, Kathy/2306 Jones Dr, Dunedin, FL.........813-734-1382
Lester, Mike/8890 River Trace Dr, Duluth, GA
(P 1060,1061)...**404-447-5332**
Levine, Arlene/1107 S Peters #508, New Orleans, LA.........504-522-1520
Lewczak, Scott/1600 E Jefferson Ct, Sterling, VA.........703-435-5982
Lewis, Chris/1155 N Virginia Ave NE, Atlanta, GA
(P 585)...**404-874-7227**
Little, Pam/321 Niagara St, Orange City, FL.........904-755-2919
Loehle, Don/2574 Sherbrooke Dr NE, Atlanta, CA.........404-633-7145
Loehle, Richard/2608 River Oak Dr, Decatur, GA.........404-325-9580
Long, Jim/4415 Briarwood Court N, Annandale, VA.........703-354-8052
Lovell, Rick/1270 W Peachtree St #8C, Atlanta, GA
(P 735)...**404-873-2287**
Lubsen, Laurie J Perkins/333 N Edison St, Arlington, VA.........703-528-2667
Lukens, Jan/2354 Chaucer Lane, Winston-Salem, NC.........919-788-5451
Lunsford, Annie/515 N Hudson St, Arlington, VA.........703-527-7696

M

Maddox, Kelly/328 Greenwood Ave, Decatur, GA
(P 228,229)...**404-377-0519**
Madson, Steven/4129 Hampstead Lane, Woodbridge, VA.........703-590-4341
Mahoney, Ron/2400 E Commercial Blvd #420,
Ft Lauderdale , FL (P 420)...**412-261-3824**
Majewski, Chuck/10075 Paradise Blvd, Treasure Island, FL.........813-367-3954
Marks, David/726 Hillpine Dr NE, Atlanta, GA.........404-872-1824
Martin, Don/5110 S W 80th St, Miami, FL.........305-665-2376
Martin, Lyn/PO Box 51972, Knoxville, TN.........615-588-1760
Matthews, Lu/547 Mount Hermon Rd, Ashland, VA
(P 380)...**804-798-9144**
Mattos, John/1408 S Sixth St, Louisville, KY
(P 662,772,773)...**502-561-0737**
Mayberry, Douglas/1315 Oakhill Ave, Gulfport, MS.........601-688-1884
Mayer, Bill/240 Forkner Dr, Decatur, GA (P 758,759).........**404-378-0686**
McCall, Paul Illustration/2403 Renseller Pl, Marietta, GA.........404-953-1599
McGinness, Jim/3822 Jancie Rd, Fairfax, VA.........703-691-0758
McGrail, Rollin/12470 West Hampton Circle, West Palm Beach, Fl.........407-795-9525
McKeever, Michael/1240 NE 171 Terrace, N Miami Beach, FL.........305-652-6668
McKelvey, David/1270 W Peachtree St #8C,
Atlanta, GA (P 736)..**404-873-2287**
McKelvey, Shawn/666 Bantry Lane, Stone Mountain,
GA (P 545)...**404-296-9666**
McKissick, Randall/PO Box 21811, Columbia, SC.........803-739-9080
McMahon, Mike/PO Box 1325, Charlotte, NC.........704-372-6007
McManus, Eugenia/PO Box 39, Mayhew, MS.........601-328-5534
Melrath, Susan/1211 Reading Terrace, W Palm Beach, FL.........407-790-1561
Miller, A J/2207 Bay Blvd #201, Indian Rocks Bch, FL.........813-596-6384
Miller-Sniady, Daphne/910 Enderby Dr, Alexandria, VA.........703-548-0408
Mitchell, Bono/2118 N Oakland St, Alexandria, VA.........703-276-0612
Mitchell, Charlie/666 Bantry Lane, Atlanta,
GA (P 543)...**404-296-9666**
Mollica, Pat/1270 W Peachtree St #8C, Atlanta,
GA (P 734)...**404-873-2287**
Montgomery, Michael/7765 Fielder Rd, Jonesboro, GA.........404-478-2929
Moore, Connie Illus/4242 Inverness Rd, Duluth, GA.........404-449-9553
Moore, Cyd/3465 Fernway Dr, Montgomery, AL.........205-281-4818
Moore, Larry/1635 Delaney St, Orlando, FL.........407-648-0832
Moore, William "Casey"/4242 Inverness Rd, Duluth, GA.........404-449-9553
Moses, David/1728 N Rock Springs Rd, Atlanta, GA.........404-874-2014
Myers, Sherwood/9770 Sterling Dr, Miami, FL.........305-238-0488

NO

Nelson, Bill/107 E Cary St, Richmond, VA (P 240,241).........**804-783-2602**
Nelson, Merri/Rt 1/ Box 38, Purcellville, VA.........703-478-8747
Neuhaus, David/2727 Duke St #709, Alexandria, VA.........703-461-8710
Norvell, Jill/2123 Cabots Point Lane, Reston, VA.........703-264-0600
O'Connor, John/2010 Scott Dr, Blacksburg, VA.........703-953-2744
Of Mice & Graphics/3930 Hancock Circle, Atlanta, GA.........404-934-1249
Oh, Beth/2292 F Dunnwoody Crossing, Atlanta, GA.........404-457-5924
Oliphant, Tim/200 MCHS Dr #2K, Lewisburg, TN.........615-359-7430
Olsen, Greg/666 Bantry Lane, Stone Mountain, GA.........404-296-9666
Overacre, Gary/3802 Vinyard Trace, Marietta, GA.........404-973-8878
Ovies, Joe/3500 Piedmont St #430, Atlanta, GA.........404-462-1209

P

Pack, John/2342 N Fillmore St, Arlington, VA (P 1100) **703-243-4024**
Pardue, Jack/2307 Sherwood Hall Ln, Alexandria, VA 703-765-2622
Parker, Suzy/1000 Wilson Blvd, Arlington, VA 703-276-3458
Pate, Martin/571 Dutch Valley Rd, Atlanta, GA...................404-881-6627
Pawelka, Rick/5720 E North Blvd, Raleigh, NC...................919-878-7883
Peeke, Kevin/5851 Sunset Dr, Miami, FL...................305-667-3252
Peery, Joe/3561 Ebenezer Rd, Marietta, GA (P 1103) **404-973-0010**
Penca, Gary/8335 NW 20th St, Coral Springs, FL...................305-752-4699
Pentard, Alton/2911 Dumaine, New Orleans, LA 504-486-0633
Perry, Phil/968 Homewood Ct, Decatur, GA 404-634-2349
Pico, Steve/2433 Keene Park Dr, Largo, FL 813-530-4266
Pitt, Bob/503 Emory Circle, Atlanta, GA 404-378-0694
Pomeroy, Bradley/4720 N 20th Rd #207, Arlington, VA 703-920-7765
Poole, Colin/817 Mackall Ave, McLean, VA (P 1108) **703-893-0759**
Powell, Rick/523 W 24th St, Norfolk, VA 804-626-1301
Primeau, Chuck/4960 Avenida Del Sol, Raleigh, NC 919-876-5529
Pygmy Design Group/1951 SW 23rd St, Miami, FL 305-856-5663

R

Rabon, Elaine Hearn/573 Hill St, Athens, GA...................404-353-8479
Rainock, Norman/10226 Purcell Rd, Glen Allen, VA...................804-264-8123
Ramirez, Roberto/2718 W Mountain St #41, Kernersville, NC...................919-748-1768
Ramsey, Ted/1623 Stowe Rd, Reston, VA 703-481-9424
Rauchman, Bob/5210 SW 60th Pl, Miami, FL...................305-445-5628
Richards, Barbara/10607 Kennel Lane, Charlotte, NC...................704-846-3944
Robinette, John/1270 W Peachtree St #8C, Atlanta, GA (P 737) **404-873-2287**
Robinson, Mark/9050 Loreleigh Way, Fairfax, VA...................703-280-4123
Rogers, Nip/93 Ashby Ct, Marshall, VA 703-364-1247
Romeo, Richard/1066 NW 96th Ave, Ft Lauderdale, FL...................305-472-0072
Roolaart, Harry/6449 Montpelier Rd, Charlotte, NC (P 1118) **704-552-6311**
Rudnak, Theo/166 Beverly Rd NE, Atlanta, GA (P 853,91) **404-876-4058**
Ruegger, Rebecca/4244 Pate, Franklin, TN (P 602) **615-794-9984**

S

Saffold, Joe/719 Martina Dr NE, Atlanta, GA (P 804,805) **404-231-2168**
Salmon, Paul/5826 Jackson's Oak Ct, Burke, VA...................703-250-4943
Sampson, Ronnie/1306 E Cary St, Richmond, VA 804-788-1358
Sams, B B/PO Box A, Social Circle, GA 404-464-2956
Sawyer, Peter A/7768 Clifton Rd, Fairfax, VA...................703-250-3117
Scheffer Studios/PO Box 2276, Clearwater, FL 813-736-6777
Schmidt, John F/7308 Leesville Blvd, Springfield, VA...................703-750-0927
Schneider, Wendi/4209 Canal St, New Orleans, LA...................504-486-9011
Scott, Robert/4108 Forest Hill Ave, Richmond, VA (P 1128) **804-232-1627**
Seif, Sue Solomon/4050 Innslake Dr, Glen Allen, VA...................804-747-9684
Selvage, Roger/2148 Cartwright Pl, Reston, VA...................703-264-5325
Shelley, G A/3204 Winchelsea Dr, Charlotte, NC...................704-536-6510
Shelly, Ron/6396 Manor Lane, S Miami, FL...................305-667-0154
Shelton, Dean/7632 Crow Cut Rd, Fairview, TN...................615-799-0409
Short, Robbie/2903 Bentwood Dr, Marietta, GA...................404-565-7811
Simmons, Keith/6125 River Meadow Court, Raleigh, NC 919-876-6236
Sipp, Geo/380 Garden Lane NW, Atlanta, GA...................404-876-0312
Sloan, Michael/PO Box 1397, Madison, TN...................615-865-7018
Smith, Donald/PO Box 391, Athens, GA...................404-543-5555
Smythe, Danny/6103 Knight Arnold, Memphis, TN (P 1147) **901-794-5883**
Soper, Patrick/214 Stephens, Lafayette, LA 318-233-1635
Spence, Jim/4260 60th St, Vero Beach, FL...................407-778-8859
Spetseris, Steve/571 Dutch Valley Road, Atlanta, GA...................404-881-6627
Spirduso, Kenneth/3811-9 Cornerwood Ln, Charlotte, NC...................704-366-4346
Spisak, Matt/968 Homewood Ct, Decatur, GA...................404-634-2349
Stanton, Mark/67 Jonesboro St, McDonough, GA...................404-957-5966
Stanton, Reggie/411 Park Ave N #11, Winter Park, FL...................305-645-1661
Steadham, Richard/14085 Ryon Court, Woodbridge, VA...................703-590-9464
Steiner, Peter/1948 Rockingham St, McLean, VA...................703-237-9576
Stewart, Greg/Route 28, Knoxville, TN 615-577-3345
Stieferman, Guy/5715 Lonacre Cove, Memphis, TN...................901-372-2902
Stone, David K/106 Stoneybrook, Chapel Hill, NC...................919-929-0853

Stork, Bill/7325 W Friendly Ave #D-1, Greensboro, NC 919-299-3640
Story, Michael/PO Box 50492, Columbia, SC 803-256-8813
Street, Renee & David/1414 S Pollard St, Arlington, VA...................703-521-6227
Streetworks Studio/1414 S Pollard St, Arlington, VA...................703-521-6227
Suplee, David/7328 Dartford Dr #9, McLean, VA...................703-848-4550

TUV

Tamara & Assoc/3565 Piedmont Rd #200, Atlanta, GA...................404-262-1209
Teague, Tom/617 Hillcrest Drive SW, Vienna, VA...................703-281-7036
Textured Graphics Studio/719 Martina Dr NE, Atlanta, GA...................404-231-2168
Thompson, Del/PO Box 7016 #225, Greenville, SC...................803-232-5444
Tinney, Robert/PO Box 778, Washington, LA...................318-826-3003
Torp, Cynthia/1408 S Sixth St, Louisville, KY (P 662,206) **502-561-0737**
Traynor, Elizabeth/Rt12 Box 32 Barbee Chapel Rd, Chapel Hill, NC 919-968-6573
Tull, Bobbi/6103 Beachway Dr, Falls Church, VA 703-998-9292
Turner, Cynthia/3 Old Miller Pl, Santa Rosa Bch, FL...................904-231-4112
Turner, Jeanne/6900 Chestnut Ave, Falls Church, VA...................703-237-1108
Turner, Pete/938 Pamlico Dr, Cary, NC...................919-467-8466
Ulan, Helen Cerra/4227 San Juan Dr, Fairfax, VA...................703-691-0474
Vaughn, Rob/600 Curtis Pkwy/Box 660706, Miami Springs, FL...................305-885-1292
Verzaal, Dale/1270 W Peachtree St #8C, Atlanta, GA (P 739) **404-873-2287**
Vincent, Wayne/957 N Livingston St, Arlington, VA...................703-532-8551
Vintson, Sherry/4860 Dover St NE, St Petersburg, FL...................813-822-2512
Voide, Raymond H/3419 Braddock Dr, Woodbridge, VA...................703-878-2585

WXY

Wagner, Stephen R/Rt 1/Box 978, Washington, VA...................703-675-3046
Walsh, Pat/8801 McNair Dr, Alexander, VA...................703-780-5578
Walsh, Taly/2481 Windbreak Dr, Alexandria, VA...................703-765-6154
Walthall, Jeffrey/2031 Rockingham St, McLean, VA...................703-538-2738
Wariner, David/1408 S Sixth St, Louisville, KY (P 661) **502-561-0737**
Warnock, Ted/4141 N Henderson Rd #913, Arlington, VA...................202-333-4141
Wasilowski, Bob/ 3258 Kinross Circle, Herndon, VA...................703-742-6658
Watts, David/1407 Brooks Ave, Raleigh, NC...................919-783-5133
Webber, Warren/571 Dutch Valley Rd, Atlanta, GA...................404-881-6627
Wetzel, Marcia/755 Virginia Ave NE, Atlanta, GA (P 586) **404-872-7980**
Whitver, Harry K/208 Reidhurst Ave, Nashville, TN (P 653) **615-320-1795**
Wilgus, David/PO Box 971, Davidson, NC...................704-892-7738
Wilkinson, Joel/707 E McBee Ave, Greenville, SC...................803-235-4483
Williams, Tim/520 Country Glen Rd, Alpharetta, GA...................404-475-3146
Wink, David/864 Charles Allen Dr, Atlanta, GA (P 1182) **404-874-3389**
Winslow, Terese/714 S Fairfax St, Alexandria, VA...................703-836-9121
Woodle, Arthur/169 Forest Ave, Marietta, GA...................404-429-1432
Woolridge, Anthony/5530 Ascot Ct #22, Alexandria, VA...................703-578-0790
Xenakis, Thomas/523 W 24th St #25, Norfolk, VA...................804-622-2061
Yarnell, David Andrew/PO Box 286, Occoquan, VA...................703-690-2987
Young, Bruce/1262 Pasadena Ave NE, Atlanta, GA...................404-892-8509

MIDWEST

A

Ahearn, John D/151 S Elm, St Louis, MO...................314-781-3389
AIR Studio/203 E Seventh St, Cincinnati, OH...................513-721-1193
Allen, David W/18108 Martin Ave #2F, Homewood, IL...................708-798-3283
Allen, Jim/Box 8454, Moline, IL...................309-799-3366
Allen, Rick/2216 E 32nd St, Minneapolis, MN (P 731) .**612-721-8832**
Allison, John/3747 Washington, Kansas City, MO (P 898) **816-561-7782**
Ambre, Matt/3222 N Clifton #2F, Chicago, IL...................312-935-5170
Anastas, Nicolette/307 N Michigan Ave #1008, Chicago, IL...................312-704-0500
Andrews, Bob/2100 W Big Beaver Rd, Troy, MI (P 1139) **303-643-6000**
Appleoff, Sandy/1809 Westport Rd, Kansas City, MO...................816-753-5421
Archer, Doug/512 South Oak POB 307, Garnett, KS (P 520) **913-448-3841**
Art Factory Ltd/925 Elmgrove, Elmgrove, WI...................414-785-1940
Art Force Inc/21700 NW Hwy #570, Southfield, MI...................313-569-1074

Edsey, Michael/6040 N Avondale, Chicago, IL 312-988-2703
Ehlert, Lois/839 N Marshall, Milwaukee, WI (P 678)....414-276-8336
Eisbrenner, Robert/422 W Melrose #207, Chicago, IL 312-528-0236
Eldridge, Gary/117 West Main St, Lowell, MI 616-897-6668
Ellis, Christy/914 N Winchester, Chicago, IL 312-342-6343
Ellithorpe, Chris/4207 N Kedvale #2D, Chicago, IL 708-924-7938
Elmore, Larry/490 Rockside Rd, Cleveland, OH 216-661-4222
English, M John/4601 Rockhill Rd, Kansas City, MO (P 569)....816-931-5648
English, Mark/512 Lakeside Ct, Liberty, MO 816-781-0056
Erdmann, Dan/3301-A S Jefferson Ave, St Louis, MO (P 491)....314-773-2600
Evans, Sid/1533 N Mohawk, Chicago, IL 312-751-1177

F

Fanning, Jim/10 E 66th St, Kansas City, MO 816-361-5191
Faust, Leslie A/1329 Maclind, St Louis, MO 314-647-2228
Ferraro, Sandra/6057 Hillside Ave, E Dr, Indianapolis, IN....317-255-6335
Flock, Mary/905 S Laflin #3, Chicago, IL 312-733-0459
Flood, Dick/1603 Sheridan Rd, Champaign, IL....217-352-8356
Fogle, David W/1257 Virginia Ave, Lakewood, OH....216-521-2854
Ford, Dan/8025 Watkins Dr, St Louis, MO 314-862-3005
Foster, Jack/650 N Willow, Elmhurst, IL 708-279-3040
Foster, Stephen/894 Grove St, Glencoe, IL (P 808,809)....708-835-2783
Foty, Tom/3836 Shady Oak Rd, Minnetonka, MN....612-933-5570
France, Jeff/4970 Fyler Ave, St Louis, MO 314-587-3426
Fredrickson, Mark/3286 Ivanhoe, St Louis, MO (P 394)....314-781-7377
Frueh, Mark/5329 N Glenwood, Chicago, IL (P 306)....312-561-6584
Fuka, Ted/8037 S Kirkland Ave, Chicago, IL 312-585-2314

G

Gadecki, Ted/5068 N Wolcott, Chicago, IL (P 892)....312-769-6566
Garbot, Dave/8422 Westberry Ln, Tinley Park, IL (P 1003)....708-532-8722
Garner, Hjordis/1834 Lincoln Park W, Chicago, IL 312-664-8673
Garrett, Tom/PO Box 3635, Minneapolis, MN (P 514)....612-374-3169
Gast, Josef/68 E Franklin St, Dayton, OH (P 286)....513-433-8383
Gauthier, Corbert/510 Marquette Ave #200, Minneapolis, MN....612-339-0947
Gelb, Jacki/3345 Seminary, Chicago, IL 312-988-2866
Gellman, Sim/475 N Prince Rd, St Louis, MO 314-994-3045
Gieseke, Thomas A/7909 W 61st St, Merriam, KS (P 1006)....913-677-4593
Gillis, Chuck/2100 W Big Beaver Rd, Troy, MI (P 1140)....303-643-6000
Gin, Byron/4 E Ohio #11, Chicago, IL (P 565)....312-944-1130
Girouard, Patrick/306 Beverly Pl, Munster, IN....219-836-0816
Goldammer, Ken/120 W Illinois St #5W, Chicago, IL (P 294,295)....312-878-7914
Goldschmidt, Rick/9627 S 50th Court, Oak Lawn, IL....708-499-1414
Gonnella, Rick/200 E Ohio 2nd fl, Chicago, IL....312-337-6692
Goodman-Willy, April/3301-A S Jefferson Ave, St Louis, MO (P 485)....314-773-2600
Grace, Rob/7516 Lamar Ave #81, Prarie Village, KS....913-341-9135
Graef, Renee/2952 N Maryland, Milwaukee, WI 414-276-7807
GraFX Creative Imaging/Franklin Park, IL 800-633-7887
Graham, Bill/116 W Illinois, Chicago, IL....312-467-0330
Grandpré, Mary/475 Cleveland Ave N #222, St Paul, MN (P 1014)....612-645-3463
Graning, Ken/1975 Cragin Dr, Bloomfield Hills, MI 313-851-3665
Grasch, Karen/405 N Wabash, Chicago, IL 312-822-9632
Graziano, Krafft & Zale/333 N Michigan #401, Chicago, IL....312-368-4355
Groff, David/68 E Franklin St, Dayton, OH (P 280)....513-433-8383
Grow, Jean/2301 W Nordale Dr, Appleton, WI 414-739-4224
Gumble, Gary/803 Elmwood #3N, Evanston, IL....708-475-4712
Gustafson, Glenn/1300 Ivy Ct, Westmont, IL....708-810-9527

H

Hackett, Michael/20789 Millard, Taylor, MI 313-358-2660
Hagel, Mike/PO Box 610, Arlington Heights, IL....312-253-0638
Halbert, Michael/2419 Big Ben, St Louis, MO (P 159,1021)....314-645-6480
Hall, Kate Brennan /1594 Wellesley Ave, St Paul, MN (P 823)....612-698-7858
Hamblin, George/944 Beach St, LaGrange Pk, IL 708-352-1780
Hannan, Peter/1341 W Melrose, Chicago, IL 312-883-9029
Hansen, Clint/405 N Wabash #3112, Chicago, IL....312-321-1336
Hanson, Eric/PO Box 3635, Minneapolis, MN (P 515)....612-374-3169
Hargreaves, Greg/1225 W 4th St, Waterloo, IA (P 353)....319-234-7055
Harman, Richard/207 S Cottonwood, Republic, MO 417-732-2914
Harmony Visuals/6641A W Burleigh St, Milwaukee, WI 414-449-2081
Harris, Jim/2310 E 101st Ave, Crown Point, IN....219-769-4460
Harris, John/3584 Normandy 1st Fl, Shaker Heights, OH (P 694)....216-838-1362
Harris, Scott/820 Gaffield Pl, Evanston, IL....312-440-2360
Harrison, William/324 W State St, Geneva, IL (P 832,82,83)....708-232-7733
Harritos, Peter/68 E Franklin St, Dayton, OH (P 285)....513-433-8383
Harvey, Ray/3037 Willow Creek Estates Dr, St Louis, MO....314-837-2141
Hatala, Dan/1225 W 4th St, Waterloo, IA (P 356)....319-234-7055
Hatcher, Lois/32 W 58th St, Kansas City, MO....816-361-6230
Havlicek, Karel/405 N Wabash #3203, Chicago, IL (P 550)....312-329-1370
Hawthorne, Bob/421 Springdale Dr, Belleville, IL 618-234-3052
Hayes, Cliff/PO Box 1239, Chicago Hts, IL 708-755-7115
Hayes, John/1121 W George St, Chicago, IL (P 882)....312-787-1333
Haynes, Bryan/2401 S 13th St, St Louis, MO (P 28)....314-771-0055
Haynes, Michael P/3070 Hawthorn Blvd, St Louis, MO 314-772-3156
Hays, Michael/324 S Maple Ave, Oak Park, IL....708-383-4229
Heinze, Mitchell/1225 W 4th St, Waterloo, IA (P 359)....319-234-7055
Henke, Matthew/310 Mansion House Ctr, St Louis, MO 314-421-6485
Higgins, Dave/2100 W Big Beaver Rd, Troy, MI (P 1140)....303-643-6000
Hockerman, Dennis/6024 W Chapel Hill Rd, Mequon, WI....414-242-4103
Hodde, Julie/68 E Franklin St, Dayton, OH....513-433-8383
Hodge, Gerald/1241 Bending Rd, Ann Arbor, MI 313-764-6163
Holladay Prints/5315 Tremont Ave #3, Davenport, IA 319-386-5645
Holton, Susan V/1512 W Jonquil, Chicago, IL....312-973-6429
Horn, Robert/405 N Wabash #2815, Chicago, IL....312-644-0058
Hosner, William/11440 Oak Dr., Shelbyville, MI 616-672-5756
Howard, Deborah/PO Box 178 197, Toledo, OH....419-335-3340
Hrabe, Curtis/2944 Greenwood Ave, Highland Park, IL 708-432-4632
Hranilovich, Barbara/1200 N Jenison, Lansing, MI 517-487-6474
Hughes, Dralene "Red"/19750 W Observatory Rd, New Berlin, WI (P 1041)....414-542-5547
Hullinger, C D/4436 South River Rd, West Lafayette, IN....317-743-3690
Hunn, John/508 Sunnyside, St Louis, MO 314-968-1061
Hunt, Harlan/900 W Jackson #7W, Chicago, IL 312-944-5680
Hunter, Steve/1225 W 4th St, Waterloo, IA (P 354)....319-234-7055

IJ

Illustrated Alaskan Moose/5 W Main St, Westerville, OH 614-898-5316
Izold, Donald/20475 Bunker Hill Dr, Fairview Park, OH....216-333-9988
Jackson, Kelly/982 Paradrome St #2, Cincinnati, OH 513-651-0258
Jackson-Zender Studio/1101 Southeastern Ave, Indianapolis, IN 317-639-5124
Jacobsen, Ken/5230 13th Ave S, Minneapolis, MN....612-822-0650
James, Bob/68 E Franklin St, Dayton, OH (P 272,273)....513-433-8383
James, Verzell/1521 W Sunnyside, Chicago, IL....312-784-2352
Jarvis, Nathan Y/708-A Main St, Grand View, MO....816-765-0617
Jay/17858 Rose St, Lansing, IL 708-474-9704
JK Art Direction/200 N Jefferson St, Milwaukee, WI....414-273-8194
Jobst, T S/2351 Woodbrook Circle, Columbus, OH 614-276-9921
Johannes, Greg/3713 N Racine #3 , Chicago, IL (P 488)....312-528-7941
Johnna/4502 Francis, Kansas City, KS (P 547)....913-722-0687
Johnson, BJ/540 N Lake Shore Dr #610, Chicago, IL....312-836-1166
Johnson, Diane/4609 N Claremont, Chicago, IL....312-728-5874
Johnson, Rick/1212 W Chase, Chicago, IL 708-790-1744
Johnson, Steve/440 Sheridan Ave South, Minneapolis, MN....612-377-8728
Jones, Jan/2332 N Halstead, Chicago, IL....312-929-1851
Jones, Mary/4511 N Campbell, Chicago, IL 312-769-1196
Jones, Michael Scott/1944 N Wilmot, Chicago, IL 312-278-4652
Jonke, Tim/88 Jefferson Lane, Streamwood, IL 708-213-3934
Juenger, Richard/1324 S 9th St, St Louis, MO 314-231-4069
Juett, Christine/501 W 11th St, Traverse City, MI....616-929-4424

K

Kalisch, John W/1330 S 33rd St, Omaha, NE....402-342-2572
Kargus, Jo Ann/5300 Old Lemay Ferry Rd, Imperial, MO 314-942-4159
Karl, Kevin/6730 Garner Ave, St Louis, MO 314-781-9494

Kars, Norman/13827 Olive St Rd, Chesterfield, MO 314-878-1780
Kasnot, Keith/3286 Ivanhoe, St Louis, MO (P 402) **314-781-7377**
Kasperski, Tom/1752 Atmore, St Louis, MO............314-522-3739
Kastaris, Rip/3301-A S Jefferson Ave, St Louis, MO
(P 489)............**314-773-2600**
Kasun, Mike/405 N Wabash #3112, Chicago, IL
(P 633)............**312-321-1336**
Kay, Michael/222 S Morgan #1A, Chicago, IL............312-738-1835
Kecman, Milan/2730 Somia Dr, Cleveland, OH............216-741-8755
Kelen, Linda/1922 W Newport, Chicago, IL............312-975-9696
Kessler Hartsock Assoc/5624 Belmont Ave, Cincinnati, OH ...513-542-8775
Kessler, Clifford/6642 West H Ave, Kalamazoo, MI............616-375-0688
Killeen, Tom/916 Olive #300, St Louis, MO............314-231-6800
Kirk, Rainey/11440 Oak Dr, Shelbyville, MI (P 704) **616-672-5756**
Kirov, Lydia/4008 N Hermitage Ave, Chicago, IL............312-248-8764
Klanderman, Leland/3286 Ivanhoe, St Louis, MO
(P 401)............**314-781-7377**
Kleber, John/211 E Ohio #621, Chicago, IL (P 563)......**312-784-2343**
Kleman, Gary B/809 S Florissant Rd, St Louis, MO............314-521-5065
Klimt, Kathy/3415 N Hoyne, Chicago, IL............312-525-1837
Knaak, Dale/c/o Dufour/633 St Clair, Sheboygan, WI 414-457-9191
Knutson, Doug/1225 W 4th St, Waterloo, IA............319-234-7055
Kock, Carl/2076 N Elston, Chicago, IL............312-342-8833
Kordic, Vladimir/35351 Grovewood Dr, Eastlake, OH............216-951-4026
Kortendick, Susan/2611 Eastwood, Evanston, IL............708-864-6062
Kotik, Kenneth William/9 Last Chance Ct,
St Peter, MO (P 1052,1053)............**314-441-1091**
Krainik, David/4719 Center Ave, Lisle, IL............708-963-4614
Kriegshauser, Shannon/3286 Ivanhoe, St Louis,
MO (P 397)............**314-781-7377**
Kueker, Don /829 Ginger Wood Court, St Louis, MO
(P 1056)............**314-225-1566**
Kulov, Dean/733 W Irving Park Rd #2, Chicago, IL............312-664-6040

L

Lackner, Paul/1225 W 4th St, Waterloo, IA (P 357) **319-234-7055**
Ladden, Randee/1200 W Waveland, Chicago, IL............312-327-8003
LaFever, Greg/68 E Franklin St, Dayton, OH
(P 278,279)............**513-433-8383**
Lambert, John/1911 E Robin Hood Ln, Arlington Heights, IL ...708-392-6349
Lange, Denis K/1545 Country Rd #995, Ashland, OH............419-289-0181
Langenderfer, Tim/631 Colona, Dayton, OH............513-298-5133
Langeneckert, Donald/4939 Ringer Rd, St Louis, MO............314-487-2042
Langeneckert, Mark/704 Dover Pl, St Louis, MO............314-752-0199
Larson, Seth/1315 Hathaway Ave, Lakewood, OH............216-228-2172
Lattimer, Evan/4203 Holly, Kansas City, MO............816-561-0103
Lawson, Robert/1523 Seminole St, Kalamazoo, MI............616-345-7607
Lederman, Marsha/4 Alpine Ct, East Brunswick, NJ............908-257-9324
Lee, Denis Charles/1120 Heatherway, Ann Arbor, MI............313-973-2795
Lee, Jared D/2942 Old Hamilton Rd, Lebanon, OH
(P 839)............**513-932-2154**
Lesh, David/5693 N Meridan St, Indianapolis, IN
(P 471)............**317-253-3141**
Letostak, John/7801 Fernhill Ave, Parma, OH............216-885-1753
Lochray, Tom/3225 Oakland Ave, Minneapolis, MN............612-823-7630
Lodderhose, Bill/6716 Sutherland, St Louis, MO............314-647-7738
Long, Bill/1580 Courtship Dr, Lancaster, OH............614-653-7058
Lord, David/1449 N Pennsylvania, Indianapolis, IN............317-634-1244
Loveless, Jim/4137 San Francisco Ave, St Louis, MO............314-533-7914
Luce, Ben/405 N Wabash #3112, Chicago, IL (P 634)......**312-321-1336**

M

Mach, Steven/515 N Halstead, Chicago, IL............312-243-4239
MacNair, Greg/7515 Wayne, University City, MO............314-721-3781
Maggard, John/68 E Franklin St, Dayton, OH
(P 274,275)............**513-433-8383**
Mahan, Benton/PO Box 66, Chesterville, OH............419-768-2204
Mallet, Kim/301 E Armour Blvd #315, Kansas City, MO............816-561-4473
Mark, Roger Illustration/8518 Alden, Lenexa, KS
(P 1074)............**913-492-4444**
Marlaire, Dennis/311 Kingston Dr, Frankfort, IL............708-819-4750
Martin, Larry/68 E Franklin St, Dayton, OH
(P 276,277)............**513-433-8383**
Matthews, Scott/6643 Devonshire St, St Louis, MO............314-481-7677
May, Jeff/7351 Tulane, St Louis, MO (P 1081)............**314-727-1476**
Mayerik, Val/20466 Drake Rd, Strongsville, OH............216-238-9492

Mayes, Kevin/1202 Tulsa St, Wichita, KS............316-522-6742
Mayse, Steve/7515 Allman, Lenexa, KS............913-599-5440
McDermott, Teri/38W563 Koshare Trail, Elgin, IL............708-888-2206
McFarland, Tom F/7300 Belleview, Kansas City, MO............816-363-5699
McKee-Anderson Group/919 Springer Dr, Lombard, IL............708-953-8706
McMahon, Mark/321 S Ridge Rd, Lake Forest, IL............708-295-2604
McNally, Jim/120 W Illinois, Chicago, IL............312-222-9504
McNamara Associates/1250 Stephenson Hwy, Troy,
MI (P 806,807)............**313-583-9200**
McNicholas, Michael/7804 W College Dr, Palos Hts, IL............708-361-2850
Meade, Roy/216 W Wayne St, Maumee, OH............419-666-1168
Mendheim, Mike/2916 W Estes, Chicago, IL............312-274-0077
Meredith, Jane/333 E Ontario #4010B-B, Chicago, IL............312-944-0731
Miller, Dave/727 Shady Oaks Ct, Elgin, IL............312-476-4429
Miller, David/PO Box 474, Elkhart, IN............219-295-1492
Miller, Kristen/3448 Hennepin Ave, Minneapolis, MN............612-827-1845
Miller, William (Bill)/1355 N Sandburg Ter #2002, Chicago, IL............312-787-4093
Mitchell, Kurt/3004 W 66th St, Chicago, IL............312-476-4429
Moline, Robin/2116 E 32nd St, Minneapolis, MN
(P 730)............**612-721-8832**
Molloy, Jack A/1645 Hennepin Ave South,
Minneapolis, MN (P 510)............**612-374-3169**
Monley, Jerry/2100 W Big Beaver Rd, Troy, MI
(P 1138)............**303-643-6000**
Moore, Stephen/1077 Country Creek Dr, Lebanon, OH............513-932-4295
Mora, Eddy/210 S Water St #44, Olathe, KS............913-782-7983
Morgan, Leonard/730 Victoria Ct, Bowlingbrook, IL............708-739-7705
Muchmore, Pat/1225 W 4th St, Waterloo, IA (P 362)......**319-234-7055**
Mundy, C W/8609 Manderley Dr, Indianapolis, IN............317-848-1330
Munger, Nancy/11440 Oak Drive, Shelbyville, MI............616-672-5756
Murakami, Tak/1535 E Juneway Terrace, Chicago, IL............312-764-7845
Murphy, Charles/4146 Pillsbury, Minneapolis, MN............612-926-4123
Musgrave, Steve/202 S State, Chicago, IL............312-939-4717

N

Nagel, Mike/PO Box 610, Arlington Hts, IL............312-253-0638
Neidigh, Sherry/325 W Huron #310, Chicago, IL............312-787-6826
Nelson Studios/10565 Widmer, Lenexa, KS............913-338-1330
Nelson, Diane/2816 Birchwood, Wilmette, IL............708-256-6200
Nelson, Fred/3 E Ontario #25, Chicago, IL............312-935-1707
Nichols, Gary/1449 N Pennsylvania St, Indianapolis, IN............317-637-0250
Niehaus, Dave/c/o Ramin/6239 Elizabeth Ave, St Louis, MO ...314-781-8851
Nighthawk Studio/1250 Riverbed Rd, Cleveland, OH............216-522-1809
Nixon, Tony/5552 Santa Fe, Overland, KS............913-384-5444
Nobles, Kelly/2625 N Clark St, Chicago, IL............312-975-0536
Noche, Mario/1449 N Pennsylvania, Indianapolis,
IN (P 665)............**317-299-8221**
Nolte, Larry/4021 Nebraska, St Louis, MO............314-481-6983
Norcia, Ernest/3451 Houston Rd, Waynesville, OH............513-862-5761
Northerner, Will/1551 W Thomas St, Chicago, IL............312-486-8098
Novak, Bob/6878 Fry Rd, Middlebury Hts, OH
(P 1096)............**216-234-1808**
Noyes, Mary Albury/716 First St N #245, Minneapolis, MN 612-338-1270
Nyberg, Tim/1012 Trillium Ln, Sister Bay, WI............414-854-4464

OP

O'Connell, Dave/2100 W Big Beaver Rd, Troy, MI
(P 1137)............**313-643-6000**
O'Connell, Mitch/6425 N Newgard #3N, Chicago, IL............312-743-3848
O'Donnell, William/6239 Elizabeth Ave, St Louis ,
MO (P 715)............**314-781-8851**
O'Malley, Kathy/4510 N Paulina #1W, Chicago, IL............312-334-7637
Oakley, Mark/2928 Wisconsin, St Louis, MO............314-772-0820
Odyssey Artworx/1324-B Skyridge Dr, Crystal Lake, IL............815-455-5554
Olds, Scott/2100 W Big Beaver Rd, Troy, MI
(P 1137)............**313-643-6000**
Oliveros, Edmond/5800 Monroe St, Sylvania, OH............419-882-7131
Olson, Robert A/15215 Buchanan Ct, Eden Prairie, MN............612-934-5767
Olson, Stan/PO Box 3635, Minneapolis, MN (P 513)......**612-374-3169**
Olsson, David/1225 W 4th St, Waterloo, IA (P 358)......**319-234-7055**
Ostresh, Michael/2034 13th St, Granite City, IL............618-876-8861
Otto, Brian/2216 E 32nd St, Minneapolis, MN............612-721-8832
Owsley, Patrick S/1 Buckingham Ct #5, Michigan
City, IN (P 1099)............**219-872-6570**
Palencar, John Jude/6763 Middlebrook Blvd,
Middleburg Heights, OH (P 822)............**216-845-8163**

Palnik, Paul/2357 Bixley Pk Rd, Bixley, OH 614-239-8710
Pappas, Chris/350 W Ontario #603, Chicago, IL 312-787-0455
Patterson/Thomas/1002 E Washington St, Indianapolis, IN 317-638-1002
Pauling, Galen T/PO Box 3150, Southfield, MI 313-356-5614
Pauly, Thomas Allen/4224 N Hermitage Ave, Chicago, IL 312-477-0440
Pepera, Fred/405 N Wabash #3203, Chicago, IL
(P 551) **312-329-1370**
Perreault, Alison Marie/1121 Wellington Ave, Chicago, IL 312-935-5326
Petan, Greg J/253 E Delaware Pl, Chicago, IL
(P 40) **312-787-9490**
Peters, David/1208 DuBois Court, St Louis, MO 314-821-8701
Peterson, Bryan/207 E Buffalo #543, Milwaukee, WI 414-291-0300
Peterson, Keith/7 W Campbell #2, Arlington Hts, IL 708-577-2279
Petrauskas, Kathy/1660 N Lasalle #2001,
Chicago, IL (P 531) **312-642-4950**
Philippidis, Evangelia/68 E Franklin St, Dayton, OH
(P 272,273) **513-433-8383**
Picasso, Dan/PO Box 3635, Minneapolis, MN (P 511) ..612-374-3169
Pitt Studios/1370 Ontario St #1430, Cleveland, OH 216-241-6720
Pitts, Ted/68 E Franklin St, Dayton, OH (P 287) **513-433-8383**
Pope, Giles/4222 Lindenwood, Matteson, IL 708-747-2056
Pope, Kevin/3286 Ivanhoe, St Louis, MO (P 406,407)....**314-781-7377**
Porazinski, Rob/777 N Michigan Ave #706,
Chicago, IL (P 652) **312-337-7770**
Porfirio, Guy/3286 Ivanhoe, St Louis, MO (P 395).........**314-781-7377**
Post, Bob/2144 Lincoln Pk W, Chicago, IL 312-549-6725
Post, Tom/2160 Julie Terr, Cincinnati, OH 513-769-0364
Pozwozd, Sally/124 N Park, Westmont, IL 708-969-5854
Prado, Hugo/3323 W Berteau Ave, Chicago, IL 312-583-7627
Pranica, John/5702 W Henderson, Chicago, IL 312-685-1207
Probert, Jean/3286 Ivanhoe, St Louis, MO (P 399) **314-781-7377**
Provenzano, Anthony/1046 Cora St, Des Plaines, IL 708-297-4560

QR

Quinn, Colleen/307 N Michigan Ave #1008, Chicago, IL 312-704-0500
Racer-Reynolds Illust/120 W Illinois 5th Fl, Chicago, IL 312-836-0099
Radencich, Michael/3016 Cherry, Kansas City, MO
(P 171,1114,1115) **816-756-1992**
RadenStudio/3016 Cherry, Kansas City, MO
(P 1114,1115,171) **816-756-1992**
Rasmussen, Bonnie/8828 Pendleton, St Louis, MO 314-962-1842
Ravenelli, Terry/2483 Waterman, Granite City, IL 618-931-7459
Rawley, Don/7520 Blaisdell Ave S, Richfield, MN 612-866-1023
Rawson, Jon/1225 S Hamilton, Lockport, IL (P 846)....**815-838-4462**
Rea, Tracy/3301-A S Jefferson Ave, St Louis, MO
(P 487) **314-773-2600**
Redner, Ann/2100 W Big Beaver Rd, Troy, MI
(P 1140) **313-643-6000**
Reed, Mike/1314 Summit Ave, Minneapolis, MN 612-374-3164
Renaud, Phill/2830 W Leland, Chicago, IL 312-583-2681
Reynolds, Bill/433 Thomas Ave South, Minneapolis, MN 612-374-3169
Riedy, Mark/68 E Franklin St, Dayton, OH
(P 270,271) **513-433-8383**
Roberts, A Hardy/6512 Charlotte, Kansas City, MO 816-444-8210
Roberts, Michael/3406 Valley Ridge Rd #305, Middleton, WI 608-241-1557
Rockwell, Steven P/1613 Leytonstone Dr, Wheaton, IL 708-690-6979
Rogers, Buc/405 N Wabash #3203, Chicago, IL
(P 552) **312-329-1370**
Rosco, Delro/405 N Wabash #3203, Chicago, IL
(P 553) **312-329-1370**
Ross, Bill/11440 Oak Drive, Shelbyville, MI 616-672-5756
Rossi, Pam/908 Main St #3, Evanston, IL 708-475-2533
Roth, Hy/1300 Ashland St, Evanston, IL 708-491-1937
Rownd, Jim/5230 13th Ave S, Minneapolis, MN 612-822-0650
Ruddell, Gary/405 N Wabash #2709, Chicago, IL 312-222-0337
Rybka, Stephen/3119 W 83rd St, Chicago, IL 312-737-1981

S

Sanford, John/5038 W Berteau, Chicago, IL 312-685-0656
Sapulich, Joe/8454 W 161st Pl, Tinley Park, IL 708-532-8766
Sayles, John/308 Eighth St, Des Moines, IA
(P 232,233) **515-243-2922**
Schmelzer, J P/1002 S Wesley Ave, Oak Park, IL 708-386-4005
Schriner, John/1347 Glacier Lane N, Maple, MN 612-559-5529
Schuler, Mark/5410 W 68th St, Prairie Village, KS 913-384-0646
Schultz, Diana/PO Box 1170, Westmont, IL 708-515-8467

Schweitzer, David/1140 Oak Dr, Shelbyville
MI (P 703) **616-672-5762**
Scibilia, Dom/8277 Broadview Rd, Broadview, OH 216-526-2036
Scott, Jerry/152 W Wisconsin Ave, Milwaukee, WI 414-271-5210
Selfridge, MC/817 Desplaines St, Plainfield, IL 815-436-7197
Sellars, Joseph/2423 W 22nd St, Minneapolis, MN 612-377-8766
Seltzer, Meyer Design & Illust/744 W Buckingham Pl, Chicago, IL 312-348-2885
Sereta, Bruce/3010 Parklane Dr, Cleveland, OH 216-241-5355
Shaw, Ned/2770 N Smith Pike, Bloomington, IN
(P 1130) **812-333-2181**
Shay, RJ/3301 S Jefferson Ave, St Louis, MO
(P 1131) **314-773-9989**
Sheban, Chris/1807 W Sunnyside #1G, Chicago,
IL (P 1132) **312-271-2720**
Sheldon, David/20 Lynnray Circle, Dayton, OH 513-433-8383
Shuta, Joanne/700 3rd St S #301, Minneapolis, MN 612-343-0432
Sienkowski, Laurie/3660 Newcastle SE, Grand Rapids, MI 616-247-0127
Signorino, Slug/3587 No Cross Trail, LaPort, IN 219-879-5221
Silvers, Bill/1496 Westford Ctr #212, Westlake, OH 516-422-1915
Simon, William/9431 Bonhomme Woods, St Louis, MO 314-993-3522
Sirrell, Terry/768 Red Oak Dr, Bartlett, IL (P 893) **708-213-9003**
Sisson-Schlesser, Kathryn/707 W Wrightwood Ave, Chicago, IL 312-472-3877
Skeen, Keith D/3228 Prairie Dr, Deerfield, WI 608-423-3020
Skidmore Sahratian Inc/2100 W Big Beaver Rd,
Troy, MI (P 1136-1141) **313-643-6000**
Slack, Chuck/9 Cambridge Ln, Lincolnshire, IL
(P 37) **708-948-9226**
Slonim, David/232 South Street, Chesterfield, IN
(P 1143) **317-378-6511**
Smallish, Craig/777 N Michigan Ave #706,
Chicago, IL (P 654) **312-337-7770**
Smallwood, Steve/2496 Bridgeport Lane SE, Grand Rapids, MI 616-698-9312
Snodgrass, Steve/1919 N Sheffield, Chicago, IL 312-868-0900
Solovic, Linda/3509 Humphrey, St Louis, MO 314-773-7897
Songero, Jay/17858 Rose St, Lansing, IL 708-849-5676
Soukup, James/Route 1, Seward, NE 402-643-2339
Speer, Terry/181 Forest St, Oberlin, OH 216-774-8319
Spiece, Jim/1811 Wood Haven #9, Ft Wayne, IN 219-747-3916
Staake, Bob/1009 S Berry Rd, St Louis, MO 314-961-2303
Stasiak, Krystyna/5421 N E River Rd #507, Chicago, IL 312-380-4038
Stearney, Mark/405 N Wabash #2809, Chicago, IL 312-644-6669
Steger, John J/4124 Humphrey, St Louis, MO 314-664-2348
Storyboard Studio/1348 W Thorndale, Chicago, IL 312-266-1417
Strandell Design Inc/218 E Ontario, Chicago, IL 312-661-1555
Strawn, Leo/52 W Wheeling St, Lancaster, OH 614-653-1487
Streff, Michael/2766 Wasson Rd, Cincinnati, OH 513-731-0360
Stroster, Maria/2057 N Sheffield, Chicago, IL (P 428) ...**312-525-2081**
Styrkowicz, Tom/3801 Olentangy Blvd, Columbus, OH 614-261-6952
Sumichrast, Józef/465 S Beverly Rd, Lake Forest,
IL (P 794,795) **708-295-0255**
Svolos, Maria/1936 W Estes, Chicago, IL 312-338-4675
Swafford, Chris/RR7 Box 336-5, Joplin, MO 417-781-5881
Swansen, Becky/815 N Marion, Oak Park, IL 312-383-0141
Swanson, James/815 North Marion, Oak Park, IL
(P 1156) **708-383-0141**
Syska, Richard/1905 W Foster, Chicago, IL 312-728-2738

T

Tate, Clark/301 Woodford St, Gridley, IL 800-828-3008
Tate, Don/557 N Park Blvd, Glen Ellyn, IL 708-469-0085
Taylor, David/1449 N Pennsylvania St, Indianapolis, IN 317-634-2728
Taylor, Joseph/2117 Ewing Ave, Evanston, IL
(P 1159) **708-328-2454**
Thiewes, Sam/111 N Andover Ln, Geneva, IL 708-232-0980
Thomas, Bob/68 E Franklin St, Dayton, OH 513-433-8383
Thomas, Pat/711 Carpenter, Oak Park, IL 708-383-8505
Thomas, Paul/4999 Orion Rd, Rochester, MI 313-656-2828
Thompson, John/1225 W 4th St, Waterloo, IA (P 360)..**319-234-7055**
Thompson, Lowell/10 E Ontario #1104, Chicago, IL 312-664-1362
Thomssen, Kate/2216 E 32nd St, Minneapolis, MN 612-721-8832
Thornton, Shelley/1600 S 22nd St, Lincoln, NE 212-683-1362
Thrun, Rick/11440 Oak Dr, Shelbyville, MI (P 702)........**616-672-5756**
Tipton, Beth/6164 Westminster Pl, St Louis, MO 314-727-5657
Tipton, Bill/1762 Sparrow Pt Ln, Fenton, MO 314-343-9961
Treadway, Todd/1225 W 4th St, Waterloo, IA (P 355)......**319-234-7055**
Trillion Inc/Anderson/5989 Tahor Dr SE, Grand Rapids, MI 616-940-9944
Truxaw, Dick/7709 W 97th St, Overland Park, KS 319-383-1555

Tull, Jeff/3301-A S Jefferson Ave, St Louis, MO (P 483) **314-773-2600**
Turgeon, James/405 N Wabash #1413, Chicago, IL 312-644-1444

UV

Utley, Tom/490 Rockside Rd, Cleveland, OH 216-661-4222
Utterback, Bill/6105 Kingston Ave, Lisle, IL 708-852-9764
Vaccarello, Paul/1133 N Dearborn, Chicago, IL 312-664-2233
Van Hamersfeld, Jon/916 Olive #300, St Louis, MO 314-231-6800
Van Kanegan, Jeff/Box 60-B RR1, Camp Point, IL 214-455-4171
Vanderbeek, Don/68 E Franklin St, Dayton, OH (P 281,283) **513-433-8383**
Vann, Bill/1706 S 8th St, St Louis, MO (P 802,803) **314-231-2322**
Vanselow, Holly/2701 N Southport, Chicago, IL 312-975-5880
VanZanten, Hugh/116 W Illinois St #5W, Chicago, IL 312-644-2890
Von Haeger, Arden/233 E Wacker Dr., Chicago, IL (P 818) **312-565-2701**
Von Haeger, Arden/606 W Washington Ave, Kirkwood, MO 314-965-5273
Voo, Rhonda/4 E Ohio #11, Chicago, IL (P 564,531) **312-944-1130**
Vuksanovich, Fran/3224 N Nordica, Chicago, IL 312-283-2138

W

Wald, Carol/217 Farnsworth Ave, Detroit, MI 313-832-5805
Walker, John/4423 Wilson Ave, Downer's Grove, IL 708-963-8359
Walker, Ken/19 W Linwood, Kansas City, MO 816-561-9405
Walter, Nancy Lee/PO Box 611, Elmhurst, IL 708-833-3898
Walters, Ching/13451 Conway Rd, St Louis, MO 314-275-2248
Watford, Wayne/3286 Ivanhoe, St Louis, MO (P 405) **314-781-7377**
Watkinson, Brent/12904 Piccadilly Cir, Lenexa, KS (P 33) **913-888-2047**
Wawiorka, Matt/1510 E Marion St, Shorewood, WI 414-765-7531
Weber, Mark/c/o Dufour/633 St Clair, Sheboygan, WI 414-457-9191
Wells, Peter/207 E Buffalo #543, Milwaukee, WI 414-272-5525
Werrmayer, Arthur/15 N Gore, St Louis, MO 314-963-0677
Wesley, Carl/2401 Clinton Ave S #304, Minneapolis, MN 612-871-4983
Westphal, Ken/7616 Fairway, Prairie Village, KS 913-381-8399
Whaley, Kevin/2116 E 32nd St, Minneapolis, MN 612-721-8832
Whitney, Bill/116 W Illinois 5th Fl, Chicago, IL 312-527-2455
Whitney, Jack/6239 Elizabeth Ave, St Louis, MO (P 716) **314-781-8851**
Whitney, Mike/7833 Kenridge Lane, St Louis, MO 314-968-1255
Wickart, Mark/6293 Surrey Ridge Rd, Lisle, IL (P 894) **708-369-0164**
Wickart, Terry/3881 64th St, Holland, MI 616-335-3511
Wild Onion Studio/431 S Dearborn #403, Chicago, IL (P 1180) **312-663-5595**
Willey, Chris/3202 Windsor #2E, Kansas City, MO 816-483-1475
Williams, Gary/7045 California Ave, Hammond, IN 219-844-8002
Williams, Gordon/1030 Glenmoor Ln, Glendale, MO 314-821-2032
Williams, Jim/225 N Michigan Ave #310, Chicago, IL 312-565-2580
Willson Graphics/100 E Ohio #314, Chicago, IL 312-642-5328
Wilson, Donald/405 N Wabash #3203, Chicago, IL 312-329-1370
Wimmer, Chuck/7760 Oakhurst Circle, Cleveland, OH (P 1181) **216-526-2820**
Winger, Jody/1039 13th Ave SE, Minneapolis, MN 612-378-0444
Winstein, Merryl/200 Oak St, St Louis, MO 314-968-2596
Wojkovich, Ron/116 W Illinois St 6th fl E, Chicago, IL 312-467-0330
Wolf, Leslie/1812 Clayborne, Chicago, IL 312-935-1707
Woolery, Lee/2231 S Patterson Blvd, Dayton, OH 513-433-7912
Worcester, Mary/5230 13th Ave S, Minneapolis, MN 612-822-0650
Worman, Brian/4507 Glenway Ave, Cincinnati, OH 513-661-7881
Wright, Ted/3286 Ivanhoe, St Louis, MO (P 404,408) ...**314-781-7377**
Wrobel, Cindy/415 Alta Dena, St Louis, MO (P 385) **314-721-4467**

YZ

Yemm, Dale/2419 S 11th St, St Louis, MO 314-481-2964
York, Jeffrey L/111 E Chestnut #18J, Chicago, IL (P 1187) **312-664-8849**
Young & Laramore/310 E Vermont, Indianapolis, IN 317-264-8000
Youssi, John/17 N 943 Powers Rd, Gilberts, IL 708-428-7398
Zadnik, Pat/9215 Woods Way Dr, Kirtland, OH 216-256-6273
Zale, David/6703 Marshall Ave, Hammond, IN 219-838-0622
Zaresky, Don/41 Leonard Ave, Northfield Center, OH 216-467-5917
Zavell, Bonnie/1007 Gulf Rd, Elyria, OH 216-365-3477
Zielinski, John/c/o Ramin/6239 Elizabeth Ave, St Louis, MO 314-781-8851

Zimnicki Design/774 Parkview Ct, Roselle, IL 708-893-2666
Zumpfe, Rosemary/825 M St, Lincoln, NE 402-476-6480

SOUTHWEST

AB

Abramson, Elaine/PO Box 330008, Ft Worth, TX 817-292-1855
Allen, Harrison/5811 Braes Heather, Houston, TX 713-729-3938
Andrew, Bill/1709 Dryden #709, Houston, TX 713-791-4924
Andrews, Chris/1515 N Beverly Ave, Tucson, AZ 602-325-5126
Bailey, Craig/1508 Bayou Oak, Friendswood, TX 713-996-6984
Baker, David R/7254 Laurie Dr, Ft Worth, TX 817-429-4777
Bates, Greg/2811 McKinney #342, Dallas, TX 214-855-0055
Bleck, Cathie/1019 N Clinton, Dallas, TX (P 60,61) **214-942-4639**
Boatwright, Phil/7150 E Grand St #715, Dallas, TX 214-324-3256
Bowman, Douglas/3030 NW Expressway #400, Oklahoma City, OK (P 928) **405-942-4868**
Brazeal, Lee Lee/3525 Mockingbird Lane, Dallas, (P 568) **214-521-5156**
Brisker, Robin/4100 Commerce, Dallas, TX 214-824-8087
Brown, Charlie/1669 S Voss #392, Houston, TX 713-782-3447
Brown, Sue Ellen/3527 Oak Lawn Ave #269, Dallas, TX 214-827-6140
Burkey, J W/1526 Edison St, Dallas, TX (P 847) **214-559-0802**
Burns, Kevin/400 W Sam Houston Pkwy S #1137, Houston, TX 713-978-3343

C

Chambers, Lindy/RR 1 Box 7, Hockley, TX 713-467-6819
Chappell, Ellis/3525 Mockingbird Lane, Dallas, TX 214-521-5156
Cherry, Jim/2310 N 10th St, Phoenix, AZ 602-253-6589
Chinchar, Alan/1718 Capstan, Houston, TX 713-480-3227
Cleveland, Thomas/15622 Canterbury Forrest, Tomball, TX 713-370-8450
Collins, Rick/110 Clearview Dr #403, Friendswood, TX 713-996-5200
Connally, Connie/1107 Hilton, Richardson, TX 214-340-7818
Cooper, Karla Tuma/3333 Elm St #105, Dallas, TX 214-871-1956
Cornelius, Ray-Mel/2811 McKinney Ave, Dallas, TX (P 616) **214-855-0055**
Craig, Kacy/7201 Woodhollow #424, Austin, TX 512-345-3784
Crampton, Michael/5429 Miller Ave, Dallas, TX 214-573-5626
Criswell, Ron/2929 Wildflower, Dallas, TX 214-620-9109
Cruz, Jose/4810 Cedar Springs #2210, Dallas, TX (P 122,123) **214-520-7004**
Cumming, Moira/9754 Parkford Dr, Dallas, TX 214-343-8655
Curry, Tom/302 Lakehills Dr, Austin, TX 512-263-3407

DEF

Dean, Michael/2001 Sul Ross, Houston, TX 713-527-0295
Depew, Bob/2755 Rollingdale, Dallas, TX 214-241-9206
Dolphens, Tom/3525 Mockingbird Lane, Dallas, TX 214-521-5156
Draper, Chad/413 N Tyler, Dallas, TX 214-526-4668
Drayton, Richard/PO Box 20053, Village of Oak Creek, AZ 602-284-1566
Durbin, Mike/4034 Woodcraft, Houston, TX 713-667-8129
Edwards, John/2356 E Broadway, Tucson, AZ (P 989) **602-623-4325**
Engel, Norman/4316 Durango, Odessa, TX 915-368-7713
English, M John/3525 Mockingbird Lane, Dallas, TX (P 569) **214-521-5156**
Eubank, Mary Grace/6222 Northwood, Dallas, TX 214-692-7579
Evans, Eleanor/965 Slocum, Dallas, TX 214-760-8232
Forbes, Bart/2706 Fairmount, Dallas, TX (P 74,75) **214-748-8436**
Ford, Cindy/2508 E 21 St, Tulsa, OK 918-743-3673
Forsbach, Robert/2811 McKinney Ave #206, Dallas, TX (P 617) **214-855-0055**
Franklin, Jeff/2729 Carter Ave, Fort Worth, TX 817-535-6360

GH

Gaber, Brad/4946 Glen Meadow, Houston, TX 713-723-0030
Gamble, Kent/7010 Vicksburg, Lubbock, TX 806-793-1389
Garns, G Allen/4 E Second Ave, Mesa, AZ (P 432,433) **602-835-5769**
Giangregorio, Laurie/6847 La Pasada, Hereford, AZ 602-378-3183
Gillespie, Mike/519 Gene Dr, Seagoville, TX 214-287-8151
Gilliam, Charles/3903 San Ramon, Arlington, TX 817-861-1988

Girden, J M/2125 Cerrada Nopal E, Tucson, AZ..............602-628-2740
Gormaday, Thomas/1221 W Ben White Blvd #208A,
Austin, TX (P 1013)..**512-326-8383**
Graham, Jack/217 E McKinley #4, Phoenix, AZ.............602-257-0097
Graves, Keith/905 W 29th St, Austin, TX.....................512-478-3338
Griego, Tony/10609 W Seldon Lane, Peoria, AZ.............602-242-5492
Grimes, Don/3514 Oak Grove, Dallas, TX (P 885).........**214-526-0040**
Hall, Bill/1235-B Colorado Ln, Arlington, TX
(P 780,781)...**817-467-1013**
Harr, Shane/637 Hawthorne, Houston, TX....................713-523-8186
Harris, Jennifer/3333 Elm St #105, Dallas, TX...............217-871-1956
Hartman, Daniel/409 W Hwy 3040 #602, Louisville, TX......214-315-1740
Haverfield, Mary/3333 Elm St #105, Dallas, TX..............214-871-1956
Heck, Cathy...915-686-9343
High, Richard/4500 Montrose #D, Houston, TX
(P 227)...**713-521-2772**
Hill, Henry/2356 East Broadway, Tucson, AZ
(P 1036)...**602-623-4325**
Huey, Kenneth/5320 Richard Ave, Dallas, TX................214-821-3042
Huffaker, Sandy/2501 W Zia Rd, Santa Fe, NM.............505-438-9586

JKL

Jenkins, Bill/3000 McKinney, Dallas, TX......................214-744-4421
Jones, Marilyn/7 Dunlin Meadow Court, The Woodlands, TX........713-292-7529
Jones, Rusty/2312 Heatherworks Way, Carrollton, TX......214-306-3835
Kaplan, Kari/1507 W Lynn St, Austin, TX......................512-476-6876
Karas, G Brian/4126 North 34th St, Phoenix, AZ............602-956-5666
Kasnot, Keith/9228 N 29th St, Phoenix, AZ (P 402).....**602-482-6501**
Keene, Donald/2811 McKinney Ave #206, Dallas,
TX (P 619)...**214-855-0055**
Kenny, Kathleen/815 N First Ave #1, Phoenix, AZ..........602-252-2332
Kenyon, Liz/4225 N 36th St #6, Phoenix, AZ.................602-954-8824
Kinkopf, Kathleen/Dallas, TX......................................214-324-4801
Kirkman, Rick/PO Box 11816, Phoenix, AZ....................602-257-1634
Knox, David/2424 N Rose, Mesa, AZ............................602-827-9339
Krejca, Gary/1203 S Ash Ave, Tempe, AZ (P 476)........**602-829-0946**
Kriebel, Nancy/354 Los Lentes Rd NE, Los Lunas, NM......505-865-6428
Kubricht, Mary Charles/637 Hawthorne, Houston, TX......713-522-1862
Lapsley, Bob/3707 Nottingham, Houston, TX.................713-667-4393
Lewis, Maurice/3704 Harper St, Houston, TX.................713-664-1807
Lindlof, Ed/603 Carolyn Ave, Austin, TX......................512-472-0195
Lisieski, Peter/2921 N Pecan St, Nacogdoches, TX..........409-564-4244

MNOP

MacFarland, Jean/126 Martinez St, Santa Fe, NM...........505-983-2226
MacPherson, Kevin/4160 N Craftsman Ct #202, Scottsdale, AZ........602-423-1500
Maloney, Dave/637 Hawthorne, Houston, TX.................713-522-1862
Martini, John/8742 Welles Dale, San Antonio, TX............512-699-9318
McClain, Lynn/8730 Vinewood, Dallas, TX....................214-321-9374
McCullough, Greg/5203 Villa Del Mar Ave #104, Arlington, TX........817-472-5173
McCullough, Lendy/111 E Santa Fe Ave #2, Santa Fe, NM........505-982-1964
McDonald, Mercedes/2811 McKinney Ave #206,
Dallas, TX (P 620)...**214-855-0055**
McElhaney, Gary/5205 Airport Blvd #201, Austin, TX......512-451-3986
McGar, Michael/3330 Irwindell Blvd, Dallas, TX.............214-339-0672
Miller, Lyle/3100 Carlisle St #112, Dallas, TX................214-871-1195
Mosberg, Hilary/2811 McKinney Ave #206, Dallas,
TX (P 618)...**214-855-0055**
Mozley, Peggy/17914 Hillcrest, Dallas, TX....................214-248-2704
Nelson, John/936 W Catalina Dr, Phoenix, AZ...............602-279-1131
Nelson, R Kenton/2811 McKinney Ave #206, Dallas,
TX (P 621,707)...**214-855-0055**
Osiecki, Lori L/123 W 2nd St, Mesa, AZ (P 1098)........**602-962-5233**
Parker, Curtis/4160 N Craftsman Ct #202, Scottsdale, AZ........602-423-1500
Pendleton, Nancy/4160 N Craftsman Ct #202, Scottsdale, AZ........602-423-1500
Phillips, Barry/128 N Clark St, Burleson, TX.................817-295-2007
Pietzsch, Steve/3057 Larry Drive, Dallas, TX.................214-279-8851
Poli, Kristina/4211 Pebblegate Ct, Houston, TX.............713-353-6910
Porea, Sean/22715 Imperial Valley #1702, Houston, TX........713-821-5159
Porfirio, Guy/2310 E 6th St, Tuscon, AZ (P 395)...........**602-323-0518**
Porter, Walter/4010 W El Camino del Cerro,
Tucson, AZ (P 1109)...**602-743-9821**
Powell, Terry/8502-D Lyndon Ln, Austin, TX.................512-335-0253
Pullen, John/3030 NW Expressway #400, Oklahoma City, OK........405-942-4868
Punchatz, Don Ivan/2605 Westgate Dr, Arlington, TX........817-469-8151

RS

Raff, Lyne/9501 Rolling Oaks Trl, Austin, TX (P 1116)....**512-219-1208**
Reed, Lynn Rowe/3333 Elm St #105, Dallas, TX............214-871-1956
Reed, William/2438 W 10th, Dallas, TX........................214-333-2884
Reimisch, Robert/545 S 7th Ave, Yuma, AZ..................602-783-7732
Ricks, Thom/6511 Adair Dr, San Antonio, TX.................512-680-6540
Roberts, Ray(P 796,797)...**602-991-8568**
Robins, Mike/637 Hawthorne, Houston, TX...................713-522-1862
Rodriguez, Laura/5417 E 8th St, Tucson, AZ..................602-625-7700
Rogers, Randy/1214 Post Oak St, Houston, TX..............713-688-0637
Rose, Lee/4250 TC Jester Blvd, Houston, TX.................713-686-4799
Ross, Eileen/6736 N 11th St, Phoenix, AZ....................602-234-1598
Salem, Kay/13418 Splintered Oak, Houston, TX.............713-469-0996
Sanchez, Pat/8603 Baumgarten, Dallas, TX..................214-328-2942
Senkarik, Mickey/PO Box 104, Helotes, TX...................512-695-9327
Shaw, Robin/3730 Kirby #1150, Houston, TX................713-520-5715
Shukan, Luis/123 Hummingbird, Livingston, TX.............409-327-2666
Singleton, Bill/809 W Wedwick St, Tucson, AZ...............602-294-1667
Sketch Pad/2605 Westgate Dr, Arlington, TX.................817-469-8151
Skistmas, Jim/2730 N Stemmons Frwy #400, Dallas, TX........214-630-2574
Slattery, Jack/5911 Inwood #4, Houston, TX.................713-785-6764
Smith, James Noel/1011 North Clinton, Dallas, TX..........214-946-4255
Smithson, David/3760 E Presidio, Tucson, AZ................602-323-8651
Stribling-Sutherland, Kelly/933 East Harpole, Argyle, TX........214-855-0055
Sturdivant, Ray/4114 McMillan, Dallas, TX (P 1152)....**214-821-8111**

TVWY

Thelen, Mary/5907 Llano, Dallas, TX (P 235).................**214-827-8073**
Tomas, Luis/419 E Continental Dr, Tempe, AZ...............602-945-6515
Tracy, Libba/329 W Vernon Ave, Phoenix, AZ................602-254-8232
Turk, Stephen/3525 Mockingbird Lane, Dallas, TX..........214-521-5156
VAS Communications/4800 N 22nd St, Phoenix, AZ........602-955-1000
Verzaal, Dale/2445 E Pebble Beach, Tempe, AZ (P 739)....**602-839-5536**
Waltman, Lynne/PO Box 470889, Ft Worth, TX..............817-738-1545
Walton, Paul R/8602 Santa Clara, Dallas, TX.................214-327-7889
Warner, Michele/1011 North Clinton, Dallas, TX.............214-946-4255
Washington, Bill/5114 Blanco Rd #1, San Antonio, TX........512-340-0021
Weakley, Mark/105 N Alamo #618, San Antonio,
TX (P 435)...**512-222-9543**
Williams, Michall Janes/546 S Country Club, Mesa, AZ........602-461-8220
Wilson, Raymond/2120 Arthur Dr, Ft Worth, TX.............817-293-0093
Yost, Mo/2008 Laws St #1A, Dallas, TX.......................214-720-4024

ROCKY MTN

ABCD

Alavezos, Gus/2215 Ptarmigan, Colorado Springs,
CO (P 174)...**719-528-6821**
Alexander, Hugh/215 15th St #1300, Denver, CO...........303-825-4440
Arnold, Jean/1220 E 400 S, Salt Lake City, UT...............801-582-4148
Boddy, Joe/5375 Skyway Dr, Missoula, MT...................406-251-3587
Botero, Kirk/396 Fifth St, Idaho Falls, ID......................208-524-3959
Brown, Craig McFarland/410 E Washington St, Colorado Springs, CO........719-471-2457
Colvin, Rob/1351 N 1670 W, Farmington, UT (P 669)....**801-451-6858**
Dolack, Monte/132 W Front St, Missoula, MT................406-549-3248
Donahue, Michael/PO Box 26090, Colorado Springs, CO........719-591-1958
Donovan, David/437 Engel Ave, Henderson, NV.............702-564-3598

FGH

Farley, Malcolm/6823 Swadley Ct, Arvada, CO..............303-420-9135
French, Bob/8304 W 71st Ave, Arvada, CO...................303-966-4768
Hardiman, Miles/30 Village Dr, Littleton, CO..................303-798-9143
Harris, Ralph/PO Box 1091, Sun Valley, ID...................208-726-8077
Heiner, Joe & Kathy/850 N Grove Dr, Alpine, UT
(P 203)...**801-756-6444**
Hirokowa, Masami/3144 W 26th Ave, Denver, CO..........303-458-1381
Ho, Quang/1553 Platte St #306, Denver, CO.................303-477-4574
Hoffman, Kate/822 W Oak Street, Ft Collins, CO
(P 1037)...**303-493-1492**
Hull, Richard/776 W 3500 South, Bountiful, UT..............801-298-1632

KLMN

Kaemmer, Gary/1724 Ogden, Denver, CO............................303-832-1579
Labadie, Ed/2309 Mt View #130, Boise, ID 208-377-2447
Lane, Tammy/PO Box 212, Aspen, CO............................303-925-9213
Millard, Dennis/3345 S 300 W #A, Salt Lake City, UT....................801-485-9782
Miller Group Ltd/250 Bell St #230, Reno, NV............................702-333-9009
Morrison, Kathy/775 E Panama Dr, Littleton, CO............................303-798-0424
Neeper Illustration & Concept Inc/737 Clarkson, Denver, CO............303-860-1857
Nelsen, Randy/15243 W Bayaud Ct, Golden, CO......................303-278-9166
Nelson, Will/10535 Saranac Dr, Boise, ID............................208-345-3131
Newsom, Tom/7713 Redrock Cr, Larkspur, CO............................303-681-2472
Norby, Carol H/192 South 600 East, Alpine, UT 801-756-1096

PRST

Peterson, Marty/918 55th St, Boulder, CO............................303-499-0900
Price, Jeannette/1164 E 820 N, Provo, UT............................801-377-3958
Ragland, Greg/2106 Lucky John Dr, Park City, UT............................801-645-9232
Regester, Sheryl/PO Box 478, Silver Plume, CO............................303-569-3374
Roush, Ragan/745 Poplar Ave, Boulder, CO............................303-440-6582
Sauter, Ron/16738 E Crestline Ln, Denver, CO............................303-680-5636
Stinson, Don/PO Box 7784, Breckenridge, CO............................303-453-0663
Strawn, Susan/1216 W Olive St, Ft Collins, CO............................303-493-0679
Sullivan, John/912 S Telluride St, Aurora, CO............................303-671-9257
Thomas, Charles/4617 W Lost Horizon Dr, Tucson, AZ............................602-743-3613
Twede, Brian L/435 S 300 E, Salt Lake City, UT 801-534-1459

UVWZ

Uhl, David/1501 Boulder, Denver, CO (P 1164,1165)....303-455-3535
Valero, Wayne/11244 Corona Dr, North Glen, CO............................303-452-3468
Van Schelt, Perry L/4495 Balsam Ave, Salt Lake City, UT....................801-266-7097
Veal, David/1534 S Columbine St, Denver, CO............................303-777-2458
Weller, Don/2240 Monarch Dr, Park City, UT (P 455)....801-649-9859
Whitesides, Kim/PO Box 2189, Park City, UT............................801-649-0490
Zilberts, Ed/7249 S Perry Park Blvd, Larkspur, CO............................303-220-5040

WEST COAST

A

**Abe, George/2125 Western Ave #400, Seattle, WA
(P 444)..206-443-0326**
Ace, Katherine/50 Claremont Ave, Orinda, CA............................415-254-0705
Adaberry, Craig/1812 Wallam St, Los Angeles, CA............................213-227-9224
Addad, Roland/2435 Polk St #21, San Francisco, CA............................415-474-3763
Aguilar, Kevin/900 Oxford Dr, Redlands, CA............................714-793-1126
Aizawa, Kaz/95 Hurlbut #11, Pasadena, CA............................818-441-3306
Ajern, Larry/1212 22nd St, Sacramento, CA............................916-442-5654
Akers, Deborah/21 Lafayette Cir #201, Lafayette, CA............................415-283-7793
Alleman, Annie/1183 E Main St #E, El Cajon, CA............................619-495-2554
Allen, Mark/9605 Sepulveda #5, Los Angeles, CA............................818-894-9123
Allen, Pat/4510 Alpine Rd, Portola Valley, CA............................415-851-3116
Allison, Gene/1232 Glen Lake Ave #314, Brea, CA............................213-690-8382
Alvin, John/15942 Londelius, Sepulveda, CA............................213-471-0232
Ambler, Barbara Hoopes/2769 Nipoma St, San Diego, CA............................619-222-7535
Amit, Emmanuel/4322 Sunset Ave, Montrose, CA(P 149)....213-249-1739
Anderson, Kevin/1267 Orkney Ln, Cardiff, CA............................619-753-8410
Anderson, Sara/3131 Western Ave #516, Seattle, WA............................206-285-1520
Anderson, Terry/5902 W 85th Pl, Los Angeles, CA............................213-645-8469
Angel, Scott/21051 Barbados Circle, Huntington Bch, CA............................714-557-5090
**Ansley, Frank/Pier 33 North, San Francisco,
CA (P 643)..415-956-4750**
Anthony, Mitchell/960 Maddux Dr, Palo Alto, CA............................415-494-3240
Apel, Eric/49269 Vista Hts Ln #202, Oakland, CA............................209-642-2801
Archey, Rebecca/80 Wellington/Box 307, Ross, CA............................415-456-7711
Arkle, Dave/259 W Orange Grove, Pomona, CA............................714-865-2967
Arruda, Richard/6010 Wilshire Blvd #505, Los Angeles, CA............................213-931-7449
Arshawsky, David/9401 Alcott St, Los Angeles, CA............................213-276-6058
Ash, Melissa/1329 Taylor St #4, San Francisco, CA............................415-563-0723
Atkins, Bill/PO Box 1091, Laguna Beach, CA............................714-499-3857
**August, Bob/183 N Martel Ave #240, Los Angeles,
CA (P 311)..213-934-3395**
Ayriss, Linda Holt/1700 E Beverly Dr, Pasadena, CA............................818-798-1535

B

Babasin, Pierre/1207 Bunkerhill Dr, Roseville, CA............................916-782-2956
**Backus, Michael/286 E Montecito, Sierra Madre, CA
(P 549)..818-449-3840**
**Baker, Don/2125 Western Ave #400, Seattle, WA
(P 445)..206-443-0326**
**Banthien, Barbara/127 Leland, Tiburon, CA
(P 204,205)..415-381-0842**
Banyai, Istvan/13220 Valleyheart Dr #305, Studio City, CA............818-906-7748
Barbaria, Steve/1990 Third St #400, Sacramento, CA............................916-442-3200
Barbee, Joel/209 Avenida San Pablo, San Clemente, CA............................714-498-0067
Barber, Karen/3444 21st St, San Francisco, CA............................415-647-1256
Barnet, Nancy/8928 Shady Vista Ct, Elk Grove, CA............................916-685-4147
Bartczak, Peter/PO Box 7709, Santa Cruz, CA............................408-426-4247
Batcheller, Keith/1438 Calle Cecilia, San Dimas, CA............................818-331-0439
Battles, Brian/6316 Dissinger Ave, San Diego, CA............................619-267-3182
**Beach, Lou/1114 S Citrus Ave, Los Angeles, CA
(P 712)..213-934-7335**
**Beck, David/183 N Martel Ave #240, Los Angeles,
CA (P 296,297)..213-934-3395**
Becker, Cary/3443 Wade St, Los Angeles, CA............................213-390-9595
Becker, Pamela/509 20th Ave, San Francisco, CA............................415-387-8372
Beckerman, Carol/3950 Long Beach Blvd, Long Beach, CA............213-595-5896
Beerworth, Roger/1723 S Crescent Hts Blvd, Los Angeles, CA............213-933-9692
Bell, Karen/1700 Decker Canyon Rd, Malibu, CA............................213-457-2476
**Bennett, Diane/240-1/2 Poinsetta Pl, Los Angeles,
CA (P 458)..213-280-0270**
Benny, Mike/3704 Norris Ave, Sacramento, CA............................916-447-8629
Bergendorff, Roger/17106 Sims St #A, Huntington Beach, CA............714-840-7665
Bettoli, Delana/737 Vernon Ave, Venice, CA............................213-396-0296
**Biers, Nanette/123 Willow Ave, Corte Madera,
CA (P 104,105)..415-668-6080**
Bilmes, Semyon/460 Rock St, Ashland, OR............................503-488-0924
Bingham, Sid/2550 Kemper Ave, La Crescenta, CA............................818-957-0163
Biomedical Illustrations/804 Columbia St, Seattle, WA............................206-682-8197
Birnbaum, Dianne/17301 Elsinore Circle, Huntington Beach, CA............714-847-7631
**Bishop, David/610 22nd St #311, San Francisco, CA
(P 840)..415-558-9532**
**Bjorkman, Steve/2402 Michelson, Irvine, CA
(P 760,761,80)..714-261-1411**
**Blackshear, Thomas/1428 Elm Dr, Novato, CA
(P 258,259)..415-897-9486**
Blair, Barry/27461 Calle Arroyo #207, San Juan Capistrno, CA............714-248-2527
Blank, Jerry/1048 Lincoln Ave, San Jose, CA............................408-289-9095
Blechman, Laurel/7853 Mammoth Ave, Panorama City, CA............................818-785-7904
Blonder, Ellen/91 Woodbine Dr, Mill Valley, CA............................415-388-9158
Boddy, William/609 N 10th St, Sacramento, CA............................916-443-5001
**Boehm, Roger C/Pier 33 North, San Francisco,
CA (P 645)..415-956-4750**
Boge, Garrett/6606 Soundview Dr, Gig Harbor, WA............................206-851-5158
Bohn, Richard/595 W Wilson St, Costa Mesa, CA............................714-548-6669
Bolourchian, Flora/12485 Rubens Ave, Los Angeles, CA............................213-827-8457
Booth/950 Klish Way, Del Mar, CA (P 558)............................619-259-5774
Booth, Margot/11604 104th Ave NE, Kirkland, WA............................206-820-2047
Borders, Jane/3632 Kalsman Dr #2, Los Angeles, CA............................213-836-7598
**Bowles, Doug/716 Sanchez St, San Francisco, CA
(P 721)..415-285-8267**
Bradley, Barbara/750 Wildcat Canyon Rd, Berkeley, CA............................415-673-4200
**Bradley, James/183 N Martel Ave #240,
Los Angeles, CA (P 308)..213-934-3395**
**Bramsen, Dave/644 North Hope Ave, Santa
Barbara, CA (P 929)..805-687-6864**
Braun, Marty/271 Otsego Ave, San Francisco, CA............................415-334-4106
**Brice, Jeff/2125 Western Ave #400, Seattle, WA
(P 446)..206-443-0326**
Bringham, Sherry/244 Ninth St, San Francisco, CA............................415-621-2992
Broad, David/100 Golden Hinde Blvd, San Rafael, CA............................415-479-5505
Brown, Bill & Assoc/1531 Pontius Ave #200, Los Angeles, CA............213-652-9380
Brown, Bill Illus/4621 Teller #108, Newport Beach, CA............................714-474-6002
**Brown, Michael David/PO Box 45969, Los Angeles,
CA (P 118,119)..213-379-7254**
Brown, Rick/1502 N Maple, Burbank, CA............................818-842-0726
Brown, Susan/2456 Riverplace, Los Angeles, CA............................213-662-5035
Brownd, Elizabeth/6955 Fernhill Dr, Malibu, CA............................213-457-4816
Browne, Rob/541 Winterberry Way, San Jose, CA............................408-255-8843
Bruce, Taylor/946-B St, Petaluma, CA (P 941)............................707-765-6744

Brugger, Bob/1132 Loma #4, Hermosa Beach, CA..................213-372-0135
Buechler, Barbara/13929 Marquessa Way Marina Del Ray, CA..........213-827-5106
Buerge, Bill/734 Basin Dr, Topanga, CA.................................213-455-3181
Bull, Michael/2350 Taylor, San Francisco, CA.........................415-776-7471
Burg, Randall/2803 Main St, Santa Monica, CA........................213-399-7267
Burgio, Trish/8205 Santa Monica Blvd, Los Angeles, CA.............213-657-1469
Burns, Rhonda/6010 Wilshire Blvd #505, Los Angeles, CA.............213-931-7449
Burnside, John E/4204 Los Feliz Blvd, Los Angeles, CA...............213-665-8913
Busacca, Mark/269 Corte Madera Ave, Mill Valley, CA................415-381-9048
Butler, Callie/2270 Del Mar Heights Rd #295,
Del Mar, CA (P 942)...**619-755-5539**

C

Cagle, Dary 805-967-4529
Caldwell, Kirk/66 Broadway, San Francisco, CA
(P 672,673)...**415-398-7553**
Calhoun, Dia/116 W Denny Way, Seattle, WA.......................206-932-9092
Calsbeek, Craig/1316 3rd St Promenade, Santa Monica, CA.............213-394-6037
Camarena, Miguel/445 W Lexington Dr, Glendale, CA 818-246-8081
Cantor, Jeremy/1441 12th St #B, Manhattan Beach, CA..............213-545-9826
Cappello, Fred/58 Brookmont St, Irvine, CA.........................714-559-5050
Capstone Studios/3408 W Burbank Blvd, Burbank, CA................818-985-8181
Carroll, Justin/1118 Chautauqua, Pacific Palisades,
CA (P 396)...**213-459-3104**
Case, Carter/3921 Palisades Pl W, Tacoma, WA....................206-566-9292
Casey, Sean/1705 Belmont Ave #300, Seattle, WA..................206-329-4273
Cash-Walsh, Tina/2803 Main St, Santa Monica, CA.................415-457-0698
Ceccarelli, Chris/3427 Folsom Blvd, Sacramento, CA...............916-455-0569
Chaffee, James/540 Colusa Way, Sacramento, CA
(P 871)...**916-348-6345**
Chan, Ron/32 Grattan St, San Francisco, CA (P 835)...**415-681-0646**
Chang, Warren/15120 Magnolia Blvd #211, Sherman Oaks, CA..........818-783-4573
Chase, Margo/2255 Bancroft Ave, Los Angeles, CA..................213-668-1055
Chewning, Randy/13051 Springarden Ln, Westminster, CA 213-433-7665
Chiodo, Joe/2556 Chicago St #40, San Diego, CA...................619-275-6383
Chorney, Steven/18686 Cumnock Pl, Northridge, CA................818-366-7779
Chouinard, Roger/1233 S La Cienega Blvd, Los Angeles, CA..........213-855-8855
Christman, Michael/104 S El Molino, Pasadena, CA.................818-793-1358
Chui, John/1962 San Pablo Ave #3, Berkeley, CA...................415-841-2238
Chun, Milt/816 Queen St, Honolulu, HI.............................808-537-1406
Chung, Helen/94 Ocean Park #2, Santa Monica, CA.................213-451-2078
Clark, Tim/8800 Venice Blvd, Los Angeles, CA.....................213-202-1044
Clarke, Greg/844 9th St #10, Santa Monica, CA
(P 959)...**213-395-7958**
Clemons, David/1425 East Orange Grove Blvd, Pasadena, CA 818-797-8998
Coe, Wayne/12623 C Sherman Way, N Hollywood, CA................818-764-7918
Cohen, Elaine/2125 Western Ave #400, Seattle, WA
(P 447)...**206-443-0326**
Cole, Dick/25 Hotaling Pl, San Francisco, CA......................415-986-8163
Commander, Bob/8800 Venice Blvd, Los Angeles, CA................213-202-6765
Conrad, Jon/6010 Wilshire Blvd #505, Los Angeles,
CA (P 482,798,799)...**213-931-7449**
Conrad, Jon/CA (P 798,799,482).................................**818-301-9662**
Consani, Chris/2601 Walnut Ave, Manhattan Beach, CA 213-546-6622
Cook, Anne/96 Rollingwood Dr, San Rafael, CA....................415-454-5799
Coons, Byron/Pier 33 North, San Francisco, CA....................415-956-4750
Cooper, Daniel E/17346 Chatsworth St #112, Granada Hills, CA..........818-368-3919
Cormier, Wil/911 E Elizabeth St, Pasadena, CA....................818-797-7999
Court, Rob/4621 Teller #108, Newport Beach, CA...................714-474-6002
Creative Source/6671 W Sunset Blvd #1519, Los Angeles, CA 213-462-5731
Criss, Keith/1005 Camelia St, Berkeley, CA 415-525-8703
Crowther, Katherine-Rose/332 Lennox #6, Oakland, CA.............415-465-7134
Cuneo, John/120 Parnassus #1D, San Francisco,
CA (P 591)...**415-664-3083**
Curtis, Cheryl/821 Madison Ave, Escondido, CA....................619-713-8443
Curtis, Todd/2032 14th St #7, Santa Monica, CA...................213-452-0738

D

Dalaney, Jack/3030 Pualei Circle #317, Honolulu, HI 808-924-7450
Darold, Dave/PO Box 5000, Davis, CA.............................916-758-1379
Darrow, David R/9655 Derald Rd, Santee, CA......................619-697-7408
Darrow, Whitney/950 Klish Way, Del Mar, CA......................203-227-7806
DaVault, Elaine/4621 Teller #108, Newport Beach, CA..............714-474-6002
Davidson, Kevin/505 S Grand St, Orange, CA......................714-633-9061
Davis, David M/737 SE Sandy Blvd, Portland, OR...................503-235-6878
Davis, Diane Kay/4621 Teller #108, Newport Beach, CA 714-474-6002

Davis, Jeff/13343 Victory Blvd #12, Van Nuys, CA..................818-764-5002
Day, Adrian/2022 Jones St, San Francisco, CA.....................415-928-0457
Day, Bruce/8141 Firth Green, Buena Park, CA......................714-994-0338
Dayal, Antar/1596 Wright St, Santa Rosa, CA
(P 800,801)...**707-544-8103**
Deal, Jim/3451 24th Ave West #120, Seattle, WA (P 986)...**206-285-2986**
Dean, Bruce/23211 Leonora Dr, Woodland Hills, CA................818-716-5632
Dean, Donald/2560 Bancroft Way #14, Berkley, CA................415-644-1139
DeAnda, Ruben/550 Oxford St #407, Chula Vista, CA..............619-427-7765
Dearstyne, John/22982 LaCadena Dr, Laguna Hills, CA.............714-768-5619
Deaver, Georgia/123 Townsend #410, San Francisco, CA............415-974-6173
Dedini, Eldon/950 Klish Way, Del Mar, CA.........................203-227-7806
DeLeon, Cam/1168 E Claremont, Pasadena, CA.....................818-797-8890
Dellorco, Chris/8575 Wonderland Ave, Los Angeles, CA 213-650-1370
Dennewill, Jim/5823 Autry Ave, Lakewood, CA.....................213-920-3895
Devaud, Jacques/1165 Bruin Tr/Box 260, Fawnskin,
CA (P 418)...**714-866-4563**
Dickey, Burrell/4975 Elmwood Dr, San Jose, CA....................408-866-0820
Dietz, Jim/2203 13th Ave E, Seattle, WA (P 640)...**206-325-2857**
Dietz, Mike/PO Box 3145, San Clemente, CA (P 988)...**714-496-3021**
Diffenderfer, Ed/32 Cabernet Ct, Lafayette, CA 415-254-8235
Dillon, Tom/1986 Stonecroft Ct, Westlake Village, CA..............805-495-5116
Dininno, Steve/Pier 33 North, San Francisco,
CA (P 644)...**415-956-4750**
Dismukes, John Taylor/2820 Westshire Dr, Hollywood, CA 213-467-2787
DiSpenza, John/PO Box 113, Roy, WA.............................206-894-3000
Doe, Bart/6304 Day St, Tujunga, CA 818-352-3673
Doney, Todd/183 N Martel Ave #240, Los Angeles,
CA (P 309)...**213-934-3395**
Doty, Eldon/3435 260th Ave NE, Redmond, WA....................206-868-9550
Dowlen, James/PO Box 475, Cotati, CA...........................707-579-1535
Downs, Richard/24294 Saradella Court, Murrieta, CA...............714-677-3452
Duell, Nancy/1042 Oakwood Ave, Venice, CA......................213-399-6903
Duffus, Bill/1745 Wagner, Pasadena, CA 818-792-7921
Dumaway, Suzanne Shimek/10333 Chrysanthemum Ln, LA, CA..........213-279-2006
Durfee, Tom/25 Hotaling Pl, San Francisco, CA.....................415-781-0527

E

Eastman, Jody/1116 Philadelphia St, Ontario, CA 714-983-2515
Eastside Illustration/737 SE Sandy Blvd, Portland, OR 503-235-6878
Eckart, Chuck/PO Box 1090, Point Reyes Sta, CA..................415-663-9016
Ecklund, Rae/14 Wilmot St, San Francisco, CA.....................415-923-0741
Eddington, Michael/10355 Eighth Ave NW, Seattle, WA.............206-781-7997
Edelson, Wendy/215 Second Ave S, Seattle, WA....................206-728-1300
Eden, Terry/510 Emerson, Palo Alto, CA...........................415-326-5263
Egan, Tim/12200 Emelita St, N Hollywood, CA......................818-995-4303
Ellescas, Richard/321 N Martel, Hollywood, CA.....................213-939-7396
Ellmore, Dennis/3245 Orange Ave, Long Beach, CA.................213-424-9379
Elstad, Ron/18253 Solano River Ct, Fountain Valley, CA.............714-964-7753
Elwood, Don/24205 E First, Liberty Lake, WA.......................509-255-6670
Emmart, Carter/471 Victory Ave, Mountain View, CA................415-961-3271
Endicott, James R/3509 N College, Newberg, OR...................503-538-5466
Ericksen, Marc/1045 Sansome St #306, San Francisco, CA 415-362-1214
Erickson, Kerne/Box 2175, Mission Viejo, CA.......................714-831-2818
Erramouspe, David/8800 Venice Blvd, Los Angeles, CA.............213-558-4914
Etow, Carole/18224 Herbold St, Northridge, CA.....................818-772-7501
Evans, Bill/101 Yesler #502, Seattle, WA...........................206-447-1600
Evans, Robert/1045 Sansome St #306, San Francisco, CA............415-397-5322
Evenson, Stan/445 Overland Ave, Culver City, CA...................213-204-1771
Everitt, Betsy/582 Santa Rosa, Berkeley, CA (P 992)...**510-527-3239**

F

Farrell, Rick/183 N Martel Ave #240, Los Angeles,
CA (P 298,299)...**213-934-3395**
Farris, Joe/950 Klish Way, Del Mar, CA............................203-227-7806
Fennel Graphics/1530 Ellis St #411, Concorde, CA 415-671-7814
Fijisaki, Tuko/1260 Sundance, San Diego, CA.......................619-424-2211
Fijosaki, Tuko/1260 Sundance, San Diego, CA.......................619-484-2211
Finger, John/1581 Boulevard Way, Walnut Creek, CA................415-945-0612
Fitting, Cynthia/2131 1/2 Pine St, San Francisco, CA...............415-567-3353
Florczak, Robert/3408 W Burbank Blvd, Burbank, CA................818-985-8181
Forrest, William/817 12th St #2, Santa Monica, CA.................213-458-9114
Fox, Mark/3006 Gough #102, San Francisco, CA....................415-673-4811
Fraze, Jon/14160 Red Hill Ave #89, Tustin, CA.....................714-731-8493
Frazee, Marla/183 N Martel Ave #240, Los Angeles,
CA (P 301)...**213-934-3395**

French, Lisa/1069 Gardenia Ave, Long Beach, CA 213-599-0361
Friel, Bryan/5648 Case Ave #1, N Hollywood, CA 818-769-3140
**Frueh, Mark/183 N Martel Ave #240, Los Angeles,
CA (P 306) 213-934-3395**
Fulp, Jim/50 Divisadero St #50, San Francisco, CA 415-621-5462
**Funkhouser, Kristen/716 Sanchez St, San Francisco,
CA (P 725) 415-285-8267**

G

**Gal, Susan Illustration/639 Third Ave, San Francisco,
CA (P 1002) 415-668-9262**
Galloway, Nixon/755 Marine Ave, Manhattan Beach, CA 213-545-7709
Garcia, Manuel/716 Sanchez St, San Francisco, CA 415-285-8267
Garner, Tracy/1830 S Robertson Blvd, Los Angeles, CA 213-204-1771
**Garvie, Ben/118 Wyndham Dr, Portola Valley, CA
(P 884) 415-851-9520**
Gay, Garry/109 Minna St #567, San Francisco, CA 415-626-6005
Gayles, James/2200 Powell St/Twr 2 #325, Emeryville, CA 415-653-3753
Gellos, Nancy/20 Armour St, Seattle, WA 206-285-5838
Germain, Frank/2870 Calle Heraldo, San Clemente, CA 714-498-7234
**Gerns, Laurie/6010 Wilshire Blvd #505,
Los Angeles, CA (P 478) 213-931-7449**
Giambarba, Paul/5851 Vine Hill Rd, Sebastapol, CA 707-829-8895
Giles, Charles F/300 Wai Nani Way #1618, Honolulu, HI 808-931-1766
**Girvin, Tim Design/1601 Second Ave 5th Fl,
Seattle, WA (P 98,99) 206-623-7808**
Gisko, Max/2629 Wakefield Dr, Belmont, CA 415-595-1893
**Glass, Randy/2706 Creston Dr, Los Angeles, CA
(P 151) 213-462-2706**
Gleeson, Tony/2525 Hyperion Ave #4, Los Angeles, CA 213-668-2704
Gleis, Linda/6671 Sunset Blvd #1519, Los Angeles, CA 213-461-6376
Glover, Gary/75 Brookview, Dana Point, CA 714-248-0232
Goddard, John/2774 Los Alisos Dr, Fallbrook, CA 619-728-5473
Goethals, Raphaelle/1674 Rotary Dr, Los Angeles, CA 213-666-3189
**Goldammer, Ken/183 N Martel Ave #240,
Los Angeles, CA (P 294,295) 213-934-3395**
Goldstein, Howard/7031 Aldea Ave, Van Nuys, CA 818-987-2837
**Gomez, Ignacio/812 Kenneth Rd, Glendale, CA
(P 607) 818-243-2838**
Gonzales, Danilo/1760 State St #21, S Pasadena, CA 818-441-2787
**Gordon, David/4120 Emerald St #3, Oakland,
CA (P 1012) 415-954-1240**
**Gordon, Emily/2022 Jones St, San Francisco, CA
(P 579) 415-928-0457**
Gottlieg, Dale/2821 Victor St, Belingham, WA 206-647-2598
Grant, Stan/432 Misson St #A, South Pasadena, CA 818-799-4697
Graphic Designers Inc/3325 Wilshire Blvd #610, Los Angeles, CA 213-381-3977
**Gray, Steve/307 Bayview Dr, Manhattan Beach, CA
(P 609) 213-372-7844**
Greenberg, Sheldon/218 Second Ave, San Francisco, CA 415-221-4970
Griffith, Linda/13972 Hilo Ln, Santa Ana, CA 714-832-8536
Grossman, Myron/12 S Fair Oaks Ave, Pasadena, CA 818-795-6992
Grove, David/382 Union St, San Francisco, CA 415-433-2100
Guidice, Rick/9 Park Ave, Los Gatos, CA 408-354-7787
Guitteau, Jud/2506 NE 49th St, Portland, OR (P 821,86) 503-282-0445
**Gunn, Robert/183 N Martell Ave #240, Los Angeles,
CA (P 304) 213-934-3395**
**Gunsaullus, Marty/716 Sanchez St, San Francisco,
CA (P 718) 415-285-8267**
Gurvin, Abe/31341 Holly Dr, Laguna Beach, CA (P 738) 714-499-2001

H

Haasis, Michael/941 N Croft Ave, Los Angeles, CA 213-654-5412
Hagio, Kunio/3408 W Burbank Blvd, Burbank, CA 818-985-8181
Hagner, Dirk/30723 Calla Chueca, San Juan Capistrano, CA 714-493-5596
Haig, Nancy A/2645 Sacramento #3A, San Francisco, CA 415-921-2415
Hale, Bruce/421 Bryant St, San Francisco, CA 415-882-9695
Hall, Patricia/5402 Ruffin Rd #103, San Diego, CA 619-268-0176
Hally, Greg/911 Victoria Dr, Arcadia, CA 818-574-0288
Hamagami, John/11409 Kingsland St, Los Angeles, CA 213-390-6911
Hamilton, Pamela/4900 Overland Ave #216, Culver City, CA 213-837-1784
Hammond, Cris/410 Johnson St, Sausalito, CA 415-332-7556
**Hampton, Gerry Inc/4792 Tiara Dr. #204,
Huntington Harbour, CA (P 1025) 714-840-8239**
Handelsman, Bud/950 Klish Way, Del Mar, CA 619-259-5774
Hanna, Gary/3827 La Crescenta, La Cresenta, CA 818-249-1380

Hannah, Halsted (Craig)/2525 8th St #14, Berkeley, CA 415-841-2273
Hardesty, Debra S/1017 Vallejo Way, Sacramento, CA 916-446-1824
Harris, Michael/Future Fonts/5841 Columbus Ave, Van Nuys, CA 818-908-1237
Hasselle, Bruce/8691 Heil Rd, Westminster, CA 714-848-2924
**Havlicek, Karel/183 N Martel Ave #240,
Los Angeles, CA (P 305) 213-934-3395**
Haydock, Robert/49 Shelley Dr, Mill Valley, CA 415-383-6986
Hays, Jim/3809 Sunnyside Blvd, Marysville, WA 206-334-7596
**Heavner, Obadinah/900 1st Ave S #404, Seattle,
WA (P 728) 206-467-1616**
Hegedus, James C/11850 Otsego, N Hollywood, CA 818-985-9966
Heimann, Jim/1548 18th St, Santa Monica, CA 213-828-1041
Heinecke, Stu/9665 Wilshire Blvd #400, Los Angeles, CA 213-837-3212
**Heinze, Mitchell/721 E Maxwell Ln, Lathrop, CA
(P 359) 209-858-5220**
**Henderson, Louis/1140 S Pasadena, Pasadena, CA
(P 532) 818-441-7703**
Hendricks, Steve/1050 Elsiemae Dr, Boulder Creek, CA 408-338-6639
**Hernandez, Oscar/5708 Case Ave #3, N Hollywood,
CA (P 604) 818-506-4541**
Herrero, Lowell/433 Bryant St, San Francisco, CA 415-543-6400
Hershey, John/2350 Taylor St, San Francisco, CA 415-928-6553
**Hewitson, Jennifer/859 Sandcastle Dr, Cardiff, CA
(P 1033) 619-944-6154**
Hienze, Mitchell/40751 Witherspoon Terrace, Fremont, CA 415-657-8124
Hilliard, Fred/5425 Crystal Springs Dr NE, Bainbridge Island, WA 206-842-6003
**Hilton-Putnam, Denise/716 Sanchez St,
San Francisco, CA (P 723) 415-285-8267**
Hinton, Hank/6118 W 6th St, Los Angeles, CA 213-938-9893
Hitch, Jeff/3001 Redhill Ave #6-210, Costa Mesa, CA 714-432-1802
Hobb, David/8818 Lamesa Blvd, Lamesa, CA 619-469-8106
Hodges, Ken/12401 Bellwood Rd, Los Alamitos, CA 213-431-4343
Hoff, Terry/1525 Grand Ave, Pacifica, CA 415-359-4081
Hogan, Jamie (Ms)/2858 Bush St, San Francisco, CA 415-929-0795
Hohman, Suzie/PO Box 594, Davis, CA 916-756-3016
Holder, Jimmy/920-K N 6th St, Burbank, CA 818-563-2162
**Holmes, Matthew/8412 Gaylord Way, Carmichael,
CA (P 844) 916-944-7270**
**Hom & Hom/6010 Wilshire Blvd #505, Los Angeles,
CA (P 480) 213-931-7449**
Homad, Jewell/1250 Long Beach Ave #309, Los Angeles, CA 213-627-6270
Hoover, Anne Nelson/8457 Paseo Del Ocaso, La Jolla, CA 714-454-4294
Hopkins, Christopher/2932 Wilshire #202, Santa Monica, CA 818-985-8181
Hord, Bob/1760 Monrovia #B-9, Costa Mesa, CA 714-631-3890
**Horjes, Peter/3647 India St #1, San Diego, CA
(P 1038) 619-299-0729**
Hosmer, Rick/720 West Mallon Ave #E, Spokane, WA 509-326-6769
**Hovland, Gary/3408 Crest Dr, Manhattan Beach, CA
(P 1039) 310-545-6808**
Hovland, Sylvia/346 Obispo Ave, Long Beach, CA 213-439-4175
Howe, Philip/540 First Ave S, Seattle, WA 206-682-3453
Hubbard, Roger/27520 Sierra Hwy #P206 , Santa Clarita, CA 805-251-2161
Hudson, Dav 213-5354621
Teller #108, Newport Beach, CA 714-474-6002
Hudson, Ron/725 Auahi St, Honolulu, HI 808-536-2692
Hughes, April/210 Columbus Ave #606, San Francisco, CA 415-826-5072
Huhn, Tim/4718 Kester Ave #208, Sherman Oaks, CA 818-986-2352
Hull, John/2356 Fair Park Ave, Los Angeles, CA 213-254-4647
Hulsey, Kevin/3141 Hollywood Dr, Los Angeles, CA 818-501-7105
Hume, Kelly/912 S Los Robles, Pasadena, CA 818-793-8344
Humphrey, Lin/14510A Big Basin Way #200, Saratoga, CA 408-741-1010
Humphries, Michael/11241 Martha Ann Dr, Los Alamitos, CA 213-493-3323
**Hunt, Robert/107 Crescent Rd, San Anselmo, CA
(P 639) 415-824-1824**
Hunt, Stan/950 Klish Way, Del Mar, CA 203-227-7806
Hunter, Alan/328-B Paseo De La Playa, Redondo Beach, CA 213-373-9468
Huston, Steve/85 N Raymond Ave #250, Pasadena, CA 818-578-0140
Huxtable, John/416 S 7th St, Burbank, CA 818-841-7114
Hwang, Francis/999 Town & Country Rd, Orange, CA 714-538-1727
Hyatt, John/80 Wellington Ave/Box 307, Ross, CA 415-456-7711

IJ

**Ibusuki, James/2920 Rosanna St,
Los Angeles, CA (P 185) 818-244-1645**
Irvine, Rex John/6026 Dovetail Dr, Agoura, CA 818-991-2522
**Ishioka, Haruo/6010 Wilshire Blvd #505,
Los Angeles, CA (P 477) 213-931-7449**

**Mezzapelle, Bruno/251 Kearny St #511,
San Francisco, CA (P 859)**..**415-441-4384**
Miller, Gregory/7317 Loch Aleme Ave, Pico Rivera, CA......................213-948-2915
Miller, Warren/950 Klish Way, Del Mar, CA.......................................619-259-5774
Mills, Diane Bogush/PO Box 162430, Sacramento, CA.....................916-454-9286
Millsap, Darrel/1744 6th Ave, San Diego, CA....................................619-543-0122
Mitchell, Briar Lee/6749 Babcock Ave, North Hollywood, CA 818-982-8594
Mitoma, Tim/4865 Doyle St #9, Emeryville, CA..................................415-547-1343
Moch, Paul/1414 Oakland Blvd #4, Walnut Creek, CA........................415-932-5815
**Moline-Kramer, Bobbie /20901 Abalar St,
Woodland Hills, CA (P 426)**...**818-884-1361**
Mollering, David/2250 Caminito Pescado #3, San Diego, CA.............619-225-0752
Monahan, Leo/721 S Victory Blvd, Burbank, CA 818-843-6115
Montoya, Ricardo/5416 Agnes Pl, Riverside, CA................................714-533-0507
Morrow, JT/220 Cavanaugh Way, Pacifica, CA...................................415-355-7899
Morse, Bill/173 18th Ave, San Francisco, CA (P 376) **415-221-6711**
Mortensen, Cristine/140 University Ave #102, Palo Alto, CA...............415-321-4787
Mortensen, Gordon/140 University Ave #102, Palo Alto, CA...............415-321-4787
Mouri, Gary/25002 Reflejo, Mission Viejo, CA...................................714-951-8136
Moyna, Nancy/1125 6th St #4, Santa Monica, CA..............................213-458-1291
Mukai, Dennis/Los Angeles, CA...213-452-9060
Mulhauser & Young/544 Pacific, San Francisco, CA...........................415-392-0542
Murphy, Michael/2630 Washington St, Alameda, CA...........................415-523-8796
Murray, Joe/14531 Big Basin Way, Saratoga, CA................................408-867-7520
Muzick, Terra/1805 Pine St #21, San Francisco, CA...........................415-346-6141
Myers, Matt/900 1st Ave S #404, Seattle, WA (P 727) **206-467-1616**

N

**Nagata, Mark/1660 11th Ave, San Francisco, CA
(P 498)**..**415-661-7528**
Nagle, Candace/230 S Oakland Ave #C, Pasadena, CA 818-793-0342
Nahas, Margo Zafer/1233 S La Cienega Blvd, Los Angeles, CA...........213-855-8855
**Nakamura, Joel/Pier 33 North, San Francisco, CA
(P 646,482)**..**415-956-4750**
**Nakamura, Joel/6010 Wilshire Blvd #505,
Los Angeles, CA (P 482,646)**..**213-931-7449**
Navarro, Arlene & Larry/1921 Comstock Ave, Los Angeles, CA...........213-201-4744
Neila, Anthony/14 Patricia Ln, Mill Valley, CA...................................415-383-7580
**Nelson, Craig/11943 Nugent Dr, Granada Hills, CA
(P 41)**..**818-363-4494**
Nelson, Mike/1836 Woodsdale Ct, Concord, CA................................707-746-0800
**Nelson, R Kenton/12 South Fair Oaks Ave,
Pasadena, CA (P 621,707)**..**818-792-5252**
Nelson, Susan/2363 N Fitch Mtn Rd, Healdsburg, CA.........................707-431-7166
Nelson, Will/716 Montgomery St, San Francisco, CA..........................415-433-1222
Nethery, Susan/1548 18th St, Santa Monica, CA................................213-828-1931
Nicholson, Norman/132 Leona Ct, Alamo, CA...................................415-837-0695
Nikosey, Tom/188 Dapplegrey Rd, Canoga Park, CA..........................213-937-2994
Nishimura, Masato/39571 Holmstead Ave, North Branch, MN..............612-674-8039
Noble, Larry/PO Box 229, Crestline, CA..714-338-5218
Norman, Gary/7825 Manchester Ave #8, Playa Del Rey, CA 213-578-2191
Nugent, Denise/PO Box 61, Burton, WA..206-463-5412
Nunez, Manuel/1018 W 13th St, San Pedro, CA.................................213-832-2471
Nye, Linda S/2482 Alto Cerro Cir, San Diego, CA...............................619-272-1305

O

**O'Brien, Kathy/401 Alameda del Prado, Navato, CA
(P 202)**..**415-883-2964**
O'Malley, Peg/275 25th Ave, San Francisco, CA 415-725-5231
O'Mary, Tom/8418 Menkar Rd, San Diego, CA..................................619-578-5361
O'Neil, Sharron/409 Alberto Way #6, Los Gatos, CA..........................408-354-3816
Oakley, Kevin/1123 N Glen Oaks, Burbank, CA.................................818-443-6162
Obrero, Rudy/3400 Barham, Los Angeles, CA...................................213-850-5700
Oden, Richard/PO Box 415, Laguna Beach, CA.................................714-760-7001
Olson, Rik/749 Circle Court, San Francisco,,CA.................................415-589-4392
Oppenheimer, Jennie/85 Liberty Ship Way #112, Sausalito, CA 415-331-0834
Orvidas, Ken/1 Microsoft Way Bldg 9, Redmond, WA.........................206-885-7437
Osborn, Jacqueline/710 Palo Alto, Palo Alto, CA...............................415-326-2275
Osborn, Stephen/710 Palo Alto, Palo Alto, CA..................................415-326-2275

P

Pace, Julie/PO Box 491, Skyforest, CA 213-837-5300
Padilla, Anthony/624 La Paloma Ave, Alhambra, CA..........................818-289-1932
Palay/Beaubois/124 University #200, Palo Alto, CA............................415-322-8456
Palermo, David/3359 Calle San Tiheo, Carlsbad, CA..........................619-452-0600

Paluso, Christopher/3217 Sweetwater Springs #89, Rancho
San Diego, CA...619-670-4907
Pansini, Tom/16222 Howland Ln, Huntington Bch, CA.......................714-847-9329
Paris Productions/2207 Garnet, San Diego, CA.................................619-272-4992
Parkinson, Jim/6170 Broadway Terrace, Oakland, CA.........................415-547-3100
Passey, Kim/115 Hurlbut #17, Pasadena, CA 818-441-4384
Pavesich, Vida/1152 Arch St, Berkeley, CA.......................................415-528-8233
Peck, Everett/716 Sanchez St, San Francisco, CA.............................415-285-8267
Pederson, Sharleen/101 California St #1107, Santa Montica, CA.........213-306-7847
Peringer, Stephen/17808 184th Ave NE, Woodinville, WA...................206-788-5767
Perini, Ben/1113 Clayton Ct, Novato, CA..415-892-6535
Petersen, Jeff/2956 Nicada Dr, Los Angeles, CA................................213-470-0140
Peterson, Barbara/2629 W Northwood, Santa Ana, CA.......................714-546-2786
Peterson, Eric/270 Termino Avenue, Long Beach, CA.........................213-438-2785
Phillips, Laura/1770 E Sonoma St, Altadena, CA................................818-794-6138
Pickard, Morgan/4621 Teller 3108, Newport Beach, CA......................714-474-6002
Pierazzi, Gary/331 Leland Ave, Menlo Park, CA.................................415-854-8765
Pina, Richard/600 Moulton #401, Los Angeles, CA.............................213-227-5213
Plagen, Bracey/21870 Grenada Ave, Cupertino, CA...........................408-252-6420
Platz, Henry III/15922 118th Pl NE, Bothell, WA.................................206-488-9171
**Podevin, Jean-Francois/5812 Newlin Ave, Whittier,
CA (P 895)**...**213-945-9613**
Ponte, Don/845 Broadway, Sonoma, CA...707-935-6335
Porcuna, Ramon/3183 Wayside Plaza #218, Walnut Creek, CA...........415-932-4739
Pound, John/5587 Noe Ave, San Diego, CA.......................................707-445-3769
**Powers, Teresa/6010 Wilshire Blvd #505,
Los Angeles, CA (P 481)**...**213-931-7449**
**Pryor, Robert/183 N Martel Ave #240, Los Angeles,
CA (P 310)**...**213-934-3395**
**Przewodek, Camille/4029 23rd St, San Francisco,
CA (P 142,143)**...**415-826-3238**
Puchalski, John/1311 Centinela Ave, Santa Monica, CA 213-828-0841
Putnam, Jamie/882 S Van Ness Ave, San Francisco, CA.....................415-641-0513
Pyle, Charles S/946 B St, Petaluma, CA (P 207) **707-765-6734**

R

Rabin, Cheryl/1562 44th Ave, San Francisco, CA...............................415-665-9057
Raess Design/424 N Larchmont Blvd, Los Angeles, CA......................213-461-9206
Read, Elizabeth/2000 Vallejo St #19, San Francisco, CA.....................415-929-7323
**Renwick/183 N Martell Ave #240, Los Angeles,
CA (P 302)**...**213-934-3395**
Renz, Mike/2223 Franklin Ave East, Seattle, WA................................206-323-9257
Rhodes, Barbara/2402 Sonora Ct, Carlsbad, CA................................619-729-4228
Richardson, Nelva/2619 American River Dr, Sacramento, CA 916-482-7438
Richter, Mische/950 Klish Way, Del Mar, CA.....................................619-259-5774
Rictor, Lew/3 Damon Ct, Alameda, CA...415-769-7130
**Rieser, William/2906 Hermosa View Dr, Hermosa
Beach, CA (P 816)**..**213-318-1837**
Rinaldi, Linda/5717 Chicopee, Encino, CA..818-881-1578
Roady, Suzanne/244 9th St, San Francisco, CA.................................415-621-2992
Robertson, Chris/PO Box 84391, Los Angeles, CA.............................213-207-5712
Robles, Bill/3443 Wade St, Los Angeles, CA.....................................213-390-9595
Rogers, Mike/8000 Owensmouth St #9, Canoga Park, CA...................818-344-8609
**Rogers, Paul/183 N Martel Ave #240,
Los Angeles, CA (P 290,291)**...**213-934-3395**
Rosco, Delro/1420 E 4th St, National City, CA (P 553) **213-464-1575**
Rosenberg, Kenneth/9710 E Lemon Ave, Arcadia, CA........................818-574-1631
Rother, Sue/19 Brookmont Circle, San Anselmo, CA..........................415-454-3593
Russo, Dave/613-D Fell St, San Francisco, CA...................................415-431-8080

S

Sakahara, Dick/28826 Cedarbluff Dr, Rancho Palos Verdes, CA..........213-541-8187
**Salentine, Katherine/2022 Jones St, San Francisco,
CA (P 581)**..**415-928-0457**
Salk, Larry/5455 Wilshire Blvd #1212, Los Angeles, CA......................213-934-1975
Salvati, Jim/1091 Wesley Ave, Pasadena, CA (P 732)....**818-441-2544**
**Sano, Kazuhiko/105 Stadium Ave, Mill Valley, CA
(P 788,789)**..**415-381-6377**
Saputo, Joe/4024 Jasper Rd, Springfield, OR 503-746-1737
Sarn/1201 Howard St, San Francisco, CA...415-928-1602
Sassooni, Maral/1416 Queens Rd, West Hollywood, CA.....................213-656-9323
Sava, Judy/813 R St, Sacramento, CA..916-444-7844
**Sawyer, Scott/508 4th St, San Francisco,
CA (P 830)**..**415-277-0539**
Scanlon, Dave/1600 18th St, Manhattan Beach, CA...........................213-545-0773
Schaefer, Robert/6010 Wilshire Blvd #505, Los Angeles, CA...............213-931-7449

Schftenaar, Johanna/2457 Wellsley Ave, Los Angeles, CA 213-479-6014
Schields, Gretchen/4556 19th St, San Francisco, CA 415-558-8851
Schmidt, Eric/1852 Kirkby Rd, Glendale, CA 818-507-0263
Schneider, Doug/4201 Cleveland #12, San Diego, CA 619-692-0545
Schroeder, Mark/Pier 33 North, San Francisco, CA 415-421-3691
Schumaker, Ward/466 Green St #203, San Francisco, CA 415-398-7295
Scoggins, Timothy/207 N Juanita #5, Redondo Beach, CA 213-543-3569
Scribner, Jo Anne L/3314 N Lee, Spokane, WA (P 810,811) 509-484-3208
Scudder, Brooks/281 41st St #36, Oakland, CA 415-652-9246
Seckler, Judy/12 S Fair Oaks Ave, Pasadena, CA 818-508-8778
Shachat, Andrew/121 Kennan St #A, Santa Cruz, CA 408-458-0566
Sharp, Bruce/2125 Western Ave #400, Seattle, WA (P 449) 206-443-0326
Shed, Greg/716 Sanchez St, San Francisco, CA (P 722) 415-285-8267
Shek, W E/1315 Ebener St #4, Redwood City, CA 415-363-0687
Shepherd, Roni/1 San Antonio Pl, San Francisco, CA 415-421-9764
Shields, Bill/14 Wilmot, San Francisco, CA 415-346-0376
Shigley, Neil/1549 Moraga Way, Moraga, CA 415-631-9255
Short, Kevin/PO Box 4037, Mission Viejo, CA 714-472-1035
Siboldi, Carla/252 Juanita Way, San Francisco, CA (P 1135) 415-681-4731
Sigala, Anthony/1681 Amberwood Dr #209, S Pasadena, CA 818-799-1448
Sigwart, Forrest/1033 S Orlando Ave, Los Angeles, CA 213-655-7734
Silberstein, Simon/1131 Alta Loma Rd #516, W Hollywood, CA 213-652-5226
Siu, Peter/559 Pacific Ave #6, San Francisco, CA 415-398-6511
Skaar, Al/2125 Western Ave #400, Seattle, WA 206-443-0326
Sloan, Rick/9432 Appalachian Dr, Sacramento, CA 916-364-5844
Smith, J J/4239 1/2 Lexington Ave, Los Angeles, CA 213-668-2408
Smith, J Randall/130 Maple St #10, Auburn, CA 916-823-5535
Smith, Jere/2125 Western Ave #400, Seattle, WA (P 450) 206-443-0326
Smith, John C/101 Yesler #502, Seattle, WA 206-441-0606
Smith, Terry/14333 Tyler St, Sylmar, CA 818-362-3599
Snyder, Teresa & Wayne/25727 Mountain Dr, Arlington, WA 206-435-8998
Solie, John/202 W Channel Rd, Santa Monica, CA 213-454-8147
Solvang-Angell, Diane/425 Randolph Ave, Seattle, WA 206-324-1199
South, Randy/3731 Cahuenga Blvd W, Studio City, CA (P 608) 818-766-3877
Spaulding, Kevin/21025 Lemarsh St #31, Chatsworth, CA 818-998-6091
Spear, Jeffrey A/2590 S Centinela Ave #7, Los Angeles, CA 213-395-3939
Spear, Randy/4532 Toucan St, Torrance, CA 213-370-6071
Speidel, Sandra/14 Wilmot, San Francisco, CA 415-923-1363
Spencer, Joe/11201 Valley Spring Ln, Studio City, CA 818-760-0216
Spengler, Kenneth/780 Parklin Ave, Sacramento, CA 916-399-9830
Steam/Dave Willardson/Glendale, CA (P 102) 818-242-5688
Stearwalt, Terri/275 S Marengo Ave #312, Pasadena, CA 818-795-3413
Steele, Robert Gantt/14 Wilmot, San Francisco, CA (P 192,193) 415-923-0741
Stein, Mike/4340 Arizona, San Diego, CA 619-295-2455
Steine, Debra/6561 Green Gables Ave, San Diego, CA 619-698-5854
Steirnagle, Michael/8100 Paseo del Ocaso, La Jolla, CA 619-454-7280
Stepp, Don/275 Marguerita Ln, Pasadena, CA 818-799-0263
Stermer, Dugald/1844 Union St, San Francisco, CA (P 819) 415-777-0110
Stevenson, Dave/522 Colonial Circle, Vacaville, CA 707-447-5720
Stewart, Barbara/1640 Tenth Ave #5, San Diego, CA 619-238-0083
Stramler, Gwyn/24294 Saradella Ct, Murrieta, CA 714-677-3452
Stuart, Walter/716 Sanchez St, San Francisco, CA (P 724) 415-285-8267
Stubbs, Barbara/8447 Mica Way, Citrus Hts, CA 916-722-9982
Sullivan, Donna/5959 Riverside Blvd #13, Sacramento, CA 916-786-3800
Sullivan, Melinda May/834 Moultrie St, San Francisco, CA 415-648-2376
Suma, Doug/605 Third St #204, San Francisco, CA (P 455) 415-777-2120
Suvityasiri, Sarn/1811 Leavenworth St, San Francisco, CA 415-928-1602
Swan, Sara/5904-B W 2nd St, Los Angeles, CA (P 1154) 213-935-4781
Swendsen, Paul/4630 Fulton St, San Francisco, CA 415-668-1077
Swimm, Tom/33651 Halyard Dr, Laguna Niguel, CA 714-496-6349
Syme, Hugh/11270 Houston St #210, N Hollywood, CA 818-508-7137
Syntax International/1790 5th St, Berkeley, CA 415-849-0560

T

Tachiera, Andrea/7416 Fairmount Ave, El Cerrito, CA 415-525-3484
Talaro, Lionel/2124 Froude St, San Diego, CA (P 578) 619-222-2476
Tanenbaum, Robert/5505 Corbin Ave, Tarzana, CA (P 161) 818-345-6741
Tank, Darrell/716 Montgomery St, San Francisco, CA 415-433-1222
Tarleton, Suzanne/1740 Stanford St, Santa Monica, CA 213-859-7563
Tarrish, Laura/123 Townsend St #215, San Francisco, CA 415-442-1866
Taylor, C Winston/17008 Lisette St, Granada Hills, CA 818-363-5761
Taylor, George/95 Hurlbut #2, Pasadena, CA 818-799-3435
Teach, Buzz/1874 27th St, Sacramento, CA 916-454-3556
Teebken, Tim/1618 W Lomita Blvd #5, Harbor City, CA 213-325-8789
Tenud, Tish/3427 Folsom Blvd, Sacramento, CA 916-455-0569
Tessler, John/614 N 10th St #200, Sacramento, CA 916-442-4600
Thayn, Ellayn/PO Box 8505, Victorville, CA 619-241-9794
The Committee/4741 Laurel Canyon Blvd, N Hollywood, CA 818-902-1440
Thomas, Mary Ann/18620 Hatteras St #222, Tarzana, CA 818-705-0289
Thompson, Brian/183 E Palm, Altadena, CA 818-798-5901
Thon, Bud/410 View Park Ct, Mill Valley, CA 415-332-5319
Thornton, Blake/18780 Melvin Ave, Sonoma, CA 707-935-9716
Thornton, Sandra/3129 Root Ave, Carmichael, CA 916-489-2877
Tiessen, Ken/311 Quincy Ave, Long Beach, CA 213-438-1346
Tilley, Debbie/2821 Camino Del Mar #78, Del Mar, CA 619-481-3251
Tillinghast, David/Pier 33 North, San Francisco, CA (P 647) 415-956-4750
Tilly, Debra/2051 Shadetree, Escondido, CA 619-432-6282
Tom, Ket/1810 Sunset Ave, Santa Barbara, CA (P 1161) 805-687-0249
Tomita, Tom/3568 E Melton, Pasadena, CA 818-796-4213
Tosch, Jamie S/8732 Fair Oaks Blvd #44, Carmichael, CA 916-944-2097
Truesdale Art & Design/5482 Complex St #112, San Diego, CA 619-268-1026
Tsuchiya, Julie/Pier 1/LOPR, San Francisco, CA 415-986-5365
Tucker, Ezra/1865 Old Mission Dr, Solvang, CA(P 877) 818-905-0758
Turchyn, Sandie/156 N Hamel Dr, Beverly Hills, CA 213-652-9561
Turner, David/3970 Atlantic #206, Long Beach, CA 213-490-9558

UV

Unger, Joe/17120 NE 96th St, Redmond, WA 206-883-1419
Unger, Judy/14160 Oro Grande St, Sylmar, CA (P 520) 818-362-6470
Unruh, Jack/716 Montgomery St, San Francisco, CA (P 438,439) 415-433-1222
Uyehara, Elizabeth/1020 Westchester Pl, Los Angeles, CA 213-731-4168
Van der Palen, Erik/3443 Wade St, Los Angeles, CA 212-390-9595
Van Overloop, Chris J/1714 Capitol Ave, Sacramento, CA 916-444-2840
Vance, Steve/1955 Vero Gordo St, Los Angeles, CA 213-662-3441
Vanderpalen, Eric/1507 Glyndon Ave, Venice, CA 213-396-1661
Vandervoort, Gene/3201 S Ramona Dr, Santa Ana, CA 714-549-3194
Varah, Monte/18052 Rayen St, North Ridge, CA 818-886-2820
Vibbert, Carolyn/3911 Bagley Ave N, Seattle, WA (P 1171) 206-634-3473
Vigon, Jay/708 S Orange Grove Ave, Los Angeles, CA 213-937-0355
Von Schmidt, Eric/1852 Kirkby Rd, Glendale, CA 818-507-0263
Voo, Rhonda/8800 Venice Blvd, Los Angeles, CA (P 531,564) 213-859-1532
Voss, Tom/7584 Charmant Dr #2121, San Diego, CA 619-457-2055

W

Wack, Jeff/3614 Berry Dr, Studio City, CA 818-508-0348
Waldron, Sarah/3690 Primrose Ave, Santa Rosa, CA (P 825) 707-778-0848
Walstead, Curt/398 Via Colinas, Westlake Village, CA 818-595-2981
Walters, Steve/6010 Wilshire Blvd #505, Los Angeles, CA (P 481) 213-931-7449
Walton, Brenda/910 2nd Ave 2nd FL, Sacramento, CA 916-448-4998
Warnick, Elsa/812 SW St Clair #7, Portland, OR 503-228-2659
Warren, Shari/2037 Belle Monti Ave, Belmont, CA (P 1174) 415-591-1229
Washington, Romeo/1567 19th Ave #2, San Francisco, CA 415-282-4847
Waters Art Studio/1820 E Garry St #207, Santa Ana, CA 714-250-4466
Watson, Richard Jesse/PO Box 1470, Murphys, CA 209-728-2701
Watts, Stan/28310 Foothill Dr, Agoura Hills, CA 805-499-4747
Weber/950 Klish Way, Del Mar, CA (P 558) 619-259-5774
Weiss, Stacy/19551 Turtle Ridge Lane, Northridge, CA 213-939-9797
Welch, Michael/1312 25th St, Sacramento, CA 916-446-5691
Welch, W John/2020 Santa Clara Ave #204, Alameda, CA 415-523-9054
Werner, Jerry/PO Box 8000, Black Butte, OR 503-595-2038
Westlight/2223 S Carmelina Ave, Los Angeles, CA (P 867) 800-872-7872

Weston, Will/135 S LaBrea, Los Angeles, CA...................213-854-3666
Wetmore, Barry/1840 Hanscom Dr, S Pasadena, CA.........213-254-5438
Wexler, Ed/4701 Don Pio Dr, Woodland Hills, CA.............818-505-7121
Wheaton, Liz/80 Wellington Ave/Box 307, Ross, CA...........415-456-7711
White, Charlie III/1725 Berkeley St, Santa Monica, CA.......213-453-4418
Wicks, Ren/3443 Wade St, Los Angeles, CA 213-390-9595

**Willardson + Assoc/103 W California, Glendale,
CA (P 103)**...**818-242-5688**
Williams, John C/5100 N Muscatel Ave, San Gabriel, CA....818-286-7949
Williams, Wayne/15423 Sutton St, Sherman Oaks, CA.......213-937-2882

**Wilson, Bill/183 N Martel Ave #240, Los Angeles,
CA (P 300)**..**213-934-3395**
Wilson, Gahan/950 Klish Way, Del Mar, CA (P 558) **619-259-5774**
Wilson, Rob/4729 Eighth Ave, Sacramento, CA.................916-451-0449
Wilson, Rowland/7501 Solano St, Rancho La Costa, CA.....619-944-3631
Wilton, Nicholas/85 Liberty Ship Way #112, Sausalito, CA...415-331-0834
Wilton/Oppenheimer/85 Liberty Ship Way, Sausalito, CA.....415-331-0834

**Wiltse, Kris/2125 Western Ave #400, Seattle,
WA (P 451)**...**206-443-0326**
Winston, Jeannie/8800 Venice Blvd, Los Angeles, CA 213-558-0141

**Winterbauer, Michael James/1220 Lyndon St #22,
South Pasadena, CA (P 1183)** **818-799-4998**
Winters, Greg/2139 Pinecrest Dr, Altadena, CA................818-798-7666
Witus, Edward/634 W Knoll Dr, Los Angeles, CA...............213-828-6521

Wolf, Paul/900 First Ave S #208, Seattle, WA (P 660) ..**206-623-1459**
Wolfe, Bruce/206 El Cerrito Ave, Piedmont, CA.................415-655-7871
Wolin, Ron/4501 Firmament, Encino, CA.........................213-214-6207
Woodman, Bill/950 Klish Way, Del Mar, CA 619-259-5774
Woodward, Teresa/544 Paseo Miramar, Pacific Palisades, CA 213-459-2317

**Wray, Greg/183 N Martel Ave #240, Los Angeles,
CA (P 292,293)**...**213-934-3395**
Wright, Carol/2500 Angie Way, Rancho Cordova, CA.........916-635-4705
Wright, Jonathan/2110 Holly Dr, Los Angeles, CA.............213-461-1091

XYZ

Xavier, Roger/3227 Del Amo Blvd, Lakewood, CA..............213-531-9631
Yadin, Hannan/5827 Hickory Dr #F, Agoura, CA................818-879-9099
Yamada, Kenny/2330 Haste St #306, Berkeley, CA............415-841-4415
Yenne, Bill/111 Pine St, San Francisco, CA 415-989-2450
Yeomans, Jeff/3838 Kendall, San Diego, CA 619-274-2855
Yoshiyama, Glenn/2125 Western Ave #400, Seattle, WA....206-443-0326
Zaslavsky, Morris/228 Main St #6, Venice, CA 213-399-3666
Zick, Brian/3251 Primera Ave, Los Angeles, CA................213-876-0402

**Ziemienski, Dennis/414 First St East, Sonoma, CA
(P 784,785)**...**707-935-0357**
Zinc, Debra/Pier 33 North, San Francisco, CA...................415-956-4750
Zito, Andy/135 S La Brea Ave, Los Angeles, CA 213-931-1181

I N T E R N A T I O N A L

**Barnett, David/41 Midcote Rd, Oadby, Leicaster,
England,(P 907)** **44-015-33717-658**
Baviera, Rocco/21 Mountwood Ave #7, Hamilton, ON........416-385-0047
Berkson, Nina/2 Silver Ave, Toronto, ON (P 556)...........**416-530-1500**
Broda, Ron/361 Dundas St, London, ON 519-672-2538
Cantin, Charles/809 Cartier, Quebec, QC........................418-524-1931

**Cousineau, Normand/2 Silver Ave, Toronto, ON
(P 554)**..**416-530-1500**
Dawson, John/116 Bedford Rd #1, Toronto, ON 416-926-0730
Dionisi, Sandra/859 King St W, Toronto, ON....................416-867-1771
Edmunds, David/1312 Monmouth Dr, Burlington, ON 416-332-6047

Frampton, Bill/49 Henderson, Toronto, ON (P 457) **416-535-1931**
Gabbana, Marc/1540 Westcott Rd, Windsor, ON 519-948-7705

**Geras, Audra/53-A Gloucester St, Toronto, ON
(P 574,575)**...**416-928-2965**
Hammond, Franklin/1 Alderton Ct, Etobicoke, ON.............416-538-4387
Heda, Jackie/3 Playter Blvd #3, Toronto, ON 416-463-8692
Johnston, WB/572 Mountain Ave, Winnipeg, MB...............204-582-1686
Jones, Danielle/55 W Charles St #1003, Toronto, ON........416-968-6277
Krb, Vladimir/PO Box 2955/Drumheller Sta, Alberta, AB 403-823-6385
Kunz, Anita/230 Ontario St, Toronto, ON.........................416-364-3846
Kurisu, Jane/97 Air Drie Rd, Toronto, ON 416-424-2524
Levine, Ron/1619 Williams St #202, Montreal, QU.............212-727-1967
Liss, Julius/446 Lawrence Ave W, Toronto, ON 416-784-1416

**MacLeod, Ainslie/33 Long Acre, London, England
WC2, (P 1069)** **44-071-240-1812**

MacDougall, Rob/2049 Lakeshore Rd W, Oakville, ON........416-847-7663

**Marsh, James/21 Elms Rd, London
SW 4 9 ER, UK (P 1075)**..**44-071-622-9350**
Miller, Jean/350 Esna Park Dr, Markham, ON...................416-883-4114
Nicol, Brock/889 Wingate Dr, Ottawa, ON.......................613-733-6026
Olthuis, Stan/524 Queen St E, Toronto, ON 416-860-0300
Ormond, Rick/42 Portland Crscnt, Newmarket, ON............416-961-4098
Pariseau, Pierre Paul/9067 Place do Montgoitier, Montreal, QU............514-388-7192
Pastucha, Ron/336 McNeans Ave, Winnipeg, MB..............204-222-3178

Pratt, Pierre/2 Silver Ave, Toronto, ON (P 557).............**416-530-1500**
Reed, Barbara/37 Strathmore Blvd, Toronto, ON 416-461-9793
Rivoche, Paul/2 Silver Ave, Toronto, ON (P 555)...........**416-530-1500**
**Rubess, Balvis/260 Brunswick Ave, Toronto, ON
(P 834)**..**416-927-7071**
Sekeris, Pim/570 Milton St #10, Montreal, QU..................514-844-0510

**Shumate, Michael/198 Chelsea Rd, Kingston, ON
(P 1134)**..**613-384-5019**
**Sinclair, Valerie/17 Bellwoods Pl, Toronto, ON
(P 94,95)**...**416-594-3400**
Snider, Jackie/RR 7/Hwy 30, Brighton, ON (P 234) **613-475-4551**
Vowles, Bob/Box 25 RR #2, Lisle, ON 519-925-6643
Van Ginkel, Paul/40 Edgehart Estates Rd NW, Calgary, AB 403-241-0516

**Zwolak, Paul/11 Prince Rupert Ave, Toronto, ON
(P 495)**..**416-531-6253**

G R A P H I C
D E S I G N E R S
N Y C

A

Abramson, Michael R Studio/401 Lafayette St 7th Fl	212-683-1271
Adams, Gaylord Design/236 E 36th St	212-684-4625
Adlemann, Morton/30 W 32nd St	212-564-8258
Adler, Stan Assoc/1140 Ave of Americas	212-719-1944
Adlerblum, Marleen/1133 Broadway #1225	212-807-8429
Adzema, Diane/17 Bleecker St	212-982-5657
AKM Associates/41 E 42nd St	212-687-7636
Alastair Brown Benjamin Assoc/419 Park Ave S	212-213-8719
Aliman, Elie/134 Spring St	212-925-9621
Allied Graphic Arts/1515 Broadway	212-730-1414
ALZ Design/11 Waverly Pl #1J	212-473-7620
American Express Publishing Co/1120 Ave of Americas	212-382-5600
Anagram Design Group/10-40 Jackson Ave, Long Island City	718-786-2020
Anagraphics Inc/104 W 29th St 2nd Fl	212-279-2370
Ancona Design Atelier/524 W 43rd St	212-947-8287
Anspach Grossman Portugal/711 Third Ave, 12th flr	212-692-9000
Antler & Baldwin Graphics/7 E 47th St	212-751-2031
Antupit and Others Inc/16 E 40th St	212-686-2552
Appelbaum Company/176 Madison Ave 4th Fl	212-213-1130
Ariel Peeri Design/135 E 27th St	212-686-0131
Arkadia Group/41 W 25th St	212-645-6226
Arnell-Bickford Assoc/100 Grand St	212-219-8400
Art Department/2 W 46th St	212-391-1826
Athey, Diane/425 W 23rd St	212-787-7415
Avanti Graphics/568 Broadway	212-966-6661

B

Balasas, Cora/651 Vanderbilt St	718-633-7753
Balch, Barbara/One Union Sq #903	212-242-0026
Bantam Books Inc/666 Fifth Ave	212-765-6500
Barnes, Miriam/2 Tudor City Pl #7D South	212-697-0441
Barnett Design Group/270 Lafayette St #801	212-431-7130
Barry David Berger Assoc/9 E 19th St	212-477-4100
Barry, Jim/69 W 68th St	212-873-6787
Becker Hockfield Design Assoc/35 E 21st St	212-505-7050
Beckerman, Ann Design/50 W 29th St	212-684-0496
Bel Air Assoc/745 Fifth Ave 17th Fl	212-838-1060
Benvenutti, Chris/12 W 27th St 12t Fl	212-696-0880
Bergman, Eliot/362 W 20th St #201 (P 918,919)	**212-645-0414**
Bernhardt/Fudyma/133 E 36th St	212-889-9337
Bernstein, Harvey/160 Fifth Ave #804	212-243-4149
Besalel, Ely/235 E 49th St	212-759-7820
Bessen Tully & Lee/220 E 23rd St 12th Fl	212-213-1911
Binns & Lubin/80 Fifth Ave	212-989-0090
Biondo, Charles Design Assoc/389 W 12th St	212-645-5300
Black, Roger/PO Box 860/Radio City Sta	212-459-7553
Blackburn, Bruce/331 Park Ave South 10th Fl	212-777-5335
Bloch, Graulich & Whelan, Inc/333 Park Ave S	212-473-7033
Boker Group/37 W 26th St	212-686-1132
Bonnell Design Associates Inc/409 W 44th St	212-757-4420
Bordnick, Jack & Assoc/224 W 35th St	212-563-1544
Borejko, Barbara/124 W 24th St 4th Fl	212-463-9292
Botero, Samuel Assoc/150 E 58th St	212-935-5155
Bradford, Peter/11 E 22nd St	212-982-2090
Brainchild Designs/108 E 16th St	212-420-1222
Braswell, Lynn/320 Riverside Dr	212-222-8761
Bree/Taub Design/648 Broadway #703	212-254-8383
Brochure People/14 E 38th St #1466	212-696-9185
Brodsky Graphics/270 Madison Ave #605	212-684-2600
Brown, Kirk Q/1092 Blake Ave, Brooklyn	718-346-8281
Bryant & Co/2 Astor Pl	212-254-5122
Buckley Designs Inc/310 E 75th St	212-861-0626
Burns, Tom Assoc Inc/330 E 42nd St	212-594-9883
By Design/14 E 38th St	212-684-0388
Byrde Richard & Pound/251 Park Ave S 14th Fl	212-777-7000
Byrne, Susan/133 W 19th St 10th Fl	212-807-6671

C

Cain, David/200 W 20th St #607 (P 851)	**212-633-0258**
Calfo/Aron Inc/20 W 20th St 9th Fl	212-627-4054
Cannan, Bill & Co Inc/529 W 42nd St #2Q	212-563-1004
Cantor, Andrew/4 W 37th St 6th Fl	212-629-0130
Canzani Graphics/11 W 30th St	212-643-1050
Caravello Studios/165 W 18th St	212-620-0620
Carlo & Associates/900 Broadway - 5th Floor	212-420-1110
Carnase, Inc/30 E 21st St	212-679-9880
Carpenter Graphic Design/72 Spring St	212-431-6666
Carson, Carol/138 W 88th St	212-580-0514
Casey, Jim/26 W 23rd St 5th Fl	212-627-3321
Cavanagh, John/306 Eighth Ave	212-741-0047
Cetta, Al/111 Bank St	212-989-9696
Chajet Design Group Inc/148 E 40th St	212-684-3669
Chang, Ivan/30 E 10th St	212-777-6102
Chapman, Sandra S/122 Ashland Pl #7E, Brooklyn	718-855-7396
Charles, Irene Assoc/104 E 40th St #206	212-765-8000
Chermayeff & Geismar/15 E 26th St 12th Fl	212-532-4499
Chin, E T Assoc/1160 Third Ave	212-645-6800
Chu, H L & Co Ltd/39 W 29th St	212-889-4818
Cliffer, Jill/9 E 16th St	212-691-7013
Cohen, Hayes Design/36-35 193rd St #3, Flushing, (P 890)	**718-321-7307**
Cohen, Norman Design/201 E 28th St #8K	212-679-3906
Collins, Thomas/156 Fifth Ave #1035	212-627-1656
Comart Assoc/360 W 31st St	212-714-2550
Condon, J & M/126 Fifth Ave	212-242-7811
Corchia Woliner Assoc/130 W 56th St	212-977-9778
Corey & Company/155 Sixth Ave 15th Fl	212-924-4311
Corpographics, Inc/47 West St	212-483-9065
Corporate Annual Reports Inc/112 E 31st St	212-889-2450
Corporate Graphics Inc/655 Third Ave	212-599-1820
Cosgrove Assoc Inc/223 E 31st St	212-889-7202
Cotler, Sheldon Inc/80 W 40th St	212-719-9590
Cousins, Morison S & Assoc/599 Broadway 8th Fl	212-751-3390
Cranner, Brian Inc/454 W 46th St #2D South	212-582-2030
Craven Design/234 Fifth Ave	212-696-4680
Creamer Dickson Basford/1633 Broadway	212-887-8670
Crow, John/34 W 37th St	212-594-2636
Csoka/Benato/Fleurant Inc/134 W 26th St	212-242-6777
Curtis Design Inc/928 Broadway #1104	212-475-3680

D

D'Astolfo, Frank Design/80 Warren St #32	212-732-3052
Daniels Design/150 E 35th St	212-889-0071
Danne, Richard & Assoc/126 Fifth Ave	212-645-7400
Davis, Jed/303 Lexington Ave	212-481-8481
Davis-Delaney-Arrow Inc/141 E 25th St	212-686-2500
Deharek & Poulin Assoc/320 W 13th St	212-929-5445
Delgado, Lisa/22 W 21st St	212-645-0097
Delphan Company/515 Madison Ave #3300	212-371-6700
DeMartin-Marona-Cranstoun-Downes/630 Third Ave 14th Fl	212-682-9044
DeMartino Design/584 Broadway	212-941-9200
Design Five/2637 Broadway	212-222-8133
Design Loiminchay/503 Broadway 5th Fl	212-941-7488
Design Plus/156 Fifth Ave #1232	212-645-2686
Designed to Print/130 W 25th St	212-924-2090
Designers Three/25 W 43rd St	212-221-5900
Designframe/1 Union Square	212-924-2426
Deutsch Design/530 Broadway	212-966-7710
Diamond Art Studio/11 E 36th St	212-685-6622
DiComo, Charles & Assoc/120 E 4th St #12K	212-689-8670
DiFranza Williamson Inc/16 W 22nd St	212-463-8302
Displaycraft/41-21 28th St, Long Island City	718-784-8186
Dixon, Ted/594 Broadway #902	212-226-5686
Donovan & Green Inc/1 Madison Ave	212-725-2233
Doret, Michael/12 E 14th St #4D (P 766)	**212-929-1688**
Douglas, Barry Design/300 E 71st St #4H	212-734-4137
Downey Weeks + Toomey/519 Eighth Ave 22nd Fl	212-564-8260
Drate, Spencer/160 Fifth Ave #613	212-620-4672
Dreyfuss, Henry Assoc/423 W 55th St	212-957-8600
Dubins, Milt Designer Inc/353 W 22nd St	212-691-0232
Dubourcq, Hilaire/110 Christopher St	212-924-1564
Dubrow, Oscar Assoc/18 E 48th St	212-688-0698

Duffy, William R/201 E 36th St 212-682-6755
Dvorak Goodspeed & Assoc/165 Lexington Ave..........................212-475-4580
Dwyer, Tom/420 Lexington Ave...212-986-7108

E

Eckstein, Linda/534 Laguardia Pl #5S....................................212-522-2552
Edgar, Lauren/26 E 20th St 8th Fl 212-673-6060
Edge, Dennis Design/36 E 38th St 212-679-0927
Eichinger, Inc/595 Madison Ave 212-421-0544
Emerson/Wajdowicz/1123 Broadway 212-807-8144
Environetics Inc/145 E 32nd St 8th Fl 212-481-9700
Environment Planning Inc/342 Madison Ave 212-661-3744
Erikson Assoc/345 Park Ave 212-688-0048
Etheridge, Palombo, Sedewitz/1500 Broadway 212-944-2530
Eucalyptus Tree Studio/73 Leonard St....................................212-226-0331

F

Falkins, Richard Design/15 W 44th St 212-840-3045
FDC Planning & Design Corp/434 E 57th St 212-355-7200
Fineberg Associates/333 E 68th St 212-734-1220
Flaherty, David/449 W 47th St #3 (P 865).....................212-262-6536
Florville, Patrick Design Research/94-50 39 Ave, Rego Park 718-475-2278
Flying Eye Graphics/208 Fifth Ave/Unit 2 212-725-0658
Forman, Yale Designs Inc/11 Riverside Dr 212-799-1665
Fredy, Sherry/111 W 24th St..212-627-1867
Freyss, Christina/267 Broadway 2nd Fl 212-571-1130
Friday Saturday Sunday Inc/210 E 15th St...............................212-353-2060
Friedlander, Ira/502 E 84th St..212-580-9800
Friedman, Adam/820 Second Ave 6th Fl 212-682-6300
Froom, Georgia/62 W 39th St #803 212-944-0330
Fulgoni, Louis/233 W 21st St #4D...212-243-2959
Fulton & Partners/330 W 42nd St, 11th Fl..............................212-695-1625
Fultz, Patrick/166 Lexington Ave..212-545-7483

G

Gale, Robert A Inc/970 Park Ave..212-535-4791
Gamarello, Paul/21 E 22nd St #4G...212-485-4774
Gardner, Beau Assoc Inc/541 Lexington Ave 18th Fl 212-832-2426
Gaster, Joanne/201 E 30th St #43 212-686-0860
Gentile Studio/333 E 46th St 212-986-7743
George, Hershell/30 W 15th St...212-929-4321
Gerstman & Meyers Inc/60 W 55th St.....................................212-586-2535
Gianninoto Assoc, Inc/133 E 54th St #2D 212-759-5757
Giber, Lauren/152 E 22nd St..212-473-2062
Giovanni Design Assoc/230 E 44th St #2L...............................212-972-2145
Gips & Balkind & Assoc/244 E 58th St 212-421-5940
Girth, Marcy/213 E 34th St #3A...212-685-0734
Glaser, Milton/207 E 32nd St...212-889-3161
Glazer & Kalayjian/301 E 45th St 212-687-3099
Glusker Group/154 W 57th St 212-757-4438
Goetz Graphics/60 Madison Ave...212-679-4250
Gold, Susan/136 W 22nd St...212-645-6977
Goldman, Neal Assoc/230 Park Ave #1507 212-687-5058
Goodman/Orlick Design, Inc/20 West 20th St. 9th Fl................212-620-9142
Gorbaty, Norman Design/14 E 38th St.....................................212-684-1665
Gordon, Sam & Assoc/226 W 4th St 212-741-9294
Gorman, Chris Assoc/305 Madison Ave 212-983-3375
Graphic Art Resource Assoc/257 W 10th St 212-929-0017
Graphic Chart & Map Co/236 W 26th St #8SE
(P 1015) 212-463-0190
Graphic Expression/330 E 59th St...212-759-7788
Graphic Media/12 W 27th St 12th Fl.......................................212-696-0880
Graphics by Nostradamus/250 W 57th St #1128A....................212-581-1362
Graphics for Industry/8 W 30th St 212-889-6202
Graphics Institute/1633 Broadway..212-887-8670
Graphics to Go/133 E 36th St 212-889-9337
Gray, George/385 West End Ave...212-873-3607
Green, Douglas/251 E 51st St...212-752-6284
Grid, Steve C/118 E 28th St #908 212-889-1888
Griffler Designs/17 E 67th St..212-794-2625
Grunfeld Graphics Ltd/80 Varick St...212-431-8700
Gucciardo & Shapokas/244 Madison Ave 212-683-9378
Guth, Marcy/213 E 34th St #3A..212-685-0734

H

Halle, Doris/355 South End Ave #4C 212-321-2671
Halversen, Everett/874 58th St, Brooklyn................................718-438-4200
Handler Group Inc/55 W 45th St...212-391-0951
Haynes, Leslie/134 E 22nd St...212-777-7390
HBO Studio Productions Inc/120A E 23rd St............................212-512-7800
Head Productions/267 Wycoff St, Brooklyn..............................718-624-1906
Hecker, Mark Studio/321 W 11th St 212-620-9050
Heimall, Bob Inc/250 W 57th St #1206...................................212-245-4525
Hernandez, Raymond/994 Ocean Ave, Brooklyn 718-462-9072
Hixson, Jeff/244 E 58th St 212-421-5888
Holzsager, Mel Assoc Inc/275 Seventh Ave.............................212-741-7373
Hopkins/Baumaun Group/236 W 26th St.................................212-727-2929
Horvath & Assoc Studios Ltd/93-95 Charles St.........................212-741-0300
Hub Graphics/18 E 16th St 4th Fl 212-675-8500
Human Factors/Industrial Design Inc/575 8th Ave 212-730-8010
Hunter, Rona Fischer/25 Fifth Ave #12F..................................212-598-4390
Huttner & Hillman/19 W 21st St 10th Fl 212-463-0776

IJ

Image Communications Inc/85 Fifth Ave..................................212-807-9677
Inkwell Inc/5 W 30th St..212-279-2066
Inner Thoughts/118 E 25th St...212-674-1277
Intersight Design Inc/419 Park Ave S 212-696-0700
Jaben, Seth Design/47 E 3rd St #3 (P 774,775)............212-673-5631
Jaffe Communications, Inc/122 E 42nd St................................212-697-4310
Jensen Assoc/145 6th Ave PH...212-645-3115
Johnston, Shaun & Susan/890 West End Ave #11E...................212-663-4686
Jonson Pedersen Hinrichs & Shakery/141 Lexington Ave............212-889-9611

K

Kaeser & Wilson Design/330 Seventh Ave................................212-563-2455
Kahn, Al Group/221 W 82nd St...212-580-3517
Kahn, Donald/39 W 29th St 12th Fl 212-889-8898
Kallir Phillips Ross Inc/605 Third Ave......................................212-878-3700
Kaplan, Barbara/875 Ave of Americas #1606...........................212-564-7706
Karlin, Bernie/41 E 42nd St #PH...212-687-7636
Kass Communications/505 Eighth Ave 19th Fl..........................212-868-3133
Kass, Milton Assoc Inc/1966 Broadway #35.............................212-874-0418
Kauftheil, Henry/220 W 19th St #1200....................................212-633-0222
Kaye Graphics/151 Lexington Ave...212-924-7800
Keithley & Assoc/32 W 22nd St 6th Fl 212-807-8388
Kleb Associates/25 W 45th St 212-246-2847
KLN Publishing Services Inc/36 E 30th St 212-686-8200
Kneapler, John/99 Lexington Ave 2nd Fl..................................212-696-1150
Ko Noda and Assoc International/950 Third Ave 212-759-4044
Kollberg-Johnson Assoc Inc/254 Fifth Ave...............................212-686-3648
Koppel & Scher Inc/156 Fifth Ave 13th Fl East.........................212-627-9330
Kosarin, Linda/400 W 58th St #5F 212-889-3050

L

Lake, John/38 E 57th St 7th Fl 212-644-3850
Lamlee, Stuart/55 W 86th St..212-772-2200
Leach, Richard/62 W 39th St #803 212-869-0972
Lee & Young Communications/One Park Ave 212-689-4000
Lesley-Hille Inc/32 E 21st St...212-677-7570
Lester & Butler/437 Fifth Ave..212-889-0578
Levine, William V & Assoc/31 E 28th St...................................212-683-7177
Levirne, Joel/151 W 46th St 212-869-8370
Lieber/Brewster Corp Design/324 W 87th St............................212-874-2874
Lieberman, Ron/109 W 28th St 212-947-0653
Liebert Studios Inc/6 E 39th St #1200.....................................212-686-4520
Lika Association/160 E 38th St..212-490-3660
Lind Brothers Inc/111 Eighth Ave 7th Fl 212-924-9280
Lippincott & Margulies Inc/499 Park Ave 212-832-3000
Little Apple Art/409 Sixth Ave, Brooklyn, NY 718-499-7045
Lombardo, Joe/98 Riverside Dr #15-G.....................................212-580-7611
Lukasiewicz Design Inc/119 W 57th St....................................212-581-3344
Lundgren, Ray Graphics/122 E 42nd St #216...........................212-370-1686
Luth & Katz Inc/40 E 49th St 9th Fl 212-644-5777

M

M & Co Design Group/50 W 17th St 12th Fl......212-243-0082
Madridejos, Fernando/130 W 67th St #1B......212-724-7339
Maggio, Ben Assoc Inc/420 Lexington Ave #1650......212-697-8600
Maggio, J P Design Assoc Inc/561 Broadway......212-725-9660
Maleter, Mari/25-34 Crescent St, Astoria......718-726-7124
Marchese, Frank/444 E 82nd St......212-988-6267
Marcus, Eric/386 Waverly Ave, Brooklyn......718-789-1799
Masuda, Coco/541 Hudson St #2 (P 782)......212-727-1599
Mauro, Frank Assoc Inc/18 W 45th St......212-719-5570
Mayo-Infurna Design/10 E 21st St 13th Fl......212-888-7883
McDonald, B & Assoc/1140 Ave of the Americas......212-869-9717
McGovern & Pivoda/39 W 38th St......212-840-2912
McNicholas, Florence/1419 8th Ave, Brooklyn......718-965-0203
Mendola Design/420 Lexington Ave......212-986-5680
Mentkin, Robert/51 E 97th St......212-534-5101
Merrill, Abby Studio Inc/153 E 57th St......212-753-7565
Metzdorf, Lyle/821 Broadway 3rd Fl......212-353-0101
Meyers, Ann/118 E 37th St......212-689-3680
Mirenburg, Barry/413 City Island Ave, City Island......718-885-0835
Mitchell, E M Inc/820 Second Ave......212-986-5595
Mizerek Design/48 E 43rd St 2nd Fl......212-986-5702
Modular Marketing Inc/1841 Broadway......212-581-4690
Monczyk, Allen/210 Fifth Ave......212-385-6633
Mont, Howard Assoc Inc/132 E 35th St......212-683-4360
Morris, Dean/307 E 6th St #4B......212-420-0673
Moshier, Harry & Assoc/18 E 53rd St......212-873-6130
Moskof & Assoc/154 W 57th St #133......212-333-2015
Mossberg, Stuart Design Assoc/11 W 73rd St......212-873-6130
Muir, Cornelius, Moore/79 5th Ave......212-463-7715
Mulligan, Donald/418 Central Pk W #81 (P 1091)......212-666-6079
Murtha Desola Finsilver Fiore/800 Third Ave......212-832-4770

N

N B Assoc Inc/435 Fifth Ave......212-684-8074
Nelson, George & Assoc Inc/PO Box 243 Madison Sq Sta......212-777-4300
Nichols, Mary Ann/80 Eighth Ave #900......212-727-9818
Nicholson Design/148 W 24th St 12th Fl......212-206-1530
Noneman & Noneman Design/230 E 18th St......212-473-4090
Notovitz & Perrault Design Inc/47 E 19th St 4th Fl......212-677-9700
Novus Visual Communications Inc/18 W 27th St......212-689-2424

OP

O & J Design/9 W 29th St 5th Fl......212-779-9654
O'Neil, Brian/95 Fifth Ave 8th Fl......212-691-1510
Oak Tree Graphics Inc/570 Seventh Ave......212-398-9355
Offenhartz, Harvey Inc/1414 Ave of Americas......212-751-3241
Ong & Assoc/11 W 19th St 6th Fl......212-633-6702
Orlov, Christian/42 W 69th St......212-873-2381
Ortiz, Jose Luis/66 W 77th St......212-877-3081
Oz Communications Inc/36 E 30th St......212-686-8200
Page Arbitrio Resen Ltd/305 E 46th St......212-421-8190
Pahmer, Hal/8 W 30th St 7th Fl......212-889-6202
Palladino, Tony/400 E 56th St......212-751-0068
Paragraphics/427 3rd St, Brooklyn......718-965-2231
Parsons School of Design/66 Fifth Ave......212-741-8900
Patel, Harish Design Assoc/218 Madison Ave......212-686-7425
Peckolick & Prtnrs/112 E 31st St......212-532-6166
Pellegrini & Assoc/16 E 40th St......212-686-4481
Pencils Portfolio Inc/333 E 49th St......212-355-2468
Penpoint Studio Inc/444 Park Ave S......212-243-5435
Penraat Jaap Assoc/315 Central Park West......212-873-4541
Pentagram/212 Fifth Ave 17th Fl......212-683-7000
Performing Dogs/45 E 19th St......212-260-1880
Perlman, Richard Design/305 E 46th St......212-935-2552
Perlman-Withers/305 E 46th St 15th Fl......212-935-2552
Perlow, Paul/123 E 54th St #6E (P 872)......212-758-4358
Peterson Blythe & Cato/216 E 45th St......212-557-5566
Pettis, Valerie/88 Lexington Ave #17G......212-683-7382
Pirman, John/57 W 28th St......212-679-2866
Platinum Design Inc/14 W 23rd St 2nd Fl......212-366-4000
Plumb Design Group Inc/57 E 11th St 7th Fl......212-673-3490
Pouget, Evelyn/23 E 7th St......212-228-7935
Prendergast, J W & Assoc Inc/605 Third Ave......212-687-8805

Pushpin Group/215 Park Ave S #1300......212-674-8080

QR

**Quon, Mike Design Office/568 Broadway #703
(P 1112,1113)......212-226-6024**
RC Graphics/157 E 57th St......212-755-1383
RD Graphics/151 Lexington Ave #5F......212-889-5612
Regn-Califano Inc/330 W 42nd St #1300......212-239-0380
Riss, Micha/25 W 45th St 2nd Fl......212-704-4000
Robinson, Mark/904 President St, Brooklyn......718-638-9067
Rogers, Ana/20 W 20th St 7th Fl......212-741-4687
Rogers, Richard Inc/300 E 33rd St......212-685-3666
**Romero, Javier/9 W 19th St 5th Fl
(Inside Front Flap/Book 2)......212-727-9445**
Rosebush Visions/154 W 57th St #826......212-398-6600
Rosenthal, Herb & Assoc Inc/207 E 32nd St......212-685-1814
Ross Culbert Lavery Russman/15 W 20th St 9th Fl......212-206-0044
Ross/Pento Inc/301 W 53rd St......212-757-5604
Rothschild, Joyce/305 E 46th St 15th Fl......212-888-8680
Rudoy, Peter/1619 Broadway 10th Fl......212-265-7600
Russell, Anthony Inc/170 Fifth Ave 11th Fl......212-255-0650
Russo, Rocco Anthony/31 W 21st St 6th Fl......212-213-4710

S

**Sabanosh, Michael/433 W 34th St #18B
(P 1122,1123)......212-947-8161**
Saiki & Assoc/154 W 18th St #2D......212-255-0466
Sakin, Sy/17 E 48th St......212-688-3141
Saks, Arnold/350 E 81st St 4th Fl......212-861-4300
Saksa Art & Design/41 Union Sq W #1001 (P 831)......212-255-5539
Salavetz, Judith/160 Fifth Ave #613......212-620-4672
Salisbury & Salisbury Inc/15 W 44th St......212-575-0770
Salpeter, Paganucci, Inc/142 E 37th St......212-683-3310
Sandgren Associates Inc/60 E 42nd St......212-679-4650
Sarda, Thomas/875 Third Ave 4th Fl......212-303-8326
Sawyer, Arnie Studio/15 W 28th St 4th Fl......212-685-4927
Say It In Neon/434 Hudson St......212-691-7977
**Sayles, John Design/420 Lexington Ave #2760
(P 232,233)......212-697-8525**
Schaefer-Cassety Inc/42 W 39th St......212-840-0175
Schaeffer/Boehm Ltd/315 W 35th St......212-947-4345
Schecht, Leslie/505 Henry St, Brooklyn......718-834-1843
Schechter Group Inc/212 E 49th St......212-752-4400
Schecterson, Jack Assoc Inc/274 Madison Ave......212-889-3950
Scheinzeit, Teri/27 W 24th St......212-627-5355
Schumach, Michael P/159-10 Sanford Ave, Flushing......718-539-5328
SCR Design Organization/1114 First Ave......212-752-8496
Seidman, Gene/20 W 20th St #703......212-741-4687
Shapiro, Ellen Assoc/141 Fifth Ave 12th Fl......212-460-8544
Shareholders Reports/600 Third Ave 14th Fl......212-686-9099
Shaw, Paul/785 West End Ave......212-666-3738
Sherin & Matejka Inc/404 Park Ave S......212-686-8410
Sherowitz, Phyllis/310 E 46th St......212-532-8933
Shreeve, Draper Design/28 Perry St......212-675-7534
Siegel & Gale Inc/1185 Ave of Americas 8th Fl......212-730-0101
Siegel, Marion/87 E 2nd St #4A......212-460-9817
Silberlicht, Ira/210 W 70th St......212-595-6252
Silverman, Bob Design/216 E 49th St 2nd Fl......212-371-6472
Singer, Paul Design/494 14th St, Brooklyn......718-449-8172
Sloan, William/236 W 26th St #805 (P 1142)......212-463-7025
Smith, Edward Design/1133 Broadway #1211......212-255-1717
Smith, Laura/12 E 14th St #4D (P 767)......212-206-9162
Sochynsky, Ilona/200 E 36th St......212-686-1275
Solay/Hunt/28 W 44th St 21st Fl......212-840-3313
Solazzo Design/928 Broadway #700......212-529-3320
Sorvino Ligasan Design Assoc/1616 York Ave #5......212-879-8197
St Vincent Milone & McConnells/1156 Sixth Ave......212-921-1414
Stern & Levine/12 W 27th St......212-545-0450
Stevenson, Bob/48 W 21st St 9th Fl......212-206-1724
Stewart Design Group/1 Union Sq W #814......212-979-2248
Stillman, Linda/1556 Third Ave......212-410-3225
Stuart, Gunn & Furuta/95 Madison Ave......212-689-0077
Studio 42/1472 Broadway #506......212-354-7298
Swatek and Romanoff Design Inc/156 Fifth Ave #1100......212-807-0236
Systems Collaborative Inc/52 Duane St......212-608-0584

T

Taurins Design Assoc/280 Madison Ave 212-679-5955
Tauss, Jack George/484 W 43rd St #40H 212-279-1658
Taylor & Ives/989 Sixth Ave 212-244-0750
Taylor, Stan Inc/6 E 39th St..212-685-4741
Tercovich, Douglas Assoc Inc/575 Madison Ave 212-838-4800
The Design Office/38 E 23rd St..212-420-1722
The Lamplight Group/342 Madison Ave 212-682-6270
Three/444 East 82nd St #12C 212-988-6267
Tibbot, Randy/838 Broadway 6th Fl 212-505-8565
Tobias, William/6 W 18th St 212-741-1712
Todd, Ann/317 W 87th St #PH..212-799-1016
Toomey, Michael/345 W 88th St 212-877-5817
Toriello, Steven/846 Carroll St, Brooklyn 718-230-4867
Tribich/Glasman Design/150 E 35th St 212-679-6016
Tscherny, George Design/238 E 72nd St....................................212-734-3277
Tunstull Studio/201 Clinton Ave #14G, Brooklyn 718-834-8529

UV

Ultra Arts Inc/150 E 35th St 212-679-7493
Un, David/130 W 25th St 212-924-2090
Valk, John/245 E 24th St...212-889-4490
Viewpoint Graphics/10 Park Ave 212-685-0560
Visible Studio Inc/99 Lexington Ave 212-683-8530
Visual Accents Corp/30 Irving Pl 212-777-7766

W

Wallace/Church Assoc/330 E 48th St 212-755-2903
Waters, John Assoc Inc/3 W 18th St 8th Fl..................................212-807-0717
Waters, Pamela Studio Inc/320 W 13th St 212-620-8100
Webster, Robert Inc/331 Park Ave S..212-677-2966
Weissman, Walter/463 West St #B332..212-989-9694
Whelan Design Office/144 W 27th St...212-691-4404
Wijtvliet, Ine/440 E 56th St 212-319-4444
Wilson, Rex Co/330 Seventh Ave...212-594-3646
Winterson, Finn/401 Eighth Ave #43, Brooklyn 212-219-2711
Wizard Graphics Inc/36 E 30th St 212-686-8200
Wolf, Henry Production Inc/167 E 73rd St 212-472-2500
Wolff, Rudi Inc/135 Central Park West 212-873-5800
Word-Wise/325 W 45th St 212-246-0430
Works/45 W 27th St 212-696-1666
Wurman, Richard Saul/59 Wooster St...212-219-8993

YZ

Yoshimura-Fisher Graphic Design/284 Lafayette St......................212-431-4776
Young Goldman Young Inc/320 E 46th St 212-697-7820
Zahor & Bender/200 E 33rd St 212-686-1121
Zazula, Hy Inc/2 W 46th St 2nd Fl..212-581-2747
Zeitsoff, Elaine/241 Central Park West 212-580-1282
Zimmerman & Foyster/22 E 21st St 212-674-0259
Zuzzolo Graphics/99-31 64th Ave #F2, Rego Pk 718-830-7116

NORTHEAST

A

Action Incentive/2 Townlake Cir, Rochester, NY 716-427-2410
Adam Filippo & Moran/1206 Fifth Ave, Pittsburgh, PA..................412-261-3720
Adler-Schwartz Graphics/6 N Park Dr Park Ctr, Hunt Valley, MD...........410-628-0600
Advertising Design Assoc Inc/1220 Ridgley St, Baltimore, MD.............301-752-2181
Altschul, Charles/356 Riverbank Rd, Stamford, CT.......................203-329-7251
American Tech Systems/5 Suburban Park Dr, Billerica, MA 617-272-8890
Anderson, Bill/27 Minkel Rd, Ossining, NY..................................914-762-4867
Aries Graphics/Massabesic, Manchester, NH 603-668-0811
Arts and Words/1025 Conn Ave NW #300, Washington, DC.................202-463-4880
Ashton, David & Co/611 Cathedral St, Baltimore, MD 301-727-1151

B

Baese, Gary/2229 N Charles St, Baltimore, MD.............................410-235-2226
Bain, S Milo/3 Shaw Lane, Hartsdale, NY.....................................914-946-0144

BAIRDesign/38 Sunset Ave, W Bridgewater, MA..........................508-580-9903
Baker, Arthur/PO Box 29, Germantown, NY 518-537-4438
Baldassini, Paul/234 Clarendon St, Boston, MA...........................617-236-0190
Baldwin, James/1467 Jordan Ave, Crofton, MD............................301-721-1896
Bally Design Inc/420 N Craig St, Pittsburgh, PA...........................412-621-9009
Barton-Gillet/10 S Gay St, Baltimore, MD 301-685-6800
Belser, Burkey/1818 N St NW #110, Washington, DC...................202-775-0333
Bennardo, Churik Design/1311 Old Freeport Rd, Pittsburgh, PA.........412-963-0133
Blake + Barancik Design/135 S 18th St, Philadelphia, PA.............215-977-9540
Bodzioch, Leon/59 Smith St, Chelmsford, MA..............................617-250-0265
Bogus, Sidney A & Assoc/22 Corey St, Melrose, MA....................617-662-6660
Bomzer Design Inc/66 Canal St, Boston, MA................................617-227-5151
Bowers, John D/PO Box 101, Radnor, PA 215-688-5541
Bradbury, Robert & Assoc/26 Halsey Ln, Closter, NJ...................201-768-6395
Brady, John Design Consultants/130 7th St, Pittsburgh, PA..........412-288-9300
Breckenridge Designs/2025 I St NW #300, Washington, DC.........202-833-5700
Breiner, Joanne/11 Webster St, Medford, MA...............................617-354-8378
Bressler, Peter Design Assoc/301 Cherry St, Philadelphia, PA.....215-925-7100
Bridy, Dan/625 Stanwix St #2402, Pittsburgh, PA........................412-531-4044
Brier, David/38 Park Ave, Rutherford, NJ......................................201-896-8476
Brown and Craig Inc/407 N Charles St, Baltimore, MD 301-837-2727
Brownstone Group/8 Raymond St, S Norwalk, CT.........................203-866-9970
Buckett, Bill Assoc/137 Gibbs St, Rochester, NY.........................716-546-6580
Byrne, Ford/100 N 20th St, Philadelphia, PA.................................215-564-0500

C

Cable, Jerry Design/133 Kuhl Rd, Flemington, NJ........................908-788-6750
Calingo, Diane/3711 Lawrence Ave, Kensington, MD 301-949-3557
Cameron Inc/9 Appleton St, Boston, MA.......................................617-338-4408
Campbell Harrington & Brear/352 W Market St, York, PA..............717-846-2947
Carmel, Abraham/7 Peter Beet Dr, Peekskill, NY..........................914-737-1439
Cascio, Chris/456 Glenbrook Rd, Stamford, CT.............................203-358-0519
Case/11 Dupont Circle NW #400, Washington, DC 202-328-5900
Chaparos Productions Limited/1112 6th St NW, Washington, DC.........202-289-4838
Charysyn & Charysyn/Route 42, Westkill, NY................................518-989-6720
Chase, David O Design Inc/E Genesee St, Skaneateles, NY.........315-685-5715
Chronicle Design/1333 New Hampshire Ave NW, Washington, DC........202-828-3519
Cleary Design/118-A N Division St, Salisbury, MD.........................301-546-1040
Cliggett, Jack/703 Redwood Ave, Yeadon, PA..............................215-623-1606
Colangelo, Ted/340 Pemberwick Rd (The Mill), Greenwich, CT.........203-531-3600
Colopy Dale Inc/850 Ridge Ave, Pittsburgh, PA.............................412-332-6706
Concept Packaging Inc/5 Horizon Rd, Ft Lee, NJ...........................201-224-5762
Consolidated Visual Center Inc/2529 Kenilworth Ave, Tuxedo, MD......301-772-7300
Cook & Shanosky Assoc/103 Carnegie Ctr #203, Princeton, NJ.........609-452-1666
Cooper, Steven/39 Bancroft Ave, Reading, MA..............................617-944-8080
Corey & Company/ Boston, MA...617-266-1850
Cundy, David/82 Main St, New Caanan, CT....................................203-972-3350
Curran & Connors Inc/333 Marcus Blvd, Hauppauge, NY...............516-433-6600

D

D'Art Studio Inc/PO Box 299, N Scituate, MA................................617-545-7313
Dakota Design/900 W Valley Rd #601, Wayne, PA..........................215-293-0900
Dale, Terry/2824 Hurst Terrace NW, Washington, DC.....................202-244-3866
Dawson Designers Associates/21 Dean St, Assonet, MA................617-644-2940
Dean, Jane/13 N Duke St, Lancaster, PA.......................................717-295-4638
DeCesare, John/1091 Post Rd, Darien, CT.....................................203-655-6057
DeMartin-Marona-Cranstoun-Downes/911 Washington St,
Wilmington, DE..302-654-5277
Design Comp Inc/5 Colony St #303, Meriden, CT............................203-235-6696
Design for Medicine Inc/301 Cherry St, Philadelphia, PA................215-925-7100
Design Group of Boston/437 Boylston St, Boston, MA.....................617-437-1084
Design Resource/700 S Henderson Rd #308B, King of Prussia, PA......215-265-8585
Design Trends/4 Broadway PO Box 119, Valhalla, NY......................914-948-0902
Designed Images/25 Chicopee St, Chicopee, MA............................413-594-2681
Dever, Jeffrey L/7619 S Arbory Lane, Laurel, MD............................301-776-2812
Dezinno, Richard/348 Neipsic Rd, Glastonbury, CT.........................203-659-1624
DiFiore Associates/625 Stanwix St #2507, Pittsburgh, PA...............412-471-0608
Dimensional Illustrators Inc/362 2nd St Pike, Southampton, PA.........215-953-1415
Dimmick, Gary/47 Riverview Ave, Pittsburgh, PA............................412-321-7225
DJV & Assoc/Rt 102, Chester, NH..603-887-3585
Dohanos, Steven/271 Sturges Highway, Westport, CT.....................203-227-3541
Downing, Allan/50 Francis St, Needham, MA..................................617-449-4784

EF

Educational Media/Graphics Division/GU Med Ctr

3900 Reservoir Rd, Washington, DC 202-625-2211
Egress Concepts/20 Woods Bridge Rd, Katonah, NY 914-232-8433
Endres, Michael/7100 Central Ave, Takoma Park, MD 301-891-1000
Erickson, Peter/46 Pleasant St, Marlboro, MA 508-481-2288
Eucalyptus Tree Studio/2221 Morton St, Baltimore, MD...................410-243-0211
Evans Garber & Paige/2631 Genesee St, Utica, NY 315-733-2313
Fader Jones & Zarkades/797 Boylston St, Boston, MA 617-267-7779
Falcone & Assoc/13 Watchung Ave Box 637, Chatham, NJ 201-635-2900
Fannell Studio/298-A Columbus Ave, Boston, MA 617-267-0895
Finnin, Teresa/655 Washington Blvd #602, Stamford, CT...................203-348-4104
Forum Inc/1226 Post Rd, Fairfield, CT 203-259-5686
Fossella, Gregory Assoc/479 Commonwealth Ave, Boston, MA...................617-267-4940
Foster, Stephen Design/17 51st St #5, Weehawken , NJ...................201-866-9040
Fraser, Robert & Assoc Inc/1101 N Calvert St, Baltimore, MD 301-685-3700
Freelance Studio/271 Rte 46 W #F109, Fairfield, NJ 201-227-3904
Fresh Produce/328-B S Broadway, Baltimore, MD 301-821-1815
Froelich Advertising Service/8 Wanamaker Ave, Mahwah, NJ...................201-529-1737
Frohman, Al/2277 4th St, East Meadow, NY 516-735-2771
Full Circle Design/726 Pacific St, Baltimore, MD 301-523-5903

G

Galeano, Margaret/35 Burwell Ave, Milford, CT 203-877-4313
Garrett, JB Studios/2050 W Stanton St, York, PA...................717-846-7056
Gasser, Gene/300 Main St, Chatham, NJ 201-635-6020
Gateway Studios/225 Ross St, Pittsburgh, PA...................412-471-7224
Gatter Inc/68 Purchase St, Rye, NY 914-967-5600
GK+D Communications/2311 Calvert St NW #300, Washington, DC ...202-328-0414
Glass, Al/3312 M St NW, Washington, DC...................202-333-3993
Glenn, Raymond/39 Edgerton Rd, Wallinford, CT...................203-269-5643
Glickman, Frank Inc/180 Mosshill Rd, Boston, MA...................617-524-2200
Goldner, Linda/709 Rittenhouse Savoy, Philadelphia, PA 215-735-8370
Gonzalez, Andres/1435 Bedford St #8C, Stamford, CT...................212-909-9358
Good, Peter Graphic Design/Pequot Press Bldg, Chester, CT...................203-526-9597
Gorelick, Alan Design/High St Court, Morristown, NJ 201-898-1991
Graham Associates Inc/1899 L St NW, Washington, DC 202-833-9657
Grant Marketing Assoc/1100 E Hector St, Conshohocken, PA...................215-834-0550
Graphicenter/1101 2nd St NE, Washington, DC 202-544-0333
Graphics By Gallo/1800-B Swann St NW, Washington, DC...................202-234-7700
Graphicus Corp/2025 Maryland Ave, Baltimore, MD...................301-727-5553
Graves Fowler & Assoc/14532 Carona Dr, Silver Spring, MD...................301-236-9808
Grear, Malcolm Designers Inc/391 Eddy St, Providence, RI 401-331-5656
Green, Mel/31 Thorpe Rd, Needham Hts, MA 617-449-6777
Greenebaum Design/86 Walnut St, Natick, MA 617-655-8146
Greenfield, Peggy/2 Lewis Rd, Foxboro, MA 617-543-6644
Gregory & Clyburne/59 Grove St, New Canaan, CT 203-966-8343
Groff, Jay Michael/515 Silver Spring Ave, Silver Spring, MD...................301-565-0431
Groth, Donna/13 Seventh Ave E, East Northport, NY...................516-757-1182
Group Four Design/PO Box 717, Avon, CT 203-678-1570
Guancione, Karen/262 DeWitt Ave, Belleville, NJ 201-450-9490
Guerrette, Muriel/97-A Perry St, Unionville, CT...................203-675-9866
Gunn Associates/275 Newbury St, Boston, MA 617-267-0618

H

Hain, Robert Assoc/346 Park Ave, Scotch Plains, NJ...................908-322-1717
Hammond Design Assoc/35 Amherst St, Milford, NH...................603-673-5253
Harvey, Ed/PO Box 23755, Washington, DC 703-671-0880
Hegemann Associates/One S Franklin St, Nyack, NY...................914-358-7348
Helms, Nina/25 Forest Ln, Westbury, NY...................516-997-6567
Herbick & Held/1117 Wolfendale St, Pittsburgh, PA...................412-321-7400
Herman, Sid & Assoc/930 Massachusetts Ave, Cambridge, MA...................617-876-6464
Heyck, Edith/36 Liberty St, Newburyport, MA 508-462-9027
Hill, Michael/2433 Maryland Ave, Baltimore, MD 410-366-8338
Hillmuth, James/3613 Norton Pl, Washington, DC...................202-244-0465
Holl, RJ/ Art Directions/McBride Rd/Box 44, Wales, MA 413-245-5024
Holloway, Martin/56 Mt Horeb Rd, Plainfield, NJ...................908-563-0169
Hough, Jack Inc/25 Seirhill Rd, Norwalk, CT...................203-846-2666
Hrivnak, James/10822 Childs Ct, Silver Spring, MD 301-681-9090
Huerta, Gerard/45 Corbin Dr, Darien, CT
(Inside Back Flap/Books 1 & 2)...................203-656-0505
Huyssen, Roger/45 Corbin Dr, Darien, CT
(Inside Back Flap/Books 1 & 2)...................203-656-0200

IJ

Image Consultants/3 Overlook Dr, Amherst, NH 603-673-5512
Image Factory/2229 N Charles St, Baltimore, MD 301-235-2226

Impress/PO Box 761, Williamsburg, MA...................413-268-3040
Independent Design/451 D St #811, Boston, MA 617-439-4944
Inkstone Design/32 Laurel St, Fairfield, CT 203-336-9599
Innovations & Development Inc/115 River Rd, Edgewater, NJ...................201-941-5500
Irish, Gary Graphics/45 Newbury St, Boston, MA...................617-247-4168
Itin, Helen/100 Cutler Rd, Greenwich, CT...................203-869-1928
Jarrin Design Inc/PO Box 421, Pound Ridge, NY 914-764-4625
Jensen, R S/819 N Charles St, Baltimore, MD...................301-727-3411
Jezierny, John Michael/20 Kenter Pl, Westville, CT...................203-689-8170
Johnson & Simpson Graphic Design/49 Bleeker St, Newark, NJ...................201-624-7788
Johnson Design Assoc/403 Massachusetts Ave, Acton, MA...................617-263-5345
Jones, Jerry/36 S Paca St #108, Baltimore, MD...................301-727-4222
Jones, Tom & Jane Kearns/2803 18th ST NW, Washington, DC...................202-232-1921

K

Kahana Associates/419 Benjamin Fox Pavilion, Jenkintown, PA...................215-887-0422
Karp, Rudi/28 Dudley Ave, Landsowne, PA 215-284-5949
Katz-Wheeler Design/37 S 20th St, Philadelphia, PA 215-567-5668
Kaufman, Henry & Assoc/2233 Wisconsin Ave NW, Washington, DC.....202-333-0700
KBH Graphics/1023 St Paul Street, Baltimore, MD 301-539-7916
Keats, Debby/23 Washington Ave, Schenectady, NY...................518-382-7560
Ketchum International/4 Gateway Ctr, Pittsburgh, PA...................412-456-3693
King-Casey Inc/199 Elm St, New Canaan, CT 203-966-3581
Klim, Matt & Assoc/PO Box Y, Avon Park N, Avon, CT...................203-678-1222
Klotz, Don/296 Millstone Rd, Wilton, CT...................203-762-9111
Knabel, Lonnie/34 Station St, Brookline, MA 617-566-4464
Knox, Harry & Assoc/9914 Locust St, Glenndale, MD...................304-464-1665
Kostanecki, Andrew Inc/47 Elm St, New Canaan, CT...................203-966-1681
Kovanen, Erik/102 Twin Oak Lane, Wilton, CT...................203-762-8961
Kramer/Miller/Lomden/Glossman/1528 Waverly, Philadelphia, PA...................215-545-7077
Krohne, David/2727 29th St NW, Washington, DC...................202-265-2371
Krone Graphic Design/426 S 3rd St, Lemoyne, PA...................717-774-7431
Kulhanek, Paul/Letter Perfect/167 Cherry St #177, Milford, CT 203-876-0697

L

LAM Design Inc/661 N Broadway, White Plains, NY...................914-948-4777
Langdon, John/4529 Pine St, Philadelphia, PA 215-476-4312
Lapham/Miller Assoc/34 Essex St, Andora, MA...................617-367-0110
Latham Brefka Associates/833 Boylston St, Boston, MA...................617-536-8787
Laufer, Joseph Mark/2308 Lombard St #1B, Philadelphia, PA 215-545-2191
Lausch, David Graphics/2613 Maryland Ave, Baltimore, MD 301-235-7453
Lebbad, James A/24 Independence Way, Titusville, NJ...................212-645-5260
Lebowitz, Mo/2599 Phyllis Dr, N Bellemore, NY 516-826-3397
Leeds, Judith K Studio/14 Rosemont Ct, N Caldwell, NJ...................201-226-3552
Lees, John & Assoc/930 Massachusetts Ave, Cambridge, MA...................617-876-6465
Lenney, Ann/2737 Devonshire Pl NW, Washington, DC...................202-667-1786
Leotta Designers Inc/303 Harry St, Conshohocken, PA...................215-828-8820
Lester Associates Inc/100 Snake Hill Rd Box D, West Nyack, NY...................914-358-6100
Levinson Zaprauskis Assoc/15 W Highland Ave, Philadelphia, PA...................215-248-5242
Lewis, Hal Design/104 S 20th St, Philadelphia, PA...................215-563-4461
Lion Hill Studio/1233 W Mt Royal Ave, Baltimore, MD...................301-837-6218
Livingston Studio/29 Robbins Ave, Elmsford, NY...................914-592-4220
Lizak, Matt/Blackplain Rd RD #1, N Smithfield, RI...................401-766-8885
Logan, Denise/203 Rugby Ave, Rochester, NY...................716-235-0893
Lose, Hal/533 W Hortter St, Philadelphia, PA (P 887)....215-849-7635
Loukin, Serge Inc/PO Box 425, Solomons, MD...................212-645-2788
Luebbers Inc/2300 Walnut St #732, Philadelphia, PA...................215-567-2360
Luma/702 N Eutaw St, Baltimore, MD...................301-523-5903
Lussier, Mark/38 Cove Ave, E Norwalk, CT...................203-852-0363
Lyons, Lisa/9 Deanne St, Gardiner, ME...................207-582-1602

M

MacIntosh, Rob Communication/93 Massachusetts, Boston, MA...................617-267-4912
Magalos, Christopher/3308 Church Rd, Cherry Hill, NJ 609-667-7433
Maglio, Mark/PO Box 872, Plainville, CT...................203-793-0771
Major Assoc/1101 N Calvert #1703, Baltimore, MD...................301-752-6174
Mandala/520 S Third St, Philadelphia, PA 215-923-6020
Mandle, James/300 Forest Ave, Paramus, NJ...................201-967-7900
Mansfield, Malcolm/20 Aberdeen St, Boston, MA...................617-437-1922
Marcus, Sarna/4720 Montgomery Ln #903, Bethesda, MD...................301-951-7044
Mariuzza, Pete/146 Hardscrabble Rd, Briarcliff Manor, NY 914-769-3310
Martucci Studio/116 Newbury St, Boston, MA...................617-266-6960
MDB Communications Inc/932 Hungerford Dr #23, Rockville, MD...................301-279-9093
Media Concepts/25 N Main St, Assonet, MA...................617-437-1382
Melanson, Donya Assoc/437 Main St, Charlestown, MA...................617-241-7300

Melone, Michael/RD 3 Box 123, Canonsburg, PA................412-746-5165
Mendez, Nancy/9816 Rosensteel Ave, Silver Spring, MD..................301-608-8075
Merry, Ann (Merry Men)/246 Western Ave, Sherborn, MA................508-655-4955
Meyer, Bonnie/259 Collignon Way #2A, River Vale, NJ................201-666-5763
Micolucci, Nicholas Assoc/515 Schumaker Rd, King of Prussia, PA....215-265-3320
Miho, J Inc/46 Chalburn Rd, Redding, CT................203-938-3214
Miller, Irving D Inc/33 Great Neck Rd, Great Neck, NY................516-466-6585
Mitchell & Company/1029 33rd St NW, Washington, DC................202-342-6025
Monti, Ron/106 W University, Baltimore, MD................301-366-8952
Morlock Graphics/722 Camberly Cir #C7, Towson, MD................301-825-5080
Moss, John C/4805 Bayard Blvd, Chevy Chase, MD................301-320-3912
Mueller & Wister/1211 Chestnut St #607, Philadelphia, PA................215-568-7260
Muller-Munk, Peter Assoc/2100 Smallman St, Pittsburgh, PA................412-261-5161
Myers, Gene Assoc/5575 Hampton, Pittsburgh, PA................412-661-6314

NO

Nason Design Assoc/329 Newbury, Boston, MA................617-266-7286
Navratil Art Studio/905 Century Bldg, Pittsburgh, PA................412-471-4322
New York Design/1984 Monroe Ave, Rochester, NY................716-473-5100
Nimeck, Fran/RD 4/ 358-A Riva Ave , North Brunswick, NJ................908-821-8741
Noi Viva Design/220 Ferris Ave, White Plains, NY................914-946-1951
Nolan & Assoc/4100 Cathedral Ave NW, Washington, DC................202-363-6553
North Charles St Design/222 W Saratoga St, Baltimore, MD................301-539-4040
Odyssey Design Group/918 F St NW #200, Washington, DC................202-783-6240
Ollio Studio/Fulton Bldg, Pittsburgh, PA................412-281-4483
On Target/1185 E Putnam Ave, Riverside, CT................203-637-8300

P

Paganucci, Bob/17 Terry Ct, Montvale, NJ................201-391-1752
Paine/ Bluett/ Paine Inc/4617 Edgefield Rd, Bethesda, MD................301-493-8445
Panke, Nick/116 Wintonbury Ave, Bloomfield, CT................203-242-6576
Parry, Ivor/Eastchester, NY................914-961-7338
Parshall, C A Inc/200 Henry St, Stamford, CT................212-947-5971
Pasinski, Irene Assoc/6026 Penn Circle S, Pittsburgh, PA................412-661-9000
Patterson, Margaret/234 Clarendon St, Boston, MA................617-424-1236
Peck, Gail M/1637 Harvard St NW, Washington, DC................202-667-7448
Perspectives In Comms/1637 Harvard St NW, Washington, DC................202-667-7448
Pesanelli, David Assoc/14508 Barkwood Dr, Rockville, MD................301-871-7355
Petty, Daphne/1460 Belmont St NW, Washington, DC................202-667-8222
Phase One Graphics/315 Market St, Sudbury, PA................717-286-1111
Phillips Design Assoc/25 Dry Dock Ave, Boston, MA................617-423-7676
Picture That Inc/880 Briarwood Rd, Newtown Square, PA................215-353-8833
Pilz, Misty/324 Elm St #203B, Monroe, CT................203-261-7665
Pinkston, Steve /212 W Miner St, West Chester, PA................215-692-2939
Planert, Paul Design Assoc/4650 Baum Blvd, Pittsburgh, PA................412-621-1275
Plataz, George/516 Martin Bldg, Pittsburgh, PA................412-322-3177
Porter, Eric/37 S 20th St, Philadelphia, PA................215-563-1904
Presentation Assocs/1346 Connecticut Ave NW, Washington, DC................202-333-0080
Production Studio/382 Channel Dr, Port Washington, NY................516-944-6688
Profile Press Inc/40 Greenwood Ave, E Islip, NY................516-277-6319
Prokell, Jim/307 4th Ave #1100, Pittsburgh, PA................412-232-3636
Publication Services Inc/990 Hope St, PO Box 4625, Stamford, CT................203-348-7351

R

Rajcula, Vincent/176 Long Meadow Hill, Brookfield, CT................203-775-2420
Ralcon Inc/431 W Market St, West Chester, PA................215-692-2840
Rand, Paul Inc/87 Goodhill Rd, Weston, CT................203-227-5375
Redtree Associates/1740 N St NW, Washington, DC................202-628-2900
Renaissance Communications/7835 Eastern Ave, Silver Spring, MD................301-587-1505
Research Planning Assoc/1831 Chestnut St, Philadelphia, PA................215-561-9700
Richardson/Smith/139 Lewis Wharf, Boston, MA................617-367-1491
Richman, Mel/15 N Presidential Blvd, Bala Cynwyd, PA................215-667-8900
Rieb, Robert/10 Reichert Circle, Westport, CT................203-227-0061
Ringel, Leonard Design/18 Wheeler Rd, Kendall Park, NJ................908-297-9084
Ritter, Richard Design Inc/31 Waterloo Ave, Berwyn, PA................215-296-0400
Ritzau van Dijk Design/7 Hart Ave, Hopewell, NJ................609-466-2797
RKM Inc/5307 29th St NW, Washington, DC................202-364-0148
Robinson, John/370 State St, North Haven, CT................203-288-7957
Rogalski Assoc/186 Lincoln St, Boston, MA................617-451-2111
Romax Studio/32 Club Circle, Stamford, CT................203-324-4260
Rosborg Inc/15 Commerce Rd, Newton, CT................203-426-3171
Roth, J H Inc/13 Inwood Ln E, Peekskill, NY................914-737-6784
Roth, Judee/103 Cornelia St, Boonton, NJ................201-316-5411
Rubin, Marc Design Assoc/PO Box 440, Breesport, NY................607-739-0871
RZA Inc/122 Mill Pond Rd, Park Ridge, NJ................201-391-8500

S

Samerjan/Edigraph /45 Cantitoe St, RFD 1, Katonah, NY................914-232-3725
Sanchez/138 S 20th St, Philadelphia, PA................215-564-2223
Schneider Design/2633 N Charles St, Baltimore, MD................301-467-2611
Schoenfeld, Cal/6 Colony Ct #B, Parsippany, NJ................201-263-1635
Schrecongost, Paul/284 Liberty St, Salem, WV................304-782-3499
Selame Design Assocs/2330 Washington St, Newton Lwr Falls, MA................617-969-6690
Shapiro, Deborah/150 Bentley Ave, Jersey City, NJ................201-432-5198
Silvia, Ken/15 Story St, Cambridge, MA................617-451-1995
Simpson Booth Designers/14 Arrow St, Cambridge, MA................617-661-2630
Smarilli Graphics Inc/602 N Front St, Warmleysburg, PA................717-737-8141
Smith, Agnew Moyer/850 Ridge Ave, Pittsburgh, PA................412-322-6333
Smith, Doug/17 Althea Lane, Larchmont, NY................914-834-3997
Smith, Gail Hunter/PO Box 217, Barnegat Light, NJ................609-494-9136
Smith, Tyler Art Direction/127 Dorrance St, Providence, RI................401-751-1220
Smizer Design/59 Wareham St, Boston, MA................617-423-3350
Snowden Assocs Inc/5217 Wisconsin Ave NW, Washington, DC................202-362-8944
Soree, Sal/97 Forest Hill Rd, W Orange, NJ................201-325-3591
Sparkman & Bartholomew/1120 Connecticut Ave, Washington, DC................202-785-2414
Spectrum Boston/79-A Chestnut St, Boston, MA................617-367-1008
Stamler Design/220 Marlborough St #1, Boston, MA................617-262-6250
Stansbury Ronsaville Wood Inc/17 Pinewood St, Annapolis, MD................301-261-8662
Star Design Inc/PO Box 30, Moorestown, NJ................609-235-8150
Steel Art Co Inc/75 Brainerd Rd, Allston, MA................617-566-4079
Stettler, Wayne Design/2311 Fairmount Ave, Philadelphia, PA................215-235-1230
Stockman & Andrews Inc/684 Warren Ave, E Providence, RI................401-438-0694
Stolt, Jill Design/1239 University Ave, Rochester, NY................716-461-2594
Stuart, Neil/RD 1 Box 64, Mahopac, NY................914-618-1662
Studio Six Design/6 Lynn Dr, Springfield, NJ................201-379-5820
Studio Three/118 South St, Philadelphia, PA................215-925-4700

TV

Takajian, Asdur/17 Merlin Ave, N Tarrytown, NY................914-631-5553
Tapa Graphics/20 Bluff Rd, Thorndale, PA................215-384-7081
Taylor, Pat/3540 'S' St NW, Washington, DC................202-338-0962
Telesis/107 E 25th, Baltimore, MD................301-235-2000
Tetrad Design/21 Southgate, Annapolis, MD................410-269-1326
The Artery/12 W Biddle St, Baltimore, MD................301-752-2979
The Avit Corp/1355 15th St #100, Fort Lee, NJ................201-886-1100
The Creative Dept/130 S 17th, Philadelphia, PA................215-988-0390
The Graphic Suite/235 Shady Ave, Pittsburgh, PA................412-661-6699
The Peregrine Group/375 Sylvan Ave, Englewood Cliffs, NJ................201-567-8585
The Studio Group/1713 Lanier Pl NW, Washington, DC................202-332-3003
The Visualizers/1100 E Carson St, Pittsburgh, PA................412-488-0944
Third Millenium Comm/979 Summer St, Stamford, CT................203-325-9104
Thompson, Bradbury/Jones Park, Riverside, CT................203-637-3614
Thomson/Corcetto & Co/4 Park Plaza #205, Wyomissing, PA................215-376-5170
Toelke, Cathleen/PO Box 487, Rhinebeck, NY
(P 762,763)................914-876-8776
Torode, Barbara/2311 Lombard St, Philadelphia, PA................215-732-6792
Total Collateral Grp/992 Old Eagles School Rd, Wayne, PA................215-687-8016
Town Studios Inc/212 9th St Victory Bldg, Pittsburgh, PA................412-471-5353
Troller, Fred Assoc Inc/12 Harbor Ln, Rye, NY................914-698-1405
Van Der Sluys Graphics Inc/3303 18th St NW, Washington, DC................202-265-3443
Vance Wright Adams & Assoc/930 N Lincoln Ave, Pittsburgh, PA................412-322-1800
VanDine, Horton, McNamara, Manges/100 Ross St, Pittsburgh, PA................412-261-4280
Vann, Bob/5306 Knox St, Philadelphia, PA................215-843-4841
Vinick, Bernard Assoc Inc/211 Wethersfield Ave, Hartford, CT................203-525-4293
Viscom Inc/PO Box 10498, Baltimore, MD................301-764-0005
Visual Research & Design/360 Commonwealth Ave, Boston, MA................617-536-2111

WYZ

Warkulwiz Design/1704 Locust St, Philadelphia, PA................215-546-0880
Wasserman's, Myron Design Group/113 Arch St, Philadelphia, PA................215-922-4545
Weadock, Rutka/1627 E Baltimore St, Baltimore, MD................301-563-2100
Webb & Co/839 Beacon St, Boston, MA................617-262-6980
Weems, Samuel/One Arcadia Pl, Boston, MA................617-288-8888
Weymouth Design/234 Congress St, Boston, MA................617-542-2647
Whibley, Edward/4733 Bethesda Ave #345, Bethesda, MD................301-951-5200
Wickham & Assoc Inc/1215 Connecticut Ave NW, Washington, DC................202-296-4860
Wiggin, Gail/23 Old Kings Hwy S, Darien, CT................203-655-1920
Willard, Janet Design Assoc/4284 Route 8, Allison Park, PA................412-486-8100
Williams Associates/200 Broadway #205, Lynnfield, MA................617-599-1818
Wilke, Jerry /Amberlands 28v, Croton-on Hudson, NY................914-271-6766

Wilsonwork Graphic Design/1811 18th St NW, Washington, DC..........202-332-9016
Winick, Sherwin/115 Willow Ave #2R, Hoboken, NJ 201-659-9116
Wolf, Anita/49 Melcher St, Boston, MA 617-426-3929
Wood, William/68 Windsor Pl, Glen Ridge, NJ 201-743-5543
Wright, Kent M Assoc Inc/22 Union Ave, Sudbury, MA 617-443-9909
WW2 Design/250 Post Rd E, Westport, CT..203-454-2550
Yavorsky, Fredrick/2300 Walnut St #617, Philadelphia, PA 215-564-6690
Yeo, Robert/746 Park Ave, Hoboken, NJ...201-659-3277
Yurdin, Carl Indust Design/2 Harborview Rd, Port Washington, NY 516-944-7811
Zeb Graphics/1312 18th St NW, Washington, DC...................................202-293-1687
Zimmerman, Amy/19 Salem Lane, Port Washington,
NY (P 659)..**212-243-1333**
Zingone, Robin/32 GodmanRd, Madison, CT..212-288-8045
Zmiejko & Assoc Design Agcy/PO Box 126, Freeland, PA....................717-636-2304

SOUTHEAST

A

Ace Art/171 Walnut St, New Orleans, LA......................................504-861-2222
Alphabet Group/1441 Peachtree NE, Atlanta, GA............................404-892-6500
Alphacom Inc/14955 NE Sixth Ave, N Miami, FL 305-949-5588
Art Services/1135 Spring St, Atlanta, GA......................................404-892-2105
Arts & Graphics/4010 Justine Dr, Annandale, VA.............................703-941-2560
Arunski, Joe & Assoc/10660 NW 17th Pl, Plantation, FL...................305-473-4114
Aurelio & Friends Inc/11110 SW 128th Ave, Miami, FL......................305-385-0723
Austin, Jeremiah/1483 Chain Bridge Rd #300, McLean, VA 703-893-7004

B

Baskin & Assoc/1021 Prince St, Alexandria, VA...............................703-836-3316
Bender, Diane/2729 S Cleveland St, Arlington, VA............................703-521-1006
Beveridge and Associates, Inc/2020 N 14th St #444, Arlington, VA 202-243-2888
Blair Incorporated/5819 Seminary Rd, Bailey's Crossroads, VA...........703-820-9011
Bodenhamer, William S Inc/7380 SW 121st St, Miami, FL...................305-253-9284
Bonner Advertising Art/1315 Washington Ave, New Orleans, LA 504-895-7938
Bowles, Aaron/1686 Sierra Woods Ct, Reston, VA............................703-437-4102
Brimm, Edward & Assoc/140 S Ocean Blvd, Palm Beach, FL 305-655-1059
Brothers Bogusky/11950 W Dixie Hwy, Miami, FL.............................305-891-3642
Bugdal Group/7130 SW 48th St, Miami, FL.....................................305-665-6686
Burch, Dan Associates/2338 Frankfort, Louisville, KY 502-895-4881

C

Carlson Design/1218 NW 6th St, Gainesville, FL...............................904-373-3153
Chartmasters Inc/3525 Piedmont,7 Pdmt Ctr, Atlanta, GA 404-262-7610
Clavena, Barbara/6000 Stone Lake, Birmingham, AL 205-991-8909
Coastline Studios/489 Semoran Blvd #109, Casselberry, FL...............407-339-1166
Communications Graphics Gp/3717 Columbia Pike, Arlington, VA 703-979-8500
Cooper-Copeland Inc/1151 W Peachtree St NW, Atlanta, GA..............404-892-3472
Corporate Design/Plaza Level-Colony Sq, Atlanta, GA.......................404-876-6062
Creative Design Assoc/9330 Silver Thorn Rd, Lake Park, FL...............305-627-2467
Creative Services Inc/2317 Esplanade St, New Orleans, LA................504-943-0842
Creative Services Unlimited/3080 N Tamiami Tr #3, Naples, FL...........813-262-0201
Critt Graham & Assoc/1190 W Orvid Hills Dr #T45, Atlanta, GA 404-320-1737

DFG

DeRose, Andrea Legg/13 East Mason Ave, Alexandria, VA.................703-836-3204
Design Associates/1601 Kent St #1010, Arlington, VA 703-243-7717
Design Inc/9304 St Marks Pl, Fairfax, VA 703-273-5053
Design Workshop Inc/7430 SW 122nd St, Miami, FL..........................305-378-1099
Designcomp/202 Dominion Rd NE, Vienna, VA 703-938-1822
Dodane, Eric/8525 Richland Colony Rd, Knoxville, TN........................615-693-6857
First Impressions/4411 W Tampa Bay Blvd, Tampa, FL.......................813-875-0555
Foster, Kim A/1801 SW 11th St, Miami, FL......................................305-642-1801
Gerbino Advertising/2000 W Commercial Blvd, Ft Lauderdale, FL........305-776-5050
Gestalt Associates, Inc/1509 King St, Alexandria, VA........................703-683-1126
Get Graphic Inc/160 Maple Ave E #201, Vienna, VA 202-938-1822
Grafik Communication/300 Montgomery St, Alexandria, VA................703-683-4686
Graphic Arts Inc/1433 Powhatan St, Alexandria, VA..........................703-683-4303
Graphic Consultants Inc/5133 Lee Hwy, Arlington, VA........................703-536-8377
Graphics Group/6111 PchtreeDunwdy Rd#G101, Atlanta, GA.............404-391-9929
Graphicstudio/12305 NE 12th Ct, N Miami, FL 305-893-1015
Great Incorporated/601 Madison St, Alexandria, VA...........................703-836-6020
Gregg, Bill Advertising Design/2465 SW 18th Ave A-3309, Miami, FL..305-854-7657

Group 2 Atlanta/3500 Piedmont Rd, Atlanta, GA 404-262-3239

HIJ

Hall Graphics/2600 Douglas Rd #608, Coral Gables, FL.....................305-443-8346
Hall, Steve Graphics/14200 SW 136th St, Miami, FL 305-255-2900
Hauser, Sydney/9 Fillmore Dr, Sarasota, FL 813-388-3021
Hendrix, Jean/PO Box 5754, High Point, NC.....................................919-840-4970
Herchak, Stephen/1735 St Julian Pl, Columbia, SC............................803-799-1800
Identitia Incorporated/1000 N Ashley Dr #515, Tampa, Fl....................813-221-3326
Jensen, Rupert & Assoc Inc/1800 Peachtree Rd #525, Atlanta, GA.....404-352-1010
Johnson Design Gp/3426 N Washington Blvd #102, Arlington, VA.......703-525-0808
Jordan Barrett & Assoc/6701 Sunset Dr, Miami, FL............................305-667-7051

KLM

Kelly & Co Graphic Design Inc/7490 30th Ave N, St Petersburg, FL 813-341-1009
Kjeldsen, Howard Assoc Inc/PO Box 420508, Atlanta, GA 404-266-1897
Klickovich Graphics/1638 Eastern Parkway, Louisville, KY 502-459-0295
Landers Design/4607 NW 6th St #3F, Gainesville, FL.........................904-375-2353
Lowell, Shelley Design/1449 Bates Ct NE, Atlanta, GA 404-636-9149
Marks, David/726 Hillpine Dr NE, Atlanta, GA...................................404-872-1824
Mason, Marlise/7534 Woodberry Ln, Falls Church, VA.......................703-573-4365
Maxine, J & Martin Adv/1497 Chain Bridge Rd #204, McLean, VA.......703-356-5222
McGurren Weber Ink/705 King St 3rd Fl, Alexandria, VA......................703-548-0003
McKenney, Ron/10 Office Park Circle #100, Birmingham, AL...............205-870-5300
MediaFour Inc/7638 Trail Run Rd, Falls Church, VA............................703-573-6117
Moore, William "Casey"/4242 Inverness Rd, Duluth, GA......................404-449-9553
Morgan-Burchette Assoc/6935 Arlington Rd, Bethesda, MD 703-549-2393
Morris, Robert Assoc Inc/6015 B NW 31 Ave, Ft Lauderdale, FL.........305-973-4380
Muhlhausen, John Design Inc/1146 Green St, Roswell, GA.................404-642-1146

PQR

Parallel Group Inc/3091 Maple Dr, Atlanta, GA..................................404-261-0988
Parks, Dick Comm/500 Montgomery St #701, Alexandria, VA 202-255-5500
Pertuit, Jim & Assoc Inc/302 Magazine St #400, New Orleans, LA.......504-568-0808
Pierre, Keith Design/8000 Colony Circle S #305, Tamarac, FL.............305-726-0401
PL&P Advertising Studio/1280 SW 36th Ave, Pompano Beach, FL 307-977-9327
Platt, Don Advertising Art/1399 SE 9th Ave, Hialeah, FL 305-888-3296
Point 6/770 40th Court NE, Ft Lauderdale, FL....................................305-563-6936
Polizos, Arthur Assoc/220 W Freemason St, Norfolk, VA.....................804-622-7033
Positively Main St Graphics/290 Coconut Ave, Sarasota, FL...............813-366-4959
PRB Design Studio/1900 Howell Brnch Rd #3, Winter Park, FL............305-671-7992
Pre-Press Studio Design/1105N Royal St, Alexandria, VA....................703-548-9194
Prep Inc/2615-B Shirlington Rd, Arlington, VA 703-979-6575
Price Weber Market Comm Inc/2101 Production Dr, Louisville, KY.......502-499-9220
Quantum Communications/1730 N Lynn St #400, Arlington, VA 703-841-1400
Rasor & Rasor/1145-D Executive Cir, Cary, NC.................................919-467-3353
Reed, Veronica/503 Lake Drive, Virginia Beach, VA............................804-422-0371
Reinsch, Michael/32 Palmetto Bay Rd, Hilton Head Island, SC 803-842-3298
Richards Design Group/4722 Old Kingston Pike, Knoxville, TN............615-584-3319
Richardson, Hank/2675 Paces Ferry Rd #225, Atlanta, GA 404-433-0973
Rodriguez, Emilio Jr/8270 SW 116 Terrace, Miami, FL 305-235-4700

ST

Sager Assoc Inc/739 S Orange Ave, Sarasota, FL.............................813-366-4192
Salmon, Paul/5826 Jackson's Oak Ct, Burke, VA...............................703-250-4943
Santa & Assoc/3960 N Andrews Ave, Ft Lauderdale, FL......................305-561-0551
Schulwolf, Frank/524 Hardee Rd, Coral Gables, FL 305-665-2129
Sirrine, J E/PO Box 5456, Greenville, SC...803-298-6000
Stewart Lopez Assoc/550 W Kentucky St, Louisville, KY.....................502-583-5502
Studio + Co/13353 Sorento Valley Dr, Largo, FL................................813-595-2275
Tash, Ken/6320 Castle Pl, Falls Church, VA......................................703-237-1712
Thayer Dana Industrial Design/Route 1, Monroe, VA..........................804-929-6359
The Associates Inc/5319 Lee Hwy, Arlington, VA...............................703-534-3940
Thomas, Steve Design/409 East Blvd, Charlotte, NC..........................704-332-4624
Turpin Design Assoc/1762 Century Blvd #B, Atlanta, GA.....................404-320-6963

VW

Varisco, Tom Graphic Design Inc/1925 Esplanade, New Orleans, LA....504-949-2888
Visualgraphics Design/1211 NW Shore Blvd, Tampa, FL 813-877-3804
Whitford, Kim/242 Mead Rd, Decatur, GA...404-371-0860
Whitver, Harry K Graphic Design/208 Reidhurst Ave,
Nashville, TN (P 653) **615-320-1795**
Winner, Stewart Inc/550 W Kentucky St, Louisville, KY........................502-583-5502

Wohler, Luann/6201 Leesburg Pike #403, Falls Church, VA 703-536-1773
Wood, Tom/3925 Peachtree Rd NE, Atlanta, GA.....................................404-262-7424

MIDWEST

A

Aarons, Allan Design/666 Dundee Rd #1701, Northbrook, IL 312-291-9800
Abrams, Kym Design/711 S Dearborn #205, Chicago, IL 312-341-0709
Ades, Leonards Graphic Design/1200 Shermer Rd, Northbrook, IL.....312-564-8863
AKA Design/7380 Marietta St, St Louis, MO 314-781-3389
Album Graphics/1950 N Ruby St, Melrose Park, IL 312-344-9100
Allied Design Group/1701 W Chase, Chicago, IL 312-743-3330
Ampersand Assoc/2454 W 38th St, Chicago, IL 312-523-2282
Anderson Studios/209 W Jackson Blvd, Chicago, IL 312-922-3039
Art Forms Inc/5150 Prospect Ave, Cleveland, OH 216-361-3855
Arvind Khatkate Design/4837 W Jerome St, Skokie, IL 312-679-4129

B

Babcock & Schmid Assoc/3689 Ira Rd, Bath, OH 216-666-8826
Bagby Design/225 N Michigan #2025, Chicago, IL 312-861-1288
Banka Mango Design Inc/274 Merchandise Mart, Chicago, IL 312-467-0059
Barfuss Creative/1331 Lake Dr SE, Grand Rapids, MI 616-459-8888
Barnes, Jeff/666 N Lake Shore Dr #1408, Chicago, IL 312-951-0996
Bartels & Cartsens/3286 Ivanhoe, St Louis, MO 314-781-7377
Benjamin, Burton E Assoc/3391 Summit, Highland Park, IL 312-432-8089
Berg, Don/207 E Michigan, Milwaukee, WI 414-276-7828
Bieger, Walter Assoc/1689 W County Rd F, Arden Hills, MN 612-636-8500
Billman, Jennifer/760 Burr Oak Dr, Westmont, IL 312-323-3616
Blake, Hayward & Co/834 Custer Ave, Evanston, IL 312-864-9800
Bobel, Jane/7543 Juler Ave, Cincinnati, OH 513-791-5337
Boller-Coates-Spadero/445 W Erie, Chicago, IL 312-787-2783
Bowlby, Joseph A/53 W Jackson #711, Chicago, IL 312-922-0890
Bradford-Cout Graphic Design/9933 Lawler, Skokie, IL 312-539-5557
Brooks Stevens Assoc Inc/1415 W Donges Bay Rd, Mequon, WI 414-241-3800

C

Campbell Art Studio/2145 Luray Ave, Cincinnati, OH.........................513-221-3600
Campbell Creative Group/8705 N Port Washington, Milwaukee, WI.....414-351-4150
Carter, Don W/ Industrial Design/8809 E 59th St, Kansas City, MO.......816-356-1874
Centaur Studios Inc/310 Mansion House Ctr, St Louis, MO.................314-421-6485
Chartmasters Inc/150 E Huron St, Chicago, IL 312-787-9040
Clifford, Keesler/6642 West H Ave, Kalamazoo, MI 616-375-0688
Combined Services Inc/501 Lynnhurst Ave, St Paul, MN 612-426-4863
Contours Consulting Design Group/864 Stearns Rd, Bartlett, IL..........312-837-4100
Coons/Beirise Design Assoc/2344 Ashland Ave, Cincinnati, OH.........513-751-7459
Cox, Stephen/424 S Clay, St Louis, MO 314-965-2150
Crosby, Bart/676 St Clair St, Chicago, IL 312-951-2800

D

Day, David Design & Assoc/700 Walnut St, Cincinnati, OH.................513-621-4060
DeBrey Design/6014 Blue Circle #D, Minneapolis, MN 612-935-2292
Dektas Eger Inc/1077 Celestial St, Cincinnati, OH 513-621-7070
Design Alliance Inc/114 E 8th St, Cincinnati, OH 513-621-9373
Design Axis/12 Westerville Sq #330, Westerville, OH 614-448-7995
Design Consultants/505 N Lakeshore Dr #4907, Chicago, IL 312-642-4670
Design Factory/7543 Floyd, Overland Park, KS 913-383-3085
Design Group Three/1114 W Armitage Ave, Chicago, IL 312-337-1775
Design Marketing/900 N Franklin #610, Chicago, IL 312-787-9409
Design Marks Corp/1462 W Irving Park, Chicago, IL 312-327-3669
Design North Inc/8007 Douglas Ave, Racine, WI 414-639-2080
Design One/437 Marshman St, Highland Park, IL 312-433-4140
Design Planning Group/223 W Erie, Chicago, IL 312-943-8400
Design Train/434 Hidden Valley Ln, Cincinnati, OH 513-761-7099
Design Two Ltd/600 N McClurg Ct #330, Chicago, IL 312-642-9888
Deur, Paul/109 Ottawa NW, Grand Rapids, MI 616-458-5661
Di Cristo & Slagle Design/741 N Milwaukee, Milwaukee, WI 414-273-0980
Dickens Design Group/13 W Grand, Chicago, IL 312-222-1850
Dimensional Designs Inc/1101 Southeastern Ave, Indianapolis, IN......317-637-1353
Doty, David Design/661 W Roscoe, Chicago, IL 312-348-1200
Douglas Design/2165 Lakeside Ave, Cleveland, OH 216-621-2558
Dresser, John Design/180 Crescent Knoll E, Libertyville, IL 312-362-4222
Dynamic Graphics Inc/6000 N Forrest Park Dr, Peoria, IL 309-688-9800

EF

Egger/Assoc Inc/812 Busse Hwy, Park Ridge, IL 312-296-9100
Ellies, Dave Indstrl Design/2015 W 5th Ave, Columbus, OH 614-488-7995
Elyria Graphics/147 Winckles St, Elyria, OH 216-365-9384
Emphasis 7 Communications/43 E Ohio #1000, Chicago, IL 312-951-8887
Engelhardt Design/1738 Irving Ave S, Minneapolis, MN 612-377-3389
Environmental Graphics/1101 Southeastern Ave, Indianapolis, IN.......317-634-1458
Epstein & Assoc/11427 Bellflower, Cleveland, OH 216-421-1600
Falk, Robert Design Group/4425 W Pine, St Louis, MO 314-531-1410
Feldkamp-Malloy/180 N Wabash, Chicago, IL 312-263-0633
Ficho & Corley Inc/875 N Michigan Ave, Chicago, IL 312-787-1011
Fleishman-Hillard, Inc/1 Memorial Dr, St Louis, MO 314-982-1700
Flexo Design/57 W Grand, Chicago, IL 312-321-1368
Ford & Earl Assoc Inc/28820 Mound Rd, Warren, MI 313-536-1999
Frederiksen Design/609 S Riverside Dr, Villa Park, IL 312-343-5882
Frink, Chin, Casey Inc/505 E Grant, Minneapolis, MN 612-333-6539

G

Gellman, Stan Graphic Design Studio/4509 Laclede, St Louis, MO 314-361-7676
Gerhardt & Clemons/848 Eastman St, Chicago, IL 312-337-3443
Glenbard Graphics Inc/333 Kimberly Dr, Carol Stream, IL 312-653-4550
Goldsholl Assoc/420 Frontage Rd, Northfield, IL 312-446-8300
Goldsmith Yamasaki Specht Inc/840 N Michigan Ave, Chicago, IL.....312-266-8404
Golon, Mary/4401 Estes St, Lincolnwood, IL 312-679-0062
Gournoe, M Inc/60 E Elm, Chicago, IL 312-787-5157
Graphic Corp/727 E 2nd St PO Box 4806, Des Moines, IA 515-247-8500
Graphic House Inc/672 Woodbridge, Detroit, MI 313-259-7790
Graphic Specialties Inc/2426 East 26th St, Minneapolis, MN.............612-722-6601
Graphica Corp/3184 Alpine, Troy, MI 313-649-5050
Graphics Group/8 S Michigan Ave, Chicago, IL 312-782-7421
Graphics-Cor Associates/549 W Randolph St, Chicago, IL 312-332-3379
Greenberg, Jon Assoc Inc/2338 Coolidge, Berkley, MI......................313-548-8080
Greenlee-Hess Ind Design/750 Beta Dr, Mayfield Village, OH 216-461-2112
Greiner, John & Assoc/311 N Ravenwood, Chicago, IL 312-644-2973
Griffin Media Design/802 Wabash Ave, Chesterton, IN 219-929-8602
Grusin, Gerald Design/232 E Ohio St, Chicago, IL 312-944-4945

HI

Hans Design/663 Greenwood Rd, Northbrook, IL 312-272-7980
Hanson Graphic/301 N Water St, Milwaukee, WI 414-347-1266
Harley, Don E Associates/1740 Livingston Ave, West St Paul, MN.......612-455-1631
Harris, Judy/550 Willow Creek Ct, Clarendon Hill, IL 312-789-3821
Hawthorne/Wolfe/1818 Chouteau, St Louis, MO 314-231-1844
Herbst Lazar Rogers & Bell Inc/345 N Canal, Chicago, IL 312-454-1116
Hirsch, David Design Group Inc/205 W Wacker Dr, Chicago, IL.........312-329-1500
Hirsh Co/8051 N Central Park Ave, Skokie, IL 312-267-6777
Hoekstra, Grant Graphics/333 N Michigan Ave, Chicago, IL 312-641-6940
Hoffar, Barron & Co/11 E Hubbard 7th Fl, Chicago, IL.......................312-922-0890
Horvath, Steve Design/301 N Water St, Milwaukee, WI 414-271-3992
Hughes, Dralene "Red"/19750 W Observatory Rd,
New Berlin, WI (P 1041) **414-542-5547**
Identity Center/1340-Q Remington Rd, Schaumburg, IL 312-843-2378
IGS Design Div/Smith Hinchman & Grylls/455 W Fort St, Detroit, MI 313-964-3000
Indiana Design/102 N 3rd St 300 Rvr Cty Bldg, Lafayette, IN 317-423-5469
Industrial Technological Assoc/30675 Solon Rd, Cleveland, OH 216-349-2900
Ing, Victor Design/5810 Lincoln, Morton Grove, IL 312-965-3459
Intelplex/12215 Dorsett Rd, Maryland Hts, MO.................................314-739-9996

JK

J M H Corp/1200 Waterway Blvd, Indianapolis, IN 317-639-2535
Johnson, Stan Design Inc/21185 W Gumina Rd, Brookfield, WI 414-783-6510
Johnson, Stewart Design Studio/218 W Walnut, Milwaukee, WI..........414-265-3377
Jones, Richmond/2530 W Eastwood St, Chicago, IL..........................312-588-4900
Joss Design Group/232 E Ohio, Chicago, IL 312-828-0055
K Squared Inc/1242 W Washington, Chicago, IL 312-421-7345
Kaulfuss Design/200 E Ontario St, Chicago, IL 312-943-2161
KDA Industrial Design Consultants/1785-B Cortland Ct, Addison, IL 312-495-9466
Keller Lane & Waln/8 S Michigan #814, Chicago, IL 312-782-7421
Kerr, Joe/405 N Wabash #2013, Chicago, IL 312-661-0097
Kornick & Lindsay/161 E Erie #107, Chicago, IL 312-280-8664
Kovach, Ronald Design/719 S Dearborn, Chicago, IL 312-461-9888
Krueger Wright Design/3744 Bryant Ave S, Minneapolis, MN 612-827-7570

L

Laney, Ron/15 Fern St/Box 423, St Jacob, IL 618-644-5883
Lehrfeld, Gerald/43 E Ohio, Chicago, IL 312-944-0651
Lenard, Catherine/700 N Green St #301N, Chicago, IL................312-248-6937
Lerdon, Wes Assoc/3070 Riverside Dr, Columbus, OH....................614-486-8188
Lesniewicz/Navarre/222 N Erie St, Toledo, OH.............................419-243-7131
Lighthaus Design Grp/4050 Pennsylvania #360, Kansas City, MO.......816-931-9554
Lipson Associates Inc/2349 Victory Pkwy, Cincinnati, OH.......513-961-6225
Lipson Associates Inc/666 Dundee Rd #103, Northbrook, IL........312-291-0500
Liska & Assoc/213 W Institute Pl #605, Chicago, IL.................312-943-5910
Lubell, Robert/2946 E Lincolnshire, Toledo, OH.........................419-531-2267

M

Maddox, Eva Assoc Inc/440 North Wells, Chicago, IL.................312-670-0092
Madsan/Kuester/1 Main @ River Pl #500, Minneapolis, MN.........612-378-1895
Manning Studios Inc/613 Main St, Cincinnati, OH 513-621-6959
Marsh, Richard Assoc Inc/203 N Wabash #1400, Chicago, IL 312-236-1331
McConnell, Brian/3508 S 12th Ave, Minneapolis, MN.....................612-724-4069
McDermott, Bill Design/1410 Hanley Industrial Ct, St Louis, MO 314-962-6286
McGuire, Robert L Design/7943 Campbell, Kansas City, MO 816-523-9164
McMurray Design Inc/405 N Wabash Ave, Chicago, IL 312-527-1555
Media Corporation/3070 Riverside Dr, Columbus, OH 614-488-7767
Media Loft/333 Washington Ave N #210, Minneapolis, MN............612-375-1086
Minnick, James Design/535 N Michigan Ave, Chicago, IL............312-527-1864
Miska, John/192 E Wallings Rd, Cleveland, OH...........................216-526-0464
Moonink Inc/233 N Michigan Ave, Chicago, IL...........................312-565-0040
Murrie White Drummond Leinhart/58 W Huron, Chicago, IL............312-943-5995

NO

Naughton, Carol & Assoc/213 W Institute Pl #708, Chicago, IL 312-951-5353
Nemetz, Jeff/900 N Franklin #600, Chicago, IL..........................312-664-8112
Nottingham-Spirk Design Inc/11310 Juniper Rd, Cleveland, OH.........216-231-7830
Oak Brook Graphics, Inc/287 W Butterfield Rd, Elmhurst, IL 312-832-3200
Obata Design/1610 Menard, St Louis, MO 314-241-1710
Oberg, Richard/327 15th Ave, Moline, IL.................................319-359-3831
Osborne-Tuttle/233 E Wacker Dr #2409, Chicago, IL...................312-565-1910
Oskar Designs/616 Sheridan Rd, Evanston, IL............................312-328-1734
Overlock Howe Consulting Gp/447 Conway Meadows, St Louis, MO......314-533-4484

P

Painter/Cesaroni Design, Inc/1865 Grove St, Glenview, IL...................312-724-8840
Palmer Design Assoc/3330 Old Glenview Rd, Wilmette, IL.............312-256-7448
Paragraphs Design/414 N Orleans #310, Chicago, IL...................312-828-0200
Paramount Technical Service Inc/31811 Vine St, Cleveland, OH 216-585-2550
Payne, Geof/817 Prairie Lane, Columbia , MO............................314-443-0384
Perlstein, Warren/560 Zenith Dr, Glenview, IL.............................312-827-7884
Peterson, Ted/23 N Lincoln St, Hinsdale, IL...............................312-920-1091
Phares Associates Inc/Hills Tech Dr, Farmington Hills, MI.............313-553-2232
Picard Didier Inc/13160 W Burleigh St, Brookfield, WI..................414-783-7400
Ping, Cliff/911 Main St #1717, Kansas City, MO..........................816-474-4366
Pinzke, Herbert/1935 N Kenmore, Chicago, IL...........................312-528-2277
Pitlock Design/300 N Michigan #200, South Bend, IN...................219-233-8606
Pitt Studios/1370 Ontario St #1430, Cleveland, OH.....................216-241-6720
Porter/Matjasich Assoc/154 W Hubbard St #504, Chicago, IL.............312-670-4355
Pride and Perfomance/970 Raymond Ave, St Paul, MN....................612-646-4800
Prodesign Inc/2500 Niagara Ln, Plymouth, MN..........................612-476-1200
Purviance, George Marketing Comm/7404 Bland Dr, Clayton, MO 314-721-2765
Pycha and Associates/16 E Pearson, Chicago, IL..........................312-944-3679

QR

Qually & Co Inc/30 E Huron #2502, Chicago, IL..........................312-944-0237
Ramba Graphics/1575 Merwin Ave, Cleveland, OH.......................216-621-1776
Red Wing Enterprises/666 N Lake Shore Dr #211, Chicago, IL 312-951-0441
Redmond, Patrick Design/757 Raymond Ave, Securty, St Paul, MN.....612-291-8689
RHI Inc/213 W Institute Pl, Chicago, IL...................................312-943-2585
Richardson/Smith Inc/10350 Olentangy River Rd, Worthington, OH....614-885-3453
Roberts Webb & Co/111 E Wacker Dr, Chicago, IL.......................312-861-0060
Roth, Randall/535 N Michigan #2312, Chicago, IL........................312-467-0140
Rotheiser, Jordan I/1725 McGovern St, Highland Park, IL....................312-433-4288

S

Samata Assoc/213 W Main Street, West Dundee, IL 312-428-8600
Sargent, Ann Design/432 Ridgewood Ave, Minneapolis, MN 612-870-9995
Savlin/Petertil/1335 Dodge Ave, Evanston, IL.............................312-328-3366
Schlatter Group Inc/40 E Michigan Mall, Battle Creek, MI................616-964-0898
Schmidt, Wm M Assoc/20296 Harper Ave, Harper Woods, MI 313-881-8075
Selfridge, Mary/817 Desplaines St, Plainfield, IL..........................815-436-7197
Seltzer, Meyer Design & Illus/744 W Buckingham Pl, Chicago, IL.......312-348-2885
Sherman, Roger Assoc Inc/13530 Michigan Ave, Dearborn, MI..........313-582-8844
Shilt, Jennifer/1010 Jorie Blvd, Oak Brook, IL.............................312-325-8657
Sigalos, Alex/520 N Michigan Ave #606, Chicago, IL....................312-321-0349
Simanis, Vito/4 N 013 Randall Rd, St Charles, IL..........................312-584-1683
Simons, I W Industrial Design/975 Amberly Pl, Columbus, OH............614-451-3796
Skidmore Sahratian/2100 W Big Beaver Rd, Troy,
MI (P 1136-1141) **313-643-6000**
Skolnick, Jerome/200 E Ontario, Chicago, IL.............................312-944-4568
Slavin Assoc Inc/229 W Illinois, Chicago, IL...............................312-822-0559
Smith, Glen Co/119 N 4th St #411, Minneapolis, MN.....................612-338-8235
Sosin, Bill/415 W Superior St, Chicago, IL.................................312-751-0974
Source & Co/116 S Michigan Ave 16th Fl, Chicago, IL..................312-236-7620
Spatial Graphics Inc/7131 W Lakefield Dr, Milwaukee, WI.............414-545-4444
Speare, Ray/730 N Franklin #501, Chicago, IL............................312-943-5808
Staake, Bob Design/1009 S Berry Rd #3D, St Louis, MO.................314-961-2303
Stepan Design/52 Carlisle Rd, Hawthorne Woods, IL.....................312-364-4121
Strizek, Jan/213 W Institute Pl, Chicago, IL...............................312-664-4772
Stromberg, Gordon H Visual Design/5423 Artesian, Chicago, IL.........312-275-9449
Studio 7/2770 State St NE, Middlebranch, OH............................216-454-1622
Studio One Graphics/16329 Middlebelt, Livonia, MI......................313-522-7505
Summers Studio/222 W Ontario, Chicago, IL.............................312-943-2533
Svolos, Maria/1936 W Estes, Chicago, IL.................................312-338-4675
Swoger Grafik/12 E Scott St, Chicago, IL.................................312-943-2491
Synthesis Concepts/360 N Michigan Ave, Chicago, IL...................312-609-1111

T

T & Company/3553 W Peterson Ave, Chicago, IL 312-463-1336
Tassian, George Org/702 Gwynne Bldg, Cincinnati, OH..................513-721-5566
Taylor & Assoc/8601 Urbandale Rd, Des Moines, IA....................515-276-0992
Tepe Hensler & Westerkamp/632 Vine St #1100, Cincinnati, OH..........513-241-0100
Teubner, Peter & Assoc/2341 N Cambridge St, Chicago, IL 312-248-6797
The Design Group/2976 Triverton Pike, Madison, WI.....................608-274-5393
The Design Partnership/124 N 1st St, Minneapolis, MN..................612-338-8889
Thorbeck & Lambert Inc/1409 Willow, Minneapolis, MN 612-871-7979
Three & Assoc/2245 Gilbert Ave, Cincinnati, OH..........................513-281-1600
Toth, Joe/20000 Eldra Rd, Rocky River, OH...............................216-356-0745

UV

Unicom/4100 W River Ln, Milwaukee, WI.................................414-354-5440
UVG & N/4415 W Harrison St, Hillside, IL.................................312-449-1500
Vallarta, Frederick Assoc Inc/40 E Delaware, Chicago, IL..................312-944-7300
Vanides-Mlodock/323 S Franklin St, Chicago, IL..........................312-663-0595
Vann, Bill Studio/1706 S 8th St, St Louis, MO
(P 802,803) **314-231-2322**
Vista Three Design/4820 Excelsior Blvd, Minneapolis, MN 612-920-5311
Visual Image Studio/1599 Selby Ave #22, St Paul, MN...................612-644-7314

WXZ

Wallner Harbauer Bruce & Assoc/500 N Michigan Ave, Chicago, IL....312-787-6787
Weber Conn & Riley/444 N Michigan #2440, Chicago, IL................312-527-4260
Weiss, Jack Assoc/409 Custer Ave #3, Evanston, IL......................312-866-7480
Widmer, Stanley Assoc/Staples Airport Ind Park, Staples, MN.............218-894-3466
Willson, William/100 E Ohio St #314, Chicago, IL.........................312-642-5328
Wooster + Assoc/314 Walnut, Winnetka, IL...............................312-726-7944
Wright Design/3744 Bryant Ave S, Minneapolis, MN......................617-666-4880
Xeno/PO Box 10030, Chicago, IL...312-327-1989
Ziegler, Nancy/420 Lake Cook Rd #110, Deerfield, IL....................312-945-2225

SOUTHWEST

AB

A&M Associates Inc/2727 N Central Ave, Box 21503, Phoenix, AZ......602-263-6504

Ad-Art Studios/813 6th Ave, Ft Worth, TX........................817-335-9603
The Ad Department/1412 Texas St, Ft Worth, TX................817-335-4012
Advertising Inc/2202 E 49th St, Tulsa, OK........................918-747-8871
Alexander, Martha/1419 Kirby Drive, Houston, TX..............713-529-0133
Anderson Pearlstone & Assoc/PO Box 6528, San Antonio, TX 512-826-1897
Ark, Chuck/3825 Bowser Ave, Dallas, TX...........................214-522-5356
Arnold Harwell McClain/4131 N Central Expwy #510, Dallas, TX 214-521-6400
Art Source Design/PO Box 2193, Grapevine, TX..................817-481-2212
The Art Works/4409 Maple St, Dallas, TX..........................214-521-2121
Basham, Clay/3003 W Alabama #101, Houston, TX..............713-529-8742
Baugh, Larry/1417 N Irving Hts, Irving, TX........................214-438-5696
Beals Advertising Agency/5005 N Penn, Oklahoma City, OK 405-848-8513
The Belcher Group Inc/8300 Bissonnet #240, Houston, TX 713-271-2727
Benhase, Meg/9541 E Myra Dr, Tucson, AZ........................602-721-0330
Bleu Design Assoc/345 E Windsor, Phoenix, AZ..................602-279-1131
Boughton, Cindy/1617 Fannin #2801, Houston, TX..............713-951-9113
Brooks & Pollard Co/1650 Union Nat'L Plaza, Little Rock, AR..........501-375-5561

CD

Central Advertising Agency/1 Tandy Circle #300, Fort Worth, TX 817-390-3011
Chandler, Jeff/PO Box 224427, Dallas, TX.........................214-946-1348
Chesterfield Interiors Inc/2213 Cedar Springs, Dallas, TX..........214-747-2211
Coffee Design Inc/5810 Star Ln, Houston, TX.....................713-780-0571
Connatser & Co/30 Highland Park Vill #201, Dallas, TX..........214-522-7373
Copeland, Kyle/11744 Wilcrest Dt #201, Houston, TX............713-499-6181
Crane, Susan Inc/8197 Chancellor Row, Dallas, TX..............214-631-6490
Cranford/ Johnson & Assoc/1st Comm Bldg, Little Rock, AR........501-376-6251
Design Bank/PO Box 33459, Austin, TX............................512-445-7584
Design Enterprises, Inc/9434 Viscount Blvd #180, El Paso, TX..........915-594-7100
Designmark/1800 W Loop South #1390, Houston, TX............713-626-0953
Drebelbis, Marsha/8150 Brookriver Dr #208S, Dallas, TX..........214-951-0266

EFG

Eisenberg Inc/4924 Cole, Dallas, TX..............................214-528-5990
Executive Image/8557 Wrld Trd Ctr/Box 581342, Dallas, TX.........214-733-0496
Ford, Deborah/202 Senter Valley, Irving, TX......................214-579-9472
Friesenhahn, Michelle/717 W Ashby, San Antonio, TX...........512-342-1997
Funk, Barbara/3174 Catamore Ln, Dallas, TX....................214-350-8534
Galen, D/5335 Bent Tree Forest #192, Dallas, TX................214-385-7855
Gluth & Weaver/3911 Stony Brook, Houston, TX.................713-784-4141
The Goodwin Co/7598 N Mesa #200, El Paso, TX................915-584-1176
Gregory Dsgn Group/3636 Lemmon #302, Dallas, TX...........214-522-9360
Grimes, Don/3514 Oak Grove, Dallas, TX (P 885).........**214-526-0040**

H

Hanagriff King Design/4151 SW Freeway, Houston, TX.........714-622-4260
Harman, Gary/1025 S Jennings #403, Ft Worth, TX.............817-332-7687
Herman, Ben/701 Pennsylvania, Fort Worth, TX................817-731-9941
Hermsen Design Assoc/5626 Preston Oaks #34-D, Dallas, TX..........214-233-5090
Herring, Jerry/1216 Hawthorne, Houston, TX....................713-526-1250
High, Richard/4500 Montrose #D, Houston, TX..................713-521-2772
Hill, Chris/3512 Lake, Houston, TX................................713-523-7363
Hixo/2905 San Gabriel #302, Austin, TX..........................512-477-0050
Hood Hope & Assoc/8023 E 63rd Box 35408, Tulsa, OK 918-250-9511
Hubler-Rosenburg Assoc/1405-A Turtle Creek, Dallas, TX...........214-742-2491

IJK

Image Excellence/3312 Shore Crest, Dallas, TX..................214-352-9958
Image Group Studio/2808 Cole St, Dallas, TX...................214-745-1411
Jacob, Jim/3524 Villanova, Dallas, TX............................214-696-3953
Jettun, Carol/4212 Cumberland Rd, Ft Worth, TX................817-737-4708
Johnson, Carla/9010 Windy Crest, Dallas, TX...................214-522-1449
Jones, Donald/10529 Sinclair, Dallas, TX.........................214-327-0819
Kilmer/Geer/5650 Kirby Dr #205, Houston, TX..................713-668-1708
Konig Design Group/4001 Broadway, San Antonio, TX..........512-824-7387

LM

Ledbetter, James/10818 Ridge Spring, Dallas, TX...............214-341-4858
Lindgren Design/5350 Interfirst Two, Dallas, TX.................214-742-3573
Loucks Atelier/2900 Weslyan #685, Houston, TX................713-877-8551
Lowe Runkle Co/6801 Broadway Extension, Oklahoma City, OK..........405-848-6800
Lyons, Dan/5510 Abrams #109A, Dallas, TX.....................214-368-4890
Martin, Hardy/2540 Walnut Hill Dr #1525, Dallas, TX...........214-351-1275

Martin, Randy/701 E Plano Pkwy, Dallas, TX....................214-881-1647
Mays, Stan/5004 Mimosa, Bellaire, TX............................713-668-6575
McCulley, Mike/412 Knollwood Ct, Euless, TX...................214-528-4889
McEuen, Roby/600 Eighth Ave, Ft Worth, TX....................817-335-5153
McFarlin, Steven/208 W Keaney #103, Mesquite, TX............214-289-1893
McGrath, Michael Design/1201 Richardson Dr, Richardson, TX..........214-644-4358
Moore Co/5427 Redfield, Dallas, TX..............................214-631-9443
Morales, Frank Design/12770 Coit Rd #905, Dallas, TX.........214-233-0667
Morris, Carroll/4835 LBJ Frwy #479, Dallas, TX................214-233-6616
Morrison & Assoc/3900 Lemmon #2, Dallas, TX................214-528-7410

NOPR

Neumann, Steve & Friends/3000 Richmond #103, Houston, TX 713-629-7501
Overton, Janet/2927 Bay Oaks Dr, Dallas, TX...................214-357-1272
Owens & Assoc Adv/2600 N Central Ave #1700, Phoenix, AZ..........602-264-5691
Pencil Point/14330 Midway #210, Dallas, TX.....................214-233-0776
Pirtle Design/4528 McKinney Ave #104, Dallas, TX..............214-522-7520
Richards Brock Miller Mitchell & Assoc/7007 Twin Hill, Dallas, TX 214-987-4800

S

Sawyer, Sandra/1319 Ballinger, Ft Worth, TX....................817-332-1611
Slaton, Richard/3514 Oak Grove #9, Dallas, TX.................214-231-3000
Squires, James/2913 N Canton, Dallas, TX......................214-939-9194
Strickland, Michael & Co/3000 Post Oak Blvd #140, Houston, TX 713-961-1323
Struthers, Yvonne/2110 Mossy Oak, Arlington, TX...............214-469-1377
Sullivan, Jack Design Group/1320 N 7th Ave, Phoenix, AZ.........602-271-0117
Suntar Designs/PO Box 1901, Prescott, AZ.......................602-778-2714
Sweeney, Jim/250 Decker, Irving, TX.............................214-258-1705

TUVW

Texas Art & Media/500 W 13th St #220, Ft Worth, TX 817-334-0443
Turnipseed, Allan/2719-C Laclede, Dallas, TX...................214-871-2828
Unigraphics/2700 Oak Lawn, Dallas, TX.........................214-526-0930
Vanmar Assoc/1440 Empire Central #458, Dallas, TX...........214-630-7603
Warden, Bill/438 Wellington Dr, Mesquite, TX...................214-634-8434
WW3 Papagalos/313 E Thomas #208, Phoenix, AZ...............602-279-2933

R O C K Y   M T N

ABC

Allison & Schiedt/219 E 7th Ave, Denver, CO....................303-830-1110
Ampersand Studios/315 St Paul, Denver, CO....................303-388-1211
Arnold Design Inc/1635 Ogden, Denver, CO.....................303-832-7156
Barnstorm Design/2527 W Colorado Ave, Colorado Springs, CO 303-630-7200
Brogren/Kelly & Assoc/3113 E Third Ave #220, Denver, CO 303-399-3851
CommuniCreations/2130 S Bellaire, Denver, CO.................303-759-1155
Cuerden Advertising Design/1730 Gaylord St, Denver, CO.......303-321-4163

DEFG

Danford, Chuck/1556 Williams St, Denver, CO..................303-320-1116
Design Center/734 W 800 S, Salt Lake City, UT.................801-532-6122
Duo Graphics/3907 Manhattan Ave, Ft Collins, CO.............303-463-2788
Engen, Scott/9058 Greenhills Dr, Sandy, UT...................801-942-3125
Entercom/425 S Cherry St #200, Denver, CO...................303-393-0405
Fleming, Ron/901 14th St N, Great Falls, MT (P 35) **406-761-7887**
Genesis Design/604 W 6th Ave, Denver, CO.....................617-881-2471
Gibby, John Design/1140 E 1250 N, Layton, UT................801-544-0736
Graphic Concepts Inc/145 Pierpont Ave, Salt Lake City, UT.....801-359-2191
Graphien Design/6950 E Belleview #250, Englewood, CO........303-779-5858
Gritz Visual Graphics/5595 Arapahoe Rd, Boulder, CO...........303-449-3840

MOR

Martin, Janet/1112 Pearl, Boulder, CO..........................303-442-8202
Matrix Design/100 Filmore 3240, Denver, CO...................303-388-9353
Montano, Daniel/1616 W 17th St #371, Denver, CO............303-628-5440
Multimedia/450 Lincoln #100, Denver, CO.......................303-777-5480
Okland Design Assoc/1970 SW Temple, Salt Lake City, UT 801-484-7861
Radetsky Design Associates/2342 Broadway, Denver, CO..........303-629-7375

TVW

Tandem Design Group Inc/217 E 7th Ave, Denver, CO 303-831-9251
Taylor, Robert W Design Inc/2260 Baseline Rd #205, Boulder, CO.......303-443-1975
Visual Communications/4475 E Hinsdale Pl, Littleton, CO......................303-773-0128
Visual Images Inc/1626 Franklin, Denver, CO 303-388-5366
Weller Institute for Design/2240 Monarch Dr, Park City, UT 801-649-9859
Worthington, Carl A Partnership/1309 Spruce St, Boulder, CO 303-449-8900

WEST COAST

A

A & H Graphic Design/11844 Rncho Brndo, Rancho Bernardo, CA.....619-486-0777
Ace Design/310 Industrial Ctr Bldg, Sausalito, CA 415-332-9390
Advertising Design & Prod Srvc/1929 Emerald St #3, San Diego, CA...619-483-1393
Advertising Designers/818 North La Brea Ave, Los Angeles, CA 213-463-8143
Advertising/Design Assoc/1906 Second Ave, Walnut Creek, CA.........415-421-7000
AGI/424 N Larchmont Blvd, Los Angeles, CA.....................................213-462-0821
Alatorre, Sean/1341 Ocean Ave #259, Santa Monica, CA..................213-209-3765
Alvarez Group/3171 Cadet Court, Los Angeles, CA...........................213-876-3491
Anderson, Lance/22 Margrave Pl #5, San Francisco, CA 415-788-5893
Andrysiak, Michele/13534 Cordary Ave #14, Hawthorne, CA..............213-973-8480
Antisdel Image Group/3252 De La Cruz, Santa Clara, CA....................408-988-1010
Art Works Design/3325 W Desert Inn Rd #1, Las Vegas, NV 702-365-1970
Art Zone/404 Piikoi St PH, Honolulu, HI...808-537-6647
Artists In Print/Bldg 314, Fort Mason Center, San Francisco, CA 415-673-6941
Artmaster Studios/547 Library St, San Fernando, CA..........................818-365-7188
Artworks Design/115 N Sycamore St, Los Angeles, CA 213-933-5763
Asbury & Assoc/3450 E Spring St, Long Beach, CA...........................213-595-6481

B

Bailey, Robert Design Group/0121 SW Bancroft St, Portland, OR.........503-228-1381
Banuelos Design/111 S Orange St, Orange, CA 714-771-4335
Baptiste, Bob/20360 Orchard Rd, Saratoga, CA 408-867-6569
Barnes, Herb Graphics/1844 Monterey Rd, S Pasadena, CA 213-682-2420
Basic Designs Inc/Box 479 Star Rt, Sausalito, CA 415-388-5141
Bass, Yager and Assoc/7039 Sunset Blvd, Hollywood, CA 213-466-9701
Bay Graphics/2550 9th St #101, Berkeley, CA....................................415-843-0701
Beggs Langley Design/619 Maybell Ave, Palo Alto, CA.......................415-857-9539
Bennett, Douglas Design/1966 Harvard Ave E, Seattle, WA 206-324-9966
Beuret, Janis/404 Piikoi St PH, Honolulu, HI.......................................808-537-6647
Bhang, Samuel Design Assoc/824 S Burnside, Los Angeles, CA 213-382-1126
The Blank Co/1048 Lincoln Ave, San Jose, CA...................................408-289-9095
Blik, Ty/715 'J' St #102, San Diego, CA 619-232-5707
Bloch & Associates/2800 28th St #105, Santa Monica, CA 213-450-8863
Boelter, Herbert A/1544 El Miradero, Glendale, CA.............................818-242-4206
Bohn, Richard/595 W Wilson St, Costa Mesa, CA 714-548-6669
Boyd, Douglas Design/6624 Melrose Ave, Los Angeles, CA 213-933-8383
Bramson + Assoc/7400 Beverly Blvd, Los Angeles, CA 213-938-3595
Breitmeyer & Assoc/10011 N Foothill Blvd #110, Cupertino, CA........408-257-4600
Bright & Associates, Inc/3008 Main St, Santa Monica, CA..................213-450-2488
Britton Design/1045 Sansome St #311, San Francisco, CA.................415-989-4119
Brown, Bill/1054 S Robertson Blvd #203, Los Angeles, CA.................213-652-9380
Burns & Associates Inc/2700 Sutter St, San Francisco, CA 415-567-4404
Burridge, Robert/2508 Castillo St #2, Santa Barbara, CA 805-964-2087
Business Graphics/1717 N Highland, Los Angeles, CA.......................213-467-0292
Buck, Debbie/PO Box 910438, San Diego, CA...................................619-792-6630

C

Camozzi, Teresa/770 California St, San Francisco, CA.........................415-392-1202
Carlson, Keith Advertising Art/251 Kearny St, San Francisco, CA 415-397-5130
Catalog Design & Prod/1485 Bay Shore Blvd, San Francisco, CA.......415-468-5500
Chan Design/1334 Lincoln Blvd #150, Santa Monica, CA...................213-393-3735
Chase, Margo/2255 Bancroft Ave, Los Angeles, CA 213-668-1055
Church, Jann/110 Newport Ctr Dr #160, Newport Beach, CA 714-640-6224
Churchill, Steven/4757 Cardin St, San Diego, CA...............................619-560-1225
Clark, Tim/8800 Venice Blvd, Los Angeles, CA...................................213-202-1044
Clasen, Gene/1355 Redondo Ave #10, Long Beach, CA.....................213-985-0051
Coak, Steve/2870 N Haven Lane, Altadena, CA..................................818-797-5477
The Coakley Heagerty Co/122 Saratoga Ave, Santa Clara, CA 408-249-6242
Coates Advertising/115 SW Ash St #323, Portland, OR......................503-241-1124
Cognata Associates Inc/2247 Webster, San Francisco, CA.................415-931-3800

Colorplay Design Studio/323 W 13th Ave, Eugene, OR.......................503-687-8262
Conber Creations/3326 NE 60th, Portland, OR...................................503-288-2938
Corporate Comms Group/310 Washington St, Marina Del Rey, CA 213-821-9086
Corporate Graphics/11849 W Olympic Blvd #204, Los Angeles, CA ...213-478-8211
Cowart, Jerry/1144-C S Robertson Blvd, Los Angeles, CA 213-278-5605
Crawshaw, Todd Design/345-D Folsom, San Francisco, CA 145-777-3939
Creative Source/6671 W Sunset Blvd #1519, Los Angeles, CA 213-462-5731
Crisp, Alan/1430 Mercy St, Mountain View, CA..................................415-965-8966
Cronan, Michael Patrick/1 Zoe St, San Francisco, CA 415-543-6745
Cross Assoc/455 Market St #1200, San Francisco, CA 415-777-2731
Cross, James/10513 W Pico Blvd, Los Angeles, CA 213-474-1484
Crouch + Fuller Inc/853 Camino Del Mar, Del Mar, CA.......................619-450-9200
Curtis, Todd/2032 14th St #7, Santa Monica, CA 213-452-0738

D

Dahm & Assoc Inc/26735 Shorewood Rd, Rncho Palos Verdes, CA....213-373-4408
Dancer Fitzgerald & Sample/1010 Battery St, San Francisco, CA 415-981-6250
Danziger, Louis/7001 Melrose Ave, Los Angeles, CA.........................213-935-1251
Dawson, Chris/7250 Beverly Blvd #101, Los Angeles, CA..................213-937-5867
Dayne, Jeff The Studio/731 NE Everett, Portland, OR.........................503-232-8777
Daystar Design/4641 Date Ave #1, La Mesa, CA................................619-463-5014
Dellaporta Adv & Graphic/2020 14th St, Santa Monica, CA................213-452-3832
DeMaio Graphics/7101 Baird St #3, Reseda, CA................................818-342-1800
Design & Direction/947 61st St #18, Oakland, CA..............................415-654-6282
Design Bank Graphic Design/9605 Sepulveda #5, Sepulveda, CA.......818-894-9123
Design Corps/501 N Alfred St, Los Angeles, CA 213-651-1422
Design Direction Group/595 S Pasadena Ave, Pasadena, CA.............818-792-4765
Design Element/8624 Wonderland Ave, Los Angeles, CA 213-656-3293
Design Graphics/2647 S Magnolia, Los Angeles, CA 213-749-7345
Design Group West/853 Camino Del Mar, Del Mar, CA.......................619-450-9200
Design Office/55 Stevenson, San Francisco, CA 415-543-4760
Design Projects Inc/16133 Ventura Blvd #600, Encino, CA.................818-995-0303
Design Vectors/408 Columbus Ave #2, San Francisco, CA.................415-391-0399
The Design Works/2205 Stoner Ave, Los Angeles, CA........................213-477-3577
The Designory Inc/351 E 6th St, Long Beach, CA...............................213-432-5707
Detanna & Assoc/12400 Wilshire Blvd #1160, Los Angeles, CA 213-207-1778
Diniz, Carlos/676 S Lafayette Park Pl, Los Angeles, CA 213-387-1171
Doane, Dave Studio/215 Riverside Dr, Orange, CA.............................714-548-7285
Doerfler Design/8742 Villa La Jolla Dr #29, La Jolla, CA......................619-455-0506
Dupre Design/415 2nd St, Coronado, CA 619-435-8369
Dyer-Cahn/8360 Melrose Ave 3rd Fl, Los Angeles, CA 213-937-4100
Dyna Pac/7926 Convoy St, San Diego, CA 619-560-0280

EF

Ehrig & Assoc/4th & Vine Bldg 8th Fl, Seattle, WA.............................206-623-6666
Engle, Ray & Assoc/626 S Kenmore, Los Angeles, CA 213-381-5001
Faia, Don/39 E Main St #6, Los Gatos, CA...408-354-1530
Farber, Melvyn Design Group/406 Bonhill Rd, Los Angeles, CA...........213-829-2668
Finger, Julie Design Inc/8467 Melrose Pl, Los Angeles, CA 213-653-0541
Floyd Design & Assoc/3451 Golden Gate Way, Lafayette, CA.............415-283-1735
Follis, Dean/2124 Venice Blvd, Los Angeles, CA 213-735-1283
Fox, BD & Friends Advertising/6671 Sunset Blvd, Los Angeles, CA.....213-464-0131
Frazier, Craig/173 7th St, San Francisco, CA 415-863-9613
Furniss, Stephanie Design/1327 Via Sessi, San Rafael, CA 415-459-4730
Fusfield, Robert/8306 Wilshire Blvd #2550, Beverly Hills, CA..............213-933-2818

G

Garnett, Joe/12121 Wilshire Blvd #322, Los Angeles, CA...................213-826-9378
Georgopoulos/Imada Design/5410 Wilshire Blvd #405, LA, CA 213-933-6425
Gerber Advertising Agency/1305 SW 12th Ave, Portland, OR.............503-221-0100
Gillian/Craig Assoc/165 Eighth St #301, San Francisco, CA 415-558-8988
Girvin, Tim Design/1601 Second Ave 5th Fl, Seattle, WA 206-623-7808
Gladych, Marianne/10641 Missouri Ave, Los Angeles, CA 213-474-1915
Global West Studio/201 N Occidental Blvd, Los Angeles, CA..............213-384-3331
The Gnu Group/2200 Bridgeway Blvd, Sausalito, CA..........................415-332-8010
Gold, Judi/8738 Rosewood Ave, West Hollywoood, CA......................213-659-4690
Gordon, Roger/10799 N Gate St, Culver City, CA...............................213-559-8287
Gould & Assoc/10549 Jefferson, Culver City, CA 213-879-1900
Graformation/5233 Bakman Ave, N Hollywood, CA 818-985-1224
Graphic Data/804 Tourmaline POB 99991, San Diego, CA 619-274-4511
Graphic Designers Inc/3325 Wilshire Blvd #610, Los Angeles, CA 213-381-3977
Graphic Studio/811 N Highland Ave, Los Angeles, CA........................213-466-2666
Graphicom Design/201 Castro St 2nd Fl, Mountain View, CA 415-969-5611

H

Harrington and Associates/11480 Burbank Blvd, N Hollywood, CA 818-508-7322
Harte-Yamashita & Forest/5735 Melrose Ave, Los Angeles, CA............213-462-6486
Hauser, S G Assoc Inc/24009 Ventura Blvd #200, Calabasas, CA 818-884-1727
Hausman, Joan/247 High St, Palo Alto, CA.......................................415-325-7957
Helgesson, Ulf Ind Dsgn/4285 Canoga Ave, Woodland Hills, CA..........818-883-3772
Holden, Cynthia/275 S Oakland Ave #308, Pasadena, CA 818-584-6944
Hornall Anderson Design/1008 Western Ave 6th Fl, Seattle, WA 206-467-5800
Hosick, Frank Design/PO Box H, Vashon Island, WA 206-463-5454
Hubert, Laurent/850 Arbor Rd, Menlo Park, CA 415-321-5182
Humangraphic/4015 Ibis St, San Diego, CA 619-299-0431
Hyde, Bill/751 Matsonia, Foster City, CA 415-345-6955

IJ

Ikkanda, Richard/2800 28th St #105, Santa Monica, CA 213-450-4881
Imag'Inez/5 Oak Flat Rd, Orinda, CA 415-254-2444
Image Stream/5450 W Washington Blvd, Los Angeles, CA...................213-933-9196
Imagination Creative Services/80 Justin, San Francisco, CA.................408-988-8696
Imagination Graphics/2760 S Harbor Blvd #A, Santa Ana, CA 714-662-3114
J J & A/405 S Flower, Burbank, CA..213-849-1444
Jaciow Design Inc/201 Castro St, Mountain View, CA 415-962-8860
Jerde Partnership/2798 Sunset Blvd, Los Angeles, CA.......................213-413-0130
Johnson Rodger Design/704 Silver Spur Rd, Rolling Hills, CA..............213-377-8860
Johnson, Iskra/1605 12th St, Seattle, WA....................................206-323-8256
Johnson, Paige Graphic Design/535-B Ramona St, Palo Alto, CA..........415-327-0488
Joly Major Product Design/4773 Sonoma Hwy, Santa Rosa, CA............415-641-1933
Jones, Brent Design/328 Hayes St, San Francisco, CA.......................415-626-8337
Jones, Jacqueline/Pier 9, San Francisco, CA..................................415-982-8484
Jones, Steve/1081 Nowita Pl, Venice, CA 213-396-9111
Jonson Pedersen Hinrichs & Shakery/620 Davis St,
San Francisco, CA..415-981-6612
Juett, Dennis & Assoc/672 S Lafayette Pk Pl #48, Los Angeles, CA.....213-385-4373

KL

K S Wilshire Inc/10494 Santa Monica Blvd, Los Angeles, CA 213-879-9595
Kageyama, David Designer/2119 Smith Tower, Seattle, WA 206-622-7281
Kessler, David & Assoc/1300 N Wilton Pl, Hollywood, CA...................213-462-6043
Klein/1111 S Robertson Blvd, Los Angeles, CA...............................213-278-5600
Kleiner, John A Graphic Design/2627 10th Ct #4, Santa Monica, CA ...216-472-7442
Kuey, Patty/20341 Ivy Hill Ln, Yorba Linda, CA 714-970-5286
Lacy, N Lee Assoc Ltd/8446 Melrose Pl, Los Angeles, CA 213-852-1414
Lancaster Design/1810 14th St, Santa Monica, CA 213-450-2999
Landes & Assoc/20313 Mason Court, Torrance, CA 213-540-0907
Landor Associates/Ferryboat Klamath Pier 5, San Francisco, CA 415-955-1200
Larson, Ron/940 N Highland Ave, Los Angeles, CA 213-465-8451
Leimer Cross Design/140 Lakeside Ave #310, Seattle, WA 206-325-8504
Leong, Russell Design/524-A Ramona St, Palo Alto, CA 415-321-2443
Leonhardt Group/411 First Ave S #400, Seattle, WA..........................206-624-0551
Lesser, Joan/Etcetera/3565 Greenwood Ave, Los Angeles, CA............213-397-4575
Letter Perfect/6606 Soundview Dr, Gig Harbor, WA...........................206-851-5158
Levine, Steve & Co/228 Main St, #5, Venice, CA 213-399-9336
Logan Carey & Rehag/353 Folsom St, San Francisco, CA 415-543-7080
Loveless, J R Design/3617 MacArthur Blvd #511, Santa Ana, CA 714-754-0886
Lumel-Whiteman/4721 Laurel Canyon #203, N. Hollywood, CA 818-769-5332

M

Mabry, Michael/212 Sutter St, San Francisco, CA............................415-982-7336
Maddu, Patrick & Co/1842 Third Ave, San Diego, CA 619-238-1340
Malone, Julie/5 Hutton Centre Dr #840, Santa Anna, CA.....................714-557-5011
Manwaring, Michael Office/1005 Sansome St, San Francisco, CA........415-421-3595
Marketing Comm Grp/124 S Arrowhead Ave, San Bernadino, CA........714-885-4976
Marketing Tools/384 Trailview Rd, Encinitas, CA...............................619-942-6042
Markofski, Don/525 S Myrtle #212, Monrovia, CA.............................818-446-1222
Marra & Assoc/2800 NW Thurman, Portland, OR 503-227-5207
Matthews, Robert/1101 Boise Dr, Campbell, CA...............................408-378-0878
Mayeda, Scott/3115 Felton St, San Diego, CA.................................619-284-9692
McCargar Design/2915 Redhill Ave #A-202, Costa Mesa, CA...............415-363-2130
McKee, Dennis/350 Townsend St, San Francisco, CA 415-543-7107
Media Services Corp/10 Aladdin Ter, San Francisco, CA.....................415-928-3033
Meek, Kenneth/90 N Berkeley, Pasadena, CA..................................818-449-9722
Miller, Marcia/425 E Hyde Park, Ingelwood, CA...............................213-677-4171
Mize, Charles Adv Art/300 Broadway #29, San Francisco, CA.............415-421-1548
Mizrahi, Robert/6256 San Harco Circle, Buena Park, CA....................714-527-6182

Mobius Design Assoc/7250 Beverly Blvd #101, Los Angeles, CA.........213-937-0331
Molly Designs Inc/15 Chrysler, Irvine, CA......................................714-768-7155
Murphy, Harry & Friends/58 Hickory Rd, Fairfax, CA..........................415-454-1672
Murray/Bradley Inc/1904 Third Ave #432, Seattle, WA 206-622-7082

N

N Graphic/480 2nd St #101, San Francisco, CA................................415-896-5806
Naganuma, Tony K Design/1100 Montgomery St, San Francisco, CA 415-433-4484
Nagel & Degastaldi Co/530 Lytton Ave #309, Palo Alto, CA 415-328-0251
Neill, Richard/9724 Olive St, Bloomington, CA.................................714-877-5824
Nicholson Design/662 Ninth Ave, San Diego, CA..............................619-235-9000
Nicolini Associates/4046 Maybelle Ave, Oakland, CA.........................415-531-5569
Niehaus, Don/2380 Malcolm Ave, Los Angeles, CA...........................213-279-1559
Nine West/9 West State St, Pasadena, CA.....................................818-799-2727
Nordenhook Design/901 Dove St #115, Newport Beach, CA................714-752-8631

OP

Olson Design Inc/853 Camino Del Mar, Del Mar, CA..........................619-450-9200
Orr, R & Associates Inc/22282 Pewter Ln, El Toro, CA........................714-770-1277
Osborn, Michael Design/105 South Park, San Francisco, CA...............415-495-4292
Oshima, Carol/1659 E Sachs Place, Covina, CA 818-966-0796
Package Deal/18211 Beneta Way, Tustin, CA..................................714-541-2440
Pease, Robert & Co/11 Orchard St, Alamo, CA................................415-820-0404
Pentagram Design/620 Davis St, San Francisco, CA 415-981-6612
Persechini & Co/357 S Robertson Blvd, Beverly Hills, CA...................213-657-6175
Peterson, Scott Design/13965 SW Linda Lane, Beaverton, OR 503-641-8685
Petzold & Assoc/11830 SW Kerr Pkwy #350, Lake Oswego, OR...........503-246-8320
Pittard, Billy/6335 Homewood Ave, Hollywood, CA...........................213-462-2300
Popovich, Mike/15428 E Valley Blvd, City of Industry, CA...................818-336-6958
Powers Design International/822 Production Pl, Newport Beach, CA......714-645-2265
Primo Angeli Graphics/590 Folsom St, San Francisco, CA 415-974-6100

QR

The Quorum/305 NE Mapleleaf Pl, Seattle, WA................................206-522-6872
Rankin, Bob Assoc/103rd St NE #4, Bellevue, WA............................206-641-4020
Reid, Scott/432 State St, Santa Barbara, CA...................................805-963-8926
Reineck & Reineck/1425 Cole St, San Francisco, CA.........................415-566-3614
Reis, Gerald & Co/560 Sutter St #301, San Francisco, CA..................415-421-1232
Rickabaugh Design/213 SW Ash #209, Portland, OR.........................503-223-2191
Ritola, Roy Inc/714 Sansome St, San Francisco, CA..........................415-788-7010
RJL Design Graphics/44110 Old Warm Springs Blvd, Fremont, CA.....415-657-2038
Roberts, Eileen/PO Box 1261, Carlsbad, CA...................................619-439-7800
Robinson, David/3607 Fifth Ave #6, San Diego, CA 619-298-2021
Rogow & Bernstein Dsgn/5971 W 3rd St, Los Angeles, CA 213-936-9916
Rolandesign/21833 De La Luz Ave, Woodland Hills, CA......................818-346-9752
Runyan, Richard Design/12016 Wilshire Blvd, W Los Angeles, CA 213-477-8878
Runyan, Robert Miles/200 E Culver Blvd, Playa Del Rey, CA...............213-823-0975
Rupert, Paul Design/708 Montgomery St, San Francisco, CA.............415-391-2966

S

Sackheim, Morton Ent/170 N Robertson Blvd, Beverly Hills, CA............213-652-0220
San Diego Art Prdctns/2752 Imperial Ave, San Diego, CA...................619-239-6666
Sanchez/Kamps Assoc/60 W Green St, Pasadena, CA 213-793-4017
Schaefer, Robert Television Art/738 N Cahuenga, Hollywood, CA........213-462-7877
Schockner, Jan/80 Wellington Ave/Box 307, Ross, CA........................415-456-7711
Schorer, R Thomas/27580 Silver Spur Rd #201, Palos Verdes, CA.......213-377-0207
Schwab, Michael Design/118 King St, San Francisco, CA....................415-546-7559
Schwartz, Bonnie/Clem/2941 4th Ave, San Diego, CA........................619-291-8878
Seiniger & Assoc/8201 W 3rd, Los Angeles, CA...............................213-653-8665
Shenon, Mike/576 Cambridge Ave, Palo Alto, CA 415-493-6878
Shimokochi/Reeves Design/4465 Wilshire Blvd, Los Angeles, CA.........213-937-3414
Sidjakov, Nicholas/3727 Buchanan, San Francisco, CA......................415-931-7500
Signworks/7710 Aurora Ave N, Seattle, WA....................................206-525-2718
Slavin, David/400 S Beverly Dr #305, Beverly Hills, CA......................213-277-7036
Smidt, Sam/666 High St, Palo Alto, CA...415-327-0707
The Smith Group/520 NW Davis St #325, Portland, OR.......................503-224-1905
Sorensen, Hugh Industrial Design/841 Westridge Way, Brea, CA..........714-529-8493
Soyster & Ohrenschall Inc/575 Sutter St, San Francisco, CA...............415-956-7575
Spear, Jeffrey A/1228 11th St #201, Santa Monica, CA......................213-395-3939
Sperling, Lauren/128 S Bowling Green Way, Los Angeles, CA.............213-472-9957
The Stansbury Co/9304 Santa Monica Blvd, Beverly Hills, CA.............213-273-1138
Starr Seigle McCombs/1001 Bishop Sq #19 Pcfc Twr, Honolulu, HI.....808-524-5080
Stephenz Group/300 Orchard City Dr #133, Campbell, CA.................408-379-4883
Strong, David Design Group/2030 First Ave #201, Seattle, WA............206-447-9160

Studio A/5801-A S Eastern Ave, Los Angeles, CA.................................213-721-1802
The Studio/45 Houston, San Francisco, CA 415-928-4400
Sugi, Richard Design & Assoc/844 Colorado Blvd #202, LA, CA 213-385-4169
Superior Graphic Systems/1700 W Anaheim St, Long Beach, CA........213-433-7421
Sussman & Prejza/1651 18th St, Santa Monica, CA 213-829-3337

TV

Tackett/Barbaria/1990 3rd St #400, Sacramento, CA 916-442-3200
Teague, Walter Dorwin Assoc/14727 NE 87th St, Redmond, WA..........206-883-8684
Thomas & Assoc/532 Colorado Ave, Santa Monica, CA 213-451-8502
Thomas, Greg/2238 1/2 Purdue Ave, Los Angeles, CA.........................213-479-8477
Thomas, Keith M Inc/3211 Shannon, Santa Ana, CA.............................714-261-1161
Torme, Dave/1868 Buchanan St, San Francisco, CA.............................415-931-3322
Trade Marx/1100 Pike St, Seattle, WA 206-623-7676
Tribotti Designs/15234 Morrison St, Sherman Oaks, CA.......................818-784-6101
Tycer Fultz Bellack/1731 Embarcadero Rd, Palo Alto, CA.....................415-856-1600
VanNoy & Co Inc/19750 S Vermont, Torrance, CA................................213-329-0800
Vantage Adv & Mktg Assoc/433 Callan Ave POB 3095,
San Leandro, CA..415-352-3640
Visual Resources Inc/1556 N Fairfax, Los Angeles, CA 213-851-6688
Voltec Associates/560 N Larchmont, Los Angeles, CA 213-467-2106

WYZ

Walton, Brenda/910 2nd St 2nd Fl, Sacramento, CA 916-448-4998
Weideman and Associates/4747 Vineland Ave, N Hollywood, CA........818-769-8488
Wells, John/407 Jackson St, San Francisco, CA....................................415-956-3952
Wertman, Chuck/559 Pacific Ave, San Francisco, CA............................415-433-4452
West, Suzanne Design/124 University Ave #201, Palo Alto, CA............415-324-8068
White + Assoc/137 N Virgil Ave #204, Los Angeles, CA 213-380-6319
Whitely, Mitchell Assoc/716 Montgomery St, San Francisco, CA 415-398-2920
Wiley, Jean/1700 I St #200, Sacramento, CA 916-447-4633
Wilkins & Peterson Design/206 Third Ave S #300, Seattle, WA 206-624-1695
Willardson + Assoc/103 W California, Glendale, CA 818-242-5688
Williams & Ziller Design/330 Fell St, San Francisco, CA.......................415-621-0330
Williams, John/330 Fell St, San Francisco, CA......................................415-621-0330
Williamson & Assoc Inc/8800 Venice Blvd, Los Angeles, CA................213-836-0143
Winters, Clyde Design/2200 Mason St, San Francisco, CA...................415-391-5643
Wong, Rick/379-A Clementina, San Francisco, CA 415-243-0588
Woo, Calvin Assoc/4015 Ibis St, San Diego, CA...................................619-299-0431
Workshop West/9720 Wilshire Blvd #700, Beverly Hills, CA.................213-278-1370
Yanez, Maurice & Assoc/901 S Sixth Ave #448, Hacienda Hts, CA......818-792-0778
Yee, Ray/424 Larchmont Blvd, Los Angeles, CA 213-465-2514
Young & Roehr Adv/6415 SW Canyon Ct, Portland, OR.......................503-297-4501
Yuguchi Krogstad/3378 W 1st St, Los Angeles, CA..............................213-383-6915
Zamparelli & Assoc/1450 Lomita Dr, Pasadena, CA.............................818-799-4370

INTERNATIONAL

Chen, Shih-chien/2839 35th St, Edmonton, AB......................................403-462-8617
Design Innovations Inc/75 Berkeley St, Toronto, ON 416-362-8470
Levine, Ron/1619 Williams St #202, Montreal, QU................................212-727-1967
Pacific Rim Design/720 E 27th Ave, Vancouver, BC 604-879-6689